The Wadsworth Handbook

Eighth Edition

Laurie G. Kirszner
University of the Sciences in Philadelphia

Stephen R. Mandell
Drexel University

Australia • Brazil • Japan • Korea • Mexico • Singapore • Spain • United Kingdom • United States

The Wadsworth Handbook, Eighth Edition
Laurie G. Kirszner,
Stephen R. Mandell

Publisher: Lyn Uhl
Senior Acquisitions Editor:
  Star MacKenzie Burruto
Development Editor: Karen Smith
Editorial Assistant: Elliot Sanchez
Senior Technology Project Manager: Stephanie Gregoire
Managing Marketing Manager:
  Mandee Eckersley
Marketing Assistant: Kate Remsberg
Senior Marketing Communications Manager: Stacey Purviance
Senior Content Project Manager:
  Lianne Ames
Senior Art Director: Cate Rickard Barr
Senior Print Buyer:
  Mary Beth Hennebury
Permissions Editor:
  Ronald Montgomery
Permissions Researcher:
  Timothy Sisler
Production Service: Nesbitt Graphics, Inc.
Text Designer: Nesbitt Graphics, Inc.
Photo Manager: Sheri Blaney
Photo Researcher: Sharon Donahue
Cover Designer: Brian Salisbury
Compositor: Nesbitt Graphics, Inc.

© 2008, 2005, 2002, 1999, 1995, 1992, 1989, 1986 Wadsworth Cengage Learning

ALL RIGHTS RESERVED. No part of this work covered by the copyright herein may be reproduced, transmitted, stored or used in any form or by any means graphic, electronic, or mechanical, including but not limited to photocopying, recording, scanning, digitizing, taping, Web distribution, information networks, or information storage and retrieval systems, except as permitted under Section 107 or 108 of the 1976 United States Copyright Act, without the prior written permission of the publisher.

> For product information and technology assistance, contact us at **Cengage Learning Academic Resource Center, 1-800-354-9706**
>
> For permission to use material from this text or product, submit all requests online at **cengage.com/permissions**
> Further permissions questions can be emailed to **permissionrequest@cengage.com**

Library of Congress Control Number: 2007920772
ISBN-13: 978-1-4390-8182-2
ISBN-10: 1-4390-8182-4

Wadsworth
20 Channel Center Street
Boston, MA 02210
USA

Cengage Learning is a leading provider of customized learning solutions with office locations around the globe, including Singapore, the United Kingdom,
Australia, Mexico, Brazil, and Japan. Locate your local office at: **international.cengage.com/region**

Cengage Learning products are represented in Canada by Nelson Education, Ltd.

For your course and learning solutions, visit
academic.cengage.com

Purchase any of our products at your local
college store or at our preferred online store **www.ichapters.com**

Credits appear on pages 757–760, which constitute an extension of this copyright page.

Printed in the United States of America
1 2 3 4 5 6 7 12 11 10 09

Chapter 20
Chicago Documentation Style 310
20a Using Chicago Style 310
20b Chicago-Style Manuscript Guidelines 321
20c Sample Chicago-Style Research Paper (Excerpts) 323

Chapter 21
CSE and Other Documentation Styles 330
21a Using CSE Style 330
21b CSE-Style Manuscript Guidelines 335
21c Sample CSE-Style Research Paper (Excerpts) 336
21d Using Other Documentation Styles 339

PART 6 Writing in the Disciplines 341

Chapter 22
Writing in the Humanities 342
22a Understanding Purpose, Audience, and Tone 342
22b Writing Assignments 343
22c Conventions of Style, Format, and Documentation 348
22d Avoiding Plagiarism 348
22e Using Visuals and Technology 348
22f Research Sources 349

Chapter 23
Writing a Literary Analysis 352
23a Reading Literature 352
23b Writing about Literature 353
23c Sample Literary Analysis (without Sources) 355
23d Sample Literary Analysis (with Sources) 359

Chapter 24
Writing a Literary Argument 366
24a Planning a Literary Argument 366
24b Supporting Your Literary Argument 368
24c Organizing a Literary Argument 371
24d Sample Literary Argument 372

Chapter 25
Writing in the Social Sciences 380
25a Understanding Purpose, Audience, and Tone 380
25b Writing Assignments 381
25c Conventions of Style, Format, and Documentation 388
25d Avoiding Plagiarism 388
25e Using Visuals and Technology 388
25f Research Sources 389

Chapter 26
Writing in the Natural and Applied Sciences 392
26a Understanding Purpose, Audience, and Tone 392
26b Writing Assignments 393
26c Conventions of Style, Format, and Documentation 397
26d Avoiding Plagiarism 398
26e Using Visuals and Technology 398
26f Research Sources 398

PART 7 Developing Strategies for Academic Success 401

Chapter 27
Ten Habits of Successful Students 402
27a Learn to Manage Your Time Effectively 402
27b Put Studying First 404
27c Be Sure You Understand School and Course Requirements 405
27d Be an Active Learner in the Classroom 407
27e Be an Active Learner Outside the Classroom 408
27f Take Advantage of College Services 409
27g Use the Library 410
27h Use Technology 411
27i Make Contacts 412
27j Be a Lifelong Learner 413

Chapter 28
Writing Essay Exams 415
28a Planning an Essay Exam Answer 416
28b Shaping an Essay Exam Answer 419
28c Writing and Revising an Essay Exam Answer 420
28d Writing Paragraph-Length Essay Exam Answers 426

Chapter 29
Writing for the Workplace 428
29a Writing Letters of Application 428
29b Designing Print Résumés 430
29c Designing Electronic Résumés 433
29d Writing Memos 438
29e Writing Emails and Sending Faxes 440

Chapter 30
Designing Effective Documents 442
30a Creating an Effective Visual Format 442
30b Using Headings 445
30c Constructing Lists 447
30d Using Visuals 449
30e Using Desktop Publishing 453

Chapter 31
Designing a Web Site 456
31a Planning Your Web Site 456
31b Creating Your Web Site 457
31c Selecting and Inserting Visuals 458
31d Planning Navigation 460
31e Linking Your Content 462
31f Editing and Proofreading Your Web Site 463
31g Posting Your Web Site 463

Chapter 32
Making Oral Presentations 464
32a Getting Started 464
32b Planning Your Speech 465
32c Preparing Your Notes 466
32d Preparing Visual Aids 467
32e Rehearsing Your Speech 470
32f Delivering Your Speech 470

PART 8 Sentence Style 473

Chapter 33
Building Simple Sentences 474
33a Constructing Simple Sentences 474
33b Identifying Phrases and Clauses 477
33c Expanding Simple Sentences 479

Chapter 34
Building Compound and Complex Sentences 488
34a Building Compound Sentences 488
34b Building Complex Sentences 491

Chapter 35
Writing Varied Sentences 494
35a Varying Sentence Length 494
35b Combining Choppy Simple Sentences 495
35c Breaking Up Strings of Compound Sentences 497
35d Varying Sentence Types 498
35e Varying Sentence Openings 500
35f Varying Standard Word Order 501

Chapter 36
Writing Emphatic Sentences 503
36a Conveying Emphasis through Word Order 503
36b Conveying Emphasis through Sentence Structure 506
36c Conveying Emphasis through Parallelism and Balance 509
36d Conveying Emphasis through Repetition 509
36e Conveying Emphasis through Active Voice 510

Chapter 37
Writing Concise Sentences 513
37a Eliminating Wordiness 513
37b Eliminating Unnecessary Repetition 516
37c Tightening Rambling Sentences 517

PART 9 Solving Common Sentence Problems 521

Chapter 38
Revising Sentence Fragments 522
38a Recognizing Sentence Fragments 522
38b Revising Dependent Clause Fragments 524
38c Revising Phrase Fragments 525
38d Revising Compounds 529
38e Using Fragments Intentionally 530

Chapter 39
Revising Run-ons 532
39a Recognizing Comma Splices and Fused Sentences 532
39b Revising with Periods 533
39c Revising with Semicolons 533
39d Revising with Coordinating Conjunctions 534
39e Revising with Subordinating Conjunctions or Relative Pronouns 534

Chapter 40
Revising Misplaced and Dangling Modifiers 537
40a Revising Misplaced Modifiers 537
40b Revising Intrusive Modifiers 541
40c Revising Dangling Modifiers 542

Chapter 41
Using Parallelism 544
41a Using Parallelism Effectively 544
41b Revising Faulty Parallelism 546

Chapter 42
Revising Awkward or Confusing Sentences 548
42a Revising Unwarranted Shifts 548
42b Revising Mixed Constructions 551
42c Revising Faulty Predication 552
42d Revising Incomplete or Illogical Comparisons 553

PART 10 Using Words Effectively 555

Chapter 43
Choosing Words 556
43a Choosing an Appropriate Level of Diction 556
43b Choosing the Right Word 559
43c Using Figures of Speech 561
43d Avoiding Inappropriate Language 563
43e Avoiding Offensive Language 566

Chapter 44
Using a Dictionary 570
44a Understanding a Dictionary Entry 570
44b Surveying Dictionaries 574

Chapter 45
Improving Spelling 575
45a Understanding Spelling and Pronunciation 575
45b Learning Spelling Rules 577
45c Developing Spelling Skills 581

PART 11 Understanding Grammar 583

Chapter 46
Using Parts of Speech 584
46a Using Nouns 584
46b Using Pronouns 584
46c Using Verbs 586
46d Using Adjectives 588
46e Using Adverbs 589
46f Using Prepositions 590
46g Using Conjunctions 591
46h Using Interjections 592

Chapter 47
Using Nouns and Pronouns 593
47a Understanding Case 593
47b Determining Pronoun Case in Special Situations 594
47c Revising Pronoun Reference Errors 596

Chapter 48
Using Verbs 600
48a Understanding Verb Forms 600
48b Understanding Tense 604
48c Understanding Mood 609
48d Understanding Voice 610

Chapter 49
Revising Agreement Errors 613
49a Making Subjects and Verbs Agree 613
49b Making Pronouns and Antecedents Agree 619

Chapter 50
Using Adjectives and Adverbs 623
50a Understanding Adjectives and Adverbs 623
50b Using Adjectives 623
50c Using Adverbs 624
50d Using Comparative and Superlative Forms 625
50e Avoiding Illogical Comparatives and Superlatives 627

PART 12 Understanding Punctuation and Mechanics 629

Chapter 51
Using End Punctuation 630
51a Using Periods 630
51b Using Question Marks 632
51c Using Exclamation Points 633

Chapter 52
Using Commas 634
52a Setting Off Independent Clauses 634
52b Setting Off Items in a Series 635
52c Setting Off Introductory Elements 637
52d Setting Off Nonessential Material 639
52e Using Commas in Other Conventional Contexts 643
52f Using Commas to Prevent Misreading 645
52g Editing Misused Commas 646

Chapter 53
Using Semicolons 649
53a Separating Independent Clauses 649
53b Separating Independent Clauses Introduced by Transitional Words and Phrases 651
53c Separating Items in a Series 652
53d Editing Misused Semicolons 654

Chapter 54
Using Apostrophes 656
54a Forming the Possessive Case 656
54b Indicating Omissions in Contractions 658
54c Forming Plurals 660
54d Editing Misused Apostrophes 661

Chapter 55
Using Quotation Marks 663
55a Setting Off Quoted Speech or Writing 663
55b Setting Off Long Prose Passages and Poetry 665
55c Setting Off Titles 667
55d Setting Off Words Used in Special Ways 668
55e Using Quotation Marks with Other Punctuation 668
55f Editing Misused Quotation Marks 669

Chapter 56
Using Other Punctuation Marks 672
56a Using Colons 672
56b Using Dashes 674
56c Using Parentheses 675
56d Using Brackets 677
56e Using Slashes 677
56f Using Ellipses 678

Chapter 57
Knowing When to Capitalize 681
57a Capitalizing the First Word of a Sentence 681
57b Capitalizing Proper Nouns 681
57c Capitalizing Important Words in Titles 685
57d Capitalizing the Pronoun *I*, the Interjection *O*, and Other Single Letters in Special Constructions 685
57e Capitalizing Salutations and Closings of Letters 686
57f Editing Misused Capitals 686

Chapter 58
Using Italics 688
58a Setting Off Titles and Names 688
58b Setting Off Foreign Words and Phrases 689
58c Setting Off Elements Spoken of as Themselves and Terms Being Defined 689
58d Using Italics for Emphasis 690

Chapter 59
Using Hyphens 691
59a Breaking a Word at the End of a Line 691
59b Dividing Compound Words 691

Chapter 60
Using Abbreviations 695
60a Abbreviating Titles 695
60b Abbreviating Organization Names and Technical Terms 695
60c Abbreviating Dates, Times of Day, and Temperatures 696
60d Editing Misused Abbreviations 697

Chapter 61
Using Numbers 700
61a Spelled-Out Numbers versus Numerals 700
61b Conventional Uses of Numerals 701

PART 13 Bilingual and ESL Writers 705

Chapter 62
Adjusting to the US Classroom 706
62a Understanding the Writing Process 706
62b Understanding English Language Basics 708
62c Learning to Edit Your Work 708

Chapter 63
Grammar and Style for ESL Writers 713
63a Using Verbs 713
63b Using Nouns 720
63c Using Pronouns 723
63d Using Adjectives and Adverbs 726
63e Using Prepositions 727
63f Understanding Word Order 730

Glossary of Usage 733

Glossary of Grammatical and Rhetorical Terms 743

Credits 757

Index 761

Contents

Note to Students xi
Note to Instructors xv

PART 1
Writing Essays 1

Chapter 1
Understanding Purpose, Audience, and Tone 2
1a Determining Your Purpose 2
1b Identifying Your Audience 9
1c Setting Your Tone 12

Chapter 2
Reading Texts 15
2a Previewing a Text 15
2b Highlighting a Text 16
2c Annotating a Text 16

Chapter 3
Reading Visuals 22
3a Interpreting a Visual 24
3b Previewing a Visual 25
3c Highlighting and Annotating a Visual 26

Chapter 4
Planning an Essay 29
4a Understanding the Writing Process 29
4b Computers and the Writing Process 30
4c Analyzing Your Assignment 31
4d Choosing and Narrowing a Topic 32
4e Finding Something to Say 34

Chapter 5
Using a Thesis to Shape Your Material 41
5a Understanding Thesis and Support 41
5b Developing a Thesis 42
5c Constructing an Informal Outline 46
5d Constructing a Formal Outline 47
5e Constructing a Storyboard 49

Chapter 6
Drafting and Revising 52
6a Writing a Rough Draft 52
6b Moving from Rough Draft to Final Draft 55
6c Using Specific Revision Strategies 58
6d Editing and Proofreading 68
6e Preparing a Final Draft 71

Chapter 7
Writing Paragraphs 78
7a Writing Unified Paragraphs 79
7b Writing Coherent Paragraphs 82
7c Writing Well-Developed Paragraphs 88
7d Patterns of Paragraph Development 90
7e Writing Special Kinds of Paragraphs 99

PART 2
Thinking Critically and Writing Arguments 105

Chapter 8
Thinking Critically 106
8a Distinguishing Fact from Opinion 106
8b Evaluating Supporting Evidence 108
8c Detecting Bias 109

iii

Chapter 9
Using Logic 113
9a Understanding Inductive Reasoning 113
9b Understanding Deductive Reasoning 115
9c Using Toulmin Logic 117
9d Recognizing Logical Fallacies 120

Chapter 10
Writing Argumentative Essays 125
10a Planning an Argumentative Essay 125
10b Using Evidence Effectively 129
10c Organizing an Argumentative Essay 132
10d Writing and Revising an Argumentative Essay 133

Chapter 11
Using Visuals to Support Your Arguments 142
11a Using Visuals 142
11b Evaluating Visuals 145

Chapter 12
Writing Electronic Arguments 149
12a Considering Audience and Purpose 149
12b Shaping Electronic Arguments 150
12c Writing and Revising Electronic Arguments 151

PART 3
Doing Research 153

Chapter 13
Writing a Research Paper 154
13a Moving from Assignment to Topic 155
13b Doing Exploratory Research and Formulating a Research Question 158
13c Assembling a Working Bibliography 159
13d Developing a Tentative Thesis 162
13e Doing Focused Research 163
13f Taking Notes 164
13g Fine-Tuning Your Thesis 169
13h Constructing an Outline 171
13i Writing a Rough Draft 173
13j Revising Your Drafts 176
13k Preparing a Final Draft 180

Chapter 14
Using and Evaluating Library Sources 181
14a Doing Exploratory Library Research 181
14b Doing Focused Library Research 187
14c Evaluating the Library's Print and Electronic Sources 193
14d Doing Research Outside the Library 196

Chapter 15
Using and Evaluating Internet Sources 198
15a Understanding the Internet 198
15b Using the World Wide Web for Research 199
15c Using Other Internet Tools 207
15d Evaluating Internet Sites 208

Chapter 16
Summarizing, Paraphrasing, Quoting, and Synthesizing Sources 213
16a Writing a Summary 213
16b Writing a Paraphrase 215
16c Quoting Sources 217
16d Integrating Source Material into Your Writing 219
16e Synthesizing Sources 223

Chapter 17
Avoiding Plagiarism 224
17a Defining Plagiarism 224

Contents v

17b Avoiding Unintentional Plagiarism 225
17c Revising to Eliminate Plagiarism 226

PART 4
Documenting Sources: MLA Style 233

Chapter 18
MLA Documentation Style 239
18a Using MLA Style 239
18b MLA-Style Manuscript Guidelines 264
18c Sample MLA-Style Research Paper 266

PART 5
Documenting Sources: APA and Other Styles 281

Chapter 19
APA Documentation Style 284
19a Using APA Style 284
19b APA-Style Manuscript Guidelines 294
19c Sample APA-Style Research Paper 297

Chapter 20
Chicago Documentation Style 310
20a Using Chicago Style 310
20b Chicago-Style Manuscript Guidelines 321
20c Sample Chicago-Style Research Paper (Excerpts) 323

Chapter 21
CSE and Other Documentation Styles 330
21a Using CSE Style 330
21b CSE-Style Manuscript Guidelines 335
21c Sample CSE-Style Research Paper (Excerpts) 336
21d Using Other Documentation Styles 339

PART 6
Writing in the Disciplines 341

Chapter 22
Writing in the Humanities 342
22a Understanding Purpose, Audience, and Tone 342
22b Writing Assignments 343
22c Conventions of Style, Format, and Documentation 348
22d Avoiding Plagiarism 348
22e Using Visuals and Technology 348
22f Research Sources 349

Chapter 23
Writing a Literary Analysis 352
23a Reading Literature 352
23b Writing about Literature 353
23c Sample Literary Analysis (without Sources) 355
23d Sample Literary Analysis (with Sources) 359

Chapter 24
Writing a Literary Argument 366
24a Planning a Literary Argument 366
24b Supporting Your Literary Argument 368
24c Organizing a Literary Argument 371
24d Sample Literary Argument 372

Chapter 25
Writing in the Social Sciences 380
25a Understanding Purpose, Audience, and Tone 380
25b Writing Assignments 381
25c Conventions of Style, Format, and Documentation 388
25d Avoiding Plagiarism 388
25e Using Visuals and Technology 388
25f Research Sources 389

Chapter 26
Writing in the Natural and Applied Sciences 392
26a Understanding Purpose, Audience, and Tone 392

Contents

- **26b** Writing Assignments 393
- **26c** Conventions of Style, Format, and Documentation 397
- **26d** Avoiding Plagiarism 398
- **26e** Using Visuals and Technology 398
- **26f** Research Sources 398

PART 7
Developing Strategies for Academic Success 401

Chapter 27
Ten Habits of Successful Students 402
- **27a** Learn to Manage Your Time Effectively 402
- **27b** Put Studying First 404
- **27c** Be Sure You Understand School and Course Requirements 405
- **27d** Be an Active Learner in the Classroom 407
- **27e** Be an Active Learner Outside the Classroom 408
- **27f** Take Advantage of College Services 409
- **27g** Use the Library 410
- **27h** Use Technology 411
- **27i** Make Contacts 412
- **27j** Be a Lifelong Learner 413

Chapter 28
Writing Essay Exams 415
- **28a** Planning an Essay Exam Answer 416
- **28b** Shaping an Essay Exam Answer 419
- **28c** Writing and Revising an Essay Exam Answer 420
- **28d** Writing Paragraph-Length Essay Exam Answers 426

Chapter 29
Writing for the Workplace 428
- **29a** Writing Letters of Application 428
- **29b** Designing Print Résumés 430
- **29c** Designing Electronic Résumés 433
- **29d** Writing Memos 438
- **29e** Writing Emails and Sending Faxes 440

Chapter 30
Designing Effective Documents 442
- **30a** Creating an Effective Visual Format 442
- **30b** Using Headings 445
- **30c** Constructing Lists 447
- **30d** Using Visuals 449
- **30e** Using Desktop Publishing 453

Chapter 31
Designing a Web Site 456
- **31a** Planning Your Web Site 456
- **31b** Creating Your Web Site 457
- **31c** Selecting and Inserting Visuals 458
- **31d** Planning Navigation 460
- **31e** Linking Your Content 462
- **31f** Editing and Proofreading Your Web Site 463
- **31g** Posting Your Web Site 463

Chapter 32
Making Oral Presentations 464
- **32a** Getting Started 464
- **32b** Planning Your Speech 465
- **32c** Preparing Your Notes 466
- **32d** Preparing Visual Aids 467
- **32e** Rehearsing Your Speech 470
- **32f** Delivering Your Speech 470

PART 8
Sentence Style 473

Chapter 33
Building Simple Sentences 474
- **33a** Constructing Simple Sentences 474
- **33b** Identifying Phrases and Clauses 477
- **33c** Expanding Simple Sentences 479

Contents **vii**

Chapter 34
Building Compound and Complex Sentences 488
34a Building Compound Sentences 488
34b Building Complex Sentences 491

Chapter 35
Writing Varied Sentences 494
35a Varying Sentence Length 494
35b Combining Choppy Simple Sentences 495
35c Breaking Up Strings of Compound Sentences 497
35d Varying Sentence Types 498
35e Varying Sentence Openings 500
35f Varying Standard Word Order 501

Chapter 36
Writing Emphatic Sentences 503
36a Conveying Emphasis through Word Order 503
36b Conveying Emphasis through Sentence Structure 506
36c Conveying Emphasis through Parallelism and Balance 509
36d Conveying Emphasis through Repetition 509
36e Conveying Emphasis through Active Voice 510

Chapter 37
Writing Concise Sentences 513
37a Eliminating Wordiness 513
37b Eliminating Unnecessary Repetition 516
37c Tightening Rambling Sentences 517

PART 9
Solving Common Sentence Problems **521**

Chapter 38
Revising Sentence Fragments 522
38a Recognizing Sentence Fragments 522
38b Revising Dependent Clause Fragments 524
38c Revising Phrase Fragments 525
38d Revising Compounds 529
38e Using Fragments Intentionally 530

Chapter 39
Revising Run-ons 532
39a Recognizing Comma Splices and Fused Sentences 532
39b Revising with Periods 533
39c Revising with Semicolons 533
39d Revising with Coordinating Conjunctions 534
39e Revising with Subordinating Conjunctions or Relative Pronouns 534

Chapter 40
Revising Misplaced and Dangling Modifiers 537
40a Revising Misplaced Modifiers 537
40b Revising Intrusive Modifiers 541
40c Revising Dangling Modifiers 542

Chapter 41
Using Parallelism 544
41a Using Parallelism Effectively 544
41b Revising Faulty Parallelism 546

Chapter 42
Revising Awkward or Confusing Sentences 548
42a Revising Unwarranted Shifts 548
42b Revising Mixed Constructions 551
42c Revising Faulty Predication 552
42d Revising Incomplete or Illogical Comparisons 553

PART 10
Using Words Effectively **555**

Chapter 43
Choosing Words 556
43a Choosing an Appropriate Level of Diction 556
43b Choosing the Right Word 559

43c Using Figures of Speech 561
43d Avoiding Inappropriate Language 563
43e Avoiding Offensive Language 566

Chapter 44
Using a Dictionary 570
44a Understanding a Dictionary Entry 570
44b Surveying Dictionaries 574

Chapter 45
Improving Spelling 575
45a Understanding Spelling and Pronunciation 575
45b Learning Spelling Rules 577
45c Developing Spelling Skills 581

PART 11
Understanding Grammar 583

Chapter 46
Using Parts of Speech 584
46a Using Nouns 584
46b Using Pronouns 584
46c Using Verbs 586
46d Using Adjectives 588
46e Using Adverbs 589
46f Using Prepositions 590
46g Using Conjunctions 591
46h Using Interjections 592

Chapter 47
Using Nouns and Pronouns 593
47a Understanding Case 593
47b Determining Pronoun Case in Special Situations 594
47c Revising Pronoun Reference Errors 596

Chapter 48
Using Verbs 600
48a Understanding Verb Forms 600
48b Understanding Tense 604
48c Understanding Mood 609
48d Understanding Voice 610

Chapter 49
Revising Agreement Errors 613
49a Making Subjects and Verbs Agree 613
49b Making Pronouns and Antecedents Agree 619

Chapter 50
Using Adjectives and Adverbs 623
50a Understanding Adjectives and Adverbs 623
50b Using Adjectives 623
50c Using Adverbs 624
50d Using Comparative and Superlative Forms 625
50e Avoiding Illogical Comparatives and Superlatives 627

PART 12
Understanding Punctuation and Mechanics 629

Chapter 51
Using End Punctuation 630
51a Using Periods 630
51b Using Question Marks 632
51c Using Exclamation Points 633

Chapter 52
Using Commas 634
52a Setting Off Independent Clauses 634
52b Setting Off Items in a Series 635
52c Setting Off Introductory Elements 637
52d Setting Off Nonessential Material 639
52e Using Commas in Other Conventional Contexts 643
52f Using Commas to Prevent Misreading 645
52g Editing Misused Commas 646

Chapter 53
Using Semicolons 649
53a Separating Independent Clauses 649

53b Separating Independent Clauses Introduced by Transitional Words and Phrases 651
53c Separating Items in a Series 652
53d Editing Misused Semicolons 654

Chapter 54
Using Apostrophes 656
54a Forming the Possessive Case 656
54b Indicating Omissions in Contractions 658
54c Forming Plurals 660
54d Editing Misused Apostrophes 661

Chapter 55
Using Quotation Marks 663
55a Setting Off Quoted Speech or Writing 663
55b Setting Off Long Prose Passages and Poetry 665
55c Setting Off Titles 667
55d Setting Off Words Used in Special Ways 668
55e Using Quotation Marks with Other Punctuation 668
55f Editing Misused Quotation Marks 669

Chapter 56
Using Other Punctuation Marks 672
56a Using Colons 672
56b Using Dashes 674
56c Using Parentheses 675
56d Using Brackets 677
56e Using Slashes 677
56f Using Ellipses 678

Chapter 57
Knowing When to Capitalize 681
57a Capitalizing the First Word of a Sentence 681
57b Capitalizing Proper Nouns 681
57c Capitalizing Important Words in Titles 685
57d Capitalizing the Pronoun *I*, the Interjection *O*, and Other Single Letters in Special Constructions 685
57e Capitalizing Salutations and Closings of Letters 686
57f Editing Misused Capitals 686

Chapter 58
Using Italics 688
58a Setting Off Titles and Names 688
58b Setting Off Foreign Words and Phrases 689
58c Setting Off Elements Spoken of as Themselves and Terms Being Defined 689
58d Using Italics for Emphasis 690

Chapter 59
Using Hyphens 691
59a Breaking a Word at the End of a Line 691
59b Dividing Compound Words 691

Chapter 60
Using Abbreviations 695
60a Abbreviating Titles 695
60b Abbreviating Organization Names and Technical Terms 695
60c Abbreviating Dates, Times of Day, and Temperatures 696
60d Editing Misused Abbreviations 697

Chapter 61
Using Numbers 700
61a Spelled-Out Numbers versus Numerals 700
61b Conventional Uses of Numerals 701

PART 13
Bilingual and ESL Writers 705

Chapter 62
Adjusting to the US Classroom 706
62a Understanding the Writing Process 706
62b Understanding English Language Basics 708
62c Learning to Edit Your Work 708

Chapter 63
Grammar and Style for ESL Writers 713
- **63a** Using Verbs 713
- **63b** Using Nouns 720
- **63c** Using Pronouns 723
- **63d** Using Adjectives and Adverbs 726
- **63e** Using Prepositions 727
- **63f** Understanding Word Order 730

Glossary of Usage 733

Glossary of Grammatical and Rhetorical Terms 743

Credits 757

Index 761

Note to Students

We would like to introduce you to the eighth edition of *The Wadsworth Handbook*, a comprehensive writing guide for college students. Our goal in this text remains the same as it was in the first edition: to help you produce sound academic writing. To this end, we provide practical support for the writing and research projects that will be important to you in your academic careers and in your professional careers as well.

The Wadsworth Handbook, which comes out of our many years of hands-on experience as teachers of writing, offers full coverage of all the topics we see as essential for writers: the writing process, critical thinking, argumentation, the research process, common sentence errors, grammar and style, punctuation and mechanics, and English for speakers of other languages. We also explain specific academic success strategies as well as conventions of writing in various disciplines. In addition, the book includes the most up-to-date information on writing in an electronic environment; visual rhetoric; MLA, APA, Chicago, and CSE documentation; writing in the disciplines; document design; and Web page design. Throughout the text, practice exercises are provided to reinforce writing skills.

As writers, you already know that to express your ideas clearly, you need to understand the basic principles of grammar, mechanics, and style. In addition, however, writers in the digital age also need to know how computers can help them communicate their ideas to others more effectively, whether they are writing for an academic audience or on the job for a business audience. In fact, in all the writing you do—regardless of your purpose or audience—technology plays an ever-increasing role in helping you to convey your ideas. For this reason, it is very important that you have a clear understanding of the relationship between technology and writing.

We revised *The Wadsworth Handbook* with this idea in mind. The result is a book that you can depend on to give you sound, sensible advice about writing as well as about the electronic tools that define the twenty-first-century writing environment. We hope you will find *The Wadsworth Handbook* a resource that you can turn to again and again as you write in college and beyond.

Laurie Kirszner
Steve Mandell
March 2007

Features of This Book

- **Frequently Asked Questions (FAQs)** appear at the beginning of each chapter. A marginal FAQ icon appears in the chapter beside each answer.

- **Computer tips** highlight specific ways in which technology can help you throughout the writing, revising, and editing processes. Each computer tip includes the URL for the book's companion Web site, <http://cengage.com/english/kirsznermandell>, which contains a wealth of online resources.

- **Grammar checker boxes** illustrating sample errors show the advantages and disadvantages of using a grammar checker.

- **Numerous checklists** summarize key information that you can quickly access as needed.

- **Close-up boxes** provide an in-depth look at some of the more perplexing writing-related issues you will encounter.

- **Parts 4–5** include the most up-to-date documentation and format guidelines from the Modern Language Association, the American Psychological Association, the University of Chicago Press, and the Council of Science Editors.

- **Newly designed documentation directories** make it easy for you to locate models for various kinds of sources, including those found in online databases such as *Academic Search Premier* and *LexisNexis*. In addition, annotated diagrams of sample works-cited entries clearly illustrate the elements of proper documentation.

- **Marginal cross-references** throughout the book allow you to flip directly to other sections that treat topics in more detail.

- **Marginal ESL cross-references** throughout the book direct you to sections of Part 13, "Bilingual and ESL Writers," where concepts are presented as they apply specifically to second-language writers.

- **ESL tips** are woven throughout the text to explain concepts in relation to the unique experiences of bilingual students.

- **Getting Help from the Dictionary boxes** appear throughout Chapter 63, "Grammar and Style for ESL Writers," offering bilingual students practical advice for using a dictionary effectively.

- **Numerous exercises** throughout the text allow you to practice at each stage of the writing, revising, and editing processes.

- **Numerous annotated sample documents**, created by both student and professional writers, illustrate the principles of effective print and electronic document design.

- **An extensive writing-centered treatment of grammar, punctuation, and mechanics**, including hand-edited examples, explains and illustrates specific strategies for improving your writing.

Note to Instructors

In this eighth edition of *The Wadsworth Handbook*, our goal is to show students how they can become more effective and confident writers. To this end, the first half of the book focuses on writing and research as well as strategies for academic success. Here we also include material to help students create and interpret visual texts as well as a chapter that guides students through the process of writing effective and compelling literary arguments. The second half of *The Wadsworth Handbook*, which deals with grammar, punctuation, and mechanics, has also been reworked to reflect our focus on student writing. Grammar checker boxes, which include sample screen shots, appear in almost every chapter, acknowledging the role computer technology plays in the revising and editing processes. Finally, we illustrate how the rules of grammar, punctuation, and mechanics operate in real-world contexts—for example, in advertisements, emails, and text messages.

Despite our focus on the electronic tools that students have at their disposal, we have not forgotten the fundamental reason students consult a handbook: to become more effective, more confident writers. Accordingly, in addition to adding checklists and revising close-up boxes, we have strengthened basic discussions of the writing process, research, grammar, style, and mechanics. For example, we have streamlined our coverage of writing essays and research papers, and we have added more examples of electronic sources and redesigned the documentation directories to make them easier to navigate. Finally, we have expanded our treatment of English for speakers of other languages in Part 13, "Bilingual and ESL Writers," by adding a new Chapter 62, "Adjusting to the US Classroom."

Although *The Wadsworth Handbook*, Eighth Edition, is grounded in the most up-to-date research in composition and rhetoric, it is also informed by our many years of classroom teaching. We began our careers as teachers of composition as graduate students in Temple University's basic writing program; years later, we both still teach first-year students. We were colleagues before we became textbook writers, and our struggle to create useful instructional materials for the students we were teaching was our first collaboration. Today, we continue to search for what works for our students—for what they will need to succeed in college and on the job. Our goal with this new edition of *The Wadsworth Handbook* is to define the challenges that real writers will encounter in the digital writing environment of the twenty-first century and to provide students with clear choices and pragmatic advice. The result, we hope, is a book that both students and instructors will trust—and one that they will use with ease and, perhaps, even with pleasure.

New to the Eighth Edition

- An expanded Part 2, "Thinking Critically and Writing Arguments," includes even more coverage of using logic, using visuals to support arguments, and writing electronic arguments.

- Newly designed documentation directories make it much easier for students to locate models for print and electronic sources—including online sources from library subscription services such as InfoTrac® and Lexis-Nexis™.

- A new Chapter 24, "Writing a Literary Argument," walks students through the steps of planning, organizing, and writing an effective literary argument.

- A new Chapter 62, "Adjusting to the US Classroom," provides strategies for bilingual and ESL writers to understand the writing process, English language basics, and the value of editing their work.

- New grammar checker boxes illustrating sample errors show the advantages and limitations of using a grammar checker.

- A streamlined new design makes the book easier to navigate.

Acknowledgments

We thank the following reviewers for their advice, which helped us develop the eighth edition:

Joan K. Anderson, *Southeastern Louisiana University*
Clay Armstrong, *East Mississippi Community College*
Nancy G. Barron, *Northern Arizona University*
Carole O. Beasley, *East Mississippi Community College*
Linda Boyd, *Houston Baptist University*
Wayne Christensen, *Florida Memorial University*

Vicki Covington, *Isothermal Community College*
Nate Gordon, *Kishwaukee College*
Barbara Hanna, *East Mississippi Community College*
Jonathan B. Himes, *John Brown University*
Steven H. Jobe, *Hanover College*
Bill Koch, *University of Northern Iowa*
Kay Kolb, *University of Texas, Permian Basin*
Kathleen Lazarus, *Daytona Beach Community College*
Jill LeRoy-Frazier, *Milligan College*
Mary Ann Macartney, *Rosemont College*
Rachel A. Mournian, *Point Loma Nazarene University*
Nancy Parker, *LeTourneau University*
Tammy Parkes, *East Mississippi Community College*
Alix Paschkowiak, *Westfield State College*
Barbara Peterson, *Isothermal Community College*
Lynn Pifer, *Mansfield University of Pennsylvania*
Norman Prinsky, *Augusta State University*
Diane Putzel, *University of Maryland, Baltimore County*
Gerald J. Pyle Jr., *Paul D. Camp Community College*
Bernard Quetchenbach, *Florida Southern College*
Mark Sandona, *Hood College*
Steve Sansom, *North Harris College*
Joan Schell, *Pennsylvania College of Technology*
James T. Simmons, *Mount Marty College*
Ron Smith, *University of North Alabama*
Nelson Stone, *Mount Marty College*
Jamie Sullivan, *Mount Marty College*
Michael Travers, *Southeastern Baptist Theological Seminary*
Natasha Whitton, *Southeastern Louisiana University*
Diana Yeager, *Hillsborough Community College*
Holly W. Young, *Heritage Christian University*
Gary Zacharias, *Palomar College*

 Any revision as extensive as this one depends on the combined talents and expertise of many people, such as those who generously contributed student essays to this book: Bryan Burke, Washington State University; Fiona Glade, Washington State University; Melinda Lipani, The University of Texas at Austin; Roger Rouland, The University of Texas at Austin; and Jessie Swigger, The University of Texas at Austin.

 We are particularly grateful to the panel of expert advisors who worked with us to develop our treatment of specific topics and features. We would like to thank Patricia Arnott, University of Delaware, for her cogent advice about library research; Bill Bolin, Texas A&M University, Commerce, for his work on Toulmin logic; Kristine Blair

Note to Instructors

and Cheryl Hoy, Bowling Green State University, for their insights on technology and visual rhetoric; and Melinda Reichelt, The University of Toledo, for her work on the ESL section.

At Wadsworth, we thank Michael Rosenberg, who provided the guidance and support that made this revision possible. He assembled an editorial team whose commitment, enthusiasm, and personal involvement made this revision a pleasure to work on, and for this—as well as for his friendship—we are very grateful.

The true star of our editorial team is Karen Smith, who is, without a doubt, the best development editor we have ever worked with. Insightful, intelligent, well organized, astute, and unflappable, the awe-inspiring Karen remained in control in all situations—no matter how difficult. We predict great things for her.

Also at Wadsworth, we would like to thank Lyn Uhl, Publisher; Star MacKenzie Burruto, Senior Acquisitions Editor; Elliot F. Sanchez, Editorial Assistant; Lianne Ames, Senior Content Product Manager; Sheri Blaney, Senior Permissions Account Manager; Mandee Eckersley, Marketing Manager; and Mary Beth Hennebury, Senior Print Buyer. We also very much appreciate Brian Salisbury's eye-catching cover design.

At Nesbitt Graphics, we remain very grateful to Susan McIntyre, our outstanding Project Manager; Jerilyn Bockorick, who created the attractive interior design; and the rest of the team, all of whom worked hard and did their usual great job.

Once again, we would like to thank our families—Mark, Adam, and Rebecca Kirszner and Demi, David, and Sarah Mandell—the people we care about the most. Finally, we would like to thank each other for making this book a collaboration in the truest sense.

Laurie Kirszner
Steve Mandell
February 2007

PART 1

Writing Essays

1 Understanding Purpose, Audience, and Tone 2
- 1a Determining Your Purpose 2
- 1b Identifying Your Audience 9
- 1c Setting Your Tone 12

2 Reading Texts 15
- 2a Previewing a Text 15
- 2b Highlighting a Text 16
- 2c Annotating a Text 16

3 Reading Visuals 22
- 3a Interpreting a Visual 24
- 3b Previewing a Visual 25
- 3c Highlighting and Annotating a Visual 26

4 Planning an Essay 29
- 4a Understanding the Writing Process 29
- 4b Computers and the Writing Process 30
- 4c Analyzing Your Assignment 31
- 4d Choosing and Narrowing a Topic 32
- 4e Finding Something to Say 34

5 Using a Thesis to Shape Your Material 41
- 5a Understanding Thesis and Support 41
- 5b Developing a Thesis 42
- 5c Constructing an Informal Outline 46
- 5d Constructing a Formal Outline 47
- 5e Constructing a Storyboard 49

6 Drafting and Revising 52
- 6a Writing a Rough Draft 52
- 6b Moving from Rough Draft to Final Draft 55
- 6c Using Specific Revision Strategies 58
- 6d Editing and Proofreading 68
- 6e Preparing a Final Draft 71

7 Writing Paragraphs 78
- 7a Writing Unified Paragraphs 79
- 7b Writing Coherent Paragraphs 82
- 7c Writing Well-Developed Paragraphs 88
- 7d Patterns of Paragraph Development 90
- 7e Writing Special Kinds of Paragraphs 99

1

Understanding Purpose, Audience, and Tone

❓ FAQs

Exactly why am I writing? (p. 2)
Who is my audience? (p. 9)
What does my instructor expect? (p. 9)
What kind of tone should I use? (p. 12)

Everyone who sets out to write confronts a series of choices. In the writing you do in school, on the job, and in your personal life, your understanding of purpose and audience is essential, influencing the choices you make about content, emphasis, organization, style, and tone.

Every written text you create addresses a particular audience and sets out to achieve one or more specific purposes.

See Ch. 3, 30d

NOTE: Like written texts, **visual texts**—fine art, charts and graphs, photographs, maps, advertisements, and so on—are also created with specific purposes and audiences in mind.

1a Determining Your Purpose

In simple terms, your **purpose** for writing is what you want to accomplish. For instance, your purpose may be to **reflect,** to express private feelings, as in the introspective or meditative writing that appears in personal journals, diaries, and memoirs. Or, your purpose may be to **inform,** to convey factual information as accurately and as logically as possible, as in the informational or expository writing that appears in reports, news articles, encyclopedias, and textbooks. At other times, your purpose may be to **persuade,** to convince your readers, as in advertising, proposals, editorials, and some business communications. Finally, your purpose may be to **evaluate,** to make a judgment about something, as in a recommendation report or a comparative analysis.

1 Writing to Reflect

In diaries and journals, writers explore ideas and feelings to make sense of their experiences; in autobiographical memoirs and in personal correspondence, they communicate their emotions and reactions to others.

> At the age of five, six, well past the time when most other children no longer easily notice the difference between sounds uttered at home and words spoken in public, I had a different experience. I lived in a world magically compounded of sounds. I remained a child longer than most; I lingered too long, poised at the edge of language—often frightened by the sounds of *los gringos*, delighted by the sounds of Spanish at home. I shared with my family a language that was startlingly different from that used in the great city around us. (Richard Rodriguez, *Aria: A Memoir of a Bilingual Childhood*)

2 Writing to Inform

In newspaper articles, writers report information, communicating factual details to readers; in reference books, instruction manuals, textbooks, and the like (as well as in catalogs, cookbooks, and government-sponsored Web sites), writers provide definitions and explain concepts or processes, trying to help readers see relationships and understand ideas.

> Most tarantulas live in the tropics, but several species occur in the temperate zone and a few are common in the southern U.S. Some varieties are large and have powerful fangs with which they can inflict a deep wound. These formidable-looking spiders do not, however, attack man; you can hold one in your hand, if you are gentle, without being bitten. Their bite is dangerous only to insects and small mammals such as mice; for man it is no worse than a hornet's sting. (Alexander Petrunkevitch, "The Spider and the Wasp")

3 Writing to Persuade

In proposals and editorials, as well as in advertising, writers try to convince readers to accept their positions on various issues.

> Testing and contact tracing may lead to a person's being deprived of a job, health insurance, housing and privacy, many civil libertarians fear. These are valid and grave concerns. But we can find ways to protect civil rights without sacrificing public health. A major AIDS-prevention campaign ought to be accompanied by intensive public education about the ways the illness is *not* transmitted, by additional safeguards on data banks and by greater penalties for those who abuse HIV victims. It may be harsh to say, but the fact that an individual may suffer as a result of doing what is right does not make doing so less of an imperative. (Amitai Etzioni, "HIV Sufferers Have a Responsibility")

4 Writing to Evaluate

In reviews of books, films, or performances and in reports, critiques, and program evaluations, writers assess the validity, accuracy, and quality of information, ideas, techniques, products, procedures, or services, perhaps assessing the relative merits of two or more things.

> ★★★★★ **One of Grisham's Best**, April 29, 2003
>
> Reviewer: **CHARLES H. PETERSON** from METAIRIE, LOUISIANA, United States
>
> Grisham is not going to win any prizes for literature, but when he tries, he can sure win a prize for page turners. This one was better thought out than most of his recent efforts. He clearly knew how he was going to end it before he started writing, which is not always the case with Grisham. While there may be literary flaws in his character development, the book proceeds at a lively and generally logical pace. It also sheds some light on the problems associated with the "class action" mentality in our legal system these days.
>
> It is what it is, and it is an excellent read. (Amazon.com customer review of John Grisham's *The King of Torts*)

CLOSE-UP

PURPOSE AND CONTENT

Your purpose for writing determines the material you choose and the way you organize and express your ideas.

- A memoir *reflecting* on the negative aspects of summer camp might focus on mosquitoes, poison ivy, homesickness, institutional food, and so on.
- A magazine article about summer camps could *inform*, presenting facts and statistics to show how camping has changed over the years.
- An advertising brochure designed to recruit potential campers could *persuade*, enumerating the benefits of the camping experience.
- A nonprofit camping association's Web site could *evaluate* various camps, assessing facilities, costs, staff-to-camper ratios, and activities in order to assist parents in choosing a camp.

Although writers write to reflect, to inform, to persuade, and to evaluate, these purposes are certainly not mutually exclusive, and writers may have other purposes as well. And, of course, in any piece of writing a writer may have a primary aim and one or more secondary purposes. In fact, a writer may even have different purposes in different sections—or different drafts—of a single document.

Determining Your Purpose ▪ **purp** **1a**

CHECKLIST

DETERMINING YOUR PURPOSE

Is your purpose to . . .
- ☐ reflect?
- ☐ inform?
- ☐ persuade?
- ☐ evaluate?
- ☐ explain?
- ☐ amuse or entertain?
- ☐ discover?
- ☐ analyze?
- ☐ debunk?
- ☐ draw comparisons?
- ☐ make an analogy?
- ☐ define?
- ☐ criticize?
- ☐ motivate?
- ☐ satirize?
- ☐ speculate?
- ☐ warn?
- ☐ reassure?
- ☐ take a stand?
- ☐ identify problems?
- ☐ suggest solutions?
- ☐ identify causes?
- ☐ predict effects?
- ☐ reflect?
- ☐ interpret?
- ☐ instruct?
- ☐ inspire?

▪ EXERCISE 1

Read the following excerpts carefully. Try to put yourself in each writer's position, considering the purpose or purposes he or she had in mind when writing. For what purpose or purposes do you think each passage was written? What makes you think so?

1. Of course, short people have been looked down upon for years. In the matter of language, for example . . . one does not wish to be found short-tempered, short-winded or shortsighted. One does not wish to be left with the short end, caught short-handed or given short shrift. Shortages, short circuits and shortfalls are universally deplored. On the other hand, one takes pride in filling a tall order, gapes at the tall ships, admires a tall tale and—out here in the Wild West—sits tall in the saddle. Although brevity is the soul of wit and one strives to make a long story short, this quality is not equally appreciated when manifested in human form. Just as we habitually use the masculine gender to denote all people, we use tallness to measure height. Thus there are those who say they are "4 feet tall" when they are clearly 4 feet short. (Beth Luey, "Short Shrift," *Newsweek*)
2. Radio began with the transatlantic "wireless" communication of Guglielmo Marconi (1874–1937) in 1901 and the development of the vacuum tube in 1904, which permitted the transmission of speech and music. But it was only in 1920 that the first major broadcasts of special events were made in Great Britain and the

United States. Lord Northcliffe, who had pioneered in journalism with the inexpensive, mass-circulation *Daily Mail*, sponsored a broadcast of "only one artist . . . the world's very best, the soprano Nellie Melba." Singing from London in English, Italian and French, Melba was heard simultaneously all over Europe on June 16, 1920. This historic event captured the public's imagination. The meteoric career of radio was launched. (McKay, Hill, Buckler, *A History of Western Society*, Vol. II)

■ **EXERCISE 2**

The two student paragraphs that follow treat the same general subject, but their purposes are different. What do you see as the primary purpose of each paragraph? What other purposes might each writer have had?

1. Answer to an essay examination question: "Identify the Boston Massacre."

    The Boston Massacre refers to a 1770 confrontation between British soldiers and a crowd of colonists. Encouraged by Samuel Adams, the citizens had become more and more upset over issues like the British government's stationing troops and customs commissioners in Boston. When angry colonists attacked a customhouse sentry on March 5, 1770, a fight broke out. Soldiers fired into the crowd, and five civilians were killed. Although the soldiers were found guilty only of manslaughter and given only a token punishment, Samuel Adams's propaganda created the idea of a "massacre" in the minds of many Americans.

2. From "The Ohio Massacre: 1770 Revisited" (student essay):

    In two incidents that occurred exactly two hundred years apart, civilian demonstrators were shot and killed by armed troops. Although civilians were certainly inciting the British troops, starting scuffles and even brawls, these actions should not have led the Redcoats to fire blindly into the crowd. Similarly, the Ohio National Guard should not have allowed themselves to be provoked by students who were calling names, shoving, or throwing objects, and Governor Rhodes should not have authorized the troops to fire their weapons. The deaths—five civilians in Boston, Massachusetts, in 1770, and four students in Kent, Ohio, in 1970—were all unnecessary.

■ **EXERCISE 3**

The primary purpose of the following article from the *New York Times* is to present information. Suppose you were using the information in an orientation booklet aimed at students entering your school, and your purpose was to persuade students of the importance of maintaining a good credit rating. How would you change the original article to help you achieve this purpose? Would you reorder any details? Would you add or delete anything?

What Makes a Credit Score Rise or Fall?
BY JENNIFER BAYOT

Your financial decisions can affect your credit score in surprising ways. Two credit-scoring simulators can help consumers understand the potential impact.

The Fair Isaac Corporation, which puts out the industry-standard FICO scores, offers the myFICO simulator. A consumer with a score of 707 (considered good) and three credit cards would be likely to add or lose points from his score by making various financial moves. Following are some examples:

- By making timely payments on all his accounts over the next month or by paying off a third of the balance on his cards, he could add as many as 20 points.
- By failing to make this month's payments on his loans, he could lose 75 to 125 points.
- By using all of the credit available on his three credit cards, he could lose 20 to 70 points.
- By getting a fourth card, depending on the status of his other debts, he could add or lose up to 10 points.
- By consolidating his credit card debt into a new card, also depending on other debts, he could add or lose 15 points.

The other simulator, the What-If, comes from CreditXpert, which designs credit management tools and puts out its own, similar credit score. A consumer with a score of 727 points (also considered good) would be likely to have her score change in the following ways:

- Every time she simply applied for a loan, whether a credit card, home mortgage or auto loan, she would lose five points. (An active appetite for credit, credit experts note, is considered a bad sign. For one thing, taking on new loans may make borrowers less likely to repay their current debts.)
- By getting a mortgage, she would lose two points.
- By getting an auto loan or a new credit card (assuming that she already has several cards) she would lose three points.
- If her new credit card had a credit limit of $20,000 or more, she would lose four points, instead of three. (For every $10,000 added to the limit, the score drops a point.)
- By simultaneously getting a new mortgage, auto loan and credit card, she would lose seven or eight points.

■ EXERCISE 4

Look closely at the visuals reproduced in Figures 1.1, 1.2, and 1.3, and consider for what purpose or purposes each might have been created. (You can consult the checklist on page 5 to help you identify the purpose or purposes that best apply.)

8 1a purp ■ Understanding Purpose, Audience, and Tone

FIGURE 1.1 Billboard for United Way of America.

FIGURE 1.2 New Orleans refugees after Hurricane Katrina, 2005.

FIGURE 1.3 Magazine ad for Birds Eye Foods.

1b Identifying Your Audience

When you are in the early stages of a writing project, staring at an empty computer screen or a blank sheet of paper, it is easy to forget that what you write will have an audience. But except for diaries and private journals, you always write for an **audience,** a particular reader or group of readers. In this sense, writing is a public rather than a private activity.

1 Writing for an Audience

In our increasingly global society, we all need to communicate with diverse audiences. Even in your own daily life, at different times, in different roles, you will address a variety of audiences:

- **In your personal life,** you may send notes, emails, or text messages to friends and family.
- **As a citizen,** consumer, or member of a community, civic, political, or religious group, you may respond to pressing social, economic, or political issues by writing letters or emails to newspapers, public officials, or representatives of special interest groups.
- **As an employee,** you may write letters, memos, and reports to your superiors, to staff members you supervise, or to coworkers; you may also be called on to address customers or critics, board members or stockholders, funding agencies or the general public.
- **As a student,** you write essays, reports, and other papers for your instructors, and you may also participate in **peer review,** writing evaluations of classmates' essays and writing responses to their comments about your own work.

As you write, you shape your writing in terms of what you believe your audience needs and expects. Your assessment of your readers' interests, educational level, biases, and expectations determines not only the information you include, but also what you emphasize and how you arrange your material.

See 8c

2 The College Writer's Audience

Writing for Your Instructor. As a student, you usually write for an audience of one: the instructor who assigns the paper. Instructors want to know what you know and whether you can express what you know clearly and accurately. They assign written work to encourage you to think critically, so the way you organize and express your ideas can be as important as the ideas themselves.

See Ch. 8

As a group, instructors have certain expectations. Because they are trained as careful readers and critics, your instructors expect accurate information, standard grammar and correct spelling, logically presented ideas, and a reasonable degree of stylistic fluency. They also expect you to define your terms and to support your generalizations with specific examples. Finally, every instructor expects you to draw your own conclusions and to provide full and accurate **documentation** for ideas that are not your own.

See Pts. 4–5

If you are writing in an instructor's academic field, you can omit long overviews and basic definitions. Remember, however, that outside their areas of expertise, most instructors are simply general readers. If you think you may know more about a subject than your instructor does, be sure to provide background and to supply the definitions, examples, and analogies that will make your ideas clear.

> **ESL TIP**
>
> If you did not attend school in the US, you may have trouble understanding your instructor's expectations. You may also have difficulty determining how much your instructor knows about a specific topic, especially if that topic relates to your own cultural background, native language, or home country. In these situations, it is usually a good idea to ask your instructor for advice.

See 6c2

Writing for Other Students. Before you submit a paper to an instructor, you may have an opportunity to participate in **peer review**, sharing your work with your fellow students and responding in writing to their work. Before you begin, you need to see your classmates as an audience whose needs you must take into account.

- **Writing Drafts** If you know that other students will read a draft of your paper, you need to consider how they might react to your ideas. For example, are they likely to disagree with you? To be shocked or offended by your paper's language or content? To be confused, or even mystified, by any of your references? Even if your readers are your own age, you cannot assume they share your values, political opinions, or cultural frame of reference. It is therefore very important that you maintain an appropriate tone and use moderate language in your paper and that you be prepared to explain any historical, geographical, or cultural references that might be unfamiliar to your audience.

- **Writing Comments** When you respond in writing to another student's paper, you need to take into account how your audience will react to your comments. Here too, your **tone** is important:

See 1c

you want to be as encouraging (and as polite) as possible. In addition, keep in mind that your purpose is not to show how clever you are, but to offer constructive comments that can help your classmate write a stronger essay.

> ### CHECKLIST
>
> **AUDIENCE CONCERNS FOR PEER-REVIEW PARTICIPANTS**
>
> To get the most out of a peer-review session, keep the following guidelines in mind:
>
> ☐ **Know your audience.** To be sure you understand what the student writer needs and expects from your comments, read the paper several times before you begin writing your response.
>
> ☐ **Focus on the big picture.** Don't get bogged down by minor problems with punctuation or mechanics or become distracted by a paper's proofreading errors.
>
> ☐ **Look for a positive feature.** Zero in on what you think is the paper's greatest strength.
>
> ☐ **Be positive throughout.** Try to avoid words like *weak*, *poor*, and *bad*; instead, try using a compliment before delivering the "bad news": "Paragraph 2 is very well developed; can you add this kind of support in paragraph 4?"
>
> ☐ **Show respect.** It is perfectly acceptable to tell a student that something is confusing or inaccurate, but don't go on the attack.
>
> ☐ **Be specific.** Avoid generalizations like "needs more examples" or "could be more interesting"; instead, try to offer helpful, focused suggestions: "You could add an example after the second sentence in paragraph 2"; "Explaining how this process operates would make your discussion more interesting."
>
> ☐ **Don't give orders.** Ask questions, and make suggestions.
>
> ☐ **Include a few words of encouragement.** Emphasize the paper's strong points.

■ **EXERCISE 5**

Look again at the excerpts and visuals in Exercises 1 through 4 on pages 5–8. This time, try to decide what audience or audiences each seems to be aimed at. Then, consider what (if anything) might have to be changed to address the needs of each of the following audiences:

- College students
- Middle-school students
- The elderly
- People with limited English skills
- People who do not live in the US

1c Setting Your Tone

Tone conveys your attitude. The attitude, or mood, that you adopt as you write may be serious or frivolous, respectful or condescending, intimate or detached. Because tone tells your readers how you feel about your material, it must remain consistent with your purpose and your audience as you write and revise.

When your general purpose is to present information, you choose words and construct sentences that make your writing objective and informative. Your choice of a factual, straightforward, reasonable—even impersonal—tone will convey your no-nonsense attitude. In such a situation, a sarcastic or playful tone would be inappropriate. When, however, your primary purpose is to influence your readers—for example, to sway their opinions or appeal to their emotions, to make them angry or sympathetic—you select words and shape sentences that serve this end. Your tone can be ironic or harsh, sentimental or cold, bitter or compassionate: whatever best reflects your attitude and serves your purpose.

Your tone also reveals how you feel toward your readers—sympathetic or superior, concerned or indifferent, friendly or critical. For instance, if you identify with your readers or feel close to them, you use a personal and conversational tone. When you address a general reader indirectly or anonymously, you use a more distant, formal tone.

When your audience is an instructor and your purpose is to inform (as is often the case in college writing situations), you should generally use an objective tone—neither too personal and informal nor too detached and formal—as the following student paragraph does.

> One of the major characteristics of streptococci is that they are gram-positive. This means that after a series of dyes and rinses they take on a violet color. (Gram-negative organisms take on a red color.) Streptococci are also nonspore forming and nonmotile. Most strains produce a protective shield called a capsule. They use organic substances instead of oxygen for their metabolism. This process is called fermentation.

An English composition assignment asking students to write an informal essay expressing their feelings about the worst job they ever had calls for an entirely different tone. In the paragraph that follows, the student's tone effectively conveys his attitude toward his job, and his use of the first person encourages his audience to identify with him. Sarcastic comments ("good little laborer," "Now here comes the excitement!") contribute to the informal effect.

Every day I followed the same boring, monotonous routine. After clocking in like a good little laborer, I proceeded over to a gray file cabinet, forced open the half-caved-in doors, and removed a staple gun, various packs of size cards, and a blue ballpoint pen. Now here comes the excitement! Each farmer had a specific number assigned to his name. As his cucumbers were being sorted according to their particular size, they were loaded into two-hundred-pound bins, which I had to label with a stapled size card with the farmer's number on it. I had to complete a specific size card for every bin containing that size cucumber. Doesn't it sound wonderful? Any second grader could have handled it. And all the time I worked, the machinery moaned and rattled, and the odor of cucumbers filled the air.

In a letter applying for a job, however, the same student would have a different purpose—and would, therefore, use a different tone. In this situation, his distance from his audience and his desire to impress readers with his qualifications would call for a much more objective and straightforward tone.

My primary duty at Germaine Produce was to label cucumbers as they were sorted into bins. I was responsible for making sure each two-hundred-pound bin bore the name of the farmer who had grown those cucumbers and also for keeping track of the cucumbers' sizes. Accuracy was extremely important in this task.

COMPUTER TIP academic.cengage.com/eng/kirsznermandell

CONVEYING YOUR TONE

Your computer gives you options—such as different type sizes and typefaces—that can help you convey a particular tone. For example, if you are applying for a job in business or industry and want to write a résumé, you would select a conservative typeface such as Times New Roman rather than a more decorative font. A plain, businesslike typeface tells readers that you are a serious applicant.

See 29b–c

■ EXERCISE 6

1. Focus on a book that you liked or disliked very much. How would you write about the book in each of the following writing situations? Consider how each writing situation would affect your choice of content, style, organization, tone, and emphasis.

    - A journal entry reflecting on your impressions of the book
    - An exam question that asks you to summarize the book's ideas

- A book review for a composition class in which you evaluate the book's strengths and weaknesses
- A letter in which you try to convince your local school board that the book should (or should not) be purchased for a public high school's library
- An editorial for your school newspaper in which you try to persuade other students that the book is worth reading
- An email to a friend recommending (or criticizing) the book

2. Choose two of the writing situations listed above, and write a paragraph in response to each specified assignment.

2

Reading Texts

FAQs

What is active reading? (p. 15)
How do I preview a text? (p. 15)
How do I highlight a text? (p. 16)
How do I annotate a text? (p. 16)

Central to becoming a writer is learning the techniques of **active reading.** Being an active reader means being actively involved with the text: reading with pen in hand and physically marking the text in order to identify parallels, question ambiguities, distinguish important points from not-so-important ones, and connect causes with effects and generalizations with specific examples. The understanding you gain from active reading prepares you to think (and write) critically about a text.

> **ESL TIP**
>
> When you read a text for the first time, don't worry about understanding every word. Instead, just try to get a general idea of what the text is about and how it is organized. Later on, you can use a dictionary to look up any unfamiliar words.

2a Previewing a Text

Before you actually begin reading a text, you should **preview** it—that is, skim it to get a sense of the writer's subject and emphasis.

When you preview a **book,** start by looking at its table of contents; then, turn to its index. A quick glance at the index will reveal the amount of coverage the book gives to subjects that may be important to you. As you leaf through the chapters, look at pictures, graphs, or tables and the captions that appear with them.

When you preview a **periodical article,** scan the introductory and concluding paragraphs for summaries of the writer's main points. (Journal articles in the sciences and social sciences often begin with summaries called **abstracts.**) Thesis statements, topic sentences, repeated key terms, transitional words and phrases, and transitional paragraphs can also help you to identify the points a writer is making. In addition, look for the **visual cues**—such as headings—that writers use to emphasize ideas.

See 30b

> ### CLOSE-UP
> #### VISUAL CUES
>
> When you preview a text, don't forget to note its use of color and of various typographical elements—such as typeface and type size, boldface and italics—to emphasize ideas.

2b Highlighting a Text

When you have finished previewing a work, you should **highlight** it, using a system of graphic symbols and underlining to identify the writer's key points and their relationships to one another. (If you are working with library material, photocopy the pages before you highlight them.) Be sure to use symbols that you will understand when you reread your material later on.

> ### CHECKLIST
> #### USING HIGHLIGHTING SYMBOLS
>
> - ☐ Underline to indicate information you should read again.
> - ☐ Box or circle key words or important phrases.
> - ☐ Put question marks next to confusing passages, unclear points, or words you need to look up.
> - ☐ Draw lines or arrows to show connections between ideas.
> - ☐ Number points that are discussed in sequence.
> - ☐ Draw a vertical line in the margin to set off an important section.
> - ☐ Star especially important ideas.

2c Annotating a Text

After you have read through a text once, read it again—this time, more critically. At this stage, you should **annotate** the pages, recording your responses to what you read. This process of recording notes in the margins or between the lines will help you understand the writer's ideas and your own reactions to those ideas.

> **ESL TIP**
>
> You may find it useful to use your native language when you annotate a text.

Some of your annotations may be relatively straightforward. For example, you may define new words, identify unfamiliar references, or jot down brief summaries. Other annotations may be more personal: you may identify a parallel between your own experience and one described in the reading selection, or you may record your opinion of the writer's position.

> **CLOSE-UP**
>
> **READING CRITICALLY**
>
> When you start to **think critically** about a text, your annotations may identify points that confirm (or dispute) your own ideas, question the appropriateness or accuracy of the writer's support, uncover the writer's biases, or even question (or challenge) the writer's conclusion.

See Ch. 8

The following passage illustrates a student's highlighting and annotations on an article about the decline of American public schools.

One of the most compelling arguments about the Vietnam War is that it lasted as long as it did because of its "classist" nature. The central thesis is that because neither the decision makers in the government *nor anyone they knew* had children fighting and dying in Vietnam, they had no personal incentive to bring the war to a halt. The government's generous college-deferment system, steeped as it was in class distinctions, allowed the white middle class to avoid the tragic consequences of the war. And the people who did the fighting and dying in place of the college-deferred were those whose voices were least heard in Washington: the poor and the disenfranchised.

Is this comparison valid? (seems forced)

I bring this up because I believe that the decline of the public schools is rooted in the same cause. Just as with the Vietnam War, as soon as the middle class no longer had a stake in the public schools, the surest pressure on school systems to provide a decent education instantly disappeared. Once the middle class was gone, no mayor was going to get booted out of office because the schools were bad. No incompetent teacher had to worry about angry parents calling for his or her head "downtown." No third-rate educationalist at the local teachers college had to fear having his or her methods criticized by anyone that mattered.

The analogy to the Vietnam War can be extended even to the extent of the denial. It amuses me sometimes to hear people like myself decry the state of the public schools. We bemoan the lack of money, the decaying facilities, the absurd credentialism, the high foolishness of the school boards. We applaud the burgeoning reform movement. And everything we say is deeply, undeniably true. We can see every problem with the schools clearly except one: the fact that our decision to abandon the schools has helped create all the other problems. One small example: In the early 1980s, Massachusetts passed one of those tax cap measures, called Proposition 2 1/2, which has turned out to be a force for genuine evil in the public schools. Would Proposition 2 1/2 have passed had the middle class still had a stake in the schools? I wonder. I also wonder whether 20 years from now, in the next round of breast-beating memoirs, the exodus of the white middle class from the public schools will finally be seen for what it was. Individually, every parent's rationale made impeccable sense—"I can't deprive my children of a decent education"—but collectively, it was a deeply destructive act.

The main reason the white middle class fled, of course, is race, or more precisely, the complicated admixture of race and class and good intentions gone awry. The fundamental good intention—which even today strikes one as both moral and right—was to integrate the public classroom, and in so doing, to equalize the resources available to all school children. In Boston, this was done through enforced busing. In Washington, it was done through a series of judicial edicts that attempted to spread the good teachers and resources throughout the system. In other big city districts, judges weren't involved; school committees, seeing the handwriting on the wall, tried to do it themselves.

However moral the intent, the result almost always was the same. The white middle class left. The historic parental vigilance I mentioned earlier had had a lot to do with creating the two-tiered system—one in which schools attended by the kids of the white middle class had better teachers, better equipment, better everything than those attended by the kids of the poor. This did not happen because the white middle-class parents were racists, necessarily; it happened because they knew how to manipulate the system and were willing to do so on behalf of their kids. Their neighborhood schools became little havens of decent education, and they didn't much care what happened in the other public schools.

In retrospect, this behavior, though perfectly understandable, was tragically short-sighted. When the judicial fiats made those safe havens untenable, the white middle class quickly discovered what the poor had always known: There weren't enough good teachers, decent equipment, and so forth to go around. For that matter, there weren't even enough good students to go around; along with everything else, middle-class parents had to start worrying about whether their kids were going to be mugged in school.

Faced with the grim fact that their children's education was quickly deteriorating, middle-class parents essentially had two choices: They could stay and pour the energy that had once gone into improving the neighborhood school into improving the entire school system—a frightening task, to be sure. Or they could leave. Invariably, they chose the latter.

And it wasn't just the white middle class that fled. The black middle class, and even the black poor who were especially ambitious for their children, were getting out as fast as they could too, though not to the suburbs. They headed mainly for the parochial schools, which subsequently became integration's great success story, even as the public schools became integration's great failure. (Joseph Nocera, "The Case Against Joe Nocera: How People Like Me Helped Ruin the Public Schools")

Margin annotations: Interesting point—but is it true? / Slanted language (over-emotional) / Generalization / Slanted language (over-emotional) / Either/or fallacy? Were there other choices? / Oversimplification? No exceptions?

■ EXERCISE 1

Preview the following passage, and then read it more carefully, highlighting and annotating it to help you understand the writer's ideas. Then, compare your highlighting and annotations with a classmate's. When you are satisfied that you have identified the most important ideas and that you both understand the passage, work together to answer the following questions.

- What is the writer's general subject?
- What is the writer's most important idea?
- How does he support this key idea?
- How does the writer make connections among related points clear?

"Go to Wall Street," my classmates said.
"Go to Wall Street," my professor advised.

"Go to Wall Street," my father threatened.

Whenever I tell people about my career indecisiveness, their answer is always the same: Get a blueprint for life and get one fast. Perhaps I'm simply too immature, but I think 20 is far too young to set my life in stone.

Nobody mentioned any award for being the first to have a white picket fence, 2.4 screaming kids, and a spanking new Ford station wagon.

What's wrong with uncertainty, with exploring multiple options in multiple fields? What's wrong with writing, "Heck, I don't know," under the "objective" section of my résumé?

Parents, professors, recruiters and even other students seem to think there's a lot wrong with it. And they are all pressuring me to launch a career prematurely.

My sociology professor warns that my generation will be the first in American history not to be more successful than our parents' generation. This depressing thought drives college students to think of success as something that must be achieved at all costs as soon as possible.

My father wants me to emulate his success: Every family wants its children to improve the family fortune. I feel that desire myself, but I realize I don't need to do it by age 25.

This pressure to do better, to compete with the achievements of our parents in a rapidly changing world, has forced my generation to pursue definitive, lifelong career paths at far too young an age. Many of my friends who have graduated in recent years are already miserably unhappy.

My professors encourage such pre-professionalism. In upper level finance classes, the discussion is extremely career-oriented. "Learn to do this and you'll be paid more" is the theme of many a lecture. Never is there any talk of actually enjoying the exercise.

Nationwide, universities are finally taking steps in the right direction by re-emphasizing the study of liberal arts and a return to the classics. If only job recruiters for Wall Street firms would do the same.

"Get your M.B.A. as soon as possible and you'll have a jump on the competition," said one overly zealous recruiter from Goldman Sachs. Learning for learning's sake was completely forgotten: Goldman Sachs refused to interview anybody without a high grade-point average, regardless of the courses composing that average.

In other interviews, it is expected that you know exactly what you want to do or you won't be hired. "Finance?" they say, "What kind of finance?"

A recruiter at Dean Witter Reynolds said investment banking demands 80 to 100 hours of work per week. I don't see how anyone will ever find time to enjoy the gobs of money they'll be making.

The worst news came from a partner at Salomon Brothers. He told me no one was happy there, and if they said they were, they're lying. He said you come in, make a lot of money and leave as fast as you can.

Two recent Wharton alumni, scarcely two years older than I, spoke at Donaldson, Lufkin & Jenrette's presentation. Their jokes about not having a life outside the office were only partially in jest.

Yet, students can't wait to play this corporate charade. They don ties and jackets and tote briefcases to class.

It is not just business students who are obsessed with their careers. The five other people who live in my house are not undergraduate business majors, but all five plan to attend graduate school next year. How is it possible that, without one iota of real work experience, these people are willing to commit themselves to years of intensive study in one narrow field?

Mom, dad, grandpa, recruiters, professors, fellow students: I implore you to leave me alone.

Now is my chance to explore, to spend time pursuing interests simply because they make me happy and not because they fill my wallet. I don't want to waste my youth toiling at a miserable job. I want to make the right decisions about my future.

Who knows, I may even end up on Wall Street. (Michael Finkel, "Undecided—and Proud of It")

CHECKLIST

READING TEXTS

As you read a text, keep the following questions in mind:

- ☐ Does the writer provide any information about his or her background? If so, how does this information affect your reading of the text?
- ☐ Are there parallels between the writer's experiences and your own?
- ☐ What is the writer's **purpose**? How can you tell?
- ☐ What **audience** is the text aimed at? How can you tell?
- ☐ What is the most important idea? What support does the writer provide for that idea?
- ☐ What information can you learn from the introduction and conclusion?
- ☐ What information can you learn from the **thesis statement**?
- ☐ What information can you learn from the **topic sentences**?
- ☐ What key words are repeated? What does this repetition tell you about the writer's purpose and emphasis?
- ☐ How would you characterize the writer's tone?
- ☐ Where do you agree with the writer? Where do you disagree?
- ☐ What, if anything, is not clear to you?

See 1a–b

See 5b

See 7a1

3

Reading Visuals

❓ FAQ
How do I interpret a visual image? (p. 24)

The texts you read in college courses—books, newspapers, and articles, in print or online—are often accompanied by visuals. For example, textbooks often include illustrations to make complex information more accessible, and newspapers use photographs to break up columns of written text as well as to add interest. Currently, more and more information is being presented in visual form—not just in magazines and other print media, but also on the Web and even on cell phones.

CLOSE-UP

READING VISUALS

Visuals are used to persuade as well as to entertain and to convey information that supplements written text.

Maps

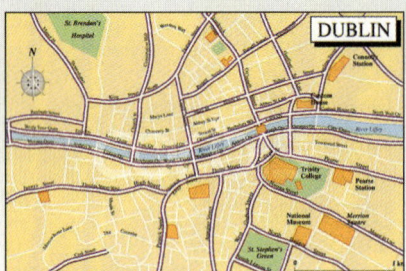

Map of Dublin, Ireland.

Photographs

Photo of university student preparing backstage at Beijing Opera.

Reading Visuals 3

Cartoons

Cartoon by Jen Sorensen.

Tables

	Location	
Employees	Madison	St. Paul
Plant	461	254
Warehouse	45	23
Outlet Stores	15	9

Table from student paper.

Fine Art

Profile of a Woman Wearing a Jabot (pastel on paper) by Mary Stevenson Cassatt (1844–1926).

Advertisements

Mercedes-Benz ad.

Scientific Diagrams

Plant engineering diagram.

Bar Graphs

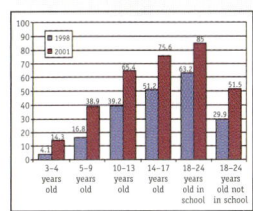

Bar graph from student's MLA research paper.

3a Interpreting a Visual

Because the world audience is becoming increasingly visual, it is important for you to acquire the skills needed to read and interpret visuals as well as to use them in your own written work. (For information on incorporating visuals into your own writing, **see 6b3**.)

The powerful newspaper photograph shown in Figure 3.1, which depicts a Marine in front of the Vietnam Veterans Memorial, uses a variety of techniques to convey its message. To **interpret** this photograph, you need to determine what strategies it uses to achieve its effect.

You might notice right away that contrasts are very important in this picture. In the background is the list of soldiers who died in the war; in the foreground, a lone member of a Marine honor guard stands in silent vigil, seemingly as static as the names carved in granite. Still, those who view this photo know that the Marine is motionless only in the picture; when the photographer puts the camera down, the Marine lives on, in contrast to those whose

The whole world is watching

Member of Marine honor guard passes the Vietnam memorial on which names of casualties of the war are inscribed

FIGURE 3.1 Newspaper photograph taken at the Vietnam Veterans Memorial.

names are listed behind him. The large close-up of the Marine set against the smaller names in the background also suggests that the photographer's purpose is at least in part to capture the contrast between the past and the present, the dead and the living. Thus, the photograph has a persuasive purpose: it suggests, as its title states, that "the whole world is watching" (and, in fact, *should* be watching) this scene in order to remember the past and honor the dead.

To convey their ideas, visuals often rely on contrasting light and shadow and on the size and placement of individual images (as well as on the spatial relationship of these images to one another and to the whole). In addition, visuals often use words (captions, slogans, explanatory text), and they may also include color, animation, audio narration, and even musical soundtracks. Given the complexity of many visuals and the number of individual elements each may use to convey its message, analyzing (or "reading") visual texts can be challenging. This task will be easier, however, if you follow the same **active reading** process you use when you read a written text.

3b Previewing a Visual

Just as with a written text, the first step in analyzing a visual text is to preview it, scanning it to get a sense of its subject and emphasis. At this stage, you may notice little more than the visual's major features: its central image, its dominant colors, its use of blank space, and the most prominent blocks of written text. Still, even these elements can give you a general idea of what the focus of the visual is and what purpose it might have.

See 2a

For example, the New Balance ad shown in Figure 3.2 shows two large images—a foot and a shoe—both with the distinctive New Balance *N* logo. This logo also appears in the slogan "N is for fit," which has a prominent central position. The slogan is allowed to speak for itself, with the text that explains the visual message appearing in very small type at the bottom of the page. Yellow is used to highlight the logo, the shoe's tread, and the word *fit*.

FIGURE 3.2 **Magazine ad for New Balance sneakers.**

3c Highlighting and Annotating a Visual

When you **highlight** a visual text, you mark it up to help you identify key images and their relationship to one another. You might, for example, use arrows to point to important images, or you might circle key words or details. When you **annotate** a visual text, you record your reactions to the images and words you see. (If a visual's background is dark, or if you are not permitted to write directly on it, you can do your highlighting and annotating on small self-stick notes.)

A student in a composition class was asked to analyze the magazine advertisement for Mercedes-Benz automobiles shown in Figure 3.3. When she visited the company Web site, she saw that Mercedes was appealing not just to those who value performance and safety but also to those interested in owning a classic, a car whose reputation is well established and well known. Moreover, with the slogan "Imagine the possibilities," the company was also appealing to those who dream of owning a luxury automobile. The student's highlighting and annotating focus on how the ad's written text and visuals work together to present the company's message: that Mercedes symbolizes safety, style, and status.

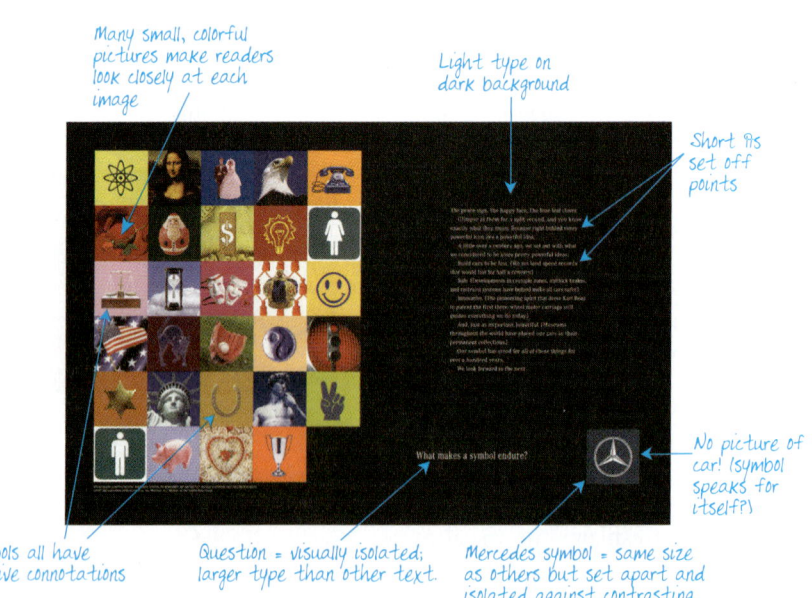

FIGURE 3.3 Mercedes-Benz ad.

Highlighting and Annotating a Visual   3c

CHECKLIST

READING VISUALS

As you highlight and annotate visual texts, keep the following questions in mind:

- ☐ Who created the visual?
- ☐ For what purpose was the visual created? For example, does it seem to be designed primarily to inform? To persuade? To entertain or amuse?   *See 1a*
- ☐ Where did the visual originally appear? What is the target audience for this publication?   *See 1b*
- ☐ What does the visual depict?
- ☐ What individual images are included in the visual? What associations do these images have for you?
- ☐ Do any people appear in the visual? What are they doing? What do they suggest about the visual's target audience?
- ☐ How would you describe the people's facial expressions? Their positions? Their body language?
- ☐ Does the visual include a lot of blank space?
- ☐ How large are the various elements (words and images)?
- ☐ Is the background light or dark? Clear or blurred? What individual elements stand out most clearly against this background?
- ☐ What general mood is suggested by the visual's use of color and shadow?
- ☐ Does the visual include any written text? What is its purpose?
- ☐ In general terms, what is the visual's message? How do its individual elements help to communicate this message?
- ☐ How would the visual's message or impact be different if something were added? If something were deleted?

■ EXERCISE 1

Use the checklist above to help you write a paragraph in response to each of the following:

1. On your way to campus or work, locate a billboard or a prominent sign (for example, on a train platform or bus shelter). What product or service does it promote? To what audience is it directed? How do you know? What does the image seem to assume about its intended audience (age, class, gender, and so on)?
2. Compare and contrast two magazine, television, or Internet advertisements for the same type of product (an automobile or cologne,

for instance) that are aimed at two different audiences. How are the two ads different? How does each aim to reach its audience? What elements contribute to the persuasive message of each ad?
3. Select a Web site related to your major or to a paper you are currently working on. What elements of the site—visuals, typeface and type size, color, and so on—contribute to the site's usefulness as an information resource? How might the site benefit from additional (or fewer) visual features?
4. Select a chapter from a textbook in your major, and examine the way in which content is arranged on the pages. What visual elements (headings, lists, charts, tables, photographs, and so on) can you identify? How do these elements highlight important information?

■ EXERCISE 2

Write a paragraph in which you analyze the ad shown in Figure 3.4. Consider the following questions: What audience is being addressed? What is the ad's primary purpose? What message is being conveyed? How do the various visual elements work together to appeal to the ad's target audience?

FIGURE 3.4 Billboard for 1-800-NO-BUTTS, the California Smokers' Helpline.

4

Planning an Essay

FAQs
Where do I start? (p. 31)
How do I choose a topic? (p. 32)
How do I find ideas to write about? (p. 34)

4a Understanding the Writing Process

Writing is a complex process of decision making—of selecting, deleting, and rearranging material.

> **CLOSE-UP**
>
> **THE WRITING PROCESS**
>
> The writing process includes the following stages:
>
> **Planning:** Consider your purpose, audience, and tone; choose your topic; discover ideas to write about.
>
> **Shaping:** Decide how to organize your material.
>
> **Drafting:** Write your first draft.
>
> **Revising:** "Re-see" what you have written; write additional drafts.
>
> **Editing:** Check grammar, spelling, punctuation, and mechanics.
>
> **Proofreading:** Reread every word, checking for any remaining errors.

The neatly defined stages listed above communicate neither the complexity nor the flexibility of the writing process. These stages actually overlap: as you look for ideas, you begin to shape your material; as you shape your material, you begin to write; as you write a draft, you reorganize your ideas; as you revise, you continue to discover new material. Moreover, these stages may be repeated again and again throughout the writing process. During your college years and in the years that follow, you will develop your own version of the writing process and use it whenever you write, adapting it to the audience, purpose, and writing situation at hand.

4b plan ■ Planning an Essay

> **ESL TIP**
>
> In many high school and college writing classes in the US, classroom activities and homework are organized around the stages of the writing process outlined in Chapters 4 through 6.

■ **EXERCISE 1**

1. Write a paragraph in which you describe your own writing process. (If you prefer, you may draw a diagram that represents your process.) What do you do first? What steps do you return to again and again? Which stages do you find most satisfying? Which do you find most frustrating?
2. Write a paragraph in which you focus on the visual aspects of your writing process. For example, do you find yourself making charts or diagrams as you write? Do you use arrows to connect ideas? How do these strategies help you to generate ideas and identify connections between them?

4b Computers and the Writing Process

See Ch. 29
See 32d2

Computers have changed the way we write and communicate in both academic and <u>workplace</u> settings. In addition to using word-processing applications for typical writing tasks, writers may rely on programs such as <u>PowerPoint</u>® for giving presentations and *Publisher*® for creating customized résumés or brochures, as well as Web-page authoring software such as *FrontPage*® for creating Internet-accessible documents that include images, movies, and a wide range of visual effects.

With the expanding role of the Internet in professional, academic, and personal communication, it is becoming increasingly likely that the feedback you receive on your writing will be electronic. For example, you may receive an email from your instructor about a draft that you have submitted to a digital drop box, a tool often associated with course management software such as *WebCT*™ or *Blackboard*™. Or, you may use discussion boards for attaching or sharing your documents with other students. Chat room and Net meeting software also allow you to discuss ideas collaboratively and to offer and receive feedback on drafts. Although the tools you use may be course- or workplace-specific, your writing process will be similar.

■ **EXERCISE 2**

To what extent does your writing process rely on the computer? Look back at the two paragraphs you wrote for Exercise 1, and add details about how you use the computer in your writing process.

4c Analyzing Your Assignment

Planning your essay—thinking about what you want to say and how you want to say it—begins well before you actually start recording your thoughts in any organized way. This planning is as important a part of the writing process as the writing itself. During this planning stage, you determine your **purpose** for writing and identify your **audience**. Then, you go on to focus on your assignment, choose and narrow your topic, and gather ideas.

See 1a–b

Before you begin writing, be sure you understand the exact requirements of your **assignment**. Ask questions, and be sure you understand the answers.

CHECKLIST

ANALYZING YOUR ASSIGNMENT

To help you understand your assignment, consider the following questions:

- ☐ Has your instructor assigned a specific topic, or can you choose your own?
- ☐ What is the word or page limit?
- ☐ How much time do you have to complete your assignment?
- ☐ Will you get feedback from your instructor? Will you have an opportunity to participate in **peer review**?

See 6c2

- ☐ Does your assignment require research?
- ☐ What format (for example, **MLA**) are you supposed to follow? Do you know what its conventions are?

See Ch. 18

- ☐ If your assignment has been given to you in writing, have you read it carefully and highlighted key words?

Kimberly Romney, a first-year composition student, was given the following assignment.

> College broadens your horizons and exposes you to new people, places, and experiences. At the same time, it can also create problems. Write an essay (about 5–7 pages long) about a problem you (and perhaps others) have encountered since coming to college. Be sure that your essay has a clearly stated thesis and that it helps readers to understand your problem.

The class was given two weeks to complete the assignment. Students were expected to do some research and to have the instructor and other students read and comment on at least one draft.

4d Choosing and Narrowing a Topic

Sometimes your instructor will allow you to choose your own topic; more often, however, you will be given a general assignment, which you will have to narrow to a **topic** that suits your purpose and audience.

Narrowing a Topic

Course	Assignment	Topic
American History	Analyze the effects of a social program on one segment of American society.	How did the GI Bill of Rights affect American servicewomen?
Sociology	Identify and evaluate the success of one resource available to the homeless population of one major American city.	The role of the Salvation Army in meeting the needs of Chicago's homeless
Psychology	Write a three- to five-page paper assessing one method of treating depression.	Animal-assisted therapy for severely depressed patients

Kimberly had no trouble thinking of problems she had encountered as a small-town student at a large urban university. One particular problem she faced was her lack of confidence with computers. Although she had learned to use email and *Word* and to do basic Internet searches, other students seemed much more proficient. Unlike her high school, her university expected students to have a high degree of computer literacy. Because the gap between what she was expected to know and what she actually knew seemed so problematic, she decided to make her lack of computer skills the topic of her paper.

Course	Assignment	Topic
Composition	Write an essay about a problem you have encountered since coming to college.	Overcoming my computer illiteracy

Choosing and Narrowing a Topic ■ **plan** **4d** 33

■ **EXERCISE 3**

Read the following excerpt, and study the photograph on page 34 (Figure 4.1). Then, list ten possible essay topics about your own childhood suggested by the writer's memories or by the photo. (Your assignment is to write a three-page essay about your childhood; your purpose is to give your audience—your composition instructor and possibly members of your peer-review group—a vivid sense of what some aspect of your childhood was like.) Finally, choose the one topic that you feel best qualified to write about, and write a few sentences explaining why you selected it.

When we weren't down at the field or watching the Yankees on TV, we were playing whiffle ball and climbing trees checking out birds' nests, going down to Fly Beach in Mrs. Zimmer's old car that honked the horn every time it turned the corner, diving underwater with our masks, kicking with our rubber frog's feet, then running in and out of our sprinklers when we got home, waiting for our turn in the shower. And during the summer nights we were all over the neighborhood, from Bobby's house to Kenny's, throwing gliders, doing handstands and backflips off fences, riding to the woods at the end of the block on our bikes, making rafts, building tree forts, jumping across the streams with tree branches, walking and balancing along the back fence like Houdini, hopping along the slate path all around the back yard seeing how far we could go on one foot.

And I ran wherever I went. Down to school, the candy store, to the deli, buying baseball cards and Bazooka bubblegum that had the little fortunes at the bottom of the cartoons.

When the Fourth of July came, there were fireworks going off all over the neighborhood. It was the most exciting time of year for me next to Christmas. Being born on the exact same day as my country I thought was really great. I was so proud. And every Fourth of July, I had a birthday party and all my friends would come over with birthday presents and we'd put on silly hats and blow these horns my dad brought home from the A&P. We'd eat lots of ice cream and watermelon and I'd open up all the presents and blow out the candles on the big red, white, and blue birthday cake and then we'd all sing "Happy Birthday" and "I'm a Yankee Doodle Dandy." At night everyone would pile into Bobby's mother's old car and we'd go down to the drive-in, where we'd watch the fireworks display. Before the movie started, we'd all get out and sit up on the roof of the car with our blankets wrapped around us watching the rockets and Roman candles going up and exploding into fountains of rainbow colors, and later after Mrs. Zimmer dropped me off, I'd lie on my bed feeling a little sad that it all had to end so soon. As I closed my eyes I could still hear strings of firecrackers and cherry bombs going off all over the neighborhood. . . . (Ron Kovic, *Born on the Fourth of July*)

34 **4e** plan ■ Planning an Essay

FIGURE 4.1 Children on the beach, posing for the camera.

4e Finding Something to Say

Once you have a topic, you can begin to collect ideas for your paper, using one (or several) of the strategies discussed in the pages that follow.

> **ESL TIP**
>
> Don't use all your time making sure you are writing grammatically correct sentences. Remember, the purpose of writing is to communicate ideas. If you want to write an interesting, well-developed essay, you will need to devote plenty of time to the activities described in this section.

1 Reading and Observing

As you read textbooks, magazines, and newspapers and browse the Internet, be on the lookout for ideas that relate to your topic. Films, television programs, interviews, telephone calls, letters, emails, and questionnaires can also provide material. But be sure your instructor permits such research—and remember to **document** ideas that are not your own. If you do not, you will be committing **plagiarism**.

See Ch. 17

When students in Kimberly's composition class were assigned to read Henry Louis Gates's essay "One Internet, Two Nations" in their textbook, she learned about the division that exists between those who are Internet savvy and those who are not. This reading assignment gave her a wider perspective on her topic and encouraged her to look beyond her own experience.

EXERCISE 4

List all the potential sources you can think of for the essay you are writing. Include specific newspapers and magazines, television shows, conversations you might have, Web sites, assigned reading, emails, and so on. Exchange lists with a classmate, and add two sources to his or her list.

2 Keeping a Journal

Many professional writers keep print or electronic **journals,** writing in them regularly whether or not they have a specific project in mind. Journals, unlike diaries, do more than simply record personal experiences and reactions. In a journal, you explore ideas, ask questions, and draw conclusions. You might, for example, analyze your position on a political issue, try to solve an ethical problem, or trace the evolution of your ideas about an academic assignment. One of Kimberly's journal entries appears below.

Journal Entry

> I'm not really comfortable writing about my own poor computer skills, but I have to admit it's a good topic for a paper about a problem I have. What I really want to focus on, though, is the ways in which computer illiteracy is a big problem not just for me but for college students in general. I don't want to write about the hours it took me to register for classes online or the fact that it took me an hour to figure out how to email my professor and then save that email. I don't want this paper to be about me and my problems. What I want to do is write about the difficulties students with weak computer skills have and mention a few things about my own life to illustrate these general ideas.

3 Freewriting

When you **freewrite,** you write nonstop about anything that comes to mind, moving as quickly as you can. Give yourself a set period of time—say, five minutes—and don't stop to worry about punctuation, spelling, or grammar, or about where your freewriting takes you. This strategy encourages your mind to make free associations; thus, it helps you to discover ideas you probably aren't even aware you have. When your time is up, look over what you have written, and underline, circle, bracket, star, boldface, or otherwise highlight the most promising ideas. You can then use one or more of these ideas as the center of a focused freewriting exercise.

When you do **focused freewriting,** you zero in on your topic. Here too you write without stopping to reconsider or reread, so you have no time to be self-conscious about style or form, to worry about the relevance of your ideas, or to count how many words you have (and panic about how many more you think you need). At its best, focused freewriting can suggest new details, a new approach to your topic, or even a more interesting topic. Excerpts from Kimberly's freewriting and focused freewriting exercises appear below.

Freewriting (Excerpt)

This isn't so bad because I finally don't have to worry about typing perfectly. I can make mistakes, and I won't have to stop writing and then correct myself. That's how I feel using computers: anxious. We had a few computers at my high school, but we didn't have to take a computer class, or even a typing class. When I got to college, I felt like such an idiot. Everyone else seemed to have no trouble using the Internet for research, creating *PowerPoint* presentations for class projects, and even creating their own Web sites. All of a sudden I was expected to use computers to register, for research, and to communicate with my professors. It was horrible! Most other students didn't ever have to ask a question about computers. It's like there are two groups when you get to college: the people who are really computer literate and those who aren't.

Focused Freewriting (Excerpt)

The first day of orientation we were told to use computers to register. It's not like I'd never used a computer before or seen the Internet. Still, I had to raise my hand and get the proctor in the computer room to come help me click on the right icon. And then I had to ask a lot of questions to figure out how to access two Web sites at the same time so that I could look at both the online course catalog and the registration Web site. Meanwhile, most of the other students were already finished and on their way to dinner. When I asked if I could get a copy of the course schedule on paper, the proctor told me that the university had recently gone "paperless." I realized then and there that I was going to have to do a lot of extra work to make myself computer literate.

4 Brainstorming

One of the most useful ways to accumulate ideas is by brainstorming (either on your own or in a group). This strategy enables you to recall bits of information and to see connections among them.

When you **brainstorm,** you list all the points you can think of that seem pertinent to your topic, recording ideas—comments, questions, single words, symbols, or diagrams—as quickly as you can, without pausing to consider their relevance or trying to understand their significance. An excerpt from Kimberly's brainstorming notes appears below.

Brainstorming Notes (Excerpt)

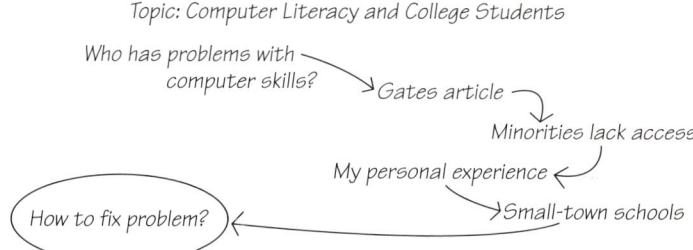

5 Clustering

Clustering—sometimes called *webbing* or *mapping*—is similar to brainstorming. However, clustering encourages you to explore your topic in a more systematic (and more visual) manner.

Begin your cluster diagram by writing your topic in the center of a sheet of paper. Then, surround your topic with related ideas as they occur to you, moving outward from the general topic in the center and writing down increasingly specific ideas and details as you move toward the edges of the page. Following the path of one idea at a time, draw lines to create a diagram (often lopsided rather than symmetrical) that arranges ideas on spokes or branches radiating out from the center (your topic). Kimberly's cluster diagram appears below.

Cluster Diagram

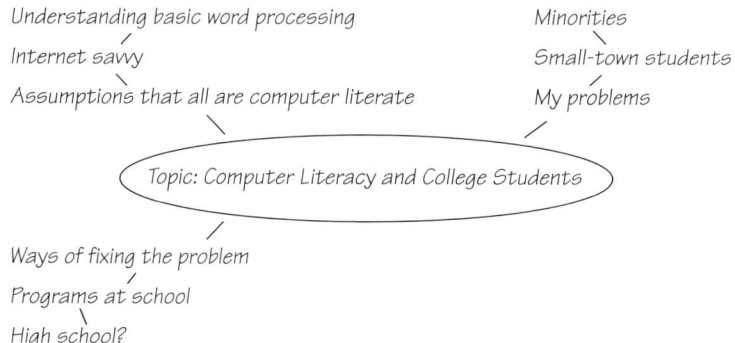

4e plan ■ Planning an Essay

> **COMPUTER TIP** academic.cengage.com/eng/kirznermandell
>
> **FINDING IDEAS**
>
> You can use your computer to help you find material to write about.
>
> - When you **freewrite**, try turning down the brightness of the monitor, leaving the screen dark to eliminate distractions and encourage spontaneity. When you reread what you have written, you can boldface or underline important ideas (or highlight them in color).
> - When you **brainstorm**, type your notes randomly. Later, after you print them out, you can add more notes and graphic elements (arrows, circles, and so on) by hand to indicate parallels and connections.

■ **EXERCISE 5**

Make a cluster diagram and brainstorming notes for the topic you chose in Exercise 3. If you have trouble thinking of ideas, try freewriting. Then, write a journal entry assessing your progress and evaluating the different strategies you used to find material for your essay. Which strategy worked best for you? Why?

6 Asking Journalistic Questions

Journalistic questions offer an orderly, systematic way of finding material to write about. Journalists ask the questions *Who? What? Why? Where? When?* and *How?* to ensure that they have explored all angles of a story, and you can use these questions to make sure you have considered all aspects of your topic. Kimberly's list of journalistic questions appears below.

Journalistic Questions

- Who is familiar with computers and the Internet, and who is not?
- What is computer literacy? What are the effects of weak computer skills? What kinds of programs exist to help college students improve computer skills?
- When did computers become essential for college students?
- Where are students most likely to learn computer skills?
- Why is familiarity with the Internet so important in college? Why are some students' computer skills so much better than others'?
- How can we help students who lag behind?

> **ESL TIP**
>
> Using your native language for planning activities has both advantages and disadvantages. On the one hand, if you do not have to contend with the strain of trying to think in English, you may be able to come up with better ideas. Additionally, using your native language may help you record your ideas more quickly and keep you from losing your train of thought. On the other hand, using your native language while planning may make it more difficult for you to move from the planning stages of your writing to drafting. After all, you will eventually have to write your paper in English.

7 Asking In-Depth Questions

If you have time, you can ask a series of more focused questions about your topic. These **in-depth questions** can give you a great deal of information, and they can also suggest ways for you to eventually shape your ideas into paragraphs and essays.

IN-DEPTH QUESTIONS

Questions	Suggested Approach
What happened? When did it happen? Where did it happen?	Suggest narration (an account of your first day of school; a summary of Emily Dickinson's life)
What does it look like? What does it sound like, smell like, taste like, or feel like?	Suggest description (of the Louvre; of the electron microscope; of a Web site)
What are some typical cases or examples of it?	Suggests exemplification (three infant day-care settings; four popular fad diets)
How did it happen? What makes it work? How is it made?	Suggest process (how to apply for financial aid; how a bill becomes a law)
Why did it happen? What caused it? What does it cause? What are its effects?	Suggest cause and effect (the events leading to the Korean War; the results of global warming; the impact of a new math curriculum on slow learners)
How is it like other things? How is it different from other things?	Suggest comparison and contrast (of the popular music of the 1970s and 1980s; of two paintings)

(continued)

IN-DEPTH QUESTIONS *(continued)*

What are its parts or types? Can they be separated or grouped? Do they fall into a logical order? Can they be categorized?	Suggest division and classification (components of the catalytic converter; kinds of occupational therapy; kinds of dietary supplements)
What is it? How does it resemble other members of its class? How does it differ from other members of its class?	Suggest definition (What is Marxism? What is photosynthesis? What is a MOO?)

An excerpt from Kimberly's list of in-depth questions appears below.

In-Depth Questions (Excerpt)

What causes the gap between those who are computer savvy and those who are not? Differences in family income, parents' education level, quality of public education, regional differences.

What are the effects of the gap? Differences in achievement in college and performance on the job; differences in access to information; differences in earning power.

Once you have gathered ideas for your essay—and perhaps begun to see the direction these ideas are taking—you are ready to decide how to shape your material.

See Ch. 5

■ EXERCISE 6

Using the two question strategies described and illustrated on pages 38–40 to supplement the work you did in Exercises 4 and 5, continue generating material for your essay-in-progress.

■ EXERCISE 7

Consider what kinds of visual images might enhance your essay-in-progress. For example, would a photograph of a particular person or place be helpful? List several possibilities, and write a few sentences explaining what each visual might add to your essay.

■ EXERCISE 8

Choose one visual to use in your essay. Using the visual as a focus, brainstorm to find additional ideas for your essay.

5

Using a Thesis to Shape Your Material

❓ FAQs

What is a thesis? (p. 41)
How do I know if I have an effective thesis? (p. 42)
Do I need an outline? (p. 46)

After you have collected possible ideas for your essay, you start to sift through these ideas and choose those you can use. As you do this, you begin to **shape** your material into a thesis-and-support essay.

5a   Understanding Thesis and Support

Your **thesis** is the main idea of your essay, the central point your essay supports. The concept of **thesis and support**—stating the thesis and then supplying information that explains and develops it—is central to much of the writing you will do in college.

As the following diagram illustrates, the essays you will write will consist of an <u>introductory paragraph</u>, which opens your essay and states your thesis; a <u>concluding paragraph</u>, which reviews your essay's major points and gives it a sense of closure, perhaps restating your thesis; and a number of **body paragraphs,** which provide the support for your thesis statement.

See 7e2–3

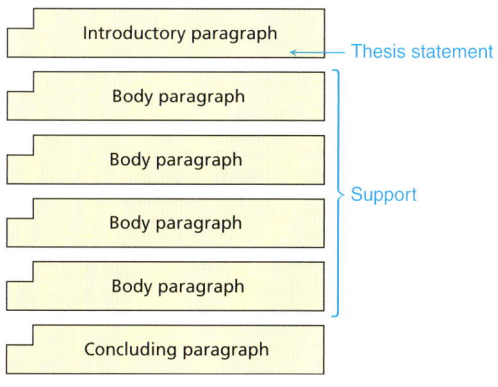

41

5b Developing a Thesis

1 Stating Your Thesis

An effective **thesis statement** has four characteristics:

1. **An effective thesis statement clearly communicates your essay's main idea.** It tells readers what your essay's topic is and suggests what you will say about it. Thus, your thesis statement reflects your essay's **purpose**.

2. **An effective thesis statement is more than a general subject, a statement of fact, or an announcement of your intent.**

Subject	Statement of Fact	Announcement
The Military Draft	The United States currently has no military draft.	In this essay, I will reconsider our country's need for a draft.

   Thesis Statement: Although today's all-volunteer force has replaced the draft, a draft may eventually be necessary.

3. **An effective thesis statement is carefully worded.** Because it communicates your paper's main idea, your thesis statement should be clearly and accurately worded. Your thesis statement—usually expressed in a single concise sentence—should be direct and straightforward. It should not include abstract language, overly complex terminology, or unnecessary details that might confuse or mislead readers. Be particularly careful to avoid vague, wordy phrases—*centers on, deals with, involves, revolves around, has a lot to do with, is primarily concerned with,* and so on.

   > The real problem in our schools ~~does~~ *is* not ~~revolve around~~ the absence of nationwide goals and standards; the problem is ~~primarily concerned with~~ the absence of resources.

   Finally, an effective thesis statement should not include phrases such as "I hope to demonstrate" and "It seems to me," which weaken your credibility by suggesting that your conclusions are tentative or are based solely on opinion rather than on reading, observation, and experience.

4. **An effective thesis statement suggests your essay's direction, emphasis, and scope.** Your thesis statement should not make promises that your essay will not fulfill. It should suggest how your ideas are related, in what order your major points will be discussed, and where you will place your emphasis, as the following thesis statement does.

Effective Thesis Statement
Widely ridiculed as escape reading, romance novels are important as a proving ground for many never-before-published writers and, more significantly, as a showcase for strong heroines.

This thesis statement is effective because it tells readers that the essay to follow will focus on two major roles of the romance novel: providing markets for new writers and (more important) presenting strong female characters. It also suggests that the essay will briefly treat the role of the romance novel as escapist fiction. As the following diagram shows, this effective thesis statement also indicates the order in which the various ideas will be discussed.

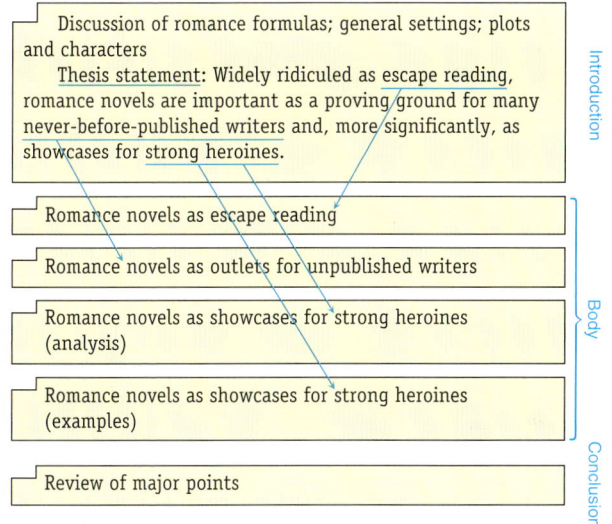

Kimberly Romney came up with the following thesis statement for her essay about her problems with computers.

> I was at a real disadvantage when I entered college because I lacked important computer skills.

2 Revising Your Thesis Statement

At this point, the thesis statement that you develop is only **tentative**. As you write and rewrite, you may modify your essay's direction, emphasis, and scope several times; if you do so, you must reword your thesis statement to reflect these modifications.

5b thesis ■ Using a Thesis to Shape Your Material

Notice how the following thesis statement changed as the student writer moved through successive drafts of his essay.

Tentative Thesis Statement (rough draft)
Professional sports can easily be corrupted by organized crime.

Revised Thesis Statement (final draft)
Although some people argue that organized crime cannot make inroads into professional sports, the way underworld figures fixed the 1919 World Series suggests the opposite.

When Kimberly revised her essay, her thesis statement changed. Compare her tentative thesis on page 43 with her revised thesis statement in her paper's final draft in **6e** on page 72.

CLOSE-UP

USING A THESIS STATEMENT TO SHAPE YOUR ESSAY

The wording of your thesis statement often suggests not only a possible order and emphasis for your essay's ideas, but also a specific pattern of development—*narration, description, exemplification, process, cause and effect, comparison and contrast, division and classification,* or *definition.* (These familiar **patterns of development** may also shape individual paragraphs of your essay.)

See 7d

Thesis Statement	Pattern of Development
As the months went by and I grew more and more involved with the developmentally delayed children at the Learning Center, I came to see how important it is to treat every child as an individual.	Narration
Looking around the room where I spent my childhood, I realized that every object I saw told me I was now an adult.	Description
The risk-taking behavior that has characterized recent years can be illustrated by the increasing interest and involvement in such high-risk sports as mountain biking, ice climbing, sky diving, and bungee jumping.	Exemplification
Armed forces basic training programs take recruits through a series of tasks designed to build camaraderie as well as skills and confidence.	Process

Thesis Statement	Pattern of Development
The gap in computer literacy between rich and poor has had many significant social and economic consequences.	Cause and Effect
Although people who live in cities and people who live in small towns have some similarities, their views on issues like crime, waste disposal, farm subsidies, and educational vouchers tend to be very different.	Comparison and Contrast
The section of the proposal that recommends establishing satellite health centers is quite promising; unfortunately, however, the sections that call for the creation of alternative educational programs, job training, and low-income housing are seriously flawed.	Division and Classification
Many people once assumed that rape was an act perpetrated by a stranger, but today's definition is much broader.	Definition

■ EXERCISE 1

Analyze each of the following items, and explain why none of them qualifies as an effective thesis statement. How could each be improved?

1. In this essay, I will examine the environmental effects of residential and commercial development on the coastal regions of the United States.
2. Residential and commercial development in the coastal regions of the United States
3. How to avoid coastal overdevelopment
4. Coastal Development: Pro and Con
5. Residential and commercial development of America's coastal regions benefits some people, but it has a number of disadvantages.
6. The environmentalists' position on coastal development
7. More and more coastal regions in the United States are being overdeveloped.
8. Residential and commercial development guidelines need to be developed for coastal regions of the United States.
9. Coastal development is causing beach erosion.
10. At one time I enjoyed walking on the beach, but commercial and residential development ruined the experience for me.

EXERCISE 2

For three of the following topics, formulate a clearly and carefully worded thesis statement.

1. A local or national event that changed your life
2. Cheating in college
3. US immigration laws
4. Should women in the military serve in combat?
5. Private versus public education
6. Should college health clinics provide birth control services?
7. Is government censorship of the Internet justified?
8. What individuals can do to save the earth
9. The portrayal of an ethnic group in film or television
10. Should smoking be banned in bars?

EXERCISE 3

Review all the notes you have accumulated so far, and use them to help you develop a thesis for an essay on the topic you chose in Chapter 4, Exercise 3.

5c Constructing an Informal Outline

Once you have decided on a thesis statement, you may want to construct an informal outline to guide you as you write. An **informal outline** arranges your essay's main points and major supporting ideas in an orderly way. Kimberly's informal outline appears below.

Informal Outline

Thesis statement: I was at a real disadvantage when I entered college because I lacked important computer skills.

Students' computer needs

- Basic word-processing programs
- Internet
- Email

Unprepared students

- No access at home
- No access at school

Consequences of computer illiteracy

- Difficulty with everyday tasks
- Embarrassment
- Missed opportunities

Possible solutions to problem
- Classes
- ??????

Personal experience
- Poor computer skills
- Classes in computer lab

5d Constructing a Formal Outline

Sometimes—particularly when you are writing a long or complex essay—you will need to construct a **formal outline,** which indicates both the exact order and the relative importance of all the ideas you will explore. (Note that formal outlines can be especially helpful in the revision stage of the writing process; **see 6c4.**)

Formal outlines conform to specific conventions of structure, content, and style. If you follow the conventions of outlining carefully, your formal outline can help you make sure that your paper presents all relevant ideas in an effective order, with appropriate emphasis.

1 Structure

Outline format should be followed strictly, as in the example below.

I. First major point of your paper
   A. First subpoint
   B. Next subpoint
      1. First supporting example
      2. Second supporting example
         a. First specific detail
         b. Second specific detail
II. Second major point

Headings should not overlap. No heading should have a single subheading (after all, a category cannot be subdivided into one part). Each entry should be preceded by an appropriate letter or number, followed by a period, and the first word of each entry should be capitalized.

2 Content

The outline, which should include the paper's thesis statement, should cover only the body of the essay, not the introductory and concluding paragraphs. Headings should be concise, specific, and descriptive, and they should also be clearly related to the material in the section of the paper to which they refer.

Style

Entries in a **sentence outline** should be complete sentences, with all sentences in the same tense. Each entry should end with a period. Entries in a **topic outline** should be words or short phrases. In a topic outline, entries should not end with periods.

NOTE: In both sentence outlines and topic outlines, all headings of the same rank (all roman numerals, all capital letters, all Arabic numerals, and so on) in each section of the outline should be grammatically *parallel*.

Kimberly decided that at this stage of the writing process, an informal outline was all she needed to guide her as she wrote a first draft. Later on, she might decide to construct a formal topic or sentence outline. Compare the following three types of outlines that could be used for one section of Kimberly's paper.

Informal Outline

Consequences of computer illiteracy

- Difficulty with everyday tasks
- Embarrassment
- Missed opportunities

Formal (Topic) Outline

III. Consequences of computer illiteracy
  A. Trouble completing everyday tasks
     1. Hard to email professors or other students
     2. Hard to write papers
     3. Unable to access listservs
  B. Embarrassment
     1. Afraid to ask questions in class
     2. Unable to exchange ideas with classmates
  C. Missed opportunities
     1. No opportunity to take exciting classes
     2. No opportunity to do advanced research
     3. No opportunity to develop advanced computer skills

Formal (Sentence) Outline

III. Without solid computer skills, students may encounter problems.
  A. Students may have trouble completing everyday tasks.
     1. They may be unable to email professors or other students.

2. They may have trouble writing papers.

   3. They may be unable to access listservs.

  B. Students may be embarrassed.

   1. They may be afraid to ask questions in class.

   2. They may be unable to exchange information with classmates.

  C. Most important, students may miss out on opportunities.

   1. They may miss the opportunity to take exciting classes.

   2. They may be unable to do advanced research.

   3. They may be unable to develop advanced computer skills.

For additional examples of topic outlines, **see 6c4** and **13h**; for another example of a sentence outline, **see 13j**.

COMPUTER TIP academic.cengage.com/eng/kirsznermandell

OUTLINING

Although you may be used to constructing outlines for your written work by hand, a number of software applications and formatting features can help in this process, including the outlining feature in some desktop publishing and word-processing programs (such as *Microsoft Word*). Another useful tool for outlining (particularly for <u>oral presentations</u>), is *Microsoft PowerPoint*, presentation software that enables you to format information on individual slides with major headings, subheadings, and bulleted lists.

See Ch. 32

■ **EXERCISE 4**

Find an editorial in the newspaper or on the Internet. Then, prepare an informal outline that includes all the writer's main points and major supporting ideas.

■ **EXERCISE 5**

Prepare an informal outline for the paper you have been developing in Chapters 4 and 5.

5e Constructing a Storyboard

Storyboarding is a way of graphically organizing material in a series of boxes or panels. This technique has long been used for outlining scenes in films and commercials, and it can be adapted, with some modifications, into a useful outlining tool for an essay or a Web site.

thesis ■ Using a Thesis to Shape Your Material

Unlike a strictly text-based outline, which uses words, phrases, or sentences to plot the organization of material in a linear way, a storyboard uses pictures and diagrams, either electronically generated or drawn by hand, to map out an arrangement of material. As a tool for shaping an essay, a storyboard can use blocks of text as well as pictures.

Storyboarding can help you plan the placement of your ideas; in addition, it can help you visualize the placement of potential source information and illustrations. Kimberly's storyboard appears below.

Storyboard

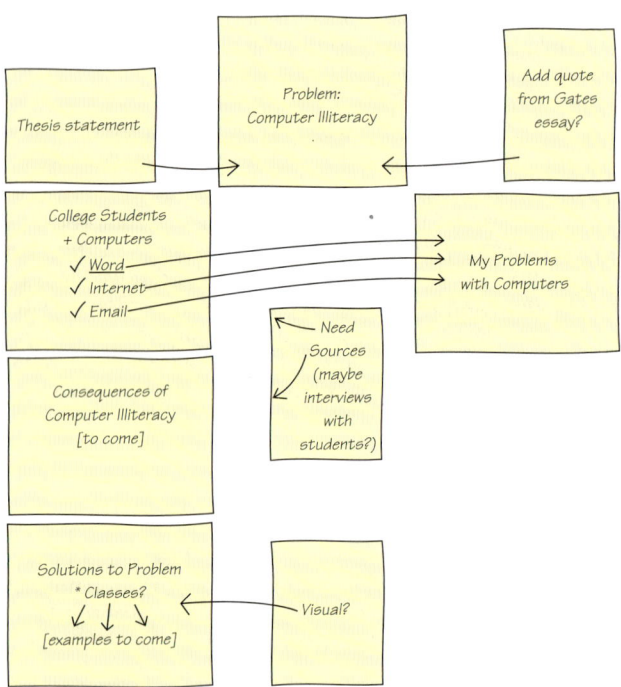

CHECKLIST

CONSTRUCTING A STORYBOARD

- ☐ Use a large sheet of paper to represent your essay.
- ☐ On the paper, draw a box to represent each major section of the paper; or, use self-stick notes or index cards as boxes.
- ☐ Fill in each box with a combination of words, shapes, and symbols to represent key ideas, sources, and visuals.

Constructing a Storyboard ■ **thesis** 5e

- ☐ If you like, use the visuals themselves—such as printouts of clip art or images cut from magazines—in your boxes.
- ☐ Leave blank space (or even a blank box) for undeveloped sections; label blank spaces "to come."
- ☐ Rearrange boxes on the page if necessary.
- ☐ Number the boxes if necessary.
- ☐ Use arrows to indicate possible relocation of elements within boxes.

■ **EXERCISE 6**

Construct a storyboard for the paper you have been developing in Chapters 4 and 5. Use the model storyboard on page 50 as a guide.

■ **EXERCISE 7**

Which did you find most useful in helping you shape your ideas—your informal outline or your storyboard? Write a paragraph explaining the strengths and weaknesses of each strategy.

Once you are able to see a clear order for your ideas, you are ready to write a <u>rough draft</u> of your paper.

See 6a

6

Drafting and Revising

❓ FAQs

How do I add a visual to my paper? (p. 57)
How do I revise my drafts? (p. 58)
How does peer review work? (p. 59)
How do I find a title for my paper? (p. 67)
What's the difference between revising *and* editing? *(p. 68)*
How much can I rely on spell checkers and grammar checkers? (p. 70)

6a   Writing a Rough Draft

A **rough draft** is far from perfect; in fact, it usually includes false starts, irrelevant information, and unrelated details. At this stage, though, the absence of focus and order is not a problem. You write your rough draft simply to get your ideas down so that you can react to them. You should expect to add or delete words, to reword sentences, to rethink ideas, and to reorder paragraphs. You should also expect to discover some new ideas—or even to take an unexpected detour.

When you write your rough draft, concentrate on the body of your essay, and don't waste time mapping out an introduction and conclusion. (These paragraphs are likely to change substantially in subsequent drafts.) For now, focus on drafting the support paragraphs of your essay.

> **ESL TIP**
>
> Using your native language occasionally as you draft your paper may keep you from losing your train of thought. However, writing most or all of your draft in your native language and then translating it into English is generally not a good idea. This process will take a long time, and the translation into English may sound awkward.

> **CHECKLIST**
>
> **DRAFTING STRATEGIES**
>
> The following suggestions should help you revise effectively:
>
> ☐ **Prepare your work area.** Once you begin to write, you should not have to stop because you need better lighting, important notes, or anything else.

Writing a Rough Draft   6a

- ☐ **Fight writer's block.** An inability to start (or continue) writing, writer's block is usually caused by fear that you will not write well or that you have nothing to say. If you really don't feel ready to write, take a short break. If you decide that you really don't have enough ideas to get you started, use one of the strategies for finding something to say.   *See 4e*

- ☐ **Get your ideas down on paper as quickly as you can.** Don't worry about sentence structure, about spelling and punctuation, or about finding exactly the right word—just write. Writing quickly helps you uncover new ideas and new connections between ideas. You may find that following an informal outline enables you to move smoothly from one point to the next, but if you find this structure too confining, go ahead and write without consulting your outline.   *See 5c*

- ☐ **Write notes to yourself.** As you type your drafts, get into the habit of including bracketed, boldfaced notes to yourself. These comments, suggestions, and questions can help you later, when you revise.

- ☐ **Take regular breaks as you write.** Try writing one section of your essay at a time. When you have completed a section—for example, one paragraph—take a break. Your mind will continue to focus on your assignment while you do other things. When you return to your essay, writing will be easier.

- ☐ **Leave yourself enough time to revise.** All writing benefits from revision, so be sure you have time to reconsider your work and to write as many drafts as you need.

- ☐ **Save your drafts.** Using the Save option in your word processor's file menu saves only your most recent draft. If you prefer to save every draft you write (so you can return to an earlier draft to locate a different version of a sentence or to reconsider a section you have deleted), use the Save As option instead.

- ☐ **Label your files.** To help you keep track of which version of your paper is which, label every file in your folder by content and date (for example, **First draft, 10/20**).

- ☐ **Don't delete material.** If you revise directly on the computer, be very careful not to delete material that you may need later. Instead, move such material to the end of your document so you can retrieve it later if necessary.

Using her informal outline and her storyboard to guide her, Kimberly Romney wrote the following rough draft. Notice that she included boldfaced and bracketed notes to remind herself to add or check information later.

Rough Draft

College Students and Computer Literacy

Today, most colleges expect their entering students to be familiar with computers. From registering for courses to contacting professors, students are required to use computers on a daily basis. I was at a real disadvantage when I entered college because I lacked important computer skills. **[Add more here? Maybe use Gates?]**

Computers have become increasingly important on college campuses. When I arrived at school, I was asked to use *Microsoft Word* to type my papers. I was also encouraged to use the Internet for research. **[Do I document this?]** In fact, many professors posted their syllabi on Web pages. I also quickly learned the importance of email. Although I'd been exposed to email in high school, I'd never had to learn how to use an email program like *Eudora* or how to download it to my computer. I had to call the help desk and it was really embarrassing. All of my friends seemed to have few problems doing this.

If you don't have high computer literacy skills, there are many consequences. Students have a lot of difficulty completing everyday tasks. It may take them a long time to email a professor or register for a course simply because they are unfamiliar with the software being used. Students who feel uncomfortable using computers also feel embarrassed. They may not want to admit that they don't understand how to use particular software programs. If they don't seek help, they miss out on a lot of opportunities. Computers are so important in school that students who don't understand them may avoid taking exciting classes that require a working knowledge of specific computer programs.

The reality is that a lot of students don't have a lot of experience with computers. Students who do understand computers are usually math and science people. If you're interested in English, you probably aren't familiar with computers. Even if they are familiar with computers, he or she may have never used the Internet. In small towns, students probably don't have access to a computer at home. Many high schools also have trouble providing their students with computer access, which is a big problem for many students. **[Need more/better support here]**

Our school does provide students with several opportunities to improve their computer skills, but most students don't know about them. The library offers several classes that teach students how to access useful information online. The computer lab also holds classes on how to use software programs like *Microsoft Word* and *Microsoft Publisher*. Students can even learn how to design their own Web pages. Unfortunately, these classes are not well advertised. Course listings appear on the Information Technology Web site, but for those students who avoid using the Internet, finding out when and where to take classes is difficult. Ironically, students who need these classes will probably not be using the Internet a lot to get information about the university. **[Check on all of this to make sure]**

When I arrived at college, I had very few computer skills. Our high school had a couple of computers, but I didn't have Internet access at home. My first required class was a writing course and was held in a computer lab. I was forced to learn how to use computers and the Internet to write my papers. After a few weeks of pretending to know what I was doing, I decided to try to find some help. I was too embarrassed to ask my professor where to go for help, so it took me a few days to find out when and where the classes were. I ended up going to the library and asking the librarian. She was really helpful and I enrolled in a couple of them. After a course on *Microsoft Word* and the Internet, I felt much more comfortable using computers.

It is important to remember that some students arrive at college with few computer skills and that they are at a significant disadvantage. **[Add more!]**

■ EXERCISE 1

Write a rough draft of the essay you began planning in Chapter 4.

6b Moving from Rough Draft to Final Draft

As you **revise** successive drafts of your essay, you should narrow your focus from larger elements, such as overall structure and content, to increasingly smaller elements, such as sentence structure and word choice.

1 Revising Your Rough Draft

After you finish your rough draft, set it aside for a day or two if you can. When you return to it, focus on only a few areas at a time. As you review this first draft, begin by evaluating the thesis-and-support structure of your essay and your paper's general organization. Once you feel satisfied that your thesis statement says what you want it to say and that your essay's content supports this thesis and is logically arranged, you can turn your attention to other matters. For example, you can make sure that you have included all the **transitional words and phrases** that readers will need to follow your discussion.

See 7b2

COMPUTER TIP academic.cengage.com/eng/kirsznermandell

MOVING TEXT

Use the Copy, Cut, and Paste features found under your word processor's Edit menu to help you move text within a single document or between documents.

---

2 Writing and Revising Additional Drafts

After you have read over your rough draft several times, making notes about your plans for revision, you are ready to write a second draft.

Because it can be more difficult to read text on the computer screen than on hard copy, you should print out every draft. This will enable you to make revisions by hand on printed pages and then return to the computer to type these changes into your document. (As you type your draft, you may want to triple-space. This will make any errors or inconsistencies more obvious and at the same time give you plenty of room to write questions, add new material, or try out new versions of sentences.)

If you write your revisions by hand on hard copy, you will find it helpful to develop a system of symbols. For instance, you can box groups of words (or even entire paragraphs) that you want to relocate, using an arrow to indicate the new location. When you want to add words, use a caret like ^*this*^. An excerpt from one of Kimberly's drafts, with her handwritten revisions, appears on the following page.

Draft with Handwritten Revisions (Excerpt)

Despite the necessity of a strong working knowledge of computers and the Internet, many students arrive at college with very little to no experience of either.

The reality is that a lot of students don't have a lot of experience with computers. Students ^*might not, for example, have had access to a computer in their home.* ~~who do understand computers are usually math and science people. If you're interested in English, you probably aren't familiar with computers~~. Even if they are familiar with computers, ~~he or she~~ *they* may have never used the Internet.

3 Adding Visuals

As you write and revise, you should consider whether one or more **visuals** might strengthen your paper by providing support for the points you are making. Sometimes you may want to use a visual that appears in one of your sources; at other times, you may be able to create a visual (for example, a photograph or a chart) yourself; at still other times, you may need to search a clip-art database to find an appropriate visual.

Once you have decided to add a particular visual to your paper, the next step is to determine where to insert it. (In general, you should place the visual in the part of the essay where it will have the greatest impact in terms of conveying information or persuading your audience.) Then, you need to format the visual. (Within *Microsoft Word*, you can double-click on an image to call up a picture-editing menu that allows you to alter the size, color, and position of the image within your essay—and even permits you to wrap text around the image.) Next, you should make sure that the visual stands out in your paper: surround it with white space, add ruled lines, or enclose it in a box.

Once the visual has been inserted where you want it, you need to integrate it into your paper. You can include a sentence that introduces the visual (**The following table illustrates the similarities between the two health plans**), or you can refer to it in your text (**Figure 1 shows Kennedy as a young man**) to give it some context and explain why you are using it. You should also identify the visual by labeling it (**Fig. 1. Photo of John F. Kennedy, 1937**). In addition, if the visual is not one you have created yourself, you must **document** it. In most academic disciplines, this means including full source information directly below the image and sometimes in the list of references as well. (To see how Kimberly integrated a visual into her paper, **see 6e**.)

See Pts. 4–5

CHECKLIST

ADDING VISUALS

To add a visual to your paper, follow these steps:
- ☐ Find an appropriate visual.
- ☐ Place the image in a suitable location.
- ☐ Format the image, and make sure it is clearly set off from the written text.
- ☐ Introduce the visual with a sentence (or refer to it in the text).
- ☐ Label the visual.
- ☐ Document the visual (if necessary).

■ EXERCISE 2

Look carefully at the visual you chose in Chapter 4, Exercise 8. In one sentence, state the main idea that this visual communicates to its audience. Then, list the individual images and details in the visual that support this main idea. Does this visual reinforce the points you are trying to make in your essay? If it does not, look for one that does.

6c Using Specific Revision Strategies

Everyone revises differently, and every writing task calls for a slightly different process of revision. Five strategies in particular can help you revise at any stage of the writing process.

1 Using Word-Processing Tools

Your word-processing program includes a variety of tools designed to make the revision process easier. For example, *Microsoft Word*'s **Track Changes** feature allows you to make changes to a draft electronically and to see the original version of the draft and the changes simultaneously. Changes appear in color as underlined or crossed out text, and writers have the option of viewing the changes on the screen or in print. This feature also allows you to accept or reject all changes or just specific changes.

Another useful revision tool is the **Compare** feature. Whereas Track Changes allows you to keep track of changes to a single document, the Compare feature allows you to analyze the changes in two completely separate versions of a document, usually an original and its most recent update. Changes appear in color as highlighted text.

Kimberly used Track Changes as she revised her rough draft. An excerpt from her rough draft, along with her changes, appears on the following page.

Rough Draft with Track Changes (Excerpt)

> Computers have become increasingly important ~~on college campuses~~ <ins>in today's society. Consequently, many scholars and public officials are concerned that those without access to computers will be at a disadvantage. Henry Louis Gates Jr., for example, argues in "One Internet, Two Nations" that the content on the Internet, which is primarily aimed at whites, threatens to leave African Americans behind. Similarly, college students who arrive with low computer literacy skills are at a disadvantage.</ins>
>
> When I arrived at school, I was asked to use computers <ins>in several ways. First, I was required to use *Microsoft Word* when typing</ins>~~to type~~ my papers. I was also encouraged to use the Internet for research. In fact, many professors posted their syllabi on Web pages. I also quickly learned the importance of email. Although I'd been exposed to email in high school, I'd never had to learn how to use an email program like *Eudora* or download it to my computer. I had to call the help desk and it was really embarrassing. All of my friends seemed to have few problems doing this.

COMPUTER TIP   academic.cengage.com/eng/kirsznermandell

TRACKING CHANGES VS. COMPARING DOCUMENTS

Where you are in the writing process can help you decide whether to track your changes or to compare one complete version of your document with another. Tracking changes is especially useful in helping you follow sentence-level changes as you draft and revise; it can also be helpful later on, when you edit words and phrases. Comparing documents is most helpful when you are comparing global changes, such as paragraph unity and thesis-and-support structure, between one draft and another.

---

2 Participating in Peer Review

Peer review—a collaborative revision strategy that enables you to get feedback from your classmates—is another useful activity. With peer review, instead of trying to imagine an audience for your paper, you address a real audience, exchanging drafts with classmates and commenting on their drafts. Such collaborative work can be formal or informal, conducted in person or electronically. For example, you and a classmate may email drafts back and forth, perhaps using *Word*'s Comment feature (see p. 60), or your instructor may conduct the class as a workshop, assigning students to work in groups to critique other students' essays.

> **COMPUTER TIP** academic.cengage.com/eng/kirsznermandell
> **PEER REVIEW**
> Certain features in word-processing programs are particularly useful for peer review. For example, the **Comment** tool allows several readers to insert comments at any point or to highlight a particular portion of the text they would like to comment on and then insert annotations. To write comments, a reviewer clicks the Insert menu and selects Comment.
>   A particular advantage of this function for peer-review groups is that a single paper can receive comments from multiple readers. Comments are identified by the initials of the reviewer and by a color assigned to the reviewer.

An excerpt from Kimberly's second draft with peer reviewers' comments appears below.

Second Draft with Peer Reviewers' Comments (Excerpt)

When I arrived at school, I was asked to use computers in several ways. First, I was required to use *Microsoft Word* when typing my papers. I was also encouraged to use the Internet for research. In fact, many professors posted their syllabi on Web pages. I also quickly learned the importance of email. Although I'd been exposed to email in high school, I'd never had to learn how to use an email program like *Eudora* or download it to my computer. I had to call the help desk and it was really embarrassing. All of my friends seemed to have few problems doing this.

Comment [KL1]: That's for sure ☺!

Comment [KL2]: Talking w/profs. is another imp. use of email.

Comment [BR1]: Yes! I emailed Prof. Wilson when I couldn't make office hrs.

Comment [CB1]: There's a lot more to talk about here. What about listservs? *PowerPoint*?

> **CHECKLIST**
> **QUESTIONS FOR PEER REVIEW**
> The following questions can help guide you through the peer-review process:
> ☐ What is the essay about? Does the topic fulfill the requirements of the assignment?

Using Specific Revision Strategies ■ **rev** **6c** 61

- ☐ What is the essay's main idea? Is the thesis clearly worded? If not, how can the wording be improved?
- ☐ Is the essay arranged logically? Do the body paragraphs appear in an appropriate order?
- ☐ What ideas support the thesis? Does each body paragraph develop one of these ideas?
- ☐ Is any necessary information missing? Identify any areas that seem to need further development. Is any information irrelevant? If so, suggest possible deletions.
- ☐ Can you think of any ideas or examples from your own reading, experience, or observations that would strengthen the writer's essay?
- ☐ Can you follow the writer's ideas? If not, would clearer connections between sentences or paragraphs be helpful? Where are such connections needed?
- ☐ Is the introductory paragraph interesting to you? Would another opening strategy be more effective?
- ☐ Does the conclusion leave you with a sense of closure? Would another concluding strategy be more effective?
- ☐ Is anything unclear or confusing?
- ☐ What is the essay's greatest strength?
- ☐ What is the essay's greatest weakness?

3 Using Instructors' Comments

Instructors' comments—in correction symbols, in marginal comments, or in conferences—can also help you revise.

Correction Symbols. Your instructor may indicate concerns about style, grammar, mechanics, or punctuation by using the correction symbols listed on the inside back cover of this book. Instead of correcting a problem, the instructor will simply identify it and supply the number of the section in this handbook that deals with the error. After reading the appropriate pages, you should be able to make the necessary corrections on your own. For example, the symbol and number beside the following sentence referred a student to **43e2**, the section in this handbook that discusses sexist language.

Instructor's Comment: Equal access to jobs is a desirable goal for all ⟨mankind⟩.   *Sxt—see 43e2*

After reading the appropriate section in the handbook, the student made the following change.

Revised: Equal access to jobs is a desirable goal for everyone.

Marginal Comments. Instructors frequently write marginal comments on your essays to suggest changes in content or structure. Such comments may ask you to add supporting information or to arrange paragraphs differently within the essay, or they may recommend stylistic changes, such as more varied sentences. Marginal comments may also question your logic, suggest a more explicit thesis statement, ask for clearer transitions, or propose a new direction for a discussion. In some cases, you can consider these comments to be suggestions rather than corrections. You may decide to incorporate these ideas into a revised draft of your essay, or you may not. In all instances, however, you should take your instructor's comments seriously.

An excerpt from Kimberly's second draft, along with her instructor's comments, follows. (Note that her instructor used *Microsoft Word*'s Comment tool to insert comments.)

Second Draft with Instructor's Comments (Excerpt)

When I arrived at school, I was asked to use computers in several ways. First, I was required to use *Microsoft Word* when typing my papers. I was also encouraged to use the Internet for research. In fact, many professors posted their syllabi on Web pages. I also quickly learned the importance of email. Although|I'd|been exposed to email in high school, |I'd|never had to learn how to use an email program like *Eudora* or download it to my computer. I had to call the help desk and it was really |embarrassing.| All of my friends seemed to have few problems doing this.

Comment [PW1]: In your final draft, edit out all contractions. (Contractions are too informal for most college writing.) See 54b1.

Comment [PW2]: Consider making this point less personal. Use this paragraph to talk about all of the reasons a student might use a computer in college. Remember, you are moving from general to specific. See 7b1.

Conferences. Many instructors require or encourage one-on-one conferences, and you should certainly schedule a conference if you can. During a conference, you can respond to your instructor's questions and ask for clarification of marginal comments. If a certain section of your paper presents a problem, use your conference time to focus on it, perhaps asking for help in sharpening your thesis or choosing more accurate words.

CHECKLIST

GETTING THE MOST OUT OF A CONFERENCE

- ☐ **Make an appointment.** If you are unable to keep your appointment, be sure to call or email your instructor to reschedule.

- ☐ **Review your work carefully.** Before the conference, reread your notes and drafts, and go over all your instructor's comments and suggestions. Make all the changes you can on your draft.

- ☐ **Bring a list of questions.** Preparing a list in advance will enable you to get the most out of the conference in the allotted time.

- ☐ **Bring your paper-in-progress.** If you have several drafts, you may want to bring them all, but be sure you bring any draft that has your instructor's comments on it.

- ☐ **Take notes.** As you discuss your paper, write down any suggestions that you think will be helpful so you won't forget them when you revise.

- ☐ **Participate actively.** A successful conference is not a monologue; it should be an open exchange of ideas.

CLOSE-UP

WRITING CENTER CONFERENCES

If you are unable to meet with your instructor—and, in fact, even if you are—it is always a good idea to make an appointment with a tutor in your school's writing center. A writing tutor (who may be either a professional or a student) is likely to know a good deal about what your instructor expects and is trained to help you produce an effective essay.

What a writing tutor can do is help you find ideas to write about and develop a thesis statement, identify parts of your essay that need more support (and help you decide what kind of support to include), and coach you as you revise your essay. What a tutor will *not* do is write your paper for you or act as a proofreader.

When you meet in conference with a writing tutor, follow the guidelines in the checklist above. In addition, be sure to bring a copy of your assignment and any drafts that include your instructor's comments.

Conferences can also take place online—most commonly, through email. If you send emails to your instructor, to your writing center tutor, or to members of your peer-review group, include a specific subject line that clearly identifies the message as coming from a student writer (for example, "question about assignment"). This is especially important if your email address does not include your name. When you attach a document to an email and send it for comments, mention the attachment in your subject line (for example, "first draft—see attachment")—and be sure your name appears on the attachment itself, not just on the email.

4 Using a Formal Outline

See 5d

Outlining can be helpful early in the revision process, when you are reworking the larger structural elements of your essay, or later on, when you are checking the logic of a completed draft. A **formal outline** reveals at once whether points are irrelevant or poorly placed—or, worse, missing. It also reveals the hierarchy of your ideas—which points are dominant and which are subordinate.

As part of her revision process, Kimberly made the following topic outline to help her check her paper's organization.

Topic Outline

<u>Thesis statement:</u> I was at a real disadvantage when I entered college because I lacked important computer skills.

I. Importance of computers
   A. Those with access to Internet vs. those without (Gates)
   B. "Digital divide" among college students
II. College students' computer needs
   A. Running basic programs
   B. Using the Internet
   C. Using email
III. Reasons for some students' poor computer skills
   A. Lack of access to computers at home
   B. Limited access to computers in elementary or high school
IV. Consequences for students with poor computer skills
   A. Difficulty with everyday tasks, such as registering for classes or contacting professors or classmates
   B. Embarrassment
   C. No access to Internet or sophisticated software
V. Possible solutions on our campus
   A. Classes
   B. More publicity

VI. My personal experience
   A. Weak computer skills
   B. Writing class in computer lab
   C. Classes on *Word*, email, and the Internet
VII. Future
   A. High schools
   B. Colleges

> **COMPUTER TIP** academic.cengage.com/eng/kirsznermandell
>
> **FORMATTING AN OUTLINE**
>
> If you use your computer's word-processing program to construct a formal outline, the Bullets and Numbering feature and the Auto Format feature will help you to format it properly. Usually found in the Format menu, Bullets and Numbering allows you to select the format type of your outline, including styles that use roman numerals, letters, and/or numbers. Once you have selected your outline style, Auto Format will arrange what you type in the selected format and allow you to customize the formatting further.

■ **EXERCISE 3**

Outline your rough draft, and use this outline to help you check the arrangement of your essay's ideas. Make any structural revisions you think are necessary. (Try not to worry at this point about stylistic issues, such as sentence variety and word choice.)

5 Using Checklists

The revision checklist that follows is keyed to sections of this text. Moving from global to specific concerns, it parallels the actual revision process. As your understanding of the writing process increases and you become better able to assess the strengths and weaknesses of your writing, you may want to add items to (or delete items from) this checklist. You can also use your instructors' comments to tailor the checklist to your own needs.

> **CHECKLIST**
>
> **REVISING YOUR ESSAY**
>
> **The whole essay**
> ☐ Do you understand your essay's purpose? **(See 1a.)**
> ☐ Have you taken your audience's needs into account? **(See 1b.)**
>
> *(continued)*

REVISING YOUR ESSAY *(continued)*

- ☐ Are thesis and support logically related, with each body paragraph supporting your thesis statement? **(See 5a.)**
- ☐ Is your thesis statement clearly and specifically worded? **(See 5b1.)**
- ☐ Have you discussed everything promised in your thesis statement? **(See 5b1.)**
- ☐ Have you presented your ideas in a logical sequence? Can you think of a different arrangement that might be more appropriate for your purpose? **(See 5c.)**

Paragraphs

- ☐ Does each body paragraph have just one main idea? **(See 7a.)**
- ☐ Are topic sentences clearly worded and logically related to your thesis? **(See 7a1.)**
- ☐ Does each body paragraph have a clear organizing principle? **(See 7b1.)**
- ☐ Are the relationships between sentences within your paragraphs clear? **(See 7b2–4.)**
- ☐ Are your body paragraphs developed fully enough to support your points? **(See 7c.)**
- ☐ Does your introductory paragraph arouse reader interest and prepare readers for what is to come? **(See 7e2.)**
- ☐ Are your paragraphs arranged according to familiar patterns of development? **(See 7d.)**
- ☐ Have you provided transitional paragraphs where necessary? **(See 7e1.)**
- ☐ Does your concluding paragraph sum up your main points? **(See 7e3.)**

Sentences

- ☐ Have you used correct sentence structure? **(See Chs. 38 and 39.)**
- ☐ Have you avoided potentially confusing shifts in tense, voice, mood, person, or number? **(See 42a1–4.)**
- ☐ Are your sentences constructed logically? **(See 42b–d.)**
- ☐ Have you placed modifiers clearly and logically? **(See Ch. 40.)**
- ☐ Are your sentences varied? **(See Ch. 35.)**
- ☐ Have you combined sentences where ideas are closely related? **(See 35b.)**
- ☐ Have you used emphatic word order? **(See 36a.)**
- ☐ Have you used sentence structure to signal the relative importance of clauses in a sentence and their logical relationship to one another? **(See 36b.)**
- ☐ Have you strengthened your sentences with repetition, balance, and parallelism? **(See 36c–d, 41a.)**

- ☐ Have you eliminated nonessential words and unnecessary repetition? (See **37a–b**.)
- ☐ Have you avoided overloading your sentences with too many words, phrases, and clauses? (See **37c**.)

Words

- ☐ Is your level of diction appropriate for your audience and your purpose? (See **43a–b**.)
- ☐ Have you selected words that accurately reflect your intentions? (See **43b1**.)
- ☐ Have you chosen words that are specific, concrete, and unambiguous? (See **43b3–4**.)
- ☐ Have you enriched your writing with figures of speech? (See **43c**.)
- ☐ Have you eliminated jargon, neologisms, pretentious diction, clichés, and offensive language from your writing? (See **43d–e**.)

■ **EXERCISE 4**

Review the second draft of your paper, this time focusing on paragraphing, topic sentences, and transitions and on the way you structure your sentences and select your words. (Use the appropriate items in the checklist above as a guide.)

■ **EXERCISE 5**

Using the revision checklist above as a model, create a ten-item customized checklist—one that reflects the specific concerns that you need to consider when you revise an essay. Then, use this checklist to help you in your revision.

CLOSE-UP

CHOOSING A TITLE

When you are ready to decide on a title for your essay, keep these criteria in mind:

- A title should be descriptive, giving an accurate sense of your essay's focus. Whenever possible, use one or more of the key words and phrases that are central to your paper.
- A title can echo the wording of your assignment, reminding you (and your instructor) that you have not lost sight of it.
- Ideally, a title should arouse interest, perhaps by using a provocative question or a quotation or by taking a controversial position.

(continued)

> **CHOOSING A TITLE** *(continued)*
>
> **Assignment:** Write about a problem faced on college campuses today.
> **Topic:** Free speech on campus
> **Possible titles:**
>
> Free Speech: A Problem for Today's Colleges (echoes wording of assignment and includes key words of essay)
>
> How Free Should Free Speech on Campus Be? (provocative question)
>
> The Right to "Shout 'Fire' in a Crowded Theater" (quotation)
>
> Hate Speech: A Dangerous Abuse of Free Speech on Campus (controversial position)

6d Editing and Proofreading

Once you have revised your drafts to your satisfaction, two final tasks remain: **editing** and **proofreading**.

> **COMPUTER TIP**   academic.cengage.com/eng/kirsznermandell
>
> **EDITING AND PROOFREADING**
>
> - As you edit and proofread, try looking at only a small portion of text at a time. Reduce the size of your window so that you can see only one or two lines of text at a time. By using this technique, you can dramatically reduce the number of surface-level errors in your paper.
> - Use the Search or Find command to look for usage errors you commonly make—for instance, confusing *it's* with *its*, *lay* with *lie*, *effect* with *affect*, *their* with *there*, or *too* with *to*. You can also uncover sexist language by searching for words like *he*, *his*, *him*, or *man*.
> - Finally, keep in mind that neatness does not equal correctness. The clean text that your computer produces can mask flaws that might otherwise be apparent; for this reason, it is up to you to make sure spelling errors and typos do not slip by.

See 43e2

1 Editing

When you **edit**, you concentrate on grammar and spelling, punctuation and mechanics. Although you have dealt with these issues as you revised previous drafts of your paper, editing is now your primary focus. As you edit, read each sentence carefully, consulting the items on the Editing Checklist on page 69. Keep your preliminary notes and drafts and your reference books (such as this handbook and a dictionary) nearby as you work. Some reference works (such as *Dictionary.com* and *Merriam-Webster Online*) are also available online.

CHECKLIST
EDITING YOUR ESSAY
Grammar
- ☐ Do subjects and verbs agree? (**See 49a.**)
- ☐ Do pronouns and antecedents agree? (**See 49b.**)
- ☐ Are verb forms correct? (**See 48a.**)
- ☐ Are tense, mood, and voice of verbs logical and appropriate? (**See 48b–d.**)
- ☐ Have you used the appropriate case for each pronoun? (**See 47a–b.**)
- ☐ Are pronoun references clear and unambiguous? (**See 47c.**)
- ☐ Are adjectives and adverbs used correctly? (**See Ch. 50.**)

Punctuation
- ☐ Is end punctuation used correctly? (**See Ch. 51.**)
- ☐ Are commas used correctly? (**See Ch. 52.**)
- ☐ Are semicolons used correctly? (**See Ch. 53.**)
- ☐ Are apostrophes used correctly? (**See Ch. 54.**)
- ☐ Are quotation marks used where they are required? (**See Ch. 55.**)
- ☐ Are quotation marks used correctly with other punctuation marks? (**See 55e.**)
- ☐ Are other punctuation marks—colons, dashes, parentheses, brackets, slashes, and ellipses—used correctly? (**See Ch. 56.**)

Spelling
- ☐ Are all words spelled correctly? (**See Ch. 45.**)

Mechanics
- ☐ Is capitalization consistent with standard English usage? (**See Ch. 57.**)
- ☐ Are italics used correctly? (**See Ch. 58.**)
- ☐ Are hyphens used where required and placed correctly within and between words? (**See Ch. 59.**)
- ☐ Are abbreviations used where convention calls for their use? (**See Ch. 60.**)
- ☐ Are numerals and spelled-out numbers used appropriately? (**See Ch. 61.**)

2 Proofreading

After you have completed your editing, print out a final draft and **proofread**, rereading every word carefully to make sure neither you nor your computer missed any typos or other errors. Finally, make sure the final typed copy of your paper conforms to your instructor's format requirements.

6d Drafting and Revising

> **CLOSE-UP**
>
> **PROOFREADING STRATEGIES**
>
> To help you proofread more effectively, try using these strategies:
> - Read your paper aloud.
> - Have a friend read your paper aloud to you.
> - Read silently word by word, using your finger or a sheet of paper to help you keep your place.
> - Read your paper's sentences in reverse order, beginning with the last sentence.

> **COMPUTER TIP** academic.cengage.com/eng/kirszpermandell
>
> **USING SPELL CHECKERS AND GRAMMAR CHECKERS**
>
> Although spell checkers and grammar checkers can make the process of editing and proofreading your papers easier, they have limitations. For this reason, neither a spell checker nor a grammar checker is a substitute for careful editing and proofreading.
>
> - **Spell Checkers** A spell checker simply identifies strings of letters it does not recognize; it does *not* distinguish between homophones or spot every typographical error. For example, it does not recognize *there* in "They forgot *there* books" as incorrect, nor does it identify a typo that produces a correctly spelled word, such as *word* for *work* or *thing* for *think*. Moreover, a spell checker may not recognize every technical term, proper noun, or foreign word you may use.
> - **Grammar Checkers** Grammar checkers scan documents for certain features (the number of words in a sentence, for example); however, they are not able to read a document to see if it makes sense. For this reason, grammar checkers are not always accurate. For example, they may identify a long sentence as a run-on when it is, in fact, grammatically correct, and they generally advise against using passive voice—even in contexts where it is appropriate. Moreover, grammar checkers do not always supply answers; often, they ask questions—for example, whether *which* should be *that* or whether *which* should be preceded by a comma—that you must answer. In short, grammar checkers can guide your editing and proofreading, but you must be the one who decides when a sentence is (or is not) correct.

■ **EXERCISE 6**

Using the checklist on page 69 as a guide, edit your essay. Then, proofread it carefully, give it an appropriate title, and print out your final draft.

■ **EXERCISE 7**

Review your responses to Exercises 1 and 2 in Chapter 4. Then, write a paragraph explaining how your personal writing process has changed since you wrote those responses.

6e Preparing a Final Draft

The annotated essay that follows is the final draft of Kimberly Romney's essay, which you first saw on pages 54–55. It incorporates the suggestions that her peer reviewers and her instructor made on her second draft.

This final draft is very different from the rough draft of the essay. As she revised, Kimberly moved from a focus on her own problems to a broader view of the issue, and she revised her thesis statement accordingly. She also added specific information from sources to support her points, including parenthetical documentation and a works-cited list that conform to **MLA** documentation style. Finally, she added a **visual** (accompanied by a caption) to illustrate the progress made in her high school since she graduated.

See Ch. 18

See 6b3

Romney 1

Kimberly Romney
Professor Wilson
English 101
10 November 2006

Computer Illiteracy: A Problem
for College Students

Introduction

Today, most colleges expect entering students to be familiar with computers. From registering for courses to contacting professors, students are required to use computers on a daily basis. For this reason, students who

Thesis statement

enter college with weak computer skills are at a significant disadvantage.

Importance of computers in society

Computers are increasingly important in today's society. As Henry Louis Gates Jr. writes in his article "One Internet, Two Nations," many people are concerned that there is a division between those who have access to the Internet and those who do not. He writes, "Today we stand at the brink of becoming two societies, one largely white and plugged in and the other black and unplugged" (500). The gap between those who are technologically literate and those who are not (although it has narrowed since Gates wrote in 2002) extends beyond race and ethnicity to include the elderly, the disabled, and those who live in rural areas. This "digital divide" can cause serious problems for college students.

Importance of computers in college

Entering college students are expected to be familiar with a variety of software programs. Most professors, for example, require their students to use *Microsoft Word* to write their papers, and many instructors expect their students to use *PowerPoint* to present their papers or research projects.

Students are also expected to be familiar with the Internet. For example, registration for classes is often conducted online. Professors and administrators use the Internet to post information about campuswide events, and many professors create their own Web pages where they post their syllabi and class assignments. Finally, professors expect their students to use the Internet when conducting research.

Importance of the Internet

A good understanding of how email works is also necessary for college success. If a student wants to communicate with someone in the class, email is one of the most efficient ways to do so. Email is also vital for communicating with professors. For example, if a student cannot attend office hours, he or she can still ask the professor a question.

Importance of email

Despite the importance of a strong working knowledge of computers and the Internet, many students (particularly older students who have been out of school for a few years) arrive at college with very little experience with either. In fact, computer illiteracy can be a real problem for entering college students. Some students have poor computer skills because they did not have access to a computer at home. Some families cannot afford computers, and others simply do not see a computer as a necessity.

Reason for students' poor skills: lack of access at home

Other students may not have been taught computer skills in elementary or high school. A recent study of efforts to bridge the "digital divide" in elementary and high schools reported that although many schools are improving their access to computers, teachers still might not use them in the classroom:

Reason for students' poor skills: lack of access at school

Only 54 percent of respondents said they integrate computers into their daily curriculum, and more than 61 percent of them said they do not have enough computers in their classrooms. More than half of teachers believe there should be one computer for each student, and nearly one-third of them say there should be one computer for every five students. (Jones)

Problems caused by weak computer skills

Those students who arrive at college with weak computer skills face serious consequences. For example, registering for classes on the Internet and contacting professors or other students via email become time-consuming (rather than timesaving) tasks. Students may be so embarrassed by their weak computer skills that they do not ask for help. Without help, they have difficulty improving their skills. As a result, they do not benefit from the opportunities offered by the Internet (such as faster and more thorough research) or by sophisticated software programs (such as professional-looking papers and presentations).

Possible solution to problems: classes

Colleges and universities recognize the problems these students face and offer programs to help them. For example, our campus has an outreach program aimed at students with sub-par computer skills. Once a week, the computer lab offers classes on software programs such as *Microsoft Word*, *PowerPoint*, and *Dreamweaver*. A class about email not only gives students basic information (such as how to send and open attachments), but also tells them how to use programs (such as *Outlook Express*) to track their daily schedules and appointments. The library also offers several classes, both general and more discipline-specific, about how to use the Internet for research.

However, while this outreach program can provide students with opportunities to improve their skills, many do not know about it. Students are not given information about these classes at orientation, and they are not well advertised in the student newspaper, or even in the computer lab and library. In addition, some staff members are not very sensitive to the embarrassment that many students feel about having poor computer skills. Many students might avoid asking a librarian or computer lab proctor for help, and this is a problem that a good advertising campaign would remedy.

Limitations of classes

As a student from a small town where computer classes were not a part of the high school curriculum, I have personal experience with this problem. I came to college with very limited computer skills. Although I had some knowledge of *Microsoft Word* and had used the Internet and email, I was not very comfortable using computers. One of my first classes here was a writing class that was held in a computer lab. I was confronted with my problem every Monday, Wednesday, and Friday, and because I was embarrassed about my poor computer skills, I did not want to ask the professor for help. Trying to find help on my own was difficult. It took me two weeks to figure out when and where classes on *Microsoft Word* and the Internet were held. However, after taking these classes, my skills were greatly improved.

Personal experience: problems in college

Through my own experience, I have come to realize that more efforts need to be made at the high school level to educate students about technology. In my own

Personal experience: changes in high school

hometown, such efforts are already underway: my high school now has a computer lab (see fig. 1), and the school district instituted a computer literacy class for all high school freshmen the year after I graduated.

Fig. 1. Student in the Woodrow Wilson High School computer lab, personal photograph by Vicky Wellborn; 5 Oct. 2006.

According to my high school English teacher, Vicky Wellborn, students really enjoy this class: they go to the new computer lab during breaks or after school, and the lab is frequently full. In addition, the district now requires teachers to take a computer literacy class so that they are better prepared to answer students' questions (Wellborn).

Despite my own frustrating experiences, I am optimistic about the future. As high schools continue to make efforts to incorporate technology into the classroom, students entering college will be better prepared for the technological challenges they will face. And as they become more computer literate, the "digital divide" will close.

Works Cited

Gates, Henry Louis, Jr. "One Internet, Two Nations." *The Blair Reader*. Ed. Laurie G. Kirszner and Stephen R. Mandell. 4th ed. Upper Saddle River: Prentice, 2002. 499-501. Print.

Jones, K. C. "Survey Says." *Technology & Learning* 26.3 (2005): 5. *Expanded Academic ASAP*. Web. 7 Oct. 2006.

Wellborn, Vicky. "Re: Computer Literacy." Message to the author. 23 Oct. 2006. E-mail.

7

Writing Paragraphs

❓ FAQs

When do I begin a new paragraph? (p. 78)
What transitional words and phrases can I use to make my paragraphs flow? (p. 83)
How do I know if I have enough information to support my paragraph's main idea? (p. 88)
How do I write a good introductory paragraph for my paper? (p. 100)
How do I write an effective concluding paragraph? (p. 102)

A **paragraph** is a group of related sentences. It may be complete in itself or part of a longer piece of writing.

CHECKLIST

When to Paragraph

- ☐ Begin a new paragraph whenever you move from one major point to another.
- ☐ Begin a new paragraph whenever you move your readers from one time period or location to another.
- ☐ Begin a new paragraph whenever you introduce a new step in a process or sequence.
- ☐ Begin a new paragraph when you want to emphasize an important idea.
- ☐ Begin a new paragraph every time a new person speaks.
- ☐ Begin a new paragraph to signal the end of your introduction and the beginning of your conclusion.

ESL TIP

Indent the first line of each paragraph one-half inch. When you type, set the margin at one-half inch, and press the return key on your computer every time you start a new paragraph. Do not add extra lines of space between paragraphs.

7a Writing Unified Paragraphs

A paragraph is **unified** when it develops a single main idea. The **topic sentence** states the main idea of the paragraph, and the other sentences in the paragraph support that idea.

1 Using Topic Sentences

Topic sentences can be placed at the beginning or at the end of a paragraph. In some cases, the paragraph's main idea may even be implied; if so, there is no explicitly stated topic sentence.

Topic Sentence at the Beginning. A topic sentence at the beginning of a paragraph tells readers what to expect and helps them to understand your paragraph's main idea immediately.

> I was a listening child, careful to hear the very different sounds of Spanish and English. Wide-eyed with hearing, I'd listen to sounds more than words. First, there were English (*gringo*) sounds. So many words were still unknown that when the butcher or the lady at the drugstore said something to me, exotic polysyllabic sounds would bloom in the midst of their sentences. Often the speech of people in public seemed to me very loud, booming with confidence. The man behind the counter would literally ask, "What can I do for you?" But by being so firm and so clear, the sound of his voice said that he was a gringo; he belonged in public society. (Richard Rodriguez, *Aria: A Memoir of a Bilingual Childhood*)

Topic Sentence at the End. If you are presenting an unusual or hard-to-accept idea, you may decide to place the topic sentence at the end of a paragraph. If you present a logical chain of reasoning and then state your conclusion in the topic sentence, you are more likely to convince readers that your conclusion is reasonable.

> These sprays, dusts, and aerosols are now applied almost universally to farms, gardens, forests, and homes—nonselective chemicals that have the power to kill every insect, the "good" and the "bad," to still the song of birds and the leaping of fish in the streams, to coat the leaves with a deadly film, and to linger on in soil—all this though the intended target may be only a few weeds or insects. Can anyone believe it is possible to lay down such a barrage of poisons on the surface without making it unfit for life? They should not be called "insecticides," but "biocides." (Rachel Carson, "The Obligation to Endure," *Silent Spring*)

Main Idea Implied. In some cases, you may not need a topic sentence. For example, in some narrative or descriptive paragraphs, an explicit topic sentence might seem forced or unnatural. In the following paragraph, the writer wants readers to conclude for themselves (as she did) that because she was female, she was considered inferior.

> I am eight years old and a tomboy. I have a cowboy hat, cowboy boots, checkered shirt and pants, all red. My playmates are my brothers, two and four years older than I. Their colors are black and green, the only difference in the way we are dressed. On Saturday nights we all go to the picture show, even my mother; Westerns are her favorite kind of movie. Back home, "on the ranch," we pretend we are Tom Mix, Hopalong Cassidy, Lash LaRue (we've even named one of our dogs Lash LaRue); we chase each other for hours rustling cattle, being outlaws, delivering damsels from distress. Then my parents decide to buy my brothers guns. These are not "real" guns. They shoot "BBs," copper pellets my brothers say will kill birds. Because I am a girl, I do not get a gun. Instantly I am relegated to the position of Indian. Now there appears a great distance between us. They shoot and shoot at everything with their new guns. I try to keep up with my bow and arrows. (Alice Walker, "Beauty: When the Other Dancer Is the Self," *In Search of Our Mothers' Gardens*)

2 Testing for Unity

Each sentence in a paragraph should support the main idea that is stated in the topic sentence. The following paragraph is not unified because it includes sentences that do not support the main idea.

Paragraph Not Unified

<u>One of the first problems I had as a college student was learning to use a computer.</u> All students were required to buy a computer before school started. Throughout the first semester, we took a special course to teach us to use a computer. *My laptop has a lot of memory and can do word processing and spreadsheets. It has a large screen and a DVD drive. My parents were happy that I had a computer, but they were concerned about the price. Tuition was high, and when they added in the price of the computer, it was almost out of reach. To offset expenses, I got a part-time job in the school library.* I am determined to overcome "computer anxiety" and to master my computer by the end of the semester. (student writer)

Sentences do not support main idea

When he revised, the writer deleted the sentences about his parents' financial situation and the computer's characteristics and added details related to his main idea.

Revised Paragraph

<u>One of the first problems I had as a college student was learning to use a computer.</u> All first-year students were required to buy a

computer before school started. Throughout the first semester, we took a special course to teach us to use the computer. In theory this system sounded fine, but in my case it was a disaster. In the first place, I had never owned a computer before. The closest I had ever come to a computer was the computer lab in high school. In the second place, I could not type well. And to make matters worse, many of the people in my computer orientation course already knew everything there was to know about operating a computer. By the end of the first week, I was convinced that I would never be able to keep up with them.

Sentences now support main idea

■ **EXERCISE 1**

Each of the following paragraphs is unified by one main idea, but that idea is not explicitly stated. Identify the main idea of each paragraph, write a topic sentence that expresses it, and decide where in the paragraph to place it.

A. The narrator in Ellison's novel leaves an all-black college in the South to seek his fortune—and his identity—in the North. Throughout the story, he experiences bigotry in all forms. Blacks as well as whites, friends as well as enemies, treat him according to their preconceived notions of what he should be, or how he can help to advance their causes. Clearly this is a book about racial prejudice. However, on another level, *Invisible Man* is more than the account of a young African American's initiation into the harsh realities of life in the United States before the civil rights movement. The narrator calls himself invisible because others refuse to see him. He becomes so alienated from society—black and white—that he chooses to live in isolation. But, when he has learned to see himself clearly, he will emerge demanding that others see him too.

B. "Lite" can mean that a product has fewer calories, or less fat, or less sodium, or it can simply mean that the product has a "light" color, texture, or taste. It may also mean none of these. Food can be advertised as 86 percent fat free when it is actually 50 percent fat because the term "fat free" is based on weight, and fat is extremely light. Another misleading term is "no cholesterol," which is found on some products that never had any cholesterol in the first place. Peanut butter, for example, contains no cholesterol—a fact that manufacturers have recently made an issue—but it is very high in fat and so would not be a very good food for most dieters. Sodium labeling presents still another problem. The terms "sodium free," "very low sodium," "low sodium," "reduced sodium," and "no salt added" have very specific meanings, frequently not explained on the packages on which they appear.

7b Writing Coherent Paragraphs

A paragraph is **coherent** when all its sentences are logically related to one another. You can create coherence by arranging details according to an organizing principle, by using transitional words and phrases, by using parallel structure, and by repeating key words and phrases.

1 Arranging Details

Even if all its sentences are about the same subject, a paragraph lacks coherence if the sentences are not arranged according to a general organizing principle—that is, if they are not arranged *spatially*, *chronologically*, or *logically*.

Spatial order establishes the way in which readers will "see" details. For example, an object or scene can be viewed from top to bottom or from near to far. Spatial order is central to **descriptive paragraphs**.

See 7d2

Chronological order presents events in sequence, using transitional words and phrases to establish the time order of events—*at first*, *yesterday*, *later*, *in 1930*, and so on. Chronological order is central to **narrative paragraphs** and **process paragraphs**.

See 7d1, 4

Logical order presents details or ideas in terms of their logical relationships to one another. Transitional words and phrases such as *first*, *second*, and *finally* establish these relationships and lead readers through the paragraph. For example, the ideas in a paragraph may move from *general to specific*, as in the conventional topic-sentence-at-the-beginning paragraph, or the ideas may progress from *specific to general*, as they do when the topic sentence appears at the end of the paragraph. A writer may also choose to begin with the *least important* idea and move to the *most important*. Logical order is central to **exemplification paragraphs** and **comparison-and-contrast paragraphs**.

See 7d3, 6

2 Using Transitional Words and Phrases

Transitional words and phrases clarify the relationships between sentences by identifying the spatial, chronological, and logical organizing principles discussed above. The following paragraph, which has no transitional words and phrases, illustrates just how important these words and phrases are.

Paragraph without Transitional Words and Phrases

Napoleon certainly made a change for the worse by leaving his small kingdom of Elba. He went back to Paris, and he abdicated for a second time. He fled to Rochefort in hope of escaping to America. He gave himself up to the English captain of the ship *Bellerophon*. He suggested that the Prince Regent grant him asylum, and he was refused. All he saw of England was the Devon coast and Plymouth Sound as he passed on to the remote island of St. Helena. He died on May 5, 1821, at the age of fifty-two.

In the narrative paragraph above, the topic sentence states the main idea of the paragraph, and the rest of the sentences support this idea. Because of the absence of transitional words and phrases, however, readers cannot tell exactly how one event in the paragraph relates to another in time. Notice how much easier it is to read this passage once transitional words and phrases (such as *after, finally, once again,* and *in the end*) have been added.

Paragraph with Transitional Words and Phrases

Napoleon certainly made a change for the worse by leaving his small kingdom of Elba. After Waterloo, he went back to Paris, and he abdicated for a second time. A hundred days after his return from Elba, he fled to Rochefort in hope of escaping to America. Finally, he gave himself up to the English captain of the ship *Bellerophon*. Once again, he suggested that the Prince Regent grant him asylum, and once again, he was refused. In the end, all he saw of England was the Devon coast and Plymouth Sound as he passed on to the remote island of St. Helena. After six years of exile, he died on May 5, 1821, at the age of fifty-two. (Norman Mackenzie, *The Escape from Elba*)

FREQUENTLY USED TRANSITIONAL WORDS AND PHRASES

To Signal Sequence or Addition

again	in addition
also	moreover
besides	one . . . another
first . . . second . . . third	too
furthermore	

To Signal Time

afterward	earlier
as soon as	finally
at first	in the meantime
at the same time	later
before	meanwhile

(continued)

FREQUENTLY USED TRANSITIONAL WORDS AND PHRASES *(continued)*

next
now
soon

subsequently
then
until

To Signal Comparison

also
by the same token
in comparison

likewise
similarly

To Signal Contrast

although
but
despite
even though
however
in contrast
instead
meanwhile

nevertheless
nonetheless
on the contrary
on the one hand . . .
  on the other hand
still
whereas
yet

To Introduce Examples

for example
for instance
namely

specifically
thus

To Signal Narrowing of Focus

after all
indeed
in fact
in other words

in particular
specifically
that is

To Introduce Conclusions or Summaries

as a result
consequently
in conclusion
in other words

in summary
therefore
thus
to conclude

To Signal Concession

admittedly
certainly
granted

naturally
of course

To Introduce Causes or Effects

accordingly
as a result
because
consequently
hence

since
so
then
therefore

3 Using Parallel Structure

<u>Parallelism</u>—the use of matching words, phrases, clauses, or sentence structures to emphasize similar ideas—can increase coherence in a paragraph. Note in the following paragraph how parallel constructions beginning with *He was* link Thomas Jefferson's accomplishments.

See 36c, 41a

> Thomas Jefferson was born in 1743 and died at Monticello, Virginia, on July 4, 1826. During his eighty-four years, he accomplished a number of things. Although best known for his draft of the Declaration of Independence, Jefferson was a man of many talents who had a wide intellectual range. He was a patriot who was one of the revolutionary founders of the United States. He was a reformer who, when he was governor of Virginia, drafted the Statute for Religious Freedom. He was an innovator who drafted an ordinance for governing the West and devised the first decimal monetary system. He was a president who abolished internal taxes, reduced the national debt, and made the Louisiana Purchase. And, finally, he was an architect who designed Monticello and the University of Virginia. (student writer)

4 Repeating Key Words and Phrases

Repeating **key words and phrases**—those essential to meaning—throughout a paragraph connects the sentences to one another and to the paragraph's main idea. The following paragraph repeats the key word *mercury* to keep readers focused on the subject. (Notice that to avoid monotony the writer sometimes refers indirectly to the subject of the paragraph with phrases such as *similarly affected* and *this problem.*)

> Mercury poisoning is a problem that has long been recognized. "Mad as a hatter" refers to the condition prevalent among nineteenth-century workers who were exposed to mercury during the manufacturing of felt hats. Workers in many other industries, such as mining, chemicals, and dentistry, were similarly affected. In the 1950s and 1960s, there were cases of mercury poisoning in Minamata, Japan. Research showed that there were high levels of mercury pollution in streams and lakes surrounding the village. In the United States, this problem came to light in 1969, when a New Mexico family got sick from eating food tainted with mercury. Since then, pesticides containing mercury have been withdrawn from the market, and chemical wastes can no longer be dumped into the ocean. (student writer)

5 Achieving Coherence between Paragraphs

The same methods you use to establish coherence within paragraphs may also be used to link paragraphs in an essay. (You can also use a <u>transitional paragraph</u> as a bridge between two paragraphs.)

See 7e

The following group of related paragraphs shows how some of the strategies discussed in 7b1–4 work together to create a coherent unit.

> A language may borrow a word directly or indirectly. A direct borrowing means that the borrowed item is a native word in the language it is borrowed from. *Festa* was borrowed directly from French and can be traced back to Latin *festa*. On the other hand, the word *algebra* was borrowed from Spanish, which in turn borrowed it from Arabic. Thus *algebra* was indirectly borrowed from Arabic, with Spanish as an intermediary.
>
> Some languages are heavy borrowers. Albanian has borrowed so heavily that few native words are retained. On the other hand, most Native American languages have borrowed little from their neighbors.
>
> English has borrowed extensively. Of the 20,000 or so words in common use, about three-fifths are borrowed. Of the 500 most frequently used words, however, only two-sevenths are borrowed, and because these "common" words are used over and over again in sentences, the actual frequency of appearance of native words is about 80 percent. Morphemes such as *and, be, have, it, of, the, to, will, you, on, that,* and *is* are all native to English. (Victoria Fromkin and Robert Rodman, *An Introduction to Language*)

These paragraphs are arranged according to a logical organizing principle, moving from the general concept of borrowing words to a specific discussion of English. In addition, each topic sentence repeats a variation of the word group *A language may borrow.* Throughout the three paragraphs, some form of this word group (as well as *word* and the names of various languages) appears in almost every sentence.

■ EXERCISE 2

A. Read the following paragraph, and determine how the author achieves coherence. Identify parallel elements, repeated words, and transitional words and phrases that link sentences.

> Some years ago the old elevated railway in Philadelphia was torn down and replaced by the subway system. This ancient El with its barnlike stations containing nut-vending machines and scattered food scraps had, for generations, been the favorite feeding ground of flocks of pigeons, generally one flock to a station along the route of the El. Hundreds of pigeons were dependent upon the system. They flapped in and out of its stanchions and steel work or gathered in watchful little audiences about the feet of anyone who rattled the peanut-vending machines. They even watched people who jingled change in their hands, and prospected for food under the feet of the crowds who gathered between trains. Probably very few among the waiting people who tossed a crumb to an eager pigeon realized that

this El was like a food-bearing river, and that the life which haunted its banks was dependent upon the running of the trains with their human freight. (Loren Eiseley, *The Night Country*)

B. Revise the following paragraph to make it more coherent.

> The theory of continental drift was first put forward by Alfred Wegener in 1912. The continents fit together like a gigantic jigsaw puzzle. The opposing Atlantic coasts, especially South America and Africa, seem to have been attached. He believed that at one time, probably 225 million years ago, there was one supercontinent. This continent broke into parts that drifted into their present positions. The theory stirred controversy during the 1920s and eventually was ridiculed by the scientific community. In 1954, the theory was revived. The theory of continental drift is accepted as a reasonable geological explanation of the continental system. (student writer)

EXERCISE 3

Read the following group of related paragraphs. Then, revise as necessary to increase coherence among paragraphs.

> *Leave It to Beaver* and *Father Knows Best* were typical of the late 1950s and early 1960s. Both were popular during a time when middle-class mothers stayed home to raise their children while fathers went to "the office." The Beaver's mother, June Cleaver, always wore a dress and high heels, even when she vacuumed. So did Margaret Anderson, the mother on *Father Knows Best*. Wally and the Beaver lived a picture-perfect, small-town life, and Betty, Bud, and Kathy never had a problem that father Jim Anderson couldn't solve.
>
> *The Brady Bunch* featured six children and the typical Mom-at-home and Dad-at-work combination. Of course, Carol Brady did wear pants, and the Bradys were what today would be called a "blended family." Nevertheless, *The Brady Bunch* presented a hopelessly idealized picture of upper-middle-class suburban life. The Brady kids lived in a large split-level house, went on vacations, had two loving parents, and even had a live-in maid, the ever-faithful, wisecracking Alice. Everyone in town was heterosexual, employed, able-bodied, and white.
>
> *The Cosby Show* was extremely popular. It featured two professional parents, a doctor and a lawyer. They lived in a townhouse with original art on the walls, and money never seemed to be a problem. In addition to warm relationships with their siblings, the Huxtable children also had close ties to their grandparents. *The Cosby Show* did introduce problems, such as son Theo's dyslexia, but in many ways it replicated the 1950s formula. Even in the post-1980s family, it seemed, father still knew best.

EXERCISE 4

Consider the possible use of a visual in each of the three paragraphs in Exercise 3. What visuals would you use? How might these visuals increase the coherence of the entire passage?

7c Writing Well-Developed Paragraphs

A paragraph is **well developed** when it includes all the supporting information—examples, statistics, expert opinion, and so on—that readers need to understand and accept its main idea.

> **CLOSE-UP**
>
> **WELL-DEVELOPED PARAGRAPHS**
>
> Keep in mind that length does not determine whether a paragraph is well developed. To determine the amount and kind of support you need, consider your audience, your purpose, and your paragraph's main idea.
>
> - **Consider your audience.** Will readers be familiar with your subject, or will it be new to them? Should the paragraph give readers detailed information, or should it just present a general overview of the topic? Given the needs of your audience, is your paragraph well developed?
>
> - **Consider your purpose.** Is your purpose to inform or to persuade, or is it something else? Given your purpose, is your paragraph well developed?
>
> - **Consider your paragraph's main idea.** Do you need to explain this idea more fully? Do you need another example, a statistic, an anecdote, or expert opinion? Given the complexity and scope of your main idea, is your paragraph well developed?

At first glance, the following paragraph may seem adequately developed.

Underdeveloped Paragraph

From Thanksgiving until Christmas, children and their parents are bombarded by ads for violent toys and games. Toy manufacturers persist in thinking that only toys that appeal to children's aggressiveness will sell. Despite claims that they (unlike action toys) have educational value, video games have escalated the level of violence. The real question is why parents continue to buy these violent toys and games for their children. (student writer)

In reality, however, the paragraph does not contain enough support to convince readers that children and parents are "bombarded by ads for violent toys." What kinds of toys appeal to a child's aggressive tendencies? What particular video games does the writer object to?

You can strengthen underdeveloped paragraphs such as the one on the previous page by adding specific examples that illustrate the statement made in the topic sentence.

Revised Paragraph (Examples Added)

From Thanksgiving until Christmas, children and their parents are bombarded by ads for violent toys and games. Toy manufacturers persist in thinking that only toys that appeal to children's aggressiveness will sell. **One television commercial praises the merits of a commando team that attacks and captures a miniature enemy base. Toy soldiers wear realistic uniforms and carry automatic rifles, pistols, knives, grenades, and ammunition. Another commercial shows laughing children shooting one another with plastic rocket launchers and tanklike vehicles.** Despite claims that they (unlike action toys) have educational value, video games have escalated the level of violence. **The most popular video games involve children in strikingly realistic combat simulations. One game lets children search out and destroy enemy fighters on the ground and in the air. Other best-selling games graphically simulate hand-to-hand combat on city streets and feature dismembered bodies and the sound of breaking bones.** The real question is why parents continue to buy these violent toys and games for their children.

Examples

Examples

You can also use expert opinion and statistics to develop the paragraph further.

Revised Paragraph (Expert Opinion and Statistics Added)

From Thanksgiving to Christmas, children are bombarded by ads for violent toys and games. Toy manufacturers persist in thinking that only toys that appeal to children's aggressiveness will sell. **The president of one large toy company recently observed that in spite of what people may say, they buy action toys. This is why toy companies spend so much money on commercials that promote them** (Wilson 54). One such television commercial features a commando team that attacks and captures a miniature enemy base. Toy soldiers wear realistic uniforms and carry automatic rifles, pistols, knives, grenades, and ammunition. Another commercial shows laughing children shooting one another with plastic rocket launchers and tanklike vehicles. Despite claims that they (unlike action toys) have educational value, video games have escalated the level of violence.

Expert opinion

Statistics A parents' watchdog group has estimated that during the past three years, violent video games have increased sales by almost 20 percent ("Action Toys Sell" 17). The most popular video games involve children in strikingly realistic combat situations. One game lets children search out and destroy enemy fighters on the ground and in the air. Other best-selling games graphically simulate hand-to-hand combat on city streets and feature dismembered bodies and chilling sound effects. The real question is why parents continue to buy these violent toys and games for their children.

Along with several specific examples, this revised paragraph now includes an expert opinion—a statement by a toy manufacturer—and a statistic that shows the extent to which sales of violent video games have increased.

See 18a

NOTE: The writer **documents** both the expert opinion and the statistic because they are not her own ideas.

■ **EXERCISE 5**

Write a paragraph for two of the following topic sentences. Be sure to include all the examples and other support necessary to develop the paragraph adequately. Assume that you are writing your paragraph for the students in your composition class.

1. First-year students can take specific steps to make sure that they are successful in college.
2. Setting up a first apartment can be quite a challenge.
3. Whenever I get depressed, I think of _____, and I feel better.
4. The person I admire most is _____.
5. If I won the lottery, I would do three things.

7d Patterns of Paragraph Development

Patterns of paragraph development—*narration, exemplification,* and so on—reflect the way a writer arranges material to express ideas most effectively.

1 Narration

A **narrative** paragraph tells a story by presenting events in chronological (time) order. Most narratives move in a logical, orderly sequence from beginning to end, from first event to last. Clear transitional words and phrases (*later, after that*) and time markers (*in 1990, two years earlier, the next day*) establish the chronological sequence.

Patterns of Paragraph Development ¶ **7d**

FIGURE 7.1 Student in pledge cap; one event in narrative sequence.

My academic career almost ended as soon as it began when, three weeks after I arrived at college, I decided to pledge a fraternity. By midterms, I was wearing a pledge cap and saying "Yes, sir" to every fraternity brother I met. When classes were over, I ran errands for the fraternity members, and after dinner I socialized and worked on projects with the other people in my pledge class. In between these activities, I tried to study. Somehow I managed to write papers, take tests, and attend lectures. By the end of the semester, though, my grades had slipped, and I was exhausted. It was then that I began to ask myself some important questions. I realized that I wanted to be popular, but not at the expense of my grades and my future career. At the beginning of my second semester, I dropped out of the fraternity and got a job in the biology lab. Looking back, I realize that it was then that I actually began to grow up. (student writer)

Topic sentence identifies subject of narrative

Sequence of events

2 Description

A **descriptive** paragraph communicates how something looks, sounds, smells, tastes, or feels. The most natural arrangement of details in a description reflects the way you actually look at a person, scene, or object: near to far, top to bottom, side to side, or front to back. This arrangement of details is made clear by transitions that identify precise spatial relationships: *next to, near, beside, under, above,* and so on.

NOTE: Sometimes a descriptive paragraph does not have an explicitly stated topic sentence. In such cases, it is unified by a **dominant impression**—the effect created by all the details in the description.

FIGURE 7.2 Vividly detailed close-up of Blue Morpho butterfly in Costa Rican rainforest.

When you are inside the jungle, away from the river, the trees vault out of sight. It is hard to remember to look up the long trunks and see the fans, strips, fronds, and sprays of glossy leaves. Inside the jungle you are more likely to notice the snarl of climbers and creepers round the trees' boles, the flowering bromeliads and epiphytes in every bough's crook, and the fantastic silk-cotton tree trunks thirty or forty feet across, trunks buttressed in flanges of

Details convey dominant impression

wood whose curves can make three high walls of a room—a shady, loamy-aired room where you would gladly live, or die. Butterflies, iridescent blue, striped, or clear-winged, thread the jungle paths at eye level. And at your feet is a swath of ants bearing triangular bits of green leaf. The ants with their leaves look like a wide fleet of sailing dinghies—but they don't quit. In either direction they wobble over the jungle floor as far as the eye can see. I followed them off the path as far as I dared, and never saw an end to ants or to those luffing chips of green they bore. (Annie Dillard, "In the Jungle")

3 Exemplification

An **exemplification** paragraph supports a topic sentence with a series of specific examples (or, sometimes, with a single extended example). These examples can be drawn from personal observation or experience or from research.

Topic sentence identifies paragraph's main idea

Series of examples

Illiterates cannot travel freely. When they attempt to do so, they encounter risks that few of us can dream of. They cannot read traffic signs and, while they often learn to recognize and to decipher symbols, they cannot manage street names which they haven't seen before. The same is true for bus and subway stops. While ingenuity can sometimes help a man or woman to discern directions from familiar landmarks, buildings, cemeteries, churches, and the like, most illiterates are virtually immobilized. They seldom wander past the streets and neighborhoods they know. Geographical paralysis becomes a bitter metaphor for their entire existence. They are immobilized in almost every sense we can imagine. They can't move up. They can't move out. They cannot see beyond. Illiterates may take an oral test for drivers' permits in most sections of America. It is a questionable concession. Where will they go? How will they get there? How will they get home? Could it be that some of us might like it better if they stayed where they belong? (Jonathan Kozol, *Illiterate America*)

FIGURE 7.3 Street signs illustrate one area of confusion for illiterates.

4 Process

Process paragraphs describe how something works, presenting a series of steps in strict chronological order. The topic sentence identifies the process, and the rest of the paragraph presents the steps involved. Transitional words such as *first, then, next, after this,* and *finally* link steps in the process.

Patterns of Paragraph Development ¶ **7d** 93

FIGURE 7.4 US Supreme Court justices after final step in process (handing down opinion in Gideon v. Wainwright, November 1962).

Members of the court have disclosed, however, the general way the conference is conducted. It begins at ten a.m. and usually runs on until late afternoon. At the start each justice, when he enters the room, shakes hands with all others there (thirty-six handshakes altogether). The custom, dating back generations, is evidently designed to begin the meeting at a friendly level, no matter how heated the intellectual differences may be. The conference takes up, first, the applications for review—a few appeals, many more petitions for certiorari. Those on the Appellate Docket, the regular paid cases, are considered first, then the pauper's applications on the Miscellaneous Docket. (If any of these are granted, they are then transferred to the Appellate Docket.) After this the justices consider, and vote on, all the cases argued during the preceding Monday through Thursday. These are tentative votes, which may be and quite often are changed as the opinion is written and the problem thought through more deeply. There may be further discussion at later conferences before the opinion is handed down. (Anthony Lewis, *Gideon's Trumpet*)

Topic sentence identifies process

Steps in process

> **CLOSE-UP**
>
> **INSTRUCTIONS**
>
> When a process paragraph presents instructions to enable readers to actually perform the process, it is written in the present tense and in the imperative mood— "*Remove* the cover . . . and *check* the valve."

5 Cause and Effect

A **cause-and-effect** paragraph explores causes or predicts or describes results; sometimes a single cause-and-effect paragraph does both. Clear, specific transitional words and phrases such as *one cause, another cause, a more important result, because,* and *as a result* convey the cause-and-effect relationship.

Some paragraphs examine causes.

The main reason that a young baby sucks his thumb seems to be that he hasn't had enough sucking at the breast or bottle to satisfy his sucking needs. Dr. David Levy pointed out that babies who are fed every 3 hours don't suck their thumbs as much as babies fed every

Topic sentence establishes major cause

Cause explored in detail

4 hours, and that babies who have cut down on nursing time from 20 minutes to 10 minutes . . . are more likely to suck their thumbs than babies who still have to work for 20 minutes. Dr. Levy fed a litter of puppies with a medicine dropper so that they had no chance to suck during their feedings. They acted just the same as babies who don't get enough chance to suck at feeding time. They sucked their own and each other's paws and skin so hard that the fur came off. (Benjamin Spock, *Baby and Child Care*)

FIGURE 7.5 Baby sucking thumb.

Other paragraphs focus on effects.

Topic sentence establishes major effect

On December 8, 1941, the day after the Japanese attack on Pearl Harbor in Hawaii, my grandfather barricaded himself with his family—my grandmother, my teenage mother, her two sisters and two brothers—inside of his home in La'ie, a sugar plantation village on Oahu's North Shore. This was my maternal grandfather, a man most villagers called by his last name, Kubota. It could mean either "Wayside Field" or else "Broken Dreams," depending on which ideograms he used. Kubota ran La'ie's general store, and the previous night, after a long day of bad news on the radio, some locals had come by, pounded on the front door, and made threats. One was said to have brandished a machete. They were angry and shocked, as the whole nation was in the aftermath of the surprise attack. Kubota was one

Discussion of other effects

of the few Japanese Americans in the village and president of the local Japanese language school. He had become a target for their rage and suspicion. A wise man, he locked all his doors and windows and did not open his store the next day, but stayed closed and waited for news from some official. (Garrett Hongo, "Kubota")

FIGURE 7.6 Headline announcing attack on Pearl Harbor.

6 Comparison and Contrast

Comparison-and-contrast paragraphs examine the similarities and differences between two subjects. **Comparison** focuses on similarities; **contrast** emphasizes differences.

Comparison-and-contrast paragraphs can be organized in one of two ways. Some paragraphs, **point-by-point** comparisons, discuss two subjects together, alternating points about one subject with comparable points about the other.

There are two Americas. One is the America of Lincoln and Adlai Stevenson; the other is the America of Teddy Roosevelt and the modern superpatriots. One is generous and humane, the other narrowly egotistical; one is self-critical, the other self-righteous; one is sensible, the other romantic; one is good-humored, the other solemn; one is inquiring, the other pontificating; one is moderate, the other filled with passionate intensity; one is judicious and the other arrogant in the use of great power. (J. William Fulbright, *The Arrogance of Power*)

Topic sentence establishes comparison

Alternating points about the two subjects

FIGURE 7.7 Abraham Lincoln (left) and Theodore Roosevelt (right) symbolize the contrast between the two Americas.

Other paragraphs, **subject-by-subject** comparisons, treat one subject completely and then move on to the other subject. In the following paragraph, notice how the writer shifts from one subject to the other with the transitional word *however*.

FIGURE 7.8 Man using mute button to halt conversation (illustrates contrast between conversation styles of men and women).

First, it is important to note that men and women regard conversation quite differently. For women it is a passion, a sport, an activity even more important to life than eating because it doesn't involve weight gain. The first sign of closeness among women is when they find themselves engaging in endless, secretless rounds of conversation with one another. And as soon as a woman begins to relax and feel comfortable in a relationship with a man, she tries to have that type of conversation with him as well. However, the first sign that a man is feeling close to a woman is when he admits that he'd rather she please quiet down so he can hear the TV. A man who feels truly intimate with a woman often reserves for her and her alone the precious gift of one-word answers. Everyone knows that the surest way to spot a successful

Topic sentence establishes comparison

First subject discussed

Second subject discussed

long-term relationship is to look around a restaurant for the table where no one is talking. Ah . . . now that's real love. (Merrill Markoe, "Men, Women, and Conversation")

An **analogy** is a special kind of comparison that explains an unfamiliar concept or object by likening it to a familiar one. In the following paragraph, the writer uses the behavior of people to explain the behavior of ants.

Topic sentence establishes analogy

Analogy explained in detail

Ants are so much like human beings as to be an embarrassment. They farm fungi, raise aphids as livestock, launch armies into wars, use chemical sprays to alarm and confuse enemies, capture slaves. The families of weaver ants engage in child labor, holding their larvae like shuttles to spin out the thread that sews the leaves together for their fungus gardens. They exchange information ceaselessly. They do everything but watch television. (Lewis Thomas, "On Societies as Organisms")

FIGURE 7.9 Tailor ants sewing leaves together illustrates analogy between ants and people.

7 Division and Classification

Division paragraphs take a single item and break it into its component parts.

Topic sentence identifies categories

Categories discussed

The blood can be divided into four distinct components: plasma, red cells, white cells, and platelets. One component, plasma, is ninety percent water and holds a great number of substances in suspension. It contains proteins, sugars, fat, and inorganic salts. Plasma also contains urea and other by-products from the breaking down of proteins, hormones, enzymes, and dissolved gases. The red cells, another component of blood, give blood its distinctive color. The red cells are most numerous; they get oxygen from the lungs and release it in the tissues. The less numerous white cells are a component of blood that defends the body against invading organisms. Finally, the platelets, which occur in almost the same number as white cells, are responsible for clotting. (student writer)

FIGURE 7.10 Components of blood—blood cells and platelets—in vein.

Classification paragraphs take many separate items and group them into categories according to qualities or characteristics they share.

Charles Babbage, an English mathematician, reflecting in 1830 on what he saw as the decline of science at the time, distinguished among three major kinds of scientific fraud. He called the first "forging," by which he meant complete fabrication—the recording of observations that were never made. The second category he called "trimming"; this consists of manipulating the data to make them look better, or, as Babbage wrote, "in clipping off little bits here and there from those observations which differ most in excess from the mean and in sticking them on to those which are too small." His third category was data selection, which he called "cooking"—the choosing of those data that fitted the researcher's hypothesis and the discarding of those that did not. To this day, the serious discussion of scientific fraud has not improved on Babbage's typology. (Morton Hunt, *New York Times Magazine*)

Topic sentence establishes categories

Categories discussed

FIGURE 7.11 The FeJee mermaid illustrates "forging," one of three categories of scientific fraud.

8 Definition

Definition paragraphs develop a formal definition by means of other patterns—for instance, defining *happiness* by telling a story (narration) or defining a diesel engine by telling how it works (process).

The following definition paragraph is developed by means of exemplification: it begins with a straightforward definition of *gadget* and then cites an example.

FIGURE 7.12 Rural mailbox with semaphore (term defined by exemplification).

A gadget is nearly always novel in design or concept and it often has no proper name. For example, the semaphore which signals the arrival of the mail in our rural mailbox certainly has no proper name. It is a contrivance consisting of a piece of shingle. Call it what you like, it saves us frequent frustrating trips to the mailbox in winter when you have to dress up and wade through snow to get there. That's a gadget! (*Smithsonian*)

Topic sentence gives general definition

Definition expanded with an example

EXERCISE 6

Determine one possible pattern of development for a paragraph on each of these topics. Then, write a paragraph on one of the topics.

1. What success is (or is not)
2. How to prepare for a job interview

3. The kinds of people who appear on television reality shows
4. My worst experience
5. American vs. British spelling
6. The connection between coffee consumption and heart disease
7. Budgeting money wisely
8. Junk food
9. Dressing for success
10. The dangers of using a cell phone while driving

■ **EXERCISE 7**

A. Read each of the following paragraphs, and then answer these questions: In general terms, how could each paragraph be developed further? What pattern of development might be used in each case?

B. Choose one paragraph, and rewrite it to develop it further.

1. Many new words and expressions have entered the English language in the last ten years or so. Some of them come from the world of computers. Others come from popular music. Still others have politics as their source. There are even some expressions that have their origins in films or television shows.

2. Making a good spaghetti sauce is not a particularly challenging task. First, assemble the basic ingredients: garlic, onion, mushrooms, green pepper, and ground beef. Sauté these ingredients in a large saucepan. Then, add canned tomatoes, tomato paste, and water, and stir. At this point, you are ready to add the spices: oregano, parsley, basil, and salt and pepper. Don't forget a bay leaf! Simmer for about two hours, and serve over spaghetti.

3. High school and college are not at all alike. Courses are a lot easier in high school, and the course load is lighter. In college, teachers expect more from students; they expect higher quality work, and they assign more of it. Assignments tend to be more difficult and more comprehensive, and deadlines are usually shorter. Finally, college students tend to be more focused on a particular course of study—even a particular career—than high school students are.

■ **EXERCISE 8**

Choose one of the four visuals on the following page, and write a paragraph developed according to a pattern the visual suggests. (Note that each visual may suggest more than one pattern.)

FIGURE 7.13 New college graduate pondering his future.

FIGURE 7.14 Goldilocks eating porridge.

FIGURE 7.15 Japanese geisha in front of soda machine.

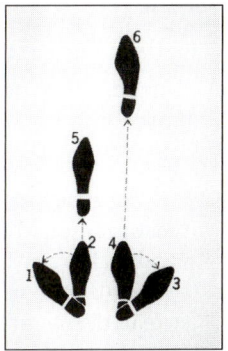

FIGURE 7.16 Basic steps of the hustle.

7e Writing Special Kinds of Paragraphs

So far, this chapter has focused on **body paragraphs,** the paragraphs that carry the weight of your essay's discussion. Other kinds of paragraphs—*transitional paragraphs, introductory paragraphs,* and *concluding paragraphs*—have special functions in an essay.

1 Transitional Paragraphs

A **transitional paragraph** connects one section of an essay to another. At their simplest, transitional paragraphs can be single sentences that move readers from one point to the next.

What is true for ants is also true for people.

This idea works better in theory than in practice.

More often, writers use transitional paragraphs to present concise summaries of what they have already said before they move on to a new point. The following transitional paragraph uses a series of questions to sum up some of the ideas the writer has been discussing. In the next part of his essay, he goes on to answer these questions.

> Can we bleed off the mass of humanity to other worlds? Right now the number of human beings on Earth is increasing by 80 million per year, and each year that number goes up by 1 and a fraction percent. Can we really suppose that we can send 80 million people per year to the Moon, Mars, and elsewhere, and engineer those worlds to support those people? And even so, nearly remain in the same place ourselves? (Isaac Asimov, "The Case against Man")

2 Introductory Paragraphs

An **introductory paragraph** prepares readers for the essay to follow. It typically introduces the subject, narrows it, and then states the essay's thesis.

> Christine was just a girl in one of my classes. I never knew much about her except that she was strange. She didn't talk much. Her hair was dyed black and purple, and she wore heavy black boots and a black turtleneck sweater, even in the summer. She was attractive—in spite of the ring she wore through her left eyebrow—but she never seemed to care what the rest of us thought about her. Like the rest of my classmates, I didn't really want to get close to her. It was only when we were assigned to do our chemistry project together that I began to understand why Christine dressed the way she did. (student writer)

ESL TIP

A **thesis statement** is a sentence that communicates your essay's main idea. Thesis statements, which usually appear in introductory paragraphs, are an important part of US academic writing.

To arouse their audience's interest, writers may vary this direct approach by using one of the following introductory strategies.

Strategies for Effective Introductions

Quotation or Series of Quotations

When Mary Cassatt's father was told of her decision to become a painter, he said: "I would rather see you dead." When Edgar Degas saw a show of Cassatt's etchings, his response was: "I am not willing to admit that a woman can draw that well." When she returned to Philadelphia after twenty-eight years abroad, having achieved renown as an Impressionist painter and the esteem of Degas, Huysmans, Pissarro, and Berthe Morisot, the *Philadelphia Ledger* reported: "Mary Cassatt, sister of Mr. Cassatt, president of the Pennsylvania Railroad, returned from Europe yesterday. She has been studying painting in France and owns the smallest Pekingese dog in the world." (Mary Gordon, "Mary Cassatt")

Question or Series of Questions

Of all the disputes agitating the American campus, the one that seems to me especially significant is that over "the canon." What should be taught in the humanities and social sciences, especially in introductory courses? What is the place of the classics? How shall we respond to those professors who attack "Eurocentrism" and advocate "multiculturalism"? This is not the sort of tedious quarrel that now and then flutters through the academy; it involves matters of public urgency. I propose to see this dispute, at first, through a narrow, even sectarian lens, with the hope that you will come to accept my reasons for doing so. (Irving Howe, "The Value of the Canon")

Definition

Moles are collections of cells that can appear on any part of the body. With occasional exceptions, moles are absent at birth. They first appear in the early years of life, between ages two and six. Frequently, moles appear at puberty. New moles, however, can continue to appear throughout life. During pregnancy, new moles may appear and old ones darken. There are three major designations of moles, each with its own unique distinguishing characteristics. (student writer)

Controversial Statement

Something had to replace the threat of communism, and at last a workable substitute is at hand. "Multiculturalism," as the new menace is known, has been denounced in the media recently as the new McCarthyism, the new fundamentalism, even the new totalitarianism—take your choice. According to its critics, who include a flock of tenured conservative scholars, multiculturalism

(continued)

STRATEGIES FOR EFFECTIVE INTRODUCTIONS (continued)

aims to toss out what it sees as the Eurocentric bias in education and replace Plato with Ntozake Shange and traditional math with the Yoruba number system. And that's just the beginning. The Jacobins of the multiculturalist movement, who are described derisively as P.C., or politically correct, are said to have launched a campus reign of terror against those who slip and innocently say "freshman" instead of "freshperson," "Indian" instead of "Native American" or, may the Goddess forgive them, "disabled" instead of "differently abled." (Barbara Ehrenreich, "Teach Diversity— with a Smile")

CLOSE-UP

INTRODUCTORY PARAGRAPHS

An introductory paragraph should make your readers want to read further. For this reason, you should avoid introductions that begin by simply announcing your subject ("In my paper, I will talk about Lady Macbeth") or by undercutting your credibility ("I don't know much about alternative energy sources, but I would like to present my opinion about the subject").

3 Concluding Paragraphs

A **concluding paragraph** typically begins with specifics—reviewing the essay's main points, for example—and then moves to more general statements. Whenever possible, it should end with a sentence that readers will remember.

> As an Arab-American, I feel I have the best of two worlds. I'm proud to be part of the melting pot, proud to contribute to the tremendous diversity of cultures, customs and traditions that makes this country unique. But Arab-bashing—public acceptance of hatred and bigotry—is something no American can be proud of. (Ellen Mansoor Collier, "I Am Not a Terrorist")

Writers may also use one of the following concluding strategies.

STRATEGIES FOR EFFECTIVE CONCLUSIONS

Prediction

Looking ahead, [we see that] prospects may not be quite as dismal as they seem. As a matter of fact, we are not doing so badly. It is something of a miracle that creatures who evolved as nomads in an intimate, small-band, wide-open-spaces context manage to get along at all as villagers or surrounded by strangers in cubicle apartments. Considering that our genius as a species is adaptability, we may yet learn to live closer and closer to one another, if not in utter peace, then far more peacefully than we do today. (John Pheiffer, "Seeking Peace, Making War")

Warning

The Internet is the twenty-first century's talking drum, the very kind of grassroots communication tool that has been such a powerful source of education and culture for our people since slavery. But this talking drum we have not yet learned to play. Unless we master the new information technology to build and deepen the forms of social connection that a tragic history has eroded, African-Americans will face a form of cybersegregation in the next century as devastating to our aspirations as Jim Crow segregation was to those of our ancestors. But this time, the fault will be our own. (Henry Louis Gates Jr., "One Internet, Two Nations")

Recommendation for Action

Computers have revolutionized learning in ways that we have barely begun to appreciate. We have experienced enough, however, to recognize the need to change our thinking about our purposes, methods, and outcome of higher education. Rather than resisting or postponing change, we need to anticipate and learn from it. We must harness the technology and use it to educate our students more effectively than we have been doing. Otherwise, we will surrender our authority to those who can. (Peshe Kuriloff, "If John Dewey Were Alive Today, He'd Be a Webhead")

Quotation

When we let freedom ring, when we let it ring from every village and every hamlet, from every state and every city, we will be able to speed up that day when all of God's children, black men and white men, Jews and Gentiles, Protestants and Catholics, will be able to join hands and sing in the words of the old Negro spiritual, "Free at last! Free at last! Thank God almighty, we are free at last!" (Martin Luther King Jr., "I Have a Dream")

> CLOSE-UP
>
> **CONCLUDING PARAGRAPHS**
>
> Because a dull conclusion can weaken an otherwise strong essay, try to make your conclusion as interesting as you can. Don't waste time repeating your introduction in different words or apologizing or undercutting your credibility ("I may not be an expert" or "At least, this is my opinion"). And remember, your conclusion should not introduce any new points or go off in new directions.

PART 2

Thinking Critically and Writing Arguments

8 Thinking Critically 106
8a Distinguishing Fact from Opinion 106
8b Evaluating Supporting Evidence 108
8c Detecting Bias 109

9 Using Logic 113
9a Understanding Inductive Reasoning 113
9b Understanding Deductive Reasoning 115
9c Using Toulmin Logic 117
9d Recognizing Logical Fallacies 120

10 Writing Argumentative Essays 125
10a Planning an Argumentative Essay 125
10b Using Evidence Effectively 129
10c Organizing an Argumentative Essay 132
10d Writing and Revising an Argumentative Essay 133

11 Using Visuals to Support Your Arguments 142
11a Using Visuals 142
11b Evaluating Visuals 145

12 Writing Electronic Arguments 149
12a Considering Audience and Purpose 149
12b Shaping Electronic Arguments 150
12c Writing and Revising Electronic Arguments 151

8

Thinking Critically

❓ FAQs

What is critical thinking? (p. 106)
How do I tell the difference between a fact and an opinion? (p. 106)
How do I evaluate the evidence a writer presents? (p. 108)
How can I tell if a writer is biased? (p. 110)

See Ch. 10

As you read and write essays, you should carefully consider the ideas they present. This is especially true in **argumentative essays**—those that take a stand on a debatable topic. Although some writers try their best to be fair, others are less scrupulous. They attempt to convince readers by using emotionally charged language, by emphasizing certain facts over others, and by intentionally using flawed logic. For this reason, it is particularly important that you apply **critical thinking** strategies when you read, learning to distinguish fact from opinion, evaluate supporting evidence, detect bias, evaluate visuals, and understand the basic principles of inductive and deductive reasoning.

> **ESL TIP**
>
> This chapter outlines ideas about thinking critically that are common in academic settings in the US. In such settings, people read texts with a critical eye, testing the author's claims to see if they seem true. Reading this chapter will help you understand how your instructor expects you to read and evaluate texts.

8a Distinguishing Fact from Opinion

A **fact** is a verifiable statement that something is true or that something occurred. An **opinion** is a personal judgment or belief that can never be substantiated beyond any doubt and is, therefore, debatable.

Fact: Measles is a potentially deadly disease.

Opinion: All children should be vaccinated against measles.

An opinion may be *supported* or *unsupported*.

Unsupported Opinion: All children in Pennsylvania should be vaccinated against measles.

Supported Opinion: Despite the fact that an effective measles vaccine is widely available, several unvaccinated Pennsylvania children have died of measles each year since 1992. States that have instituted vaccination programs have had no deaths in the same time period. For this reason, all children in Pennsylvania should be vaccinated against measles.

As these examples show, supported opinion is more convincing than unsupported opinion. Remember, however, that support can only make a statement more convincing; it cannot turn an opinion into a fact.

CLOSE-UP

SUPPORTING YOUR OPINIONS

Opinions can be supported with **examples**, **statistics**, or **expert opinion**.

Examples

The American Civil Liberties Union is an organization that has been unfairly characterized as left wing. It is true that it has opposed prayer in the public schools, defended conscientious objectors, and challenged police methods of conducting questioning and searches of suspects. However, it has also backed the antiabortion group Operation Rescue in a police brutality suit and presented a legal brief in support of a Republican politician accused of violating an ethics law.

Statistics

A recent National Institute of Mental Health study concludes that mentally ill people account for more than 30 percent of the homeless population (Young 27). Because so many homeless people have psychiatric disabilities, the federal government should seriously consider expanding the state mental hospital system.

Expert Opinion

No soldier ever really escapes the emotional consequences of war. As William Manchester, noted historian and World War II combat veteran, observes in his essay "Okinawa: The Bloodiest Battle of All," "the invisible wounds remain" (72).

8b Thinking Critically

■ EXERCISE 1

Some of the following statements are facts; others are opinions. Identify each fact with the letter *F* and each opinion with the letter *O*. Then consider what kind of information, if any, could support each opinion.

1. The incidence of violent crime fell in the first six months of this year.
2. New gun laws and more police officers led to a decrease in crime early in the year.
3. The television rating system uses a system similar to the familiar movie rating codes to let parents know how appropriate a certain show might be for their children.
4. The new television rating system would be better if it gave specifics about the violence, sexual content, and language in rated television programs.
5. Affirmative action laws and policies have helped women and minority group members advance in the workplace.
6. Affirmative action policies have outlived their usefulness.
7. Women who work are better off today than they were twenty years ago.
8. The wage gap between men and women in similar jobs is smaller now than it was twenty years ago.
9. The Charles River and Boston Harbor currently test much lower for common pollutants than they did ten years ago.
10. We do not need to worry about environmental legislation anymore because we have made great advances in cleaning up our environment.

8b Evaluating Supporting Evidence

The examples, statistics, or expert opinions that a writer uses to support a statement are called **evidence**. The more reliable the supporting evidence, the more willing readers will be to accept a statement.

See 10b1

All evidence—no matter what kind—must be *accurate*, *sufficient*, *representative*, and *relevant*.

- Evidence is likely to be **accurate** if it comes from a trustworthy source. Such a source quotes exactly and does not present remarks out of context. It also presents examples, statistics, and expert testimony fairly, drawing them from other reliable sources.
- Evidence is likely to be **sufficient** if a writer presents an adequate amount of information. It is not enough, for instance, for a writer to cite just one example in an attempt to demonstrate that most

poor women do not receive adequate prenatal care. Similarly, the opinions of a single expert, no matter how reputable, are not enough to support this position.

- Evidence is likely to be **representative** if it reflects a fair range of sources and viewpoints. Writers should not just choose evidence that supports their position and ignore evidence that does not. In other words, they should not permit their biases to govern their choice of evidence. For example, a writer who is making the point that Asian immigrants have had great success in achieving professional status in the United States must draw from a range of Asian immigrant groups—Vietnamese, Chinese, Japanese, Indian, and Korean, for example—not just one.
- Evidence is likely to be **relevant** if it specifically applies to the case being discussed. For example, a writer cannot support the position that the United States should send medical aid to developing nations by citing examples that apply only to our own nation's health-care system.

■ EXERCISE 2

Read the following student paragraph, and evaluate its supporting evidence.

> The United States is becoming more and more violent every day. I was talking to my friend Gayle, and she mentioned that a guy her roommate knows was attacked at dusk and had his skull crushed by the barrel of a gun. Later she heard that he was in the hospital with a blood clot in his brain. Two friends of mine were walking home from a party when they were attacked by armed men right outside the A-Plus Mini Market. These two examples make it very clear to me how violent our nation is becoming. My English professor, who is in his fifties, remembers a few similar violent incidents occurring when he was growing up, and he was even mugged in London last year. He believes that if more London police carried guns, the city would be safer. Two of the twenty-five people in our class have been the victims of violent crime, and I feel lucky that I am not one of them.

8c Detecting Bias

Bias is the tendency to base conclusions on preconceived ideas rather than on evidence. As a critical reader, you should be aware that bias may sometimes lead writers to see what they want to see and therefore to select only that evidence that is consistent with their own biases.

Thinking Critically

CLOSE-UP

DETECTING BIAS

When you read, look for the following kinds of bias:

- **The Writer's Stated Beliefs** If a writer declares herself to be a strong opponent of childhood vaccinations, this statement should alert you to the possibility that the writer may not present a balanced view of the subject.
- **Sexist or Racist Statements** A writer who assumes all engineers are male or all nurses are female reflects a clear bias. A researcher who assumes certain racial or ethnic groups are intellectually superior to others is also likely to present a biased view.
- **Slanted Language** Some writers use **slanted language**—language that contains value judgments—to influence readers' reactions. For example, a newspaper article that states "The politician gave an impassioned speech" gives one impression; the statement "The politician delivered a diatribe" gives another.
- **Biased Tone** The tone of a piece of writing indicates a writer's attitude toward readers or toward his or her subject. An angry tone might indicate that the writer is overstating his or her case.
- **Biased Choice of Evidence** Frequently, the examples or statistics cited in a piece of writing reveal the writer's bias. For instance, a writer may include only examples that support a point and omit examples that may contradict it.
- **Biased Choice of Experts** A writer should cite experts who represent a fair range of opinion. If, for instance, a writer assessing the president's policy on stem-cell research includes only statements by experts who vehemently oppose this procedure, he or she is presenting a biased case.

See 1c

NOTE: Don't forget that your own biases can also affect your response to a text. When you read, it is important to remain aware of your own values and beliefs and to be alert to how they affect your reactions.

■ **EXERCISE 3**

Read the following essay about home schooling, a movement supported by parents who have abandoned traditional schools in favor of teaching their children at home. After evaluating the quality of the writer's supporting evidence, identify her biases, and decide if these biases undercut her argument in any way. Use the questions in the "Detecting Bias" Close-up box as a guide.

Questioning the Motives of Home-Schooling Parents

America's most famous home-schooling parents at the moment are Andrea Yates and JoAnn McGuckin. Yates allegedly drowned her five children in a Houston suburb. McGuckin was arrested and charged with child neglect in Idaho. Her six kids barricaded themselves in the family's hovel when child-care workers came to remove them.

The intention here is not to smear the parents who instruct 1.5 million mostly normal children at home. But a social phenomenon that isolates children from the outside world deserves closer inspection.

The home-schooling movement runs an active propaganda machine. It portrays its followers in the most flattering terms—as bulwarks against the moral decay found in public, and presumably private, schools. Although now associated with conservative groups, modern home-schooling got its start among left-wing dropouts in the '60s.

Home-schooled students do tend to score above average on standardized tests. The most likely reason, however, is that most of the parents are themselves upper income and well educated. Students from those backgrounds also do well in traditional schools.

Advocates of home-schooling have become a vocal lobbying force in Washington, D.C. Children taught at home may be socially isolated, but the parents have loads of interaction. Membership in the anti-public-education brigade provides much comradeship.

The mouthpiece for the movement, the Home School Legal Defense Association (*www.hslda.org*), posts articles on its Web site with headlines like, "The Clinging Tentacles of Public Education." Trashing the motivations of professional teachers provides much sport.

Perhaps the time has come to question the motives of some home-schooling parents. Are the parents protecting their children from a cesspool of bad values in the outside world? Or are the parents just people who can't get along with others? Are they "taking charge" of their children's education? Or are they taking their children captive?

Yates and McGuckin are, of course, extreme cases and probably demented. But a movement that insists on parents' rights to do as they wish with their children gives cover for the unstable, for narcissists and for child-abusers.

In West Akron, Ohio, reporters would interview Thomas Lavery on how he successfully schooled his five children in their home. The kids all had top grades and fine manners. They recalled how their father loved to strut before the media.

Eventually, however, the police came for Lavery and charged him with nine counts of child endangerment. According to his children, Lavery smashed a daughter over the head with a soda can after she did poorly in a basketball game. Any child who wet a bed would spend the night alone, locked in the garage.

A child who spilled milk had to drop on his or her knees and lick it up from the floor. And in an especially creepy attempt to establish himself as master, Lavery would order his children to damn the name of God.

The best way to maintain the sanctity of a family madhouse is to keep the inmates inside. Allowing children to move about in the world could jeopardize the deal.

In some cases, it might also prevent tragedy. Suppose one of Andrea Yates' children had gone to a school and told a teacher of the mother's spiraling mental state. The teacher could have called a child-welfare officer and five little lives might have been saved.

Putting the horror stories aside, there's something sad about home-schooled children. During the New Hampshire presidential primary race, I attended an event directed at high-school and college students. The students were a lively bunch, circulating around the giant room, debating and arguing. Except for my table.

About four young people and a middle-aged woman were just sitting there. The teenagers were clearly intelligent and well behaved. I tried to chat, but they seemed wary of talking with strangers. The woman proudly informed me that they were her children and home-schooled.

The Home School Legal Defense Association condemns government interference in any parent's vision of how a child might be educated. The group's chairman, Michael Farris, says things like, "We just want to say to the government: We are doing a good job, so leave us alone."

Could that be where JoAnn McGuckin found her twisted sense of grievance? "Those are my kids," she said as Idaho removed her children from their filthy home. "The state needs to mind its own business." (Froma Harrop, *Seattle Times*)

9

Using Logic

❓ FAQs

What is inductive reasoning? (p. 113)
What is deductive reasoning? (p. 115)
What is a logical fallacy? (p. 120)

Argumentative essays rely primarily on **logic.** Logical reasoning enables you to construct arguments that reach conclusions in a persuasive and systematic way. Before you can read and evaluate argumentative writing (and write an argumentative essay of your own), it is essential that you understand the basic principles of *inductive* and *deductive reasoning* on which arguments are based.

See Ch. 10

9a   Understanding Inductive Reasoning

1 Moving from Specific to General

Inductive reasoning moves from specific facts, observations, or experiences to a general conclusion. Writers use inductive reasoning when they address a skeptical audience that requires a lot of evidence before it will accept a conclusion. You can see how inductive reasoning operates by studying the following list of specific statements about the relationship between SAT scores and admissions at one particular college:

- The SAT is an admission requirement for all applicants.
- High school grades and rank in class are also examined.
- Nonacademic factors, such as sports, activities, and interests, are taken into account as well.
- Special attention is given to the applications of athletes, minorities, and children of alumni.
- Fewer than 52 percent of applicants for a recent class with SAT verbal scores between 600 and 700 were accepted.
- Fewer than 39 percent of applicants with similar math scores were accepted.
- Approximately 18 percent of applications with SAT verbal scores between 450 and 520 and about 19 percent of applicants with similar SAT math scores were admitted.

After reading the statements on page 113, you can use inductive reasoning to draw the general conclusion that although they are important, SAT scores are not the single factor that determines whether or not a student is admitted.

2 Making Inferences

No matter how much evidence is presented, an inductive conclusion is never certain, only probable. You arrive at an inductive conclusion by making an **inference**, a statement about the unknown based on the known. In order to bridge the gap that exists between your specific observations and your general conclusion, you have to make an **inductive leap.** If you have presented enough specific evidence, this gap will be relatively small and your readers will readily accept your conclusion. If the gap is too big, your readers will accuse you of making a <u>hasty generalization</u> and will not accept your conclusion. Even with the most effective support, absolute certainty is not possible with inductive reasoning. The best you can do is present a convincing case to readers.

See 9d1

■ **EXERCISE 1**

Read the paragraph below, and then determine which of the statements that follow it can be inferred from the paragraph.

Americans are becoming more ecologically aware with each passing year, but their awareness may be limited. Most people know about the destruction of rain forests in South America, for example, or the vanishing African elephant, but few realize what is going on in their own backyards in the name of progress. Even people who are knowledgeable about such topics as the plight of the wild mustang, the dangers of toxic waste disposal, and acid rain frequently fail to realize either the existence or the importance of "smaller" ecological issues. The wetlands are a good case in point. In recent decades, more than 500,000 acres of wetlands a year have been filled, and it seems unlikely that the future will see any great change. What has happened in recent times is that United States wetlands are filled in one area and "restored" in another area, a practice that is legal according to Section 404 of the Clean Water Act and one that does in fact result in "no net loss" of wetlands. Few see the problems with this. To most, wetlands are mere swamps, and getting rid of swamps is viewed as something positive. In addition, the wetlands typically contain few spectacular species—the sort of glamour animals, such as condors and grizzlies, that easily attract publicity and sympathy. Instead, they contain boring specimens of flora and fauna unlikely to generate great concern among the masses. Yet the delicate balance of the ecosystem is upset by the elimination or "rearrangement" of such marshy areas. True, cosmically speaking, it matters little if one organism (or many) is wiped out. But even obscure subspecies might provide some much-needed product or information in the future. We should not forget that penicillin was made from a lowly mold.

1. The loss of even a single species may be disastrous to the ecosystem of the wetlands.
2. Even though the wetlands are considered swamps, most people are very concerned about their fate.
3. Section 404 of the Clean Water Act is not sufficient to protect the wetlands.
4. Few Americans are concerned about environmental issues.
5. Most people would agree that the destruction of rain forests is worse than the destruction of the wetlands.

9b Understanding Deductive Reasoning

1 Moving from General to Specific

Deductive reasoning moves from a generalization believed to be true or self-evident to a more specific conclusion. Writers use deductive reasoning when they address an audience that is more likely to be influenced by logic than by evidence. The process of deduction has traditionally been illustrated with a **syllogism**, a three-part set of statements or propositions that includes a **major premise**, a **minor premise**, and a **conclusion**.

> **Major Premise:** All books from that store are new.
> **Minor Premise:** These books are from that store.
> **Conclusion:** Therefore, these books are new.

The major premise of a syllogism makes a general statement that the writer believes to be true. The minor premise presents a specific example of the belief that is stated in the major premise. If the reasoning is sound, the conclusion should follow from the two premises. (Note that these two premises contain all the information expressed in the conclusion; that is, the conclusion introduces no terms that have not already appeared in the major and minor premises.) The advantage of a deductive argument is that if readers accept the premises, they usually grant the conclusion.

NOTE: When you write an <u>argument</u>, you can use a syllogism during the planning stage (to test the validity of your points), or you can use it as a revision strategy (to test your logic). In either case, the syllogism enables you to express your deductive argument in its most basic form and to see whether it makes sense.

See Ch. 10

2 Constructing Sound Syllogisms

A syllogism is **valid** (or logical) when its conclusion follows from its premises. A syllogism is **true** when it makes accurate claims—that is, when the information it contains is consistent with the facts. To be **sound,** a syllogism must be both valid and true. However, a syllogism may be valid without being true or true without being valid. The following syllogism, for example, is valid but not true.

> **Major Premise:** All politicians are male.
> **Minor Premise:** Barbara Boxer is a politician.
> **Conclusion:** Therefore, Barbara Boxer is male.

As odd as it may seem, this syllogism is valid. In the major premise, the phrase *all politicians* establishes that the entire class *politicians* is male. After Barbara Boxer is identified as a politician, the conclusion that she is male automatically follows—but, of course, she is not. Because the major premise of this syllogism is not true, no conclusion based on it can be true. Even though the logic of the syllogism is correct, its conclusion is not. Therefore, the syllogism is not sound.

3 Recognizing Enthymemes

An enthymeme is a syllogism in which one of the premises—often the major premise—is unstated. Enthymemes often occur as sentences containing words that signal conclusions—*therefore, consequently, for this reason, for, so, since,* or *because.*

> Melissa is on the Dean's List; therefore, she is a good student.

The preceding sentence contains the minor premise and the conclusion of a syllogism. The reader must fill in the missing major premise in order to complete the syllogism and see whether or not the reasoning is logical.

> **Major Premise:** All those on the Dean's List are good students.
> **Minor Premise:** Melissa is on the Dean's List.
> **Conclusion:** Therefore, Melissa is a good student.

Bumper stickers often take the form of enthymemes, stating just a conclusion ("Eating meat is murder") and leaving readers to supply both the major and minor premises. Careful readers, however, are not so easily fooled. They supply the missing premise (or premises), and then determine if the resulting syllogism is sound.

EXERCISE 2

Read the following two enthymemes:

- Because tax cuts help the economy, we should support the president's tax proposals.
- Eating meat is murder.

Now, supply the missing premises, and determine if the resulting syllogisms are sound—in other words, if they are both valid and true.

9c Using Toulmin Logic

Stephen Toulmin, a contemporary philosopher and rhetorician, has formulated another way of analyzing arguments. According to Toulmin, the traditional syllogistic approach, while useful for identifying flaws in logic, is not useful for analyzing arguments that occur in the real world because these arguments tend to be far more complex than a three-part syllogism suggests. To address this shortcoming, Toulmin created a system that enables writers and readers of argument to compose or analyze arguments at a deeper level than the traditional syllogism permits.

According to Toulmin, most arguments contain the following elements: *the claim, the qualifiers, the support, the warrant,* and *the backing*. The Toulmin model of argument is illustrated in the box below.

THE TOULMIN MODEL OF ARGUMENT

Claim (the point a writer is trying to prove): College athletes should receive salaries for the time they spend competing in sports.

Qualifiers (words or phrases that limit the claim): College athletes *who participate in programs that bring money into the school* should receive salaries for the time they spend competing in sports.

Support (facts, examples, and expert opinion that support the claim): Colleges and universities make a great deal of money from their sports programs.

Warrant (underlying assumption that connects the support with the claim): Athletic scholarships do not fairly compensate student athletes in successful sports programs.

Backing (facts and examples that support the warrant): Studies show that the compensation given to student athletes in major football and basketball programs is small in comparison to the millions of dollars the teams raise for their schools.

In an argumentative essay, the **claim** is the thesis, an opinion that must be supported with **evidence**. For example, in the Toulmin argument in the box on page 117, the claim is "College athletes should receive salaries for the time they spend competing in sports."

The **qualifiers** are words (*probably, sometimes, many,* and *few,* for example) or phrases that limit the claim. Qualifiers demonstrate to readers that you have not overstated your claim. In the argument on page 117, for example, the qualifier limits the claim by saying that only student athletes who participate in programs that make money for the school (not all student athletes) should receive a salary.

The **support** convinces readers that the claim is worth considering. For example, in the argument on page 117, the claim would be supported with facts, examples, and expert opinion that establish that colleges can make a great deal of money from their sports programs.

The **warrant** (or **warrants**) is an assumption that readers must accept in order for the argument to succeed. Sometimes a writer will think that a warrant is so obvious (or self-evident) that it need not be stated. In this case, readers would have to infer the unstated warrant in order to evaluate the argument. At other times, a writer will explicitly state the warrant.

Whether the warrant is implied or explicit, readers have to determine if the writer has supplied the **backing**, the facts and examples needed to support it. For example, in the argument on page 117, the underlying assumption is that athletic scholarships do not fairly compensate student athletes. To establish the validity of this assumption, you would have to provide data to show that sports scholarships do not equitably compensate student athletes.

■ EXERCISE 3

Read this newspaper editorial carefully.

> A nation succeeds only if the vast majority of its citizens succeed. It therefore stands to reason that with immigrants accounting for about 40 percent of our population growth, the future economic and social success of the United States is bound up with the success of these new Americans. Demography, in a word, is destiny.
>
> This is an important principle to keep in mind as we try to come to grips with the problems and opportunities presented by the flood of legal and illegal immigrants from Mexico and other parts of South and Central America, who now constitute by far our largest immigrant group.
>
> How are we doing in our efforts to assimilate these largely Hispanic newcomers and provide them with a bright future? Some signs are disturbing.
>
> John Garcia, associate professor of political science at the University of Arizona, writing in *International Migration Review,* finds that the average rate of naturalization of Mexican immigrants is one-tenth that of other immigrant naturalization rates. The Select Commission on Immigration

and Refugee Policy made a similar finding. Increasingly, immigrants are separated from everyone else by language, geography, ethnicity and class.

The future success of this country is closely linked to the ability of our immigrants to succeed. Yet 50 percent of our children of Hispanic background do not graduate from high school. Hispanic students score 100 points under the average student on Scholastic Aptitude Test scores. Hispanics have much higher rates of poverty, illiteracy and need for welfare than the national average. This engenders social crisis.

Not all the indicators of assimilation are pessimistic: the success of many Indochinese immigrants has been gratifying. But the warning signs of nonassimilation are increasing and ominous.

America must make sure the melting pot continues to melt: immigrants must become Americans. Seymour Martin Lipset, professor of political science and sociology at the Hoover Institution, Stanford University, observes: "The history of bilingual and bicultural societies that do not assimilate are histories of turmoil, tension and tragedy. Canada, Belgium, Malaysia, Lebanon—all face crises of national existence in which minorities press for autonomy, if not independence. Pakistan and Cyprus have divided. Nigeria suppressed an ethnic rebellion. France faces difficulties with its Basques, Bretons and Corsicans."

The United States is at a crossroads. If it does not consciously move toward greater integration, it will inevitably drift toward more fragmentation. It will either have to do better in assimilating all of the other peoples in its boundaries or it will witness increasing alienation and fragmentation. Cultural divisiveness is not a bedrock upon which a nation can be built. It is inherently unstable.

The nation faces a staggering social agenda. We have not adequately integrated blacks into our economy and society. Our education system is rightly described as "a rising tide of mediocrity." We have the most violent society in the industrial world; we have startlingly high rates of illiteracy, illegitimacy and welfare recipients.

It bespeaks a hubris to madly rush, with these unfinished social agendas, into accepting more immigrants and refugees than all of the rest of the world and then to still hope to keep a common agenda.

America can accept additional immigrants, but we must be sure that they become American. We can be a Joseph's coat of many nations, but we must be unified. One of the common glues that hold us together is language—the English language.

We should be color-blind but linguistically cohesive. We should be a rainbow but not a cacophony. We should welcome different peoples but not adopt different languages. We can teach English through bilingual education, but we should take great care not to become a bilingual society. (Richard D. Lamm, "English Comes First")

A. Answer the following questions about the essay.

1. Former Colorado governor Richard D. Lamm relies on a number of unstated premises about his subject that he expects his audience to accept. What are some of these premises?

2. What kinds of information does Lamm use to support his position?
3. Where does Lamm state his conclusion? Restate the conclusion in your own words.
4. In paragraph 1, Lamm uses deductive reasoning. Express this reasoning as a syllogism.
5. Express the syllogism in paragraph 1 in terms of Toulmin logic.

B. Evaluate the reasoning in each of the following statements. (If the statement is in the form of an enthymeme, supply the missing term before evaluating it.)

1. All immigrants should speak English. If they do not, they are not real Americans.
2. Richard D. Lamm was born in the United States and grew up in an English-speaking household. Therefore, he has no credibility on the subject of bilingualism.
3. Spanish-speaking immigrants should be required by law to learn English. After all, most eastern European immigrants who came to this country early in the twentieth century learned English.
4. If immigrants do not care enough about our country to learn English, we should not allow them to become citizens.
5. Some immigrants have become financially successful even though they did not learn English. Obviously, then, learning English does not increase an immigrant's chances for success.
6. All Cuban immigrants speak Spanish. Former Secretary of Housing and Urban Development Henry Cisneros speaks Spanish, so he must be a Cuban immigrant.
7. As sociologist Seymour Martin Lipset points out, bilingual societies can be threatened by tension and political unrest. Therefore, it is important that immigrants not be bilingual.

9d Recognizing Logical Fallacies

Fallacies are flawed arguments. A writer who inadvertently uses logical fallacies is not thinking clearly or logically; a writer who intentionally uses them is trying to deceive readers. It is important that you learn to recognize fallacies—to challenge them when you read and to avoid them when you write.

ESL TIP

In many cultures, people present arguments in order to persuade others to believe something. However, the rules for constructing such arguments are different in different cultures. In US academic settings, writers are discouraged from using the types of arguments listed in the Close-up box on pages 121–22 because they are not considered fair.

CLOSE-UP

LOGICAL FALLACIES

- **Hasty Generalization** Drawing a conclusion based on too little evidence

  The person I voted for is not doing a good job in Congress. Therefore, voting is a waste of time. (One disappointing experience does not warrant the statement that you will never vote again.)

- **Sweeping Generalization** Making a generalization that cannot be supported no matter how much evidence is supplied

  Everyone should exercise. (Some people, for example those with severe heart conditions, might not benefit from exercise.)

- **Equivocation** Shifting the meaning of a key word or phrase during an argument

  It is not in the public interest for the public to lose interest in politics. (Although clever, the shift in the meaning of the term *public interest* clouds the issue.)

- **Non Sequitur (Does Not Follow)** Arriving at a conclusion that does not logically follow from what comes before

  Kim Williams is a good lawyer, so she will make a good senator. (Kim Williams may be a good lawyer, but it does not necessarily follow that she will make a good senator.)

- **Either/Or Fallacy** Treating a complex issue as if it has only two sides

  Either we institute universal health care, or the health of all Americans will decline. (Good health does not necessarily depend on universal health care.)

- **Post Hoc** Establishing an unjustified link between cause and effect

  The United States sold wheat to Russia. This must be what caused the price of wheat to rise. (Other factors, unrelated to the sale, could have caused the price of wheat to rise.)

- **Begging the Question** (circular reasoning) Stating a debatable premise as if it were true

  Stem-cell research should be banned because nothing good can come from something so inherently evil. (Where is the evidence that stem-cell research is "inherently evil"?)

- **False Analogy** Assuming that because things are similar in some ways, they are similar in other ways

  When forced to live in crowded conditions, people act like rats. They turn on each other and act violently. (Both people and rats might dislike living in crowded conditions, but unlike rats, people do not necessarily resort to violence in this situation.)

(continued)

Logical Fallacies (continued)

- **Red Herring** Changing the subject to distract readers from the issue

    Our company may charge high prices, but we give a lot to charity each year. (What does charging high prices have to do with giving to charity?)

- **Argument to Ignorance** Saying that something is true because it cannot be proved false, or vice versa

    How can you tell me to send my child to a school where there is a child who has AIDS? After all, doctors can't say for sure that my child won't catch AIDS, can they? (Just because a doctor cannot prove the speaker's claim to be false, it does not follow that the claim is true.)

- **Bandwagon** Trying to establish that something is true because everyone believes it is true

    Everyone knows that eating candy makes children hyperactive. (Where is the evidence to support this claim?)

- **Argument to the Person** *(Ad Hominem)* Attacking the person and not the issue

    Of course the congressman supports drilling for oil in the Arctic wildlife preserve. He worked for an oil company before he was elected to Congress. (By attacking his opponent, the speaker attempts to sidestep the issue.)

- **Argument to the People** Appealing to people's prejudices

    Because foreigners are attempting to overrun our shores, we should cut back on immigration. (By introducing prejudice, the speaker attempts to distract the audience.)

EXERCISE 4

Identify the logical fallacies in the following statements. In each case, name the fallacy, and then rewrite the statement to correct the problem.

1. Membership in the Coalition against Pornography has more than quadrupled since the 1990s. Convenience stores in many parts of the country have limited their selection of pornography and, in many cases, taken pornography off the shelves. In 1995, the defense appropriations bill included a ban on the sale of pornography on military installations. The American public clearly believes that pornography has a harmful effect on its audience.
2. With people like Larry Flynt and Hugh Hefner arguing that pornography is harmless, you know that pornography is causing its readers to live immoral lifestyles.

3. The Republican Party and conservative thinkers are all for the free market when the issue is environmental degradation, but they will be the first ones to call for a limit to what can be shown on movies, television, and the Internet.
4. Television is out of control. There is more foul language, sex, and sexual innuendo on television than there has ever been before. The effects of this obscene and pornographic material have been clearly documented in studies that proved that serial killers and other criminals were much more likely to be regular consumers of pornographic materials.
5. We know that television causes children to be more violent. So what can we use to control television? The V-chip, television ratings, and more governmental control of television content will help us reduce violence.
6. Study after study has been completed, and none of the researchers has presented incontrovertible evidence that rap music causes an increase in violent behavior among its listeners.
7. A boy in Idaho set fire to his family's home after watching a television stunt show. From this incident, we can see that television has a negative influence on children's behavior.
8. We want our children to grow up in safe neighborhoods. We would like to see less violence in the schools and on the playgrounds. We would like to be less fearful when we have to go out at night. If we stop polluting our culture with violent images from television and popular music, we can reclaim our communities and our children.
9. Ted Bundy and Richard Ramirez, two of the most violent serial killers ever caught, both viewed pornography regularly. Pornography caused them to kill women.
10. Some people believe that violence on television affects children and want the government to find ways to limit violence. Others believe that children are unaffected by the violence they see on television. I do not think violence on television causes children to become violent.

■ EXERCISE 5

Read the following excerpt. Identify as many logical fallacies as you can. Then, write a letter to the author pointing out the fallacies and explaining how they weaken his argument.

Hunting and eating a free-roaming wild deer is one thing; slaughtering and eating a [wounded] deer is another.
The point . . . is that—despite what our enemies are saying—hunters are just as compassionate as the next fellow. It hurts us to see an animal suffer, and when we can help an animal in need, we go out of our way to do whatever we can.

A case in point is the story . . . about SCI Alaska vice president Dave Campbell's efforts to help a cow moose. That animal had carried a poorly shot arrow in its body for weeks until Campbell saw it and made certain it got help.

Despite how some media handled that story, there is no irony in hunters coming to the rescue of the same species we hunt.

We do it all the time.

A story of hunters showing compassion for an animal is something you'll never see in *The Bunny Huggers' Gazette* (yes, there is such a publication. It's a bimonthly magazine produced on newsprint. According to the publisher's statement, it provides information about vegetarianism, and "organizations, protests, boycotts or legislation on behalf of animal liberation . . .").

Among the protests announced in the June issue of *BHG* are boycotts against the countries of Ireland and Spain, the states and provinces of the Yukon Territory, Alberta, British Columbia, Pennsylvania and Alaska, the companies of American Express, Anheuser-Busch, Bausch & Lomb, Bloomingdale's, Coca-Cola Products, Coors, Gillette, Hartz, L'Oreal, McDonald's, Mellon Bank, Northwest Airlines, Pocono Mountain resorts and a host of others.

Interestingly, *BHG* tells how a subscribing group, Life Net of Montezuma, New Mexico, has petitioned the US Forest Service to close portions of the San Juan and Rio Grande National Forests between April and November to all entry "to provide as much protection as possible" for grizzly bears that may still exist there. Another subscriber, Predator Project of Bozeman, Montana, is asking that the entire North Cascades region be closed to coyote hunting because gray wolves might be killed by "sportsmen (who) may not be able to tell the difference between a coyote and a wolf."

Although it's not a new idea, another subscriber, Prairie Dog Rescue, is urging persons who are opposed to hunting to apply for limited quota hunting permits because "one permit in peaceful hands means one less opportunity for a hunter to kill."

And if you ever doubted that the vegetarian/animal rights herd is a wacko bunch, then consider the magazine's review of *Human Tissue, A Neglected Experimental Resource*. According to the review, the 24-page essay encourages using human tissues to test "medicines and other substances, any of which would save animals' lives." (Bill Roberts, "The World of Hunting")

10

Writing Argumentative Essays

❓ FAQs

How do I know if a topic is suitable for an argumentative essay? (p. 125)
How do I make sure that I have an argumentative thesis? (p. 126)
How should I deal with opposing arguments? (p. 128)
How can I convince readers that I'm someone they should listen to? (p. 129)
How can I be sure I'm being fair? (p. 131)
How should I organize my argumentative essay? (p. 132)

For most people, the true test of their critical thinking skills comes when they write an **argumentative essay,** one that takes a stand on an issue and uses logic and evidence to convince readers. When you write an argument, you follow the same process you use when you write any essay. However, because the purpose of an argument is to change the way readers think, you need to use some additional strategies to present your ideas to your audience.

See Chs. 4–6

10a Planning an Argumentative Essay

1 Choosing a Debatable Topic

Because an argumentative essay attempts to change the way people think, it must focus on a **debatable topic,** one about which reasonable people may disagree. **Factual statements**—verifiable assertions about which reasonable people do *not* disagree—are, therefore, not suitable as topics for argument.

> **Fact:** First-year students are not required to purchase a meal plan from the university.
>
> **Debatable Topic:** First-year students *should be* required to purchase a meal plan from the university.

Your topic should be narrow enough so that you can write about it within your page limit. Remember, in your argumentative essay, you will have to develop your own ideas and present convincing support while also pointing out the strengths and weaknesses of opposing arguments. If your topic is too broad, you will not be able to treat it in enough detail.

In addition, your topic should be interesting to you and to your readers. Keep in mind that some topics—such as "The Need for Gun Control" or "The Fairness of the Death Penalty"—have been discussed and written about so often that you may not be able to say anything new or interesting about them. Instead of relying on an overused topic, choose one that enables you to contribute something to the debate.

2 Developing an Argumentative Thesis

After you have chosen a topic, your next step is to state your position in an **argumentative thesis,** one that takes a strong stand. Properly worded, this thesis statement lays the foundation for the rest of your argument.

See 5b

One way to make sure that your **thesis statement** actually does take a stand is to formulate an **antithesis,** a statement that takes the opposite position. If you can state an antithesis, your thesis statement takes a stand.

> **Thesis Statement:** Term limits would improve government by bringing people with fresh ideas into office every few years.
>
> **Antithesis:** Term limits would harm government because elected officials would always be inexperienced.

CLOSE-UP

DEVELOPING AN ARGUMENTATIVE THESIS

To make sure your argumentative thesis is effective, ask the following questions:

- Is your thesis one with which reasonable people would disagree?
- Can you formulate an antithesis?
- Can your thesis be supported by evidence?
- Does your thesis make clear to readers what position you are taking?

---

3 Defining Your Terms

You should always define the key terms you use in your argument—especially those you use in your thesis statement. After all, the soundness of an entire argument may hinge on the definition of a word that may mean one thing to one person and another thing to someone else. For example, in the United States, democratic elections involve the selection of government officials by popular vote; in other countries, the word *democratic* may be used to describe elections in which only one candidate is running or in which all candidates represent the same party. For this reason, if your argument hinges on a key term like *democratic*, you should make sure that your readers know exactly what you mean.

> **CLOSE-UP**
>
> **USING PRECISE LANGUAGE**
>
> Be careful to use precise language in your thesis statement. Avoid vague and judgmental words, such as *wrong*, *bad*, *good*, *right*, and *immoral*.
>
> **Vague:** Censorship of the Internet would be wrong.
> **Clearer:** Censorship of the Internet would unfairly limit free speech.

4 Considering Your Audience

As you plan your essay, keep a specific audience in mind. Are your readers unbiased observers or people deeply concerned about the issue you plan to discuss? Can they be cast in a specific role—concerned parents, victims of discrimination, irate consumers—or are they so diverse that they cannot be categorized?

See 1b

   Always assume that your audience will question your assumptions. Even if your readers are sympathetic to your position, you cannot assume that they will accept your ideas without question; they will still need to see that your argument is logical and that your evidence is solid. More skeptical readers will need reassurance that you understand their concerns and that you concede some of their points. However, no matter what you do, you may never be able to convince hostile readers that your conclusion is valid. The best you can hope for is that these readers will acknowledge the strengths of your argument even if they reject your conclusion.

> **ESL TIP**
>
> If you have not lived in the United States very long, it may be difficult for you to assess what your readers know and believe. Since your instructor is one of your primary readers, consult him or her about this issue.

5 Refuting Opposing Arguments

As you develop your argument, you should briefly summarize and then **refute**—that is, disprove—opposing arguments by showing that they are untrue, unfair, illogical, unimportant, or irrelevant. (If an opponent's position is so strong that it cannot be refuted, concede the point, and then identify its limitations.) In the following paragraph, a student refutes the argument that Sea World is justified in keeping whales in captivity.

> Of course, some will say that Sea World wants to capture only a few whales, as George Will points out in his commentary in *Newsweek*. Unfortunately, Will downplays the fact that Sea World wants to capture a hundred whales, not just "a few." And, after releasing ninety of these whales, Sea World intends to keep ten for "further work." At hearings in Seattle last week, several noted marine biologists went on record as condemning Sea World's research program.

NOTE: When you acknowledge an opposing view, be careful not to distort or oversimplify it. This tactic, known as creating a **straw man,** can seriously undermine your credibility.

COMPUTER TIP academic.cengage.com/eng/kirsznermandell

REFUTING OPPOSING ARGUMENTS

As you formulate an argument, you can use your computer to create a table or chart that organizes all the arguments against your position. Using the Table menu in your word-processing program, create a two-column table. Label the first column "Opposing Arguments" and the second column "Refutations." List the arguments against your position in the first column and your refutations of these arguments in the second column. When you are finished, delete the weakest opposing arguments. When you write your essay, discuss only those opposing arguments and refutations that remain.

■ **EXERCISE 1**

Choose one of the following five statements, and list the arguments in favor of it. Then, list the arguments against it. Finally, choose one position (pro or con), and write a paragraph or two supporting it. Be sure to refute the arguments against your position.

1. Public school students who participate in extracurricular activities should have to submit to random drug tests.
2. The federal government should limit the amount of violence shown on television.

3. A couple applying for a marriage license should be required to take AIDS tests.
4. Retirees making more than $50,000 a year should not be eligible for Social Security benefits.
5. Colleges and universities should provide free day care for students' children.

10b Using Evidence Effectively

1 Supporting Your Argument

Most arguments are built on **assertions**—statements that you make about a debatable topic—backed by <u>evidence</u>—supporting information, in the form of examples, statistics, or expert opinion. If, for instance, you asserted that law-enforcement officials are winning the war against violent crime, you could then support this assertion by referring to a government report stating that violent crime—especially murder—has dramatically decreased during the past decade. This report would be one piece of persuasive evidence.

See 8b

Only assertions that are **self-evident** ("All human beings are mortal"), **true by definition** (2 + 2 = 4), or **factual** ("The Atlantic Ocean separates England and the United States") need no proof. All other kinds of assertions require support.

NOTE: Remember that you can never prove a thesis conclusively—if you did, there would be no argument. The best you can do is to provide enough evidence to establish a high probability that your thesis is reasonable or valid.

2 Establishing Credibility

Clear reasoning, compelling evidence, and strong refutations go a long way toward making an argument solid. But these elements in themselves are not sufficient to create a convincing argument. In order to convince readers, you have to satisfy them that you are someone they should listen to—in other words, that you have **credibility**.

Some people, of course, bring credibility with them every time they speak. When a Nobel Prize winner in physics makes a speech about the need to control proliferation of nuclear weapons, we assume that he or she speaks with authority. But most people do not have this kind of credibility. When you write an argument, you must work to establish your credibility by *establishing common ground, demonstrating knowledge, maintaining a reasonable tone,* and *presenting yourself as someone worth listening to.*

Establishing Common Ground. When you write an argument, it is tempting to go on the attack, emphasizing the differences between your position and those of your opponents. Writers of effective arguments, however, know they can gain a greater advantage by establishing common ground between their opponents and themselves.

> **CLOSE-UP**
>
> **USING ROGERIAN ARGUMENT**
>
> One way to establish common ground is to use the techniques of **Rogerian argument.** According to the psychologist Carl Rogers, you should think of the members of your audience as colleagues with whom you must collaborate to find solutions to problems. Instead of verbally assaulting them, you should emphasize points of agreement. In this way, rather than taking a confrontational stance, you establish common ground and work toward a resolution of the problem you are discussing.

Demonstrating Knowledge. Including relevant personal experiences in your argumentative essay can show readers that you know a lot about your subject; demonstrating this kind of knowledge gives you authority. For example, describing what you observed at a National Rifle Association convention can give you authority in an essay arguing for (or against) gun control.

See Pts. 4–5

You can also establish credibility by showing you have done research into a subject. By referring to important sources of information and by providing accurate **documentation** for your information, you show readers that you have done the necessary background reading. Including references to a range of sources—not just one—suggests that you have a balanced knowledge of your subject. However, questionable sources, inaccurate (or missing) documentation, and factual errors can undermine an argument. For many readers, an undocumented quotation or even an incorrect date can call an entire argument into question.

See 1c

Maintaining a Reasonable Tone. Your **tone** is almost as important as the information you convey. Talk *to* your readers, not *at* them. If you lecture your readers or appear to talk down to them, you will alienate them. Remember that readers are more likely to respond to a writer who is conciliatory than to one who is strident or insulting.

As you write your essay, use moderate language, and qualify your statements so that they seem reasonable. Try to avoid words and phrases such as *never, all,* and *in every case,* which can make your claims seem exaggerated and unrealistic. The statement "Euthanasia is never acceptable," for example, leaves you no room for compromise. A more conciliatory statement might be "In cases of extreme suffering, a patient's desire for death is certainly understandable, but in most cases, the moral, social, and legal implications of euthanasia make it unacceptable."

Presenting Yourself as Someone Worth Listening To. When you write an argument, you should make sure you present yourself as someone your readers will want to listen to. Present your argument in positive and forceful terms, and don't apologize for your views. For example, do not rely on phrases—such as "In my opinion" and "It seems to me"—that undercut your credibility. Be consistent, and be careful not to contradict yourself. Finally, limit your use of the first person ("I"), and avoid slang and colloquialisms.

3 Being Fair

Argument promotes one point of view, so it is seldom objective. However, college writing requires that you stay within the bounds of fairness and avoid **bias**. To be sure that the support for your argument is not misleading or distorted, you should take the following steps.

See 8c

Avoid Distorting Evidence. You **distort** evidence when you misrepresent it. Writers sometimes intentionally misrepresent their opponents' views by exaggerating them and then attacking this extreme position. For example, a senator of a northeastern state proposed requiring unmarried mothers receiving welfare to identify their children's fathers and to supply information about them. Instead of challenging this proposal directly, a critic distorted the senator's position and attacked it unfairly.

> What is the senator's next idea in his headlong rush to embrace the extreme right-wing position? A program of tattoos for welfare mothers? A badge sewn on to their clothing identifying them as welfare recipients? Creation of colonies in which welfare recipients would be forced to live like lepers? How about an involuntary relocation program into concentration camps?

Avoid Quoting Out of Context. A writer or speaker **quotes out of context** by taking someone's words from their original setting and using them in another. When you select certain statements and ignore others, you can change the meaning of what someone has said or suggested.

> **Mr. N, Township Resident:** I don't know why you are opposing the new highway. According to your own statements, the highway will increase land values and bring more business into the area.
>
> **Ms. L, Township Supervisor:** I think you should look at my statements more carefully. I have a copy of the paper that printed my interview, and what I said was [*reading*]: "The highway will increase land values a bit and bring some business to the area.

But at what cost? One hundred and fifty families will be displaced, and the highway will divide our township in half." My comments were not meant to support the new highway but to underscore the problems that its construction will cause.

Avoid Slanting. You **slant** information when you select only information that supports your case and ignore information that does not. Slanting also occurs when you use inflammatory language to create bias. For example, a national magazine slanted its information when it described a person accused of a crime as "a hulk of a man who looks as if he could burn out somebody's eyes with a propane torch." Although one-sided presentations frequently appear in tabloids and some popular magazines, you should avoid such distortions in your argumentative essays.

Avoid Using Unfair Appeals. Traditionally, writers of arguments use three kinds of appeals to influence readers: **logical appeals** address an audience's sense of reason; **emotional appeals** play on the emotions of a reader; and **ethical appeals** call the reader's attention to the credibility of the writer.

See 9d

Problems arise when these appeals are used unfairly. For example, writers can use **fallacies** to fool readers into thinking that a conclusion is logical when it is not. Writers can also employ inappropriate emotional appeals—to prejudice or fear, for example—to influence readers. And finally, writers can unfairly use their credentials in one area of expertise to bolster their stature in another area that they are not qualified to discuss.

10c Organizing an Argumentative Essay

See 9a–b

In its simplest form, an argument consists of a thesis statement and supporting evidence. However, argumentative essays frequently use **inductive and deductive reasoning** and other specialized strategies to win audience approval and overcome potential opposition.

> **CLOSE-UP**
>
> **ELEMENTS OF AN ARGUMENTATIVE ESSAY**
>
> **Introduction**
>
> See 7e2
>
> The  of your argumentative essay orients your readers to your subject. Here you can show how your subject concerns your audience, establish common ground with your readers, and perhaps explain how your subject has been misunderstood.

Thesis Statement

Your thesis statement can appear anywhere in your argumentative essay. Most often, you state your thesis in your introduction. However, if you are presenting a highly controversial argument—one to which you believe your readers might react negatively—you may postpone stating your thesis until later in your essay.

See 5b, 10a2

Background

In this section, you can briefly present a narrative of past events, an overview of others' opinions on the issue, definitions of key terms, or a review of basic facts.

Arguments in Support of Your Thesis

Begin with your weakest argument, and work up to your strongest. If all your arguments are equally strong, you might begin with those with which your readers are already familiar and therefore perhaps more likely to accept.

Refutation of Opposing Arguments

If the opposing arguments are relatively weak, summarize and refute them after you have made your case. However, if the opposing arguments are strong, concede their strengths and then discuss their limitations before you present your own arguments.

Conclusion

Often, the conclusion restates the major arguments in support of your thesis. Your conclusion can also summarize key points, restate your thesis, remind readers of the weaknesses of opposing arguments, or underscore the logic of your position. Many writers like to end their arguments with a strong last line, such as a quotation or a statement that sums up the argument.

See 7e3

10d Writing and Revising an Argumentative Essay

1 Writing an Argumentative Essay

The following student essay includes many of the elements discussed in this chapter. The writer, Samantha Masterton, was asked to write an argumentative essay on a topic of her choice, drawing her supporting evidence from her own knowledge and experience as well as from other sources.

Masterton 1

Samantha Masterton
Professor Egler
English 102
4 April 2007

The Returning Student: Older Is Definitely Better

Introduction — After graduating from high school, young people must decide what they want to do with the rest of their lives. Many graduates (often without much thought) decide to continue their education uninterrupted, and they go on to college. This group of teenagers makes up what many see as typical first-year college students. Recently, however, this stereotype has been challenged by an influx of older students, including myself, into American colleges and universities. Not only do these students make a valuable contribution to the schools they attend, but they also offer an alternative to young people who go to college simply because they do not know what else to do. *Thesis statement* — A few years off between high school and college can give many—perhaps most—students the life experience they need to appreciate the value of higher education and to gain more from it.

Background — The college experience of an eighteen-year-old is quite different from that of an older "nontraditional" student. The typical high school graduate is often concerned with things other than cracking books—for example, going to parties, dating, and testing personal limits. However, older students—those who are twenty-five years of age or older—take seriously the idea of returning to college. Although many high school students do not think twice about whether or not to attend college, older students have much more to consider when they think about returning to college. For example, they must decide how much time they can spend getting their degree and

Masterton 2

consider the impact attending college will have on their families and on their finances.

In the United States, the demographics of college students is changing. According to a 2002 US Department of Education report titled *Nontraditional Undergraduates*, the percentage of students who could be classified as "nontraditional" has increased over the last decade (see fig. 1). So, in spite of the challenges that older students face when they return to school, more and more are choosing to make the effort.

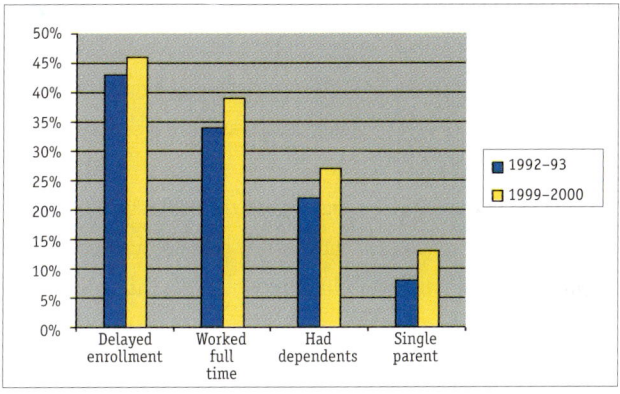

Fig. 1. United States, Dept. of Educ., Office of Educ. Research and Improvement, Natl. Center for Educ. Statistics; *Nontraditional Undergraduates*, by Susan Choy; 2002; National Center for Education Statistics; Web; 27 Feb. 2007.

Most older students return to school with well-defined goals. The US Department of Education's *Nontraditional Undergraduates* report shows that more than one-third of nontraditional students decided to attend college because it was required by their job, and eighty-seven percent enrolled in order to gain skills (10). Getting a college degree is often a requirement for professional advancement, and older students are therefore more likely to take college seriously. In general, older students enroll in college with a definite course of study in mind. For older students, college is an extension of work rather than a place to discover what they want to be when they graduate. A study by psychologists R. Eric Landrum, Je T'aime Hood, and Jerry M. McAdams concluded, "Nontraditional students seemed to be more appreciative of their opportunities, as indicated by their higher enjoyment of school and appreciation of professors' efforts in the classroom" (744). Clearly defining their goals enables older students to take advantage of the opportunities presented by professors as well as to make use of career offices and other services colleges provide.

Older students also understand the actual benefits of doing well in school and successfully completing a degree program. Older students I have known rarely cut lectures or put off studying. This is because older students are often balancing the demands of home and work, and they know how important it is to do well. The difficulties of juggling school, family, and work compel older students to be disciplined and focused—especially concerning their schoolwork. This pays off; older students tend to devote more hours per week to studying and tend to have higher grade point averages than younger students do (Landrum, Hood, and McAdams 742-43).

My observations of older students have convinced me that many students would benefit from delaying entry into college. Given their greater maturity and experience, older students bring more into the classroom than younger students do. Eighteen-year-olds are immature and inexperienced. They cannot be expected to have formulated definite goals or developed firm ideas about themselves or about the world in which they live. In contrast, older students have generally had a variety of real-life experiences. Most have worked for several years, and many have started families. Their years in the "real world" have helped them become more focused and more responsible than they were when they graduated from high school. As a result, they are better prepared for college than they would have been when they were young.

Personal experience used as evidence in support of thesis

Of course, postponing college for a few years is not for everyone. Certainly some teenagers have a definite sense of purpose and maturity well beyond their years, and these individuals would benefit from an early college experience, so that they can get a head start on their careers. Charles Woodward, a law librarian, went to college directly after high school, and for him the experience was positive. "I was serious about learning, and I loved my subject," he said. "I felt fortunate that I knew what I wanted from college and from life." Many younger students, however, are not like Woodward; they graduate from high school without any clear sense of purpose. For this reason, it makes sense for them to postpone college until they are mature enough to benefit from the experience.

Refutation of opposing argument

Granted, some older students have difficulties when they return to college. Because these students have been out of school so long, they may have difficulty studying and adapting to the routines of academic life. As I have seen, though, these problems disappear after an initial period of adjustment, and older students quickly adapt to college. Of course, it is true that many older students find

Refutation of opposing argument

it difficult to balance the needs of their family with college and to cope with the financial burden of tuition. However, this challenge is becoming easier with the growing number of online courses and the introduction of governmental programs, such as educational tax credits, to ease the financial burden of returning to school (Agbo 164-65).

Conclusion

All things considered, higher education is often wasted on the young, who are either too immature or too unfocused to take advantage of it. Taking a few years off between high school and college would give these students the time they need to make the most of a college education. The increasing number of older students returning to college seems to indicate that many students are taking this path. According to a US Department of Education report, *Digest of Education Statistics, 2001*, forty percent of students enrolled in American colleges in 2000 were twenty-five years of age or older. Older students such as these have taken time off to serve in the military, to gain valuable work experience, or to raise a family. By the time they get to college, they have defined their goals and made a commitment to achieve them. It is clear that postponing college for a few years can result in a better educational experience.

Masterton 6

Works Cited

Agbo, S. "The United States: Heterogeneity of the Student Body and the Meaning of 'Nontraditional' in U.S. Higher Education." *Higher Education and Lifelong Learners: International Perspectives on Change*. Ed. Hans G. Schuetze and Maria Slowey. London: Routledge, 2000. 149-69. Print.

Landrum, R. Eric, Je T'aime Hood, and Jerry M. McAdams. "Satisfaction with College by Traditional and Nontraditional College Students." *Psychological Reports* 89.3 (2001): 740-46. Print.

United States. Dept. of Educ. Office of Educ. Research and Improvement. Natl. Center for Educ. Statistics. *Digest of Education Statistics, 2001*. By Thomas D. Snyder. 2002. *National Center for Education Statistics*. Web. 27 Feb. 2007.

---. ---. ---. ---. *Nontraditional Undergraduates*. By Susan Choy. 2002. *National Center for Education Statistics*. Web. 27 Feb. 2007.

Woodward, Charles B. Personal interview. 21 Mar. 2007.

10d rev ■ Writing Argumentative Essays

2 Revising an Argumentative Essay

See 6c

When you <u>revise</u> your argumentative essay, you use the same strategies you use for any essay. In addition, you concentrate on some specific concerns, which are listed in the following checklist.

CHECKLIST

ARGUMENTATIVE ESSAYS

- ☐ Is your topic debatable?
- ☐ Does your essay have an argumentative thesis?
- ☐ Have you defined the key terms you use in your argument?
- ☐ Have you considered the opinions, attitudes, and values of your audience?
- ☐ Have you summarized and refuted opposing arguments?
- ☐ Have you supported your assertions with evidence?
- ☐ Have you used relevant visuals to strengthen your argument?
- ☐ Have you documented all information that is not your own?
- ☐ Have you established your credibility?
- ☐ Have you been fair?
- ☐ Have you avoided logical fallacies?
- ☐ Have you constructed your argumentative essay logically?
- ☐ Have you provided your readers with enough background information?
- ☐ Have you presented your points clearly and organized them logically?
- ☐ Have you written an interesting introduction and a strong conclusion?

CLOSE-UP

USING TRANSITIONS IN ARGUMENTATIVE ESSAYS

Argumentative essays should include transitional words and phrases to indicate which paragraphs are arguments in support of the thesis, which are refutations of arguments that oppose the thesis, and which are conclusions.

Arguments in support of thesis	accordingly, because, for example, for instance, in general, given, generally, since

Refutations	although, admittedly, certainly, despite, granted, in all fairness, naturally, nonetheless, of course
Conclusions	all things considered, as a result, in conclusion, in summary, therefore, thus

EXERCISE 2

Samantha Masterton deleted the following paragraph from her essay "The Returning Student: Older Is Definitely Better." Do you think Samantha was right to delete it? If it belongs in the essay, where would it go? Would it need any revision?

> The dedication of adult students is evident in the varied roles they must play. Many of the adults who return to school are seeking to increase their earning power. They have established themselves in the working world, only to find they cannot advance without more education or a graduate degree. The dual-income family structure enables many of these adults to return to school, but it is unrealistic for them to put their well-established lives on hold while they pursue their education. In addition to the rigors of college, older students are often juggling homes, families, and jobs. However, adult students make up in determination what they lack in time. In contrast, younger students often lack the essential motivation to succeed in school. Teenagers in college often have no clear idea of why they are there and, lacking this sense of purpose, may do poorly even though they have comparatively few outside distractions.

11

Using Visuals to Support Your Arguments

❓ FAQs

How can visuals make an argumentative essay more persuasive? (p. 142)
How do I evaluate a visual? (p. 145)
How can a photograph be misleading? (p. 145)
How can a chart or graph misrepresent data? (p. 147)

11a Using Visuals

See 6b3, 30d

Visuals can add a persuasive dimension to your argumentative essays. Because visual images can have such an immediate impact, they can make a good argumentative essay even more persuasive.

In a sense, visuals are another type of evidence that can support your thesis statement. For example, the addition of a photograph of a roadway work zone choked with traffic (Figure 11.1) could help support your assertion that your township should provide more effective work-zone strategies to reduce congestion. In addition, a graph or chart could easily establish the fact that traffic congestion has gotten considerably worse over the past twenty years (Figure 11.2).

FIGURE 11.1 Traffic jam in a roadway work zone.

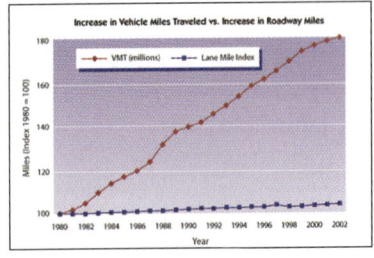

FIGURE 11.2 Chart showing the increase in vehicle miles traveled versus the increase in roadway miles from 1980 to 2002.

FIGURE 11.3 Cartoon from the *Honolulu Advertiser*.

To persuade readers, visuals rely on elements such as images, written text, white space, and color. Consider, for example, the editorial cartoon in Figure 11.3 (above). This cartoon was drawn in response to a US Supreme Court ruling that upheld the Children's Internet Protection Act, which mandated filters on all Internet computers in public libraries. The goal of this law was to prevent children from accessing sexually explicit material online. This cartoon criticizes the Supreme Court's ruling. The two figures (one a child and the other an adult) that dominate the cartoon are staring intently at a computer screen. The use of written text in the cartoon is limited to the labels "Supreme Court" and "Public Library." Thus, with just a few words, this visual forcefully makes the cartoonist's point: that Americans—even minors—do not need the Supreme Court looking over their shoulders and deciding what information they can access in the library. If you were writing an argument that took the same position as this cartoon, it could certainly help you make your point.

Remember, visuals should not be used simply for decoration or to break up the text of your paper. To be effective, they must contribute something useful to your discussion. Irrelevant or inappropriate visuals will not only distract readers, but also confuse them. Moreover, misleading or unfair visuals will damage your credibility, thereby undercutting your argument. For this reason, when you select visuals, remember your purpose and audience and the tone you wish to establish. Just as you would with any other evidence in an argumentative essay, you should **evaluate** the visuals you use to make sure that they are not taken out of context and that they do not make their points unfairly.

See 11b

11a Using Visuals to Support Your Arguments

CHECKLIST

SELECTING VISUALS

- [ ] Does the visual clearly support your argument?
- [ ] In what way do the various elements of the visual reinforce your point?
- [ ] What point does the visual make?
- [ ] Is the visual aimed at a particular type of audience?
- [ ] Could the visual confuse or distract your readers in any way?
- [ ] Could the visual seem unfair to readers?

■ EXERCISE 1

Look carefully at the political cartoon in Figure 11.4.

FIGURE 11.4 Cartoon from Arizona *Tribune*.

Now, use the questions in the checklist above to help you determine whether or not the cartoon would provide useful evidence to support the following argumentative thesis statements:

- Because public opinion seems to be turning against the death penalty, it should be abolished as soon as possible.
- If the death penalty is abolished, violent criminals will be more likely to commit violent crimes.
- Because the death penalty seems to be carried out in such an unfair and arbitrary way, it should be abolished as soon as possible.
- Until an exhaustive study of the death penalty can be carried out, state governors should declare a moratorium on capital punishment.
- Although many consider the death penalty to be "cruel and unusual punishment," it is still appropriate for particularly heinous crimes.

EXERCISE 2

Visit two Web sites that take opposing positions on a controversial topic. What visuals are used on each site, and how are they used to support each site's position?

11b Evaluating Visuals

Just as you have to think critically about the ideas you read, you also have to think critically about the visuals that accompany these texts. Whether they are photographs, advertisements, or statistical charts and graphs, visuals are often designed to influence readers—for example, to encourage them to support a cause or to buy a product. And, like other kinds of evidence, visuals can also distort or misrepresent facts and mislead readers.

1 Misleading Photographs

FIGURE 11.5 **Elvis sighting.**

Almost all photographs that appear in print have been altered in some way. The most common changes involve cropping a picture to eliminate distracting background objects, re-coloring a background to emphasize subjects in the foreground, and altering the brightness and contrast of an image to enhance its overall quality. There is a difference, however, between adjusting an image to make it clearer or more appealing and altering an image for the purpose of misrepresenting facts—for example, in advertisements that show "dramatic" before-and-after weight loss results and in pictures "proving" Elvis is still alive (see Figure 11.5). People usually recognize such photographs for what they are—visual fakes—and do not take them seriously.

Problems arise, however, when an overly zealous editor, reporter, or photographer alters a serious news photograph in order to support a particular point of view or when a scientist alters a photograph to misrepresent data. For example, most people would agree that cropping a photograph of a battle so that it fits within the boundaries of a two-column newspaper article is acceptable. However, cropping the photograph to eliminate wounded civilians on one side of the image—especially when this tactic is used to make a case for or against a war—is more than just misleading; it is dishonest. The same holds true for researchers who write a report in which they include photos that have been altered to support their conclusions.

11b Using Visuals to Support Your Arguments

Another questionable tactic is the use of **staged photographs,** visual images that purport to be spontaneous when they are actually posed. Even the hint of staging can discredit a visual image. One of the most famous examples of this concerns the flag-raising photograph at the battle of Iwo Jima during World War II (see Figure 11.6). Photographer Joe Rosenthal's Pulitzer Prize–winning image is perhaps the most famous war photograph ever taken. When it appeared in newspapers on February 25, 1945, it immediately captured the attention of the American public, so much so that it became the model for the Marine Corps monument in Washington, DC. Almost immediately, however, people began to question whether or not the photograph was staged. Rosenthal did not help matters when he seemed to admit to a correspondent that it was. Later, however, he said that he had been referring to a posed shot he took the same day (see Figure 11.7), not the famous flag-raising picture. Historians now agree that the flag-raising picture was not staged, but this charge haunted Rosenthal his entire life and is still repeated by some as if it were fact.

FIGURE 11.6 Soldiers raise a flag at the battle of Iwo Jima, February 1945.

FIGURE 11.7 Soldiers pose before the camera at Iwo Jima, February 1945.

COMPUTER TIP academic.cengage.com/eng/kirsznermandell

ALTERING IMAGES

With the advent of desktop digital imaging programs, altering images is no longer something only professionals can do. Programs such as *Adobe Photoshop*® give users access to a wide range of digital image editing techniques. If you do decide to alter an image, however, be careful not to distort or misrepresent it.

■ **EXERCISE 3**

Compare and contrast the two Iwo Jima photographs. How do various elements of the two images convey the photographer's purpose, tone, and theme? What elements suggest that the second photo is staged?

EXERCISE 4

Look at the following photograph in its original and cropped form (Figures 11.8 and 11.9). Compare the two representations of the events taking place. How does the cropped image differ from the original image? Do you think cropping misrepresents the photographer's original intention in any significant way?

FIGURE 11.8 **Couple kissing while women argue.**

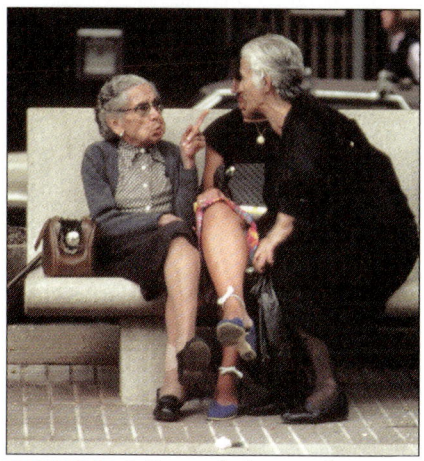

FIGURE 11.9 **Cropped photograph.**

2 Misleading Charts and Graphs

Charts and graphs are effective tools for showing relationships among statistical data in science, business, and other disciplines, where they are often used as supporting evidence. However, charts can skew results and mislead readers when their components (titles, labels, and so on) are manipulated—for example, to show just partial or mislabeled data. Whenever you encounter a chart or graph in a document, make certain that visual information is labeled clearly and accurately and that data increments are large enough to be significant.

Consider, for example, the potentially misleading nature of the two salary charts below. At first glance, it appears as if the salaries in the "Salaries Up!" chart (Figure 11.10) rose dramatically and those in the "Salaries Stable!" chart (Figure 11.11) remained almost the same. A closer analysis of the two charts, however, reveals that the salaries in the two charts are nearly identical across the six-year period. The data on the two charts seem to differ so dramatically because of the different ways the two charts display salary increases: in the first chart, salary increases are given in $500 increments; in the second chart, salary increases are given in $5,000 increments. For this reason, a $1,000 increase on the first chart registers quite visibly, whereas on the second chart it hardly shows at all.

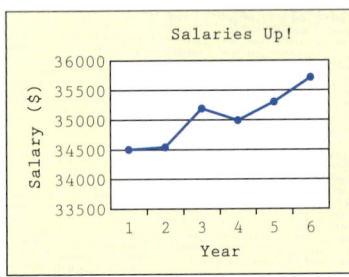
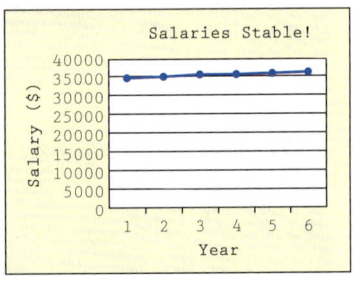

FIGURE 11.10 Salary chart 1 from the *CPIT Maths2Go* online tutorial.

FIGURE 11.11 Salary chart 2 from the *CPIT Maths2Go* online tutorial.

■ **EXERCISE 5**

Find a chart or graph (in a report or advertisement, for instance) that you think is misleading. Identify the elements that seem to distort the data being portrayed.

12

Writing Electronic Arguments

❓ FAQs

What is the most obvious difference between electronic and print arguments? (p. 149)

How do electronic arguments use hyperlinks? (p. 150)

What are the special challenges of writing an electronic argument? (p. 152)

In email, discussion boards, newsgroups, electronic classroom environments, blogs, and chat rooms, electronic arguments occur daily on a wide variety of topics. Because of the nature of Internet-based communication, these arguments are somewhat different from standard print arguments. In order to write an effective argument for an online audience, you should be aware of the demands of writing in an electronic environment.

NOTE: For a glossary of common computer and Internet terms, go to http://academic.cengage.com/eng/kirsznermandell ▶ *The Wadsworth Handbook* ▶ Book Resources ▶ Glossary of Computer and Internet Terms.

12a   Considering Audience and Purpose

The most obvious difference between electronic arguments and print arguments is the nature of the **audience**. Audiences for print arguments are relatively passive: they read an argument from beginning to end, form their own ideas about it, and then stop. Depending on the writing situation, however, audiences for electronic arguments can respond differently. In some cases, readers may be passive; in other cases, they can be quite active, posting responses in chat rooms and directly communicating with the writer (sometimes in real time) as well as with one another.

The **purpose** of electronic arguments is also quite different from that of print arguments. Unlike print arguments, which appear as carefully crafted finished products in newspapers and magazines, electronic arguments are frequently written in immediate response to other people's arguments or ideas. In fact, by including links to a writer's email address or to a chat room, many online arguments encourage readers to respond. For this reason, in addition to trying to convince, the purpose of electronic arguments may also be to engage, respond, refute, react, clarify, or instruct.

12b Shaping Electronic Arguments

Because of the dynamic environment of the Internet, electronic arguments (for example, those found on blogs) are often brief and relatively informal. Much like a conversation, these arguments frequently begin by making a single point, which they then develop over time as the situation warrants (see Figure 12.1). In order to follow an argument, a reader often has to scroll through several pages of online postings. In this sense, electronic arguments are more like works in progress than finished products.

Even when electronic arguments physically resemble print arguments (as they do in online journal articles and in newsgroup postings), the way they present information may be different from the way print arguments do. Print arguments are **linear**; that is, readers move in a straight line from the beginning of an argument to the end. Also, in order to be effective, a print argument must be **self-contained**. It must include all the background information, explanations, supporting evidence, and visuals necessary to make its point.

Electronic arguments, however, may not be linear. They often contain **hyperlinks** (design elements or highlighted text that readers can click to access other Web sites) as well as graphics, sound, and video. Because writers of electronic arguments (such as the one shown in Figure 12.2) rely on

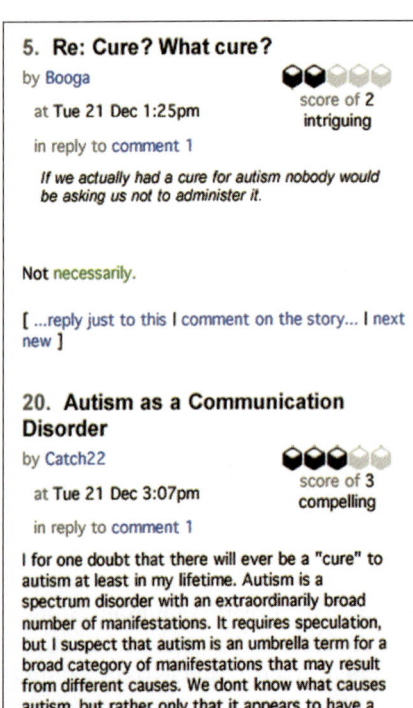

FIGURE 12.1 Plastic.com blog postings.

hyperlinks to supplement their discussions, an electronic argument will often address just the main points of an argument. Links then encourage readers to go to other sites to obtain the facts, statistical data, and other articles that supplement the discussion. When readers access these sites, they can take in as much or as little information as they want or need. For example, readers of the electronic argument about gun control pictured in Figure 12.2 could link to FBI data about the connection between "concealed carry laws" and violent crime. Once they access this material, they can choose to carefully analyze it, to skim it, or to ignore it completely.

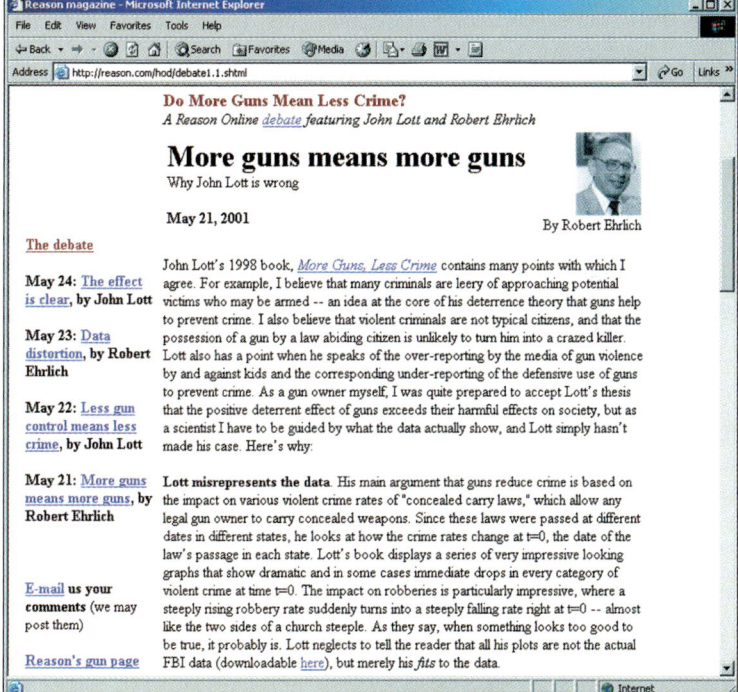

FIGURE 12.2 Excerpt from "Do More Guns Mean Less Crime? A *Reason Online* Debate."

12c Writing and Revising Electronic Arguments

If you write an argument for a Web site or for an online discussion group, you should use the same strategies you use when you write and revise a print argument. In addition, you should keep in mind the specific challenges of writing in an electronic environment. The checklist on page 152 will help you address these issues.

CHECKLIST

WRITING AND REVISING ELECTRONIC ARGUMENTS

When you write electronic arguments, follow these guidelines:
- ☐ Don't overload readers with excess information.
- ☐ Provide links to Web sites, film clips, articles, and so on.
- ☐ If a debate is taking place through email, discussion groups, or chat rooms, consider the positions that have been presented.
- ☐ Consider posting two versions of your argument: a condensed Web-based version for online reading and a longer word-processed version that can be downloaded and read in print form.
- ☐ Before posting an argument to a discussion group, read through the group's list of Frequently Asked Questions (FAQs) to make sure that you do not inadvertently violate any posting guidelines and thereby damage your credibility with the group.
- ☐ Use a balanced, reasonable tone rather than one that is dismissive or potentially insulting.
- ☐ Consider how color, typeface, type size, visuals, and overall design can make your argument clearer.
- ☐ Consider whether to present any information in the form of tables, charts, or graphs.
- ☐ Edit and proofread carefully.

■ EXERCISE 1

Look back at the excerpt from *Reason Online* magazine (Figure 12.2). Identify the elements of the excerpt (such as its hyperlinks) that indicate that it is part of an online argument. What do these elements add to the argument? In what way, if any, do they detract from the argument's effectiveness?

■ EXERCISE 2

Suppose you are an editor of a print magazine that is going to publish the article from *Reason Online* (Figure 12.2). Make a list of the specific changes the writer will have to make to the Web version to make his argument suitable for print.

PART 3

Doing Research

13 Writing a Research Paper 154
- 13a Moving from Assignment to Topic 155
- 13b Doing Exploratory Research and Formulating a Research Question 158
- 13c Assembling a Working Bibliography 159
- 13d Developing a Tentative Thesis 162
- 13e Doing Focused Research 163
- 13f Taking Notes 164
- 13g Fine-Tuning Your Thesis 169
- 13h Constructing an Outline 171
- 13i Writing a Rough Draft 173
- 13j Revising Your Drafts 176
- 13k Preparing a Final Draft 180

14 Using and Evaluating Library Sources 181
- 14a Doing Exploratory Library Research 181
- 14b Doing Focused Library Research 187
- 14c Evaluating the Library's Print and Electronic Sources 193
- 14d Doing Research Outside the Library 196

15 Using and Evaluating Internet Sources 198
- 15a Understanding the Internet 198
- 15b Using the World Wide Web for Research 199
- 15c Using Other Internet Tools 207
- 15d Evaluating Internet Sites 208

16 Summarizing, Paraphrasing, Quoting, and Synthesizing Sources 213
- 16a Writing a Summary 213
- 16b Writing a Paraphrase 215
- 16c Quoting Sources 217
- 16d Integrating Source Material into Your Writing 219
- 16e Synthesizing Sources 223

17 Avoiding Plagiarism 224
- 17a Defining Plagiarism 224
- 17b Avoiding Unintentional Plagiarism 225
- 17c Revising to Eliminate Plagiarism 226

13

Writing a Research Paper

❓ FAQs

How do I plan a research project? (p. 154)
How do I keep track of all my sources? (p. 159)
What system should I use for taking notes? (p. 164)
Why can't I just photocopy or print out the information I need instead of taking notes? (p. 168)
How do I turn my notes into an outline? (p. 171)

Research is the systematic investigation of a topic outside your own knowledge and experience. However, doing research means more than just reading other people's ideas. When you undertake a research project, you become involved in a process that requires you to **think critically**: to evaluate and interpret the ideas explored in your sources and to develop ideas of your own. Your research will be most efficient if you follow a systematic process such as the one outlined below.

See Ch. 8

THE RESEARCH PROCESS		
Activity	**Date Due**	**Date Completed**
Move from an Assignment to a Topic, **13a**	_____	_____
Do Exploratory Research and Formulate a Research Question, **13b**	_____	_____
Assemble a Working Bibliography, **13c**	_____	_____
Develop a Tentative Thesis, **13d**	_____	_____
Do Focused Research, **13e**	_____	_____
Take Notes, **13f**	_____	_____
Fine-Tune Your Thesis, **13g**	_____	_____
Outline Your Paper, **13h**	_____	_____
Draft Your Paper, **13i**	_____	_____
Revise Your Paper, **13j**	_____	_____
Prepare Your Final Draft, **13k**	_____	_____

13a Moving from Assignment to Topic

1 Understanding Your Assignment

Every research paper begins with an assignment. Before you can find a direction for your research, you must be sure you understand the exact requirements of the specific assignment.

> **CHECKLIST**
>
> **UNDERSTANDING YOUR ASSIGNMENT**
> - ☐ When is the completed research paper due?
> - ☐ About how long should it be?
> - ☐ Will you be given a specific research schedule to follow, or can you set your own schedule?
> - ☐ Is your purpose to explain, to persuade, or to do something else?
> - ☐ Is your audience your instructor? Your fellow students? Both? Someone else?
> - ☐ Is collaborative work permitted? Is it encouraged? If so, at what stages of the research process?
> - ☐ Does your instructor expect you to keep your notes on note cards? In a computer file?
> - ☐ Does your instructor expect you to prepare a formal outline?
> - ☐ Are instructor–student conferences required? Are they encouraged?
> - ☐ Will your instructor review notes, outlines, or drafts with you at regular intervals?
> - ☐ Does your instructor require you to keep a research notebook?
> - ☐ What manuscript guidelines and documentation style are you expected to follow?
> - ☐ What help is available to you—from your instructor, from other students, from experts on your topic, from community resources, and from your library staff?

In Chapters 4–6 of this text, you followed the writing process of Kimberly Romney as she planned, drafted, and revised a short essay for her first-semester composition course. In her second-semester composition class, Kimberly was given the following assignment:

> Write a ten- to fifteen-page research paper that takes a position on any issue related to the Internet. Keep a research notebook that traces your progress.

Throughout this chapter, you will see examples of the work Kimberly did as she completed this assignment.

2 Choosing a Topic

Once you understand the requirements and scope of your assignment, you need to decide on a topic. In many cases, your instructor will help you choose a topic, either by providing a list of suitable topics or by suggesting a general subject area—for example, a famous trial, an event that happened on the day you were born, a problem on college campuses. Keep in mind, though, that you will still need to narrow your topic to one you can write about: one trial, one event, one problem.

If your instructor prefers that you select a topic on your own, you should consider several possible topics and weigh both their suitability for research and your interest in them. You decide on a topic for your research paper in much the same way you decide on a topic for a short essay: you read, brainstorm, talk to people, and ask questions. Specifically, you talk to friends and family, coworkers, and perhaps your instructor; read magazines and newspapers; take stock of your interests; consider possible topics suggested by your other courses (historical events, scientific developments, and so on); and, of course, browse the Internet. (Your search engine's **subject guides** can be particularly helpful to you as you look for a promising topic for your research or try to narrow a broad subject area.)

See 15b2

> ### CHECKLIST
>
> **CHOOSING A RESEARCH TOPIC**
>
> As you look for a suitable research topic, keep the following guidelines in mind:
>
> ☐ **Are you genuinely interested in your research topic?** Remember that you will be deeply involved with the topic you select for weeks—perhaps even for an entire semester. If you lose interest in your topic, you are likely to see your research as a tedious chore rather than as an opportunity to discover new information, new associations, and new insights.
>
> ☐ **Is your topic suitable for research?** Topics limited to your personal experience and those based on value judgments are not suitable for research. For example, "The superiority of Freud's work to Jung's" might sound promising, but no amount of research can establish that one person's work is "better" than another's.
>
> ☐ **Are the boundaries of your research topic appropriate?** A research topic should be neither too broad nor too narrow. "Julius

and Ethel Rosenberg: Atomic Spies or FBI Scapegoats?" is far too broad a topic for a ten-page—or even a hundred-page—treatment, and "One piece of evidence that played a decisive role in establishing the Rosenbergs' guilt" would probably be too narrow for a ten-page research paper. But how one newspaper reported the Rosenbergs' espionage trial or how a particular group of people (government employees or college students, for example) reacted at the time to the couple's 1953 execution would work well.

3 Starting a Research Notebook

Keeping a **research notebook,** a combination journal of your reactions and log of your progress, is an important part of the research process. A research notebook maps out your direction and keeps you on track; throughout the research process, it helps you define and redefine the boundaries of your assignment.

In your research notebook (which can be an actual notebook or a computer file), you can record lists of things to do, sources to check, leads to follow up on, appointments, possible community contacts, questions to which you would like to find answers, stray ideas, possible thesis statements or titles, and so on. (Be sure to date your entries and to check off and date work completed.)

As she began her research, Kimberly set up a computer file in which she planned to keep all the electronic documents for her paper. In a *Word* document that she labeled "Research Notebook," she outlined her schedule and explored some preliminary ideas.

Here is an example of an entry from Kimberly's research notebook in which she discusses how she chose a topic for her research paper.

Excerpt from Research Notebook

> Last semester, I wrote a personal essay about my difficulties using computers and the Internet when I arrived at college. In class, we'd read an essay by Henry Louis Gates Jr. that confirmed what I thought: not everyone feels comfortable using computers and the Internet. Gates says that the Internet threatens to create two societies, one that is tapped into the digital economy and one that is not, and he refers to this problem as the "digital divide." For this paper, I'd like to expand the paper I wrote for my first-semester composition course and talk more broadly about the digital divide. I asked Professor Smith if I could, and she gave me permission. (I'll check with Professor Wilson too.)

EXERCISE 1

Using your instructor's guidelines for selecting a research topic, choose a topic for your paper. Then, start a research notebook. Begin by entering information about your assignment and your schedule. Then, explore some preliminary ideas about your topic.

13b Doing Exploratory Research and Formulating a Research Question

During **exploratory research,** you develop an overview of your topic, searching the Internet and looking through general reference works such as encyclopedias, bibliographies, and specialized dictionaries (either in print or online). Your goal at this stage is to formulate a **research question** that you want your research paper to answer. A research question helps you to decide which sources to seek out, which to examine first, which to examine in depth, and which to skip entirely. (The answer to your research question will be your paper's **thesis statement**.)

See 13d

Kimberly began her exploratory research with a preliminary search on *Google* (see Figure 13.1). When she entered the keywords *digital divide,* they generated thousands of hits, but she wasn't overwhelmed. She had learned in her library orientation that the first ten to twenty items would be most useful to her because the results of a *Google*

FIGURE 13.1 *Google* search engine.

search are listed in order of relevance to the topic, with the most relevant sites listed first. After a quick review of these items, she moved on to a search of the subject guides on *InfoTrac College Edition*, a database her library subscribed to (see Figure 13.2).

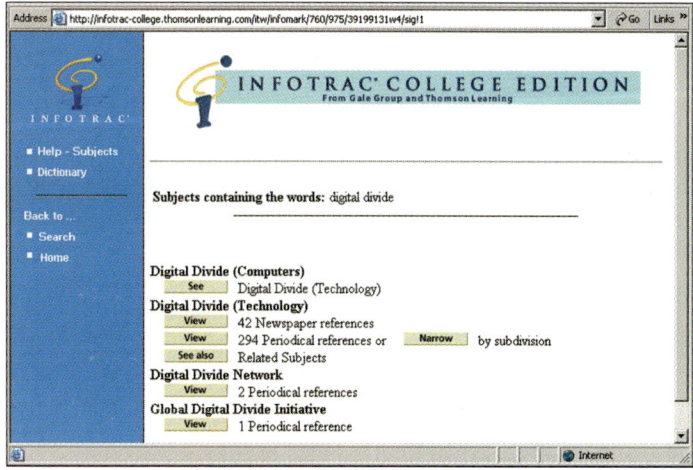

FIGURE 13.2 *InfoTrac College Edition.*

When she finished her exploratory research, Kimberly decided on the following research question:

> Do all Americans have equal access to the Internet?

13c Assembling a Working Bibliography

During your exploratory research, you begin to assemble a **working bibliography** for your paper. This working bibliography will be the basis for your <u>works-cited</u> list, which will include all the sources you cite in your paper.

See 18a2

1 Recording Bibliographic Information

As you consider each potential source, record full and accurate bibliographic information in a separate computer file designated "Bibliography" (or, if you prefer, on individual index cards). Keep records of interviews (including telephone and email interviews), meetings, lectures, films, and electronic sources as well as of books and articles. For each source, include not only basic identifying details—such as the date of an interview, the call number of a library book, the URL of an Internet source and the date you downloaded it, or the author of an article accessed from a database—but also a brief evaluation that includes comments about the kind of information the source contains, the amount of information offered, its relevance to your topic, and its limitations.

> **CLOSE-UP**
>
> **ASSEMBLING A WORKING BIBLIOGRAPHY**
>
> As you record bibliographic information for your sources, include the following information:
>
> - **Book** Author(s); title (italicized in computer file, underlined on index card); call number (for future reference); city of publication; publisher; date of publication; medium; brief evaluation
> - **Article** Author(s); title of article (in quotation marks); title of journal (italicized in computer file, underlined on index card); volume and issue numbers; date; inclusive page numbers; medium; date downloaded (if applicable); URL (if applicable); brief evaluation

As you go about collecting sources and building your working bibliography, be careful to monitor the quality and relevance of all the materials you examine. Making informed choices early in the research process will save you a lot of time in the long run. (For more information on evaluating library sources, **see 14c;** for guidelines on evaluating Internet sources, **see 15d.**)

Following are examples of records Kimberly kept for her working bibliography. In the library, she copied her source information on index cards. When she returned to her dorm room, she transferred the information from her cards into a computer file.

Information for Working Bibliography (on Index Card)

HN49.156 N69 2001	Call number
Norris, Pippa	Author
Digital Divide: Civic Engagement, Information Poverty, and the Internet Worldwide	Title
Cambridge: Cambridge UP, 2001. Print.	Publication information and medium
A book about the digital divide that explains its history and its relationship to economics and class. Published in 2001; may be outdated.	Evaluation

Information for Working Bibliography (in Computer File)

Author —	Pekow, Charles
Title —	"Community Technology Program in Crosshairs of Congress"
Publication information and medium —	*Community College Week.* 15 Aug. 2005: n. pag. *Academic Search Premier.* Web. Accessed January 30, 2006.
Evaluation —	Describes the different positions that the members of Congress have on whether the federal government should provide funding for the Community Technology Centers program.

> **COMPUTER TIP** academic.cengage.com/eng/kirsznermandell
>
> **ASSEMBLING A WORKING BIBLIOGRAPHY**
>
> Various computer software programs can make it easy for you to compile your working bibliography electronically. For example, *WriteNote*, a Web-based research and writing application, enables you to create a personal record of the sources you consult. Later, when you begin writing, you can insert a bibliographic citation from *WriteNote* directly into your *Word* document. *WriteNote* automatically formats the in-text citation and bibliography entry according to one of the many possible documentation styles from which you can choose.

2 Preparing an Annotated Bibliography

Some instructors require an **annotated bibliography,** a list of all your sources accompanied by a brief summary and evaluation of each source. The following is an excerpt from Kimberly's annotated bibliography.

Annotated Bibliography (Excerpt)

Young, Jeffrey R. "Does 'Digital Divide' Rhetoric Do More Harm than Good?" *The Chronicle of Higher Education.* Chronicle of Higher Educ., 9 Nov. 2001. Web. 10 Jan. 2006. This article explains that some scholars feel the focus on the "digital divide" among minorities actually promotes the idea that they are technologically backward. While programs aimed at closing the "digital divide" were supposed to equalize the technological playing field, the rhetoric used may actually encourage racist stereotypes.

Even though it's several years old, this article made me reconsider my views about programs working to bridge the digital divide. Also, it supports Henry Louis Gates's argument that many minorities are not using the Internet because the content does not appeal to their interests or needs.

■ EXERCISE 2

Do some exploratory research to find a research question for your paper, carefully evaluating the relevance and usefulness of each source. Then, compile a working bibliography. When you have finished, reevaluate the usefulness of your sources and plan additional research if necessary. If your instructor requires you to do so, prepare an annotated bibliography.

13d Developing a Tentative Thesis

Your **tentative thesis** is a preliminary statement of the main idea you think your research will support. This statement, which you will eventually refine into your paper's *thesis statement*, should answer your research question. Kimberly's progress from assignment to tentative thesis appears below.

Assignment	Topic	Research Question	Tentative Thesis
Issue related to the Internet	Access to the Internet	Do all Americans have equal access to the Internet?	Not all Americans have equal access to the Internet, and this is a potentially serious problem.

Because it suggests the specific direction your research will take as well as the scope and emphasis of your argument, your tentative thesis can help you generate a list of the main points you plan to develop in your paper. This list can help you narrow the focus of your research so you can zero in on a few specific categories to explore as you read and take notes. Kimberly used her tentative thesis to help her generate the following list of points to explore further.

> Tentative Thesis: Not all Americans have equal access to the Internet, and this is a potentially serious problem.
> - Give background about the Internet; tell why it's important.
> - Identify groups that don't have access to the Internet.
> - Explain problems this creates.
> - Suggest possible solutions.

■ EXERCISE 3

Following your instructor's guidelines, develop a tentative thesis for your research paper, and compile a list of the points you plan to develop.

13e Doing Focused Research

During **exploratory research,** you consult general reference works to get an overview of your topic. During **focused research,** however, you consult books, periodical articles, and other sources (in print and online) to find the specific information—facts, examples, statistics, definitions, quotations—you need to support your points. Once you have decided on a tentative thesis and made a list of the points you plan to explore, you are ready to begin your focused research.

1 Reading Sources

As you look for information, try to explore as many sources as possible. It makes sense to examine more sources than you actually intend to use so you can proceed even if one or more of your sources turns out to be biased, outdated, unreliable, superficial, or irrelevant—in other words, not suitable.

As you explore various sources, quickly evaluate each source's potential usefulness. For example, if your source is a book, skim the table of contents and the index; if your source is a journal article, read the abstract. Then, if an article or a section of a book seems useful, photocopy it for future reference. Similarly, when you find an online source that looks promising, print it out (or send it to yourself as an email attachment) so you can evaluate it further later on. (For information on evaluating print and electronic sources, **see 14c** and **15d**.)

NOTE: Do not paste online source material directly into your paper. This practice can lead to **plagiarism**. See Ch. 17

2 Balancing Primary and Secondary Sources

During your focused research, you will encounter both **primary sources** (original documents and observations) and **secondary sources** (interpretations of original documents and observations). See 14b4

> **Primary Source:** United States Constitution, Amendment XIV (Ratified July 9, 1868). Section I.
>
> All persons born or naturalized in the United States, and subject to the jurisdiction thereof, are citizens of the United States and the state wherein they reside. No state shall make or enforce any law which shall abridge the privileges or immunities of citizens of the United States; nor shall any state deprive any person of life, liberty, or property, without the process of law; nor deny to any person within its jurisdiction the equal protection of the laws.

Secondary Source: Paula S. Rothenberg, *Racism and Sexism: An Integrated Study.*

Congress passed the Fourteenth Amendment . . . in July 1868. This amendment, which continues to play a major role in contemporary legal battles over discrimination, includes a number of important provisions. It explicitly extends citizenship to all those born or naturalized in the United States and guarantees all citizens due process and "equal protection" of the law.

For some research projects, primary sources are essential; however, most research projects in the humanities rely heavily on secondary sources, which provide scholars' insights and interpretations.

PRIMARY AND SECONDARY SOURCES

Primary Source	Secondary Source
Novel, poem, play, film	Criticism
Diary, autobiography	Biography
Letter, historical document, speech, oral history	Historical analysis
Newspaper article	Editorial
Raw data from questionnaires or interviews	Social science article; case study
Observation/experiment	Scientific article

13f Taking Notes

As you locate information in the library and on the Internet, take notes (either by hand or on a computer) to create a record of exactly what you found and where you found it.

1 Recording Source Information

See Ch. 6

Each piece of information you record in your notes (whether **summarized**, **paraphrased**, or **quoted** from your sources) should be accompanied by a short descriptive heading that indicates its relevance to one of the points you will develop in your paper. Because you will use these headings to guide you as you organize your notes, you should make them as specific as possible. For example, labeling every note for a paper on the digital divide **digital divide** or **Internet** will not prove very helpful later on. More focused headings—for instance, **dangers of digital divide** or **government's steps to narrow the gap**—will be much more useful.

Also include brief comments that make clear your reasons for recording the information. These comments (enclosed in brackets so you will know they are your own ideas, not those of your source) should establish the purpose of your note—what you think it can explain, support, clarify, describe, or contradict—and perhaps suggest its relationship to other notes or other sources. Any questions you have about the information or its source can also be included in your comment.

Finally, each note should fully and accurately identify the source of the information you are recording. You do not have to write out the complete citation, but you do have to include enough information to identify your source. For example, **Gates 499** would be enough to send you back to your working bibliography card or file, where you would be able to find the complete documentation for Henry Louis Gates's essay "One Internet, Two Nations." (If you use more than one source by the same author, you need a more complete reference.)

When you take notes, your goal is flexibility: you want to be able to arrange and rearrange information easily and efficiently as your paper takes shape. If you take notes on your computer, type each individual note (accompanied by source information) under a specific heading rather than listing all information from a single source under the same heading, and be sure to divide notes from one another with extra space or horizontal lines, as illustrated on page 166. (As you revise, you can move notes around so those on the same topic are grouped together.)

If you take notes by hand, use the time-tested index-card system, taking care to write on only one side of the card and to use a separate index card for each individual note rather than running several notes together on a single card. (Later, you can enter the information from these notes into your computer file.)

Following are examples of notes that Kimberly took. When she read sources in her dorm room, she took notes on her computer. For sources that she read in the library, she used index cards to record notes. Later, she entered this information into her computer file.

Notes (on Index Card)

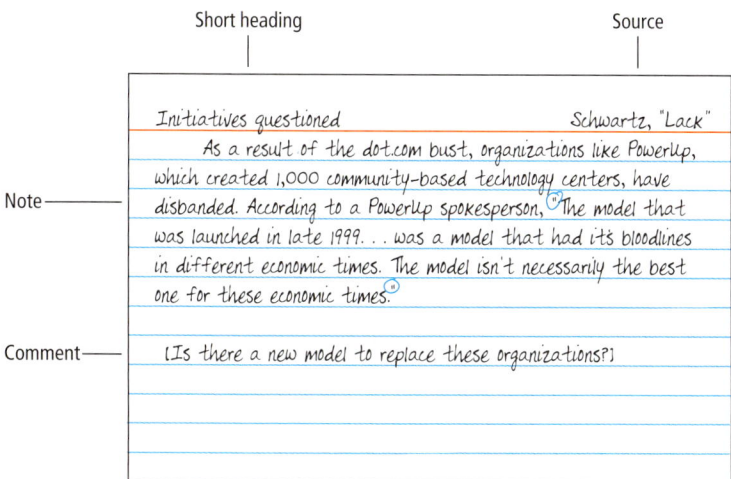

Notes (in Computer File)

Short heading → *Problems of digital divide* — Dalton, *Knight Ridder/Tribune*, 7/4/04 ← **Source**

Note (quotation) → "A recent report by the Pew Internet & American Life Project revealed that minorities are slightly more likely than whites to use the Internet at places other than home or work, with 23 percent of blacks and Hispanics using the Internet outside home or work, compared with 19 percent of whites."

Comment → [*Does this mean minorities are less likely to own computers?*]

Efforts to close gap — Dalton, *Knight Ridder/Tribune*, 7/4/04

Note (paraphrase) → 14 million Americans use the Internet at libraries, and the availability of public-access computers increased library visits by 17 percent between 1996 and 2001.

Comment → [*Are minorities more likely to use library computers to access the Internet?*]

Recommendations for the future — Dalton, *Knight Ridder/Tribune*, 7/4/04

Note (summary) → In New York, many of the computer basics classes at libraries fill up quickly. Out of 40 classes, a quarter of them were filled to capacity. Consequently, libraries need more funding to increase the availability of classes.

Comment → [*Who should provide this funding?*]

COMPUTER TIP

TAKING NOTES

Note-taking software, such as *WriteNote* (shown below), can make it easy for you to record and organize information, allowing you to create files in which you can store notes (quotations, summaries, paraphrases, your own comments), pictures, or tables; to sort and categorize your material; and even to print out the information in order on computerized note cards.

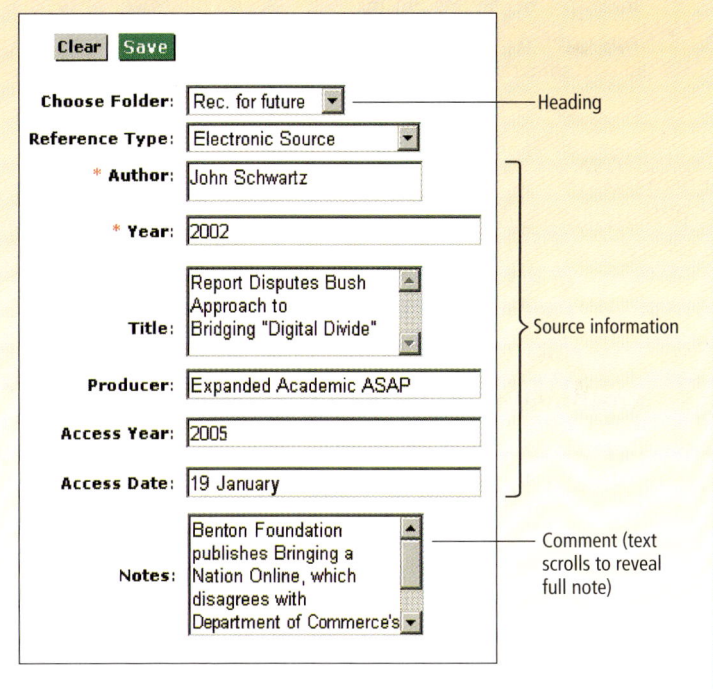

CHECKLIST

TAKING NOTES

☐ **Identify the source of each piece of information.**

☐ **Include everything now that you will need later** to understand your note—names, dates, places, connections with other notes—and to remember why you recorded it.

☐ **Distinguish quotations from paraphrases and summaries and your own ideas from those of your sources.** If you copy a source's words, place them in quotation marks. (If you take notes

(continued)

> **TAKING NOTES** *(continued)*
>
> by hand, circle the quotation marks; if you type your notes, put the quotation marks in boldface.) If you write down your own ideas, enclose them in brackets—and, if you are typing, italicize them as well. These techniques will help you avoid accidental plagiarism in your paper.
>
> ☐ **Put an author's ideas into your own words whenever possible,** summarizing and paraphrasing material as well as adding your own observations and analyses.
>
> ☐ **Copy quoted material accurately,** using the writer's exact words, spelling, punctuation marks, and capitalization.

See Ch. 17

> **ESL TIP**
>
> Taking notes in English (rather than in your native language) will make it easier for you to transfer the notes into a draft of your paper. However, you may find it faster and more effective to use your native language when writing your own comments about each note.

2 Managing Photocopies and Printouts

Much of the information you gather will be in the form of photocopies (of articles, book pages, and so on) and material printed out from the Internet. Learning to manage this source information efficiently will save you a lot of time.

First, be careful not to allow the ease of copying to encourage you to postpone decisions about the usefulness of your sources. After all, you can easily accumulate so many pages that it will be almost impossible for you to keep track of all your information.

Also, keep in mind that making copies of sources is only the first step in the process of taking thorough, careful notes. You still have to evaluate, paraphrase, and summarize your source's ideas and make connections among them.

In addition, photocopies and printouts do not have much flexibility. For example, a single page of text may include information that should be earmarked for several different sections of your paper. This lack of flexibility makes it almost impossible for you to arrange information into any meaningful order.

Remember, you should approach photocopies and material you print out from the Internet just as you approach any other source: as material that you will read, highlight, annotate, and then take notes about.

CLOSE-UP

AVOIDING PLAGIARISM

To avoid the possibility of accidental plagiarism, be sure to keep all downloaded material in a separate file—not in your Notes file. After you read this material and decide how to use it, you can move the notes you take into your Notes file (along with full source information).

See Ch. 17

CHECKLIST

WORKING WITH PHOTOCOPIES AND PRINTOUTS

To get the most out of photocopies and material printed out from the Internet, follow these guidelines:

- ☐ Record full and accurate source information—including the inclusive page numbers, electronic address (URL), and any other relevant information—on the first page of each copy.
- ☐ Clip or staple together consecutive pages of a single source.
- ☐ Do not photocopy or print out a source without reminding yourself—*in writing*—why you are doing so. In pencil or on removable self-stick notes, record your initial responses to the source's ideas, jot down cross-references to other works or notes, and highlight important sections.
- ☐ Photocopying can be time-consuming and expensive, so try to avoid copying material that is only marginally relevant to your paper.
- ☐ Keep photocopies and printouts in a separate file so you will be able to find them when you need them.

■ EXERCISE 4

Begin focused research for your paper, reading sources carefully and taking notes as you read. Your notes should include paraphrase, summary, and your own observations and analysis as well as quotations.

13g Fine-Tuning Your Thesis

After you have finished your focused research and note-taking, you should be ready to refine your tentative thesis into a carefully worded statement that expresses a conclusion your research can support. This thesis statement should be more precise than your tentative thesis, accurately conveying the direction, emphasis, and scope of your paper.

See 5a–b

Compare Kimberly's tentative thesis with her final thesis statement.

Tentative Thesis
Not all Americans have equal access to the Internet, and this is a potentially serious problem.

Thesis Statement
Although the Internet has changed our lives for the better, it has also left some people behind, creating two distinct classes—those who have access and those who do not.

If your thesis statement does not express a conclusion your research can support, you will need to revise it further. Reviewing your notes carefully, perhaps grouping information in different ways, may help you decide on a more suitable thesis. Or, you may try other techniques—for instance, using your research question as a starting point for additional freewriting or brainstorming.

See 4e3–4

■ EXERCISE 5

Read the following passages. Assume you are writing a research paper on the influences that shaped young writers in the 1920s. What possible thesis statements could be supported by the information in these passages?

1. Yet in spite of their opportunities and their achievements the generation deserved for a long time the adjective [lost] that Gertrude Stein had applied to it. The reasons aren't hard to find. It was lost, first of all, because it was uprooted, schooled away and almost wrenched away from its attachment to any region or tradition. It was lost because its training had prepared it for another world than existed after the war (and because the war prepared it only for travel and excitement). It was lost because it tried to live in exile. It was lost because it accepted no older guides to conduct and because it formed a false picture of society and the writer's place in it. The generation belonged to a period of transition from values already fixed to values that had to be created. (Malcolm Cowley, *Exile's Return*)

2. The 1920s were a time least likely to produce substantial support among intellectuals for any sound, rational, and logical program. Prewar stability and convention were condemned because all evidences of stability seemed illusory and artificial. The very lively and active interest in science was perhaps the decade's most substantial contribution to modern civilization. Yet in this case as well, achievement became a symbol of disorder and a source of disenchantment. (Frederick J. Hoffman, *The 20's*)

3. Societies do not give up old ideals and attitudes easily; the conflicts between the representatives of the older elements of traditional American culture and the prophets of the new day were at times as bitter as they were extensive. Such matters as religion, marriage, and moral standards as well as the issues over race, prohibition, and immigration were at the heart of the conflict. (Introduction to *The Twenties*, ed. George E. Mowry)

■ EXERCISE 6

Review the tentative thesis you developed for Exercise 3. Carefully read all the notes you have collected during your focused research, and develop a thesis statement for your paper.

13h Constructing an Outline

Once you have a thesis statement, you are ready to make an outline to guide you as you write your rough draft.

A formal outline is different from a list of the main points you tentatively plan to develop in your paper. A <u>formal outline</u>—which may be either a **topic outline** or a **sentence outline**—includes all the points you will develop. It indicates both the exact order in which you will present your ideas and the relationship between main points and supporting details.

See 5d

NOTE: The outline you construct at this stage is only a guide for you to follow as you draft your paper. Later on in the writing process, you may want to construct another outline as a revision strategy to help you check the logic of your paper's organization.

CHECKLIST

CONSTRUCTING A FORMAL OUTLINE

When you construct a formal outline for your research paper, follow these guidelines:

- ☐ Write your thesis statement at the top of the page.
- ☐ Review your notes to make sure each note expresses only one general idea. If this is not the case, recopy any unrelated information to create a separate note.
- ☐ Check that the heading for each note specifically characterizes that note's information. If it does not, change the heading.
- ☐ Sort your notes according to their headings, keeping a miscellaneous file for notes that do not seem to fit into any category.

(continued)

> **CONSTRUCTING A FORMAL OUTLINE** *(continued)*
> Irrelevant notes, those unrelated to your paper's thesis, should be set aside (but not discarded).
> ☐ Check your categories for balance. If most of your notes fall into just one or two categories, revise some of your headings to create narrower, more focused categories. If you have only one or two notes in a category, you may need to do additional research or treat that topic only briefly (or not at all).
> ☐ Organize the individual notes within each group, adding more specific subheads to your headings as needed. Arrange your notes in an order that highlights the most important points and subordinates lesser ones.
> ☐ Decide on a logical order in which to discuss your paper's major points.
> ☐ Construct your formal outline, using divisions and subdivisions that correspond to your headings.
> ☐ Review your completed outline to make sure you have not placed too much emphasis on a relatively unimportant idea, ordered ideas illogically, or created sections that overlap with others.

Kimberly made the following topic outline to guide her as she wrote her first draft.

Topic Outline

<u>Thesis statement</u>: Although the Internet has changed our lives for the better, it has also left some people behind, creating two distinct classes—those who have access and those who do not.

I. Development of the Internet
    A. Empowering tool
    B. Source of knowledge and prosperity
II. Problems of digital divide
    A. Lack of access by many groups
    B. Educational and economic disadvantages
    C. Widening gap between haves and have-nots
III. Efforts by government and others to close gap
    A. Community Technology Centers Program
    B. Commerce Department's Technology Opportunities Program
    C. Bill and Melinda Gates Foundation
    D. *The Digital Divide Network*

IV. Need for initiatives questioned
      A. Increase in minority computer use
      B. Bush administration view
      C. Challenges by minority groups
   V. Need for initiatives defended
      A. Benton Foundation report
      B. Popularity of public library programs
      C. Continued gap in schools
      D. Continued problems for minorities and the poor
   VI. Recommendations for the future
      A. Improve access to technology, especially the Internet
      B. Redefine "digital divide" to make it more inclusive
      C. Continue federal funding

■ **EXERCISE 7**

Carefully review your notes. Then, sort and group them into categories, and construct a topic outline for your paper.

COMPUTER TIP   academic.cengage.com/eng/kirsznermandell

OUTLINING

Before you begin writing, create a separate file for each major section of your outline. Then, copy your notes into these files in the order in which you intend to use them. You can print out each file as you need it and use it as a guide as you write.

13i Writing a Rough Draft

When you are ready to write your <u>rough draft</u>, check to be sure you have arranged your notes in the order in which you intend to use them. Follow your outline as you write, using your notes as needed. As you draft, you can write notes to yourself in brackets. In these notes, you should jot down questions and identify points that need further clarification and areas that need more development.

As you move along, leave space for material you plan to add, and identify phrases or whole sections that you think you may later decide to move or delete. In other words, lay the groundwork for revision.

As your draft takes shape, be sure to supply transitions between sentences and paragraphs to indicate how your points are related. To make it easy for you to revise later on, you might want to

See 6a

triple-space your draft. Be careful to copy source information fully and accurately on this and every subsequent draft, placing documentation as close as possible to the material it identifies.

> **COMPUTER TIP** academic.cengage.com/eng/kirsznermandell
>
> **DRAFTING**
>
> You can use a split screen or multiple windows to view your notes as you draft your paper. You can also copy the material that you need from your notes and then insert it into the text of your paper. (As you copy, be especially careful that you do not unintentionally commit **plagiarism**.)

See 17b

1 Shaping the Parts of the Paper

Like any other essay, a research paper has an introduction, a body, and a conclusion. In your rough draft, as in your outline, you focus on the body of your paper. Don't spend time planning your introduction or conclusion at this stage; your ideas will change as you write, and you will need to revise and expand your opening and closing paragraphs later to reflect those changes.

See 7e2

Introduction. In your **introduction,** you identify your topic and establish how you will approach it, perhaps presenting an overview of the problem you will discuss or summarizing research already done on your topic. Your **introduction** also includes your thesis statement, which presents the position you will support in the rest of the paper.

See 7a1

Body. As you draft the **body** of your paper, you lead readers through your discussion with strong **topic sentences** that correspond to the divisions of your outline.

> In the late 1990s, many argued that the Internet had ushered in a new age, one in which instant communication would bring people closer together and eventually eliminate national boundaries.

See 30b

You can also use **headings** if they are a convention of the discipline in which you are writing.

> Responses to Digital Divide
>
> In response, the government, corporations, nonprofit organizations, and public libraries made efforts to bridge the gap between the "haves" and the "have-nots."

Even in your rough draft, carefully worded topic sentences and headings will help you keep your discussion under control.

Use different patterns of development to shape the individual sections of your paper, and be sure to connect ideas with clear transitions. If necessary, connect two sections of your paper with a transitional paragraph that shows their relationship.

Conclusion. In the conclusion of your research paper, you may want to restate your thesis. This is especially important in a long paper because by the time your readers get to the end, they may have lost sight of your paper's main idea. Your conclusion can also include a summary of your key points, a call for action, or perhaps an apt quotation. (Remember, however, that in your rough draft, your concluding paragraph is usually very brief.)

See 7d

See 7e1

See 7e3

2 Working Source Material into Your Paper

In the body of your paper, you evaluate and interpret your sources, comparing different ideas and assessing various points of view. As a writer, your job is to draw your own conclusions, blending information from various sources into a paper that coherently and forcefully presents your own original viewpoint to your readers.

Be sure to integrate source material smoothly into your paper, clearly and accurately identifying the relationships among various sources (and between those sources' ideas and your own). If two sources present conflicting interpretations, you should be especially careful to use precise language and accurate transitions to make the contrast apparent (for instance, **Although the Bush administration remains optimistic, some studies suggest . . .**). When two sources agree, you should make this clear (for example, **Like Young, McPherson believes . . .** or **Department of Commerce statistics confirm Gates's point**). Such phrasing will provide a context for your own comments and conclusions. If different sources present complementary information about a subject, blend details from the sources carefully, keeping track of which details come from which source.

See 16d

3 Integrating Visuals

Photographs, diagrams, graphs, and other visuals can be very useful additions to your research paper because they can provide additional support for the points you make. You may be able to create a visual on your own (for example, by taking a photograph or creating a bar graph). You may also be able to scan an appropriate visual from a book or magazine or access an image database.

When Kimberly Rommey searched *Google*'s image database, she was able to find a visual to include in her paper (see Figure 13.3 on page 176).

See Ch. 3, 30d

rev ▪ Writing a Research Paper

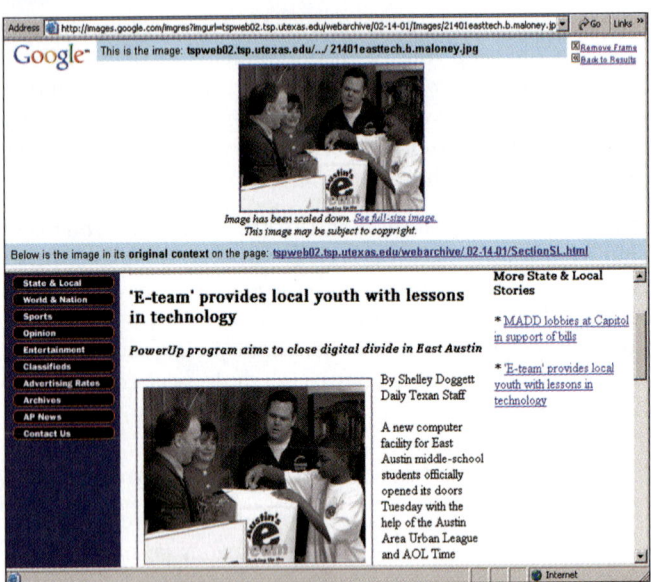

FIGURE 13.3 "Power Up" visual on *Google* image database.

■ EXERCISE 8

Write a rough draft of your paper, being careful to incorporate source material and visuals smoothly and to record source information accurately. Begin by drafting the section for which you have the most material.

13j Revising Your Drafts

See 6b–c

As you review your drafts, you follow the revision procedures that apply to any paper. In addition, you should review the questions in the checklist on page 179, which apply specifically to research papers.

See 5d

A good way to begin revising is to make an outline of your draft to check the logic of its organization and the relationships among sections. When Kimberly began to revise, the first thing she did was construct a **sentence outline** to check the structure of her paper. An excerpt from her sentence outline follows.

Sentence Outline (Excerpt)

Thesis statement: Although the Internet has changed our lives for the better, it has also left some people behind, creating two distinct classes—those who have access and those who do not.

    I. In the late 1990s, many argued that the Internet had ushered in a new age.

        A. Former Vice President Al Gore saw the Internet as an empowering tool.

B. Gore believed the Internet would bring knowledge and prosperity to the entire world.
II. Others questioned the benefits of the Internet.
  A. They argued that the Internet was out of reach for many Americans.
   1. Low-income and minority households were less likely than others to have computers.
   2. For minorities, Internet content was as much a problem as economics.

Your instructor's revision suggestions, which can come orally (in a conference) or in handwritten comments on your paper, can also help you revise. Alternatively, your instructor may use *Microsoft Word*'s Comment tool to make comments electronically on a draft that you email to him or her. When you revise, you can incorporate these suggestions into your paper, as Kimberly did.

Rough Draft with Instructor's Comments (Excerpt)

The Bill and Melinda Gates Foundation has provided libraries across the country with funding that allows them to purchase computers and connect to the Internet (Egan). Nonprofit organizations also sponsor Web sites, such as *The Digital Divide Network*, a site that posts stories about the digital divide from a variety of perspectives. By posting information on the Web site that they created, the site's sponsor hopes to raise awareness of the problems that the digital divide causes.

Comment [PS1]: You need a transition sentence before this one to show that this paragraph is about a new idea. See 7b2.

Comment [PS2]: Wordy. See 37a.

Revision Incorporating Instructor's Suggestions

Nonprofit organizations also worked to bridge the digital divide. The Bill and Melinda Gates Foundation, for example, has provided libraries across the country with funding that allows them to purchase computers and connect to the Internet (Egan). Nonprofit organizations also sponsor Web sites, such as *The Digital Divide Network*, a site that posts stories about the digital divide from a variety of perspectives. By posting information, the site's sponsor hopes to raise awareness of the problems that the digital divide causes.

Feedback you get from **peer review**—other students' comments, handwritten or electronic—can also help you revise. As you incorporate your classmates' suggestions, as well as your own changes and any suggested by your instructor, you can use *Microsoft Word*'s Track Changes tool to help you keep track of the revisions you make on your draft.

Following are two versions of an excerpt from Kimberly's paper. The first version includes comments (inserted with *Microsoft Word*'s Comment tool) from two peer reviewers. The second uses the Track Changes tool to show the revisions Kimberly made in response to these comments.

Rough Draft with Peer Reviewers' Comments (Excerpt)

A recent article observes that many African-American and other minority groups argue that digital divide rhetoric might actually stereotype minorities. The article says that digital divide rhetoric "could discourage businesses or academics from creating content or services tailored for minority communities—ultimately making the digital divide a self-fulfilling prophecy." Many scholars and leaders in the African-American community fear that a focus on the digital divide will lead to its being seen as a fact to be accepted rather than as a problem to be solved. Tara L. McPherson says that "the idea of challenging the digital divide is not about denying it's existence. But it is to ensure that the focus on the digital divide doesn't naturalize a kind of exclusion of investment."

Comment [TG1]: You need a transition sentence here!

Comment [DL1]: Ditto, this is really awk.☺

Comment [RS1]: Tell us the name and where this came from.

Comment [DL2]: Do you need a p. #?

Comment [TG2]: Use a stronger word—*asserts, claims,* etc. We're not supposed to keep using "says."☺

Comment [DL3]: I think you're supposed to have the author's last name here.

Revision with Track Changes

In other cases, the groups targeted by digital divide programs argue that they might do more harm than good. A recent article in the *Chronicle of Higher Education* observes that many African-American and other minority groups argue that digital divide rhetoric might actually stereotype minorities. The article says that digital divide rhetoric "could discourage businesses or academics from creating content or services tailored for minority communities—ultimately making the digital divide a self-fulfilling prophecy." (Young). Many scholars and leaders in the

African-American community fear that a focus on the digital divide will lead to its being seen as a fact to be accepted rather than as a problem to be solved. Tara L. McPherson agrees, arguing that "the idea of challenging the digital divide is not about denying its existence. But it is to ensure that the focus on the digital divide doesn't naturalize a kind of exclusion of investment." (qtd. in Young).

CHECKLIST

REVISING A RESEARCH PAPER

As you revise your research paper, ask yourself these questions:
- ☐ Should you do more research to find support for certain points?
- ☐ Do you need to reorder the major sections of your paper?
- ☐ Should you rearrange the order in which you present your points within sections?
- ☐ Do you need to add section headings? transitional paragraphs?
- ☐ Have you integrated source material smoothly into your paper? *See 16d*
- ☐ Have you chosen visuals carefully and integrated them smoothly into your paper?
- ☐ Are quotations blended with paraphrase, summary, and your own observations and reactions?
- ☐ Have you avoided plagiarism by carefully documenting all borrowed ideas? *See Ch. 17*
- ☐ Have you analyzed and interpreted the ideas of others rather than simply stringing those ideas together?
- ☐ Do your own ideas—not those of your sources—define the focus of your discussion?

NOTE: You will probably take your paper through several drafts, changing different parts of it each time or working on one part over and over again. After revising each draft thoroughly, print out a corrected version and make additional corrections by hand on that draft before typing the next version.

COMPUTER TIP   academic.cengage.com/eng/kirsznermandell

REVISING

When you finish revising your paper, copy the file that contains your working bibliography and insert it at the end of your paper. Delete any irrelevant entries, and then create your works-cited list. (Make sure the format of the entries in your works-cited list conforms to the documentation style you are using.)

13k Writing a Research Paper

■ **EXERCISE 9**

Following the guidelines in 13j and 4c, revise your research paper until you are ready to prepare your final draft.

13k Preparing a Final Draft

See 6d

Before you print out the final version of your paper, **edit and proofread** hard copy of both your paper and your works-cited list. Next, consider (or reconsider) your paper's **title**. It should be descriptive enough to tell your readers what your paper is about, and it should create interest in your subject. Your title should also be consistent with the **purpose** and tone of your paper. (You would hardly want a humorous title for a paper about the death penalty or world hunger.) Finally, your title should be engaging and to the point—and perhaps even provocative. Often, a quotation from one of your sources will suggest a likely title.

See 1a

When you are satisfied with your title, read your paper one last time, proofreading for grammar, spelling, or typing errors you may have missed. Pay particular attention to parenthetical documentation and works-cited entries. (Remember that every error undermines your credibility.) Once you are satisfied that your paper is as accurate as you can make it, print out your final draft. Then, fasten the pages with a paper clip (do not staple the pages or fold the corners together), and hand it in. Some instructors will allow you to email your final draft. (For the final draft of Kimberly's research paper, along with her works-cited list, **see 18c.**)

■ **EXERCISE 10**

Prepare a works-cited list for your research paper. Then, edit your paper and your works-cited list; decide on a title; and check to make sure your paper follows the format your instructor requires. Proofread your final draft carefully before you hand it in.

14

Using and Evaluating Library Sources

❓ FAQs

What electronic resources can I use to help me find information about my topic? (p. 185)
How do I get a book my school library does not own? (p. 190)
How do I find articles in the library? (p. 190)
How do I evaluate the print and electronic sources I find in the library? (p. 193)
How do I conduct an interview? (p. 197)

A modern, networked college library offers you resources that you cannot find anywhere else—even on the Internet. In the long run, you will save a great deal of time and effort, as well as gain a deeper understanding of your topic, if you begin your research with a survey of the library's print and electronic resources.

See Ch. 15

CHECKLIST

BEFORE YOU START LIBRARY RESEARCH

- ☐ Know the library's physical layout.
- ☐ Take a tour of the library if one is offered.
- ☐ Familiarize yourself with the library's holdings.
- ☐ Find out if the library has a guide to its resources.
- ☐ Meet with a librarian if you have questions.
- ☐ Be sure you know the library's hours.
- ☐ Find out if you can access some of the library's resources through your own computer at home or in your dorm room.

14a Doing Exploratory Library Research

During **exploratory research,** your goal is to formulate a **research question**—the question you want your paper to answer. At this stage, you search the library's print and electronic resources to get

14a Using and Evaluating Library Sources

See 13e

a general sense of what they contain. (Later, during your **focused research**, you will look for specific material to use in your paper.) You can begin this process by searching your college or university library's **online catalog** to see what kind of information is available about your topic. You can then look at general reference works and consult the library's electronic databases.

1 Using Online Catalogs

Most college and university libraries—and a growing number of regional and community libraries—have abandoned print catalog systems in favor of **online catalogs**—computer databases that list all the books, articles, and other materials held by the library. Figure 14.1 shows the home page of a university library's online catalog.

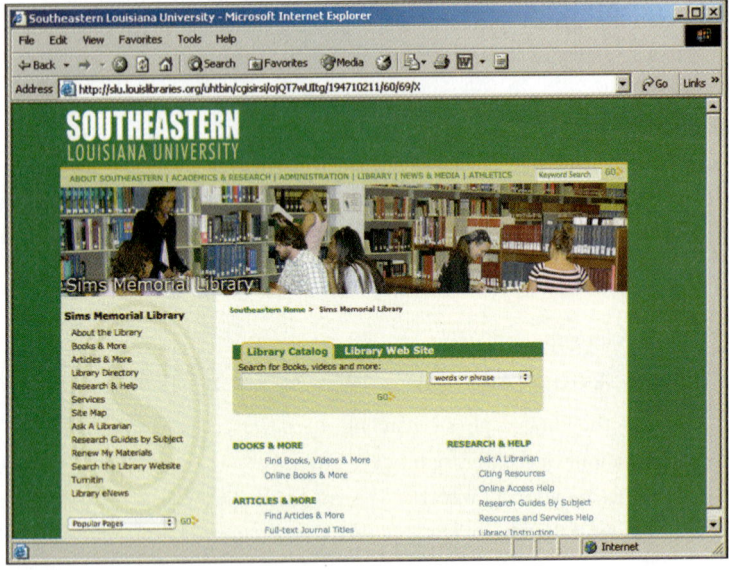

FIGURE 14.1 Home page of a university library's online catalog.

You access an online catalog (as well as other electronic library resources) by using one of the computer terminals located throughout the library and typing in specific words or phrases that enable you to find the information you need. If you have never used an online catalog, ask your reference librarian for help before you begin.

When you search the online catalog for information about your topic, you may conduct either a *keyword search* or a *subject search*. Later on in the research process, when you know more precisely what you are looking for, you can search for a particular book by entering its title, author, or call number.

Conducting a Keyword Search. When you carry out a **keyword search,** you enter into the Search box of the online catalog a word or words associated with your topic. The screen then displays a list of articles that contain those words in their bibliographic citations or abstracts. The more precise your keywords are, the more specific and useful the information you retrieve will be. (Combining keywords with AND, OR, and NOT allows you to narrow or broaden your search. This technique is called conducting a **Boolean search**.)

See 15b3

CHECKLIST

KEYWORD DOS AND DON'TS

When conducting a keyword search, remember the following hints:

☐ Use precise, specific keywords to distinguish your topic from similar topics.

☐ Enter both singular and plural keywords when appropriate—*printing press* and *printing presses,* for example.

☐ Enter both abbreviations and their full-word equivalents (for example, *US* and *United States*).

☐ Try variant spellings (for example, *color* and *colour*).

☐ Don't use too long a string of keywords. (If you do, you will retrieve large amounts of irrelevant material.)

Conducting a Subject Search. When you carry out a **subject search,** you enter specific subject headings into the online catalog. Although it may be possible to guess at a subject heading, your search will be more successful if you consult the *Library of Congress Subject Headings,* held at the reference desk of your library, to help you identify the exact words you need. Figure 14.2 on page 184 shows the results of a search in a university library's online catalog.

CLOSE-UP

KEYWORD SEARCHING VERSUS SUBJECT SEARCHING

Keyword Searching	Subject Searching
■ Searches many subject areas	■ Searches only a specific subject area
■ Any significant word or phrase can be used	■ Only the specific words listed in the *Library of Congress Subject Headings* can be used
■ Retrieves large number of items	■ Retrieves small number of items
■ May retrieve many irrelevant items	■ Retrieves few irrelevant items

14a Using and Evaluating Library Sources

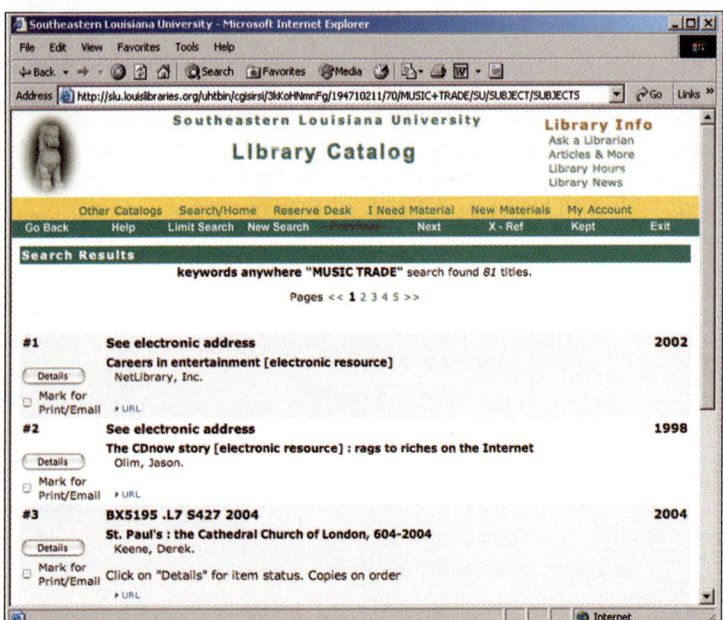

FIGURE 14.2 Online catalog search results for the subject heading *Music Trade*.

NOTE: Many college and university libraries offer remote access to their online resources. Ask at your library for the appropriate Web address and password.

2 Consulting General Reference Works

General reference works—encyclopedias, bibliographies, and so on—that provide broad overviews of particular subjects can be helpful when you are doing exploratory research. From these sources, you can learn key facts and specific terminology as well as find dates, places, and names. In addition, general reference works often include bibliographies that you can use later on when you do focused research.

> **CLOSE-UP**
>
> **GENERAL REFERENCE WORKS**
>
> **General Encyclopedias** Many general multivolume encyclopedias are available in electronic format. For example, *The New Encyclopaedia Britannica* is available on CD-ROM and DVD as well as on the World Wide Web at <http://www.britannica.com>.
>
> **Specialized Encyclopedias, Dictionaries, and Bibliographies** These specialized reference works contain in-depth articles focusing on a single subject area.

> **General Bibliographies** General bibliographies—such as *Books in Print* and *The Bibliographic Index*—list books available in a wide variety of fields.
>
> **General Biographical References** Biographical reference books—such as *Who's Who in America*, *Who's Who*, and *Dictionary of American Biography*—provide information about people's lives as well as bibliographic listings.

NOTE: Articles in general encyclopedias are usually not detailed enough for a college-level research paper. Articles in specialized encyclopedias, dictionaries, and bibliographies, however, are more likely to be appropriate for your research.

3 Using Library Databases

The same computer terminals that enable you to access the online catalog also enable you to access a variety of other electronic databases.

Online databases are collections of digital information—citations of books, reports, and journal, magazine, and newspaper articles (and sometimes the full text of articles)—arranged for easy access and retrieval by computer. Different libraries offer different databases and make them available in different ways. Many libraries have implemented Web-based systems that give users remote access to databases (and online catalogs). Some libraries may have databases on CD-ROM or DVD, but most subscribe to information service companies, such as DIALOG or Gale, that provide online access to hundreds of databases. One of your first tasks should be to determine what subscription databases your library offers. Visit your library's Web site, or ask a reference librarian for more information. Figure 14.3 on page 186 shows a partial list of databases to which one college library subscribes.

General and Specialized Subscription Databases. The databases in your college library are likely to be **subscription databases**. The library must subscribe to them in order to make them available to students and faculty.

Some library databases cover many subject areas (*Expanded Academic ASAP* or *LexisNexis Academic Universe*, for example); others cover just one subject area in great detail (*PsycINFO* or *Sociological Abstracts*, for example). Assuming that your library offers a variety of databases, how do you know which ones will be best for your research topic? One strategy is to begin by searching a general database that includes full-text articles and then move on to a more specialized database that covers your subject in more detail. The specialized databases are

14a Using and Evaluating Library Sources

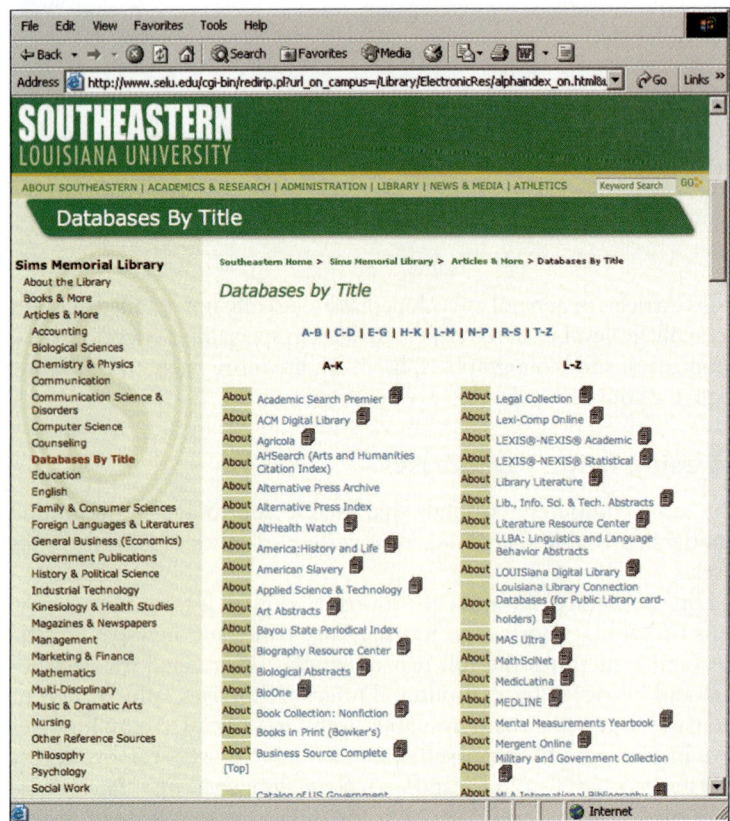

FIGURE 14.3 Partial list of databases to which one college library subscribes.

more likely to include scholarly and professional sources, but they are also less likely to include full text. They will, however, include **abstracts** (short summaries) that can help you determine the usefulness of a source. If you are in doubt about which databases would be most useful, ask a librarian for suggestions. (Figure 14.4 shows a printout from a library subscription database.)

Searching Databases. You can search library databases in two ways: by *subject headings* and by *keyword(s)*.

When you search by **subject headings**, you choose a heading from a list of terms recognized by that database. Sometimes it is easy to choose a subject heading, but sometimes it is hard to choose an appropriate term. For example, what do you call older people? Are they senior citizens? elderly? aged? (Some databases provide a print or online thesaurus to help you choose subject headings.)

```
                    Date    Volume    Issue      First page    Total number
                                     number     of article      of pages
```

Title: The Supply Side of the Digital Divide: Is There Equal Availability in the Broadband Internet Access Market?

Periodical: *Economic Inquiry,* April 2003 v41 i2 p346(18).

Author: James E. Prieger

Author's Abstract: The newest dimension of the digital divide is access to broadband (high-speed) Internet service. Using comprehensive US data covering all forms of access technology (chiefly DSL and cable modem), I look for evidence of unequal broadband availability in areas with high concentrations of poor, minority, or rural households. There is little evidence of unequal availability based on income or on black or Hispanic concentration. There is mixed evidence concerning availability based on Native American or Asian concentration. Other findings: Rural location decreases availability; market size, education, Spanish language use, commuting distance, and Bell presence increase availability. (JEL L96, J78, L51)

Subjects: Digital Divide (Technology) = Demographic Aspects

Internet = Usage

Features: tables; figures

FIGURE 14.4 Library subscription database printout.

The other option is **keyword searching,** which allows you to type in any significant term likely to be found in the title, subject headings, abstract, or (if the full text is available) text of an article. Keyword searching also allows you to link terms using **Boolean operators** (AND, OR, NOT). For example, *elderly* AND *abuse* would identify only articles that mention both elderly people and abuse; *elderly* OR *aged* OR *senior citizens* would identify articles that mention any of these terms. Keyword searching is particularly helpful when you need to narrow or expand the focus of your search.

Both subject heading and keyword searches are useful ways to find information on your topic. The most important thing is to be persistent. One good source often leads to another: abstracts and text may suggest other terms you can use, and references and footnotes may suggest additional sources. Figure 14.5 on page 188 shows a search page from a library subscription database.

14b Doing Focused Library Research

Once you have completed your exploratory research and formulated your research question, it is time to move to focused research. During **focused research,** you examine the specialized reference

14b Using and Evaluating Library Sources

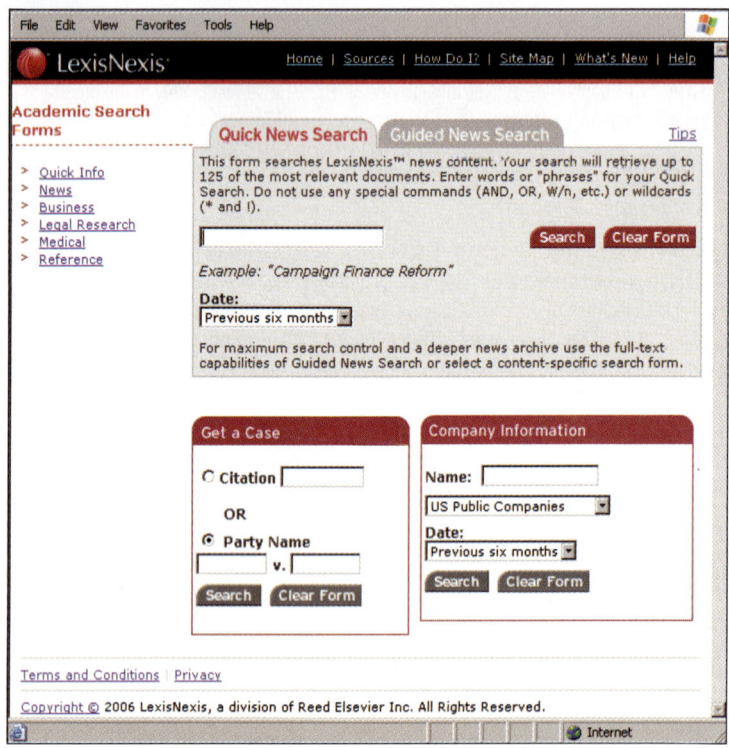

FIGURE 14.5 Search page from *LexisNexis Academic Universe*, a library subscription database.

works, books, and articles devoted specifically to your topic. At this stage, you may also need to make use of the special services that many college libraries offer.

If your library has a Web site (and most libraries do), you may find it enables you to access more than just the library catalog or the various periodicals to which it subscribes. In fact, many library Web sites are gateways to a vast amount of information, including research guides on a wide variety of topics, electronic journals and newspapers to which the library subscribes, and links to recommended Internet resources.

1 Consulting Specialized Reference Works

During your exploratory research, you use general reference works to help you narrow your topic and formulate your research question. Now, you can access **specialized reference works**—unabridged dictionaries, special dictionaries, yearbooks, almanacs, atlases, and so on—to find facts, examples, statistics, definitions, and expert opinion. (Note that many of these works are available online and in print.)

> **CLOSE-UP**
>
> **SPECIALIZED REFERENCE WORKS**
>
> **Unabridged Dictionaries** Unabridged dictionaries, such as the *Oxford English Dictionary*, are comprehensive works that give detailed information about words.
>
> **Special Dictionaries** These dictionaries may focus on topics such as usage, synonyms, slang and idioms, etymologies, and foreign terms; some focus on specific disciplines such as accounting or law.
>
> **Yearbooks and Almanacs** A **yearbook** is an annual publication that updates factual and statistical information already published in a reference source. An **almanac** provides lists, charts, and statistics about a wide variety of subjects.
>
> *World Almanac.* Includes statistics about government, population, sports, and many other subjects. Published annually since 1868.
> *Information Please Almanac.* Includes information unavailable in the *World Almanac.* Published annually since 1947.
> *Facts on File.* Covering 1940 to the present, this work offers digests of important news stories from metropolitan newspapers.
> *Editorials on File.* Reprints important editorials from American and Canadian newspapers.
> *Statistical Abstract of the United States.* Summarizes the statistics gathered by the US government. Published annually.
>
> **Atlases** An **atlas** contains maps and charts as well as historical, cultural, political, and economic information.
>
> *National Geographic Atlas of the World.* Published by the National Geographic Society. The most up-to-date atlas available.
> *Rand McNally Cosmopolitan World Atlas.* A modern and extremely legible medium-sized atlas.
> *We the People: An Atlas of America's Ethnic Diversity.* Presents information about specific ethnic groups. Maps show immigration routes and settlement patterns.
>
> **Quotation Books** A **quotation book**—such as *Bartlett's Familiar Quotations*—contains numerous quotations on a wide variety of subjects. Such quotations can be useful for your paper's introductory and concluding paragraphs.

2 Consulting Books

The online catalog gives you the information you need—the call numbers—for locating specific titles. A **call number** is like a book's address in the library: it tells you exactly where to find the book you are looking for.

Once you become familiar with the physical layout of the library and the classification system your library uses, you should find it quite simple to locate the books you need.

> **CHECKLIST**
> **TRACKING DOWN A MISSING BOOK**
>
> | Problem | Possible Solution |
> |---|---|
> | 1. Book has been checked out of library. | ☐ Consult person at circulation desk. |
> | 2. Book is not in library's collection. | ☐ Check other nearby libraries.
☐ Ask instructor if he or she owns a copy.
☐ Arrange for interlibrary loan (if time permits). |
> | 3. Journal is not in library's collection/ article is ripped out of journal. | ☐ Arrange for interlibrary loan (if time permits).
☐ Check to see whether article is available in a full-text database.
☐ Ask librarian whether article has been reprinted as part of a collection. |

3 Consulting Periodicals

A **periodical** is a newspaper, magazine, scholarly journal, or other publication published at regular intervals (weekly, monthly, or quarterly). Articles in **scholarly journals** can be the best, most reliable sources you can find on a subject; they provide current information and are written by experts on the topic. And, because these journals focus on a particular subject area, they can provide in-depth analysis.

NOTE: You cannot access most scholarly journals on the free Internet. Although you may occasionally find individual articles on the Internet, the easiest and most reliable way to access scholarly journals is through one of the subscription databases in your college library.

Periodical indexes are databases that list articles from a selected group of magazines, newspapers, or scholarly journals. Most libraries offer these indexes online. They are updated frequently and provide the most current information available.

> ## CLOSE-UP
>
> ### FREQUENTLY USED PERIODICAL INDEXES
>
> Academic libraries usually subscribe to the following periodical indexes. (Be sure to check your library's Web site or ask a librarian about those available to you.)
>
> | General Indexes | Description |
> |---|---|
> | *EBSCOhost* | Database system for thousands of periodical articles on many subjects |
> | *Expanded Academic ASAP* | A largely full-text database covering all subjects in thousands of magazines and scholarly journals |
> | *FirstSearch* | Full-text articles from many popular and scholarly periodicals |
> | *LexisNexis Academic Universe* | Includes full-text articles from national, international, and local newspapers. Also includes large legal and business sections. |
> | *Readers' Guide to Periodical Literature* | Index to popular periodicals |
>
> | Specialized Indexes | Description |
> |---|---|
> | *Dow Jones Interactive* | Full-text articles from US newspapers and trade journals |
> | *ERIC* | Largest database of education-related journal articles and reports in the world |
> | *General BusinessFile ASAP* | A full-text database covering business topics |
> | *PubMed (MEDLINE)* | Covers articles in medical journals. Some may be available in full text. |
> | *PsycINFO* | Covers psychology and related fields |
> | *Sociological Abstracts* | Covers the social sciences |

4 Finding Primary and Secondary Sources

<u>Primary sources</u> are original documents and observations. They include diaries, letters, speeches, manuscripts, memoirs, autobiographies, records of governments or organizations, newspaper articles, and even books written at the time an event occurred. Primary sources also include photographs, maps, films, tape recordings, statistics and other research data, novels, short stories, poems, and plays.

<u>Secondary sources</u> are interpretations of original documents and observations. In many cases, their purpose is to interpret or analyze primary sources. Secondary sources include textbooks, literary criticism, and encyclopedias.

See 13e2

See 13e2

CHECKLIST

Finding Primary Sources

- ☐ Do a keyword search of your online catalog. Use keywords that combine your topic with additional terms that describe the format of the primary source—for example, *slaves* AND *narratives*.
- ☐ See if the online catalog lists any bibliographies that might include primary sources. For example, a bibliography might list works *by* an author (primary sources) as well as works *about* the author (secondary sources).
- ☐ Check with a reference librarian to see if your library subscribes to any databases that contain full-text primary sources.
- ☐ Check with a reference librarian to see if your library houses government publications that may include primary sources.
- ☐ Check with a reference librarian to see if your library houses any manuscripts.
- ☐ Use the Internet to find digitized collections of primary source materials—for example, documents that relate to US history, transcripts of television shows, or video clips.

NOTE: The US Government makes available a good deal of primary source material, much of it on the Web—for example, statistical information collected by government agencies; reports issued by government agencies such as the Environmental Protection Agency, the Department of Education, and NASA; US Supreme Court decisions; and presidential papers, political speeches, treaties, and US patents. A good Web site for locating government publications is <http://www.firstgov.gov>.

CHECKLIST

Finding Secondary Sources

- ☐ Search your library's online catalog for books. Combine a term that describes your topic with terms such as *interpretation*, *criticism*, or *bibliography*.
- ☐ Search your library's subscription databases for articles in scholarly journals, popular magazines, and newspapers that discuss and interpret the causes and effects of events.
- ☐ Check the notes, bibliographies, and works-cited lists that appear in books and articles.
- ☐ Do a keyword search on the Internet—but be sure to evaluate any information you find.

5 Using Special Library Resources

As you do focused research, consult a librarian if you plan to use any of the following special library resources.

> **CLOSE-UP**
>
> **SPECIAL LIBRARY RESOURCES**
>
> - **Interlibrary Loans** Your library may be part of a library system that allows loans of books from one location to another.
> - **Special Collections** Your library may house special collections of books, manuscripts, or documents.
> - **Government Documents** A large university library may have a separate government documents area with its own catalog or index.
> - **Vertical File** The vertical file includes pamphlets from a variety of organizations and interest groups, newspaper clippings, and other material collected by librarians.

EXERCISE 1

Which library research sources would you consult to find the following information?

1. A discussion of Monica Ali's novel *Brick Lane* (2003)
2. A government publication about how to heat your home with solar energy
3. Biographical information about the American anthropologist Margaret Mead
4. Books about Margaret Mead and her work
5. Information about what is being done to prevent the killing of wolves in North America
6. Information about the theories of Albert Einstein
7. Current information about the tobacco lobby
8. The address at which to contact Edward P. Jones, an American writer
9. Whether your college library has *The Human Use of Human Beings* by Norbert Wiener
10. Current information about AmeriCorps

14c Evaluating the Library's Print and Electronic Sources

Whenever you find a source (print or electronic), take the time to **evaluate** it—to assess its usefulness and its reliability. To determine the usefulness of a library source, ask the following questions:

- **Does the source treat your topic in enough detail?** To be of any real help, a book should include a section or chapter on your topic, not simply a footnote or a brief reference. For articles, either read the abstract or skim the entire article for key facts, looking closely at section headings, information set in boldface type, and topic sentences. An article should have your topic as its central subject (or at least one of its main concerns).
- **Is the source current?** The date of publication tells you whether the information in a book or article is up to date. A source's currency is particularly important for scientific and technological subjects, but even in the humanities, new discoveries and new ways of thinking lead scholars to reevaluate and modify their ideas.
- **Is the source respected?** A contemporary review of a source can help you make this assessment. *Book Review Digest*, available in print and online, lists popular books that have been reviewed in at least three newspapers or magazines and includes excerpts from representative reviews as well as abstracts.
- **Is the source reliable?** Is the source largely fact or unsubstantiated opinion? Does the writer support his or her conclusions? Does the writer include documentation? Is the writer objective, or does he or she have a particular agenda to advance? Compare a few statements with a neutral source—a textbook or an encyclopedia, for instance—to see whether a writer seems to be slanting facts.
- **Is the source a scholarly or a popular publication?** In general, **scholarly publications**—books and journals aimed at an audience of expert readers—are more respected and reliable than **popular publications**—books, magazines, and newspapers aimed at an audience of general readers. However, assuming they are current, written by reputable authors, and documented, articles from some popular publications (such as the *Atlantic* and *Harper's*) may be appropriate for your research. But remember that most popular publications do not have the same rigorous standards as scholarly publications do. For this reason, before you use information from popular sources such as *Newsweek* or *Sports Illustrated*, check with your instructor.

CLOSE-UP

SCHOLARLY VERSUS POPULAR PUBLICATIONS

Scholarly Publications	Popular Publications
Report the results of research	Entertain and inform
Are often published by a university press or have some connection with a university or academic organization	Are published by commercial presses

Scholarly Publications

Are usually **refereed**; that is, a group of expert reviewers determines what will be published

Are usually written by someone who is a recognized authority in the field about which he or she is writing

Are written for a scholarly audience, so they often use technical vocabulary and include challenging content

Nearly always contain extensive documentation as well as a bibliography of works consulted

Are published primarily because they make a contribution to a particular field of study

Popular Publications

Are usually not refereed

May be written by experts in a particular field, but more often they are written by freelance or staff writers

Are written for general readers, so they usually use an accessible vocabulary and do not include challenging content

Rarely cite sources or use documentation

Are published primarily to make a profit

■ **EXERCISE 2**

Read the following paragraphs carefully, paying close attention to the information provided about their sources and authors as well as to their content. Decide which sources would be most useful and reliable in supporting the thesis "Winning the right to vote has (or has not) significantly changed the role of women in national politics." Which sources, if any, should be disregarded? Which would you examine first? Why?

1. Woman has been the great unpaid laborer of the world, and although within the last two decades a vast number of new employments have been opened to her, statistics prove that in the great majority of these, she is not paid according to the value of the work done, but according to sex. The opening of all industries to women, and the wage question as connected with her, are the most subtle and profound questions of political economy, closely interwoven with the rights of self-government. (Susan B. Anthony; first appeared in Vol. I of *The History of Woman Suffrage*; reprinted in *Voices from Women's Liberation*, ed. Leslie B. Tanner, NAL, 1970. *An important figure in the battle for women's suffrage, Susan B. Anthony [1820–1906] also lectured and wrote on abolition and temperance.*)

2. With women as half the country's elected representatives, and a woman President once in a while, the country's machismo problems would be greatly reduced. The old-fashioned idea that

manhood depends on violence and victory is, after all, an important part of our troubles.... I'm not saying that women leaders would eliminate violence. We are not more moral than men; we are only uncorrupted by power so far. When we do acquire power, we might turn out to have an equal impulse toward aggression. (Gloria Steinem, "What It Would Be Like If Women Win," *Time*, 1970. Steinem, *a well-known feminist and journalist, is one of the founders of* Ms. *magazine.*)

3. Nineteen eighty-two was the year that time ran out for the proposed equal rights amendment. Eleanor Smeal, president of the National Organization for Women, the group that headed the intense 10-year struggle for the ERA, conceded defeat on June 24. Only 24 words in all, the ERA read simply: "Equality of rights under the law shall not be denied or abridged by the United States or by any state on account of sex." Two major opinion polls had reported just weeks before the ERA's defeat that a majority of Americans continued to favor the amendment. (June Foley, "Women 1982: The Year That Time Ran Out," *The World Almanac & Book of Facts*, 1983.)

4. It won't happen this year. But the next chance at the White House is only four years away, and more women than you might think are already laying the groundwork for their own presidential bids. Bolstered by changing public attitudes, women in politics no longer assume that the Oval Office will always be a male bastion. In 1936, when George Gallup first asked people whether they would "vote for a woman for president if she qualified in every other respect," 65 percent said they would not. Back then, women were only slightly more open to the idea than men. Things are far different today. A recent poll shows that 90 percent of Americans, men included, say they could support a woman for president. (Eleanor Clift and Tom Brazaitis, *Madam President*, © 2000 by Eleanor Clift and Tom Brazaitis. *The authors profile the women who they say are positioning themselves to be president.*)

14d Doing Research Outside the Library

Interviews (conducted in person or by email) often give you material that you cannot always find in a library—for instance, biographical information, a firsthand account of an event, or the opinions of an expert.

The kinds of questions you ask in an interview depend on the information you want. **Open-ended questions**—questions designed to elicit general information—allow a respondent great flexibility in answering: *"Do you think students today are motivated? Why or why* *not?"* **Closed-ended questions**—questions intended to elicit specific information—enable you to zero in on a particular detail about a subject: *"How much money did the government's cost-cutting programs actually save?"*

> ### CHECKLIST
> #### CONDUCTING AN INTERVIEW
> ☐ Always make an appointment.
> ☐ Prepare a list of specific questions tailored to the subject matter and the time limit of your interview.
> ☐ Do background reading about your topic. (Do not ask for information that you can easily find elsewhere.)
> ☐ Have a pen and paper with you. If you want to record the interview, get your subject's permission in advance.
> ☐ Allow the person you are interviewing to complete an answer before you ask another question.
> ☐ Take notes, but continue to pay attention as you do so.
> ☐ Pay attention to the reactions of your interview subject.
> ☐ Be willing to depart from your prepared list of questions to ask follow-up questions.
> ☐ At the end of the interview, thank your subject for his or her time and cooperation.
> ☐ Send a brief note of thanks.

COMPUTER TIP academic.cengage.com/eng/kirsznermandell

CONDUCTING AN EMAIL INTERVIEW

Using email to conduct an interview can save you a great deal of time. Before you send your questions, make sure the person is willing to cooperate. If the person agrees, send a short list of specific questions. After you have received the answers, send a response thanking the person for his or her cooperation.

15

Using and Evaluating Internet Sources

❓ FAQs

If I use the Internet, do I still have to go to the library? (p. 198)
How do I choose the right search engine? (p. 204)
What can I do to make my Web search more productive? (p. 206)

15a Understanding the Internet

The **Internet** is a vast system of networks that links millions of computers. Because of its size and diversity, the Internet allows people from all over the world to communicate quickly and easily.

Furthermore, because it is inexpensive to publish text, pictures, and sound online, businesses, government agencies, libraries, and universities are able to make available vast amounts of information: years' worth of newspaper articles, hundreds of thousands of pages of scientific or technical papers, government reports, images of all the paintings in a museum, virtual tours of historically significant buildings or sites—even an entire library of literature.

Even with all its advantages, however, the Internet does not give you access to the high-quality print and electronic resources found in a typical college library. For this reason, you should consider the Internet to be a supplement to your library research, not a substitute for it.

CLOSE-UP

LIMITATIONS OF INTERNET RESEARCH

- Many important and useful publications are available only in print or through the library's subscription databases and not on the Internet.
- The information in your college library will almost always be more focused and more useful than much of what you will find on the Internet.
- The information you see on an Internet site—unlike information in your library's subscription databases—may not be there when you try to access it at a later time. (For this reason, MLA recommends that you print out all Internet documents you use in your research.)

- Because librarians screen the material in your college library, it is likely to meet academic standards of reliability. (Even so, you still have to *evaluate* any information before you use it in a paper.)
- Although the authorship of Internet documents can often be difficult or impossible to determine, this is not usually the case with the sources in your college library.

See 14c, 15d

15b Using the World Wide Web for Research

When most people refer to the Internet, they actually mean the **World Wide Web,** which is just a part of the Internet. (**See 15c** for other components of the Internet that you can use in your research.) The Web relies on **hypertext links,** keywords highlighted in color (and often underlined). By clicking your mouse on these links, you can move easily from one **Web page** (a single document) to another or from one **Web site** (a collection of Web pages) to another.

To carry out a Web search, you need a **Web browser,** a tool that enables you to view information on the Web. Two of the most popular browsers—*Microsoft Internet Explorer* and *Netscape Navigator*—display the full range of text, photos, sound, and video available in Web documents. (Most new computers come with one or both of these browsers already installed.)

NOTE: Some browsers are designed especially for users with disabilities. (Figure 15.1 on page 200 shows a screen from a Web browser that uses screen magnification and audio.)

Once you are connected to the Internet, you use your browser to access a **search engine,** a program that searches for and retrieves documents available on the Internet. There are three ways to use search engines to find the information you want: *entering an electronic address, using subject guides,* and *doing a keyword search.*

1 Entering an Electronic Address

The most basic way to access information on the Web is to go directly to a specific electronic address, called a **URL** (uniform resource locator). Search engines and Web browsers enable you to enter a URL into the Location text field on your browser's **home page** (the page you see when you open your browser). Once you type in a URL and click on Search (or hit Enter or the return key), you will be connected to the Web site you want. (Figure 15.2 on page 200 shows a location field.)

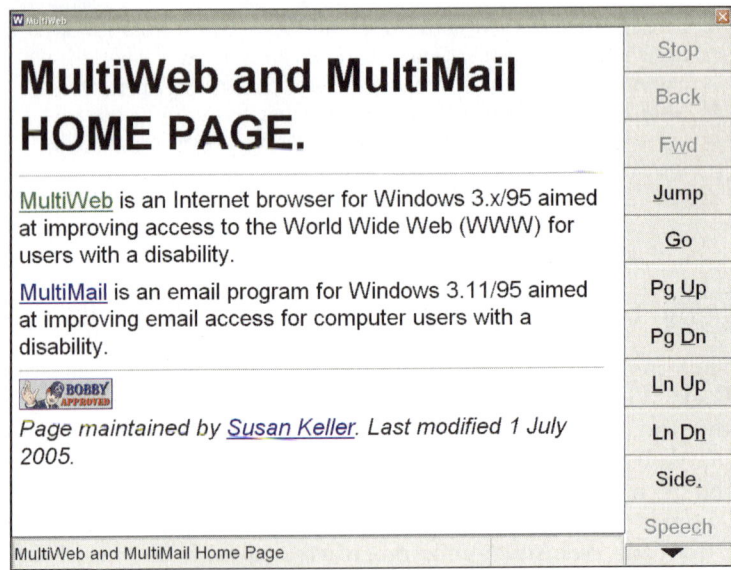

FIGURE 15.1 *MultiWeb* browser.

Location field

FIGURE 15.2 Entering an address in *Netscape Navigator*.

CLOSE-UP

WHAT TO DO IF YOU CANNOT CONNECT

If you cannot connect to the Web site that you want, do not give up. You can use the following strategies to help you connect:

- Wait a short period of time, and try again. If a Web site is extremely busy, it may block users.
- Make sure that you have typed in the URL correctly. Adding a space or omitting just a punctuation mark will send you to the wrong site—or to no site at all.
- If the URL is very long, delete a section of the end of the URL—from slash to slash—and try again.
- Try using just the base URL, deleting everything after *.com* or *.gov*. If this abbreviated URL does not take you where you want to go, you have an incorrect address.
- If you are following a link from one document to another and cannot connect, type the URL of the link into the location field of your search engine, and try again.

COMPUTER TIP academic.cengage.com/eng/kirsznermandell

UNDERSTANDING URLS

The first section of a URL indicates the type of file being accessed. In the address http://www.google.com/images, *http* indicates that the file is in hypertext transfer protocol. After the colon and the two slashes is the name of the host site where the file is stored (www.google.com). The *www* tells the user that the Web site is on the World Wide Web, *google* is the domain name, and *com* shows that this is a commercial institution. Following this section is the directory path to the file (*images*).

For links to Web sites for **exploratory and focused research,** go to http://academic.cengage.com/eng/kirsznermandell ▶ *The Wadsworth Handbook* ▶ Chapter 15 ▶ Using and Evaluating Internet Sources.

2 Using Subject Guides

You can also use subject guides to help you locate information. Some search engines, such as *Yahoo!*, *About.com*, and *Look Smart*, contain a **subject guide**—a list of general categories (*Finance, News, Sports,* and so on) from which you can choose. (Figure 15.3 on page 202 shows the home page of a search engine with a subject guide.) Each general category will lead you to a more specific list of categories and subcategories until, eventually, you get to the topic you want. For example, clicking on *Society* might lead you to *Activism* and then to *Animal Rights* and eventually to an article concerning cruelty to animals on

FIGURE 15.3 *Yahoo!* home page with subject guide.

factory farms. Although using subject guides is a time-consuming strategy for finding specific information, it can be an excellent tool during [exploratory research](), when you want to find or narrow a topic.

See 14a

3 Doing a Keyword Search

Finally, you can locate information by doing a **keyword search.** You do this by entering a keyword (or words) into your search engine's search field. (Figure 15.4 shows a search engine's keyword search page.) The search engine will identify any site in its database on which the keyword (or words) you have typed appears. (These sites are called **hits.**) If, for example, you simply type *Civil War* (say, in hope of finding information on Fort Sumter during the Civil War), the search engine will generate an enormous list of hits—well over a million. This list will likely include, along with sites that might be relevant to your research, the Civil War Reenactors home page as well as sites that focus on Civil War music.

Because searching this way is inefficient and time consuming, you need to focus your search by using **search operators,** words and symbols that tell a search engine how to interpret your keywords. One way to focus your search is to put quotation marks around your search term (type "*Fort Sumter*" rather than *Fort Sumter*). This will direct the search engine to locate only documents containing this phrase.

Using the World Wide Web for Research — 15b

Search field

FIGURE 15.4 *Google* keyword search page.

Another way to focus your search is to carry out a **Boolean search,** combining keywords with AND, OR, NOT (typed in all capital letters), or a plus or minus sign to eliminate irrelevant hits from your search. (To do this type of search, you may have to select a search engine's Advanced Search option.) For example, to find Web pages that focus on the battle of Fort Sumter in the Civil War, type *Civil War* AND *Fort Sumter*. If you do, your search will yield only items that contain *both* terms. (If you typed in *Civil War* OR *Fort Sumter*, your search will yield items that contain *either* term.) Some search engines allow you to search using three or more keywords—*Civil War* AND *Fort Sumter* NOT *national monument*, for example. In this case, your search would yield items that contained both the terms *Civil War* and *Fort Sumter*, but not the term *national monument*. By limiting your search in this way, you would just get items that discussed Fort Sumter and the Civil War and eliminate items that discussed Fort Sumter's current use as a national monument. Thus, doing a Boolean search enables you to avoid irrelevant Web pages.

COMPUTER TIP academic.cengage.com/eng/kirsznermandell

USING SEARCH OPERATORS

" " **(quotation marks)** Use quotation marks to search for a specific phrase: "*Baltimore Economy*"

AND Use AND to search for sites that contain both terms: *Baltimore* AND *Economy*

OR Use OR to search for sites that contain either term: *Baltimore* OR *Economy*

(continued)

> **USING SEARCH OPERATORS** *(continued)*
>
> **NOT** Use NOT to exclude the term that comes after the NOT:
> *Baltimore* AND *Economy* NOT *Agriculture*
>
> **+ (plus sign)** Use a plus sign to include the term that comes after it:
> *Baltimore + Economy*
>
> **− (minus sign)** Use a minus sign to exclude the term that comes after it: *Baltimore + Economy − Agriculture*

4 Choosing the Right Search Engine

The most widely used search engines are **general-purpose search engines** that focus on a wide variety of topics. Some of these search engines are more user-friendly than others; some allow for more sophisticated searching functions; some are updated more frequently; and some are more comprehensive than others. As you try out various search engines, you will probably settle on a favorite that you will turn to first whenever you need to find information.

> **CLOSE-UP**
>
> **POPULAR SEARCH ENGINES**
>
> *AllTheWeb* <www.alltheweb.com>: This excellent search engine provides comprehensive coverage of the Web. Many users think that this search engine is as good as *Google*. In addition to generating Web page results, *AllTheWeb* has the ability to search for news stories, pictures, video clips, MP3s, and FTP files.
>
> *AltaVista* <www.altavista.com>: Good, precise engine for focused searches. Fast and easy to use.
>
> *Ask.com* <www.ask.com>: Allows you to narrow your search by asking questions, such as *Are dogs smarter than pigs?*
>
> *Excite* <www.excite.com>: Good for general topics. Because it searches over 250 million Web sites, you often receive more information than you need.
>
> *Go* <http://infoseek.go.com>: Enables you to access information in a directory of reviewed sites, news stories, and Usenet groups.
>
> *Google* <www.google.com>: Arguably the best search engine available. Accesses a large database that includes both text and graphics. It is easy to navigate, and searches usually yield a high percentage of useful hits. (Google recently instituted *Google Scholar*, which searches for scholarly literature, including peer-reviewed papers, books, abstracts, and technical reports from all areas of research. It can be accessed at <www.scholar.google.com>.)

HotBot <www.hotbot.com>: Excellent, fast search engine for locating specific information. Good search options allow you to fine-tune your searches.

Lycos <www.lycos.com>: Enables you to search for specific media (graphics, for example). A somewhat small index of Web pages.

Teoma <www.teoma.com>: Although it has a smaller index of the Web than *Google* and *AllTheWeb*, it is very effective when it comes to answering questions. It contains a Refine feature that offers suggested topics to explore after you do a search. It also has a Resources section that will point you to linked resources about various topics.

WebCrawler <www.webcrawler.com>: Good for beginners. Easy to use.

Yahoo! <www.yahoo.com>: Good for exploratory research. Enables you to search using either subject headings or keywords. Searches its own indexes as well as the Web.

Because even the best search engines search only a fraction of what is on the Web, if you use only one search engine, you will most likely miss much valuable information. It is therefore a good idea to repeat each search with several different search engines or to use one of the **metasearch** or **metacrawler** engines that uses several search engines simultaneously.

CLOSE-UP

METASEARCH ENGINES

Dogpile <www.dogpile.com>

Ixquick <www.ixquick.com>

Metacrawler <www.metacrawler.com>

Profusion <www.profusion.com>

Zworks <www.zworks.com>

In addition to the popular general-purpose search engines and metasites, there are also numerous **specialized search engines** devoted entirely to specific subject areas, such as literature, business, sports, and women's issues. Hundreds of such specialized search engines are indexed at *Allsearchengines.com* <www.allsearchengines.com>. These sites are especially useful during **focused research**, when you are looking for in-depth information about your topic.

See 14b

NOTE: *Search Engine Watch* <www.searchenginewatch.com> maintains an extensive, comprehensive, and up-to-date list of the latest search engines. Not only does this site list search engines by category, it also reviews them.

15b Using and Evaluating Internet Sources

> **CLOSE-UP**
>
> **SPECIALIZED SEARCH ENGINES**
>
> *Voice of the Shuttle* (humanities search engine)
>   <http://vos.ucsb.edu/>
>
> *Pilot-Search.com* (literary search engine)
>   <http://www.pilot-search.com/>
>
> *FedWorld* (US government database and report search engine)
>   <http://www.fedworld.gov/>
>
> *HealthFinder* (health, nutrition, and diseases information for consumers)
>   <http://www.healthfinder.gov/default.htm>
>
> *The Internet Movie Database* (search engine and database for film facts, reviews, and so on)
>   <http://www.imdb.com>
>
> *SportQuest* (sports search engine)
>   <http://www.sportquest.com/>
>
> *FindLaw* (legal search engine)
>   <http://www.findlaw.com/>

> **CHECKLIST**
>
> **TIPS FOR EFFECTIVE SEARCHING**
>
> ☐ **Choose your keywords carefully.** A search engine is only as good as the keywords you use. Use quotation marks and Boolean search operators to make your searches more productive. Review the Computer Tip box on pages 203–04 before you use any search engine.
>
> ☐ **Include enough terms.** If you are looking for information on housing, for example, search for several different variations of your keyword: *housing, houses, home buyer, buying houses, residential real estate*, and so on. Some search engines, like *Infoseek*, automatically search plurals; others do not. Some, like *AltaVista*, automatically search variants of your keyword; others require you to think of the variants yourself.
>
> ☐ **Choose the right search engine.** No one all-purpose search site exists. Make sure you review the lists of search engines on pages 204–05 and 206.
>
> ☐ **Use more than one search engine.** Because different search engines index different sites, try several. If one does not yield results after a few tries, switch to another. Also, do not forget to do a metasearch with a search engine like *Metacrawler*.
>
> ☐ **Add useful sites to your Bookmarks or Favorites list.** Whenever you find a particularly useful Web site, **bookmark** it by selecting

this option on the menu bar of your browser (with some browsers, such as *Internet Explorer*, this option is called *Favorites*). If you add a site to your bookmark list, you can return to the site whenever you want to by opening the Bookmark menu and selecting it.

15c Using Other Internet Tools

In addition to the World Wide Web, the Internet includes a number of other tools that you can use to gather information for your research.

1 Using Email

Email can be useful as you do research because it enables you to exchange ideas with classmates, ask questions of your instructors, and even conduct long-distance interviews. You can follow email links in Web documents, and you can also send word-processing documents or other files as email attachments from one computer to another.

2 Using Listservs

Listservs (sometimes called **discussion lists**), electronic mailing lists to which you subscribe, enable you to communicate with groups of people interested in particular topics. (Many schools, and even individual courses, have their own listservs.) Subscribers to a listserv send emails to a main email address, and these messages are routed to all members of the group. Some listserv subscribers may be experts who can answer your queries. Keep in mind, however, that you must evaluate any information you get from a listserv before you use it in your research.

3 Using Newsgroups

Like listservs, **newsgroups** are discussion groups. Unlike listserv messages, which are sent to you as email, newsgroup messages are collected on the **Usenet** system, a global collection of news servers, where anyone who subscribes can access them. In a sense, newsgroups function as giant bulletin boards where users post messages that others can read and respond to. Thus, newsgroups can provide specific information as well as suggestions about where to look for further information. Just as you would with a listserv, you should evaluate information you get from a newsgroup before you use it.

4 Using MUDS, MOOS, IRCS, and Instant Messaging

With emails and listservs, there is a delay between the time a message is sent and the time it is received. **MUDS, MOOS, IRCS,** and **instant messaging** enable you to send and receive messages in real time. In other words, communication is **synchronous:** messages are sent and received as they are typed. Synchronous communication programs are being used more and more in college settings—for class discussions, online workshops, and collaborative projects.

> ### CHECKLIST
>
> #### OBSERVING NETIQUETTE
>
> **Netiquette** refers to the guidelines that responsible users of the Internet should follow when they communicate. When you use the Internet, especially email and synchronous communication, keep the following guidelines in mind:
>
> - ☐ **Don't shout.** All-uppercase letters indicate that a person is SHOUTING. Not only is this immature, but it is also distracting and irritating.
> - ☐ **Watch your tone.** Make sure you send the message you actually intend to convey. What may sound humorous to you may seem sarcastic or impolite to someone else.
> - ☐ **Be careful what you write.** Remember, once you hit *Send*, it is often too late to call back your message. For this reason, treat an email message or a posting as you would a written letter. Take the time to proofread and to consider carefully what you have written.
> - ☐ **Respect the privacy of others.** Do not forward or post a message that you have received unless you have permission from the sender to do so.
> - ☐ **Do not flame.** When you **flame,** you send an insulting electronic message. At best, this response is immature; at worst, it is disrespectful.
> - ☐ **Make sure you use the correct electronic address.** Be certain that your message goes to the right person. Nothing is more embarrassing than sending a communication to the wrong address.
> - ☐ **Use your computer facility ethically and responsibly.** Do not use computer labs for personal communications or for entertainment. Not only is this a misuse of the facility, but it also ties up equipment that others may be waiting to use.

15d   Evaluating Internet Sites

Web sites vary greatly in reliability. Because anyone can operate a Web site and thereby publish anything, regardless of quality, critical evaluation of Web-based material is even more important than evaluation of more traditional sources of information, such as books and journal articles.

Determining the quality of a Web site is crucial if you plan to use it as a source for your research. If you are using a Web site for personal information or entertainment, it is probably enough just to be aware of what is legal and what is illegal (for example, you should not download copyrighted material, such as software or music, that has been illegally posted on a Web site). However, if you are using the Internet to locate appropriate sources for a research project, you need to be much more careful. For this reason, you should evaluate the content of any Web site for *accuracy, credibility, objectivity, currency, scope of coverage,* and *stability.*

Accuracy. **Accuracy** refers to the reliability of the material itself and to the use of proper documentation. Factual errors—especially errors in facts that are central to the main idea of the source—should cause you to question the reliability of the material you are reading. To evaluate a site's accuracy, ask these questions:

- Is the text free of basic grammatical and mechanical errors?
- Does the site contain factual errors?
- Does the site provide a list of references?
- Are links available to other sources?
- Can information be verified by print or other sources?

Credibility. **Credibility** refers to the credentials of the person or organization responsible for the site. Web sites operated by well-known institutions (the Smithsonian or the Library of Congress, for example) have a high degree of credibility. Those operated by individuals (personal Web pages or **blogs,** for example) are often less reliable. To evaluate a site's credibility, ask these questions:

- Does the site list an author (or authors)? Are credentials (for example, professional or academic affiliations) provided for the author?
- Is the author a recognized authority in his or her field?
- Is the site **refereed?** That is, does an editorial board or a group of experts determine what material appears on the Web site?
- Does the organization sponsoring the Web site exist apart from its Web presence?
- Can you determine how long the Web site has existed?

Objectivity. **Objectivity** refers to the degree of bias that a Web site exhibits. Some Web sites make no secret of their biases. They openly advocate a particular point of view or action, or they are clearly trying to sell something. Other Web sites may try to hide their biases. For example, a Web site may present itself as a source of factual information when it is actually advocating a political point of view. To evaluate a site's objectivity, ask these questions:

- Does advertising appear in the text?
- Does a business, a political organization, or a special interest group sponsor the site?

- Does the site express a particular viewpoint?
- Does the site contain links to other sites that express a particular viewpoint?

> **CHECKLIST**
>
> **DETERMINING THE LEGITIMACY OF AN ANONYMOUS OR QUESTIONABLE WEB SOURCE**
>
> When a Web source is anonymous (or has an author whose name is not familiar to you), you have to take special measures to determine its legitimacy:
>
> ☐ **Post a query.** If you subscribe to a newsgroup or listserv, ask others in the group what they know about the source and its author.
>
> ☐ **Follow the links.** Follow the hypertext links in a document to other documents. If the links take you to legitimate sources, you know that the author is aware of these sources of information.
>
> ☐ **Do a keyword search.** Do a search using the name of the sponsoring organization or the author as keywords. Other documents (or citations in other works) may identify the author.
>
> ☐ **Look at the URL.** The last part of a Web site's URL can tell you whether the site is sponsored by a commercial entity (*.com*), a nonprofit organization (*.org*), an educational institution (*.edu*), the military (*.mil*), or a government agency (*.gov*). Knowing this information can tell you whether an organization is trying to sell you something (*.com*) or just providing information (*.edu* or *.org*).

Currency. **Currency** refers to how up-to-date the Web site is. The easiest way to assess a site's currency is to see when it was last updated. Keep in mind, however, that even if the date on the site is current, the information that the site contains may not be. To evaluate a site's currency, ask these questions:

- Does the site include the date when it was last updated?
- Are all the links to other sites still functioning?
- Is the actual information on the page up-to-date?
- Does the site clearly identify the date it was created?

Scope of Coverage. **Scope of coverage** refers to the comprehensiveness of the information on a Web site. More coverage is not necessarily better, but some sites may be incomplete. Others may provide information that is no more than common knowledge. Still others may present discussions that may not be suitable for college-level research. To evaluate the scope of a site's coverage, ask these questions:

- Does the site provide in-depth coverage?

- Does the site provide information that is not available elsewhere?
- Does the site identify a target audience? Does this target audience suggest the site is appropriate for your research needs?

Stability. **Stability** refers to whether or not the site is being maintained. A stable site will be around when you want to access it again. Web sites that are here today and gone tomorrow make it difficult for readers to check your sources or for you to obtain updated information. To evaluate a site's stability, ask these questions:

- Has the site been active for a long period of time?
- Is the site updated regularly?
- Is the site maintained by a well-known, reliable organization, committed to financing the site?

■ EXERCISE 1

Examine the home page for the *Washington Post* Web site (Figure 15.5). Use the criteria discussed in 15d to evaluate its content in terms of accuracy, credibility, objectivity, currency, scope of coverage, and stability.

FIGURE 15.5 The *Washington Post* home page
<www.washingtonpost.com>.

■ EXERCISE 2

Study the two Web pages shown in Figures 15.6 and 15.7 on page 212. Use the criteria outlined in 15d to evaluate their content. Then, write a paragraph in which you compare the two sites.

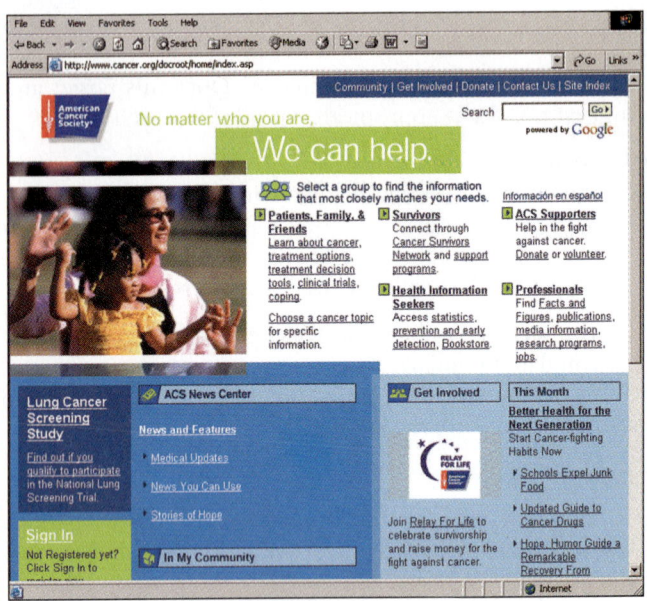

FIGURE 15.6 American Cancer Society home page.

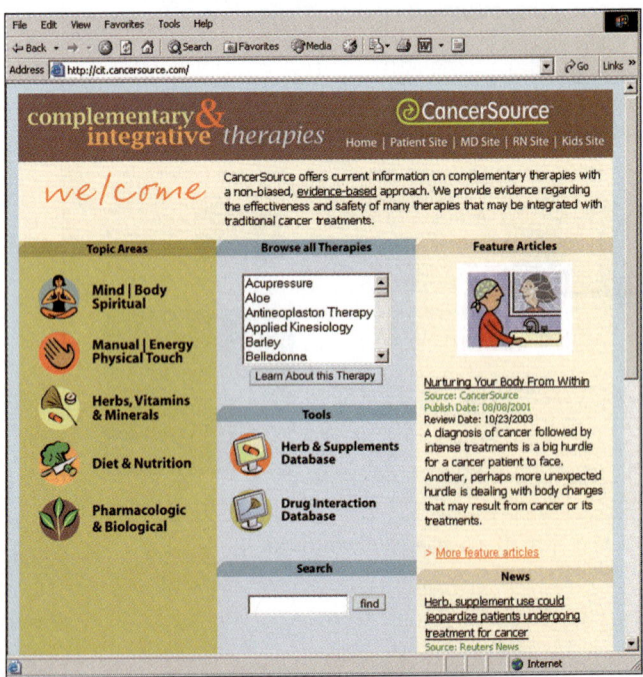

FIGURE 15.7 CancerSource Complementary & Integrative Therapies home page.

16

Summarizing, Paraphrasing, Quoting, and Synthesizing Sources

❓ FAQs

What is the difference between a paraphrase and a summary? (p. 215)
When should I quote a source? (p. 218)
How do I avoid saying "he said" or "she said" every time I use a source? (p. 219)
How can readers tell the difference between my own ideas and those of my source? (p. 222)

Although it may seem like a good strategy, copying down the words of a source is the least efficient way of **taking notes**. Experienced researchers know that a better strategy is to take notes that combine summary and paraphrase with direct quotation. By doing so, they make sure they understand the material and see its relevance to their research. This, in turn, makes it possible for them to **synthesize sources**, combining borrowed material with their own original ideas.

See 13f

See 16d3

16a Writing a Summary

A **summary** is a brief restatement, *in your own words*, of the main idea of a passage or an article. When you write a summary, you condense the writer's ideas into a few concise sentences. A summary is always much shorter than the original because it omits the examples, asides, analogies, and rhetorical strategies that writers use to add emphasis and interest.

When you summarize, use your own words, not the exact language or phrasing of your source. If you think it is necessary to reproduce a distinctive word or phrase, place it in quotation marks; otherwise, you will be committing **plagiarism**. Remember that your summary should accurately represent the writer's ideas and should include only the ideas of your source, not your own interpretations or opinions. Finally, be sure to document all quoted words and paraphrases as well as the summary itself.

See Ch. 17

213

> **CLOSE-UP**
>
> **SUMMARIES**
>
> - **Summaries are original.** They should use your own language and phrasing, not the language and phrasing of your source.
> - **Summaries are concise.** They should always be much shorter than the original.
> - **Summaries are accurate.** They should precisely express the main idea of your source.
> - **Summaries are objective.** They should not include your opinions.

Compare the following three passages. The first is an original source; the second, an acceptable summary; and the third, an unacceptable summary.

Original Source

Today, the First Amendment faces challenges from groups who seek to limit expressions of racism and bigotry. A growing number of legislatures have passed rules against "hate speech"—[speech] that is offensive on the basis of race, ethnicity, gender, or sexual orientation. The rules are intended to promote respect for all people and protect the targets of hurtful words, gestures, or actions.

Legal experts fear these rules may wind up diminishing the rights of all citizens. "The bedrock principle [of our society] is that government may never suppress free speech simply because it goes against what the community would like to hear," says Nadine Strossen, president of the American Civil Liberties Union and professor of constitutional law at New York University Law School. In recent years, for example, the courts have upheld the right of neo-Nazis to march in Jewish neighborhoods; protected cross-burning as a form of free expression; and allowed protesters to burn the American flag. The offensive, ugly, distasteful, or repugnant nature of expression is not reason enough to ban it, courts have said.

But advocates of limits on hate speech note that certain kinds of expression fall outside of First Amendment protection. Courts have ruled that "fighting words"—words intended to provoke immediate violence—or speech that creates a clear and present danger are not protected forms of expression. As the classic argument goes, freedom of speech does not give you the right to yell "Fire!" in a crowded theater. (Sudo, Phil. "Freedom of Hate Speech?" *Scholastic Update* 124.14 [1992]: 17–20. Print.)

The following acceptable summary gives an accurate, objective overview of the original without using its exact language or phrasing. (The one distinctive phrase from the source is placed in quotation marks.)

Acceptable Summary

The right to freedom of speech, guaranteed by the First Amendment, is becoming more difficult to defend. Some people think that stronger laws against the use of "hate speech" weaken the First Amendment. But others argue that some kinds of speech remain exempt from this protection (Sudo 17).

The following unacceptable summary uses words and phrases from the original without placing them in quotation marks. This use constitutes **plagiarism**. In addition, the unacceptable summary expresses the student writer's opinion (**Other people have the sense to realize . . .**).

See Ch. 17

Unacceptable Summary

Today, the First Amendment faces challenges from lots of people. Some of these people are legal experts who want to let Nazis march in Jewish neighborhoods. Other people have the sense to realize that some kinds of speech fall outside of First Amendment protection because they create a clear and present danger (Sudo 17).

> **CHECKLIST**
>
> **WRITING A SUMMARY**
> - ☐ Reread your source until you understand it.
> - ☐ Write a one-sentence restatement of the main idea.
> - ☐ Write your summary, using the one-sentence restatement as your topic sentence. Use your own words and phrasing, not those of your source. Include quotation marks where necessary.
> - ☐ Add appropriate documentation.

16b Writing a Paraphrase

A summary conveys just the main idea of a source; a **paraphrase** gives a *detailed* restatement of a source's important ideas in their entirety. It not only indicates the source's main points, but it also reflects its order, tone, and emphasis. Consequently, a paraphrase can sometimes be as long as the source itself.

When you paraphrase, make certain that you use your own words, except when you want to quote to give readers a sense of the original. If you do include quotations, circle the quotation marks in your notes so that you will not forget to document them later. Try not to look at the source as you write, use language and syntax that come naturally to you, and avoid duplicating the phrasing or sentence structure of the original. Whenever possible, use synonyms that accurately convey the meaning of the original word or phrase. If you cannot think of a synonym for an important term, quote it—but remember to document all direct quotations from your source as well as the entire paraphrase. Finally, be sure that your paraphrase reflects only the ideas of your source—not your analysis or interpretation of those ideas.

> **CLOSE-UP**
>
> **PARAPHRASES**
>
> - **Paraphrases are original.** They should use your original language and phrasing, not the language and phrasing of your source.
> - **Paraphrases are accurate.** They should precisely reflect both the ideas and the emphasis of your source.
> - **Paraphrases are objective.** They should not include your opinions.
> - **Paraphrases are complete.** They should include all the important ideas in your source.

Compare the following three passages. The first is an original source, the second is an acceptable paraphrase, and the third is an unacceptable paraphrase.

Original Passage

When you play a video game, you enter into the world of the programmers who made it. You have to do more than identify with a character on a screen. You must act for it. Identification through action has a special kind of hold. Like playing a sport, it puts people into a highly focused and highly charged state of mind. For many people, what is being pursued in the video game is not just a score, but an altered state.

The pilot of a race car does not dare to take . . . attention off the road. The imperative of total concentration is part of the high. Video games demand the same level of attention. They can give people the feeling of being close to the edge because, as in a dangerous situation, there is no time for rest and the consequences of wandering attention [are] dire. With pinball, a false move can be recuperated. The machine can be shaken, the ball repositioned. In a video game, the program has no tolerance for error, no margin for safety. Players experience their every movement as instantly translated into game action. The game is relentless in its demand that all other time stop and in its demand that the player take full responsibility for every act, a point that players often sum up [with] the phrase "One false move and you're dead." (Turkle, Sherry. *The Second Self: Computers and the Human Spirit.* New York: Simon, 1984. 83–84. Print.)

The following acceptable paraphrase conveys the key ideas of the source and maintains an objective tone. Although it follows the order and emphasis of the original—and even quotes a key phrase—its wording and sentence structure are very different from those of the source.

Acceptable Paraphrase

The programmer defines the reality of the video game. The game forces a player to merge with the character who is part of the game. The character becomes an extension of the player, who determines how he or she will think and act. According to Turkle, like sports, video games put a player into a very intense "altered state" of mind that is the most important part of the activity (83).

The total involvement they demand is what attracts many people to video games. These games can simulate the thrill of participating in a dangerous activity without any of the risks. There is no time for rest and no opportunity to correct errors of judgment. Unlike video games, pinball games are forgiving. A player can—within certain limits—manipulate a pinball game to correct minor mistakes. With video games, however, every move has immediate consequences. The game forces a player to adapt to its rules and to act carefully. One mistake can cause the death of the character on the screen and the end of the game (Turkle 83-84).

The following unacceptable paraphrase simply echoes the phrasing and syntax of the original, borrowing words and expressions without enclosing them in quotation marks. This constitutes plagiarism. In addition, the paraphrase digresses into a discussion of the student writer's own views about the relative merits of pinball and video games (**That is why I like . . .**).

See Ch. 17

Unacceptable Paraphrase

Playing a video game, you enter into a new world—one the programmer of the game made. You can't just play a video game; you have to identify with it. Your mind goes to a new level, and you are put into a highly focused state of mind.

Just as you would if you were driving a race car or piloting a plane, you must not let your mind wander. Video games demand complete attention. But the sense that at any time you could make one false move and lose is their attraction—at least for me. That is why I like video games more than pinball. Pinball is just too easy. You can always recover. By shaking the machine or quickly operating the flippers, you can save the ball. Video games, however, are not so easy to control. Usually, one slip and you're dead (Turkle 83-84).

CHECKLIST

WRITING A PARAPHRASE

- ☐ Reread your source until you understand it.
- ☐ Write your paraphrase, following the order, tone, and emphasis of the original and making sure that you do not use the words or phrasing of the original without enclosing the borrowed material within quotation marks.
- ☐ Add appropriate documentation.

16c Quoting Sources

When you **quote,** you copy a writer's statements exactly as they appear in a source, word for word and punctuation mark for punctuation mark, enclosing the borrowed material in quotation marks. As a rule, you should not quote extensively in a research paper. Numerous quotations interrupt the flow of your discussion and give readers the impression that your paper is just a collection of other people's ideas.

> **CHECKLIST**
>
> **WHEN TO QUOTE**
>
> Quote a source in the following situations:
> - ☐ Quote when a source's wording or phrasing is so distinctive that a summary or paraphrase would diminish its impact.
> - ☐ Quote when a source's words—particularly those of a recognized expert on your subject—will lend authority to your presentation.
> - ☐ Quote when a writer's words are so concise that paraphrasing would create a long, clumsy, or incoherent phrase or would change the meaning of the original.
> - ☐ Quote when you go on to disagree with a source. Using a source's exact words helps convince readers you are being fair.
>
> **NOTE:** Remember to document all quotations that you use in your paper.

■ **EXERCISE 1**

Choose a debatable issue from the following list:

- ■ Illegal immigrants' rights to medical care
- ■ Helmet requirements for motorcycle riders
- ■ Community service requirements for college students
- ■ Making English the official language of the United States
- ■ Requiring every citizen to carry a national identification card
- ■ A constitutional amendment prohibiting the defacing of the American flag

Write a one-sentence summary of your own position on the issue; then, interview a classmate and write a one-sentence summary of his or her position on the same issue. Be sure each sentence includes the reasons that support the position. Next, write a single sentence that compares and contrasts the two positions.

■ **EXERCISE 2**

Assume that in preparation for a paper on the effects of the rise of the suburbs, you read the following paragraph from the book *Great Expectations: America and the Baby Boom Generation* by Landon Y. Jones. Reread the paragraph, and write a brief summary. Then, write a paraphrase of the paragraph, quoting only those words and phrases you consider especially distinctive.

As an internal migration, the settling of the suburbs was phenomenal. In the twenty years from 1950 to 1970, the population of the suburbs doubled from 36 million to 72 million. No less than 83 percent of the total population growth in the United States during the 1950s was in the suburbs, which were growing fifteen times faster than any other segment of the country. As people packed and moved, the national mobility rate leaped by 50 percent. The only other comparable influx was the wave of European immigrants to the United States around the turn of the century. But as *Fortune* pointed out, more people moved to the suburbs every year than had ever arrived on Ellis Island.

16d Integrating Source Material into Your Writing

Weave quotations, paraphrases, and summaries smoothly into your discussion, adding your own analysis or explanation to increase coherence and to show the relevance of your source material to the points you are making.

CLOSE-UP

INTEGRATING SOURCE MATERIAL INTO YOUR WRITING

To make sure your sentences do not all sound the same, experiment with different methods of integrating source material into your paper:

- Vary the verbs you use to introduce a source's words or ideas (instead of repeating *says*).

acknowledges	discloses	implies
suggests	observes	notes
concludes	believes	comments
insists	explains	claims
predicts	summarizes	illustrates
reports	finds	proposes
warns	concurs	speculates
admits	affirms	indicates

- Vary the placement of the **identifying tag** (the phrase that identifies the source), putting it in the middle or at the end of the quoted material instead of always at the beginning.

Quotation with Identifying Tag in Middle: "A serious problem confronting Amish society from the viewpoint of the Amish themselves," observes Hostetler, "is the threat of absorption into mass society through the values promoted in the public school system" (193).

Paraphrase with Identifying Tag at End: The Amish are also concerned about their children's exposure to the public school system's values, notes Hostetler (193).

1 Integrating Quotations

Be sure to work quotations smoothly into your sentences. Use a brief introductory remark to provide a context for the quotation, and quote only those words you need to make your point. Quotations should never be awkwardly dropped into your paper, leaving the relationship between the quoted words and your point unclear.

> **Acceptable:** For the Amish, the public school system is a problem because it represents "the threat of absorption into mass society" (Hostetler 193).
>
> **Unacceptable:** For the Amish, the public school system represents a problem. "A serious problem confronting Amish society from the viewpoint of the Amish themselves is the threat of absorption into mass society through the values promoted in the public school system" (Hostetler 193).

Whenever possible, use an **identifying tag** to introduce the source of the quotation.

> **Identifying Tag:** As John Hostetler points out, the Amish see the public school system as a problem because it represents "the threat of absorption into mass society" (193).

CLOSE-UP

PUNCTUATING IDENTIFYING TAGS

Whether or not to use a comma with an identifying tag depends on where you place the tag in the sentence. If the identifying tag immediately precedes a quotation, use a comma.

> As Hostetler points out, "The Amish are successful in maintaining group identity" (56).

If the identifying tag does not immediately precede a quotation, do not use a comma.

> Hostetler points out that the Amish frequently "use severe sanctions to preserve their values" (56).

NOTE: Never use a comma after *that*: Hostetler says that Amish society is "defined by religion" (76).

Substitutions or Additions within Quotations. Indicate changes or additions that you make to a quotation by enclosing your changes in brackets.

> **Original Quotation:** "Immediately after her wedding, she and her husband followed tradition and went to visit almost everyone who attended the wedding" (Hostetler 122).

Quotation Edited to Make Verb Tenses Consistent: Nowhere is the Amish dedication to tradition more obvious than in the events surrounding marriage. Right after the wedding celebration, the Amish bride and groom "visit almost everyone who [has] attended the wedding" (Hostetler 122).

Quotation Edited to Supply an Antecedent for a Pronoun: "Immediately after her wedding, [Sarah] and her husband followed tradition and went to visit almost everyone who attended the wedding" (Hostetler 122).

Quotation Edited to Change an Uppercase to a Lowercase Letter: The strength of the Amish community is illustrated by the fact that "[i]mmediately after her wedding, she and her husband followed tradition and went to visit almost everyone who attended the wedding" (Hostetler 122).

Omissions within Quotations. When you delete unnecessary or irrelevant words, substitute an **ellipsis** (three spaced periods) for the deleted words.

See 56f1

Original Quotation: "Not only have the Amish built and staffed their own elementary and vocational schools, but they have gradually organized on local, state, and national levels to cope with the task of educating their children" (Hostetler 206).

Quotation Edited to Eliminate Unnecessary Words: "Not only have the Amish built and staffed their own elementary and vocational schools, but they have gradually organized . . . to cope with the task of educating their children" (Hostetler 206).

CLOSE-UP

OMISSIONS WITHIN QUOTATIONS

Be sure you do not misrepresent or distort the meaning of quoted material when you shorten it. For example, do not say, "the Amish have managed to maintain . . . their culture" when the original quotation is "the Amish have managed to maintain *parts* of their culture."

NOTE: If the passage you are quoting already contains ellipses, MLA style requires that you place brackets around any ellipses you add.

Long Quotations. Set off a quotation of more than four typed lines of **prose** (or more than three lines of **poetry**) by indenting it one inch from the margin. Double-space, and do not use quotation marks. If

See 55b

you are quoting a single paragraph, do not indent the first line. If you are quoting more than one paragraph, indent the first line of each complete paragraph an additional one-quarter inch. Integrate the quotation into your paper by introducing it with a complete sentence followed by a colon. Place parenthetical documentation one space after the end punctuation.

> According to Hostetler, the Amish were not always hostile to public education:
>> The one-room rural elementary school served the Amish community well in a number of ways. As long as it was a public school, it stood midway between the Amish community and the world. Its influence was tolerable, depending upon the degree of influence the Amish were able to bring to the situation. (196)

2 Integrating Paraphrases and Summaries

Introduce your paraphrases and summaries with identifying tags, and end them with appropriate documentation. By doing so, you make certain that your readers are able to differentiate your own ideas from those of your sources.

Correct (Identifying Tag Differentiates Ideas of Source from Ideas of Writer): Art can be used to uncover many problems that children have at home, in school, or with their friends. For this reason, many therapists use art therapy extensively. According to William Alschuler in *Art and Self-Image,* children's views of themselves in society are often reflected by their art style. For example, a cramped, crowded art style using only a portion of the paper shows a child's limited role (260).

Misleading (Ideas of Source Blend with Ideas of Writer): Art can be used to uncover many problems that children have at home, in school, or with their friends. For this reason, many therapists use art therapy extensively. Children's views of themselves in society are often reflected by their art style. For example, a cramped, crowded art style using only a portion of the paper shows their limited role (Alschuler 260).

EXERCISE 3

Look back at the summary and paraphrase that you wrote for Exercise 2. Write three possible identifying tags for each, varying the verbs you use for attribution and the placement of the identifying tag. Be sure to include appropriate documentation at the end of each passage.

16e Synthesizing Sources

When you write a **synthesis,** you use paraphrase, summary, and quotation to combine material from two or more sources, along with your own ideas, in order to express an original viewpoint. (In this sense, an entire research paper is a synthesis.) You begin synthesizing material by comparing your sources and determining how they are alike and different, where they agree and disagree, and whether they reach the same conclusions. As you identify connections between one source and another or between a source and your own ideas, you develop your own perspective on your subject. It is this viewpoint, summarized in a thesis statement (in the case of an entire paper) or in a topic sentence (in the case of a paragraph), that becomes the focus of your synthesis.

As you write your synthesis, make your points one at a time, and use material from your sources to support these points. Be certain to use identifying tags as well as the transitional words and phrases that your readers will need to follow your discussion. Finally, remember that your ideas, not the ideas of your sources, should be central to your discussion.

The following synthesis was written by a student as part of a research paper.

> Computers have already changed our lives. They carry out (at incredible speed) many of the everyday tasks that make our way of life possible. For example, computer billing, with all its faults, makes modern business possible, and without computers we would not have access to the telephone services or television reception that we take for granted. But computers are more than fast calculators. According to one computer expert, they are well on their way to learning, creating, and someday even thinking (Raphael 21). Another computer expert, Douglas Hofstadter, agrees, saying that someday a computer will have both "will . . . and consciousness" (423). It seems obvious, then, that computers will change our lives even more in the future.

▪ EXERCISE 4

Write a paragraph that synthesizes the two positions you worked with in Exercise 1. (If you like, you may use the sentence comparing the two positions, drafted in response to Exercise 1, as your topic sentence.)

17

Avoiding Plagiarism

❓ FAQs
What is plagiarism? (p. 224)
What material don't I have to document? (p. 225)
How can I be sure that I don't plagiarize? (p. 229)

17a Defining Plagiarism

Plagiarism is presenting another person's ideas or words as if they were your own. Most plagiarism is **unintentional plagiarism**—for example, inadvertently typing a quoted passage into a paper and forgetting to include the quotation marks and documentation. The availability on the Web of information that can be downloaded and pasted into a paper has increased the likelihood of accidental plagiarism. In fact, the freewheeling appropriation and circulation of information that routinely takes place on the Web may give the false impression that this material does not need to be documented. Whether they appear in print or in electronic form, however, the words, ideas, and images of others (including photographs, graphs, charts, and statistics) must be properly documented.

There is a difference, however, between an honest mistake and **intentional plagiarism**—for example, copying sentences from a journal article or submitting a paper that someone else has written. The penalties for unintentional plagiarism may sometimes be severe, but intentional plagiarism is almost always dealt with harshly: students who intentionally plagiarize can receive a failing grade for the paper (or the course) or can even be expelled from school.

COMPUTER TIP academic.cengage.com/eng/kirsznermandell

DETECTING PLAGIARISM

The same technology that has made unintentional plagiarism more common has also made plagiarism easier to detect. By doing a *Google* search, an instructor can quickly find the source of a phrase that has been plagiarized from an Internet source. Some software can search subscription databases and identify plagiarized passages in student papers. *InSite* is a Web-based application that compares, word for word, the information contained on the Web and in *InfoTrac*® College Edition (a subscription database) with passages in student papers. Thus, you can also use *InSite* to search your own drafts for unintentionally plagiarized material before submitting papers to your instructors. Below are the results of an *InSite* originality report indicating that certain parts of a paper have been plagiarized.

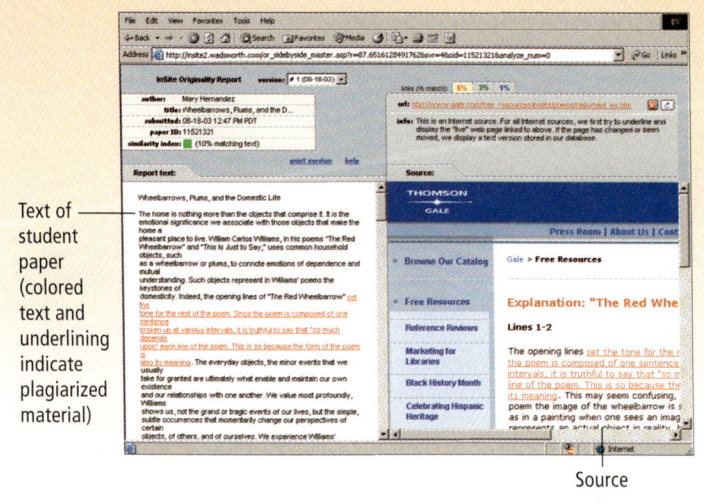

Text of student paper (colored text and underlining indicate plagiarized material)

Source

17b Avoiding Unintentional Plagiarism

The most common cause of unintentional plagiarism is sloppy research habits. To avoid this problem, start your research paper early. Do not cut and paste text from a Web site or full-text database directly into your paper. If you paraphrase, do so correctly by following the advice in 15b; changing a few words here and there is not enough.

> **ESL TIP**
>
> Because writing in a second language can be difficult, you may be tempted to closely follow the syntax and word choice of your sources. Be aware, however, that this practice constitutes plagiarism.

In addition to taking careful notes and distinguishing between your ideas and those of your sources, you must also use proper **documentation**. In general, you must document any words, ideas, and images that you borrow from your sources (whether print or electronic). Of course, certain material need not be documented: **common knowledge** (information most readers probably know), facts available from a variety of reference sources, familiar sayings

See Pts. 4–5

and well-known quotations, and your own original research (interviews and surveys, for example). Information that is another writer's original contribution, however, must be acknowledged. So, although you do not have to document the fact that John F. Kennedy graduated from Harvard in 1940 or that he was elected president in 1960, you do have to document information from a historian's evaluation of his presidency.

> **CLOSE-UP**
>
> **AVOIDING TWO SPECIAL PROBLEMS**
>
> The two following situations can also create problems:
>
> 1. In general, you should not submit a paper to one course that you have already received a grade for in another course. If you intend to substantially rework or expand the paper, however, you may be able to use it—but be sure to get permission from both course instructors.
> 2. Collaborative work presents another problem. If you participate in a collaborative research project, make sure that you clearly identify the sections that each person worked on and that you get guidelines from your instructor for how to document collaborative work.

17c Revising to Eliminate Plagiarism

You can avoid plagiarism by using documentation wherever it is required and by following these guidelines:

1 Enclose Borrowed Words in Quotation Marks

Original: Historically, only a handful of families have dominated the fireworks industry in the West. Details such as chemical recipes and mixing procedures were cloaked in secrecy and passed down from one generation to the next. . . . One effect of familial secretiveness is that, until recent decades, basic pyrotechnic research was rarely performed, and even when it was, the results were not generally reported in scientific journals. (Conkling, John A. "Pyrotechnics." *Scientific American* July 1990: 96. Print.)

Plagiarism: John A. Conkling points out that until recently, little scientific research was done on the chemical properties of fireworks, and when it was, the results were not generally reported in scientific journals (96).

Even though the student writer documents the source of his information, he uses the source's exact words without placing them in quotation marks.

Correct (Borrowed Words in Quotation Marks): John A. Conkling points out that until recently, little scientific research was done on the chemical properties of fireworks, and when it was, "the results were not generally reported in scientific journals" (96).

Correct (Paraphrase): John A. Conkling points out that the little research conducted on the chemical composition of fireworks was seldom reported in the scientific literature (96).

COMPUTER TIP academic.cengage.com/eng/kirsznermandell

Plagiarism and Internet Sources

Any time you download text from the Internet, you run the risk of committing unintentional plagiarism. To avoid the possibility of plagiarism, follow these guidelines:

- Download information into individual files so that you can keep track of your sources.
- Do not simply cut and paste blocks of downloaded text into your paper; first summarize or paraphrase this material.
- If you record the exact words of your source, enclose them in quotation marks.
- Whether your information is from emails, online discussion groups, listservs, or Web sites, give proper credit by providing appropriate documentation.
- Always document figures, tables, charts, and graphs obtained from the Internet or from any other electronic source.

---

2 Do Not Imitate a Source's Syntax and Phrasing

Original: Let's be clear: this wish for politically correct casting goes only one way, the way designed to redress the injuries of centuries. When Pat Carroll, who is a woman, plays Falstaff, who is not, casting is considered a stroke of brilliance. When Josette Simon, who is black, plays Maggie in *After the Fall*, a part Arthur Miller patterned after Marilyn Monroe and which has traditionally been played not by white women, but by blonde white women, it is hailed as a breakthrough.

But when the pendulum moves the other way, the actors' union balks. (Quindlen, Anna. "Error, Stage Left." *New York Times* 12 Aug. 1990, sec. 1: 21. Print.)

Plagiarism: Let us be honest. The desire for politically appropriate casting goes in only one direction, the direction intended to make up for the damage done over hundreds of years. When Pat Carroll, a female, is cast as Falstaff, a male, the decision is a brilliant one. When Josette Simon, a black woman, is cast as Maggie in *After the Fall*, a role that Arthur Miller based on Marilyn Monroe and that has usually been played by a woman who is not only white but also blonde, it is considered a major advance.

But when the shoe is on the other foot, the actors' union resists (Quindlen 21).

Although this student writer does not use the exact words of her source, she closely imitates the original's syntax and phrasing, simply substituting synonyms for the author's words.

Correct (Paraphrase; One Distinctive Phrase Placed in Quotation Marks): According to Anna Quindlen, the actors' union supports "politically correct casting" (21) only when it means casting a woman or minority group member in a role created for a male or a Caucasian. Thus, it is acceptable for actress Pat Carroll to play Falstaff or for black actress Josette Simon to play Marilyn Monroe; in fact, casting decisions such as these are praised. But when it comes to casting a Caucasian in a role intended for an African American, Asian, or Hispanic, the union objects (21).

NOTE: Although the parenthetical documentation at the end identifies the passage's source, the quotation requires separate documentation.

3 Document Statistics Obtained from a Source

Although many people assume that statistics are common knowledge, they are usually the result of original research and must, therefore, be documented. Moreover, providing the source of the statistics helps readers to assess their reliability.

Correct: According to one study, male drivers between the ages of sixteen and twenty-four accounted for the majority of accidents. Of 303 accidents recorded almost one half took place before the drivers were legally allowed to drive at eighteen (Schuman et al. 1027).

4 Differentiate Your Words and Ideas from Those of Your Source

Original: At some colleges and universities traditional survey courses of world and English literature . . . have been scrapped or diluted. At others they are in peril. At still others they will be. What replaces them is sometimes a mere option of electives, sometimes "multicultural" courses introducing material from Third World cultures and thinning out an already thin sampling of Western writings, and sometimes courses geared especially to issues of class, race, and gender. Given the notorious lethargy of academic decision-making, there has probably been more clamor than change; but if there's enough clamor, there will be change.

(Howe, Irving. "The Value of the Canon." *New Republic* 2 Feb. 1991: 40–47. Print.)

> **Plagiarism:** Debates about expanding the literary canon take place at many colleges and universities across the United States. At many universities, the Western literature survey courses have been edged out by courses that emphasize minority concerns. These courses are "thinning out an already thin sampling of Western writings" in favor of courses geared especially to issues of "class, race, and gender" (Howe 40).

Because the student writer does not differentiate his ideas from those of his source, it appears that only the quotations in the last sentence are borrowed when, in fact, the first sentence also owes a debt to the original. The writer should have clearly identified the boundaries of the borrowed material by introducing it with an identifying tag and ending with documentation. (Note that a quotation *always* requires its own documentation.)

> **Correct:** Debates about expanding the literary canon take place at many colleges and universities across the United States. According to critic Irving Howe, at many universities the Western literature survey courses have been edged out by courses that emphasize minority concerns (41). These courses, says Howe, are "thinning out an already thin sampling of Western writings" in favor of "courses geared especially to issues of class, race, and gender" (40).

CHECKLIST

AVOIDING PLAGIARISM

☐ **Take careful notes.** Be sure you have recorded information from your sources carefully and accurately.

☐ **In your notes, clearly identify borrowed material.** In handwritten notes, put all words borrowed from your sources inside circled quotation marks, and enclose your own comments within brackets. If you are taking notes on a computer, boldface all quotation marks.

☐ **In your paper, differentiate your ideas from those of your sources** by clearly introducing borrowed material with an identifying tag and by following it with documentation.

☐ **Enclose all direct quotations** used in your paper within quotation marks.

☐ **Review all paraphrases and summaries** in your paper to make certain they are in your own words and that any distinctive words and phrases from a source are quoted.

(continued)

> **AVOIDING PLAGIARISM** *(continued)*
> - ☐ **Document all quoted material and all paraphrases and summaries** of your sources.
> - ☐ **Document all information** that is open to dispute or that is not common knowledge.
> - ☐ **Document all opinions, conclusions, figures, tables, statistics, graphs, and charts** taken from a source.
> - ☐ **Never submit the work of another person as your own.** Do not buy a paper from an online paper mill or use a paper written by a friend. In addition, never include in your paper passages that have been written by a friend, relative, or writing tutor.
> - ☐ **Never use sources that you have not actually read (or invent sources that do not exist).**

■ EXERCISE

The following paragraph uses material from three sources, but its student author has neglected to cite them. After reading the paragraph and the three sources that follow it, identify the material that has been quoted directly from a source. Compare the wording to the original for accuracy, and insert quotation marks where necessary, making sure the quoted passages fit smoothly into the paragraph. Differentiate the ideas of the student from those of each of the three sources by using identifying tags to introduce any quotations. (If you think the student did not need to quote a passage, paraphrase it instead.) Finally, add parenthetical documentation for each piece of information that requires it.

Student Paragraph

Oral history is an important way of capturing certain aspects of the past that might otherwise be lost. While history books relate the stories of great men and great events, rarely do they include the experiences of ordinary people—slaves, concentration camp survivors, and the illiterate, for example. By providing information about the people and emotions of the past, oral history makes sense of the present and gives a glimpse of the likely future. But because any particular rendition of a life history relies heavily on personal memory, great care must be taken to evaluate and explain the context of an oral history. Like any other historical account, oral history is just one of many possible versions of an individual's past.

Source 1

Oral history relies heavily on memory, a notoriously malleable entity; people remake the past in light of present concerns and knowledge. Yet not all memories are false, and oral history gives us testimony that might otherwise be lost—stories of slaves, of concentration camp survivors, of the illiterate and the obscure, of the legion "ordinary people" who rarely find their way into the history books. Oral history gives us the human element, the thoughts and emotions and confusions that lie beneath the calm surface of written documents. Even when people remake the past because memories are faulty or unbearable, we can learn much about the ways in which the past affects the present. (Freedman, Jean R. "Never Underestimate the Power of a Bus: My Journey to Oral History." *Oral History Review* 29.2 [2002]: 30. Print.)

Source 2

[There is a] widely held view that history belongs to great men and great events, not ordinary people or ordinary life. Yet we know that "ordinary" people in our local districts have important stories to tell. . . . Local histories tell us, on the one hand, that things were done differently in the past, but on the other hand, that in essence people and emotions were much the same. We need to learn from the past to make sense of the present, and get a glimpse of the likely future. (Gregg, Alison. "Planning and Managing an Oral History Collection." *Aplis* 13.4 [2000]: 174. Print.)

Source 3

One aspect of oral history . . . concerns the way in which any particular rendition of a life history is a product of the personal present. It is well-recognized that chronicles of the past are invariably a product of the present, so that different "presents" inspire different versions of the past. Just as all historical accounts—the very questions posed or the interpretive framework imposed—are informed by the historian's present, so, too, is a life history structured by both the interviewer's and the narrator's present. . . . [O]ral history cannot be treated as a source of some narrative truth, but rather as one of many possible versions of an individual's past. . . . [and] the stories told in an oral history are not simply the source of explanation, but rather require explanation. (Honig, Emily. "Getting to the Source: Striking Lives: Oral History and the Politics of Memory." *Journal of Women's History* 9.1 [1997]: 139. Print.)

PART 4

Documenting Sources: MLA Style

18 MLA Documentation Style 239
18a Using MLA Style 239
18b MLA-Style Manuscript Guidelines 264
18c Sample MLA-Style Research Paper 266

DIRECTORY OF MLA PARENTHETICAL REFERENCES

1. A work by a single author (p. 240)
2. A work by two or three authors (p. 240)
3. A work by more than three authors (p. 241)
4. A work in multiple volumes (p. 241)
5. A work without a listed author (p. 241)
6. A work that is one page long (p. 241)
7. An indirect source (p. 241)
8. More than one work (p. 241)
9. A literary work (p. 242)
10. The Bible (p. 242)
11. An entire work (p. 243)
12. Two or more authors with the same last name (p. 243)
13. A government document or a corporate author (p. 243)
14. A legal source (p. 243)
15. An electronic source (p. 243)

DIRECTORY OF MLA WORKS-CITED LIST ENTRIES

PRINT SOURCES: *Entries for Books*

Authors

1. A book by one author (p. 246)
2. A book by two or three authors (p. 246)
3. A book by more than three authors (p. 247)
4. Two or more books by the same author (p. 247)
5. A book by a corporate author (p. 247)
6. An edited book (p. 247)

Editions, Multivolume Works, Forewords, Translations, and Sacred Works

7. A subsequent edition of a book (p. 248)
8. A republished book (p. 248)
9. A book in a series (p. 248)
10. A multivolume work (p. 248)
11. The foreword, preface, or afterword of a book (p. 248)
12. A book with a title within its title (p. 249)
13. A translation (p. 249)
14. The Bible (p. 249)

Parts of Books

15. A short story, play, or poem in an anthology (p. 249)
16. A short story, play, poem, or essay in a collection of an author's work (p. 249)
17. An essay in an anthology (p. 250)
18. More than one work from the same anthology (p. 250)
19. An article in a reference book (signed/unsigned) (p. 250)

Dissertations, Pamphlets, Government Publications, and Legal Sources

20. A dissertation (published/unpublished) (p. 250)
21. A pamphlet (p. 251)
22. A government publication (p. 251)
23. A legal source (p. 251)

PRINT SOURCES: Entries for Articles

Articles in Scholarly Journals

24. An article in a scholarly journal (p. 253)

Articles in Magazines and Newspapers

25. An article in a weekly magazine (signed/unsigned) (p. 253)
26. An article in a monthly magazine (p. 253)
27. An article that does not appear on consecutive pages (p. 253)
28. An article in a newspaper (signed/unsigned) (p. 253)
29. An editorial in a newspaper (p. 254)
30. A letter to the editor of a newspaper (p. 254)
31. A book review in a newspaper (p. 254)
32. An article with a title within its title (p. 254)

ENTRIES FOR MISCELLANEOUS PRINT AND NONPRINT SOURCES

Lectures and Interviews

33. A lecture (p. 254)
34. A personal interview (p. 254)
35. A published interview (p. 254)

Letters

36. A personal letter (p. 255)
37. A letter published in a collection (p. 255)
38. A letter in a library's archives (p. 255)

Films, Videotapes, Radio and Television Programs, and Recordings
39. A film (p. 255)
40. A videotape, DVD, or laser disc (p. 255)
41. A radio or television program (p. 255)
42. A recording (p. 255)

Paintings, Photographs, Cartoons, and Advertisements
43. A painting (p. 256)
44. A photograph (p. 256)
45. A cartoon or comic strip (p. 256)
46. An advertisement (p. 256)

ELECTRONIC SOURCES: *Entries from Internet Sites*

Internet-Specific Sources
47. An entire Web site (p. 258)
48. A document within a Web site (p. 258)
49. A home page for a course (p. 258)
50. A personal home page (p. 258)
51. A radio program accessed from an Internet archive (p. 258)
52. An email (p. 258)
53. An online posting (p. 258)

Books, Articles, Reviews, Letters, and Reference Works on the Internet
54. A book (p. 258)
55. An article in a scholarly journal (p. 258)
56. An article in a magazine (p. 259)
57. An article in a newspaper (p. 259)
58. An article in a newsletter (p. 259)
59. A review (p. 259)
60. A letter to the editor (p. 259)
61. An article in an encyclopedia (p. 259)
62. A government publication (p. 260)

Paintings, Photographs, Cartoons, and Maps on the Internet
63. A painting (p. 260)
64. A photograph (p. 260)
65. A cartoon (p. 260)
66. A map (p. 260)

ELECTRONIC SOURCES: *Entries from Online Databases*

Journal Articles, Magazine Articles, News Services, and Dissertations from Online Databases

67. A scholarly journal article (p. 261)
68. A monthly magazine article (p. 261)
69. A news service (p. 261)
70. A newspaper article (p. 261)
71. A published dissertation (p. 261)

OTHER ELECTRONIC SOURCES

DVD-ROMs and CD-ROMs

72. A nonperiodical publication on DVD-ROM or CD-ROM (p. 262)
73. A periodical publication on DVD-ROM or CD-ROM (p. 262)

18

MLA Documentation Style

❓ FAQs

When should I use MLA documentation? (p. 239)
How do I document sources I get from the Internet? (p. 256)
How do I type a works-cited list? (p. 266)
Does my paper need a title page? (p. 266)
What should an MLA paper look like? (p. 267)

Documentation is the formal acknowledgment of the sources you use in your paper. This chapter explains and illustrates the documentation style recommended by the Modern Language Association (MLA). Chapter 19 discusses the documentation style of the American Psychological Association (APA), Chapter 20 gives an overview of the format recommended by *The Chicago Manual of Style*, and Chapter 21 presents the formats recommended by the Council of Science Editors (CSE) and organizations in other disciplines.

18a Using MLA Style

MLA style* is required by instructors of English and other languages as well as by many instructors in other humanities disciplines. MLA documentation has three parts: *parenthetical references in the body of the paper (also known as in-text citations), a works-cited list, and content notes.*

1 Parenthetical References

MLA documentation uses parenthetical references in the body of the paper keyed to a works-cited list at the end of the paper. A typical parenthetical reference consists of the author's last name and a page number.

> The colony appealed to many idealists in Europe (Kelley 132).

If you state the author's name or the title of the work in your discussion, do not include it in the parenthetical reference.

> Penn's political motivation is discussed by Joseph J. Kelley in *Pennsylvania, The Colonial Years, 1681-1776* (44).

---

*MLA documentation style follows the guidelines set in the *MLA Handbook for Writers of Research Papers*, 7th ed. (New York: MLA, 2009).

To distinguish two or more sources by the same author, include the title after the author's name. If the title is long, use an abbreviated version. When you shorten a title, begin with the word by which the work is alphabetized in the list of works cited.

Penn emphasized his religious motivation (Kelley, *Pennsylvania* 116).

> **CLOSE-UP**
>
> **PUNCTUATING WITH MLA PARENTHETICAL REFERENCES**
>
> **Paraphrases and Summaries** Parenthetical references are placed *before* the sentence's end punctuation.
>
> Penn's writings epitomize seventeenth-century religious thought (Dengler and Curtis 72).
>
> **Quotations Run In with the Text** Parenthetical references are placed *after* the quotation but *before* the end punctuation.
>
> As Ross says, "Penn followed his conscience in all matters" (127).
>
> According to Williams, "Penn's utopian vision was informed by his Quaker beliefs . . ." (72).
>
> **Quotations Set Off from the Text** When you quote more than four lines of prose or more than three lines of poetry, parenthetical references are placed one space *after* the end punctuation.
>
> According to Arthur Smith, William Penn envisioned a state based on his religious principles:
>
>> Pennsylvania would be a commonwealth in which all individuals would follow God's truth and develop according to God's law. For Penn, this concept of government was self-evident. It would be a mistake to see Pennsylvania as anything but an expression of Penn's religious beliefs. (314)

See 55b

SAMPLE MLA PARENTHETICAL REFERENCES

1. A Work by a Single Author

Fairy tales reflect the emotions and fears of children (Bettelheim 23).

2. A Work by Two or Three Authors

The historian's main job is to search for clues and solve mysteries (Davidson and Lytle 6).

With the advent of behaviorism, psychology began a new phase of inquiry (Cowen, Barbo, and Crum 31-34).

3. A Work by More Than Three Authors

List only the first author, followed by et al. ("and others").

> Helping each family reach its goals for healthy child development and overall family well-being was the primary approach of Project EAGLE (Bartle et al. 35).

Or, list the last names of all authors in the order in which they appear on the work's title page.

> Helping each family reach its goals for healthy child development and overall family well-being was the primary approach of Project EAGLE (Bartle, Couchonnal, Canda, and Staker 35).

4. A Work in Multiple Volumes

If you list more than one volume of a multivolume work in your works-cited list, include the appropriate volume and page number (separated by a colon followed by a space).

> Gurney is incorrect when he says that a twelve-hour limit is negotiable (6: 128).

5. A Work without a Listed Author

Use the full title (if brief) or a shortened version of the title (if long), beginning with the word by which it is alphabetized in the works-cited list.

> The group issued an apology a short time later ("Satire Lost" 22).

6. A Work That Is One Page Long

Do not include a page reference for a one-page article.

> Sixty percent of Arab Americans work in white-collar jobs (El-Badru).

7. An Indirect Source

If you use a statement by one author that is quoted in the work of another author, indicate that the material is from an indirect source with the abbreviation qtd. in ("quoted in").

> According to Valli and Lucas, "the form of the symbol is an icon or picture of some aspect of the thing or activity being symbolized" (qtd. in Wilcox 120).

8. More Than One Work

Cite each work as you normally would, separating one citation from another with a semicolon.

> The Brooklyn Bridge has been used as a subject by many American artists (McCullough 144; Tashjian 58).

NOTE: Long parenthetical references can distract readers. Whenever possible, present them as **content notes**.

See 18a3

9. A Literary Work

When citing a work of **fiction,** it is often helpful to include more than the author's name and the page number in the parenthetical citation. Follow the page number with a semicolon, and then add any additional information that might be helpful.

> In *Moby-Dick,* Melville refers to a whaling expedition funded by Louis XIV of France (151; ch. 24).

Parenthetical references to **poetry** do not include page numbers. In parenthetical references to *long poems,* cite division and line numbers, separating them with a period.

> In the *Aeneid,* Virgil describes the ships as cleaving the "green woods reflected in the calm water" (8.124).

(In this citation, the reference is to book 8, line 124 of the *Aeneid.*) When citing *short poems,* identify the poet and the poem in the text of the paper, and use line numbers in the citation.

> In "A Song in the Front Yard," Brooks's speaker says, "I've stayed in the front yard all my life / I want a peek at the back" (lines 1-2).

NOTE: When citing lines of a poem, include the word **line** (or **lines**) in the first parenthetical reference; use just the line numbers in subsequent references.

When citing a **play,** include the act, scene, and line numbers (in arabic numerals), separated by periods. Titles of well-known literary works (such as Shakespeare's plays) are often abbreviated (*Mac.* **2.2.14-16**).

10. The Bible

MLA style requires that a biblical citation include the version of the Bible (italicized) and the book (abbreviated if longer than four letters, but not italicized or enclosed in quotation marks), followed by the chapter and verse numbers (separated by a period).

> The cynicism of the speaker is apparent when he says, "All things are wearisome; no man can speak of them all" (*New English Bible,* Eccles. 1.8).

NOTE: The first time you use a biblical citation, include the version in your parenthetical reference; after that, only include the book. If you are using more than one version of the Bible, however, include the version in each in-text citation.

11. An Entire Work
When citing an entire work, include the author's name and the work's title in the text of your paper rather than in a parenthetical reference.

> Lois Lowry's *Gathering Blue* is set in a technologically backward village.

12. Two or More Authors with the Same Last Name
To distinguish authors with the same last name, include their initials in your parenthetical references.

> Recent increases in crime have caused thousands of urban homeowners to install alarms (L. Cooper 115). Some of these alarms use sophisticated sensors that were developed by the army (D. Cooper 76).

13. A Government Document or a Corporate Author
Cite such works using the organization's name (usually abbreviated) followed by the page number (**Amer. Automobile Assn. 34**). You can avoid long parenthetical references by working the organization's name (not abbreviated) into your paper.

> According to the President's Commission for the Study of Ethical Problems in Medicine and Biomedical and Behavioral Research, the issues relating to euthanasia are complicated (76).

14. A Legal Source
Titles of acts or laws that appear in the text of your paper or in the works-cited list should not be italicized or enclosed in quotation marks. In the parenthetical reference, titles are usually abbreviated, and the act or law is referred to by sections. Include the USC (United States Code) and the year the act or law was passed (if relevant).

> Such research should include investigations into the cause, diagnosis, early detection, prevention, control, and treatment of autism (42 USC 284q, 2000).

Names of legal cases are usually abbreviated (**Roe v. Wade**). They are italicized in the text of your paper but not in the works-cited list.

> In *Goodridge v. Department of Public Health*, the court ruled that the Commonwealth of Massachusetts had not adequately provided a reasonable constitutional cause for barring homosexual couples from civil marriages (2003).

15. An Electronic Source
If a reference to an electronic source includes paragraph numbers rather than page numbers, use the abbreviation **par.** or **pars.** followed by the paragraph number or numbers.

The earliest type of movie censorship came in the form of licensing fees, and in Deer River, Minnesota, "a licensing fee of $200 was deemed not excessive for a town of 1000" (Ernst, par. 20).

If the electronic source has no page or paragraph numbers, try to cite the work in your discussion rather than in a parenthetical reference. By consulting your works-cited list, readers will be able to determine that the source is electronic and may therefore not have page numbers.

In her article "Limited Horizons," Lynne Cheney observes that schools do best when students read literature not for practical information but for its insights into the human condition.

2 Works-Cited List

The **works-cited list,** which appears at the end of your paper, is an alphabetical listing of all the research materials you cite. Double-space within and between entries on the list, and indent the second and subsequent lines of each entry one-half inch. (**See 18b** for full manuscript guidelines.)

PRINT SOURCES: Entries for Books

Book citations include the author's name; book title (italicized); and publication information (place, publisher, date, publication medium). Figures 18.1 and 18.2 show where you can find this information.

FIGURE 18.1 Title page of a book showing the location of the information needed for documentation.

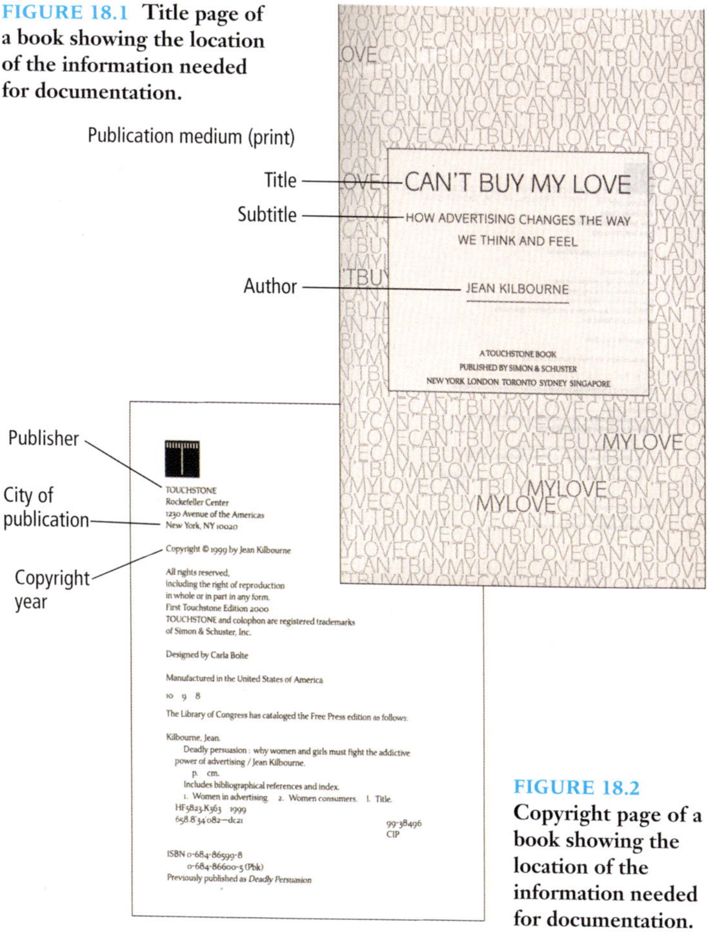

FIGURE 18.2 Copyright page of a book showing the location of the information needed for documentation.

In your works-cited list citation, capitalize all major words of the book's title except articles, coordinating conjunctions, prepositions, and the *to* of an infinitive (unless such a word is the first or last word of the title or subtitle). Do not italicize the period that follows a book title. The following is a works-cited entry for the book pictured on page 245.

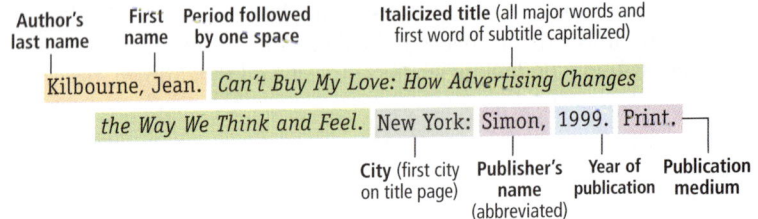

Author's last name | First name | Period followed by one space | Italicized title (all major words and first word of subtitle capitalized)

Kilbourne, Jean. *Can't Buy My Love: How Advertising Changes the Way We Think and Feel.* New York: Simon, 1999. Print.

City (first city on title page) | Publisher's name (abbreviated) | Year of publication | Publication medium

> **CLOSE-UP**
>
> **PUBLISHERS' NAMES**
>
> MLA requires abbreviated forms of publishers' names in the list of works cited. In general, omit articles; abbreviations, such as *Inc.* and *Corp.*; and words such as *Publishers*, *Books*, and *Press*. If the publisher's name includes a person's name, use the last name only. Finally, use standard abbreviations whenever you can—*UP* for University Press and *P* for Press, for example.
>
> | Name | Abbreviation |
> |---|---|
> | Basic Books | Basic |
> | Government Printing Office | GPO |
> | The Modern Language Association of America | MLA |
> | Oxford University Press | Oxford UP |
> | Alfred A. Knopf, Inc. | Knopf |
> | Random House, Inc. | Random |
> | University of Chicago Press | U of Chicago P |

Authors

1. A Book by One Author

Bettelheim, Bruno. *The Uses of Enchantment: The Meaning and Importance of Fairy Tales.* New York: Knopf, 1976. Print.

2. A Book by Two or Three Authors

List the first author with last name first. List subsequent authors with first name first in the order in which they appear on the title page.

Peters, Michael A., and Nicholas C. Burbules. *Poststructuralism and Educational Research.* Lanham: Rowman, 2004. Print.

3. A Book by More Than Three Authors

List the first author only, followed by **et al.** ("and others").

> Badawi, El Said, et al. *Modern Written Arabic.* London: Routledge, 2004. Print.

Or, include all the authors in the order in which they appear on the title page.

> Badawi, El Said, Daud A. Abdu, Mike Carfter, and Adrian Gully. *Modern Written Arabic.* London: Routledge, 2004. Print.

4. Two or More Books by the Same Author

List books by the same author in alphabetical order by title. After the first entry, use three unspaced hyphens followed by a period in place of the author's name.

> Ede, Lisa. *Situating Composition: Composition Studies and the Politics of Location.* Carbondale: Southern Illinois UP, 2004. Print.
>
> ---. *Work in Progress.* 6th ed. Boston: Bedford, 2004. Print.

NOTE: If the author is the editor or translator of the second entry, place a comma and the appropriate abbreviation after the hyphens (**---, ed.**). See entry 6 for more on edited books and entry 13 for more on translated books.

5. A Book by a Corporate Author

A book is cited by its corporate author when individual members of the association, commission, or committee that produced it are not identified on the title page.

> American Automobile Association. *Western Canada and Alaska.* Heathrow: AAA, 2004. Print.

6. An Edited Book

An edited book is a work prepared for publication by a person other than the author. If your focus is on the *author's* work, begin your citation with the author's name. After the title, include the abbreviation **Ed.** ("Edited by"), followed by the editor or editors.

> Twain, Mark. *Adventures of Huckleberry Finn.* Ed. Michael Patrick Hearn. New York: Norton, 2001. Print.

If your focus is on the *editor's* work, begin your citation with the editor's name followed by the abbreviation **ed.** ("editor") if there is one editor or **eds.** ("editors") if there are more than one. After the title, give the author's name, preceded by the word **By**.

> Hearn, Michael Patrick, ed. *Adventures of Huckleberry Finn.* By Mark Twain. New York: Norton, 2001. Print.

Editions, Multivolume Works, Forewords, Translations, and Sacred Works

7. A Subsequent Edition of a Book
When citing an edition other than the first, include the edition number that appears on the work's title page.

> Wilson, Charles Banks. *Search for the Native American Purebloods.*
> 3rd ed. Norman: U of Oklahoma P, 2000. Print.

8. A Republished Book
Include the original publication date after the title of a republished book—for example, a paperback version of a hardcover book.

> Wharton, Edith. *The House of Mirth.* 1905. New York: Scribner's, 1975. Print.

9. A Book in a Series
If the title page indicates that the book is a part of a series, include the series name, neither italicized nor enclosed in quotation marks, and the series number, followed by a period, after the publication information.

> Davis, Bertram H. *Thomas Percy.* Boston: Twayne, 1981. Print. Twayne's English Authors Ser. 313.

10. A Multivolume Work
When all volumes of a multivolume work have the same title, include the number of the volume you are using.

> Fisch, Max H., ed. *Writings of Charles S. Peirce: A Chronological Edition.*
> Vol. 4. Bloomington: Indiana UP, 2000. Print.

If you use two or more volumes that have the same title, cite the entire work.

> Fisch, Max H., ed. *Writings of Charles S. Peirce: A Chronological Edition.*
> 6 vols. Bloomington: Indiana UP, 2000. Print.

When the volume you are using has an individual title, you may cite the title without mentioning any other volumes.

> Mareš, Milan. *Fuzzy Cooperative Games: Cooperation with Vague Expectations.* New York: Physica-Verlag, 2001. Print.

If you wish, however, you may include supplemental information, such as the number of the volume, the title of the entire work, the total number of volumes, or the inclusive publication dates.

11. The Foreword, Preface, or Afterword of a Book

> Campbell, Richard. Preface. *Media and Culture: An Introduction to Mass Communication.* By Bettina Fabos. Boston: Bedford, 2005. vi-xi. Print.

12. A Book with a Title within Its Title

If the book you are citing contains a title that is normally italicized (a novel, play, or long poem, for example), do not italicize the interior title.

> Fulton, Joe B. *Mark Twain in the Margins: The Quarry Farm Marginalia and A Connecticut Yankee in King Arthur's Court.* Tuscaloosa: U of Alabama P, 2000. Print.

If the book you are citing contains a title that is normally enclosed in quotation marks, keep the quotation marks.

> Hawkins, Hunt, and Brian W. Shaffer, eds. *Approaches to Teaching Conrad's "Heart of Darkness" and "The Secret Sharer."* New York: MLA, 2002. Print.

13. A Translation

> García Márquez, Gabriel. *One Hundred Years of Solitude.* Trans. Gregory Rabassa. New York: Avon, 1991. Print.

14. The Bible

Italicize the title, and give full publication information.

> *The New English Bible with the Apocrypha.* Oxford Study ed. New York: Oxford UP, 1976. Print.

Parts of Books

15. A Short Story, Play, or Poem in an Anthology

> Chopin, Kate. "The Storm." *Literature: Reading, Reacting, Writing.* Ed. Laurie G. Kirszner and Stephen R. Mandell. 6th ed. Boston: Wadsworth, 2007. 281-85. Print.
>
> Shakespeare, William. *Othello, the Moor of Venice. Shakespeare: Six Plays and the Sonnets.* Ed. Thomas Marc Parrott and Edward Hubler. New York: Scribner's, 1956. 145-91. Print.

See entry 18 for information on how to cite more than one work from the same anthology.

16. A Short Story, Play, Poem, or Essay in a Collection of an Author's Work

> Bukowski, Charles. "lonely hearts." *The Flash of Lightning behind the Mountain: New Poems.* New York: Ecco, 2004. 115-16. Print.

NOTE: The title of the poem is not capitalized because it appears in lowercase letters in the original.

17. An Essay in an Anthology

Even if you cite only one page of an essay in your paper, supply inclusive page numbers for the entire essay.

> Crevel, René. "From *Babylon*." *Surrealist Painters and Poets: An Anthology*.
>
> Ed. Mary Ann Caws. Cambridge: MIT P, 2001. 175-77. Print.

18. More Than One Work from the Same Anthology

List each work from the same anthology separately, followed by a cross-reference to the entire anthology. Also, list complete publication information for the anthology itself.

> Agar, Eileen. "Am I a Surrealist?" Caws 3-7.
>
> Caws, Mary Ann, ed. *Surrealist Painters and Poets: An Anthology*.
>
> Cambridge: MIT P, 2001. Print.
>
> Crevel, René. "From *Babylon*." Caws 175-77.

19. An Article in a Reference Book (Signed/Unsigned)

For a signed article, begin with the author's name. For unfamiliar reference books, include full publication information.

> Drabble, Margaret. "Expressionism." *The Oxford Companion to English*
>
> *Literature*. 6th ed. New York: Oxford UP, 2000. Print.

If the article is unsigned, begin with the title. For familiar reference books, do not include full publication information.

> "Cubism." *The Encyclopedia Americana*. 2004 ed. Print.

NOTE: Omit page numbers when the reference book lists entries alphabetically. If you are listing one definition among several from a dictionary, include the abbreviation **Def.** ("Definition") along with the letter and/or number that corresponds to the definition.

> "Justice." Def. 2b. *The Concise Oxford Dictionary*. 10th ed. 1999. Print.

Dissertations, Pamphlets, Government Publications, and Legal Sources

20. A Dissertation (Published/Unpublished)

Cite a published dissertation the same way you would cite a book, but add relevant dissertation information before the publication information.

> Rodriguez, Jason Anthony. *Bureaucracy and Altruism: Managing the*
>
> *Contradictions of Teaching*. Diss. U of Texas at Arlington, 2003.
>
> Ann Arbor: UMI, 2004. Print.

NOTE: University Microfilms International (UMI), which publishes most of the dissertations in the United States, is also available online by subscription. For the proper format for citing online databases, see entries 67–71.

Use quotation marks for the title of an unpublished dissertation.

> Bon Tempo, Carl Joseph. "Americans at the Gate: The Politics of American
> Refugee Policy." Diss. U of Virginia, 2004. Print.

21. A Pamphlet

Cite a pamphlet as you would a book. If no author is listed, begin with the title (italicized).

> *Choosing the Right Digital Camera*. Rochester: Kodak, 2004. Print.

22. A Government Publication

If the publication has no listed author, begin with the name of the government, followed by the name of the agency. You may use an abbreviation if its meaning is clear: **United States. Cong. Senate.**

> United States. Office of Consumer Affairs. *2003 Consumer's Resource
> Handbook*. Washington: GPO, 2003. Print.

When citing two or more publications by the same government, use three unspaced hyphens (followed by a period) in place of the name for the second and subsequent entries. When you cite more than one work from the same agency of that government, use an additional set of unspaced hyphens in place of the agency name.

> United States. FAA. *Passenger Airline Safety in the Twenty-First Century*.
> Washington: GPO, 2003. Print.
>
> ---. ---. *Recycled Air in Passenger Airline Cabins*. Washington: GPO, 2002. Print.

23. A Legal Source

In general, you do not need a works-cited entry for familiar historical documents. Parenthetical references in the text are sufficient—for example, **US Const., art. 3, sec. 2**. If you cite an act in the works-cited list, include the name of the act, its Public Law (Pub. L.) number its Statutes at Large (Stat.) cataloging number, its enactment date, and its publication medium.

> Children's Health Act. Pub. L. 106-310. 114. Stat. 1101. 17 Oct. 2000. Print.

In works-cited entries for legal cases, abbreviate names of cases, but spell out the first important word of each party's name. Include the volume number, abbreviated name (not italicized), and inclusive page numbers of the law report; the name of the deciding court; the decision year; and publication information for the source. Do not italicize the case name in the works-cited list.

> Abbott v. Blades. 544 US 929. Supreme Court of the US. 2005. *United
> States Reports*. Washington: GPO, 2007. Print.

PRINT SOURCES: Entries for Articles

Article citations include the author's name; the title of the article (in quotation marks); the title of the periodical (italicized); the volume and issue numbers (when applicable; see below); the year or date of publication; the pages on which the full article appears, without the abbreviations *p.* or *pp.*; and the publication medium. Figure 18.3 shows where you can find this information.

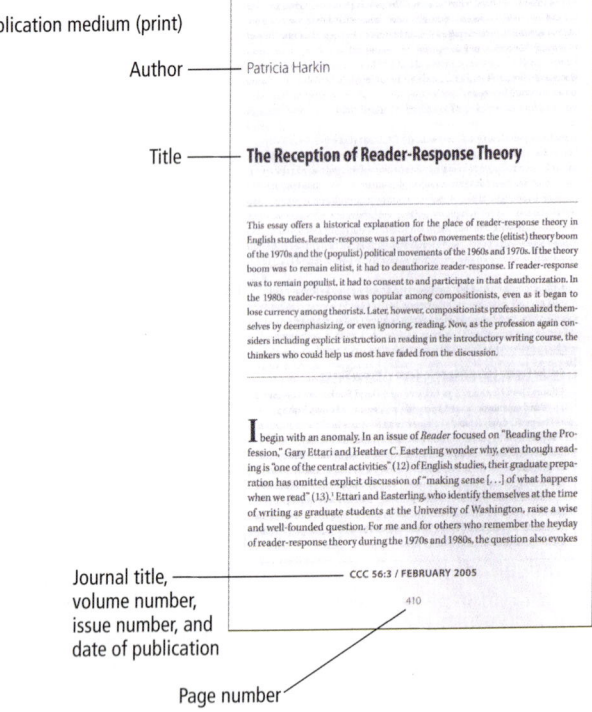

FIGURE 18.3 First page of an article showing the location of the information needed for documentation.

The following is a works-cited entry for the above article.

Harkin, Patricia. "The Reception of Reader-Response Theory." *College Composition and Communication* 56.3 (2005): 410-25. Print.

Articles in Scholarly Journals

24. An Article in a Scholarly Journal
MLA guidelines now recommend that you include both the volume number and the issue number (separated by a period) for all scholarly journal articles that you cite, regardless of whether they are paginated continuously through an annual volume or separately in each issue. Follow the volume and issue numbers with the year of publication (in parentheses), the inclusive page numbers, and the publication medium.

> Siderits, Mark. "Perceiving Particulars: A Buddhist Defense." *Philosophy East and West* 54.3 (2004): 367-83. Print.

Articles in Magazines and Newspapers

25. An Article in a Weekly Magazine (Signed/Unsigned)
For signed articles, start with the author, last name first. In dates, the day precedes the month (abbreviated except for May, June, and July).

> Corliss, Richard. "His Days in Hollywood." *Time* 14 June 2004: 56-62. Print.

For unsigned articles, start with the title of the article.

> "Ronald Reagan." *National Review* 28 June 2004: 14-17. Print.

26. An Article in a Monthly Magazine

> Thomas, Evan. "John Paul Jones." *American History* Aug. 2003: 22-25. Print.

27. An Article That Does Not Appear on Consecutive Pages
When, for example, an article begins on page 120 and then skips to page 186, include only the first page number, followed by a plus sign.

> Di Giovanni, Janine. "The Shiites of Iraq." *National Geographic* June 2004: 62+. Print.

28. An Article in a Newspaper (Signed/Unsigned)

> Krantz, Matt. "Stock Success Not Exactly Unparalleled." *Wall Street Journal* 11 June 2004: B1+. Print.

> "A Steadfast Friend on 9/11 Is Buried." *New York Times* 6 June 2002: B8. Print.

NOTE: Omit the article *the* from the title of a newspaper even if the newspaper's actual title includes the article.

29. An Editorial in a Newspaper

Brooks, David. "Living in the Age of Political Segregation." Editorial. *Dayton Daily News* 1 July 2004, final ed.: A12. Print.

30. A Letter to the Editor of a Newspaper

Chang, Paula. Letter. *Philadelphia Inquirer* 10 Dec. 2006, suburban ed.: A17. Print.

31. A Book Review in a Newspaper

Straw, Deborah. "Thinking about Tomorrow." Rev. of *Planning for the 21st Century: A Guide for Community Colleges*, by William A. Wojciechowski and Dedra Manes. *Community College Week* 7 June 2004: 15. Print.

32. An Article with a Title within Its Title

If the article you are citing contains a title that is normally enclosed in quotation marks, use single quotation marks for the interior title.

Zimmerman, Brett. "Frantic Forensic Oratory: Poe's 'The Tell-Tale Heart.'" *Style* 35 (2001): 34-50. Print.

If the article you are citing contains a title that is normally italicized, use italics for the title in your works-cited entry.

Lingo, Marci. "Forbidden Fruit: The Banning of *The Grapes of Wrath* in the Kern County Free Library." *Libraries and Culture* 38 (2003): 351-78. Print.

ENTRIES FOR MISCELLANEOUS PRINT AND NONPRINT SOURCES

Lectures and Interviews

33. A Lecture

Grimm, Mary. "An Afternoon with Mary Grimm." Visiting Writers Program. Dept. of English, Wright State U, Dayton. 16 Apr. 2004. Lecture.

34. A Personal Interview

West, Cornel. Personal interview. 28 Dec. 2005.

Tannen, Deborah. Telephone interview. 8 June 2005.

35. A Published Interview

Huston, John. "The Outlook for Raising Money: An Investment Banker's Viewpoint." *NJBIZ* 30 Sept. 2002: 2-3. Print.

Letters

36. A Personal Letter
Tan, Amy. Letter to the author. 7 Apr. 2006. TS.

37. A Letter Published in a Collection
Joyce, James. "Letter to Louis Gillet." 20 Aug. 1931. *James Joyce*. By Richard Ellmann. New York: Oxford UP, 1965. 631. Print.

38. A Letter in a Library's Archives
Stieglitz, Alfred. Letter to Paul Rosenberg. 5 Sept. 1923. MS. Stieglitz Archive. Yale U Arts Lib., New Haven.

Films, Videotapes, Radio and Television Programs, and Recordings

39. A Film
Include the title of the film (italicized), the distributor, and the date, along with other information that may be useful to readers, such as the names of the performers, the director, and the screen writer. Conclude with the publication medium.

Citizen Kane. Dir. Orson Welles. Perf. Welles, Joseph Cotten, Dorothy Comingore, and Agnes Moorehead. RKO, 1941. Film.

If you are focusing on the contribution of a particular person, begin with that person's name.

Welles, Orson, dir. *Citizen Kane*. Perf. Welles, Joseph Cotten, Dorothy Comingore, and Agnes Moorehead. RKO, 1941. Film.

40. A Videotape, DVD, or Laser Disc
Cite a videotape, DVD, or laser disc as you would cite a film, but include the original release date (when available).

Bowling for Columbine. Dir. Michael Moore. 2002. United Artists and Alliance Atlantis, 2003. DVD.

41. A Radio or Television Program
"War Feels Like War." *P.O.V.* Dir. Esteban Uyarra. PBS. WPTD, Dayton, 6 July 2004. Television.

42. A Recording
List the composer, conductor, or performer (whomever you are focusing on), followed by the title, publisher, year of issue, and publication medium.

Boubill, Alain, and Claude-Michel Schönberg. *Miss Saigon*. Perf. Lea Salonga, Claire Moore, and Jonathan Pryce. Cond. Martin Koch. Geffen, 1989. Audiocassette.

Marley, Bob. "Crisis." *Kaya*. Kava Island, 1978. LP.

Paintings, Photographs, Cartoons, and Advertisements

43. A Painting

Hopper, Edward. *Railroad Sunset*. 1929. Oil on canvas. Whitney Museum of American Art, New York.

44. A Photograph

Cite a photograph in a museum's collection in the same way you cite a painting.

Stieglitz, Alfred. *The Steerage*. 1907. Photograph. Los Angeles County Museum of Art, Los Angeles.

45. A Cartoon or Comic Strip

Trudeau, Garry. "Doonesbury." Comic strip. *Philadelphia Inquirer* 15 Sept. 2003, late ed.: E13. Print.

46. An Advertisement

Microsoft. Advertisement. *National Review* 8 June 2004: 17. Print.

ELECTRONIC SOURCES: Entries from Internet Sites

MLA style* recognizes that full source information for Internet sources is not always available. Include in your citation whatever information you can reasonably obtain: the author or editor of the site (if available); the name of the site (italicized); the version number of the source (if applicable); the name of any institution or sponsor (if unavailable, include the abbreviation **N.p.** for "no publisher); the date of electronic publication or update (if unavailable, include the abbreviation **n.d.** for "no date of publication") the publication medium (**Web**); and the date you accessed the source. (MLA style recommends omitting the URL from the citiation unless it is necessary to find the source.) Figure 18.4 shows where you can find this information.

---

*The documentation style for Internet sources presented here conforms to the most recent guidelines published in the *MLA Handbook for Writers of Research Papers* (7th ed.) and found online at <http://www.mlahandbook.org>.

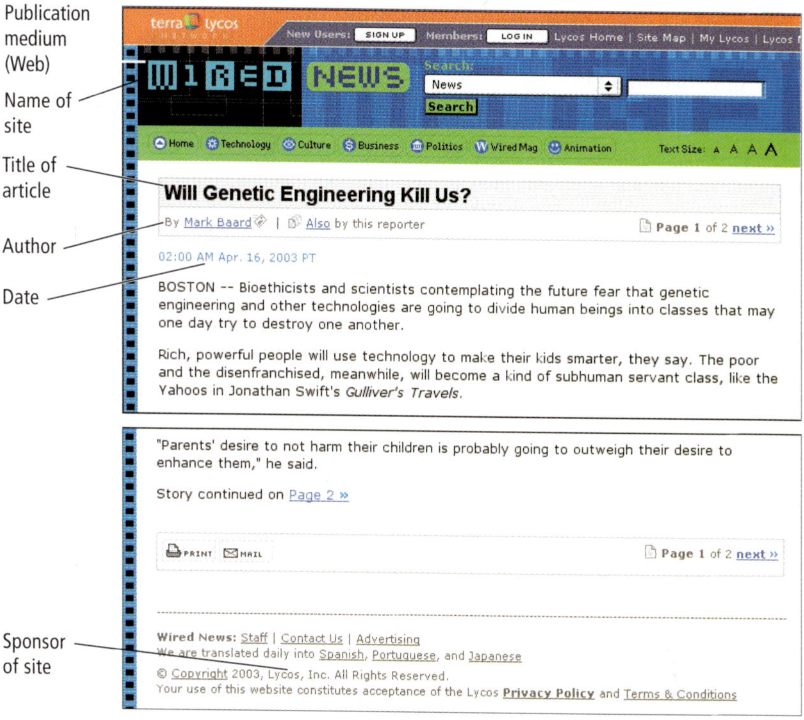

Electronic Sources: Entries from Internet Sites ■ **MLA/doc** **18a** **257**

FIGURE 18.4 Pages of an online article showing the location of the information needed for documentation.

If an electronic address (URL) is necessary, MLA requires that you enclose the URL within angle brackets to distinguish the address from the punctuation in the rest of the citation. If a URL will not fit on a line, the computer will carry the entire URL over to the next line. If you prefer to divide the URL, divide it after a slash. (Do not insert a hyphen.)

The following is a works-cited entry for the source above. Although it is not needed to locate the source, a URL has been provided in the citation to illustrate proper format.

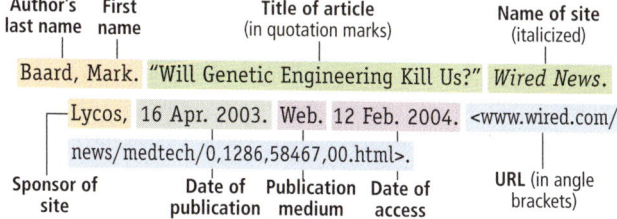

Internet-Specific Sources

47. An Entire Web Site

Nelson, Cary, ed. *Modern American Poetry*. Dept. of English, U of Illinois, Urbana-Champaign, 2002. Web. 26 May 2008.

48. A Document within a Web Site

"D Day: June 7th, 1944." *History.com*. History Channel, 1999. Web. 7 June 2002.

49. A Home Page for a Course

Walker, Janice R. Home page. *Georgia Southern University*. Dept. of Writing and Linguistics, Georgia Southern U, 5 June 2008. Web. 30 Mar. 2009.

50. A Personal Home Page

Gainor, Charles. Home page. U of Toronto, 22 July 2005. Web. 10 Nov. 2005. <http://www.chass.utoronto.ca:9094/~char>.

51. A Radio Program Accessed from an Internet Archive

"Teenage Skeptic Takes on Climate Scientists." Narr. David Kestenbaum. *Morning Edition*. Natl. Public Radio. WNYC, New York, 15 Apr. 2008. Transcript. *NPR*. Web. 30 Mar. 2009.

52. An Email

Smith, Karen. Message to the author. 28 June 2005. E-mail.

53. An Online Posting

Schiller, Stephen. "Paper Cost and Publishing Costs." Online posting. *New York Times*. New York Times, 24 Apr. 2002. Web. 11 May 2002. <www.nytimes.com/webin/webx?13A^41356.ee765e/0>.

Books, Articles, Reviews, Letters, and Reference Works on the Internet

54. A Book

Douglass, Frederick. *My Bondage and My Freedom*. Boston, 1855. *Google Book Search*. Web. 8 June 2005.

55. An Article in a Scholarly Journal

When you cite information from an electronic source that has a print version, include the publication information for the print source, the inclusive page numbers if available (if unavailable, include the abbreviation **n. pag.** for "no pagination") the publication medium, and the date you accessed it.

> DeKoven, Marianne. "Utopias Limited: Post-Sixties and Postmodern American Fiction." *Modern Fiction Studies* 41.1 (1995): 75-97. Web. 20 Jan. 2005.

56. An Article in a Magazine

> Weiser, Jay. "The Tyranny of Informality." *Time*. Time, 26 Feb. 1996. Web. 1 Mar. 2002.

57. An Article in a Newspaper

> Wyatt, Edward. "Electronic Device Stirs Unease at Book Fair." *New York Times*. New York Times, 2 June 2008. Web. 12 June 2008.

58. An Article in a Newsletter

> Sullivan, Jennifer S., comp. "Documentation Preserved, New Collections." *AIP Center for History of Physics* 39.2 (2007): n. pag. Web. 26 Feb. 2008.

59. A Review

> Ebert, Roger. Rev. of *Star Wars: Episode I—The Phantom Menace*, dir. George Lucas. *Chicago Sun-Times*. Digital Chicago, 8 June 2000. Web. 22 June 2000.

60. A Letter to the Editor

> Chen-Cheng, Henry H. Letter. *New York Times*. New York Times, 19 July 1999. Web. 1 Jan. 2009.

61. Article in an Encyclopedia

Include the article's title, the title of the database (italicized), the version number (if available), the sponsor, the date of electronic publication, the publication medium, and the date of access.

> "Hawthorne, Nathaniel." *Encyclopaedia Britannica Online*. Encyclopaedia Britannica, 2008. Web. 16 May 2008.

62. A Government Publication

Cite an online government publication as you would cite a print version; end with the information required for an electronic source.

> United States. Dept. of Justice. Office of Justice Programs. *Violence against Women: Estimates from the Redesigned National Crime Victimization Survey*. By Ronet Bachman and Linda E. Saltzman. Aug. 1995. Bureau of Justice Statistics. Web. 10 July 2003.

Paintings, Photographs, Cartoons, and Maps on the Internet

63. A Painting

> Seurat, Georges-Pierre. *Evening, Honfleur*. 1886. Oil on canvas. Museum of Mod. Art, New York. *MoMA.org*. Web. 8 Jan. 2004.

64. A Photograph

> Brady, Mathew. *Ulysses S. Grant 1822-1885*. 1864. *Mathew Brady's National Portrait Gallery*. Web. 2 Oct. 2002.

65. A Cartoon

> Stossel, Sage. "Star Wars: The Next Generation." Cartoon. *Atlantic Unbound*. Atlantic Monthly Group, 2 Oct. 2002. Web. 14 Nov. 2002.

66. A Map

> "Philadelphia, Pennsylvania." Map. *U.S. Gazetteer*. U.S. Census Bureau, n.d. Web. 17 July 2000.

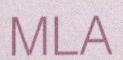

ELECTRONIC SOURCES: *Entries from Online Databases*

To cite information from an online database, supply the publication information (including page numbers, if available; if unavailable, use **n. pag.**) followed by the name of the database (italicized), the publication medium (**Web**), and the date of access.

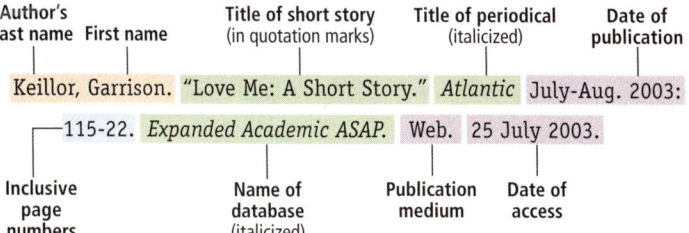

Journal Articles, Magazine Articles, News Services, and Dissertations from Online Databases

67. A Scholarly Journal Article

Schaefer, Richard J. "Editing Strategies in Television News Documentaries." *Journal of Communication* 47.4 (1997): 69-89. *InfoTrac OneFile Plus*. Web. 2 Oct. 2002.

68. A Monthly Magazine Article

Livermore, Beth. "Meteorites on Ice." *Astronomy* July 1993: 54-58. *Expanded Academic ASAP Plus*. Web. 12 Nov. 2003.

Wright, Karen. "The Clot Thickens." *Discover* Dec. 1999. *MasterFILE Premier*. Web. 10 Oct. 2003.

69. A News Service

Ryan, Desmond. "Some Background on the Battle of Gettysburg." *Knight Ridder/Tribune News Service* 7 Oct. 1993: n. pag. *InfoTrac OneFile Plus*. Web. 16 Nov. 2003.

70. A Newspaper Article

Meyer, Greg. "Answering Questions about the West Nile Virus." *Dayton Daily News* 11 July 2002: Z3-7. *LexisNexis*. Web. 17 Feb. 2003.

71. A Published Dissertation

Rodriguez, Jason Anthony. *Bureaucracy and Altruism: Managing the Contradictions of Teaching*. Diss. U of Texas at Arlington, 2003. *ProQuest*. Web. 4 Mar. 2006.

OTHER ELECTRONIC SOURCES

DVD-ROMs and CD-ROMs

72. A Nonperiodical Publication on DVD-ROM or CD-ROM

Cite a nonperiodical publication on DVD-ROM or CD-ROM the same way you would cite a book, but include the appropriate medium of publication.

> "Windhover." *The Oxford English Dictionary*. 2nd ed. Oxford: Oxford UP, 2001. DVD-ROM.
>
> "Whitman, Walt." *DiskLit: American Authors*. Boston: Hall, 2000. CD-ROM.

73. A Periodical Publication on DVD-ROM or CD-ROM

> Zurbach, Kate. "The Linguistic Roots of Three Terms." *Linguistic Quarterly* 37 (1994): 12-47. CD-ROM. *InfoTrac: Magazine Index Plus*. Information Access. Jan. 2001.

■ EXERCISE 1

The following notes identify sources used in a paper on censorship and the Internet. Following the proper format for MLA parenthetical documentation, create a parenthetical reference for each source, and then create a works-cited list, arranging the sources in the proper order.

1. Page 72 in a book called Banned in the USA by Herbert N. Foerstel. The book has 231 pages and was published in a third edition in 2006 by Greenwood Press, located in Westport, Connecticut. The author's name appears in the text of your paper.
2. A statement made by Esther Dyson in her keynote address at the Newspapers 1996 Conference. Her statement is quoted in an article by Jodi B. Cohen called Fighting Online Censorship. The speech has not been printed in any other source. The article is in the April 13, 1996, edition of the weekly business journal Editor & Publisher. Dyson's quotation appears on page 44. The article begins on page 44 and continues on page 60. Dyson's name is mentioned in the text of your paper.
3. If You Don't Love It, Leave It, an essay by Esther Dyson in the New York Times Magazine, July 15, 1995, on pages 26 and 27. Your quotation comes from the second page of the essay. No author's name is mentioned in the text of your paper.

4. An essay by Nat Hentoff titled Speech Should Not Be Limited on pages 22–26 of the book Censorship: Opposing Viewpoints, edited by Terry O'Neill. The book is published by Greenhaven Press in St. Paul, Minnesota. The publication year is 2005. The quotation you have used is from page 24, and the author is mentioned in the text of your paper.
5. An essay by Robert Cannon on the Internet called A Parent's Guide to Supervising a Child Online. The essay appeared on the Web site Internet Issues, which was updated May 10, 2002. Although the essay prints out on four pages, the pages are not numbered. In your paper, you summarize information from the second and third pages of the document. You accessed the information on January 20, 2006, from the online database *Expanded Academic ASAP Plus*.

3 Content Notes

Content notes—multiple bibliographical citations or other material that does not fit smoothly into your paper—are indicated by a **superscript** (raised numeral) in the text. Notes can appear either as footnotes at the bottom of the page or as endnotes on a separate sheet entitled **Notes**, placed after the last page of the paper and before the works-cited list. Content notes are double-spaced within and between entries. The first line is indented one-half inch, and subsequent lines are typed flush left.

For Multiple Citations

In the Paper

Many researchers emphasize the necessity of having dying patients share their experiences.[1]

In the Note

1. Kübler-Ross 27; Stinnette 43; Poston 70; Cohen and Cohen 31-34; Burke 1: 91-95.

For Other Material

In the Paper

The massacre during World War I is an event the survivors could not easily forget.[2]

In the Note

2. For a firsthand account of these events, see Bedoukian 178-81.

18b MLA-Style Manuscript Guidelines

Although MLA papers do not usually include abstracts or internal headings, this situation is changing. Be sure you know what your instructor expects.

The following guidelines are based on the latest version of the *MLA Handbook for Writers of Research Papers*.

CHECKLIST

TYPING YOUR PAPER

When typing your paper, use the student paper in **18c** as your model.

- ☐ Type your paper with a one-inch margin at the top and bottom and on both sides. Double-space your paper throughout.
- ☐ If your instructor requires a title page, use the one on page 267 as a guide. If no title page is required, your first page should follow the format of page 268.
- ☐ Capitalize all important words in your title, but not prepositions, articles, coordinating conjunctions, or the *to* in infinitives (unless they begin or end the title or subtitle). Do not underline your title or enclose it in quotation marks. Never put a period after the title, even if it is a sentence.
- ☐ Number all pages of your paper consecutively—including the first—in the upper right-hand corner, one-half inch from the top, flush right. Type your last name followed by a space before the page number on every page.
- ☐ Set off quotations of more than four lines of prose or more than three lines of poetry by indenting the whole quotation one inch. If you quote a single paragraph or part of a paragraph, do not indent the first line beyond one inch. If you quote two or more paragraphs, however, indent the first line of each paragraph an additional quarter inch. (If the first sentence does not begin a paragraph, do not indent it. Indent the first line only in successive paragraphs.)
- ☐ If you use source material in your paper, follow MLA documentation style.

See 18a

CHECKLIST

USING VISUALS

- ☐ Insert **visuals** into the text as close as possible to where they are discussed.

  See 30d

- ☐ *Above* the table, label each table with the word **Table** followed by an arabic numeral (for instance, **Table 1**). Double-space, and type a descriptive caption, with the first line flush with the left-hand margin; indent subsequent lines one-quarter inch. Capitalize the caption as if it were a title. *Below* the table, type the word **Source**, followed by a colon and all source information. Type the first line of the source information flush with the left-hand margin; indent subsequent lines one-quarter inch.

- ☐ Label other types of visual material—graphs, charts, photographs, clip art, drawings, and so on—**Fig.** (Figure) followed by an arabic numeral (for example, **Fig. 2**). Type each label and a title or caption on the same line, followed by source information, directly below the visual. Type all lines flush with the left-hand margin.

- ☐ Do not include the source of the visual in the works-cited list unless you use other material from that source elsewhere in the paper.

CHECKLIST

PREPARING THE MLA WORKS-CITED LIST

- ☐ Begin the works-cited list on a new page after the last page of text or **content notes**, numbered as the next page of the paper.

  See 18a3

- ☐ Center the title **Works Cited** one inch from the top of the page. Double-space between the title and the first entry.

- ☐ Each entry on the works-cited list has three divisions: author, title, and publication information. Separate divisions with a period and one space.

- ☐ List entries alphabetically, with last name first. Use the author's full name as it appears on the title page. If a source has no listed author, alphabetize it by the first word of the title (not counting the article).

- ☐ Type the first line of each entry flush with the left-hand margin; indent subsequent lines one-half inch.

- ☐ Double-space within and between entries.

18c Sample MLA-Style Research Paper

The following student paper, "The Great Digital Divide," uses MLA documentation style. It includes MLA-style in-text citations, a bar graph, a notes page, and a works-cited list. Although MLA does not require a title page, Kimberly's instructor required her class to include one. See page 72 for an example of the first page of an MLA-style research paper without a title page.

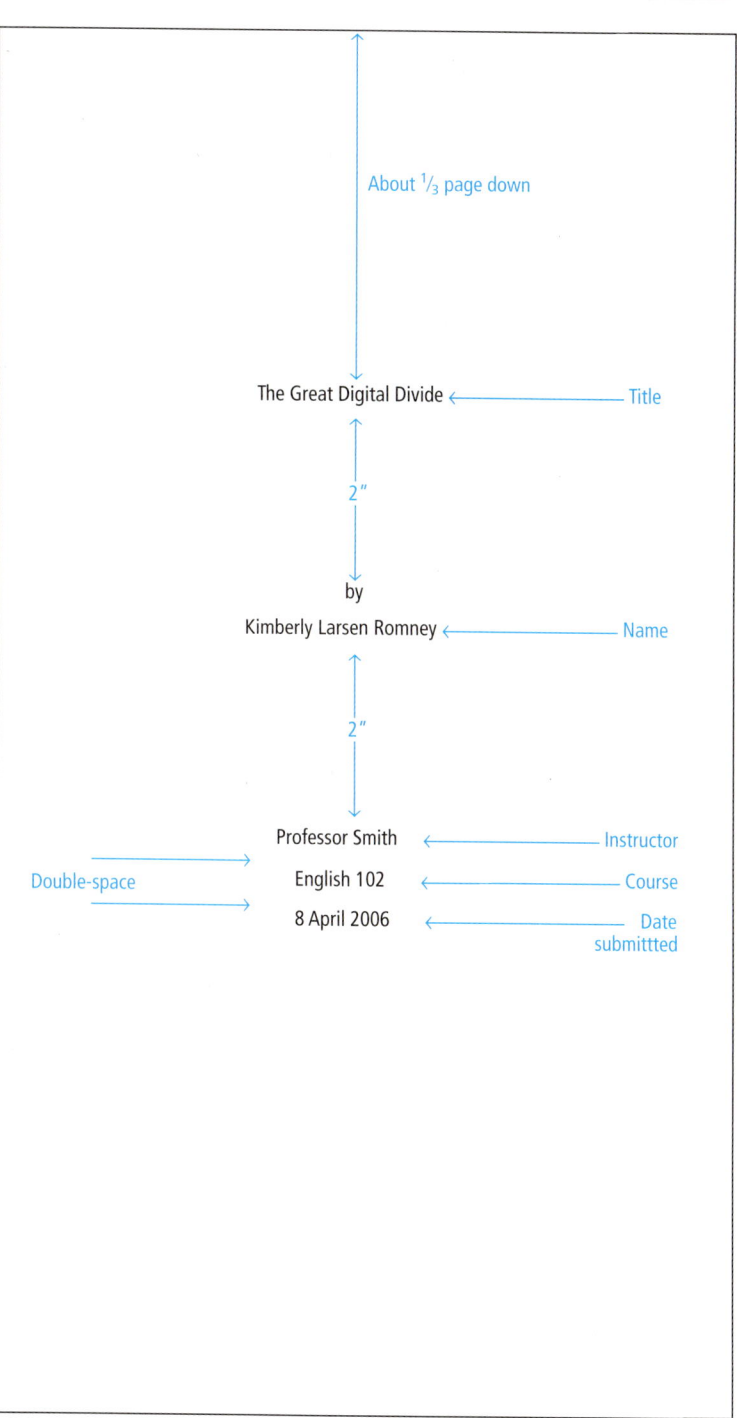

Romney 1

The Great Digital Divide

Today, a basic understanding of computers and how to use them is necessary for success. For this reason, those who are unfamiliar with modern digital technology find themselves at a great disadvantage when it comes to education and employment. One of the most exciting digital technologies available is the Internet. With its accompanying software and services, the Internet has completely changed the way we access and see information. Clearly, the Internet offers great promise, but some argue that it has created many problems as well. Although the Internet has changed our lives for the better, it has also left some people behind, creating two distinct classes—those who have access and those who do not.

In the late 1990s, many argued that the Internet had ushered in a new age, one in which instant communication would bring people closer together and eventually eliminate national boundaries. In his speech "Building a Global Community," former Vice President Al Gore took this optimistic view, seeing the Internet as a means "to deepen and extend our oldest and most cherished global values: rising standards of living and literacy, an ever-widening circle of freedom, and individual empowerment." Gore went on to say that he could imagine the day when we would "extend our knowledge and our prosperity to our most isolated inner cities, to the barrios, the favelas, the colonias, and our most remote rural villages."

Others, however, argued that for many people, the benefits of the Internet were not nearly this obvious or far-reaching. They maintained that the Internet was creating what many have called a "digital divide," which excludes a large percentage of the poor, elderly, disabled, and members of many minority groups from current technological advancements (*Digital Divide Network*).

A survey conducted by the United States Department of Commerce in 2002 showed that white people and those with higher annual incomes were more likely to own computers than minorities and people from low-income households. In households where the average income was $75,000 and over, 89% had access to a computer. In households earning $10,000-$14,999, only 25% had access to a computer. Moreover, although 61% of white households had access to a computer, only 37.1% of African-American and 40% of Hispanic households had home computers.

While the Department of Commerce study suggested that financial circumstances were largely responsible for the "digital divide," the gap in computer ownership across incomes indicated that other factors might also be contributing to the disparity. For example, in a 1999 *New York Times* op-ed article, Henry Louis Gates, Jr., argued that bridging the digital divide would "require more than cheap PC's"; it would "involve content" (500).[1] African Americans were not interested in the Internet, Gates wrote, because the content rarely appealed to them. Gates compared the lack of interest in the Internet with the history of African Americans' relationship to the recording industry. According to Gates, blacks began to buy records "only when mainstream companies . . . introduced so-called race records, blues and jazz discs aimed at a nascent African-American market" (501). Gates suggested that Web sites that address the needs of African

Americans could play the same role that race records did for the music industry. Ignoring the race problem, Gates warned, would lead to a form of "cybersegregation" that would devastate the African-American community (501).

It was clear to many that people without Internet access had difficulty at school, trouble obtaining jobs, and fewer opportunities to save money and time as consumers. They also lacked access to educational materials and to jobs posted on the Internet. With access to only a portion of available goods and services, people who were not connected did not have the advantages that people who were online could routinely get. Thus, instead of bringing people together, the Internet seemed to be widening the economic and social divide that already separated people in this country.

In response, the government, corporations, nonprofit organizations, and public libraries made efforts to bridge the gap between the "haves" and "have-nots." For example, the Education Department's Community Technology Centers Program helped finance computer activity centers for students and adults. Also, the Department of Commerce's Technology Opportunities Program (TOP) provided money and services to organizations that needed more technology to operate efficiently. One recipient was America's Second Harvest, which used the funds to track donations to its national network of food banks (Schwartz, "Report").

Nonprofit organizations also worked to bridge the digital divide. The Bill and Melinda Gates Foundation, for example, provided libraries across the country with funding that allowed them to purchase computers and connect to the Internet (Egan). Nonprofit organizations also began to sponsor Web sites, such as *The Digital Divide Network*, a site that posted stories about the digital divide from a variety of perspectives. By posting information, the site's sponsor hoped to raise awareness of the problems that the digital divide causes.

Recently, however, some people have begun to question the need for many of these initiatives. In fact, as illustrated in fig. 1, computer use by young people between the ages of three and twenty-four rose dramatically between 1998 and 2001.

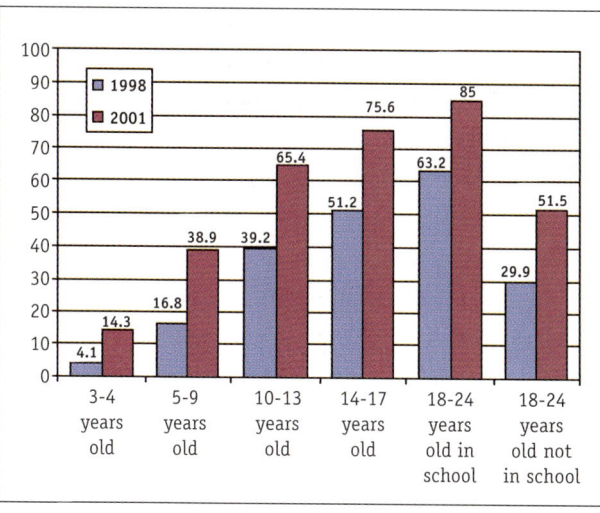

Graph summarizes relevant data. Source information is typed directly below the figure.

Fig. 1. United States, Dept. of Commerce, Economics and Statistics Admin.; Natl. Telecommunications and Information Admin.; *A Nation Online: How Americans Are Expanding Their Use of the Internet*; 2002; National Telecommunications and Information Administration; Web; 20 Jan. 2006.

Several recent studies seem to support this view. For example, a 2004 study by the Pew Research Center found that nearly 66% of whites and Hispanics and 61% of African Americans used the Internet (Nelson). Another study, conducted by the University of Texas at Dallas, also found that the digital divide seemed to be closing. According to Professor Donald Hicks, research showed that "broadband Internet [was] more readily available in minority neighborhoods than in areas that [were] home to more whites" (Nelson). Even earlier, a 2002 report by the United States Department of Commerce, using the most recent census data then available, concluded that Internet access in homes had increased significantly between 1999 and 2001, even among minorities. A more recent national study by the Pew Foundation, conducted in 2006, reported that "74 percent of whites go online, 61 percent of African Americans do and 80 percent of English-speaking Hispanic Americans report using the Internet" (Marriott).

Arguing that significant strides have been made to bridge the digital divide, the Bush administration has questioned whether programs like the Community Technology Centers Program are still needed (Pekow). At the same time, private industry has withdrawn some support for efforts to bridge the digital divide. One organization, called PowerUp, worked with corporations to create community-based technology centers. In places like Austin, Texas, PowerUp established a computer center in the city's impoverished neighborhoods by collaborating with AOL Time Warner and the Austin Urban League (Doggett). Despite its initial success, the organization was hard hit by an economic downturn. According to a PowerUp spokesperson,

"The model that was launched in late 1999 . . . was a model that had its bloodlines in different economic times. The model isn't necessarily the best one for these economic times" (Schwartz, "Lack"). In 2002, PowerUp closed its offices, leaving the community centers they created to find funding on their own.

In other cases, the groups targeted by digital divide programs argued that such programs might do more harm than good. A 2001 article in the *Chronicle of Higher Education* observed that many African-American and other minority groups argue that digital divide rhetoric actually stereotypes minorities. The article pointed out that digital divide rhetoric "could discourage businesses or academics from creating content or services tailored for minority communities—ultimately making the digital divide a self-fulfilling prophecy" (Young). Many scholars and leaders in the African-American community feared that a focus on the digital divide would lead to its being seen as a fact to be accepted rather than as a problem to be solved. Tara L. McPherson agreed, arguing that "the idea of challenging the digital divide is not about denying its existence. But it is to ensure that the focus on the digital divide doesn't naturalize a kind of exclusion of investment" (qtd. in Young).

However, despite the appearance that the digital divide is closing and the claims that digital divide rhetoric may actually be harmful, many public officials and private interest groups continued to voice their concerns that gaps in technological literacy and availability remained a problem among many populations and communities. In fact, a 2002 report published by the Benton Foundation disagreed with the United States Department of Commerce's optimistic

Qtd. in indicates that McPherson's comments were quoted in Young's article

findings. This report contended that federal funding should be key in continuing to bring more people into the digital age (Dickard et al.).

While the Department of Commerce report maintained that most people had access to computers in their homes, the Benton Foundation's report used the same statistics to argue that many people continued to have difficulty accessing the Internet. The Benton report found that 75% of people with household incomes of less than $15,000 and 66% with incomes between $15,000 and $35,000 were not yet using the Internet (Dickard et al.). Wealthier Americans, however, had significantly greater access to the Internet. Of the Americans with incomes of $50,000-$75,000 a year, 67.3% used the Internet (Dickard et al.). As a result, the Benton Foundation strongly disagreed with the Bush administration's recommendation to cut programs like the Department of Commerce's Technology Opportunities Program (TOP) and the Community Technology Centers Program (CTC):

> TOP and CTC are important engines of digital opportunity. . . . A federal retreat from that leadership role would undermine innovative efforts to bring digital opportunity to underserved communities and jeopardize many successful community programs. Rather than walking away from the investment, the federal government should build upon the success of these programs to bring digital opportunity to the entire nation. (Dickard et al.)

The popularity of programs offered by the public library system also challenges the wisdom of the federal government's desire to cut funding for programs that increase computer literacy. According to an article published in the *Knight Ridder/Tribune Business News*, the New York Public Library system's computer literacy courses drew over eighteen thousand people in 2003. The demand for these classes was so high that many classes filled up, leaving people frustrated and disappointed (Dalton). The clear conclusion is that although the gap between the haves and have-nots may be closing, continued success depends on continued financial support of successful programs.[2]

    Evidence suggests that although progress has been made in closing the digital divide, more needs to be done. As Michel Marriott points out, however, some groups that study Internet use or work to introduce young people to computers continue to believe that "[d]espite the dissolving gap . . . the digital divide is still vast in more subtle ways." For example, a coordinator for the Digital Divide Network notes that minorities and low-income Internet users are still less likely to own computers and therefore more likely to rely on school or office computers, which are not always available to them. As a result, their computer skills may not be as sophisticated as those of people who have unlimited Internet access (Marriott).

    It is not only minorities and the impoverished who are affected by the digital divide. Many people know that children in inner-city schools lack access to computer technology and to the Internet, but few know that children attending schools in rural areas are also at risk. Vicky Wellborn, a high school English teacher in a small town, reports that her school only recently instituted a computer literacy program. As they ordered computers, the

Romney 9

instructors realized that one of their biggest challenges would be training themselves. Certainly the computer literacy program has been helpful to many students, but the difficulties of teaching an unfamiliar subject continue to challenge teachers at the school (Wellborn).

> **Conclusion recommends solutions for problem of "digital divide"**

Although many strides have been made in closing the gap between those who have access to the Internet and those who do not, problems and new challenges remain. Steps must be taken to solve these problems. First, we must continue efforts to make the Internet available to the widest possible audience. We must also ensure that the rhetoric surrounding the term *digital divide* is used to close this gap, not to create a new one by establishing or reinforcing stereotypes about minorities. A broader definition of what the digital divide is might help us to see that it has the potential to marginalize many groups of people—the poor, the elderly, the disabled, and rural schoolchildren, for example—not just members of minority groups. On a practical level, the federal government should continue to fund programs that increase access to computer technology in general, and to the Internet in particular. Unless we take steps to make sure these resources are available to all, we are still in danger of becoming two separate and unequal societies: one "plugged-in" and privileged and one "unplugged" and marginalized.

> **Because concluding paragraph introduces no new material (it summarizes material already discussed and presents student's original conclusions), no documentation is necessary**

Romney 10

Notes

1. Interestingly, Gates also acknowledges that African Americans bear some of the responsibility for changing the situation.

2. An even more recent survey by the Leadership Council on Civil Rights found that low-income high-school students who have access to computers are six to eight percent more likely to graduate from high school than teenagers who do not. The study also showed a correlation between computer use and a decrease in school suspensions and criminal activities.

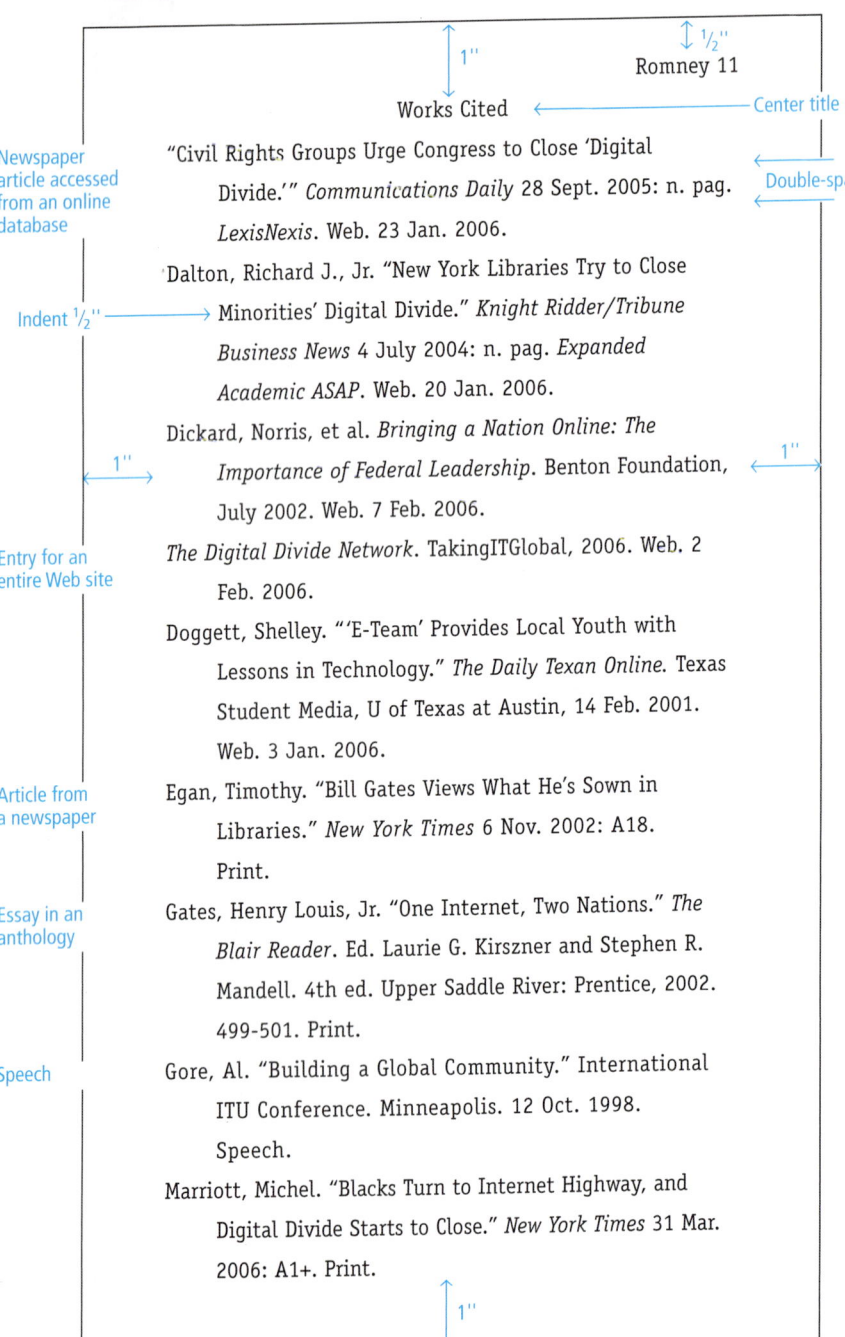

Nelson, Colleen McCain. "Ethnic Gap on Internet Narrowing, Study Says." *Knight Ridder/Tribune Business News* 10 June 2004: n. pag. *Expanded Academic ASAP*. Web. 20 Jan. 2006.

Pekow, Charles. "Community Technology Program in Crosshairs of Congress." *Community College Week* 15 Aug. 2005: n. pag. *Academic Search Premier*. Web. 30 Jan. 2006.

Schwartz, John. "A Lack of Money Forces Computer Initiative to Close." *New York Times* 30 Oct. 2002: n. pag. *Expanded Academic ASAP*. Web. 20 Jan. 2006.

---. "Report Disputes Bush Approach to Bridging 'Digital Divide.'" *New York Times* 11 July 2002: n. pag. *Expanded Academic ASAP*. Web. 19 Jan. 2006.

United States. Dept. of Commerce. Economics and Statistics Admin. Natl. Telecommunications and Information Admin. *A Nation Online: How Americans Are Expanding Their Use of the Internet*. 2002. National Telecommunications and Information Administration. Web. 20 Jan. 2006.

Wellborn, Vicky. "Re: Computer Literacy." Message to the author. 23 Jan. 2006. E-mail.

Young, Jeffrey R. "Does 'Digital Divide' Rhetoric Do More Harm than Good?" *The Chronicle of Higher Education*. Chronicle of Higher Educ., 9 Nov. 2001. Web. 10 Jan. 2006.

PART 5

Documenting Sources: APA and Other Styles

19 APA Documentation Style 284
19a Using APA Style 284
19b APA-Style Manuscript Guidelines 294
19c Sample APA-Style Research Paper 297

20 Chicago Documentation Style 310
20a Using Chicago Style 310
20b Chicago-Style Manuscript Guidelines 321
20c Sample Chicago-Style Research Paper (Excerpts) 323

21 CSE and Other Documentation Styles 330
21a Using CSE Style 330
21b CSE-Style Manuscript Guidelines 335
21c Sample CSE-Style Research Paper (Excerpts) 336
21d Using Other Documentation Styles 339

19 APA — APA Documentation Style

DIRECTORY OF APA IN-TEXT CITATIONS

1. A work by a single author (p. 285)
2. A work by two authors (p. 285)
3. A work by three to five authors (p. 285)
4. A work by six or more authors (p. 285)
5. Works by authors with the same last name (p. 286)
6. A work by a corporate author (p. 286)
7. A work with no listed author (p. 286)
8. A personal communication (p. 286)
9. An indirect source (p. 286)
10. A specific part of a source (p. 286)
11. An electronic source (p. 286)
12. Two or more works within the same parenthetical reference (p. 287)
13. A table (p. 287)

DIRECTORY OF APA REFERENCE LIST ENTRIES

PRINT SOURCES: *Entries for Books*

Authors

1. A book with one author (p. 288)
2. A book with more than one author (p. 288)
3. A book with no listed author or editor (p. 288)
4. A book with a corporate author (p. 288)
5. An edited book (p. 289)

Editions, Multivolume Works, Forewords

6. A work in several volumes (p. 289)
7. The foreword, preface, or afterword of a book (p. 289)

Parts of Books

8. A selection from an anthology (p. 289)
9. An article in a reference book (p. 289)

Government Reports

10. A government report (p. 289)

PRINT SOURCES: *Entries for Articles*

Articles in Scholarly Journals

11. An article in a scholarly journal with continuous pagination through an annual volume (p. 290)
12. An article in a scholarly journal with separate pagination in each issue (p. 290)

Articles in Magazines and Newspapers

13. A magazine article (p. 290)
14. A newspaper article (p. 291)
15. A letter to the editor of a newspaper (p. 291)

ENTRIES FOR MISCELLANEOUS PRINT SOURCES

Letters

16. A personal letter (p. 291)
17. A published letter (p. 291)

ENTRIES FOR OTHER SOURCES

Television Broadcasts, Films, CDs, Audiocassette Recordings, Computer Software

18. A television broadcast (p. 291)
19. A television series (p. 291)
20. A film (p. 292)
21. A CD recording (p. 292)
22. An audiocassette recording (p. 292)
23. Computer software (p. 292)

ELECTRONIC SOURCES: *Entries from Internet Sites*

Internet-Specific Sources

24. An Internet article based on a print source (p. 293)
25. An article in an Internet-only journal (p. 293)
26. A document from a university Web site (p. 293)
27. A Web document (no author identified, no date) (p. 293)
28. An email (p. 293)
29. A message posted to a newsgroup (p. 293)
30. A searchable database (p. 294)

Abstracts, Newspaper Articles

31. An abstract (p. 294)
32. An article in a daily newspaper (p. 294)

19

APA Documentation Style

❓ FAQs
When should I use APA documentation? (p. 284)
How do I arrange the entries in an APA reference list? (p. 297)
What should an APA paper look like? (p. 297)

19a Using APA Style

APA style* is used extensively in the social sciences. APA documentation has three parts: *parenthetical references in the body of the paper,* a *reference list,* and optional *content footnotes.*

1 Parenthetical References

APA documentation uses short parenthetical references in the body of the paper keyed to an alphabetical list of references that follows the paper. A typical parenthetical reference consists of the author's last name (followed by a comma) and the year of publication.

> Many people exhibit symptoms of depression after the death of a pet (Russo, 2000).

If the author's name appears in an introductory phrase, include the year of publication there as well.

> According to Russo (2000), many people exhibit symptoms of depression after the death of a pet.

Note that you may include the author's name and the date either in the introductory phrase or in parentheses at the end of the borrowed material.

When quoting directly, include the page number in parentheses after the quotation.

> According to Weston (1996), children from one-parent homes read at "a significantly lower level than those from two-parent homes" (p. 58).

---

*APA documentation format follows the guidelines set in the *Publication Manual of the American Psychological Association*, 5th ed. Washington, DC: APA, 2001.

284

NOTE: A long quotation (forty words or more) is not set in quotation marks. It is set as a block, and the entire quotation is double-spaced and indented one-half inch from the left margin. Parenthetical documentation is placed one space after the final punctuation.

SAMPLE APA IN-TEXT CITATIONS

1. **A Work by a Single Author**

   Many college students suffer from sleep deprivation (Anton, 1999).

2. **A Work by Two Authors**

   There is growing concern over the use of psychological testing in elementary schools (Albright & Glennon, 1982).

3. **A Work by Three to Five Authors**

If a work has more than two but fewer than six authors, mention all names in the first reference; in subsequent references in the same paragraph, cite only the first author followed by **et al.** ("and others"). When the reference appears in later paragraphs, include the year.

First Reference

   (Sparks, Wilson, & Hewitt, 2001)

Subsequent References in the Same Paragraph

   (Sparks et al.)

References in Later Paragraphs

   (Sparks et al., 2001)

4. **A Work by Six or More Authors**

When a work has six or more authors, cite the name of the first author followed by **et al.** and the year in all references.

   (Miller et al., 1995)

CLOSE-UP

CITING WORKS BY MULTIPLE AUTHORS

When referring to multiple authors in the text of your paper, join the last two names with **and**.

   According to Rosen, Wolfe, and Ziff (1988). . . .

In-text citations (as well as reference list entries) require an **ampersand (&)**.

   (Rosen, Wolfe, & Ziff, 1988)

5. Works by Authors with the Same Last Name

If your reference list includes works by two or more authors with the same last name, use each author's initials in all in-text citations.

> F. Bor (2001) and S. D. Bor (2000) concluded that no further study was needed.

6. A Work by a Corporate Author

If the name of a corporate author is long, abbreviate it after the first citation.

First Reference

> (National Institute of Mental Health [NIMH], 2001)

Subsequent Reference

> (NIMH, 2001)

7. A Work with No Listed Author

If a work has no listed author, cite the first two or three words of the title (followed by a comma) and the year. Use quotation marks around titles of periodical articles and chapters of books; use italics for titles of books, periodicals, brochures, reports, and the like.

> ("New Immigration," 2000)

8. A Personal Communication

Cite letters, memos, telephone conversations, personal interviews, emails, messages from electronic bulletin boards, and so on only in the text—*not* in the reference list.

> (R. Takaki, personal communication, October 17, 2001)

9. An Indirect Source

> Cogan and Howe offer very different interpretations of the problem (cited in Swenson, 2000).

10. A Specific Part of a Source

Use abbreviations for the words *page* (**p.**), *pages* (**pp.**), *chapter* (**chap.**), and *section* (**sec.**).

> These theories have an interesting history (Lee, 1966, chap. 2).

11. An Electronic Source

For an electronic source that does not show page numbers, use the paragraph number preceded by a ¶ symbol or the abbreviation **para**.

> Conversation at the dinner table is an example of a family ritual (Kulp, 2001, ¶ 3).

In the case of an electronic source that has neither page nor paragraph numbers, cite both the heading in the source and the number of the paragraph following the heading in which the material is located.

> Healthy eating is a never-ending series of free choices (Shapiro, 2001, Introduction section, para. 2).

If the source has no headings, you may not be able to specify an exact location.

12. Two or More Works within the Same Parenthetical Reference

List works by different authors in alphabetical order, separated by semicolons.

> This theory is supported by several studies (Barson & Roth, 1995; Rose, 2001; Tedesco, 2002).

List two or more works by the same author or authors in order of date of publication (separated by commas), with the earliest date first.

> This theory is supported by several studies (Rhodes & Dollek, 2000, 2002, 2003).

For two or more works by the same author published in the same year, designate the work whose title comes first alphabetically *a*, the one whose title comes next *b*, and so on; repeat the year in each citation.

> This theory is supported by several studies (Shapiro, 2003a, 2003b).

13. A Table

If you use a table from a source, give credit to the author in a note at the bottom of the table. Do not include this information in the reference list.

> *Note.* From "Predictors of Employment and Earnings Among JOBS Participants," by P. A. Neenan and D. K. Orthner, 1996, *Social Work Research, 20*(4), p. 233.

2 Reference List

The **reference list** gives the publication information for all the sources you cite. It should appear at the end of your paper on a new numbered page titled **References**. Entries in the reference list should be arranged alphabetically. Double-space within and between reference list entries. The first line of each entry should start at the left margin with the second and subsequent lines indented one-half inch. (**See 19b** for full manuscript guidelines.)

PRINT SOURCES: Entries for Books

Book citations include the author's name (last name first); the year of publication (in parentheses); the book title (italicized); and publication information.

Capitalize only the first word of the title and subtitle and any proper nouns. Include any additional necessary information—edition, report number, or volume number, for example—in parentheses after the title. In the publication information, write out in full the names of associations, corporations, and university presses. Include the words **Book** and **Press**, but do not include terms such as **Publishers**, **Co.**, or **Inc.**

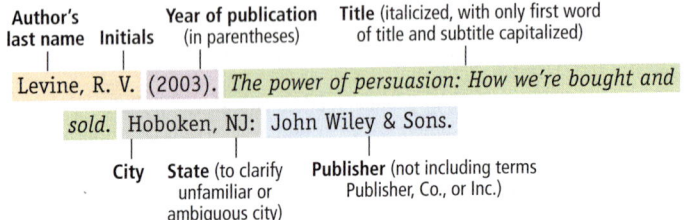

Authors

1. A Book with One Author

Maslow, A. H. (1974). *Toward a psychology of being*. Princeton: Van Nostrand.

2. A Book with More Than One Author

List up to six authors by last name and initials, using an ampersand (&) to connect the last two names. For more than six authors, add **et al.** after the sixth name.

Wolfinger, D., Knable, P., Richards, H. L., & Silberger, R. (1990). *The chronically unemployed*. New York: Berman Press.

3. A Book with No Listed Author or Editor

Writing with a computer. (2006). Philadelphia: Drexel Press.

4. A Book with a Corporate Author

When the author and the publisher are the same, include the word **Author** at the end of the citation instead of repeating the publisher's name.

League of Women Voters of the United States. (2005). *Local league handbook*. Washington, DC: Author.

5. An Edited Book

Lewin, K., Lippitt, R., & White, R. K. (Eds.). (1985). *Social learning and imitation*. New York: Basic Books.

Editions, Multivolume Works, Forewords

6. A Work in Several Volumes

Jones, P. R., & Williams, T. C. (Eds.). (1990–1993). *Handbook of therapy* (Vols. 1–2). Princeton: Princeton University Press.

7. The Foreword, Preface, or Afterword of a Book

Taylor, T. (1979). Preface. In B. B. Ferencz, *Less than slaves* (pp. ii–ix). Cambridge: Harvard University Press.

Parts of Books

8. A Selection from an Anthology

Give inclusive page numbers preceded by **pp.** (in parentheses) after the title of the anthology. The title of the selection is not enclosed in quotation marks.

Lorde, A. (1984). Age, race, and class. In P. S. Rothenberg (Ed.), *Racism and sexism: An integrated study* (pp. 352–360). New York: St. Martin's Press.

NOTE: If you cite two or more selections from the same anthology, give the full citation for the anthology in each entry.

9. An Article in a Reference Book

Edwards, P. (Ed.). (1987). Determinism. In *The encyclopedia of philosophy* (Vol. 2, pp. 359–373). New York: Macmillan.

Government Reports

10. A Government Report

National Institute of Mental Health. (1987). *Motion pictures and violence: A summary report of research* (DHHS Publication No. ADM 91-22187). Washington, DC: U.S. Government Printing Office.

PRINT SOURCES: Entries for Articles

Article citations include the author's name (last name first); the date of publication (in parentheses); the title of the article; the title of the periodical (italicized); the volume number (italicized); the issue number, if any (in parentheses); and the inclusive page numbers (including all digits).

Capitalize the first word of the article's title and subtitle as well as any proper nouns. Do not underline or italicize the title of the article or enclose it in quotation marks. Give the periodical title in full, and capitalize all words except articles, prepositions, and conjunctions of fewer than four letters. Use **p.** or **pp.** when referring to page numbers in newspapers, but omit this abbreviation when referring to page numbers in journals and popular magazines.

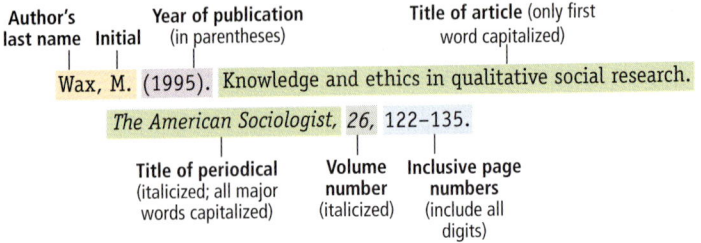

Articles in Scholarly Journals

11. An Article in a Scholarly Journal with Continuous Pagination through an Annual Volume

> Miller, W. (1969). Violent crimes in city gangs. *Journal of Social Issues, 27,* 581–593.

12. An Article in a Scholarly Journal with Separate Pagination in Each Issue

> Williams, S., & Cohen, L. R. (1984). Child stress in early learning situations. *American Psychologist, 21*(10), 1–28.

NOTE: Do not leave a space between the volume and issue numbers.

Articles in Magazines and Newspapers

13. A Magazine Article

> McCurdy, H. G. (1983, June). Brain mechanisms and intelligence. *Psychology Today, 46,* 61–63.

14. A Newspaper Article

If an article appears on nonconsecutive pages, give all page numbers, separated by commas (for example, **A1, A14**). If the article appears on consecutive pages, indicate the full range of pages (for example, **A7–A9**).

> James, W. R. (1993, November 16). The uninsured and health care. *Wall Street Journal,* pp. A1, A14.

15. A Letter to the Editor of a Newspaper

> Williams, P. (2000, July 19). Self-fulfilling stereotypes [Letter to the editor]. *Los Angeles Times,* p. A22.

ENTRIES FOR MISCELLANEOUS PRINT SOURCES

Letters

16. A Personal Letter

References to unpublished personal letters, like references to all other personal communications, should be included only in the text of the paper, not in the reference list.

17. A Published Letter

> Joyce, J. (1931). Letter to Louis Gillet. In Richard Ellmann, *James Joyce* (p. 631). New York: Oxford University Press.

ENTRIES FOR OTHER SOURCES

Television Broadcasts, Films, CDs, Audiocassette Recordings, Computer Software

18. A Television Broadcast

> Murphy, J. (Executive Producer). (2002, March 4). *The CBS evening news* [Television broadcast]. New York: Columbia Broadcasting Service.

19. A Television Series

> Sorkin, A., Schlamme, T., & Wells, J. (Executive Producers). (2002). *The west wing* [Television series]. Los Angeles: Warner Bros. Television.

20. A Film

Spielberg, S. (Director). (1994). *Schindler's list* [Motion picture]. United States: Universal.

21. A CD Recording

Marley, B. (1977). Waiting in vain. On *Exodus* [CD]. New York: Island Records.

22. An Audiocassette Recording

Skinner, B. F. (Speaker). (1972). *Skinner on Skinnerism* [Cassette recording]. Hollywood, CA: Center for Cassette Studies.

23. Computer Software

Sharp, S. (1995). *Career Selection Tests* (Version 5.0) [Computer software]. Chico, CA: Avocation Software.

APA — ELECTRONIC SOURCES: *Entries from Internet Sites*

APA guidelines for documenting electronic sources focus on Web sources, which often do not include all the bibliographic information that print sources do. For example, Web sources may not include page numbers or a place of publication. At a minimum, a Web citation should have a title, a date (the date of publication, update, or retrieval), and an electronic address (URL). If possible, also include the author(s) of a source. When you need to divide a URL at the end of a line, break it after a slash or before a period (do not add a hyphen). Do not add a period at the end of the URL. (Current guidelines for citing electronic sources can be found on the APA Web site at <www.apa.org>.)

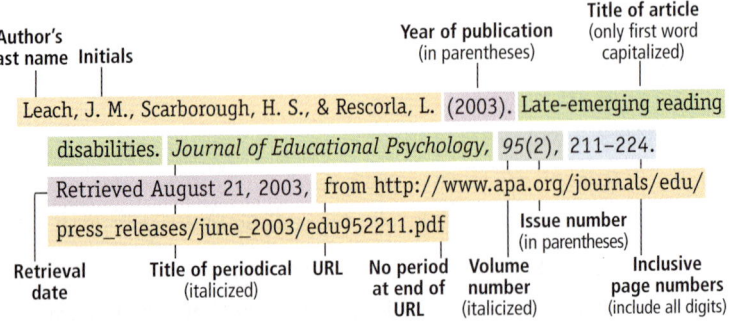

Electronic Sources: Entries from Internet Sites ■ APA/doc **19a** **293**

Internet-Specific Sources

24. An Internet Article Based on a Print Source
If you have seen the article only in electronic format, include the phrase **Electronic version** in brackets after the title.

> Winston, E. L. (2000). The role of art therapy in treating chronically depressed patients [Electronic version]. *Journal of Bibliographic Research, 5,* 54–72.

NOTE: If you think the article you retrieved may be different from the print version, add the date you retrieved it and the URL.

25. An Article in an Internet-Only Journal

> Hornaday, J., & Bunker, C. (2001). The nature of the entrepreneur. *Personal Psychology, 23,* Article 2353b. Retrieved November 21, 2001, from http://journals.apa.org/volume23/pre002353b.html

26. A Document from a University Web Site

> Beck, E. (1997, July). *The good, the bad & the ugly: Or, why it's a good idea to evaluate web sources.* Retrieved January 7, 2002, from New Mexico State University Library Web site: http://lib.nmsu.edu/instruction/evalcrit.html

27. A Web Document (No Author Identified, No Date)
A document with no author or date should be listed by title, followed by the abbreviation **n.d.** (for "no date"), the retrieval date, and the URL.

> *The stratocaster appreciation page.* (n.d.). Retrieved July 27, 2002, from http://members.tripod.com/~AFH/

28. An Email
As with all other personal communication, references to personal email should be included only in the text of your paper, not in the reference list.

29. A Message Posted to a Newsgroup
List the author's full name—or, if that is not available, the screen name. In brackets after the title, provide information that will help readers access the message.

> Shapiro, R. (2001, April 4). Chat rooms and interpersonal communication [Msg 7]. Message posted to news://sci.psychology.communication

30. A Searchable Database

Nowroozi, C. (1992). What you lose when you miss sleep. *Nation's Business, 80*(9), 73–77. Retrieved April 22, 2001, from Expanded Academic ASAP database.

Abstracts, Newspaper Articles

31. An Abstract

Guinot, A., & Peterson, B. R. (1995). *Forgetfulness and partial cognition* (Drexel University Cognitive Research Report No. 21). Abstract retrieved December 4, 2001, from http://www.Drexel.edu/~guinot/deltarule-abstract.html

32. An Article in a Daily Newspaper

Farrell, P. D. (1997, March 23). New high-tech stresses hit traders and investors on the information superhighway. *Wall Street Journal.* Retrieved April 4, 1999, from http://wall-street.news.com/forecasts/stress/stress.html

3 Content Footnotes

APA format permits content notes, indicated by **superscripts** (raised numerals) in the text. The notes are listed on a separate numbered page, titled **Footnotes**, following the appendixes (or after the reference list if there are no appendixes). Double-space all notes, indenting the first line of each note one-half inch and beginning subsequent lines flush left. Number the notes with superscripts that correspond to the numbers in your text.

19b APA-Style Manuscript Guidelines

Social science papers have internal headings. For example, internal sections may include an untitled introduction and the headings **Background**, **Method**, **Results**, and **Discussion**. Each section of a social science paper is a complete unit with a beginning and an end so that it can be read separately and still make sense out of context. The body of the paper may include charts, graphs, maps, photographs, flowcharts, or tables.

The following guidelines are based on the latest version of the *Publication Manual of the American Psychological Association.*

CHECKLIST

TYPING YOUR PAPER

When typing your paper, use the student paper in **19c** as your model.

- ☐ Leave one-inch margins at the top and bottom and on both sides. Double-space your paper throughout.
- ☐ Indent the first line of every paragraph and the first line of every content footnote one-half inch from the left-hand margin.
- ☐ Set off a **long quotation** (more than forty words) in a block format by indenting the entire quotation one-half inch from the left-hand margin. Do not indent the first line further.
- ☐ Number all pages consecutively. Each page should include a **page header** (an abbreviated title) and a page number typed one-half inch from the top and one inch from the right-hand edge of the page. Leave one-half inch between the page header and the page number.
- ☐ Center major headings, and type them with uppercase and lowercase letters. Place minor headings flush left, typed with uppercase and lowercase letters and italicized. *See 30b*
- ☐ Format items in a series as a numbered list. *See 30c*
- ☐ Arrange the pages of the paper in the following order:
  - Title page (page 1) with a page header, running head, title, byline (your name), and the name of your school. (Your instructor may require additional information.)
  - Abstract (page 2)
  - Text of paper (beginning on page 3)
  - Reference list (new page)
  - Appendixes (start each on a new page)
  - Content footnotes (new page)
- ☐ If you use source material in your paper, citations should be consistent with APA documentation style. *See 19a*

COMPUTER TIP   academic.cengage.com/eng/kirsznermandell

DOCUMENT FORMATTING

Several document formatting options in your word-processing program can help you format your research paper according to APA style. For example, you can use the Header/Footer option (see below) to place the appropriate words consistently at the top right of your pages. To use this tool, select the View menu and scroll down to Header/Footer.

CHECKLIST

USING VISUALS

APA style distinguishes between two types of visuals: **tables** and **figures** (charts, graphs, photographs, and diagrams). In manuscripts not intended for publication, tables and figures are included in the text. A short table or figure should appear on the page where it is discussed; a long table or figure should be placed on a separate page just after the page where it is discussed.

Tables
Number all **tables** consecutively. Each table should have a *label* and a *title*.

- ☐ The **label** consists of the word **Table** (not in italics), along with an arabic numeral, typed flush left above the table.
- ☐ Double-space and type a brief explanatory **title** for each table (in italics) flush left below the label. Capitalize the first letters of principal words of the title.

  Table 7

  Frequency of Negative Responses of Dorm Students to Questions

  Concerning Alcohol Consumption

Figures
Number all **figures** consecutively. Each figure should have a *label* and a *caption*.

- ☐ The **label** consists of the word **Figure** (typed flush left below the figure) followed by the figure number (both in italics).
- ☐ The **caption** explains the figure and serves as a title. Double-space the caption, but do not italicize it. Capitalize only the first word, and end the caption with a period. The caption follows the label (on the same line).

  Figure 1. Duration of responses measured in seconds.

NOTE: If you use a table or figure from an outside source, include full source information in a note at the bottom of the table or figure. This information does not appear in your reference list.

CHECKLIST

PREPARING THE APA REFERENCE LIST

- ☐ Begin the reference list on a new page after the last page of text, numbered as the next page of the paper.
- ☐ Center the title **References** at the top of the page.

- [ ] List the items in the reference list alphabetically (with author's last name first).
- [ ] Type the first line of each entry at the left margin. Indent subsequent lines one-half inch.
- [ ] Separate the major divisions of each entry with a period and one space.
- [ ] Double-space the reference list within and between entries.

CHECKLIST
ARRANGING ENTRIES IN THE APA REFERENCE LIST

- [ ] Single-author entries precede multiple-author entries that begin with the same name.

    Field, S. (1987)

    Field, S., & Levitt, M. P. (1984)

- [ ] Entries by the same author or authors are arranged according to date of publication, starting with the earliest date.

    Ruthenberg, H., & Rubin, R. (1985)

    Ruthenberg, H., & Rubin, R. (1987)

- [ ] Entries with the same author or authors and date of publication are arranged alphabetically according to title. Lowercase letters (*a*, *b*, *c*, and so on) that indicate the order of publication are placed within parentheses.

    Wolk, E. M. (1996a). Analysis . . .

    Wolk, E. M. (1996b). Hormonal . . .

19c Sample APA-Style Research Paper

The following student paper, "Sleep Deprivation in College Students," uses APA documentation style. It includes a title page, an abstract, a reference list, a table, and a bar graph.

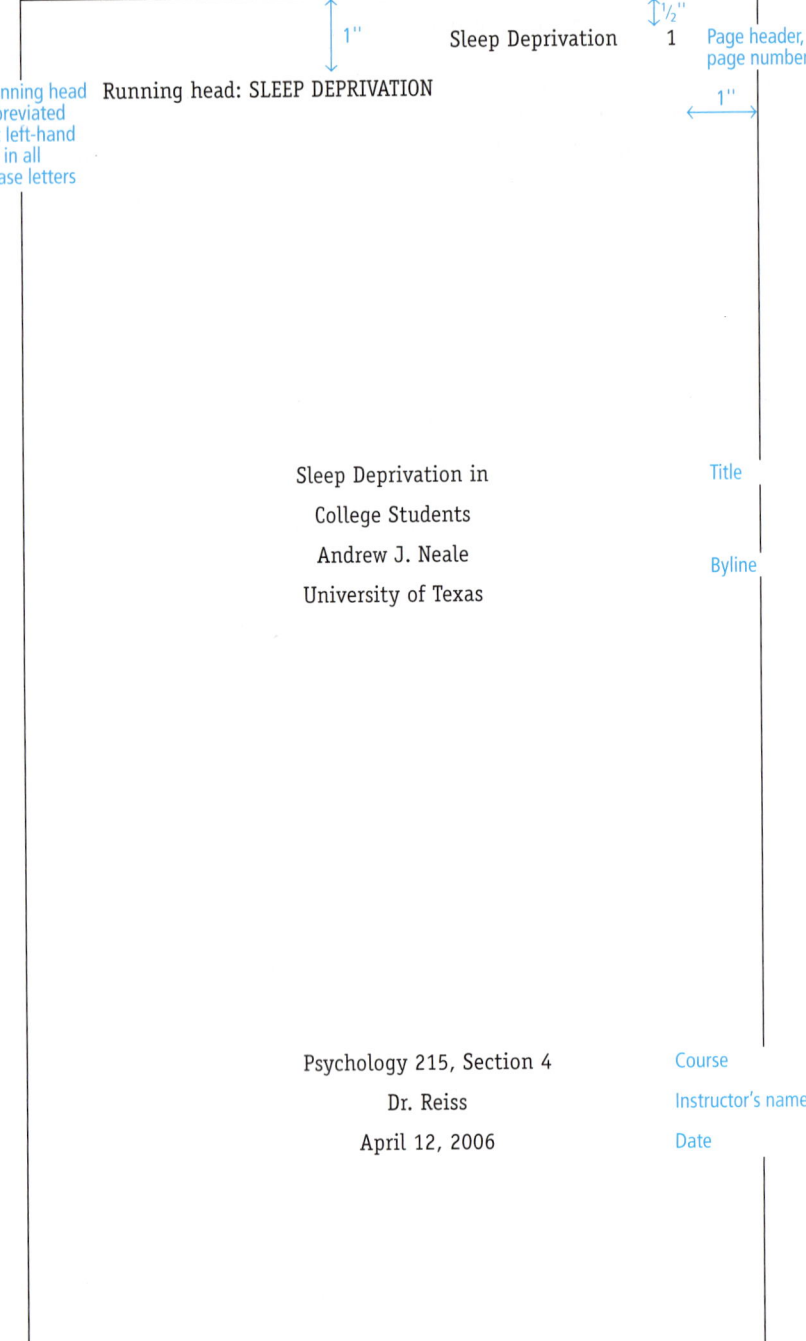

Abstract

A survey of 50 first-year college students in an introductory biology class was conducted. The survey consisted of 5 questions regarding the causes and results of sleep deprivation and specifically addressed the students' study methods and the grades they received on the fall midterm. The study's hypothesis was that although students believe that forgoing sleep to study will yield better grades, sleep deprivation may actually cause a decrease in performance. The study concluded that while only 43% of the students who received either an A or a B on the fall midterm deprived themselves of sleep in order to cram for the test, 90% of those who received a C or a D were sleep deprived.

Sleep Deprivation 3

Sleep Deprivation in College Students

For many college students, sleep is a luxury they feel they cannot afford. Bombarded with tests and assignments and limited by a 24-hour day, students often attempt to make up time by doing without sleep. Ironically, however, students may actually hurt their academic performance by failing to get enough sleep. According to several psychological and medical studies, sleep deprivation can lead to memory loss and health problems, both of which are more likely to harm a student's academic performance than to help it.

Background

Sleep is often overlooked as an essential part of a healthy lifestyle. Millions of Americans wake up daily to alarm clocks because their bodies have not gotten enough sleep. This indicates that for many people, sleep is viewed as a luxury rather than a necessity. As National Sleep Foundation Executive Director Richard L. Gelula observes, "Some of the problems we face as a society—from road rage to obesity—may be linked to lack of sleep or poor sleep" (National Sleep Foundation, 2002, ¶ 3). In fact, according to the National Sleep Foundation, "excessive sleepiness is associated with reduced short-term memory and learning ability, negative mood, inconsistent performance, poor productivity and loss of some forms of behavioral control" (2000, ¶ 2).

Sleep deprivation is particularly common among college students, many of whom have busy lifestyles and are required to memorize a great deal of material before their exams. It is common for college students to take a quick nap between classes or fall asleep while studying in the library because they are sleep deprived. Approximately

44% of young adults experience daytime sleepiness at least a few days a month (National Sleep Foundation, 2002, ¶ 6). Many students face daytime sleepiness on the day of an exam because they stayed up all night studying. These students believe that if they read and review immediately before taking a test—even though this usually means losing sleep—they will remember more information and thus get better grades. However, this is not the case.

A study conducted by professors Mary Carskadon at Brown University in Providence, Rhode Island, and Amy Wolfson at the College of the Holy Cross in Worcester, Massachusetts, showed that high school students who got adequate sleep were more likely to do well in their classes (Carpenter, 2001). According to their study of the correlation between grades and sleep, students who went to bed earlier on both weeknights and weekends earned mainly A's and B's. The students who received D's and F's averaged about 35 minutes less sleep per day than the high achievers (cited in Carpenter). Apparently, then, sleep is essential to high academic achievement.

Once students reach college and have the freedom to set their own schedules, however, many believe that sleep is a luxury they can do without. For example, students believe that if they use the time they would normally sleep to study, they will do better on exams. A recent survey of 144 undergraduate students in introductory psychology classes contradicted this assumption. According to this study, "long sleepers," those individuals who slept 9 or more hours out of a 24-hour day, had significantly higher grade point averages (GPAs) than "short sleepers," individuals who slept less than 7 hours out of a 24-hour day. Therefore, contrary to the belief of many college students, more sleep is often required to achieve a high GPA (Kelly, Kelly, & Clanton, 2001).

Many students believe that sleep deprivation is not the cause of their poor performance, but rather that a host of other factors might be to blame. A study in the *Journal of American College Health* tested the effect that several factors have on a student's performance in school, as measured by students' GPAs. Some of the factors considered included exercise, sleep, nutritional habits, social support, time management techniques, stress management techniques, and spiritual health (Trockel, Barnes, & Egget, 2000). The most significant correlation discovered in the study was between GPA and the sleep habits of students. Sleep deprivation had a more negative impact on GPAs than any other factor did (Trockel et al.).

> First reference includes all three authors; *et al.* replaces second and third authors in subsequent reference in same paragraph

Despite these findings, many students continue to believe that they will be able to remember more material if they do not sleep at all before an exam. They fear that sleeping will interfere with their ability to retain information. Pilcher & Walters (1997), however, showed that sleep deprivation actually impaired learning skills. In this study, one group of students was sleep-deprived, while the other got 8 hours of sleep before the exam. Each group estimated how well it had performed on the exam. The students who were sleep-deprived believed their performance on the test was better than did those who were not sleep-deprived, but actually the performance of the sleep-deprived students was significantly worse than that of those who got 8 hours of sleep prior to the test (Pilcher & Walters, 1997, cited in Bubolz, Brown, & Soper,

2001). This study confirms that sleep deprivation harms cognitive performance even though many students believe that the less sleep they get, the better they will do.

A survey of students in an introductory biology class at the University of Texas demonstrated the effects of sleep deprivation on academic performance and supported the hypothesis that despite students' beliefs, forgoing sleep does not lead to better test scores.

Method

To determine the causes and results of sleep deprivation, a study of the relationship between sleep and test performance was conducted. A survey of 50 first-year college students in an introductory biology class was completed, and their performance on the fall midterm was analyzed.

Each student was asked to complete a survey consisting of the following five questions about their sleep patterns and their performance on the fall midterm:

1. Do you regularly deprive yourself of sleep when studying for an exam?
2. Did you deprive yourself of sleep when studying for the fall midterm?
3. What was your grade on the exam?
4. Do you feel your performance was helped or harmed by the amount of sleep you had?
5. Will you deprive yourself of sleep when you study for the final exam?

To maintain confidentiality, the students were asked not to put their names on the survey. Also, to determine whether the students answered question 3 truthfully, the group grade distribution from the surveys was compared to the number of A's, B's, C's, and D's shown in the instructor's record of the test results. The two frequency distributions were identical.

Results

Analysis of the survey data indicated a significant difference between the grades of students who were sleep-deprived and the grades of those who were not. The results of the survey are presented in Table 1.

Table 1

Results of Survey of Students in University of Texas Introduction to Biology Class Examining the Relationship between Sleep Deprivation and Academic Performance

Grade Totals	Sleep-Deprived	Not Sleep-Deprived	Usually Sleep-Deprived	Improved	Harmed	Continue Sleep Deprivation?
A = 10	4	6	1	4	0	4
B = 20	9	11	8	8	1	8
C = 10	10	0	6	5	4	7
D = 10	8	2	2	1	3	2
Total	31	19	17	18	8	21

The grades in the class were curved so that out of 50 students, 10 received A's, 20 received B's, 10 received C's, and 10 received D's. For the purposes of this survey, an A or B on the exam indicates that the student performed well. A grade of C or D on the exam is considered a poor grade.

Of the 50 students in the class, 31 (or 62%) said they deprived themselves of sleep when studying for the fall midterm. Of these students, 17 (or 34% of the class) answered yes to the second question, reporting they regularly deprive themselves of sleep before an exam.

Of the 31 students who said they deprived themselves of sleep when studying for the fall midterm, only 4 earned A's, and the majority of the A's in the class were received by those students who were not sleep-deprived. Even more significant was the fact that of the 4 students who were sleep-deprived and got A's, only one student claimed to usually be sleep-deprived on the day of an exam. Thus, assuming the students who earn A's in a class do well in general, it is possible that sleep deprivation did not help or harm these students' grades. Not surprisingly, of the 4 students who received A's and were sleep-deprived, all said they would continue to use sleep deprivation to enable them to study for longer hours.

The majority of those who used sleep deprivation in an effort to obtain a higher grade received B's and C's on the exam. A total of 20 students earned a grade of B on the exam. Of those students, only 9, or 18% of the class, said they were deprived of sleep when they took the test.

Students who said they were sleep-deprived when they took the exam received the majority of the poor grades. Ten students got C's on the midterm, and of these 10 students, 100% said they were sleep-deprived when they took the test. Of the 10 students (20% of the class) who got D's, 8 said they were sleep-deprived. Figure 1 shows the significant relationship that was found between poor grades on the exam and sleep deprivation.

Discussion

For many students, sleep is viewed as a luxury rather than as a necessity. Particularly during the exam period,

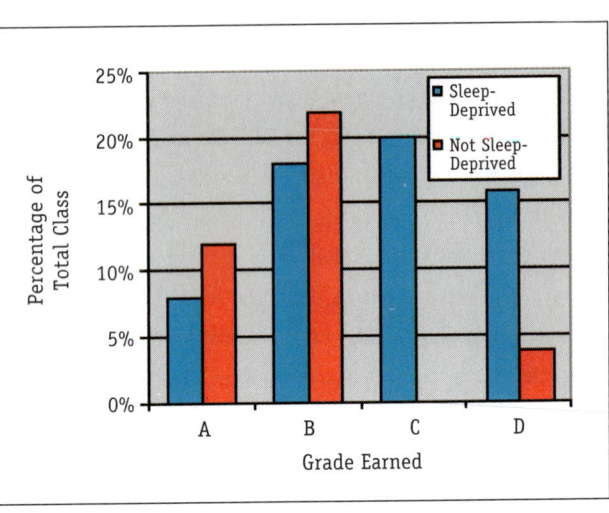

Figure 1. Results of survey of students in University of Texas introduction to biology class examining the relationship between sleep deprivation and academic performance.

students use the hours in which they would normally sleep to study. However, this method does not seem to be effective. The survey discussed here reveals a clear correlation between sleep deprivation and lower exam scores. In fact, the majority of students who performed well on the exam, earning either an A or a B, were not deprived of sleep. Therefore, students who choose studying over sleep should rethink their approach and consider that sleep deprivation may actually lead to impaired academic performance.

References

Bubolz, W., Brown, F., & Soper, B. (2001). Sleep habits and patterns of college students: A preliminary study. *Journal of American College Health, 50,* 131–135.

Carpenter, S. (2001). Sleep deprivation may be undermining teen health. *Monitor on Psychology, 32*(9). Retrieved March 9, 2006, from http://www.apa.org/monitor/oct01/sleepteen.html

Kelly, W. E., Kelly, K. E., & Clanton, R. C. (2001). The relationship between sleep length and grade-point average among college students. *College Student Journal, 35*(1), 84–90.

National Sleep Foundation. (2000). *Adolescent sleep needs and patterns: Research report and resource guide.* Retrieved March 16, 2006, from http://www.sleepfoundation.org/publications/sleep_and_teens_report1.pdf

National Sleep Foundation. (2002, April). *Epidemic of daytime sleepiness linked to increased feelings of anger, stress, and pessimism.* Retrieved March 14, 2006, from http://www.sleepfoundation.org/nsaw/pk_pollresultsmood.html

Trockel, M., Barnes, M., & Egget, D. (2000). Health-related variables and academic performance among first-year college students: Implications for sleep and other behaviors. *Journal of American College Health, 49,* 125–131.

20 Chicago ■ Chicago Documentation Style

DIRECTORY OF CHICAGO-STYLE ENDNOTES AND BIBLIOGRAPHY ENTRIES

PRINT SOURCES: *Entries for Books*

Authors

1. A book by one author (p. 312)
2. A book by two or three authors (p. 312)
3. A book by more than three authors (p. 313)
4. A book by a corporate author (p. 313)
5. An edited book (p. 313)

Editions, Multivolume Works

6. A subsequent edition of a book (p. 313)
7. A multivolume work (p. 314)

Parts of Books

8. A chapter in a book (p. 314)
9. An essay in an anthology (p. 314)

Religious Works

10. A religious work (p. 314)

PRINT SOURCES: *Entries for Articles*

Articles in Scholarly Journals

11. An article in a scholarly journal with continuous pagination through an annual volume (p. 315)
12. An article in a scholarly journal with separate pagination in each issue (p. 315)

Articles in Magazines and Newspapers

13. An article in a weekly magazine (signed/unsigned) (p. 315)
14. An article in a monthly magazine (signed/unsigned) (p. 316)
15. An article in a newspaper (signed/unsigned) (p. 316)

ENTRIES FOR MISCELLANEOUS PRINT AND NONPRINT SOURCES

Interviews

16. A personal interview (p. 317)
17. A published interview (p. 317)

Letters, Government Documents

18. A personal letter (p. 317)
19. A government document (p. 317)

Videotapes, DVDs, and Recordings

20. A videotape or DVD (p. 318)
21. A recording (p. 318)

ELECTRONIC SOURCES: *Entries from Internet Sites*

Internet-Specific Sources

22. An article in an online journal (p. 318)
23. An article in an online magazine (p. 319)
24. An article in an online newspaper (p. 319)
25. A Web site or home page (p. 319)
26. An email message (p. 320)
27. A listserv message (p. 320)

ELECTRONIC SOURCES: *Entries from Subscription Services*

Documents from a Subscription Service

28. A scholarly journal article (p. 320)

20

Chicago Documentation Style

❓ FAQs

When should I use Chicago-style documentation? (p. 310)
How do I prepare a list of endnotes? (p. 322)
How do I arrange the entries in a Chicago-style bibliography? (p. 323)
What does a Chicago-style paper look like? (p. 323)

20a   Using Chicago Style

The Chicago Manual of Style is used in history and in some social science and humanities disciplines. **Chicago style*** has two parts: *notes at the end of the paper* (**endnotes**) and *a list of bibliographic citations.* (Chicago style encourages the use of endnotes, but it allows the use of footnotes at the bottom of the page.)

1 Endnotes and Footnotes

The notes format calls for a **superscript** (raised numeral) in the text after source material you have either quoted or referred to. This numeral, placed after all punctuation marks except dashes, corresponds to the numeral that accompanies the note.

Endnote and Footnote Format: Chicago Style

In the Text

> By November of 1942, the Allies had proof that the Nazis were engaged in the systematic killing of Jews.[1]

---

*Chicago-style documentation follows the guidelines set in *The Chicago Manual of Style*, 15th ed. Chicago: University of Chicago Press, 2003. The manuscript guidelines and sample research paper at the end of this chapter follow guidelines set in Kate L. Turabian's *A Manual for Writers of Term Papers, Theses, and Dissertations*, 6th ed. Chicago: University of Chicago Press, 1993. Turabian style, which is based on Chicago style, addresses formatting concerns specific to college writers.

Print Sources: Entries for Books ■ **Chicago/doc** **20a**

In the Note

   1. David S. Wyman, *The Abandonment of the Jews: America and the Holocaust 1941–1945* (New York: Pantheon Books, 1984), 65.

> **CLOSE-UP**
>
> **SUBSEQUENT REFERENCES TO THE SAME WORK**
>
> In the first reference to a work, use the full citation; in subsequent references to the same work, list only the author's last name, followed by a comma, an abbreviated title, another comma, and a page number.
>
> **First Note on Espinoza**
>
>   1. J. M. Espinoza, *The First Expedition of Vargas in New Mexico, 1692* (Albuquerque: University of New Mexico Press, 1949), 10–12.
>
> **Subsequent Note**
>
>   5. Espinoza, *First Expedition*, 29.
>
> **NOTE:** *The Chicago Manual of Style* allows the use of the abbreviation *ibid.* ("in the same place") for subsequent references to the same work as long as there are no intervening references. *Ibid.* takes the place of the author's name and the work's title—but not the page number.
>
> **First Note on Espinoza**
>
>   1. J. M. Espinoza, *The First Expedition of Vargas in New Mexico, 1692* (Albuquerque: University of New Mexico Press, 1949), 10–12.
>
> **Subsequent Note**
>
>   2. Ibid., 23.

2 Bibliography

In addition to the heading **Bibliography**, Chicago style allows **Selected Bibliography**, **Works Cited**, and **References**. Bibliography entries are arranged alphabetically. Double-space within and between entries.

PRINT SOURCES: Entries for Books — *Chicago*

Capitalize the first, last, and all major words of titles and subtitles. Chicago style recommends the use of italics for titles, but underlining to indicate italics is also acceptable. The following is a sample bibliography entry for a book.

20a Chicago/doc ■ Chicago Documentation Style

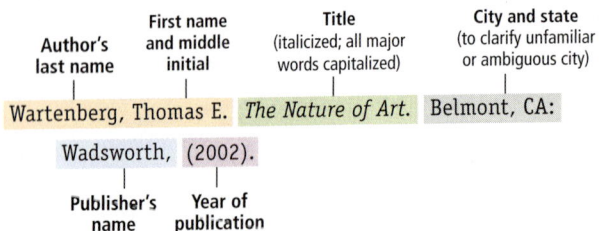

Authors

1. A Book by One Author
Endnote

    1. Robert Dallek, *An Unfinished Life: John F. Kennedy 1917–1963* (New York: Little Brown, 2003), 213.

Bibliography

    Dallek, Robert. *An Unfinished Life: John F. Kennedy 1917–1963.* New York: Little Brown, 2003.

2. A Book by Two or Three Authors
Endnote
Two Authors

    2. Jack Watson and Grant McKerney, *A Cultural History of the Theater* (New York: Longman, 1993), 137.

Three Authors

    2. Nathan Caplan, John K. Whitmore, and Marcella H. Choy, *The Boat People and Achievement in America: A Study of Economic and Educational Success* (Ann Arbor: University of Michigan Press, 1990), 51.

Bibliography
Two Authors

    Watson, Jack, and Grant McKerney. *A Cultural History of the Theater.* New York: Longman, 1993.

Three Authors

    Caplan, Nathan, John K. Whitmore, and Marcella H. Choy. *The Boat People and Achievement in America: A Study of Economic and Educational Success.* Ann Arbor: University of Michigan Press, 1990.

3. A Book by More Than Three Authors
Endnote
Chicago style favors **and others** rather than **et al.** in endnotes.

> 3. Robert E. Spiller and others, eds., *Literary History of the United States* (New York: Macmillan, 1953), 24.

Bibliography
All authors' names are listed in the bibliography.

> Spiller, Robert E., Willard Thorp, Thomas H. Johnson, and Henry Seidel Canby, eds. *Literary History of the United States*. New York: Macmillan, 1953.

4. A Book by a Corporate Author
If a publication issued by an organization does not identify an author, list the organization as the author, even if its name is repeated in the title, in the series title, or as the publisher.

Endnote

> 4. National Geographic Society, *National Parks of the United States*, 3rd ed. (Washington, DC: National Geographic Society, 1997), 77.

Bibliography

> National Geographic Society. *National Parks of the United States*. 3rd ed. Washington, DC: National Geographic Society, 1997.

5. An Edited Book
Endnote

> 5. William Bartram, *The Travels of William Bartram,* ed. Mark Van Doren (New York: Dover Press, 1955), 85.

Bibliography

> Bartram, William. *The Travels of William Bartram*. Edited by Mark Van Doren. New York: Dover Press, 1955.

Editions, Multivolume Works

6. A Subsequent Edition of a Book
Endnote

> 6. Laurie G. Kirszner and Stephen R. Mandell, *The Wadsworth Handbook,* 8th ed. (Boston: Wadsworth, 2008), 52.

Bibliography

> Kirszner, Laurie G., and Stephen R. Mandell. *The Wadsworth Handbook*. 8th ed. Boston: Wadsworth, 2008.

7. A Multivolume Work
Endnote

> 7. Kathleen Raine, *Blake and Tradition* (Princeton, NJ: Princeton University Press, 1968), 1:143.

Bibliography

> Raine, Kathleen. *Blake and Tradition*. Vol. 1. Princeton, NJ: Princeton University Press, 1968.

Parts of Books

8. A Chapter in a Book
Endnote

> 8. Roy Porter, "Health, Disease, and Cure," in *Quacks: Fakers and Charlatans in Medicine* (Gloucestershire, UK: Tempus Publishing, 2003), 182–205.

Bibliography

> Porter, Roy. "Health, Disease, and Cure." Chap. 5 in *Quacks: Fakers and Charlatans in Medicine*. Gloucestershire, UK: Tempus Publishing, 2003.

9. An Essay in an Anthology
Endnote

> 9. G. E. R. Lloyd, "Science and Mathematics," in *The Legacy of Greece,* ed. Moses Finley (New York: Oxford University Press, 1981), 270.

Bibliography

> Lloyd, G. E. R. "Science and Mathematics." In *The Legacy of Greece,* edited by Moses Finley, 256–300. New York: Oxford University Press, 1981.

Religious Works

10. A Religious Work
References to religious works (such as the Bible) are usually limited to the text or notes and not listed in the bibliography. In citing the Bible, include the book (abbreviated), the chapter (followed by a colon), and the verse numbers. Identify the version, but do not include a page number.

Endnote

> 10. Phil. 1:9–11 (King James Version).

PRINT SOURCES: Entries for Articles

Endnotes for articles include just the initial page numbers; bibliography entries supply inclusive page numbers.

The following is a sample bibliography entry for an article.

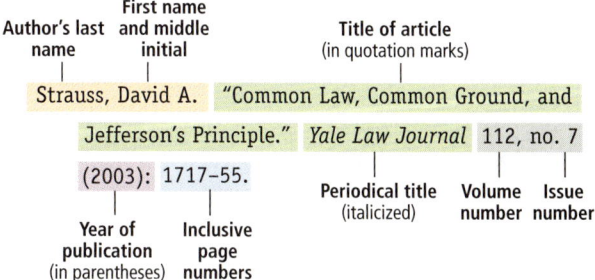

Articles in Scholarly Journals

11. An Article in a Scholarly Journal with Continuous Pagination through an Annual Volume

Endnote

    11. John Huntington, "Science Fiction and the Future," *College English* 37 (Fall 1975): 341.

Bibliography

    Huntington, John. "Science Fiction and the Future." *College English* 37 (Fall 1975): 340–58.

12. An Article in a Scholarly Journal with Separate Pagination in Each Issue

Endnote

    12. R. G. Sipes, "War, Sports, and Aggression: An Empirical Test of Two Rival Theories," *American Anthropologist* 4, no. 2 (1973): 80.

Bibliography

    Sipes, R. G. "War, Sports, and Aggression: An Empirical Test of Two Rival Theories." *American Anthropologist* 4, no. 2 (1973): 65–84.

Articles in Magazines and Newspapers

13. An Article in a Weekly Magazine (Signed/Unsigned)
Endnote
Signed

    13. Pico Iyer, "A Mum for All Seasons," *Time*, April 8, 2002, 51.

Unsigned

    13. "Burst Bubble," *NewScientist,* July 27, 2002, 24.

Bibliography
Signed

    Iyer, Pico. "A Mum for All Seasons." *Time,* April 8, 2002.

Unsigned

    "Burst Bubble." *NewScientist,* July 27, 2002, 24–25.

14. An Article in a Monthly Magazine (Signed/Unsigned)
Endnote
Signed

    14. Tad Suzuki, "Reflecting Light on Photo Realism," *American Artist,* March 2002, 47.

Unsigned

    14. "Repowering the U.S. with Clean Energy Development." *BioCycle,* July 2002, 14.

Bibliography
Signed

    Suzuki, Tad. "Reflecting Light on Photo Realism." *American Artist,* March 2002, 46–51.

Unsigned

    "Repowering the U.S. with Clean Energy Development." *BioCycle,* July 2002, 14.

15. An Article in a Newspaper (Signed/Unsigned)
Endnote
Because the pagination of newspapers can change from edition to edition, Chicago style does not require page numbers for newspaper articles.
Signed

    15. Francis X. Clines, "Civil War Relics Draw Visitors, and Con Artists," *New York Times,* August 4, 2002, national edition, sec. A.

Unsigned

    15. "Feds Lead Way in Long-Term Care," *Atlanta Journal-Constitution,* July 21, 2002, sec. E.

Bibliography
Signed

    Clines, Francis X. "Civil War Relics Draw Visitors, and Con Artists." *New York Times,* August 4, 2002, national edition, sec. A.

Unsigned

"Feds Lead Way in Long-Term Care." *Atlanta Journal-Constitution,* July 21, 2002, sec. E.

NOTE: Omit the article *the* from the newspaper's title, but include a city name in the title, even if it is not part of the actual title.

ENTRIES FOR MISCELLANEOUS PRINT AND NONPRINT SOURCES

Interviews

16. A Personal Interview
Endnote

 16. Cornel West, interview by author, tape recording, June 8, 2003.

Bibliography
Personal interviews are not listed in the bibliography.

17. A Published Interview
Endnote

 17. Gwendolyn Brooks, interview by George Stavros, *Contemporary Literature* 11, no. 1 (Winter 1970): 12.

Bibliography

 Brooks, Gwendolyn. Interview by George Stavros. *Contemporary Literature* 11, no. 1 (Winter 1970): 1–20.

Letters, Government Documents

18. A Personal Letter
Endnote

 18. Julia Alvarez, letter to the author, April 10, 2002.

Bibliography
Personal letters are not listed in the bibliography.

19. A Government Document
Endnote

 19. U.S. Department of Transportation, *The Future of High-Speed Trains in the United States: Special Study, 2001* (Washington, DC: GPO, 2002), 203.

Bibliography

 U.S. Department of Transportation. *The Future of High-Speed Trains in the United States: Special Study, 2001*. Washington, DC: GPO, 2002.

Videotapes, DVDs, and Recordings

20. A Videotape or DVD
Endnote

20. *Interview with Arthur Miller,* dir. William Schiff, 17 min., The Mosaic Group, 1987, videocassette.

Bibliography

Interview with Arthur Miller. Directed by William Schiff. 17 min. The Mosaic Group, 1987. Videocassette.

21. A Recording
Endnote

21. Bob Marley, "Crisis," *Bob Marley and the Wailers,* Kava Island Records 423 095-3, compact disc.

Bibliography

Marley, Bob. "Crisis." *Bob Marley and the Wailers.* Kava Island Records 423 095-3. Compact disc.

Chicago — ELECTRONIC SOURCES: Entries from Internet Sites

Internet citations for electronic sources include the author's name; the title of the document (enclosed in quotation marks); the title of the Internet site (italicized); the publication date (or, if no date is available, the abbreviation **n.d.**); the URL; and the date of access (in parentheses).

Gray, Christopher. "Recalling the Days of Knights and Elks." *New York Times on the Web,* August 24, 2003. http://www.nytimes.com/2003/08/24/realestate/24COV.html (accessed August 25, 2003).

- Author's last name, First name
- Title of article (in quotation marks)
- Date of publication
- Title of Internet site (italicized)
- Date of access (in parentheses)
- URL of database

Internet-Specific Sources

22. An Article in an Online Journal
Endnote

22. Robert F. Brooks, "Communication as the Foundation of Distance Education," *Kairos: A Journal of Rhetoric, Technology, and*

Pedagogy 7, no. 2 (2002), http://english.ttu.edu/kairos/index.html (accessed March 20, 2002).

Bibliography

Brooks, Robert F. "Communication as the Foundation of Distance Education." *Kairos: A Journal of Rhetoric, Technology, and Pedagogy 7,* no. 2 (2002). http://english.ttu.edu/kairos/index.html (accessed March 20, 2002).

23. An Article in an Online Magazine
Endnote

23. Steven Levy, "I Was a Wi-Fi Freeloader," *Newsweek,* October 9, 2002, http://www.msnbc.com/news/816606.asp (accessed January 9, 2004).

Bibliography

Levy, Steven. "I Was a Wi-Fi Freeloader." *Newsweek,* October 9, 2002. http://www.msnbc.com/news/816606.asp (accessed January 9, 2004).

24. An Article in an Online Newspaper
Endnote

24. William J. Broad, "Piece by Piece, the Civil War *Monitor* Is Pulled from the Atlantic's Depths," *New York Times on the Web,* July 18, 2002, http://query.nytimes.com/search/advanced (accessed June 15, 2004).

Bibliography

Broad, William J. "Piece by Piece, the Civil War *Monitor* Is Pulled from the Atlantic's Depths." *New York Times on the Web,* July 18, 2002. http://query.nytimes.com/search/advanced (accessed June 15, 2004).

25. A Web Site or Home Page
Endnote

25. David Perdue, "Dickens's Journalistic Career," *David Perdue's Charles Dickens Page,* September 24, 2002, http://www.fidnet.com/~dap1955/dickens (accessed September 10, 2003).

Bibliography

Perdue, David. "Dickens's Journalistic Career." *David Perdue's Charles Dickens Page.* September 24, 2002. http://www.fidnet.com/~dap1955/dickens (accessed September 10, 2003).

26. An Email Message
Do not include the author's email address after his or her name.

Endnote

26. Meg Halverson, "Scuba Report," email message to author, April 2, 2004.

Bibliography
Email messages are not listed in the bibliography.

27. A Listserv Message
Include the name of the list and the date of the individual posting. Include the listserv address after the date of publication.

Endnote

27. Dave Shirlaw, email to Underwater Archeology discussion list, September 6, 2002, http://lists.asu.edu/archives/sub-arch.html (accessed May 12, 2002).

Bibliography
Listserv messages are not listed in the bibliography.

Chicago — ELECTRONIC SOURCES: *Entries from Subscription Services*

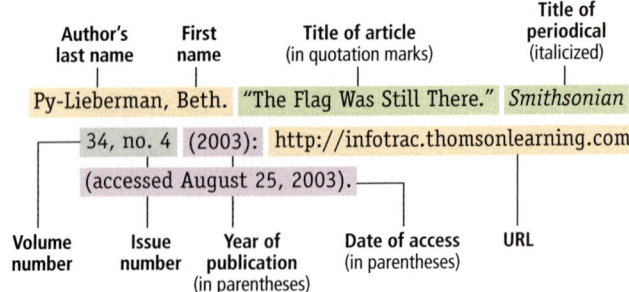

Documents from a Subscription Service

28. A Scholarly Journal Article
Include as much publication information as you can. Always give the URL of the subscription service's main page; the date of access (in parentheses) is optional.

Endnote

28. Richard J. Schaefer, "Editing Strategies in Television Documentaries," *Journal of Communication* 47, no. 4 (1997): 80, http://www.galegroup.com/onefile (accessed October 2, 2003).

Bibliography

Schaefer, Richard J. "Editing Strategies in Television Documentaries." *Journal of Communication* 47, no. 4 (1997): 80. http://www.galegroup.com/onefile (accessed October 2, 2003).

20b Chicago-Style Manuscript Guidelines

CHECKLIST

TYPING YOUR PAPER

When you type your paper, use the student paper in **20c** as your model.

- ☐ On the title page, include the full title of your paper as well as your name. Also include the course title, the instructor's name, and the date. Each element on the title page is considered a major heading and should appear entirely in capitals.
- ☐ Type your paper with a one-inch margin at the top, at the bottom, and on both sides.
- ☐ Double-space your paper throughout.
- ☐ Indent the first line of each paragraph one-half inch. Set off a long prose quotation (ten or more typed lines or more than one paragraph) from the text by indenting the entire quotation one-half inch from the left-hand margin. Do not use quotation marks. If the quotation is a full paragraph, include the paragraph indentation.
- ☐ Number all pages consecutively at the top of the page, with the number either centered or flush right. Page numbers should appear at a consistent distance (at least one-half inch) from the top edge. The title page is not numbered; the first full page of the paper is numbered page 1.
- ☐ Use superscript numbers to indicate in-text citations. Type superscript numbers at the end of cited material (quotations, paraphrases, or summaries). Leave no space between the superscript number and the preceding letter or punctuation mark. The number follows any punctuation mark except for a dash, which it precedes. The note number should be placed at the end of a sentence (or at the end of a clause).
- ☐ When you cite source material in your paper, use Chicago documentation style.

See 20a

CHECKLIST

Using Visuals

According to *The Chicago Manual of Style*, there are two types of visuals: **tables** and **figures** (or **illustrations**), including charts, graphs, photographs, maps, and diagrams.

Tables

- ☐ Give each **table** a label and an arabic number (**TABLE 1**, **TABLE 2**, and so on).
- ☐ Give each table a descriptive title in the form of a sentence. Place the title after the table number.
- ☐ Place both the label and the title above the table.
- ☐ Place source information below the table, introduced by the italicized word **Source**. (If there is more than one source, begin with **Sources**.)

   Source: David E. Fisher and Marshall Jon Fisher, *Tube: The Invention of Television* (Washington, DC: Counterpoint Press, 1996), 185.

If the sources are listed in the bibliography, use a shortened form below the table.

   Source: Fisher and Fisher 1996.

Figures

- ☐ Give each **figure** a label and an arabic number (**Figure 1**) as well as a caption. The label **Figure** may be abbreviated **Fig**. (**Fig. 1**).
- ☐ Place both the label and caption below the figure, on the same line.
- ☐ Place source information in parentheses at the end of the title or caption.

   Fig. 1. Television and its influence on young children. (Photograph from ABC Photos.)

CHECKLIST

Preparing Chicago-Style Endnotes

- ☐ Begin the endnotes on a new page (after the last page of the paper and before the bibliography).
- ☐ Type the title **NOTES** entirely in capitals, and center it two inches from the top of the page.
- ☐ Number the page on which the endnotes appear as the next page of the paper.
- ☐ Type and number notes in the order in which they appear in the paper, beginning with number 1.

- ☐ Type the note number on (not above) the line, followed by a period and one space.
- ☐ Indent the first line of each note one-half inch; type subsequent lines flush with the left-hand margin.
- ☐ Double-space within and between entries.
- ☐ Break URLs after slashes, before punctuation marks, or before or after the symbols = and &.

CHECKLIST

PREPARING A CHICAGO-STYLE BIBLIOGRAPHY

- ☐ Type entries on a separate page after the endnotes.
- ☐ Type the title BIBLIOGRAPHY entirely in capitals, and center it two inches from the top of the page.
- ☐ List entries alphabetically according to the author's last name.
- ☐ Type the first line of each entry flush with the left-hand margin. Indent subsequent lines one-half inch.
- ☐ Double-space within and between entries.

20c Sample Chicago-Style Research Paper (Excerpts)

The following pages are from a student paper, "The Flu of 1918 and the Potential for Future Pandemics," written for a history course. The paper uses Chicago-style documentation and includes a title page, a notes page, and a bibliography.

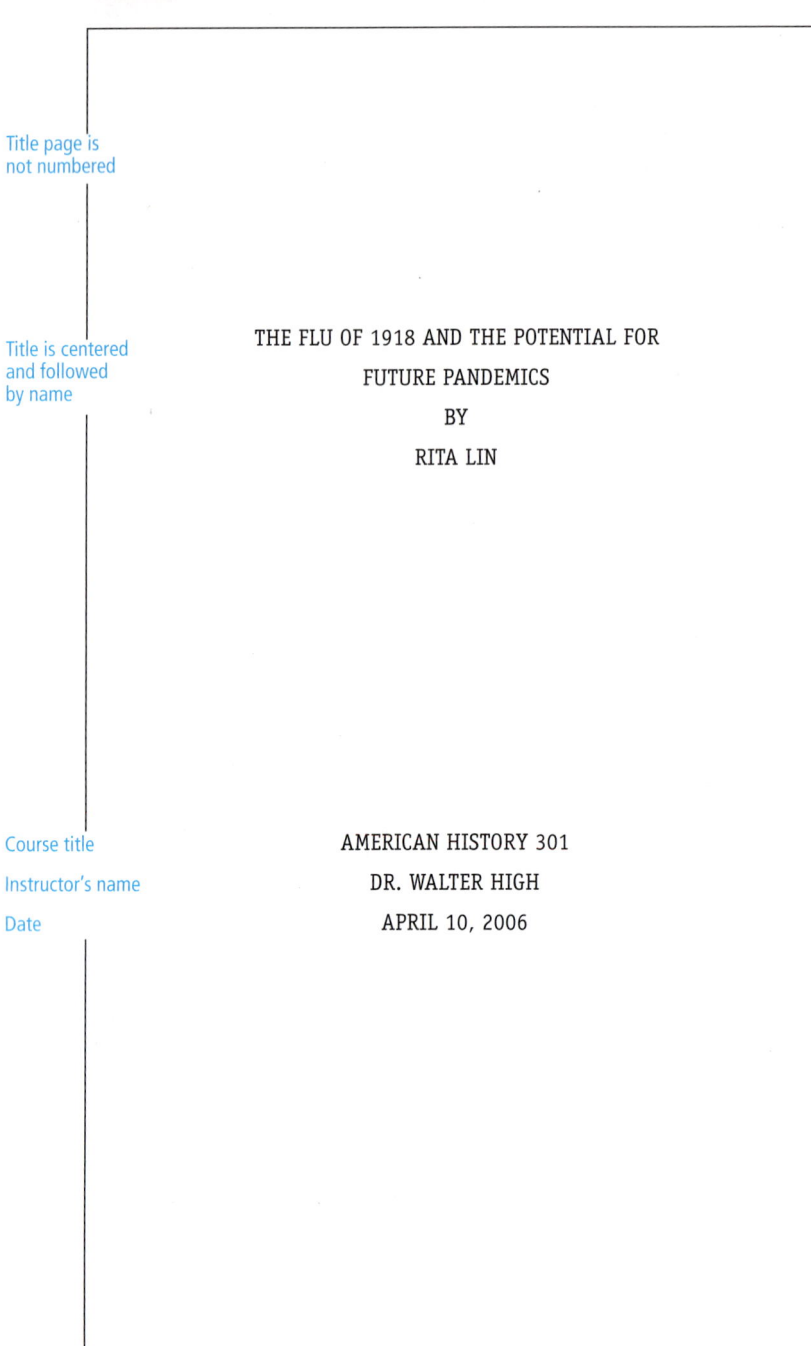

The Flu of 1918 and the Potential for Future Pandemics

In November 2002, a mysterious new illness surfaced in China. By May 2003, what became known as SARS (Severe Acute Respiratory Syndrome) had been transported by air travelers to Europe, South America, South Africa, Australia, and North America, and the worldwide death toll had grown to 250.[1] By June 2003, there were more than 8,200 suspected cases of SARS in 30 countries and 750 deaths related to the outbreak, including 30 in Toronto. Just when SARS appeared to be waning in Asia, a second outbreak in Toronto, the hardest hit of all cities outside of Asia, reminded everyone that SARS remained a deadly threat.[2] As SARS continued to claim more victims and expand its reach, fears of a new pandemic spread throughout the world.

The belief that a pandemic could occur in the future is not a far-fetched idea. During the twentieth century, there were three, and the most deadly one, in 1918, has several significant similarities to the SARS outbreak. As David Brown points out, in many ways, the 1918 influenza pandemic is a mirror reflecting the causes and symptoms, as well as the future potential, of SARS. Both are caused by a virus, lead to respiratory illness, and spread through casual contact and coughing. Outbreaks for both are often traced to one individual, quarantine is the major weapon against the spread of both, and both likely arose from mutated animal viruses. Moreover, as Brown observes, the greatest fear regarding SARS is that it will become so widespread that transmission chains will be undetectable, and health officials will be helpless to restrain outbreaks. Such was the case with the 1918 influenza, which also began mysteriously in China and was transported around the globe (at that time by World War I military ships). By the time the flu lost its power in the spring of 1919, in a year's time it had killed more than 50 million people worldwide,[3] more than twice as many as those who died during the four and a half years of World War I. Thus, if SARS is a reflection of the potential for a future flu pandemic—and experts believe it is—the international community needs to acknowledge the danger, accelerate its research, and develop an extensive virus-surveillance system.

The 1918 flu was different from anything previously known to Americans. Among the peculiarities of the pandemic was its origin and cause. In the spring of 1918,

NOTES

1. Nancy Shute, "SARS Hits Home," *U.S. News & World Report,* May 5, 2003, 42.

2. "Canada Waits for SARS News as Asia Under Control," *Sydney Morning Herald on the Web,* June 2, 2003, http://www.smh.com.au/text/articles/2003/06/01/1054406076596.htm (accessed April 2, 2006).

3. David Brown, "A Grim Reminder in SARS Fight: In 1918, Spanish Flu Swept the Globe, Killing Millions," *MSNBC News Online,* June 4, 2003, http://www.msnbc.com/news/ 921901.asp (accessed April 2, 2006).

4. Doug Rekenthaler, "The Flu Pandemic of 1918: Is a Repeat Performance Likely?—Part 1 of 2," *Disaster Relief: New Stories,* February 22, 1999, http://www.disasterrelief.org/Disasters/990219Flu/ (accessed March 9, 2006).

5. Lynette Iezzoni, *Influenza 1918: The Worst Epidemic in American History* (New York: TV Books, 1999), 40.

6. "1918 Influenza Timeline," *Influenza 1918,* 1999, http://www.pbs.org/wgbh/amex/influenza/timeline/index.html (accessed March 9, 2006).

7. Iezonni, *Influenza 1918,* 131–132.

8. Brown, "Grim Reminder."

9. Iezonni, *Influenza 1918,* 88–89.

10. Ibid, 204.

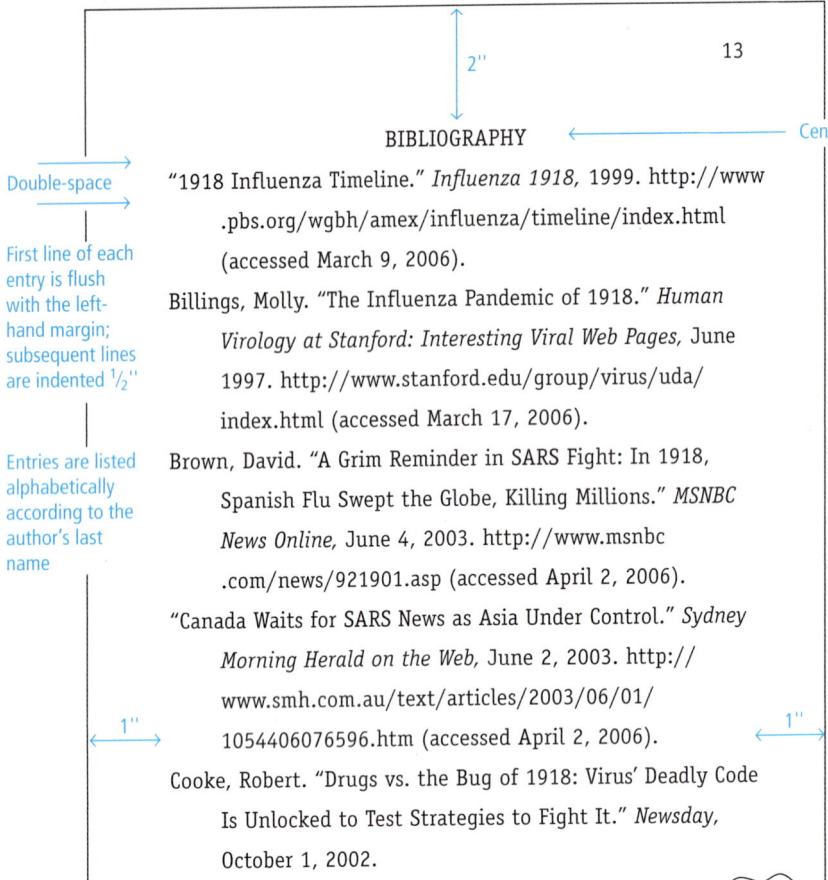

DIRECTORY OF CSE REFERENCE LIST ENTRIES

PRINT SOURCES: *Entries for Books*

Authors
1. A book with one author (p. 332)
2. A book with more than one author (p. 332)
3. An edited book (p. 332)

Parts of Books
4. A chapter or other part of a book with a separate title but with the same author (p. 332)
5. A chapter or other part of a book with a different author (p. 332)

Religious Works, Classical Literature
6. A religious work (p. 333)
7. Classical literature (p. 333)

PRINT SOURCES: *Entries for Articles*

Articles in Scholarly Journals
8. An article in a journal paginated by issue (p. 333)
9. An article in a journal with continuous pagination (p. 333)

Articles in Magazines and Newspapers
10. A magazine article (signed/unsigned) (p. 334)
11. A newspaper article (signed/unsigned) (p. 334)

ENTRIES FOR MISCELLANEOUS PRINT AND NONPRINT SOURCES

Films, Videotapes, Recordings, Maps
12. An audiocassette (p. 334)
13. A film, videotape, or DVD (p. 334)
14. A map (p. 334)

ELECTRONIC SOURCES: *Entries from Internet Sites*

Internet-Specific Sources
15. An online book (p. 335)
16. An online journal (p. 335)

21

CSE and Other Documentation Styles

❓ FAQs

When should I use CSE documentation? (p. 330)
How should I prepare a CSE reference list? (p. 336)
What should a CSE paper look like? (p. 336)
What other documentation styles can I use? (p. 339)

21a Using CSE Style

CSE style,* recommended by the Council of Science Editors (CSE), is used in biology, zoology, physiology, anatomy, and genetics. CSE style has two parts—*documentation in the text* and a *reference list.*

1 Documentation in the Text

CSE style permits either of two documentation formats: *citation-sequence format* and *name-year format.*

Citation-Sequence Format. The **citation-sequence format** calls for either **superscripts** (raised numbers) in the text of the paper (the preferred form) or numbers inserted parenthetically in the text of the paper.

> One study[1] has demonstrated the effect of low dissolved oxygen.

These numbers refer to a list of references at the end of the paper. Entries are numbered in the order in which they appear in the text of the paper. For example, if **James** is mentioned first in the text, **James** will be number 1 in the reference list. When you refer to more than one source in a single note, the numbers are separated by a hyphen if they are in sequence and by a comma if they are not.

> Some studies[2-3] dispute this claim.

> Other studies[3,6] support these findings.

---

*CSE style follows the guidelines set in the style manual of the Council of Science Editors: *Scientific Style and Format: The CSE Manual for Authors, Editors, and Publishers,* 7th ed. New York: Rockefeller UP, 2006.

NOTE: The **citation-name format** is a variation of the citation-sequence format. In the citation-name format, the names in the reference list are listed in alphabetical order. The numbers assigned to the references are used as in-text references, regardless of the order in which they appear in the paper.

Name-Year Format. The **name-year format** calls for the author's name and the year of publication to be inserted parenthetically in the text. If the author's name is used to introduce the source material, only the date of publication is needed in the parenthetical citation.

> A great deal of heat is often generated during this process (McGinness 1999).
>
> According to McGinness (1999), a great deal of heat is often generated during this process.

When two or more works are cited in the same parentheses, the sources are arranged chronologically (from earliest to latest) and separated by semicolons.

> Epidemics can be avoided by taking tissue cultures (Domb 1998) and by intervention with antibiotics (Baldwin and Rigby 1984; Martin and others 1992; Cording 1998).

NOTE: The citation **Baldwin and Rigby 1984** refers to a work by two authors; the citation **Martin and others 1992** refers to a work by three or more authors.

2 Reference List

The format of the reference list depends on the documentation format you use. If you use the **name-year** documentation format, your reference list will resemble the reference list for an **APA** paper. If you use the **citation-sequence** documentation style (as in the paper in 21c), your sources will be listed by number, in the order in which they appear in your paper, on a **References** page. Double-space within and between entries. Type each number flush left, followed by a period and one space. Align the second and subsequent lines with the first letter of the author's last name.

See Ch. 19

PRINT SOURCES:
Entries for Books

List the author or authors by last name; after one space, list the initial or initials (unspaced) of the first and middle names (followed by a period); the title (not underlined, and with only the first word capitalized); the place of publication; the full name of the publisher (followed by a semicolon); the year (followed by a period); and the total number of pages (including back matter, such as the index).

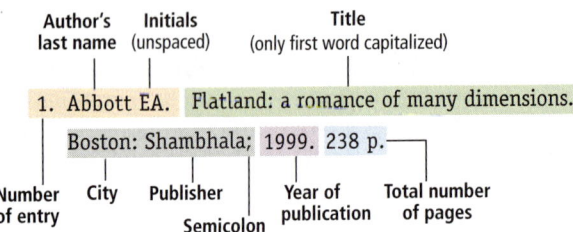

Authors

1. A Book with One Author

> 1. Hawking SW. Brief history of time: from the big bang to black holes. New York: Bantam; 1995. 198 p.

NOTE: No comma follows the author's last name, and no period separates the initials of the first and middle names.

2. A Book with More Than One Author

> 2. Horner JR, Gorman J. Digging dinosaurs. New York: Workman; 1988. 210 p.

3. An Edited Book

> 3. Goldfarb TD, editor. Taking sides: clashing views on controversial environmental issues. 2nd ed. Guilford (CT): Dushkin; 1987. 323 p.

NOTE: The publisher's state, province, or country can be added within parentheses to clarify the location. The two-letter postal service abbreviation can be used for the state or province.

Parts of Books

4. A Chapter or Other Part of a Book with a Separate Title but with the Same Author

> 4. Asimov I. Exploring the earth and cosmos: the growth and future of human knowledge. New York: Crown; 1984. Part III, The horizons of matter; p. 245-294.

5. A Chapter or Other Part of a Book with a Different Author

> 5. Gingerich O. Hints for beginning observers. In: Mallas JH, Kreimer E, editors. The Messier album: an observer's handbook. Cambridge: Cambridge Univ Pr; 1978. p. 194-195.

Religious Works, Classical Literature

6. A Religious Work

6. The New Jerusalem Bible. Garden City (NY): Doubleday; 1985. Luke 15:11-32; p. 1715-1716.

7. Classical Literature

7. Homer. Odyssey; Book 17:319-332. In: Lombardo S, translator and editor. The essential Homer: selections from the Iliad and the Odyssey. Indianapolis: Hackett; 2000. p. 391-392.

PRINT SOURCES: Entries for Articles

List the author or authors (last name first); the title of the article (not in quotation marks, and with only the first word capitalized); the abbreviated name of the journal (with all major words capitalized, but not italicized or underlined); the year (followed by a semicolon); the volume number, the issue number (in parentheses), followed by a colon; and inclusive page numbers. No spaces separate the year, the volume number, and the page numbers. Month names longer than three letters are abbreviated to their first three letters.

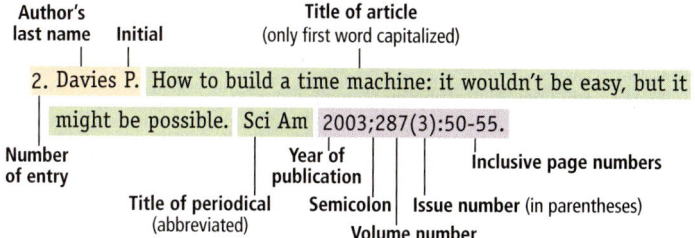

Articles in Scholarly Journals

8. An Article in a Journal Paginated by Issue

8. Sarmiento JL, Gruber N. Sinks for anthropogenic carbon. Phy Today 2002;55(8):30-36.

9. An Article in a Journal with Continuous Pagination

9. Brazil K, Krueger P. Patterns of family adaptation to childhood asthma. J Pediatr Nurs 2002;17:167-173.

NOTE: Omit the month (and day for weeklies) and issue number for journals with continuous pagination within volumes.

Articles in Magazines and Newspapers

10. A Magazine Article (Signed/Unsigned)

Signed

10. Nadis S. Using lasers to detect E.T. Astronomy 2002 Sep:44-49.

Unsigned

10. Brown dwarf glows with radio waves. Astronomy 2001 Jun:28.

11. A Newspaper Article (Signed/Unsigned)

Signed

11. Husted B. Don't wiggle out of untangling computer wires. Atlanta Journal-Constitution. 2002 Jul 21;Sect Q:1(col 1).

Unsigned

11. Scientists find gene tied to cancer risk. New York Times. 2002 Apr 22;Sect A:18(col 6).

ENTRIES FOR MISCELLANEOUS PRINT AND NONPRINT SOURCES

Films, Videotapes, Recordings, Maps

12. An Audiocassette

12. Ascent of man [audiocassette]. Bronowski J. New York: Jeffrey Norton Pub; 1974. 1 audiocassette: 2-track, 55 min.

13. A Film, Videotape, or DVD

13. Stoneberger B, Clark R, editor. Women in science [videocassette]. American Society for Microbiology, producer. Madison (WI): Hawkhill; 1998. 1 videocassette: 42 min., sound, color, 1/2 in. Accompanied by: 1 guide.

14. A Map

A Sheet Map

14. Amazonia: a world resource at risk [ecological map]. Washington: National Geographic Society; 1992. 1 sheet.

A Map in an Atlas

14. Central Africa [political map]. In: Hammond citation world atlas. Maplewood (NJ): Hammond; 1996. p. 114-115. Color, scale 1:13,800,000.

ELECTRONIC SOURCES: Entries from Internet Sites

CSE

Author's last name (unspaced) | Initials | Title of article (only first word capitalized)

3. Sarra SA. The method of characteristics with applications to conservation laws. J Online Math and Its Apps [Internet] 2003 [cited 2003 Aug 26];3. Available from: http://www.joma.org/vol3/articles/sarra/sarra.html

Number of entry | Title of periodical (abbreviated) | Description of medium (in brackets) URL | Year of publication | Date of access (abbreviated; in brackets) | Semicolon | Volume number

Internet-Specific Sources

15. An Online Book

15. Bohm D. Causality and chance in modern physics [Internet]. Philadelphia: Univ of Pennsylvania Pr; c1999 [cited 2005 Aug 17]. Available from: http://www.netlibrary.com/ebook_info.asp?product_id517169

16. An Online Journal

16. Lasko P. The *Drosophila melanogaster* genome: translation factors and RNA binding proteins. J Cell Biol [Internet]. 2000 [cited 2005 Aug 15];150(2):F51-56. Available from: http://www.jcb.org/search.dtl

21b CSE-Style Manuscript Guidelines

CHECKLIST

TYPING YOUR PAPER

When you type your paper, use the student paper in **21c** as your model.

- ☐ Type your name, the course, and the date flush left one inch from the top of the first page.
- ☐ If required, include an **abstract** (a 250-word summary of the paper) on a separate numbered page.
- ☐ Double-space throughout.
- ☐ Insert tables and figures in the body of the paper. Number tables and figures in separate sequences (**Table 1**, **Table 2**; **Figure 1**, **Figure 2**; and so on).

(continued)

TYPING YOUR PAPER *(continued)*

- ☐ Number pages consecutively in the upper right-hand corner; include a shortened title before the number.
- ☐ When you cite source material in your paper, follow **CSE documentation style**.

See 21a

CHECKLIST

PREPARING THE CSE REFERENCE LIST

- ☐ Begin the reference list on a new page after the last page of the paper, numbered as the next page.
- ☐ Center the title **References**, **Literature Cited**, or **References Cited** about one inch from the top of the page.
- ☐ List the entries in the order in which they first appear in the paper—not alphabetically.
- ☐ Number the entries consecutively; type the note numbers flush left on (not above) the line, followed by a period.
- ☐ Leave one space between the period and the first letter of the entry; align subsequent lines directly beneath the first letter of the author's last name.
- ☐ Double-space within and between entries.

21c   Sample CSE-Style Research Paper (Excerpts)

The following pages are from a student paper that explores the dangers of global warming for humans and wildlife. The paper, which cites seven sources and includes a graph, illustrates CSE citation-sequence format.

Sara Castillo
Ecology 4223.01
April 10, 2007

Polar Ice Caps Could Melt by the
End of This Century

The Arctic and Antarctica are homes to the earth's polar ice caps, and global warming appears to be melting them. When polar temperatures increase, parts of floating ice sheets and glaciers break off and melt. This process could eventually cause the ocean levels to rise and have disastrous effects on plants, animals, and human beings. There are ways to prevent this disaster, but they will only be effective if governments have the will to implement them immediately.

The polar ice caps are melting at a rapid rate, and much of the scientific community agrees that global warming is one of the causes. The greenhouse effect, the mechanism that causes global warming, occurs when molecules of greenhouse gases in the atmosphere reflect the rays of the sun back to the earth. This mechanism enables our planet to maintain a temperature adequate for life. However, as the concentration of greenhouse gases in the atmosphere increases, more heat from the sun is retained, and the temperature of the earth rises.[1]

Greenhouse gases include carbon dioxide (CO_2), methane, and nitrous oxide.[2] Since the beginning of the industrial revolution in the late 1800s, people have been burning fossil fuels that create CO_2.[3] This CO_2 has led to an increase in the greenhouse effect and has contributed to the global warming that is melting the polar ice caps. As Figure 1 shows, the surface temperature of the earth has increased by about 1 degree Celsius (1.8 degrees Fahrenheit) since the 1850s. Some scientists have predicted that temperatures will increase even further.

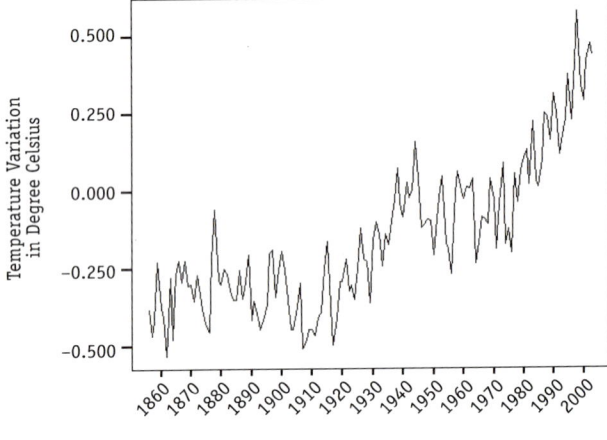

Fig. 1. Global temperature variation from the average during the base period 1961-1990 (adapted from Climatic research unit: data: temperature 2003) [Internet]. [cited 2007 Mar 11]. Available from: http://www.cru.uea.ac.uk/cru/data/temperature.

It is easy to see the effects of global warming. For example, the Pine Island Glacier in Antarctica was depleted at a rate of 1.6 meters per year between 1992 and 1999. This type of melting is very likely to increase the freshwater that drains into the oceans each year, thus

Polar Ice Caps 8

References

1. Edmonds A. A closer look at the greenhouse effect. Brookfield: Copper Beach Books; 1997. 32 p.
2. Smith RL, Smith TM. Elements of ecology. 5th ed. San Francisco: Benjamin Cummings; 2003. 534 p.
3. Pringle L. Global warming: the threat of earth's changing climate. New York: Sea and Star Books; 2001. 48 p.
4. Perkins S. Antarctic glacier thins and speeds up. Sci News 2001;159(5):70.
5. Pearce F. Arctic to lose all summer ice by 2100. New Scientist [Internet]. 2002 [cited 2007 Mar 11];70(2): 99-133. Available from: http://www.newscientist.com
6. The pacific decadal oscillation. BioSci 2000 Aug:32-39.
7. Woods M. Science on ice. Brookfield (CT): Millbrook Press; 1995. 96 p.

1"
Indent 1 space
Double-space
1"
1"
Book with one author
Book with more than one author
Entries listed in order in which they first appear in the paper
Online journal
Print journal

21d Using Other Documentation Styles

The following style manuals describe documentation formats and manuscript guidelines used in various fields.

CHEMISTRY

Dodd, Janet S. American Chemical Society. *The ACS Guide: A Manual for Authors and Editors*. 2nd ed. Washington: Amer. Chemical Soc., 1997.

GEOLOGY

United States Geological Survey. *Suggestions to Authors of the Reports of the United States Geological Survey*. 7th ed. Washington: GPO, 1991.

GOVERNMENT DOCUMENTS

Garner, Diane L. *The Complete Guide to Citing Government Information Resources: A Manual for Writers and Librarians*. Rev. ed. Bethesda: Congressional Information Service, 1993.

United States Government Printing Office. *Style Manual.* Washington: GPO, 2000.

JOURNALISM

Goldstein, Norm, ed. *Associated Press Stylebook and Briefing on Media Law.* 35th ed. New York: Associated P, 2000.

LAW

The Bluebook: A Uniform System of Citation. Comp. Editors of *Columbia Law Review* et al. 16th ed. Cambridge: Harvard Law Rev. Assn., 1996.

MATHEMATICS

American Mathematical Society. *AMS Author Handbook.* Providence: Amer. Mathematical Soc., 1998.

MEDICINE

Iverson, Cheryl. *Manual of Style: A Guide for Authors and Editors.* 9th ed. Chicago: Amer. Medical Assn., 1997.

MUSIC

Holoman, D. Kern, ed. *Writing about Music: A Style Sheet from the Editors of 19th-Century Music.* Berkeley: U California P, 1988.

PHYSICS

American Institute of Physics. *AIP Style Manual.* 5th ed. New York: Am. Inst. of Physics, 1995.

SCIENTIFIC AND TECHNICAL WRITING

Rubens, Philip, ed. *Science and Technical Writing: A Manual of Style.* 2nd ed. New York: Routledge, 2001.

PART 6

Writing in the Disciplines

22 **Writing in the Humanities** 342
- **22a** Understanding Purpose, Audience, and Tone 342
- **22b** Writing Assignments 343
- **22c** Conventions of Style, Format, and Documentation 348
- **22d** Avoiding Plagiarism 348
- **22e** Using Visuals and Technology 348
- **22f** Research Sources 349

23 **Writing a Literary Analysis** 352
- **23a** Reading Literature 352
- **23b** Writing about Literature 353
- **23c** Sample Literary Analysis (without Sources) 355
- **23d** Sample Literary Analysis (with Sources) 359

24 **Writing a Literary Argument** 366
- **24a** Planning a Literary Argument 366
- **24b** Supporting Your Literary Argument 368
- **24c** Organizing a Literary Argument 371
- **24d** Sample Literary Argument 372

25 **Writing in the Social Sciences** 380
- **25a** Understanding Purpose, Audience, and Tone 380
- **25b** Writing Assignments 381
- **25c** Conventions of Style, Format, and Documentation 388
- **25d** Avoiding Plagiarism 388
- **25e** Using Visuals and Technology 388
- **25f** Research Sources 389

26 **Writing in the Natural and Applied Sciences** 392
- **26a** Understanding Purpose, Audience, and Tone 392
- **26b** Writing Assignments 393
- **26c** Conventions of Style, Format, and Documentation 397
- **26d** Avoiding Plagiarism 398
- **26e** Using Visuals and Technology 398
- **26f** Research Sources 398

22

Writing in the Humanities

❓ FAQs

What kinds of assignments can I expect in the humanities? (p. 343)
What documentation styles are used in the humanities? (p. 348)
What research sources will I use in my humanities courses? (p. 349)

The **humanities** include art, drama, film, history, languages, literature, music, philosophy, and religion. In these disciplines, research often involves analyzing or interpreting a primary source—a literary work, a historical document, a musical composition, or a painting or piece of sculpture—or making connections between one work and another. Scholars in humanities disciplines may also cite secondary sources—commentaries on primary sources—to support their points or develop new interpretations.

See 13e2, 14b4

22a Understanding Purpose, Audience, and Tone

Writing assignments in the humanities—in subjects such as literature, philosophy, ethnic studies, and art history—may be formal or informal. While formal writing may require you to use academic discourse and MLA documentation style and format, informal writing assignments may require no more than your personal responses to your reading and observations. Each of these two types of writing has a distinct purpose and tone.

See Ch. 18

Informal writing assignments may have a variety of names: journals, response papers, or daily logs, for example. The purpose of this type of writing is generally to encourage reflection. For this reason, it is acceptable for you to use a relatively conversational, even colloquial, style and to use the first person (*I*). Often, your instructor will specify an audience: your classmates, the instructor, or someone else. Sometimes, you may be asked to share these personal writings on the Web, perhaps by posting weekly responses to a class Web page or class discussion list. At other times, you may keep these writings entirely personal—for example, in a journal that reflects on your learning throughout a semester.

More **formal** writing assignments—bibliographic essays, literary analyses, research papers, and so on—often require that you summarize, analyze, or evaluate print and electronic sources, and synthesize information from a variety of sources. Because the purpose of a formal writing assignment is often to persuade an audience to accept a particular point of view or position, such assignments require a more objective tone and a higher level of diction than informal assignments do.

See 16d3

See 43a

22b Writing Assignments

1 Response Essay

In some humanities disciplines (particularly literature, music, and art), you may be asked to write a **response essay,** an informal reaction to a literary work, a painting, a dance performance, or a concert. This kind of assignment calls for you to write a first-person account of your feelings and reactions.

> **ESL TIP**
>
> Depending on your cultural background, you may not have much experience with personal writing in a school setting. However, when you write a response essay, your instructor expects you to write about *your own reactions*, not give a general description of the subject of your essay.

Assignment (World Music)

> In preparation for writing an informal response to a musical production on campus, attend one of the performances offered by the Music and Drama Department during the upcoming month. Take notes as you watch and listen to the performance. Then, write an informal essay that communicates your response to the performance. What was memorable or remarkable? How did the audience react at particular moments? How did you feel as you were watching and listening, and then how did you feel when the performance was over?

Sample Response Essay (Excerpt)

> When I first arrived, I saw that the people in the audience were pretty much who I expected to see at a classical music recital, including quite a few faculty I recognized. (I'm sure they were shocked to see me there.) The audience was quiet as they waited for Chu's entrance; everyone just kind of sat looking at the darkened stage, which contained a very large grand piano and a cello. When Chu came on stage, the applause was almost deafening. I hadn't realized he was so famous. The

audience quieted down in expectation when he sat down and picked up his bow. The first item on the program was a solo titled *Allegretto Minimoso*. I have to admit that once he started to play his cello, I didn't even notice what was going on in the audience anymore. His music made me think of tall cliffs towering over the ocean under a bright sky during a storm. I was hooked from the first moment.

2 Summary Essay

See 16a

See Ch. 28

Instructors in the humanities may ask you to write summaries to show that you have read and understood assigned material. For this reason, summaries are often used in essay exams.

Assignment (European Philosophers)

To demonstrate your understanding of the readings in this course, write a summary of Louis Althusser's "Ideology and Ideological State Apparatuses," which discusses one of the most important concepts of European Marxism. Be sure to include the title and author in your first paragraph along with a sentence that states the main point of the article. Also include in-text citations that follow MLA guidelines.

Sample Summary Essay (Excerpt)

In "Ideology and Ideological State Apparatuses," Louis Althusser develops a general theory that defines ideology in a broad sense while explaining its role in promulgating the class system. He sees ideology as existing outside of history, as having an unchanging structure (128) and as therefore predictable in its effect. Althusser claims that ideology, whether it is political, religious, ethical, or economic, forms "imaginary" boxes, or varying "world outlooks" (130), which frame individuals' efforts to honestly assess their own living conditions. Ideology reels us in by asserting that we are free-thinking individuals, stringing us along while simultaneously stripping us of autonomy.

3 Annotated Bibliography and Bibliographic Essay

See 13c2

If you are writing a research paper that includes many sources, your instructor may ask you to prepare an annotated bibliography—a list of sources (accompanied by full source information) followed by summary and evaluation. In some cases, you may also be asked to write a bibliographic essay that discusses these sources and their relevance to your research.

Assignment (Nineteenth-Century American Literature)

Write a bibliographic essay that discusses three of the sources you use in your research paper. Do not simply describe or summarize your sources; synthesize, compare, and contrast them, developing your own point in your essay. Be sure to include paraphrases and quotations from your sources as well as a works-cited list.

Sample Bibliographic Essay (Excerpt)

The women mill operatives of Lowell, Massachusetts, produced a variety of writings in different genres that portray the ways in which they negotiated their everyday urban experiences in their boardinghouses and on the factory production line. While their descriptions of daily life in the mill town can be read as a story of their journey to financial independence, these writings also reveal the women's collective coming of political age. The *Lowell Offering*, first published in 1840, was a "monthly magazine, thirty pages long, priced at six and one-quarter cents an issue" (Eisler 33) that began as a corporately owned concern but later was bought, run, and edited by two women who were both former mill operatives. While the publishers of the *Offering* focused on presenting the working women's own creations, *The Factory Girl's Garland*, also begun in 1840 (only to fold less than one year later), was more of a "liberal reformist paper [that] spoke paternalistically in favor of the mill women, and at times even preached at them" (Vogel 791). Jean Marie Lutes explains that some labor reformists among the operatives found the "sentimental tales, romantic stories, and poetic rhyme" of the *Offering* too "neutral," accusing it of having "neglected the operative as a working being" (8). Therefore, they chose to represent their concerns through the *Voice of Industry*, a newspaper whose "case for reform," Lutes argues, was only made possible through the preliminary cultural work performed by the less critical *Offering*: while the *Voice* explicitly called for recognition of working class women's rights, it was the *Offering* that "initiate[d] the discourse of female working-class culture" (9). These periodicals demonstrate various ways in which the operatives were initiating change for white working-class women through both their physical and their literary labors.

Works Cited

Eisler, Benita. *The Lowell Offering: Writings by New England Mill Women (1840-1845)*. New York: Norton, 1998. Print.

Lutes, Jean Marie. "Cultivating Domesticity: Labor Reform and the Literary Culture of the Lowell Mill Girls." *Works and Days* 22.11 (1993): 7-27. Print.

Vogel, Lise. "Their Own Work: Two Documents from the Nineteenth-Century Labor Movement." *Signs: Journal of Women in Culture and Society* 1.3 (1976): 787-802. Print.

4 Analysis Essay

Analysis essays are common in various humanities disciplines. (For examples of literary analyses, **see Chapter 23**.)

Assignment (Advanced Composition)

Research a current ad campaign for a specific product, service, or cause. Select a poster, billboard, or other visual from the campaign, and write an essay analyzing the ad's purpose, target audience, and overall message. Describe how the ad's various elements (words and images) work together to reach the intended audience, and explain who benefits from the ad's message, and how.

Sample Analysis Essay (Excerpt)

The Teen Action Board, a nonprofit group of Massachusetts high school students, recently launched a multimedia campaign aimed at helping to prevent teen dating abuse. The "See It and Stop It!" campaign has produced posters as well as radio and television ads to alert teens to the prevalence and danger of dating abuse in America. One poster, titled "He Calls Her" (see fig. 1), shows a young woman named Angela, whose boyfriend smothers her with repeated phone calls. This ad illustrates the techniques the campaign uses to call attention to the subtle forms of dating abuse that many teens, particularly females, encounter.

The "He Calls Her" poster uses words and images to convey the campaign's overall message: that the effects of dating abuse are clear, even when the signs of abuse are not. The central image of a despondent

Fig. 1. "He Calls Her" campaign poster; *The Advertising Council*; Ad Council, 2003; Web; 26 Feb. 2006.

Angela holding her cell phone, framed on one side with more snapshots of Angela and her phone, shows the reality of a suffocating relationship. The repetition of the phrase "He calls her" reinforces the constancy of the abuse. In addition, the "cut-and-paste" design of the ad—including the hastily taped edges of the creased photos, the prominent text seemingly made from a label-maker, and the smaller, ransom-note-style slogan and logo—conveys the harsh reality and pressing urgency of teen dating abuse.

    The ad establishes a contrast between a healthy relationship ("He calls her") and an unhealthy one ("He calls her 50 times a day") and implores its teen audience to take a stand against abuse. The concluding plea to "speak up against abuse" urges the audience not just to recognize abuse but also to do something about it.

22c Conventions of Style, Format, and Documentation

1 Style and Format

Each humanities discipline has its own specialized vocabulary. You should use the terms used in the field, but be careful not to overuse technical terminology. You can use the first person (*I*) when you are expressing your own reactions and convictions—for example, in a response essay. In other situations, avoid the first person.

Although papers in the humanities do not usually include abstracts, internal headings, tables, or graphs, this situation is changing. Be sure you know what your instructor expects.

See Ch. 23, Ch. 24

NOTE: When you write papers about literature, follow the special conventions that apply to literary analysis.

2 Documentation

See Ch. 18, Ch. 20

Literature and modern and classical language scholars, as well as scholars in music and sometimes in art history, use MLA documentation style; history scholars use Chicago style.

22d Avoiding Plagiarism

See Ch. 17

Humanities sources are usually books and journal articles. When plagiarism occurs, it is often the result of inaccurate summary and paraphrase, failure to use quotation marks where they are required, and confusion between your ideas and those of your sources.

Whenever you use sources, you must be careful to document them. In this way, you acknowledge the work of others who influenced your ideas or contributed to your conclusions. Take accurate notes, avoid cutting and pasting chunks of information into your paper, and whenever you quote, summarize, or paraphrase, do so honestly. Document ideas as well as words, no matter where they come from. "Borrowing" without acknowledgment is plagiarism, and the penalties for plagiarism can be severe. (You do not have to document **common knowledge.** If you have any questions about what constitutes common knowledge in your humanities discipline, be sure to check with your instructor.)

22e Using Visuals and Technology

Many humanities disciplines rely on visual and multimedia texts as well as printed ones. As a result, you may have a great deal of flexibility and creativity in determining what visual media to include in your papers and research projects as well as in choosing a format in which to produce your work.

For example, while a response essay for a literature course may focus on a written work, a response essay for an art history, music appreciation, or theater course will likely focus on a visual image found in a gallery or museum, or on the Web; on an audio recording on CD or in concert; or even on a theatrical performance or a film or television dramatization. Following the guidelines of copyright and fair use, you may be able to include an image or brief audio excerpt—or even a digital video clip of a live or televised performance—in your paper. Similarly, if a review essay you write focuses on film, television, or theater, it may be possible for you to include media clips—or, in some cases, hyperlinks to files and Internet resources that provide a more detailed picture of the event you are reviewing.

22f Research Sources

Each discipline within the humanities has its own methodology, so it is important to know not only the sources or tools that are used by scholars in that field, but also the way students and scholars conduct research.

In literature, for example, scholars may analyze, explain, or interpret the text of a poem, short story, or novel, or the work of a particular author. They study the text itself, but often they also look in books and journal articles for evidence that will support their conclusions. They use the tools of their discipline: library resources (online catalogs, specialized databases, periodical indexes, bibliographies, and so on) and Internet resources to locate that evidence.

In other humanities disciplines—such as history—specialized databases, periodical indexes, reference works, and Web sites also exist. But **primary sources,** such as narratives, letters, diaries, or other original documents, also provide important evidence in historical research.

In some cases, you may be asked to provide your own analysis, interpretation, or criticism of an original text, work of art, or musical composition, without reading what has already been written about it. More often, however, you will be asked to use **secondary sources** to reinforce your conclusions, especially when you are an undergraduate student.

Doing library research in the humanities does not usually require that you know what the latest thinking is about a particular work, author, idea, or theory. Older books and journal articles may be as valuable as recent ones. When you begin your research, you can consult the *Humanities Index,* a general resource that lists articles from more than two hundred scholarly journals in such areas as history, language, literary criticism, philosophy, and religion. It is available in print—with entries arranged alphabetically in yearly volumes according to author and subject—and in electronic form.

Many specialized sources are also available for each humanities discipline. They include databases that cover the literature of that discipline and other sources that provide background information about people, creative works, literary or artistic movements, or historical time periods. Some of these specialized sources will be found in your library's reference collection; others may be available online.

> **CLOSE-UP**
>
> **Finding Additional Sources**
>
> Reading the lists of works cited at the ends of books, chapters, or journal articles may help you to identify other relevant sources. Reference works also frequently include lists of sources for further reading. Finally, annotated bibliographies can help you distinguish the useful sources from the irrelevant ones.

1 Reference Books

Library research is an important part of study in many humanities disciplines. When you begin your research in any subject area, the *Humanities Index* is one general source you can use. Another excellent index available in print and as a computer-searchable database is the *Arts and Humanities Citation Index*. For a list of reference books for specific humanities disciplines, go to http://academic.cengage.com/eng/kirsznermandell/ ▶ *The Wadsworth Handbook* ▶ Chapter 22 ▶ Humanities Reference Books.

2 Databases for Computer Searches

Some of the most helpful databases for humanities disciplines include *Arts and Humanities Citation Index; Art Abstracts/Art Index; MLA International Bibliography; Religion Index; Philosopher's Index, Essay and General Literature Index; Art Bibliographies Modern; America: History and Life; Historical Abstracts; Language and Language Behavior Abstracts (LLBA);* and *RILM Abstracts of Music Literature*. Ask a reference librarian about the availability of these and other databases in your library.

3 Web Sites

For links to Web sites for specific humanities disciplines, go to http://academic.cengage.com/eng/kirsznermandell/ ▶ *The Wadsworth Handbook* ▶ Chapter 22 ▶ Humanities Web Sites.

4 Other Sources of Information

Research in the humanities is not limited to print and electronic resources. For example, historians may do interviews and archival work or consult records collected in town halls, churches, or courthouses; art historians visit museums and galleries; and music scholars attend concerts.

In addition, nonprint sources, such as <u>interviews</u>, can be important resources for a paper in any humanities discipline.

See 14d

23

Writing a Literary Analysis

❓ FAQs

How do I find the real meaning of a literary work? (p. 352)
Do I put a title in quotation marks, or do I italicize it? (p. 354)
What does a literary analysis look like? (p. 355)
How do I use sources in a literary analysis? (p. 359)

Learning to read, respond to, and write about literature are important skills that can serve you while you are a college student as well as later in your life beyond the classroom.

23a Reading Literature

See Ch. 2

When you read a literary work you plan to write about, you use the same critical thinking skills and **active reading** strategies you apply to other works you read: you preview the work and highlight it to identify key ideas and cues to meaning; then, you annotate it carefully.

As you read and take notes, focus on the special concerns of **literary analysis,** considering elements like a short story's plot, a poem's rhyme or meter, or a play's staging. Look for *patterns*, related groups of words, images, or ideas that run through a work. Look for *anomalies*, unusual forms, unique uses of language, unexpected actions by characters, or original treatments of topics. Finally, look for *connections*, links with other literary works, with historical events, or with biographical information.

CLOSE-UP

READING LITERATURE

When you read a work of literature, keep in mind that you do not read to discover the one correct meaning the writer has hidden between the lines. The "meaning" of a literary work is created by the interaction between a text and its readers. Do not assume, however, that a work can mean whatever you want it to mean; ultimately, your interpretation must be consistent with the stylistic signals, thematic suggestions, and patterns of imagery in the text.

23b Writing about Literature

When you have finished your reading and annotating, you decide on a topic, and then you *brainstorm* to find ideas to write about; then, you decide on a *thesis* and use it to help you organize your material. As you arrange related material into categories, you will begin to see a structure for your paper. At this point, you are ready to start drafting your essay.

See 4e4
See 5a–b

When you write about literature, your goal is to make a point and support it with appropriate references to the work under discussion or to related works or secondary sources. As you write, you observe the conventions of literary criticism, which has its own specialized vocabulary and formats. You also respond to certain discipline-specific assignments. For instance, you may be asked to **analyze** a work, to take it apart and consider one or more of its elements—perhaps the plot or characters in a story or the use of language in a poem. Or, you may be asked to **interpret** a work, to explore its possible meanings. Finally, you may be called on to **evaluate** a work, to assess its strengths and weaknesses.

More specifically, you may be asked to trace the critical or popular reception to a work, to compare two works by a single writer (or by two different writers), or to consider the relationship between a work of literature and a literary movement or historical period. You may be asked to analyze a character's motives or the relationship between two characters or to comment on a story's setting or tone. Whatever the case, understanding exactly what you are expected to do will make your writing task easier.

CHECKLIST

CONVENTIONS OF WRITING ABOUT LITERATURE

When you write about a literary work, keep the following conventions in mind:

- ☐ Use present-tense verbs when discussing works of literature (**The character of Mrs. Mallard's husband is not developed**).
- ☐ Use past-tense verbs only when discussing historical events (**Owen's poem conveys the destructiveness of World War I, which at the time the poem was written was considered to be. . . .**); when presenting historical or biographical data (**Her first novel, published in 1811 when Austen was thirty-six, . . .**); or when identifying events that occurred prior to the time of the story's main action (**Miss Emily is a recluse; since her father died she has lived alone except for a servant**).

(continued)

WRITING ABOUT LITERATURE (continued)

- ☐ Support all points with specific, concrete examples from the work you are discussing, briefly summarizing key events, quoting dialogue or description, describing characters or setting, or paraphrasing ideas.

- ☐ Combine paraphrase, summary, and quotation with your own interpretations, weaving quotations smoothly into your paper (**see 16d1**).

- ☐ Be careful to acknowledge all the sources you use, including the literary work or works under discussion. Introduce the words or ideas of others with a reference to the source, and follow borrowed material with appropriate parenthetical documentation (**see 18a1**). Be sure you have quoted accurately and enclosed the words of others in quotation marks.

- ☐ Include a works-cited list (**see 18a2**) in accordance with MLA documentation style.

- ☐ When citing a part of a short story or novel, supply the page number (**168**). For a poem, give the line numbers (**2-4**). For a classic verse play, include act, scene, and line numbers (**1.4.29-31**). For other plays, supply act and/or scene numbers. (For guidelines on quoting more than four lines of prose or more than three lines of poetry, **see 55b2**.)

- ☐ Avoid subjective expressions such as *I feel, I believe, it seems to me,* and *in my opinion*. These weaken your paper by suggesting that its ideas are "only" your opinion and have no validity in themselves.

- ☐ Avoid unnecessary plot summary. Your goal is to draw a conclusion about one or more works and to support that conclusion with pertinent details. If a plot development supports a point you wish to make, a *brief* summary is acceptable, but plot summary is no substitute for analysis.

- ☐ Use literary terms accurately. For example, be careful not to confuse *narrator* or *speaker* with *writer*. Feelings or opinions expressed by a narrator or character do not necessarily represent those of the writer. You should not say **Frost expresses his indecision** when you mean the poem's *speaker* (not the poet) is indecisive. For a glossary of literary terms, go to http://academic.cengage.com/eng/kirsznermandell/ ▶ *The Wadsworth Handbook* ▶ Chapter 23 ▶ Glossary.

- ☐ Italicize titles of books and plays (**see 58a**); enclose titles of short stories and poems in quotation marks (**see 55c**). Book-length poems are treated as long works, and their titles should be italicized.

23c Sample Literary Analysis (without Sources)

Daniel Johanssen, a student in an introductory literature course, wrote an essay about Delmore Schwartz's 1959 poem "The True-Blue American," which appears below. Daniel's essay, which begins on page 357, includes annotations that highlight some conventions of writing about poetry. (Note that because all students in the class selected poems from the same text, Daniel's instructor did not require a works-cited list.)

> **ESL TIP**
>
> You may find English-language poetry difficult to understand, but you should know that even native English speakers may have trouble understanding poetry because of the special ways in which poets use words. Do your best, and remember that as a person who speaks more than one language, you may have a greater sensitivity to language than people who speak only one language.

THE TRUE-BLUE AMERICAN

Jeremiah Dickson was a true-blue American,
For he was a little boy who understood America, for he felt that he must
Think about *everything*; because that's all there is to think about,
Knowing immediately the intimacy of truth and comedy,
Knowing intuitively how a sense of humor was a necessity   5
For one and for all who live in America. Thus, natively, and
Naturally when on an April Sunday in an ice cream parlor Jeremiah
Was requested to choose between a chocolate sundae and a banana split
He answered unhesitatingly, having no need to think of it
Being a true-blue American, determined to continue as he began: 10
Rejecting the either-or of Kierkegaard,[1] and many another European;

(continued)

THE TRUE-BLUE AMERICAN *(continued)*

Refusing to accept alternatives, refusing to believe the choice
  of between;
Rejecting selection; denying dilemma; electing absolute
  affirmation:
knowing
  in his breast   15
    The infinite and the gold
    Of the endless frontier, the deathless West.
"Both: I will have them both!" declared this true-blue American
In Cambridge, Massachusetts, on an April Sunday, instructed
  By the great department stores, by the Five-and-Ten,   20
Taught by Christmas, by the circus, by the vulgarity and
  grandeur of Niagara Falls and the Grand Canyon,
Tutored by the grandeur, vulgarity, and infinite appetite
  gratified and
    Shining in the darkness, of the light
On Saturdays at the double bills of the moon pictures,
The consummation of the advertisements of the imagination   25
  of the light
Which is as it was—the infinite belief in infinite hope—
  of Columbus, Barnum, Edison, and Jeremiah Dickson.

---

[1] Søren Kierkegaard (1813–1855)—Danish philosopher who greatly influenced twentieth-century existentialism. *Either-Or* (1841) is one of his best-known works.

Johanssen 1

Daniel Johanssen
Professor Stang
English 1001
8 April 2006

Irony in "The True-Blue American"

    The poem "The True-Blue American," by Delmore Schwartz, is not as simple and direct as its title suggests. In fact, the title is extremely ironic. At first, the poem seems patriotic, but actually the flag-waving strengthens the speaker's criticism. Even though the poem seems to support and celebrate America, it is actually a bitter critique of the negative aspects of American culture.

    According to the speaker, the primary problem with America is that its citizens falsely believe themselves to be authorities on everything. The following lines introduce the theme of the "know-it-all" American: "For he was a little boy who understood America, for he felt that he must / Think about *everything*; because that's *all* there is to think about" (lines 2-3). This theme is developed later in a series of parallel phrases that seem to celebrate the value of immediate intuitive knowledge and a refusal to accept or to believe anything other than what is American (4-6).

    Americans are ambitious and determined, but these qualities are not seen in the poem as virtues. According to the speaker, Americans reject sophisticated "European" concepts like doubt and choices and alternatives and instead insist on "absolute affirmation" (13)—simple solutions to complex problems. This unwillingness to compromise translates into stubbornness and materialistic greed. This tendency is illustrated by the boy's asking for *both* a chocolate sundae *and* a banana split at the ice cream parlor—not "either-or" (11). Americans are characterized as pioneers who want it all, who will stop at nothing to achieve "The infinite and the gold / Of the endless frontier, the deathless West" (16-17). For the speaker, the pioneers who seek this "endless frontier" are not noble or self-sacrificing; they are like greedy little boys at an ice cream parlor.

According to the speaker, the greed and materialism of America began as grandeur but ultimately became mere vulgarity. Similarly, the "true-blue American" is not born a vulgar parody of grandeur; he learns from his true-blue fellow Americans, who in turn were taught by experts:

> By the great department stores, by the
>   Five-and-Ten,
> Taught by Christmas, by the circus, by the
>   vulgarity and grandeur of Niagara Falls
>   and the Grand Canyon,
> Tutored by the grandeur, vulgarity,
>   and infinite appetite
> gratified. . . . (20-22)

Among the "tutors" the speaker lists are such American institutions as department stores and national monuments. Within these institutions, grandeur and vulgarity coexist; in a sense, they are one and the same.

The speaker's negativity climaxes in the phrase "Shining in the darkness, of the light" (23). This paradoxical statement suggests that negative truths are hidden beneath America's glamorous surface. All the grand and illustrious things of which Americans are so proud are personified by Jeremiah Dickson, the spoiled brat in the ice cream parlor.

Like America, Jeremiah has unlimited potential. He has native intuition, curiosity, courage, and a pioneer spirit. Unfortunately, however, both America and Jeremiah Dickson are limited by their willingness to be led by others, by their greed and impatience, and by their preference for quick, easy, unambiguous answers rather than careful philosophical analysis. Regardless of his—and America's—potential, Jeremiah Dickson is doomed to be hypnotized and seduced by glittering superficialities, light without substance, and to settle for the "double bills of the moon pictures" (24) rather than the enduring truths of a philosopher such as Kierkegaard.

23d Sample Literary Analysis (with Sources)

Tim Westmoreland, a student in an introductory literature course, wrote the following analysis of John Updike's short story "A&P." The paper uses MLA documentation style.

Westmoreland 1

Tim Westmoreland
Professor Adkins
Literature 2101
25 February 2006

"A&P": A Class Act

John Updike's "A&P," like many of his other works, is a "profoundly American" story about social inequality and an attempt to bridge the gap between social classes (Steiner). The story is told by an eighteen-year-old boy who is working as a checkout clerk in an A&P in a small New England town five miles from the beach. The narrative is delivered in a slangy, colloquial voice that tells of a brief but powerful encounter with a "beautiful but inaccessible girl" from another social and economic level (Wells 128). Sammy, the narrator, is working his cash register on a slow Thursday afternoon when, as he says, "In walks these three girls in nothing but bathing suits" (Updike, "A&P" 230). Lengel, the store's manager—a Sunday school teacher and "self-appointed moral policeman"—confronts the girls, telling them that they should be decently dressed (Wells 131). It is a moment of embarrassment and insight for all parties concerned, and in an apparently impulsive act, Sammy quits his job. Although the plot is simple, what is at the heart of the story is complex: a noble gesture that serves as a futile attempt to cross social and economic boundaries.

Through Sammy's eyes, we see the class conflict that defines the story. The privileged young girls in bathing suits are very different from the few customers who are shopping in the store. Sammy refers to the customers as "sheep" (Updike, "A&P" 231) and describes one of them as

---

Title included because paper cites two sources by Updike

Thesis statement

"a witch about fifty with rouge on her cheekbones and no eyebrows" (Updike, "A&P" 230). Other customers are characterized in equally negative terms—for example, "houseslaves in pin curlers" (Updike, "A&P" 231) and "an old party in baggy gray pants" (Updike, "A&P" 232.) Unlike the other customers, the leader of the three girls is described as a "queen":

> She came down a little hard on her heels, as if she didn't walk in her bare feet that much, putting down her heels and then letting the weight move along to her toes as if she was testing the floor with every step, putting a little deliberate extra action into it. (Updike, "A&P" 230)

It seems clear that Sammy realizes that Queenie and her friends come from farther away than just the beach. They have come to test the floors of a store patronized by the less well-off and do it openly, in defiance of social rules. In a sense, they are "slumming."

Queenie, whose name suggests her superior status, understands her position in social as well as sexual terms. Sammy has to spend the summer working, but she has come to the A&P just to purchase "Kingfish Fancy Herring Snacks in Pure Sour Cream" for her parents. (The exotic and expensive herring snacks hints at their different backgrounds.) Regardless, the two act in ways that are not all that different. Both are self-consciously trying out new roles, with Sammy trying to rise above his station in life and Queenie trying to move below hers. As Queenie arrives at the register, Sammy observes, "Now her hands are empty, not a ring or a bracelet, . . . and I wonder where the money's coming from. Still with that prim look she lifts a folded dollar bill out of the hollow at the center of her nubbled pink top" (Updike, "A&P" 232). With this gesture, she not only tests her own sexual powers but also sinks to the level of the supermarket. Despite her act, though, Sammy knows how different Queenie's world is from his:

> I slid right down her voice into her living room. Her father and the other men were standing around in ice-cream coats and bow ties and the women were in sandals picking up herring snacks on toothpicks off a big plate and they were all holding drinks the color of water with olives and sprigs of mint in them. When my parents have somebody over they get lemonade and if it's a real racy affair Schlitz in tall glasses with "They'll Do It Every Time" cartoons stencilled on. (Updike, "A&P" 232)

As Updike says in an interview with writer Donald Murray, "[Sammy] is a blue-collar kid longing for a white-collar girl."

At this point in the story, as Sammy says, "everybody's luck begins to run out" (Updike, "A&P" 232). Lengel, the store manager, who represents "the cruel and unethical" rules that govern matters of social etiquette (Updike, interview), confronts the girls, telling them that they are indecently dressed. "'We *are* decent,' Queenie says suddenly, her lower lip pushing, getting sore now that she remembers her place, a place from which the crowd that runs the A&P must look pretty crummy" (Updike, "A&P" 233). Suddenly, Sammy can no longer be a detached observer and, in a gesture of defiance, he quits. The real question here is *why* he quits. In fact, Updike himself wonders "to what extent his gesture of quitting has to do with the fact that she is rich and he is poor" (Interview).

By quitting, Sammy challenges social inequality, but is his response really just heroic posturing—or simply an expression of his long-standing frustration? In other words, does Sammy quit because of what Updike calls a "misunderstanding of how the world is put together" (Interview) or because he is "a boy who's tried to reach out of his immediate environment towards something bigger and better" ("Still Afraid")? Although Sammy's action may be simply impulsive—Sammy even states it would be "fatal" (Updike, "A&P" 233) not to go through with his initial gesture—it seems likely that he is taking a deliberate stand against what he sees as social injustice. Unlike Queenie's act of defiance, Sammy's gesture will have long-term consequences (Oates). As Updike points out, in Sammy's small town everyone will find out what he has done, and he may be "known . . . as a quitter" (Interview). Sammy's understanding and acceptance of these consequences ("'You'll feel this for the rest of your life.' Lengel says, and I know that's true, . . . "), and of the limitations his social class imposes upon him, constitute his initiation into adulthood (Updike, "A&P" 234). Whether quitting is Sammy's first step toward overcoming these limitations or a romantic gesture he will live to regret remains to be seen. As Updike says, "How blind we are, as we awkwardly push outward into the world!" ("Still Afraid").

Although it is true that both Queenie and Sammy attempt to cross social boundaries, the reason for their actions are different. Queenie's provocative gesture is well thought out: she deliberately relinquishes her trappings, her clothes and jewelry. If only for a few minutes, she sheds her dignity and her wealth in order to flaunt her sexuality and her power. In contrast, Sammy chooses impulsively, in what Updike calls a "hot flash," a "moment of manly decisiveness," to take action and, ultimately, gives up both his dignity and his power (Interview). He gains only a brief moment of glory before he finds himself alone in the parking lot. In this instant, he confronts the social inequality and the unspeakable frustration it represents. According to Updike, Sammy cannot win—even though in a "noble surrender of his position," he gains an understanding of the weight he must bear (Interview).

Works Cited

Oates, Joyce Carol. "John Updike's American Comedies." *Joyce Carol Oates on John Updike*. U of San Francisco, 5 Apr. 1998. Web. 15 Jan. 2006.

Steiner, George. "Supreme Fiction: America Is in the Details." *The New Yorker*. Condé Nast, 11 Mar. 1996. Web. 20 Feb. 2006.

Updike, John. "A&P." *Literature: Reading, Reacting, Writing*. Ed. Laurie G. Kirszner and Stephen R. Mandell. 6th ed. Boston: Wadsworth, 2007. 230-34. Print.

---. Interview by Donald Murray. *The Heinle Original Film Series in Literature*. Dir. Bruce Schwartz. Thomson, 2004. DVD.

---. "Still Afraid of Being Caught." *New York Times*. New York Times, 8 Oct. 1995. Web. 16 Feb. 2006. Print.

Wells, Walter. "John Updike's 'A&P': A Return Visit to Araby." *Studies in Short Fiction* 30.2 (1993): 127-33. *Magazine Index Plus*. Web. 15 Feb. 2006.

24

Writing a Literary Argument

❓ FAQs

What kind of topic should I choose? (p. 366)
What kind of evidence should I use to support my literary argument? (p. 368)
Should I use visuals? (p. 371)
What should a literary argument look like? (p. 372)

See Ch. 23

When you write a literary argument, you follow the same process you do when you write a literary analysis. However, because the purpose of an argument is to convince readers, you need to use some additional strategies to present your ideas.

24a Planning a Literary Argument

1 Choosing a Debatable Topic

Your first step in writing a literary argument will be to decide on a specific topic to write about. Because an argumentative essay attempts to change the way readers think, it must focus on a **debatable topic,** one about which reasonable people may disagree. **Factual statements**—statements about which reasonable people do *not* disagree—are therefore inappropriate as topics for argument.

> **Factual Statement:** Linda Loman is Willy Loman's long-suffering wife in Arthur Miller's play *Death of a Salesman*.
>
> **Debatable Topic:** More than a stereotype of the long-suffering wife, Linda Loman in Arthur Miller's play *Death of a Salesman* is a multidimensional character.

2 Developing an Argumentative Thesis

After you have chosen your topic, your next step is to state your position in an **argumentative thesis**—one that takes a strong stand. Properly worded, this thesis statement will lay the foundation for the rest of your argument.

One way to make sure that your thesis actually does take a stand is to formulate an **antithesis**—a statement that takes an arguable position opposite from yours. If you can construct an antithesis, you can be certain that your thesis statement takes a stand. If you cannot, your thesis statement needs further revision to make it an argumentative thesis.

> **Thesis Statement:** The last line of Richard Wright's short story "Big Black Good Man" indicates that Jim was fully aware all along of Olaf's deep-seated racial prejudice.
>
> **Antithesis:** The last line of Richard Wright's short story "Big Black Good Man" indicates that Jim remained unaware of Olaf's feelings toward him.

3 Defining Your Terms

You should always define the key terms you use in your argument. For example, if you are using the term *narrator* in an essay, make sure that readers know whether you are referring to a first-person or a third-person narrator. In addition, you may need to clarify the distinction between an **unreliable narrator**—someone who misrepresents or misinterprets events—and a **reliable narrator**—someone who accurately describes events. Without a clear definition of the terms you are using, readers may have a very difficult time understanding the point you are making.

CLOSE-UP

DEFINING YOUR TERMS

Be especially careful to use precise terms in your thesis statement. Avoid vague and judgmental words, such as *wrong*, *bad*, *good*, *right*, and *immoral*.

Vague: The poem "Birmingham Sunday (September 15, 1963)" by Langston Hughes shows how bad racism can be.

Clear: The poem "Birmingham Sunday (September 15, 1963)" by Langston Hughes makes a moving statement about how destructive racism can be.

---

4 Considering Your Audience

As you plan your essay, keep your audience in mind. For example, if you are writing about a work that has been discussed in class, you can assume that your readers are familiar with it; include plot summary only when it is needed to explain or support a point you are making. Keep in mind that you will be addressing an academic

24b Writing a Literary Argument

audience—your instructor and possibly some students. For this reason, you should be sure to follow the **conventions of writing about literature** as well as the conventions of standard written English.

See 23b

When you write an argumentative essay, always assume that you are addressing a skeptical audience. Remember, your thesis is debatable, so not everyone will agree with you—and even if your readers are sympathetic to your position, you cannot assume that they will accept your ideas without question.

5 Refuting Opposing Arguments

See 10a5

As you develop your literary argument, you may need to **refute**—that is, to disprove—opposing arguments by demonstrating that they are false, misguided, or illogical. By summarizing and refuting opposing views, you make opposing arguments seem less credible to readers; thus, you strengthen your case.

In the following paragraph, a student refutes the argument that Homer Barron, a character in William Faulkner's short story "A Rose for Emily," is gay.

Summary of opposing argument

A number of critics have suggested that Homer Barron, Miss Emily's suitor, is gay. Certainly, there is some evidence in the story to support this interpretation. For example, the narrator points out that Homer enjoys "the company of men" (Faulkner 220) and that he is not "a marrying man" (Faulkner 220). In addition, the narrator describes Homer as wearing yellow gloves when he takes Emily for drives. According to the critic William Greenslade, in the 1890s yellow was associated with homosexuality (24).

Refutation

This evidence, however, does not establish that Homer is gay. During the nineteenth century, many men preferred the company of other men (as many do today). This, in itself, did not mean they were gay. Neither does the fact that Homer wears yellow gloves. According to the narrator, Homer is a man who likes to dress well. It is certainly possible that he wears these gloves to impress Miss Emily, a woman he is trying to attract.

24b Supporting Your Literary Argument

1 Using Evidence Effectively

Many literary arguments are built on **assertions**—statements made about a debatable topic—that are backed by **evidence**—supporting examples in the form of references to the text, quotations, and the opinions of literary critics. For example, if you stated that Torvald Helmer, Nora's husband in Henrik Ibsen's play *A Doll House*, is as much a victim of society as his wife is, you could support this assertion with relevant quotations and examples from the play. You could also paraphrase, summarize, or quote the ideas of literary critics who also hold this opinion. Remember, only assertions that are **self-evident** (**All plays include characters and dialogue**) or **factual** (***A Doll House* was published in 1879**) need no supporting evidence. All other kinds of assertions require support.

2 Establishing Credibility

Some people bring **credibility** with them whenever they write. When a well-known literary critic evaluates the contributions of a particular writer, you can assume that he or she speaks with authority. (Although you might question the critic's opinions, you do not question his or her expertise.) But most people do not have this kind of credibility. When you write a literary argument, you must constantly work to establish credibility. You do this by *demonstrating knowledge, maintaining a reasonable tone,* and *presenting yourself as someone worth listening to.*

Demonstrating Knowledge. One way to establish credibility is by presenting your own carefully considered ideas about a subject. A clear argument and compelling support can demonstrate to readers that you know what you are talking about.

You can also show readers that you have thoroughly researched your subject. By referring to important sources and by providing accurate documentation for your information, you present evidence that you have done the necessary background reading.

Maintaining a Reasonable Tone. Your **tone**—your attitude toward your readers or subject—is almost as important as the information you convey. Talk *to* your readers not *at* them. If you lecture your readers or appear to talk down to them, you will alienate them. Generally speaking, readers are more likely to respond to a writer who seems balanced and respectful than one who seems strident or condescending.

As you write your essay, use moderate language, and qualify your statements so that they seem reasonable. Try to avoid words and phrases such as *all, never, always,* and *in every case,* which can make your points seem simplistic, exaggerated, or unrealistic. Also, avoid absolute statements. For example, the statement **In "Doe Season," the ocean symbolizes Andy's attachment to her mother** leaves no room for other possible interpretations. A more measured and accurate statement might be **In "Doe Season," the ocean seems to suggest Andy's identification with her mother and her realization that she is becoming a woman.**

Presenting Yourself as Someone Worth Listening To. When you write a literary argument, you should try to present yourself as someone your readers will want to listen to. Make your argument confidently, and don't apologize for your views. For example, do not use phrases such as "In my opinion" and "It seems to me," which undercut your credibility. Finally, avoid the use of *I* (unless you are asked to give your opinion or to write a reaction statement), and avoid slang and colloquialisms.

3 Being Fair

College writing requires that you stay within the bounds of fairness and that you avoid conclusions based on **bias** (preconceived ideas) rather than on evidence. To make sure that the support for your argument is not misleading or distorted, you should follow these guidelines:

- ***Avoid distorting evidence.*** Distortion is misrepresentation. Writers sometimes misrepresent the extent to which critical opinion supports their thesis. For example, by saying that "many critics" think that something is so when only one or two do, they try to make a weak case stronger than it actually is.
- ***Avoid quoting out of context.*** When you take words from their original setting and use them in another, you are quoting out of context. When you quote a source's words out of their original context, you can change the meaning of what someone has said or suggested. For example, you are quoting out of context if you say, **Emily Dickinson's poems are so idiosyncratic that they do not appeal to readers** when your source says, "Emily Dickinson's poems are so idiosyncratic that they do not appeal to readers *who are accustomed to safe, conventional subjects.*" By eliminating a key portion of the original source's sentence, you alter its meaning.
- ***Avoid slanting.*** When you select only information that supports your position and ignore information that does not, you are guilty of slanting. You can eliminate this problem by including a full range of examples, not just examples that support your thesis.
- ***Avoid using unfair appeals.*** Writers of literary arguments rely on logic to convince readers that their ideas are worth considering. Problems arise, however, when writers use **logical fallacies**—flawed arguments—to fool readers into thinking that a conclusion is valid when it is not. Writers can also undercut their credibility if they use questionable support—books and articles by writers who have little or no expertise on the topic. This is especially true when

See 9d

information is obtained from the Internet, where the credentials of a writer may be difficult or impossible to assess.

4 Using Visuals as Evidence

Visuals—photographs, drawings, diagrams, and the like—can add a persuasive dimension to your essay. Because visual images have an immediate impact, they can sometimes make a good literary argument even better. In a sense, visuals are another type of evidence that can support your thesis.

Of course, not all visuals will be appropriate or effective for a literary argument. Before using a visual, make certain it actually supports the point you are making. If it does not, it will distract readers and thereby undercut your argument. To ensure that readers understand the purpose the visual is supposed to serve, introduce it with a sentence that establishes its context; then, discuss its significance, paying particular attention to how it helps you make your point. Finally, be sure to include full documentation for any visual that is not your original creation.

24c Organizing a Literary Argument

In its simplest form, a literary argument—like any argumentative essay—consists of a thesis statement and supporting evidence. Like other argumentative essays, however, literary arguments frequently include additional elements to win audience approval and to overcome potential opposition.

ELEMENTS OF LITERARY ARGUMENTS

- **Introduction:** The introduction should orient readers to the subject of your essay, presenting the issue you will discuss and explaining its significance.
- **Thesis statement:** In most literary arguments, you will present your thesis statement in your introduction. However, if you think your readers may not be familiar with the issue you are discussing (or if it is very controversial), you may want to postpone stating your thesis until later in the essay—perhaps until after the background section.
- **Background:** In this section, you can survey critical opinion about your topic, perhaps pointing out the shortcomings of these opinions. You can also define key terms, review basic facts, or briefly summarize the plot of the work or works you will discuss.
- **Arguments in support of your thesis:** Here you present your assertions and the evidence to support them. It makes sense to move

(continued)

ELEMENTS OF LITERARY ARGUMENTS *(continued)*

from least controversial to most controversial point or from most familiar to least familiar idea.
- **Refutation of opposing arguments:** In a literary argument, you may want to summarize and refute the most obvious arguments against your thesis. If you do not address these opposing arguments, doubts about your position will remain in your readers' minds.
- **Conclusion:** Your conclusion will often restate your thesis as well as the major arguments you have made in support of it. Your conclusion can also summarize key points, remind readers of the weaknesses of opposing arguments, or underscore the logic of your position.

24d Sample Literary Argument

The following student paper presents a literary argument about Dee, a character in Alice Walker's short story "Everyday Use." The student author supports her thesis with ideas she developed as she read the story as well as with information she found when she did research. She also includes two visuals from a DVD of the story.

Margaret Chase
Professor Sierra
English 1001
16 April 2006

The Politics of "Everyday Use"

Alice Walker's "Everyday Use" focuses on a mother, Mrs. Johnson, and her two daughters, Maggie and Dee, and how they view their heritage. The story's climax comes when Mrs. Johnson rejects Dee's request to take a hand-stitched quilt with her so that she can hang it on her wall. Knowing that Maggie will put the quilt to "everyday use," Dee is horrified, and she tells her mother and Maggie that they do not understand their heritage. Although many literary critics see Dee's desire for the quilt as materialistic and shallow, a closer examination of the social and historical circumstances in which Walker wrote this 1973 story suggests a more generous interpretation of Dee's behavior.

On the surface, "Everyday Use" is a story about two sisters, Dee and Maggie, and Mrs. Johnson, their mother. Mrs. Johnson tells the reader that "Dee, . . . would always look anyone in the eye. Hesitation was no part of her nature" (470). Unlike her sister, Maggie is shy and introverted. She is described as looking like a lame animal that has been run over by a car. According to the narrator, "She has been like this, chin on chest, eyes on ground, feet in shuffle" (470) ever since she was burned in a fire.

Unlike Dee, Mrs. Johnson never received an education. After second grade, she explains, the school closed down. She says, "Don't ask me why: in 1927 colored asked fewer questions than they do now" (470). Mrs. Johnson admits

Chase 2

that she accepts the status quo even though she knows that it is unjust. This admission further establishes the difference between Mrs. Johnson and Dee: Mrs. Johnson has accepted her circumstances, while Dee has worked to change hers. Their differences are illustrated in a film version of the story by their contrasting dress. As shown in fig. 1, Dee and her boyfriend Hakim dress in the Afrocentric style of the late 1960s, embracing their African heritage. However, Mrs. Johnson and Maggie dress in plain, conservative clothing.

Fig. 1. Dee and Hakim arrive at the family home; "Everyday Use," *Wadsworth Original Film Series in Literature,* dir. Bruce R. Schwartz; Wadsworth, 2005; DVD.

When Dee arrives home with her new boyfriend, it soon becomes obvious that her character is, for the most part, unchanged. As she eyes her mother's belongings and asks Mrs. Johnson if she can take the top of the butter churn home with her, it is clear that she is still very materialistic. However, her years away from home have also politicized her. Dee now wants to be called "Wangero" because she believes (although mistakenly) that her given name comes from whites who owned her ancestors. She wears African clothing and talks about how a new day is dawning for African Americans.

The meaning and political importance of Dee's decision to adopt an African name and wear African clothing cannot be fully understood without a knowledge of the social and political context in which Walker wrote this story. Walker's own comments about this time period explain Dee's behavior and add meaning to it.

Social and historical context used as evidence to support thesis

In an interview with her biographer, Evelyn C. White, Walker explains that the late 1960s was a time of cultural and intellectual awakening for African Americans. Many turned ideologically and culturally to Africa, adopting the dress, hairstyles, and even the names of their African ancestors. Walker admits that as a young woman she too became interested in discovering her African heritage. (In fact, she herself was given the name *Wangero* during a visit to Kenya in the late 1960s.) Walker tells White that she considered keeping this new name but eventually realized that to do so would be to "dismiss" her family and her American heritage. When she researched her American family, she found that her great-great-grandmother had walked from Virginia to Georgia carrying two children. "If that's not a Walker," she says, "I don't know what is." Thus, Walker realized that, over time, African Americans had actually transformed the names they had originally taken from their enslavers. To respect the ancestors she knew, Walker says, she decided it was important to retain her name.

Chase 4

Along with adopting symbols of their African heritage, many African Americans also worked to elevate these symbols, such as the quilt shown in fig. 2, to the status of high art. According to Kalamu Ya Salaam, one way of doing this was to put these objects in museums; another was to hang them on the walls of their homes. Such acts were aimed at convincing whites that African Americans had an old and rich culture, and that consequently, they deserved not only basic civil rights, but also respect. These gestures were also meant to improve self-esteem and pride within black communities (42-43).

Fig. 2. Traditional hand-stitched quilt; Evelyn C. White, "Alice Walker: Stitches in Time," interview, *Wadsworth Original Film Series in Literature*, dir. Bruce R. Schwartz; Wadsworth, 2005; DVD.

Admittedly, as some critics have pointed out, Dee is more materialistic than political. For example, although Mrs. Johnson makes several statements throughout the story that suggest her admiration of Dee's defiant character, she also identifies incidents that highlight Dee's materialism and selfishness. When their first house burned down, Dee watched it burn while she stood under a tree with "a look of concentration" (470) rather than remorse. Mrs. Johnson knows that Dee hated their small, dingy house, and she knows too that Dee was glad to see it destroyed. Furthermore, Walker acknowledges in the interview with Evelyn C. White that as she was writing the story, she imagined that Dee might even have set the fire that destroyed the house and scarred her sister. Even now, Dee is ashamed of the tin-roofed house her family lives in, and she has said that she would never bring her friends there. Mrs. Johnson has always known that Dee wanted "nice things" (470); even at sixteen, "she had a style of her own: and knew what style was" (470). However, although these examples indicate that Dee is materialistic and self-serving, they also show positive traits: pride and a strong will. Knowing that she will encounter strong opposition wherever she goes, she works to use her appearance to establish power. Thus, her desire for the quilt can be seen as an attempt to establish herself and her African-American culture in a society dominated by whites.

Refutation of opposing argument

Mrs. Johnson knows Dee wants the quilt, but she decides instead to give it to Maggie. According to literary critics Houston Baker and Charlotte Pierce-Baker, when Mrs. Johnson decides to give the quilt to Maggie, she is challenging Dee's understanding of her heritage. Unlike Dee, Mrs. Johnson recognizes that quilts signify "sacred generations of women who have made their own special kind of beauty separate from the traditional artistic world" (qtd. in Piedmont-Marton 45). According to Baker and Pierce-Baker, Mrs. Johnson realizes that her daughter Maggie, whom she has long dismissed because of her quiet

Analysis of Mrs. Johnson's final act

nature and shyness, understands the true meaning of the quilt in a way that Dee never will (Piedmont-Marton 45). Unlike Dee, Maggie has paid close attention to the traditions and skills of her mother and grandmother: she has actually learned to quilt. More important, by staying with her mother instead of going to school, she has gotten to know her family. She poignantly underscores this fact when she tells her mother that Dee can have the quilt because she does not need it to remember her grandmother. Even though Maggie's and Mrs. Johnson's understanding of heritage may be more emotionally profound than Dee's, it is important not to dismiss Dee's interest in elevating the quilt to the level of high art. The political stakes of defining an object as art in the late 1960s and early 1970s were high, and the fight for equality went beyond basic civil rights.

Conclusion

Although there is much in the story that demonstrates Dee's materialism, her desire to hang the quilt should not be dismissed as simply a selfish act. Like Mrs. Johnson and Maggie, Dee is a complicated character. At the time the story was written, displaying the quilt would have been not only a personal act, but also a political act—an act with important, positive results. The final message of "Everyday Use" may just be that an accurate understanding of the quilt (and, by extension, of African-American culture) requires both views—Maggie's and Mrs. Johnson's "everyday use" and Dee's elevation of the quilt to art.

Works Cited

Piedmont-Marton, Elisabeth. "An Overview of 'Everyday Use.'" *Short Stories for Students* 2 (1997): 42-45. *Literature Resource Center*. Web. 2 Apr. 2006.

Salaam, Kalamu Ya. "A Primer of the Black Arts Movement: Excerpts from *The Magic of Juju: An Appreciation of the Black Arts Movement*." *Black Renaissance/Renaissance Noire* (2002): 40-59. *Expanded Academic ASAP*. Web. 10 Apr. 2006.

Walker, Alice. "Alice Walker: Stitches in Time." Interview by Evelyn C. White. *The Wadsworth Original Film Series in Literature: "Everyday Use."* Dir. Bruce R. Schwartz. Wadsworth, 2005. DVD.

---. "Everyday Use." *Literature: Reading, Reacting, Writing*. Ed. Laurie G. Kirszner and Stephen R. Mandell. 6th ed. Boston: Wadsworth, 2007. 469-75. Print.

25

Writing in the Social Sciences

❓ FAQs

What kinds of assignments can I expect in the social sciences? (p. 381)
What documentation styles are used in the social sciences? (p. 388)
What research sources will I use in my social sciences courses? (p. 389)

The **social sciences** include anthropology, business, criminal justice, economics, education, political science, psychology, social work, and sociology. When you approach an assignment in the social sciences, your purpose is often to study the behavior of individuals or groups. You may be seeking to understand causes; predict results; define a policy, habit, or trend; or analyze a problem.

Before you can approach a problem in the social sciences, you must develop a **hypothesis,** an educated guess about what you believe your research will suggest. Then, you can gather the data that will either prove or disprove that hypothesis. Data may be quantitative or qualitative. **Quantitative data** are numerical—the "countable" results of surveys and polls. **Qualitative data** are less exact and more descriptive—the results of interviews or observations, for example.

25a Understanding Purpose, Audience, and Tone

Like writing assignments in the humanities, writing assignments in the social sciences can be *informal* or *formal*. Informal writing assignments ask you to record your personal observations and reactions. More formal writing assignments require you to analyze and synthesize data. Each of these types of assignments has its own characteristic style and tone.

Informal writing assignments encourage you to examine ideas, phenomena, and data in the world around you. One example of an informal writing assignment is a personal experience essay, in which you are asked to relate your own observations of an event or an experience. Because you are being asked for your personal reactions, it is acceptable to use the first person (*I*) as well as a conversational tone.

Formal writing assignments—such as case studies, research essays, and proposals—use an objective tone and a technical vocabulary. These assignments often require you to examine similarities and differences between what you have observed and what you have read or to evaluate terms and concepts from your course readings and lectures. While the purpose of writing in the social sciences is often to inform, it may also be to persuade—for example, to propose changes in an after-school tutoring center or to convince readers that binge drinking is a problem on campus.

Sometimes your instructor will define an audience for your assignment—your classmates, a supervisor of a social services agency, or a public official, for example—but sometimes you have to come up with your own or assume that you are addressing a general audience of readers in your field.

> **CLOSE-UP**
>
> **USING THE PASSIVE VOICE**
>
> Unlike writers in the humanities, writers in the social sciences often use the **passive voice**. The passive voice enables these writers to avoid the first person and thus to present their research in objective terms.
>
> See 48d

25b Writing Assignments

1 Personal Experience Essay

In some social science disciplines (particularly psychology, education, and sociology), you may write an informal **personal experience essay** that reports on a field trip or a site visit or even an interview with a professional working in the field. In this kind of assignment, you record specific details about an event. For example, students in a sociology class might write about their visit to a state correctional facility or a homeless shelter.

Assignment (Anthropology: Service Learning)

> Describe your first visit to your field-learning site. How did you feel as you made your way there? What expectations did you have? Record your initial impressions of the site: How did you feel as you were walking in? What were the first things you noticed? What surprises did you find?

Sample Personal Experience Essay (Excerpt)

> I walked from Main Street to River and finally onto the two-lane gravel street of Park, where I could see from the distance the dogs running around their pens at the Humane Society. As I walked by the

fenced cages, I hoped that my interaction with the animals would be beneficial for me as well as for them. I walked slowly up to the main office, not sure what to expect. At home, I volunteered at a daycare center, but this was my first time working with animals.

Working with animals was my first choice for the service-learning part of this course. I have loved animals ever since I was a child. However, normally I interact with the pets in people's homes, so I was not accustomed to the behaviors of the affection-starved animals that I encountered at the Humane Society. Each animal has its own sad story. Each has its own personality traits as well. On my first day at the Humane Society, I met Barney, a dog with an interesting personality. He had a bright blue collar around his neck and was full of energy. During our thirty-minute walk, he purposely walked around me and tangled me up in his leash. He repeated this "game" as often as I would allow him to, and he reacted well to affection. Because he wasn't hand-shy, I concluded that his owner had not abused him. Barney and I have already formed a close bond.

2 Book Review

Instructors in the social sciences may ask you to write a book review. A **book review** should include enough summary to familiarize your audience with the book's content. It should also include your evaluation of the book and your analysis of its contribution to the discipline. Be sure to include the author, date, and title of the book in your first paragraph.

Assignment (Political Science)

Who: Your audience for this assignment is your class research group.

What: Write a book review, summarizing the content and commenting on the usefulness to the field, of Steven Kelman's *Making Public Policy: A Hopeful View of American Government.*

When: Due next Tuesday.

Where: For your weekly group meeting.

Why: This book will be one of your sources for your group research project. Reviews will be evaluated according to how well they demonstrate your understanding of the book, what insights they provide into your research topic, and how well they are written.

Sample Book Review (Excerpt)

Kelman next examines the Presidency. In this section, he explores the relationship between the Presidency and the bureaucracy. Rather than dividing the Executive and the bureaucracy into the Senior Executive Service and the Civil Service, Kelman limits his discussion to the Executive Office of the President (EOP) and direct political appointments.

Kelman's observations concerning the importance of organizational structure, ground rules, and operating tradition are important. Particularly significant is how organizational characteristics affect the flow of debate, information, and decision making as well as how these characteristics eliminate certain issues from consideration. For example, when a congressional committee debates legislation, the consequences of different organizational structures become visible and are subject to debate and change. When a committee chair excludes an issue from debate, however, the different organizational structures never become visible. According to Kelman, political decision makers may not even be conscious of the exclusion.

3 Case Study

Social science courses, especially psychology, sociology, and anthropology, frequently require **case studies** that describe, analyze, and solve problems involving human and institutional interactions. Case studies usually describe a problem and suggest solutions or treatments.

In political science, case studies can examine foreign policy negotiations or analyze issues such as government infringement on civil liberties. In psychology, social work, and education, case studies typically focus on individuals and their interaction with peers or with agency professionals.

Assignment (Psychology of the Family)

Write a formal case study of the family you have been studying.

Sample Case Study

Family Profile

The Newberg family consists of Tom and Tina and their children David (8), Angela (6), and Cristina (4).

Problem

Tom has been laid off from his automobile production-line job. Tina is not employed outside the home. They have a mortgage on their home as well as $6,000 in credit card debt.

The loss of income when Tom was laid off from his job caused a change in the economic status of the Newberg family. Initially, Tom and Tina had a negative attitude toward their situation and were not resourceful. Tom tried to maintain his traditional family role, wanting to be the sole provider, while Tina continued to stay at home with their children. Both Tom and Tina saw no way to alleviate their financial difficulties. Both were heavy smokers, and this habit increased their expenses.

Observations

Tom spent so much time looking for a job that he had little time with his family—especially the children. Eventually, Tina borrowed money from her parents to try to start a door-to-door beauty products business. When this failed, she found a job driving a delivery truck, but it was only part time. Tom and Tina's financial situation severely strained the family. Even so, the couple made no plans about where the family would go if they lost their house; they just kept hoping things would improve.

Discussion

Even when both the Newbergs managed to get full-time jobs, they were unable to maintain the lifestyle they were used to. Image is very important to Tom and Tina: they thought they had to look like a traditional family in order to have self-esteem. This is especially important to Tom. The prognosis for the Newberg family, even though they now have a regular income, is not promising unless they learn to cooperate, to set goals as a family, and to share responsibilities. Both debt counseling and family counseling are strongly recommended.

4 Annotated Bibliography and Review-of-Research Essay

Social science instructors may ask you to write an **annotated bibliography** in which you summarize and evaluate each of your research sources. You may also be asked to write a **review-of-research essay** (sometimes called a **review-of-literature essay**), in which you discuss the entries in your annotated bibliography and possibly compare them. The review-of-research essay is often part of a social science research paper. By commenting on recent scholarship on a particular topic, you demonstrate knowledge of the topic as well as an understanding of different critical approaches to that topic.

Assignment (Sociology)

Research an issue of your choice, one that interests you and that has a significant impact on particular populations in your state. Then, compile an annotated bibliography of at least six sources. Finally, write a review-of-research essay that discusses these sources.

Sample Annotated Bibliography (Excerpt)

Adams, J. R. (2002). Farm bill funding boosts FMNP. *National Association of Farmers' Market Nutrition Programs.* Retrieved September 25, 2005, from http://www.nafmnp.org. This excellent article provides current information on the Farmers' Market Nutrition Program (FMNP), with particular reference to its legislative appropriation status. The author stresses the need for continued lobbying to keep FMNP and WIC programs alive.

Sample Review-of-Research Essay (Excerpt)

J. R. Adams (2002) discusses the efforts farmers and lobbyists have made in securing funding for the Farmers' Market Nutrition Program, stressing recent victories in obtaining government funding. For example, even though funding had originally been cut by half in the projected budget for 2002, this shortfall was corrected, and the program's funding was sustained at the same level as it stood in 2001 (Rosen, 2002). Farmers stand to benefit from this program and from the similar Seniors Farmers' Market Nutrition Program (SFMNP). Similarly, as S. Z. Greenberg et al. (2001) point out, these programs not only create a potential new market for farmers' products, but also may benefit from private grants to supplement government funding.

5 Proposal

A **proposal** is often the first stage of a research project. In a proposal, you define your research project and make a convincing case for it.

Assignment (Psychology of Substance Abuse)

Write a proposal to solve a problem associated with alcohol abuse. Each source you use—including Web sites, journal articles, monographs, and interviews—should be documented in APA style.

Sample Proposal (Excerpt)

Statement of the Problem

The physiological effects of alcohol can impair a person's normal functioning. The severity of these effects depends on an individual's Blood Alcohol Concentration (BAC), which is determined by the individual's weight, speed of alcohol consumption, and amount of alcohol consumed. If an individual's BAC is higher than .08, he or she can be charged with Driving Under the Influence (DUI).

As Figure 1 illustrates, the number of DUIs in Frewsdale is high, with 1067 DUI charges in the past 5 years. Of course, this number reflects

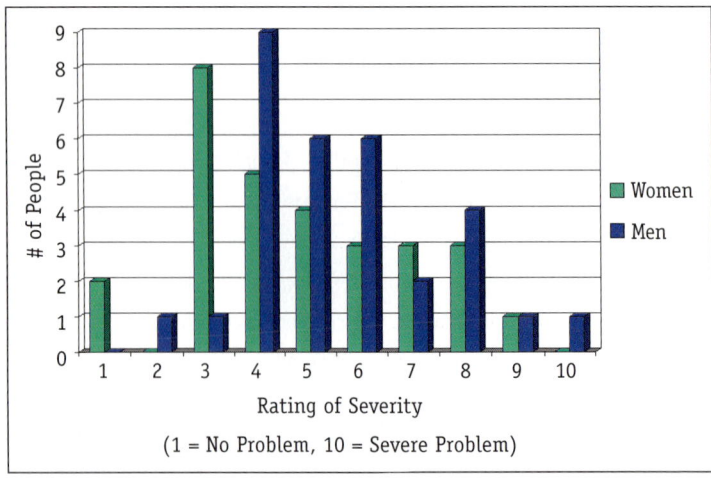

Figure 1. Drunk driving in Frewsdale.

only the individuals who were actually caught; the number of people driving with a BAC higher than .08 is probably much higher, as shown by our survey of Frewsdale University students, in which more than 80% of respondents—none of whom had ever received a DUI charge—indicated that they knew somebody who had driven drunk.

The entire community of Frewsdale would benefit from a program that would get drunk drivers off the road. An alternative transportation method available to people who have been drinking would greatly reduce the number of DUIs in Frewsdale. Furthermore, such a program would reduce the number of people who walk home alone late at night and potentially put themselves at risk.

To address this problem, we propose a safe-ride program for the city, aimed primarily at providing a free ride home on weekends (when people most frequently go out, as Figure 2 shows) for residents of Frewsdale who have been drinking.

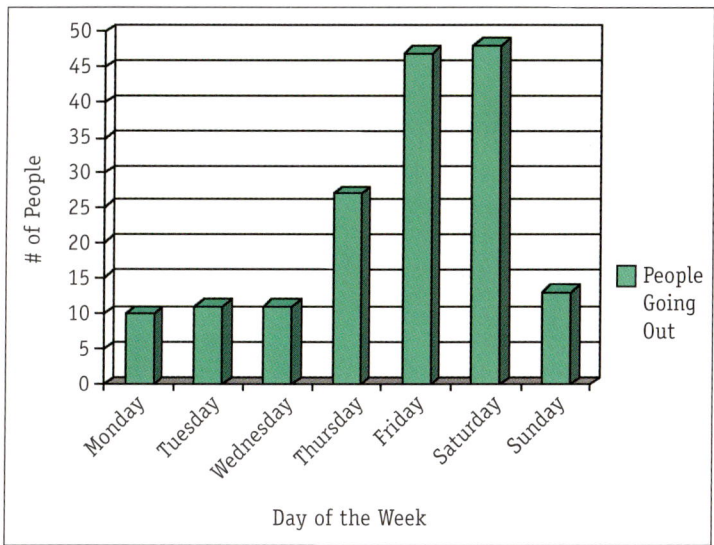

Figure 2. Nights people go out in Frewsdale.

25c Conventions of Style, Format, and Documentation

1 Style and Format

Like other disciplines, the social sciences use a technical vocabulary. Because you are addressing specialists, you should use the specialized vocabulary of the discipline and, when you discuss charts and tables, you should use statistical terms, such as *mean*, *percentage*, and *chi square*. Keep in mind, however, that you should use plain language to explain what *percentages*, *means*, and *standard deviations* signify in terms of your analysis.

See 19b

A social science research paper follows a specific format. For example, **APA manuscript guidelines** require a title page that includes a **running head**, a **title**, and a **byline** (your name, school, and so on). Every page of the paper, including the title page, should have a **page header**, an abbreviated title and page number printed at the top. Social science papers also include **internal headings** (for example, **Method, Results, Background of Problem, Description of Problem, Solutions,** and **Conclusion**). Each section of a social science paper is a complete unit with a beginning and an end so that sections can be read separately, out of context, and still make sense. The body of the paper may present and discuss graphs, maps, photographs, flowcharts, or tables.

2 Documentation

See Ch. 19

Many of the journals in the various social science disciplines use **APA documentation style**.

25d Avoiding Plagiarism

See Ch. 17

When writing in the social sciences, it is important to avoid **plagiarism** by correctly documenting the data, words, and ideas of others that you use in your paper.

In addition, social scientists are bound by ethical considerations regarding the treatment of research subjects, the protection of privacy, and the granting of credit to those who have made substantial contributions to a research project.

25e Using Visuals and Technology

Because of the many types of documents social scientists write and the varied methods of data collection, visuals and technology play an important role in all phases of the writing process.

In the data collection stage of a project, research may involve more than simply transcribing information into print. Digital cameras play an important role in capturing important interactions among subjects, and both digital video and digital audio recorders can assist in the transcription of interviews. These devices allow writers to include both images and audio files in various social science projects.

See 14d

Software available for both the PC and Macintosh—for example, *Adobe Photoshop* for image editing, Apple's *iMovie* for video editing, and *Sound Forge* and *Peak* for sound editing—can help with data representation. These programs help you edit most image, video, or audio data for Web or print delivery. Other useful software applications include statistical packages such as *SAS* and *SPSS*, which analyze quantitative data.

Various types of writing in the social sciences have specific style and formatting conventions that require attention to document design. For example, the general formatting of documents requires the use of headings and subheadings as well as other stylistic elements, such as boldface and italics. Familiarizing yourself with the various menus in your word-processing program that allow you to create and edit tables and charts, as well as with spreadsheet programs like *Microsoft Excel*, will help you design various kinds of documents.

See Ch. 30

25f Research Sources

Although library research is an important component of social science research, social scientists also engage in field research. In **library research,** social scientists consult print and electronic versions of compilations of statistics, government documents, and newspaper articles, in addition to scholarly books and articles. In **field research,** social scientists conduct interviews and surveys and observe individuals and groups. Because so much of their data are quantitative, social scientists must know how to analyze statistics and how to read and interpret tables.

See 14d

Social scientists also must analyze or evaluate the work of others in their fields. They may conduct literature reviews to discover what research has already been done, or they may analyze research reports. Social scientists are particularly interested in case studies and published reports of surveys, opinion polls, interviews, experiments, and observations that may be useful in proving or disproving a theory.

Social scientists are expected to base their studies on the most current thinking surrounding a topic. Statistics *must* be up to date. For this reason, although books may be useful for gathering background information and putting a topic in context, for the most current information, researchers turn to electronic databases to locate recent scholarly journal articles and government publications.

Some excellent databases and print indexes cover the literature of the social sciences. *Social Sciences Citation Index* is available in print and as a database titled *Web of Science*. Other databases and indexes cover specific disciplines within the social sciences. In addition to databases, the Internet may be very helpful to social scientists who are looking for government information, including census data, statistics, congressional reports, laws, and reports issued by government agencies.

See Ch. 15

If you are unsure about using the online catalog or databases to find appropriate books, government publications, statistics, or journal articles, ask for help in the reference department of your library.

1 Reference Books

For a list of social science reference sources, many of which are available on CD-ROM, DVD, or online as well as in print, go to http://academic.cengage.com/eng/kirsznermandell/ ▶ *The Wadsworth Handbook* ▶ Chapter 25 ▶ Social Sciences Reference Books.

2 Government Documents

Government documents are important resources for social scientists because they contain complete and up-to-date facts and figures on a wide variety of subjects. Government documents can be located through the *Monthly Catalog*, which contains the list of documents (in print, microfiche, and electronic form) published each month. Other useful indexes include *The Congressional Information Service Index*, *The American Statistics Index*, and *The Index to U.S. Government Periodicals*.

3 Newspaper Articles

Newspaper articles are particularly good resources for research topics in political science, economics, and business. Useful sources of information from newspapers are *NewsBank*, *National Newspaper Index*, and *LexisNexis Academic Universe*. Some major newspapers also publish indexes to their contents.

4 Databases for Computer Searches

Some of the more widely used databases for social science disciplines are *Cendata*; *General BusinessFile ASAP*; *Social Sciences Citation Index*; *Social Sciences Index*; *PsycINFO*; *ERIC*; *Sociological Abstracts*; *Information*

Science Abstracts; *PAIS International*; *Population Bibliography*; *EconLit*; *ABI/INFORM*; *Management Contents*; *LexisNexis Academic Universe*; and *Facts on File*.

Ask a reference librarian about the availability of these and other databases in your library.

5 Web Sites

For links to Web sites for specific social sciences disciplines, go to http://academic.cengage.com/eng/kirsznermandell/ ▶ *The Wadsworth Handbook* ▶ Chapter 25 ▶ Social Sciences Web Sites.

6 Other Sources of Information

Interviews, surveys, and observations of the behavior of various groups and individuals are important nonlibrary sources for social science research. For example, in a political science class, your instructor may ask you to interview a sample of college students and classify them as conservative, liberal, or moderate. You may be asked to poll each group to find out college students' attitudes on issues such as the death penalty, affirmative action, or the problems of the homeless. If you were writing a paper on educational programs for the mentally gifted, you might observe and compare two classes—one of gifted students and one of average students. You might also interview students, teachers, or parents. Similarly, research in psychology and social work may rely on your observations of clients and their families.

See 14d

26

Writing in the Natural and Applied Sciences

❓ FAQs

What kinds of assignments can I expect in the natural and applied sciences? (p. 393)

What documentation styles are used in the natural and applied sciences? (p. 397)

What research sources will I use in my natural and applied science courses? (p. 398)

26a Understanding Purpose, Audience, and Tone

See Ch. 21

Writing assignments in the natural and applied sciences—for example, in courses in biology, chemistry, geology, astronomy, mathematics, physics, engineering, nursing, and computer science—use a formal, objective tone and follow documentation guidelines such as those published by the Council of Science Editors (CSE).

Most scientific writing is aimed at readers who are familiar with the technical language and writing conventions of a particular scientific discipline, but occasionally it may be aimed at general readers. Its express purpose is to report empirical data (data that are obtained by observations and experiments), and it uses the **scientific method**.

> **CLOSE-UP**
>
> **THE SCIENTIFIC METHOD**
>
> The **scientific method** relies on empirical data to explain and solve problems. After using secondary sources to research a problem, you gather and interpret information by following these steps:
>
> 1. Propose a **hypothesis** that makes a claim about the cause and effect of the problem.
> 2. Plan a research design and methodology.
> 3. Carry out the experiment, recording observations and data.
> 4. Analyze the results of the experiment, carefully comparing the initial hypothesis with the actual results.
> 5. Make recommendations for further experiments.

26b Writing Assignments

1 Laboratory Report

One of the most frequently assigned writing tasks in the sciences is the laboratory report, which is divided into sections that reflect the stages of the scientific method. However, not every section will be necessary for every experiment, and some experiments may call for additional components, such as an abstract or reference list. In addition, lab experiments may include tables, charts, graphs, and illustrations. The exact format for a lab report is usually defined by a course's lab manual.

2 Observation Essay

Some science instructors may ask you to write about and analyze your own observations of the natural world. This is one of the few assignments in the natural and applied sciences in which you will be encouraged to use the first person (*I*). In this type of essay, you first record your observations in detail (using scientific terminology where necessary) and then provide scientific analysis of the phenomena you describe.

Assignment (Ecology)

Write an article for a local environmentalists' magazine in which you describe a natural setting and then discuss the environmental impact of human beings on the place you are describing.

Sample Observation Essay (Excerpt)

    Lake Wenatchee, part of Alpine Lakes, is in the Wenatchee National Forest, where over 700 small, freshwater lakes are scattered throughout the central Cascade region. The average annual precipitation is 40 inches; this rainfall accounts for the mixed conifers—Douglas firs, grand firs, and cedars—that thrive there. The rain-shadow effect also causes the soils in the region to be rich in organic materials as well as basalt, pumice, and volcanic ash. However, human activity—clear-cutting of old growth forest, damming of rivers, and fire suppression—is altering the area's natural ecology. These activities lead to a build-up of debris, a higher number of forest fires, severe soil erosion, and the endangerment of local species of animals and fish.

While climbing one stretch of a barely distinguishable trail, I noticed a very large area on the side of the mountain that had no trees. Because the terrain is sloped, clear-cutting the trees causes extreme soil erosion, including mudslides. Because it also destroys animal habitats, many species of owl, woodpecker, and squirrel will soon be added to the Endangered Species list.

Although clearing the land may be necessary for building new homes, for producing fuel and paper, and for developing agriculture, the trees are being cut faster than they can be replaced. For this reason, the probable future damage that the clear-cutting of so many trees will produce must be assessed.

3 Literature Survey

Literature surveys are common in the sciences, often appearing as a section of a proposal or as part of a research paper. A **literature survey** summarizes a number of studies and sometimes compares and contrasts them. By doing so, the literature survey provides a theoretical context for the paper's discussion.

A literature survey should have a formal and objective tone and be aimed at readers who are experts in your field. The purpose of a literature survey is to give these readers an overview of a range of scholarly publications about your subject. Although you may touch on the history of your topic, your primary focus should be on the most current research available.

Assignment (Biology)

Research an aspect of plant biology and write up your findings in a formal article that contains the following sections: Abstract, Introduction, Literature Survey, Materials, Methods, Results, Discussion, Conclusions, Reference List, and Appendix (if necessary).

Sample Literature Survey (Excerpt)

The cell *Myxococcus xanthus* responds to starvation by initiating a cycle that culminates with the cell forming spore-filled fruiting bodies. This developmental cycle, which is dependent upon changes in gene expression, ensures cell sporulation at the appropriate time and place. Thousands of cells are affected by this process. Recent studies strongly suggest that NtrC-like activators are a crucial component of the complex regulatory controls of *M. xanthus'* developmental program. Twelve NtrC activators were found to be most important in the process.[1] These findings led to further research that examined the specific developmental moments at which NtrC proteins activate specific sets of genes throughout the process.[2] In addition, Garza and others[3] identified two inductive components of the early part of the developmental process.

References

1. Gorski L, Kaiser D. Targeted mutagenesis of σ^{54} activator proteins in *Myxococcus xanthus.* J of Bacteriol 1998;180:5896-5905.
2. Keseler IM, Kaiser D. An early A-signal-dependent gene in *Myxococcus xanthus* has a σ^{54}-like promoter. J of Bacteriol 1995;177:4638-4644.
3. Garza AG, Pollack JS, Harris BZ, Lee A, Keseler IM, Licking EF, Singer M. SdeK is required for early fruiting body development in *Myxococcus xanthus.* J of Bacteriol 1998;180:4628-4637.

4 Abstract

An **abstract**—a concise summary of a technical article—is a standard part of many assignments in the natural sciences. In addition, many scientific indexes include abstracts so that researchers can determine whether an article is of use to them. In the natural sciences, the purpose of an abstract is to inform readers about the goals, methods, and results of the original article.

You begin writing an abstract after you have finished writing your paper. When writing an abstract, follow the organization of your paper, devoting a sentence or two to each of its major sections. State the purpose, the method of research, results, and conclusions in the order in which they appear in the paper, but include only essential information. Keep in mind that abstracts in the sciences do not use quotations or paraphrases.

The following abstract was written as part of the assignment on page 394.

Sample Abstract

This project used Wisconsin Fast Plants to determine the effect of gibberellic acid on plants. Gibberellic acid is a growth hormone that stimulates a plant to grow taller by elongation of internode length. The research tested the hypothesis that plants that are treated with gibberellic acid will grow taller than plants that are untreated, and the internode length on treated plants will be longer than that on untreated plants. Results supported this hypothesis: the internode length on treated plants was longer than that on untreated plants. Furthermore, even the dwarf plants that were treated with gibberellic acid grew longer, reaching almost the same height as the control standard plants by the last day of measurement. Therefore, the results of this experiment indicate that gibberellic acid can stimulate the growth of plants by elongation of internode length, though not by internode number.

5 Biographical Essay

In a science or math course, an instructor may ask you to write an essay about a historical figure. When writing your essay, try to relate the information you find about your subject to the work you have been doing in the course—for example, you might consider how Mendel's ideas about genetics connect to your work on heredity.

Assignment (Geometry)

Select a well-known historical figure whose life and work we have discussed in class. Then, write a biographical essay in which you summarize his or her contributions to geometry.

Sample Biographical Essay (Excerpt)

Jean-Victor Poncelet was born in Metz, northeastern France, in July 1788. He studied calculus with Gaspard Monge at the École Polytechnique and then joined the army as a lieutenant of engineers, following Napoleon to Russia. While he was a prisoner of war in Saratoff on the River Volga, he began researching projective geometry, investigating the projective properties of figures later in his great work *Traité des Propriétés Projectives des Figures*.

Projective geometry is a branch of geometry concerned with properties of geometric figures that retain their character. The basic elements of projective geometry are points, lines, and planes. The concept of parallel does not exist in projective geometry because any pair of distinct lines intersects in a point, and if these lines are parallel in the sense of Euclidean geometry, then their point of intersection is at infinity.

26c Conventions of Style, Format, and Documentation

1 Style and Format

Because writing in the sciences focuses on experiments, not on those conducting the experiments, writers often use the passive voice. For example, in a lab report, you would say, "The mixture was heated for forty-five minutes" rather than "I heated the mixture for forty-five minutes." Another stylistic convention concerns verb tense: a conclusion or a statement of generally accepted fact should be in the present tense ("Objects in motion *tend* to stay in motion"); a summary of a study, however, should be in the past tense ("Watson and Crick *discovered* the structure of DNA"). Finally, note that direct quotations are seldom used in scientific papers.

Because you are writing to inform or persuade other scientists, you should write clearly and concisely. Remember to use technical terms only when they are necessary. Too many terms can make your paper difficult to understand—even for scientists familiar with your discipline.

Keep in mind that each scientific discipline prescribes formats for tables and other visuals and the way they are to be presented. Place tables as close as possible to your discussion of them, and number and label any type of illustration or diagram so you can refer to it in your text.

See 30d1

Remember that different scientific journals may use different paper formats. For example, the *Journal of Immunology* might have a format different from that of the *Journal of Parasitology*. Your instructor may ask you to prepare your paper according to the style sheet of a journal to which you could submit your work. Although publication may seem a remote possibility to you, following a style sheet reminds you that writing in the sciences involves writing for a specific audience.

2 Documentation

Documentation style varies from one scientific discipline to another; even within a given discipline, documentation style may vary from one journal to another. For this reason, ask your instructor which documentation style is required. Many disciplines in the sciences use a number-reference format. For instance, electrical engineers use the format of the Institute for Electronics and Electrical Engineers, chemists use the format of the American Chemical Society, and mathematicians use the format of the American Mathematical Society.

26d Avoiding Plagiarism

In the sciences, it is especially important to acknowledge the work of others who contributed to your research results. If many people contribute to a research project, the work of each one must be properly cited. Falsifying data or using the experimental results, computer codes, chemical formulas, graphs, images, ideas, or words of others without proper acknowledgment is particularly serious because it undermines the integrity of your work.

See Ch. 17

If you need more information about what constitutes **plagiarism** in the sciences or how to cite the work of individual collaborators in a research report, be sure to check with your instructor.

26e Using Visuals and Technology

During the prewriting and drafting stages of your writing, much of your work will involve representing data visually—for example, compiling tables or flowcharts. During the drafting process, these visuals can help you organize information and keep track of complex cause-and-effect relationships.

You can also use your computer to help you organize your notes into files that correspond to the typical sections of a document—for example, Abstract, Introduction, Methods, Results, and References. Later on, you can expand each section and combine sections to form the final version of your document.

More than in other disciplines, research and writing in the natural and applied sciences are done collaboratively. Multiple authors for lab reports, research reports, and grants are common, and a number of electronic strategies—for example, the Comment and Track Changes features in a word processor, email, online real-time discussion, and file storage on a local network or shared computer—can make this collaborative process easier.

26f Research Sources

Although much scientific research takes place in the laboratory or in the natural world, it is also important that scientists know how to do library research. Literature surveys allow scientists to discover what research has already been done. Building on this research, they can conduct meaningful experiments that prove or disprove a theory or solve a problem. Scientists then explain the experimental process so that others can reproduce their results, communicate their findings, and add to the body of scientific knowledge. Much of this research is collaborative. It is not uncommon for several people to work on different aspects of a research problem in the laboratory or in the library and then jointly report on the results.

As in the social sciences, scientists must have the most current information. Books may provide background information, define terms, and assess what has been discovered in the past, but scholarly journal articles, conference proceedings, technical reports, and research reports are essential for locating the most up-to-date and relevant literature.

Some of the most comprehensive databases are those that cover the sciences. *Science Citation Index* covers all the natural and applied sciences. Others cover specific disciplines: *PubMed* (medicine), *Biological Abstracts* (biology), and *Chemical Abstracts* (chemistry) are examples of specialized databases that are also available in print.

1 Reference Books

For a list of science reference sources, many of which are available on DVD, on CD-ROM, in online databases, or in print, go to http://academic.cengage.com/eng/kirsznermandell/ ▶ *The Wadsworth Handbook* ▶ Chapter 26 ▶ Natural and Applied Sciences Reference Books.

2 Databases for Computer Searches

Helpful databases for research in the sciences include: *BIOSIS; Agricola; Aquatic Sciences and Fisheries Abstracts; Columbia Earthscape; CAB Abstracts; CINAHL; Compendex; NTIS; Inspec; PubMed; MATHSCI; Life Sciences Collection; GEOREF; Chemical Abstracts; Environmental Sciences and Pollution Management Abstracts; Science Citation Index; Wildlife and Ecology Studies Worldwide; GEOBASE; OceanBase;* and *Zoological Record Online.* Check with a reference librarian about the availability of these and other databases in your library.

3 Web Sites

For links to Web sites for specific natural and applied sciences disciplines, go to http://academic.cengage.com/eng/kirsznermandell/ ▶ *The Wadsworth Handbook* ▶ Chapter 26 ▶ Natural and Applied Sciences Web Sites.

4 Other Sources of Information

Opportunities for research outside the library vary widely because of the many ways in which scientists can gather information. In agronomy, for example, researchers collect soil samples; in toxicology, they test air or water quality. In marine biology, they might conduct research in a particular aquatic environment, and in chemistry, they conduct experiments to identify an unknown substance. Scientists also conduct surveys: epidemiologists study the spread of communicable diseases, and cancer researchers question populations to determine how environmental or dietary factors influence the likelihood of contracting cancer. Finally, the Internet is an important source of up-to-date scientific information. In fact, scientists have used the Internet for years to share information about their research.

PART 7

Developing Strategies for Academic Success

27 **Ten Habits of Successful Students** 402
27a Learn to Manage Your Time Effectively 402
27b Put Studying First 404
27c Be Sure You Understand School and Course Requirements 405
27d Be an Active Learner in the Classroom 407
27e Be an Active Learner Outside the Classroom 408
27f Take Advantage of College Services 409
27g Use the Library 410
27h Use Technology 411
27i Make Contacts 412
27j Be a Lifelong Learner 413

28 **Writing Essay Exams** 415
28a Planning an Essay Exam Answer 416
28b Shaping an Essay Exam Answer 419
28c Writing and Revising an Essay Exam Answer 420
28d Writing Paragraph-Length Essay Exam Answers 426

29 **Writing for the Workplace** 428
29a Writing Letters of Application 428
29b Designing Print Résumés 430
29c Designing Electronic Résumés 433
29d Writing Memos 438
29e Writing Emails and Sending Faxes 440

30 **Designing Effective Documents** 442
30a Creating an Effective Visual Format 442
30b Using Headings 445
30c Constructing Lists 447
30d Using Visuals 449
30e Using Desktop Publishing 453

31 **Designing a Web Site** 456
31a Planning Your Web Site 456
31b Creating Your Web Site 457
31c Selecting and Inserting Visuals 458
31d Planning Navigation 460
31e Linking Your Content 462
31f Editing and Proofreading Your Web Site 463
31g Posting Your Web Site 463

32 **Making Oral Presentations** 464
32a Getting Started 464
32b Planning Your Speech 465
32c Preparing Your Notes 466
32d Preparing Visual Aids 467
32e Rehearsing Your Speech 470
32f Delivering Your Speech 470

27

Ten Habits of Successful Students

❓ FAQs

What tools can I use to help me manage my time? (p. 402)
What is the best way to study? (p. 404)
What college services can help me? (p. 409)

As you have probably already observed, the students who are most successful in college are not always the ones who enter with the best grades. In fact, successful students have *learned* to be successful: they have developed specific strategies for success, and they apply these strategies to their education. If you take the time, you can learn the habits of successful students and apply them to your own college education—and, later on, to your career.

27a Learn to Manage Your Time Effectively

One of the most difficult things about college is the demands it makes on your time. It is hard, especially at first, to balance studying, coursework, family life, friendships, and a job. But if you do not take control of your schedule, it will take control of you; if you do not learn to manage your time, you will always be struggling to catch up.

❓ Fortunately, there are two tools you can use to help you manage your time: a **personal organizer** and a **monthly calendar**. (Of course, simply buying an organizer and a calendar will not solve your time-management problems—you have to *use* them. Moreover, you have to use them effectively and regularly.)

Carry your organizer with you at all times, and post your calendar in a prominent place (perhaps above your desk or on your refrigerator). Remember to record *in both places* not only school-related deadlines, appointments, and reminders (every assignment due date, study group meeting, conference appointment, and exam), but also outside responsibilities such as work hours and dental appointments. Record tasks and dates as soon as you learn of them; if you do not write something down immediately, you are likely to forget it. (If you make an entry in your organizer while you are in class, be sure to copy it onto your calendar when you get home.)

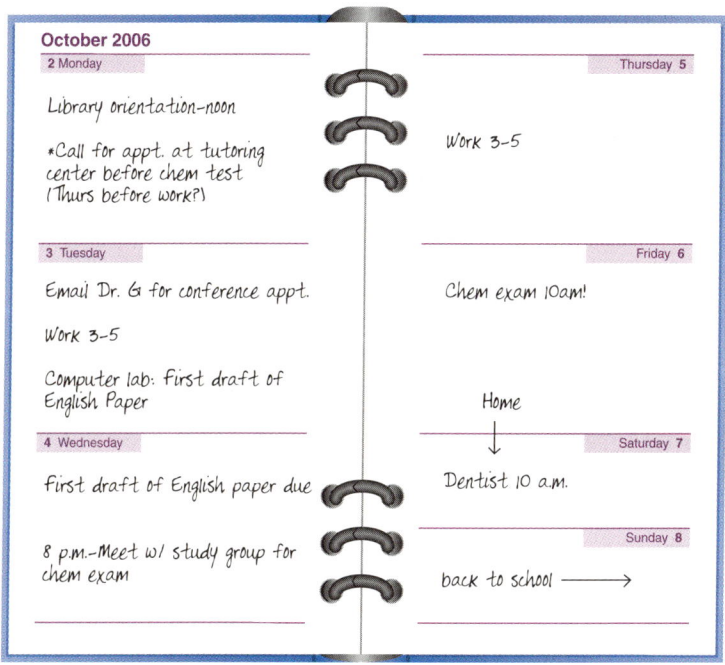

FIGURE 27.1 Sample organizer pages for one week.

You can also use your organizer to help you plan a study schedule, as illustrated in Figure 27.1. You do this by blocking out times to study or to complete assignment-related tasks—such as a library database search for a research paper—in addition to appointments and deadlines. (It is a good idea to make these entries in pencil so you can adjust your schedule as new responsibilities arise.)

> **COMPUTER TIP** academic.cengage.com/eng/kirszermandell
>
> **USING ELECTRONIC ORGANIZERS**
>
> If you prefer, you can keep your schedule on your computer (or on a handheld electronic organizer). For example, *Microsoft Outlook* enables you to set up a calendar/organizer in day-, week-, or month-at-a-glance formats. Once you have set up your calendar and organizer pages, you can easily add and delete entries, move appointments and reminders from one day to another, and print out pages.

The bottom line is this: your college years can be a very stressful time, but although some degree of stress is inevitable, it can be kept in check. If you are organized, you will be better able to handle the pressures of a college workload.

■ **EXERCISE 1**

Buy a monthly calendar and a personal organizer, and fill in the upcoming week's deadlines, appointments, and reminders. (Note that your campus bookstore may offer these items for sale at reduced prices—or even distribute them at no cost.) Bring both the calendar and the organizer to class, and exchange them with another student's. Are your classmate's entries similar to yours? How do you account for any major differences you notice? Do you have too many entries? too few? Edit your calendar and organizer pages to reflect any new insights you have gained from this exercise. Then, add graphic elements (underlining, boxes, and so on) to highlight particularly important items.

See 2b

27b Put Studying First

To be a successful student, you need to understand that studying is something you do *regularly*, not just right before an exam. You also need to know that studying does not mean simply memorizing facts; it also means reading, rereading, and discussing ideas until you understand them.

To make studying a regular part of your day, set up a study space that includes everything you need (supplies, good light, a comfortable chair) and does not include anything you do not need (clutter, distractions). Then, set up a tentative study schedule that reflects your priorities. Try to designate at least two hours each day to complete assignments due right away, to work on those due later on, and to reread class notes. When you have exams and papers to do, you can adjust your schedule accordingly.

CLOSE-UP

UNDERSTANDING YOUR LEARNING STYLE

Some students prefer to study alone; others prefer to study in groups. Some students learn best from reading material, highlighting and annotating extensively or even recopying their notes. Still others are **aural learners,** who learn most effectively by listening to instructors or other students (or to taped lectures), or **visual learners,** who understand concepts best when they can see (or draw) images. Understanding what kind of learner you are will help you achieve your goals as a student.

See 2b–c

Successful students often form **study groups,** and this is a strategy you should use whenever you can—particularly in courses you find challenging. A study group of four or five students who meet regularly (not just the night before an exam) can make studying more focused and effective as well as more enjoyable and less stressful. By discussing concepts with your classmates, you can try out your ideas and get feedback, clarify complex concepts, and formulate questions for your instructor.

CHECKLIST

WORKING IN A STUDY GROUP

Working collaboratively in a **study group** requires some degree of organization. To get the most out of your study group, you need to set some ground rules:

- ☐ Meet regularly.
- ☐ Decide in advance who will be responsible for particular tasks.
- ☐ Set deadlines.
- ☐ Listen when someone else is speaking.
- ☐ Don't reject other people's ideas and suggestions without considering them very carefully.
- ☐ Take stock of the group's problems and progress at regular intervals.
- ☐ Be mindful of other students' learning styles and special needs.

■ EXERCISE 2

1. Set up a study space in your home or your dorm room, and then draw a diagram of this space.
2. Plan a tentative study schedule for the next two weeks.
3. Set up a study group of at least three students to review material for one of your classes once or twice a week. (Begin by getting phone numbers and email addresses from everyone in your proposed group.) After your first exam, write a paragraph evaluating the group's success. Did all members attend meetings regularly, keep up with the readings and other class assignments, and contribute to the group's discussions? Consider changing the group's size, membership, schedule, or routine to help you solve any problems you observe.

27c Be Sure You Understand School and Course Requirements

To succeed in school, you need to know what is expected of you; if you are not sure, ask.

When you first arrived at school, you probably received various orientation materials—a student handbook, library handouts, and so on—that set forth the rules and policies of your school. Read these documents carefully (if you have not already done so), and be sure you understand what they ask of you. If you do not, ask your peer counselor or your adviser for clarification.

You also need to understand the specific requirements of each course you take. Education is a series of contracts between you and your instructors, and each course syllabus explains the terms of a particular contract. A **syllabus** tells you when assignments are due and when exams are scheduled. In addition, it may tell you an instructor's policies about attendance and lateness, assignments and deadlines, plagiarism, and classroom etiquette. A syllabus may also explain penalties for late assignments or missed quizzes, tell how much each assignment is worth, or note additional requirements, such as fieldwork or group projects. Requirements vary significantly from course to course, so read each syllabus carefully—and pay close attention to any supplementary handouts your instructors distribute.

> **ESL TIP**
>
> If you did not attend high school in the United States, some of your instructors' class policies and procedures may seem strange to you. To learn more about the way US college classes are run, read the syllabus for each of your courses, and talk to your instructors about your concerns. You may also find it helpful to talk to older students with cultural backgrounds similar to your own. For more information on adjusting to the US classroom, **see Chapter 62.**

As the semester progresses, your instructors will give you additional information about their expectations. For example, before an exam you will be told what material will be covered, how much time you will have to complete the test, and whether you will be expected to write an essay or fill in an answer sheet that will be graded electronically. When a paper is assigned, you may be given specific information not only about its content, length, and due date but also about its format (font size, line spacing, and margin width, for example). If your instructor does not give you this information, it is your responsibility to find out what is expected of you.

> **CLOSE-UP**
>
> **CREATING A PORTFOLIO**
>
> Some instructors may require that you submit a **portfolio,** a collection of your coursework in print or electronic form. Portfolios may be re-

viewed and graded at the end of the term or at regular intervals throughout the term. If your instructor requires you to assemble a portfolio of written work, be sure to find out exactly what material is to be included (for example, only the final draft or earlier drafts as well?) and what format is required for each assignment.

■ **EXERCISE 3**

Review all the course materials you have been given so far in one of your classes. Make a list of ten important questions that are answered in these handouts (for example, "What is the date of the midterm exam?" or "Are late papers always penalized?"). Then, exchange lists of questions with a classmate, and use your handouts to help you answer your classmate's list of questions. If you are unable to answer some of the questions on this list, be sure to find out the answers from your instructor.

27d Be an Active Learner in the Classroom

Education is not about sitting passively in class and waiting for information and ideas to be given to you. It is up to you to be an active participant in your own education.

First, take as many small classes as you can. These classes give you the opportunity to interact with other students and with your instructor. If a large course has recitation sections, be sure to attend these regularly even if they are not required. Also be sure to take as many classes as possible that require writing. Good writing skills are essential to your success as a student, and you need all the practice you can get.

Take responsibility for your education by attending class regularly and arriving on time. Listen attentively, and take careful, complete notes. (Try to review these notes later with other students to make sure you have not missed anything important.) Do your homework on time, and keep up with the reading. When you read an assignment, apply the techniques of **active reading**, interacting with the text instead of just looking passively at what is on the page. If you have time, read beyond the assignment, looking on the Internet and in books, magazines, and newspapers for related information that interests you.

See Ch. 2

As important as it is to listen and take notes in class, it is just as important (particularly in small classes and recitations) to participate in class discussions: to ask and answer questions, volunteer opinions, and give helpful feedback to other students. By participating in such discussions, you learn more about the subject matter being discussed, and you also learn to listen to other points of view, to test your ideas, and to respect the ideas of others.

ESL TIP

Especially in small classes, US instructors usually expect students to participate in class discussion. If you feel nervous about speaking up in class, you might start by expressing your support of a classmate's opinion.

EXERCISE 4

1. Working in a group of three or four students, brainstorm to devise some additional active learning strategies.
2. Consulting your class notes if necessary, work with your group to develop a list of four or five questions you could ask your instructor in order to get additional information about the topics covered in the previous day's class. (Be sure to phrase the questions so they do not elicit simple yes or no answers.)

27e Be an Active Learner Outside the Classroom

Taking an active role in your education is also important outside the classroom. Don't be afraid to approach your instructors; take advantage of their office hours, and keep in touch with them by email. Get to know your major adviser well, and be sure he or she knows who you are and where your academic interests lie. Make appointments, ask questions, discuss possible solutions to problems: this is how you learn.

ESL TIP

Visiting your instructors during office hours is a good idea. These visits give you a chance to ask questions about your course assignments and lectures, and they can also help you establish relationships with your instructors. Such relationships will be helpful in the future if you have a problem with a course or need a letter of recommendation. In many cases, you can visit your instructors during their office hours without an appointment. Check your course syllabi to find out when office hours are and whether or not appointments are required.

It is also important to participate in the life of your school. Read your school newspaper, check the college Web site regularly, join clubs, and apply for internships. This participation in life outside the classroom can help you develop new interests and friendships as well as enhance your education.

> **CLOSE-UP**
>
> **FINDING INTERNSHIPS**
>
> Many businesses, nonprofit organizations, and government agencies offer **internships** (paid or unpaid) to qualified students. These internships, which can last for a summer, a single term, or an entire academic year, give students the opportunity to learn about a particular career or field of study while earning college credit. Internships may also offer the chance to experience life in another part of the country—or in another part of the world. If your school does not have an office that coordinates internships, ask your academic adviser, a reference librarian, or your career services personnel for help.

Finally, participate in the life of your community. Take service-learning courses, if they are offered at your school, or volunteer at a local school or social agency. As successful students know, education is more than just attending classes.

EXERCISE 5

1. If you do not already have your instructors' and advisers' email addresses in your email address book, enter them now, along with their office phone numbers. (Also enter these numbers in your cell phone.)
2. Make a list of the extracurricular activities you participate in at school. Next, list three activities you would *like* to participate in. For each of these three activities, list all the benefits you might expect to gain from participating. Then, write a sentence explaining how you can become involved.
3. In a paragraph, describe your ideal internship—one that would not only prepare you for your chosen career but would also be enjoyable and perhaps even exciting.

27f Take Advantage of College Services

Colleges and universities offer students a wide variety of support services. Most students will need help of one kind or another at some point during their college careers; if help is available, it makes sense to use it.

For example, if you are struggling with a particular course, you can go to the tutoring service offered by your school's academic support center or by an individual department. Often, the tutors are students who have done well in the course, and their perspective will be very helpful. If you need help with writing or revising a paper, you can make an appointment with the writing center, where tutors will give you advice (but will *not* rewrite or edit your paper for you). If you are having trouble deciding what courses to take or what to major in, see your academic adviser. If you are having trouble adjusting to college life, your peer counselor or (if you live in a dorm) your resident adviser may be able to help you. If you have a personal or family problem you would rather not discuss with another student, make an appointment at your school's counseling center, where you can get advice from professionals who understand student problems.

Of course, other services are available—for example, at your school's computer center, job placement service, and financial aid office. Your academic adviser or instructors can tell you where to find the help you need, but it is up to you to make the appointment.

ESL TIP

Many ESL students find using their school's writing center very helpful. In fact, many writing centers have tutors who specialize in working with ESL students. Most writing centers provide assistance with assignments for any course, and they often assist with writing job application letters and résumés.

■ EXERCISE 6

Working with another student, draw a simple map of your school's campus that identifies the location (or locations) of each of the following college services:

- Tutoring center
- Writing center
- Computer lab
- Academic advising
- Counseling center
- Student health center
- Your major's department offices
- Career services office
- Financial aid office
- Bookstore
- Parking lots

27g Use the Library

See 14a–c

As more and more material becomes available on the Internet, you may begin to think of your college library as outdated or even obsolete. But learning to use the library is an important part of your education.

The library has a lot to offer. For one thing, it can provide a quiet place to study—something you may need if you have a large family or noisy roommates. The library also provides access to materials that cannot be found online—rare books, special collections, audio-visual materials—as well as electronic databases that contain articles you will not find on the free Internet.

Finally, the library is the place where you have access to the experience and expert knowledge of your school's reference librarians. These professionals can answer questions, guide your research, and point you to sources that you might never have found on your own.

■ EXERCISE 7

Visit your school library. Arrange for a library assistant to give you a tour and to introduce you to the library's print and electronic resources. Ask questions, take notes, and be sure to take copies of handouts about the library's hours and services. Also, find out the names of the reference librarians who work with students in the courses you are taking. In class, compare notes with other students; if you still have questions about how to use the library, ask your instructor where to go for additional help.

27h Use Technology

Technological competence is essential for success in college. For this reason, it makes sense to develop good word-processing skills and to become comfortable with the **Internet**. You should also know how to send and receive email from your university account as well as how to attach files to your email. Beyond the basics, you should learn how to manage the files you download, how to evaluate Web sites, and how to use the electronic resources of your library. You might also find it helpful to know how to scan documents (containing images as well as text) and how to paste text and images into your documents.

See Ch. 15

If you do not have these skills, you need to locate campus services that will help you get them. Workshops and online tutorials may be available through your school library, and individual assistance with software and hardware is available in computer labs.

COMPUTER TIP academic.cengage.com/eng/kirsznermandell

EMAILING YOUR INSTRUCTOR

If you use **email** to contact your instructor, be aware that the same etiquette you would use in a face-to-face setting applies online. You can enhance your credibility by including a specific request or question in

(continued)

> **EMAILING YOUR INSTRUCTOR** *(continued)*
>
> the subject line, by addressing your instructor in the same way he or she prefers to be addressed in the classroom, and by including your name at the end of the email, particularly when your email address does not clearly indicate your identity. Finally, be sure to check your message for grammatical and mechanical errors.

Part of being technologically savvy in college involves being aware of the online services your campus has to offer. For example, many campuses rely on customizable information-management systems called **portals.** Not unlike commercial services, such as Yahoo! or America Online, a portal requires you to log in with a user ID and password to access services, such as locating and contacting your academic adviser and viewing your class schedule or your grades.

Finally, you need to know not only how to use technology to enhance a project—for example, how to use *PowerPoint* for an oral presentation or *Excel* to make a table—but also *when* to use technology (and when *not* to).

See 30d1

■ EXERCISE 8

1. Compare your computer skills with those of a classmate. Are your skills roughly equivalent, or is one of you considerably more proficient or more confident? How do you account for any differences?
2. What computer skill would you most like to acquire? Write a paragraph explaining why you want to learn this skill and how you believe it will help you. Then, find out (from an instructor, the computer lab, or a more computer-savvy classmate) exactly how and where you can learn that skill.

27i Make Contacts

One of the most important things you can do for yourself, both for the short term and for the long term, is to make contacts while you are in school and to use them both during college and after you graduate.

Your first contacts are your fellow students. Be sure you have the names, phone numbers, and email addresses of at least two students in each of your classes. These contacts will be useful to you if you miss class, if you need help understanding your notes, or if you want to find someone to study with.

You should also build relationships with students with whom you participate in college activities, such as the college newspaper or the tutoring center. These people are likely to share your goals and interests, so you may want to get feedback from them as you move on to choose a major, consider further education, and make career choices.

Finally, develop relationships with your instructors, particularly those in your major area of study. One of the factors cited most often in studies of successful students is the importance of **mentors,** experienced individuals whose advice they trust. Long after you leave college, you will find these contacts useful.

> **CLOSE-UP**
>
> **FINDING MENTORS**
>
> The most obvious way to locate a **mentor** is to develop a relationship with an instructor you admire, perhaps taking several courses with him or her. Alternatively, you can develop a close professional relationship with a supervisor at work or in an internship. You should also consider the advantages of working for one of your professors—as a research assistant, in a work-study job, or even as a babysitter or petsitter. A professor who knows you well will be likely to take a special interest in your education and in your career.

■ **EXERCISE 9**

1. Identify a potential mentor, and write a letter that you could send to that person. In your letter, explain why you would like to work in his or her field and ask for advice about how to achieve your goals.
2. Write a profile of your ideal mentor. What personal qualities, education, experience, and professional status should this person have? How would you expect this person to help you? (Consider your short-term as well as your long-term goals, and consider the personal, educational, and employment decisions you would need to make in order to achieve these goals.)

27j Be a Lifelong Learner

Your education should not stop when you graduate from college, and this is something you should be aware of from the first day you set foot on campus. To be a successful student, you need to see yourself as a lifelong learner.

Get in the habit of reading newspapers; know what is happening in the world outside school. Talk to people outside the college community, so you don't forget there are issues that have nothing to do with courses and grades. Never miss an opportunity to learn: try to get in the habit of attending plays and concerts sponsored by your school or community and lectures offered at your local library or bookstore.

And think about your future, the life you will lead after college. Think about who you want to be and what you have to do to get there. This is what successful students do.

EXERCISE 10

See 16a

1. Find an article in a newspaper that has direct bearing on your school or your field of study. Write a one-paragraph *summary* of this article. (If you prefer, you can write an analysis of a relevant photograph.)
2. Study classified ads in a newspaper (or online) and find two advertisements: one for a job for which you believe you qualify right now, and one for your "dream job." (If you cannot locate appropriate ads, write them yourself.)

See 29b–c

3. Write your *résumé*.

CHECKLIST

BECOMING A SUCCESSFUL STUDENT

☐ Do you have a personal organizer? a calendar? Do you use them regularly?
☐ Have you set up a comfortable study space?
☐ Have you planned a study schedule?
☐ Have you joined a study group?
☐ Have you read your course syllabi and orientation materials carefully?
☐ Are you attending classes regularly and keeping up with your assignments?
☐ Do you take advantage of your instructors' office hours?
☐ Do you participate in class?
☐ Do you participate in college life?
☐ Do you know where to get help if you need it?
☐ Do you know how to use your college library? Do you use it?
☐ Are you satisfied with your level of technological expertise?
☐ Do you know where to get additional instruction?
☐ Are you trying to make contacts and find mentors?
☐ Do you see yourself as a lifelong learner?

28

Writing Essay Exams

❓ FAQs

How do I know what an exam question is really asking me to do? (p. 417)
How do I organize an essay exam answer? (p. 419)
What should I look for when I reread my answer? (p. 421)

Taking exams is a skill, one you have been developing throughout your life as a student. Although both short-answer and essay exams require you to study, to recall what you know, and to budget your time carefully as you write your answers, only essay questions ask you to **synthesize** information and to arrange ideas in a series of clear, logically connected sentences and paragraphs. To write an essay examination, or even a paragraph-length answer, you must do more than memorize facts; you must see the relationships among them. In other words, you must **think critically** about your subject.

See 16d3

See Ch. 8

CLOSE-UP

WRITING IN-CLASS ESSAYS

Many of the strategies that can help you write strong responses to essay exams can also help you plan, write, and revise other kinds of in-class essays.

If you are asked to write an in-class essay, follow the steps outlined in this chapter, and be sure you understand exactly what you are being asked to do and how much time you have in which to do it. Keep in mind, however, that in-class essays, unlike essay exams, may be evaluated on their style and structure as well as on their content. This means, for example, that they should have fully developed introductory and concluding paragraphs.

ESL TIP

Writing essay exam answers can be especially stressful because you have a short amount of time to write a thoughtful, accurate, and well-organized essay, using correct grammar and mechanics. One way to make this process easier is to have a clear plan before you begin writing. First,

(continued)

> **ESL TIP** (*continued*)
> decide what information you want to include in your answer and how you want to organize it, and then make an informal outline of your ideas to guide you as you write.

28a Planning an Essay Exam Answer

Because you are under time pressure during an exam, you may be tempted to skip the planning and revision stages of the writing process. But if you write in a frenzy and hand in your exam without a second glance, you are likely to produce a disorganized or even incoherent answer. With thoughtful planning and careful editing, you can write an answer that demonstrates your understanding of the material.

1 Review Your Material

Be sure you know beforehand the scope and format of the exam. How much of your text and class notes will be covered—the entire semester's work or only the material presented since the last exam? Will you have to answer every question, or will you be able to choose among alternatives? Will the exam be composed entirely of fill-in, multiple-choice, or true/false questions, or will it call for sentence-, paragraph-, or essay-length answers? Will the exam test your ability to recall specific facts, or will it require you to demonstrate your understanding of the course material by drawing conclusions?

All exams challenge you to recall and express in writing what you already know—what you have read, what you have heard in class, what you have reviewed in your notes. Before you take any exam, then, you must study: reread your text and class notes, highlight key points, and perhaps outline particularly important sections of your notes.

Different kinds of exams, however, require different strategies. When you prepare for a short-answer exam, you may memorize facts without analyzing their relationship to one another or their relationship to a body of knowledge as a whole: the definition of *pointillism*, the date of Queen Victoria's death, the formula for a quadratic equation, three reasons for the fall of Rome, two examples of conditioned reflexes, four features of a feudal economy, six steps in the process of synthesizing Vitamin C. When you prepare for an essay exam, however, you must do more than remember bits of information; you must also make connections among ideas.

When you are sure you know what to expect, see if you can anticipate the essay questions your instructor might ask. Try out likely questions on classmates, and see whether you can do some collaborative brainstorming to outline answers to possible questions. If you have time, you might even practice answering one or two in writing.

2 Consider Your Audience and Purpose

The <u>audience</u> for an exam is the instructor who prepared it. As you read the questions, think about what your instructor has emphasized in class. Keep in mind that your <u>purpose</u> is to demonstrate that you understand the material, not to make clever remarks or introduce irrelevant information. Also, make every effort to use the vocabulary of the particular academic <u>discipline</u> and to follow any discipline-specific stylistic conventions your instructor has discussed.

See 1a–b

See Pt. 6

3 Read through the Entire Exam

Before you begin to write, read the questions carefully to determine your priorities and your strategy. First, be sure that your copy of the test is complete and that you understand exactly what each question requires. If you need clarification, ask your instructor or proctor for help. Then, plan carefully, deciding how much time you should devote to answering each question. Often, the point value of each question or the number of questions on the exam indicates how much time you should spend on each answer. If an essay question is worth fifty out of one hundred points, for example, you will probably have to spend at least half (and perhaps more) of your time planning, writing, and proofreading your answer.

Next, decide where to start. Responding first to questions whose answers you are sure of is usually a good strategy. This tactic ensures that you will not become bogged down in a question that baffles you, left with too little time to write a strong answer to a question that you understand well. Moreover, starting with the questions that you are sure of can help build your confidence.

4 Read Each Question Carefully

To write an effective answer, you need to understand the question. As you read any essay question, you may find it helpful to underline key words and important terms.

> **Sociology:** <u>Distinguish</u> among <u>Social Darwinism</u>, <u>instinct theory</u>, and <u>sociobiology</u>, giving <u>examples</u> of each.
>
> **Music:** <u>Explain how</u> Milton <u>Babbitt</u> used the <u>computer</u> to expand <u>Schoenberg's twelve-tone</u> method.
>
> **Philosophy:** <u>Define existentialism</u> and <u>identify three</u> influential existentialist <u>works</u>, explaining <u>why</u> they are important.

Look carefully at the wording of each question. If the question calls for a comparison and contrast of two styles of management, an analysis of one style, no matter how comprehensive, will not be acceptable. If the question asks for causes and effects, a discussion of causes alone will not do.

> **CLOSE-UP**
>
> **KEY WORDS IN EXAM QUESTIONS**
>
> Pay careful attention to the words used in exam questions:
>
> - Explain
> - Compare
> - Contrast
> - Trace
> - Evaluate
> - Discuss
> - Clarify
> - Relate
> - Justify
> - Analyze
> - Interpret
> - Describe
> - Classify
> - Identify
> - Illustrate
> - Define
> - Support
> - Summarize

The wording of the question suggests what you should emphasize. For instance, an American history instructor would expect very different answers to the following two exam questions:

- Give a detailed explanation of the major <u>causes</u> of the Great Depression, noting briefly some of the effects of the economic collapse on the United States.
- Give a detailed summary of the <u>effects</u> of the Great Depression on the United States, briefly discussing the major causes of the economic collapse.

Although the two questions above look alike, the first calls for an essay that stresses *causes*, whereas the second calls for one that stresses *effects*.

> **ESL TIP**
>
> If you don't understand a word or a part of an essay question, ask your instructor for clarification.

5 Brainstorm to Find Ideas

Once you think you understand the question, you need to <u>find something to say</u>. Begin by **brainstorming,** quickly writing down all the relevant ideas you can remember. Then, identify the most important points, and delete the others. A quick review of the exam question and your supporting ideas should lead you toward a workable thesis for your essay answer.

28b Shaping an Essay Exam Answer

Like an essay, an effective exam answer has a definite structure.

1 Stating a Thesis

Often, you can rephrase the exam question as a **thesis statement**. For example, the American history exam question "Give a detailed summary of the effects of the Great Depression on the United States, briefly discussing the major causes of the economic collapse" suggests the following thesis statement.

> **Effective Thesis Statement:** The Great Depression, caused by the American government's economic policies, had major political, economic, and social effects on the United States.

This effective thesis statement addresses all aspects of the question but highlights only relevant concerns.

The following thesis statements are not effective.

> **Vague Thesis Statement:** The Great Depression, caused largely by profligate spending patterns, had a number of very important results.
>
> **Incomplete Thesis Statement:** The Great Depression caused major upheaval in the United States.
>
> **Irrelevant Thesis Statement:** The Great Depression, caused largely by America's poor response to the 1929 stock market crash, had more important consequences than World War II did.

2 Making an Informal Outline

Because time is limited, you should plan your answer before you write it. Therefore, once you have decided on a suitable thesis, you should make an **informal outline** of your major points.

On the inside cover of your exam book, or on its last sheet, list your supporting points in the order in which you plan to discuss them. Once you have completed your outline, check it against the exam question to make certain it covers everything the question calls for—and *only* what the question calls for.

An informal outline for an answer to the American history question introduced above ("Give a detailed summary of the effects of the Great Depression on the United States, briefly discussing the major causes of the economic collapse") might look like the one on the following page.

Thesis Statement: The Great Depression, caused by the American government's economic policies, had major political, economic, and social effects on the United States.

Supporting Points:

Causes

American economic policies: income poorly distributed, factories expanded too much, more goods produced than could be purchased.

Effects

1. Economic situation worsened—farmers, businesses, workers, and stock market all affected.
2. Roosevelt elected—closed banks, worked with Congress to enact emergency measures.
3. Reform—TVA, AAA, NIRA, etc.
4. Social Security Act, WPA, PWA

28c Writing and Revising an Essay Exam Answer

Referring to your outline, you can now begin to draft your answer. Don't bother crafting an elaborate or unusual **introduction;** your time is precious, and so is your reader's. A simple statement of your thesis that summarizes your answer is your best introductory strategy: this approach is efficient, and it reminds you to address the question directly.

To develop the **body** of the essay, follow your outline point by point, using clear topic sentences and transitions to indicate your progression and to help your instructor see that you are answering the question in full. Such signals, along with <u>parallel</u> sentence structure and repeated key words, make your answer easy to follow.

See 41a

The most effective **conclusion** for an essay examination is a clear, simple restatement of the thesis or a summary of the essay's main points.

Although essay answers should be complete and detailed, they should not contain irrelevant material. Every unnecessary fact or opinion increases your chance of error, so don't repeat yourself or volunteer unrequested information, and don't express your own feelings or opinions unless such information is specifically asked for. In addition, be sure to support all your general statements with specific examples.

Finally, be sure to leave enough time to revise what you have written. As you reread, try to view your answer objectively. Is your thesis statement clearly worded? Does your essay support your thesis and answer the question? Are your facts correct, and are your ideas presented in a logical order? Review your topic sentences and transitions; check sentence structure and word choice, spelling and punctuation. If a sentence—or even a whole paragraph—seems irrelevant, cross it out. If you suddenly remember something you want to add, you can insert a few additional words with a caret (∧). Neatly insert a longer addition at the end of your answer, box it, and label it so your instructor will know where it belongs.

> **ESL TIP**
>
> Because of time pressure, you will probably not be able to write in-class essay exam answers that are as polished as your out-of-class writing. Still, you should do your best to convey your ideas as clearly as you can. Especially in classes outside of the English department, instructors are usually more concerned with the accuracy of the content of your answers than with your writing style. Therefore, instead of wasting time searching for the "perfect" words or phrases, use words and grammatical constructions that are familiar to you. After you have written an answer that you feel is accurate, well developed, and well organized, you can use any remaining time to check your grammar and mechanics. (Don't waste time recopying passages unless what you have written is illegible.)

The one-hour essay exam answer that appears below follows the outline on page 420. Notice how the student restates the question in her thesis statement and keeps the question in focus by repeating words that signal her focus on causes and effects (*cause*, *effect*, *result*, *response*, and *impact*).

Effective Essay Exam Answer

Question: Give a detailed summary of the effects of the Great Depression on the United States, briefly discussing the major causes of the economic collapse.

The Great Depression, caused by the American government's economic policies, had major political, economic, and social effects on the United States. — *Introduction—thesis statement rephrases question*

The Depression was precipitated by the stock market crash of October 1929, but its actual causes were more subtle: they lay in the US government's economic policies. First, personal income was not well — *Policies leading to Depression* distributed. Although production rose during the 1920s, the farmers and other workers got too little of the profits; instead, a disproportionate amount of income went to the richest 5 percent of the population. The tax policies at this time made inequalities in income even worse. A good deal of income also went into development of new manufacturing plants. This expansion stimulated the economy but encouraged the production of more goods than consumers could purchase. Finally, during the economic boom of the 1920s, the government did not attempt to limit speculation or impose regulations on the securities market; it also did little to help build up farmers' buying power. Even after the crash began, the government made mistakes: instead of trying to address the country's deflationary economy, the government focused on keeping the budget balanced and making sure the United States adhered to the gold standard.

(¶2 summarizes causes)

The Depression, devastating to millions of individuals, had a tremendous impact on the nation as a whole. Its political, economic, and social consequences were great.

Transition from causes to effects

Between October 1929 and Roosevelt's inauguration on March 4, 1932, the economic situation grew worse. Businesses were going bankrupt, banks were failing, and stock prices were falling. Farm prices fell drastically, and hungry farmers were forced to burn their corn to heat their homes. There was massive unemployment, with millions of workers jobless and humiliated, losing skills and self-respect. President Hoover's Reconstruction Finance Corporation made loans available to banks, railroads, and businesses, but Hoover thought state and local funds (not the federal government) should finance public works programs and relief. Confidence in the president declined as the country's economic situation worsened.

Early effects (¶s 4–8 summarize important results in chronological order)

One result of the Depression was the election of Franklin Delano Roosevelt. By the time of his inauguration, most American banks had closed, thirteen million workers were unemployed, and millions of farmers were threatened by foreclosure. Roosevelt's response was immediate: two days after he took office, he closed all the remaining banks and took steps to support the stronger ones with loans and to

Additional effects: Roosevelt's emergency measures

prevent the weaker ones from reopening. During the first hundred days of his administration, he kept Congress in special session. Under his leadership, Congress enacted emergency measures designed to provide "Relief, Recovery, and Reform."

In response to the problems caused by the Depression, Roosevelt set up agencies to reform some of the conditions that had helped to cause the Depression in the first place. The Tennessee Valley Authority, created in May 1933, was one of these. Its purposes were to control floods by building new dams and improving old ones, and to provide cheap, plentiful electricity. The TVA improved the standard of living of area farmers and drove down the price of power all over the country. The Agricultural Adjustment Administration, created the same month as the TVA, provided for taxes on basic commodities, with the tax revenues used to subsidize farmers to produce less. This reform measure caused prices to rise. *[Additional effects: Roosevelt's reform measures]*

Another response to the problems of the Depression was the National Industrial Recovery Act. This act established the National Recovery Administration, an agency that set minimum wages and maximum hours for workers and set limits on production and prices. Other laws passed by Congress between 1935 and 1940 strengthened federal regulation of power, interstate commerce, and air traffic. Roosevelt also changed the federal tax structure to redistribute American income. *[Additional effects: NIRA, other laws, and so on]*

One of the most important results of the Depression was the Social Security Act of 1935, which established unemployment insurance and provided financial aid for the blind and disabled and for dependent children and their mothers. The Works Progress Administration (WPA) gave jobs to over two million workers, who built public buildings, roads, streets, bridges, and sewers. The WPA also employed artists, musicians, actors, and writers. The Public Works Administration (PWA) cleared slums and created public housing. In the National Labor Relations Act (1935), workers received a guarantee of government protection for their unions against unfair labor practices by management. *[Additional effects: Social Security, WPA, and so on]*

As a result of the economic collapse known as the Great Depression, Americans saw their government take responsibility for providing *[Conclusion—restatement of thesis]* immediate relief, for helping the economy recover, and for taking steps to ensure that the situation would not be repeated. The economic, political, and social impact of the laws passed during the 1930s is still with us, helping to keep our government and our economy stable.

Notice that in her answer the student does not include any irrelevant material: she does not, for example, describe the conditions of people's lives in detail, blame anyone in particular, discuss the president's friends and enemies, or consider parallel events in other countries. She covers only what the question asks for. Notice, too, how topic sentences (**One result of the Depression . . .** ; **In response to the problems caused by the Depression . . .** ; **One of the most important results of the Depression . . .**) keep the primary purpose of the discussion in focus and guide her instructor through the essay.

A well-planned essay like the preceding one is not easy to write. Consider the following ineffective answer to the same question.

Ineffective Essay Exam Answer

> The Great Depression is generally considered to have begun with the stock market crash of October 1929 and to have lasted until the defense buildup for World War II. It was a terrible time for millions of Americans, who were not used to being hungry or out of work. Perhaps the worst economic disaster in our history, the Depression left its scars on millions of once-proud workers and farmers who found themselves reduced to poverty. We all have heard stories of businessmen committing suicide when their investments failed, of people selling apples on the street, and of farmers and their families leaving the Dust Bowl in desperate search of work. My own great-grandfather, laid off from his job, had to support my great-grandmother and their four children on what he could make from odd carpentry jobs. This was the Depression at its worst.

No clear thesis; vague, subjective impressions of the Depression

> What else did the Depression produce? One result of the Depression was the election of Franklin Delano Roosevelt. Roosevelt immediately closed all banks. Then, Congress set up the Federal Emergency Relief Administration, the Civilian Conservation Corps, the Farm Credit Administration, and the Home Owners' Loan Corporation. The Reconstruction Finance Corporation and the Civil Works Administration were two other agencies designed to provide "Relief, Recovery, and Reform." All these agencies helped Roosevelt in his efforts to lead the nation to recovery while providing relief and reform.

Gratuitous summary

Along with these emergency measures, Roosevelt set out to reform some of the conditions he felt were responsible for the economic collapse. Accordingly, he created the Tennessee Valley Authority (TVA) to control floods and provide electricity in the Tennessee Valley. The Agricultural Adjustment Agency levied taxes and got the farmers to grow less, causing prices to rise. Thus, these agencies, the TVA and the AAA, helped to ease things for the farmers. *Unsupported generalization*

The National Industrial Recovery Act established the National Recovery Administration, which was designed to help workers. It established minimum wages and maximum hours, both of which made conditions better for workers. Other important agencies included the Federal Power Commission, the Interstate Commerce Commission, the Maritime Commission, and the Civil Aeronautics Authority. Changes in the tax structure at about this time made the tax system fairer and eliminated some inequities. Roosevelt, working smoothly with his cabinet and with Congress, took many important steps to ease the nation's economic burden. *Why were these agencies important? What did they do?*

Despite the fact that he was handicapped by polio, Roosevelt was a dynamic president. His fireside chats, which millions of Americans heard on the radio every week, helped to reassure Americans that things would be fine. This increased his popularity. But he had problems, too. Not everyone agreed with him. Private electric companies opposed the TVA, big business disagreed with his support of labor unions, the rich did not like the way he restructured the tax system, and many people saw him as dangerously radical. Still, he was one of the most popular presidents ever. *Digression: discussion of Roosevelt is irrelevant*

—Social Security Act: unemployment insurance, aid to blind and disabled and children *Undeveloped information*
—WPA: built public projects
—PWA: public housing
—National Labor Relations Act: strengthened labor unions

This essay only indirectly answers the exam question. It devotes too much space to unnecessary elements: an emotional introduction, needlessly repeated words and phrases, gratuitous summaries, and unsupported generalizations. Without a thesis statement to guide her, the writer slips into a discussion of only the immediate impact of the Depression and never discusses its causes or its long-term effects.

Although the body paragraphs do provide the names of many agencies created by the Roosevelt administration, they do not explain the purpose of most of them. Consequently, the student seems to consider the formation of the agencies, not their contributions, to be the Depression's most significant result.

Because the student took a time-consuming detour to discuss Roosevelt, she had to list some information at the end of the essay without discussing it fully; moreover, she was left with no time to sum up her main points, even in a one-sentence conclusion. Although it is better to include undeveloped information than to skip it altogether, many instructors will not give credit if you do not write your answer in full. More important, you cannot effectively show logical or causal relationships in a list.

28d Writing Paragraph-Length Essay Exam Answers

Some essay questions ask for a paragraph-length answer, not a full essay. A paragraph should be just that: not one or two sentences, not a list of points, not more than one paragraph.

See 7a

A paragraph-length answer should be **unified** by a clear topic sentence. Just as an essay answer begins with a thesis statement, a paragraph answer opens with a topic sentence that summarizes what the paragraph will cover. You should phrase this sentence so that it echoes the wording of the exam question. The paragraph should also be **coherent**—that is, its statements should be linked by transitions that move the reader along. Finally, the paragraph should be **well developed**, with enough relevant detail to convince your reader that you know what you are talking about.

See 7b–c

Effective Paragraph-Length Exam Answer

Question: In one paragraph, define the term *management by objectives*, give an example of how it works, and briefly discuss an advantage of this approach.

Definition — As defined by Horngren, <u>management by objectives</u> is an approach by which a manager and his or her superior together formulate goals, and plans by which they can achieve these goals, for a forthcoming period.

Example — For example, a manager and a superior can formulate a responsibility accounting budget, and the manager's performance can then be measured according to how well he or she meets the objectives defined by the

Advantage — budget. The advantage of this approach is that the goals set are attainable because they are not formulated in a vacuum. Rather, the objectives are based on what the entire team reasonably expects to accomplish. As a result, the burden of responsibility is shifted from the superior to the team: the goal itself defines all the steps needed for its completion.

In this answer, key phrases (**As defined by . . .** ; **For example . . .** ; **The advantage of this approach . . .**) clearly identify the various parts of the question being addressed. The writer includes just what the question asks for, and no more. His use of the wording of the question helps make the paragraph orderly, coherent, and emphatic.

The student who wrote the following response may know what *management by objectives* is, but his paragraph sounds more like a casual explanation to a friend than an answer to an exam question.

Ineffective Paragraph-Length Exam Answer

Management by objectives is when managers and their bosses get together to formulate their goals. This is a good system of management because it cuts down on hard feelings between managers and their superiors. Because they set the goals together, they can make sure they're attainable by considering all possible influences, constraints, and so on, that might occur. This way neither the manager nor the superior gets all the blame when things go wrong.

Sketchy, casual definition; no example given

Vague

Remember, no response to an exam question will be effective unless you take the time to read the question carefully, plan your response, and outline your answer before you begin to write. It is always a good idea to use the wording of the question in your answer and to reread your answer to make sure it explicitly answers the question and contains no distracting grammatical or mechanical errors.

29

Writing for the Workplace

❓ FAQs

How do I write a letter to apply for a job? (p. 428)
What should a print résumé look like? (p. 430)
What should a scannable résumé look like? (p. 433)
How do I design a résumé to be posted on a Web site? (p. 436)

Business communications should be brief and to the point, with important information placed first. Be concise, avoid digressions, and try to sound as natural as possible.

29a   Writing Letters of Application

A **letter of application** summarizes your qualifications for a specific position. Letters of application should be short and focused. When you apply for employment, your primary objective is to obtain an interview.

Begin your letter of application by identifying the job you are applying for and stating where you heard about it—in a newspaper, in a professional journal, on a Web site, or from your school's job placement service, for example. Be sure to include the date of the advertisement and the exact title of the position. End your introduction with a statement that expresses your ability to do the job.

In the body of your letter, provide the information that will convince your reader of your qualifications—for example, relevant courses you have taken and pertinent job experience. Be sure to address any specific points mentioned in the advertisement. Above all, emphasize your strengths, and explain how they relate to the specific job for which you are applying.

Conclude by saying that you have enclosed your résumé and stating that you are available for an interview, noting any dates on which you will not be available. (Be sure to include your phone number and your email address.)

Sample Letter of Application

246 Hillside Drive
Urbana, IL 61801
Kr237@metropolis.105.com

October 20, 2005

Mr. Maurice Snyder, Personnel Director
Guilford, Fox, and Morris
22 Hamilton Street
Urbana, IL 61822

Dear Mr. Snyder:

My college advisor, Dr. Raymond Walsh, has told me that you are interested in hiring a part-time accounting assistant. I believe that my academic background and my work experience qualify me for this position.

I am presently a junior accounting major at the University of Illinois. During the past year, I have taken courses in taxation, trusts, and business law. I am also proficient in *Lotus* and *ClarisWorks*. Last spring, I gained practical accounting experience by working in our department's tax clinic.

After I graduate, I hope to get a master's degree in taxation and then return to the Urbana area. I believe that my experience in taxation as well as my familiarity with the local business community would enable me to contribute to your firm.

I have enclosed a résumé for your consideration. I will be available for an interview any time after midterm examinations, which end October 25. I look forward to hearing from you.

Sincerely yours,

Sandra Kraft

Sandra Kraft
Enc: Résumé

> **COMPUTER TIP** — academic.cengage.com/eng/kirsznermandell
>
> **LETTER TEMPLATES**
>
> The templates found within your word-processing program can help you structure your letters (as well as résumés, memos, faxes, and brochures).

> **CLOSE-UP**
>
> **WRITING FOLLOW-UP LETTERS**
>
> After you have been interviewed, send a **follow-up** letter to the person (or persons) who interviewed you. First, thank your interviewer for taking the time to see you. Then, remind the interviewer of your qualifications and of your interest in the position. Because so few applicants write follow-up letters, such letters make a very positive impression.

■ **EXERCISE 1**

Look through the employment advertisements in your local newspaper or in the files of your college placement service. Choose one job, and write a letter of application in which you summarize your achievements and discuss your qualifications for the position.

29b Designing Print Résumés

A **résumé** lists relevant information about your education, your job experience, your goals, and your personal interests.

There is no single correct format for a résumé. You may decide to arrange your résumé in **chronological order** (see page 431), listing your education and work experience in sequence (beginning with the most recent) or in **emphatic order** (see page 432) beginning with the material that will be of most interest to an employer (for example, important skills). Whatever a résumé's arrangement, it should be brief—one page is usually sufficient for an undergraduate—easy to read, clear and emphatic, logically organized, and completely free of errors.

Sample Résumé: Chronological Order

KAREN L. OLSON

SCHOOL
3812 Hamilton St. Apt. 18
Philadelphia, PA 19104
215-382-0831
olsont@dunm.ocs.drexel.edu

HOME
110 Ascot Ct.
Harmony, PA 16037
412-452-2944

EDUCATION

DREXEL UNIVERSITY, Philadelphia, PA 19104
Bachelor of Science in Graphic Design
Anticipated Graduation: June 2007
Cumulative Grade Point Average: 3.2 on a 4.0 scale

COMPUTER SKILLS AND COURSEWORK

HARDWARE
Familiar with both Macintosh and PC systems
SOFTWARE
Adobe Illustrator, Photoshop, and *Type Align; QuarkXPress; CorelDRAW; Micrografx Designer*
COURSES
Corporate Identity, Environmental Graphics, Typography, Photography, Painting and Printmaking, Sculpture, Computer Imaging, Art History

EMPLOYMENT EXPERIENCE

THE TRIANGLE, Drexel University, Philadelphia, PA 19104
January 2004–present
Graphics Editor. Design all display advertisements submitted to Drexel's student newspaper.

UNISYS CORPORATION, Blue Bell, PA 19124
June–September 2004, Cooperative Education
Graphic Designer. Designed interior pages as well as covers for target marketing brochures. Created various logos and spot art designed for use on interoffice memos and departmental publications.

CHARMING SHOPPES, INC, Bensalem, PA 19020
June–December 2003, Cooperative Education
Graphic Designer/Fashion Illustrator, Created graphics for future placement on garments. Did some textile designing. Drew flat illustrations of garments to scale in computer. Prepared presentation boards.

DESIGN AND IMAGING STUDIO, Drexel University, Philadelphia, PA 19104
October 2002–June 2004
Monitor. Supervised computer activity in studio. Answered telephone. Assisted other graphic design students in using computer programs.

ACTIVITIES AND AWARDS

The Triangle, Graphics Editor: 2004–present
Kappa Omicron Nu Honor Society, vice president: 2002–present
Dean's List: spring 2001, fall and winter 2002
Graphics Group, vice president: 2002–present

REFERENCES AND PORTFOLIO

Available upon request.

Sample Résumé: Emphatic Order

Michael D. Fuller

SCHOOL
27 College Avenue
University of Maryland
College Park, MD 20742
(301) 357-0732
mful532@aol.com

HOME
1203 Hampton Road
Joppa, MD 21085
(301) 877-1437

Restaurant Experience

McDonald's Restaurant, Pikesville, MD. Cook.
Prepared hamburgers. Acted as assistant manager for two weeks while manager was on vacation. Supervised employees, helped prepare payroll and work schedules. Was named employee of the month. Summer 2003.

University of Maryland, College Park, MD. Cafeteria busboy.
Cleaned tables, set up cafeteria, and prepared hot trays. September 2004–May 2005.

Other Work Experience

University of Maryland Library, College Park, MD. Reference assistant. Filed, sorted, typed, shelved, and catalogued. Earnings offset college expenses. September 2003–May 2004.

Education

University of Maryland, College Park, MD (sophomore).
Biology major. Expected date of graduation: June 2007.
Forest Park High School, Baltimore, MD.

Interests

Member of University Debating Society.
Tutor in University's Academic Enrichment Program.

References

Mr. Arthur Sanducci, Manager
McDonald's Restaurant
5712 Avery Road
Pikesville, MD 22513

Mr. William Czernick, Manager
Cafeteria
University of Maryland
College Park, MD 20742

Ms. Stephanie Young, Librarian
Library
University of Maryland
College Park, MD 20742

ESL TIP

When describing honors received in another country that may not be familiar to potential employers, it is wise to provide explanatory information. For example, you might indicate what percentage of graduates receive the honor you have been awarded. You may also wish to indicate your visa status and your language skills on your résumé.

NOTE: In some countries, job applicants list information about their age and marital status in their job application materials. However, in the United States, this is usually not done because employers are not legally allowed to discriminate on the basis of such information.

CLOSE-UP

RÉSUMÉ STYLE

Use strong action verbs to describe your duties, responsibilities, and accomplishments:

- accomplished
- communicated
- completed
- performed
- achieved
- collaborated
- implemented
- organized
- supervised
- instructed
- proposed
- trained

NOTE: Use past tense for past positions and present tense for current positions.

COMPUTER TIP   academic.cengage.com/eng/kirsznermandell

RÉSUMÉS

When you send a résumé by email, send it as an attachment, not as part of the email itself. Résumés inserted into the body of an email can lose their formatting and be impossible to read.

29c Designing Electronic Résumés

Most résumés are still submitted on paper, but electronic résumés—scannable and Web-based—are quickly gaining in popularity.

1 Scannable Résumés

Many employers request scannable résumés that they can download into a database for future reference. If you have to prepare such a résumé, keep in mind that scanners will not pick up columns, bullets, or italics and that shaded or colored paper will make your résumé difficult to scan.

Whereas in a print résumé you use specific action verbs (**edited**) to describe your accomplishments, in a scannable résumé you use nouns (**editor**) that can be entered into a company database. These words will help employers find your résumé when they carry out a keyword search for applicants with certain skills. To facilitate keyword searches, applicants often include Key Words sections on their résumés to highlight their skills.

Sample Résumé: Scannable

Constantine G. Doukakis
2000 Clover Lane
Fort Worth, TX 76107

Phone: (817) 735-9120
Email: Douk@aol.com

Employment Objective: Entry-level position in an organization that will enable me to use my academic knowledge and the skills that I learned in my work experience.

Education:

University of Texas at Arlington, Bachelor of Science in Civil Engineering, June 2006. Major: Structural Engineering. Graduated Magna Cum Laude. Overall GPA: 3.754 on a 4.0 base.

Scholastic Honors and Awards:

Member of Phi Eta Sigma First-Year Academic Honor Society, Chi Epsilon Civil Engineering Academic Society, Tau Beta Pi Engineering Academic Society, Golden Key National Honor Society.

Jack Woolf Memorial Scholarship for Outstanding Academic Performance.

Cooperative Employment Experience:

Dallas-Fort Worth International Airport, Tarrant County, TX, Dec. 2004 to June 2005. Assistant Engineer. Supervised and inspected airfield paving, drainage, and utility projects as well as terminal building renovations. Performed on-site and laboratory soil tests. Prepared concrete samples for load testing.

Dallas-Fort Worth International Airport, Tarrant County, TX, Jan. 2005 to June 2005. Draftsperson in Design Office. Prepared contract drawings and updated base plans as well as designed and estimated costs for small construction projects.

Johnson County Electric Cooperative, Clebume, TX, Jan. 2004 to June 2004. Junior Engineer in Plant Dept. of Maintenance and Construction Division. Inspected and supervised in-plant construction. Devised solutions to construction problems. Estimated costs of materials for small construction projects. Presented historical data relating to the function of the department.

Key Words:

Organizational and leadership skills. Written and oral communication skills, C++, IBM, Macintosh, DOS, Windows XP, and Mac OS 10.3, Word, Excel, FileMakerPro, PowerPoint, WordPerfect, Internet client software. Computer model development. Technical editor.

2 Web-Based Résumés

See Ch. 31

It is becoming common to have a version of your résumé posted on a personal Web site. Usually, a Web-based résumé is an alternative to a print résumé that you have mailed or a scannable version that you have submitted to a database or as an email attachment. Figure 29.1 shows a Web-based version of a student's résumé. The student has also included on her Web site a PDF (portable document format) version of her résumé that is available for downloading and printing (see Figure 29.2). The PDF file maintains the format of the résumé, includes the use of boldface and italic type, bullets, and horizontal rules.

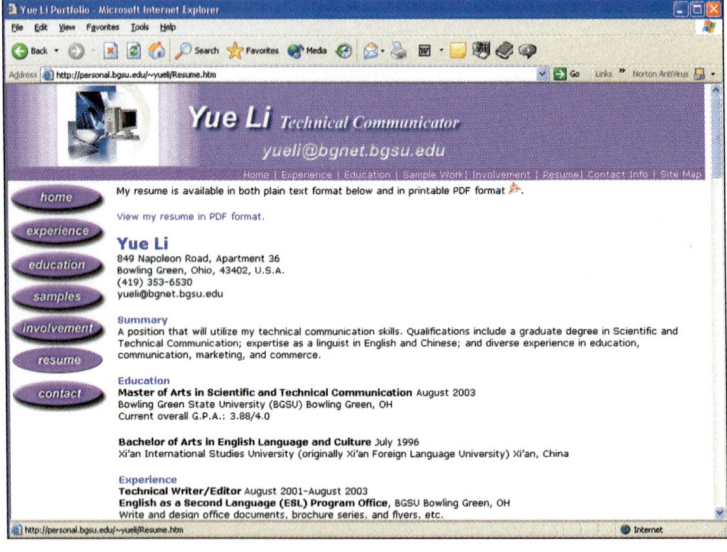

FIGURE 29.1 Student Web-based résumé.

COMPUTER TIP academic.cengage.com/eng/kirsznermandell

PDF Résumés

A PDF résumé allows you to maintain the original design of your word-processed résumé file, including the use of boldface and italic type, bullets, and horizontal rules. Another advantage of this type of résumé is that anyone can view and print a PDF file with the free, downloadable *Adobe Acrobat Reader* <http://www.adobe.com/products/acrobat/readermain.html>.

Designing Electronic Résumés 29c

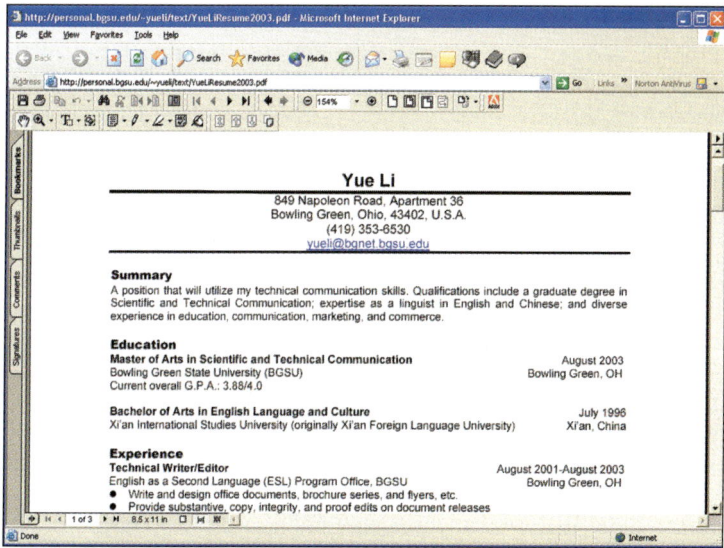

FIGURE 29.2 Student PDF résumé.

CLOSE-UP

ELECTRONIC PORTFOLIOS

Many disciplines are moving toward **electronic portfolios,** Web-based collections of materials that represent a job applicant's skills and abilities. Prospective employers can select the items in the portfolio of most interest to them, perhaps following up on a reference in a cover letter or a link in an electronic résumé. Portfolios may also include personal statements, writing samples, and even video or audio clips.

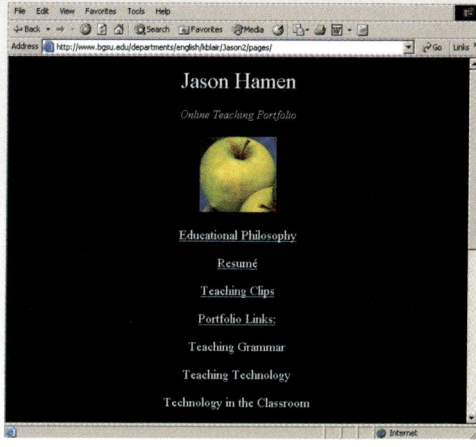

EXERCISE 2

Prepare two versions of your résumé—one print and the other scannable—that you could include with the letter of application you wrote for Exercise 1. How are these two résumés alike? How are they different?

29d Writing Memos

Memos communicate information within an organization. A memo can be short or long, depending on its purpose.

Begin your memo with a purpose statement that presents your reason for writing it. Follow this statement with a background section that gives readers the information they will need to understand the current situation. Then, in the body of your memo, present the detailed information that constitutes your support. If your document is short, use bulleted or numbered lists to emphasize information. If it is long—more than two or three paragraphs—use headings to designate the various sections of the memo (**Summary**, **Background**, **Benefits**, and so on). End your memo with a statement of your conclusions and recommendations.

Sample Memo

TO: Ina Ellen, Senior Counselor
FROM: Kim Williams, Student Tutor Supervisor
SUBJECT: Construction of a Tutoring Center
DATE: November 10, 2005

Opening component

This memo proposes the establishment of a tutoring center in the Office of Student Affairs.

Purpose statement

BACKGROUND
Under the present system, tutors must work with students at a number of facilities scattered across the university campus. As a result, tutors waste a lot of time running from one facility to another and are often late for appointments.

Body

NEW FACILITY
I propose that we establish a tutoring facility adjacent to the Office of Student Affairs. The two empty classrooms next to the office, presently used for storage of office furniture, would be ideal for this use. We could furnish these offices with the desks and file cabinets already stored in these rooms.

BENEFITS
The benefits of this facility would be the centralizing of the tutoring services and the proximity of the facility to the Office of Student Affairs. The tutoring facility could also use the secretarial services of the Office of Student Affairs.

RECOMMENDATIONS
To implement this project we would need to do the following:
1. Clean up and paint rooms 331 and 333
2. Use folding partitions to divide each room into five single-desk offices
3. Use stored office equipment to furnish the center

Conclusion

I am certain these changes would do much to improve the tutoring service. I look forward to discussing this matter with you in more detail.

29e Writing Emails and Sending Faxes

1 Writing Emails

In many workplaces, virtually all internal (and some external) communications are transmitted as email. Although personal email tends to be quite informal, business email should observe the conventions of standard written communication.

> **CHECKLIST**
>
> **WRITING EMAILS**
>
> The following guidelines can help you communicate effectively in an electronic business environment:
>
> ☐ Write in complete sentences. Avoid the slang, imprecise diction, and abbreviations that are commonplace in personal email.
> ☐ Use an appropriate tone. Address readers with respect, just as you would in a standard business letter.
> ☐ Include a subject line that clearly identifies your content. If your subject line is vague, your email may be deleted without being read.
> ☐ Make your message as short as possible.
> ☐ Use short paragraphs, and leave an extra space between paragraphs.
> ☐ Use lists and internal headings to make your message easy to read and understand.
> ☐ Take the time to edit your email and delete excess words and phrases.
> ☐ Proofread carefully before sending your email. Look for errors in grammar, spelling, and punctuation.
> ☐ Make sure that your list of recipients is accurate and that you do not send your email to unintended recipients.
> ☐ Do not send your email until you are absolutely certain your message says what you want it to say.
> ☐ Do not forward an email unless you have the permission of the sender.
> ☐ Watch what you write. Always remember that email written at work is the property of the employer, who has the legal right to access it, even without your permission.

2 Sending Faxes

In spite of the prevalence of email, businesses still routinely send and receive many faxes. Forms that need signatures, papers that cannot easily be digitized, copies of printed documents, and printed communications that must be sent immediately all are transmitted by fax.

> **CLOSE-UP**
>
> **SENDING MESSAGES BY FAX**
>
> Faxes are often received not by an individual but at a central location, so include a cover sheet that contains the recipient's name and title, the date, the company and department, the fax and telephone numbers, and the total number of pages faxed. In addition, supply your own name and telephone and fax numbers. (It is also a good idea to call ahead to alert the addressee that a fax is coming.)

> **CHECKLIST**
>
> **USING VOICE MAIL**
>
> Like email, voice mail can present challenges. The following tips will help you deliver a voice-mail message clearly and effectively:
> - ☐ Organize your message before you deliver it. Long, meandering, or repetitive messages will frustrate listeners.
> - ☐ Begin your message with your name and affiliation as well as the date and time of your call.
> - ☐ State the subject of your message first. Then, fill in the details.
> - ☐ Speak slowly. Many experts advise people to speak much more slowly than they would in normal conversation.
> - ☐ Speak clearly. Enunciate your words precisely so a listener will understand your message the first time. Be sure to spell your name.
> - ☐ Give your phone number twice—once at the beginning and again at the end of your message. No one wants to replay a long voice-mail message just to get a phone number.

30

Designing Effective Documents

❓ FAQs

What is document design? (p. 442)
When should I use headings? (p. 445)
When I list points, should I use bullets or numbers? (p. 447)
When should I use visuals in my paper? (p. 449)

Document design refers to the principles that help you determine how to design a piece of written work—a research paper, report, or Web page, for example—so that it communicates your ideas clearly and effectively. Although formatting requirements—for example, how tables and charts are constructed and how information is presented on a title page—may differ from discipline to discipline, all well-designed documents share the same general characteristics: an effective visual format, clear headings, useful lists, and helpful visuals.

30a Creating an Effective Visual Format

An effective document includes visual elements that help readers find, read, and interpret information on a page. For example, wide margins can give a page a balanced, uncluttered appearance; white space can break up a long discussion; and a distinctive type size or typeface can make a word or phrase stand out on a page.

1 Margins

Margins frame a page and keep it from looking overcrowded. Because long lines of text can overwhelm readers and make a document difficult to read, a page should have margins of at least one inch all around. If the material you are writing about is highly technical or unusually difficult, use wider margins (one and a half inches).

In most cases, you should **justify** (uniformly align, except for paragraph indentations) the left-hand margin of your pages. You can either leave a ragged edge on the right or justify your text so all the words are aligned evenly along the right margin of your page.

(A ragged edge is preferable because it varies the visual landscape of your text, making it easier to read.)

2 White Space

White space denotes the areas of a page that are intentionally left blank: the spaces between lines of text, the space between text and visuals, and, of course, the margins. Used effectively, white space can isolate material and thereby focus a reader's attention on it. You can use white space around a block of text—a paragraph or a section, for example—or around visuals such as charts, graphs, and photographs. White space can eliminate clutter, break a discussion into manageable components, and focus readers' attention on a particular element on a page.

COMPUTER TIP   academic.cengage.com/eng/kirsznermandell

BORDERS, HORIZONTAL RULES, AND SHADING

Most word-processing programs enable you to create borders, horizontal rules, and shaded areas of text. Border and shading options are usually found under the Format menu of your word-processing program. With these features, you can select line style, thickness, and color and also adjust white space, boxed text, and the degree of shading.

---

3 Color

Like white space, **color** (when used in moderation) can help to emphasize and clarify information while making it visually appealing. In addition to using color to emphasize information, you can use it to distinguish certain types of information—for example, titles can be one color and subheadings can be another, complementary color. You can also use color to differentiate the segments of a chart or the bars on a graph. Many software applications, including *Microsoft Word* and *PowerPoint*, contain design templates (such as the one shown in Figure 30.1 on page 444) that make it easy for you to choose a color scheme or to create your own. Remember, however, that too many colors can distract readers and obscure your visual emphasis.

4 Typeface and Type Size

Your computer gives you a wide variety of typefaces and type sizes (measured in **points**) from which to choose. **Typefaces** are distinctively designed sets of letters, numbers, and punctuation marks. The typeface you choose should be suitable for your purpose and

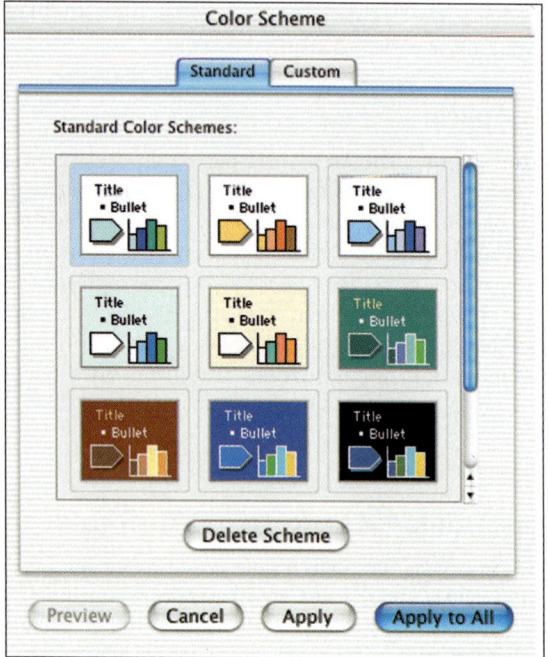

FIGURE 30.1 *Microsoft PowerPoint* Color Scheme menu.

audience. In your academic writing, avoid fancy or elaborate typefaces—script or old English, for example—that call attention to themselves and distract readers. Instead, select a typeface that is simple and direct—Courier, Times New Roman, or Arial, for example. In nonacademic documents—such as Web pages and flyers—decorative typefaces may be used to emphasize a point or attract a reader's attention.

You also have a wide variety of **type sizes** available to you. For most of your academic papers, you will use 10- or 12-point type (headings will sometimes be larger). Documents such as advertisements, brochures, and Web pages, however, may use a variety of type sizes. (Keep in mind that point size alone is not a reliable guide for size. For instance, 12-point type in **Chicago** is much larger than 12-point type in Courier or in Arial Condensed Light.)

5 Line Spacing

Line spacing refers to the amount of space between the lines of a document. If the lines are too far apart, the text will seem to lack cohesion; if the lines are too close together, the text will appear crowded and be difficult to read. The type of writing you do may determine line spacing: the paragraphs of business letters, memos, and some reports are usually single-spaced and separated by a double space, but the paragraphs of academic papers are usually double-spaced.

30b Using Headings

Used effectively, headings help readers understand information, and they also break up a text, making it inviting and easy to read. Different academic disciplines have different requirements concerning headings. For this reason, you should consult the appropriate style manual before inserting headings in a paper.

> **CLOSE-UP**
>
> **USING HEADINGS**
>
> Headings perform several functions in a document:
>
> - **Headings tell readers that a new idea is being introduced.** In this way, headings tell readers what to expect in a section before they actually read it.
> - **Headings emphasize key ideas.** By summarizing an idea and isolating it from the text around it, headings help readers identify important information.
> - **Headings indicate how information is organized in a text.** Headings use various typefaces and type sizes (as well as indentation) to indicate the relative importance of ideas. For example, the most important information in a text will be set off as first-level headings and have the same typeface and type size. The next most important information will be set off as second-level headings, also with the same typeface and type size.

1 Number of Headings

The number of headings you need depends on the document. A long, complicated document will need more headings than a shorter, less complicated one. Keep in mind that too few headings may not be of much use, but too many headings will make your document look like an outline.

2 Phrasing

Headings should be brief, descriptive, and to the point. They can be single words—**Summary** or **Introduction**, for example—or they can be phrases (always stated in parallel terms): **Traditional Family Patterns, Alternate Family Patterns, Modern Family Patterns**. Finally, headings

See Ch. 41

can be questions (**How Do You Choose a Major?**) or statements (**Choose Your Major Carefully**).

3 Indentation

Indenting is one way of distinguishing one level of heading from another. In general, the more important a heading is, the closer it is to the left-hand margin: first-level headings are justified left, second-level headings are indented one-half inch, and third-level headings are indented further. Alternatively, headings may be centered, with different levels of subheadings placed flush left or run into the text.

4 Typographical Emphasis

You can emphasize important words in headings by using **boldface**, *italics*, or ALL CAPITAL LETTERS. Used in moderation, these distinctive typefaces make a text easier to read. Used excessively, however, they slow readers down.

5 Consistency

Headings at the same level should have the same format—the same typeface, type size, and degree of indentation—as well as parallel phrasing. If one first-level heading is boldfaced and centered, all other first-level headings must be boldfaced and centered. Using consistent patterns reinforces the connection between content and ideas and makes a document easier to understand.

CLOSE-UP

SAMPLE HEADING FORMATS

Flush Left, Boldfaced, Uppercase and Lowercase
　Indented, Boldfaced, Uppercase and Lowercase
　　Indented, italicized, lowercase; run into the text at the beginning of a paragraph; ends with a period.

Or

Centered, Boldfaced, Uppercase and Lowercase

Flush Left, Underlined, Uppercase and Lowercase
　Indented, underlined, lowercase; run into the text at the beginning of a paragraph; ends with a period.

Or

ALL CAPITAL LETTERS, CENTERED

NOTE: Never separate a heading from the text that goes with it: if a heading is at the bottom of one page and the text that goes with it is on the next page, move the heading onto the next page so readers can see the heading and the text together.

30c Constructing Lists

By breaking long discussions into a series of key ideas, a list makes information easier to understand. By isolating individual pieces of information and by providing visual cues (such as bullets or numbers), a list also directs readers to important information on a page.

> **CHECKLIST**
>
> **CONSTRUCTING EFFECTIVE LISTS**
>
> When constructing lists, follow these guidelines:
>
> ☐ **Indent each item.** Each item on a list should be indented so that it stands out from the text around it.
>
> ☐ **Set off items with numbers or bullets.** Use **bullets** when items are not organized according to any particular sequence or priority (the members of a club, for example). Use **numbers** when you want to indicate that items are organized according to a sequence (the steps in a process, for example) or priority (the things a company should do to decrease spending, for example).
>
> ☐ **Introduce a list with a complete sentence.** Do not simply drop a list into a document; introduce it with a complete sentence (followed by a colon).
>
> ☐ **Use parallel structure.** Lists are easiest to read when all items are parallel and about the same length.
>
> A number of factors can cause high unemployment:
> - a decrease in consumer spending
> - a decrease in factory orders
> - a decrease in factory output
>
> ☐ **Punctuate correctly.** If the items on a list are fragments (as in the example above), begin each item with a lowercase letter, and do not end it with a period. However, if the items on a list are complete sentences (as in the example below), begin each item with a capital letter and end it with a period.
>
> Here are the three steps we must take to reduce our spending:
> 1. We must cut our workforce by 10 percent.
> 2. We must use less expensive vendors.
> 3. We must decrease overtime payments.
>
> ☐ **Do not overuse lists.** Too many lists will make a document seem cluttered. In addition, they will give readers the impression that you are simply listing points instead of discussing them.

Figure 30.2 shows a page from a student's report that incorporates some of the effective design elements discussed in 30a–c.

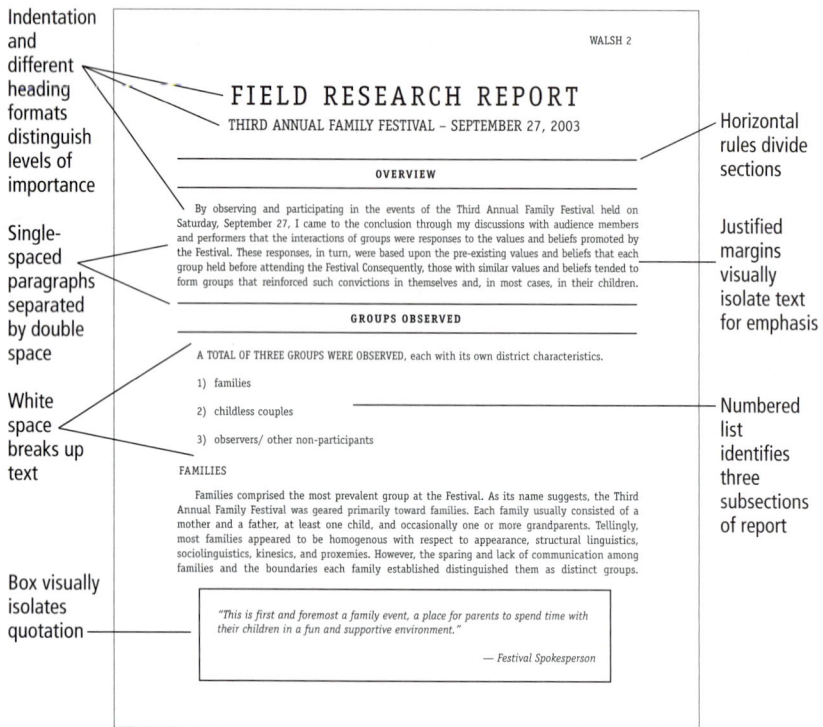

FIGURE 30.2 A well-designed page from a student's report.

■ **EXERCISE 1**

Select two different documents—for example, a page from a procedure manual and an invitation, or a report and a flyer. Then, make a list of the design elements each document contains. Finally, evaluate the relative effectiveness of the two documents, given their intended audiences.

■ **EXERCISE 2**

Look at the advertisement in Figure 30.3, noting its organization, format, and design. How does the ad make use of margins, white space, typeface and type size, line spacing, and other document design features to emphasize important elements of the text? Can any design elements be improved?

Using Visuals **30d** 449

FIGURE 30.3 Print advertisement for a radio station.

30d Using Visuals

Visuals—such as *tables, graphs, diagrams*, and *photographs*—can help you convey complex ideas that are difficult to communicate with words, and they can also help you attract readers' attention.

You can create your own tables and graphs by using applications in software packages such as *Excel, Lotus,* or *Word*. In addition, many stand-alone graphics software packages enable you to create complex charts, tables, and graphs that contain three-dimensional effects. You can also photocopy or scan diagrams and photographs from a print source or download them from the Internet or from CD-ROMs or DVDs. Remember, however, that if you use a visual from a source, you must use appropriate <u>documentation</u>.

See Pts. 4–5

1 Tables

Tables present data in a condensed, visual format—arranged in rows and columns. Tables may contain numerical data, text, or a combination of the two. When you plan your table, make sure you include only the data that you will need; discard information that is too detailed or difficult to understand. Keep in mind that tables can distract readers, so include only those necessary to support your discussion. (The table in Figure 30.4 reports the student writer's original research and therefore needs no documentation.)

As the following table shows, the Madison location now employs more workers in every site than St. Paul location.

Table 1
Number of Employees at Each Location

	Location	
Employees	Madison	St. Paul
Plant	451	254
Warehouse	45	23
Outlet Stores	15	9

Because this location has grown so quickly, steps must be taken to....

- Boldface and shading set off column headings
- Underlining sets off row headings
- Heading
- Descriptive caption
- Ruled lines improve readability

FIGURE 30.4 Table from a student paper.

2 Graphs

Like tables, **graphs** present data in visual form. Whereas tables may present specific numerical data, graphs show the general pattern or trend that the data suggest. Because graphs tend to be more general (and therefore less accurate) than tables, they are frequently accompanied by tables. Figure 30.5 is an example of a bar graph showing data from a source.

3 Diagrams

A **diagram** calls readers' attention to specific details of a mechanism or object. Diagrams are often used in scientific and technical writing to clarify concepts that are difficult to explain in words. Figure 30.6, which illustrates the sections of an orchestra, serves a similar purpose in a music education paper.

4 Photographs

Photographs enable you to show exactly what something or someone looks like—an animal in its natural habitat, a work of fine art, or an actor in costume, for example. Although computer technology that enables you to paste photographs directly into a text is widely available, you should use it with restraint. Not every photograph will support or enhance your written text; in fact, an irrelevant photo-

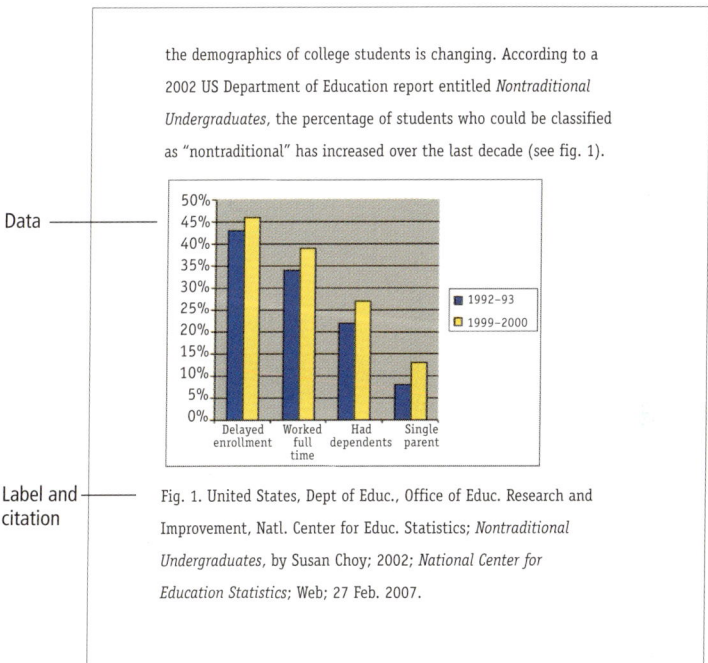

FIGURE 30.5 Bar graph from a student paper.

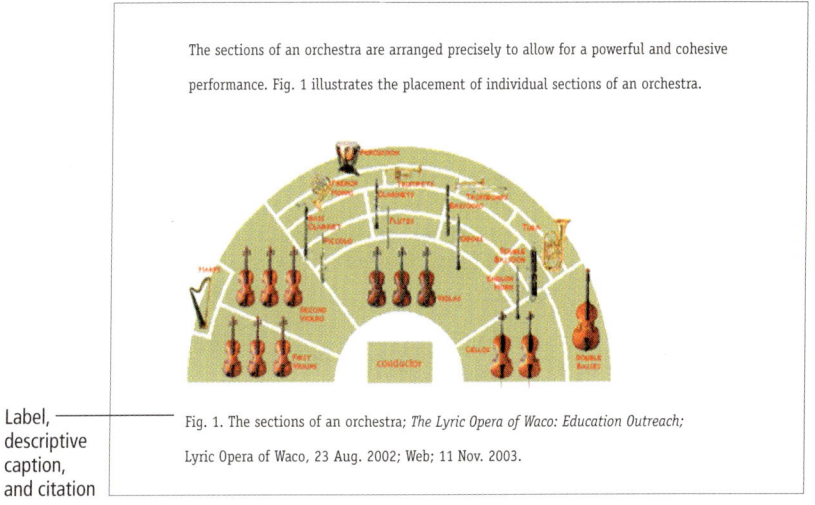

FIGURE 30.6 Diagram from a student paper.

graph will distract readers. The photograph of a wooded trail in Figure 30.7 on page 452 illustrates the student writer's description of a local recreational area.

Designing Effective Documents

> travelers are well advised to be prepared, to always carry water, and to dress for the conditions. Loose fitting, lightweight wicking material covering all exposed skin is necessary in summer, and layers of warm clothing are needed for cold-weather outings. Hats and sunscreen are always a good idea no matter what the temperature, although most of the trails are quite shady with huge oak trees. Fig. 1 shows a shady portion of the trail.
>
>
>
> Fig. 1. Greenbelt Trail in springtime (author photo).

Photo sized and placed appropriately within text with consistent white space above and below

Reference to photo provides context

Label and descriptive caption

FIGURE 30.7 Photograph from a student paper.

CLOSE-UP

VISUALS AND COPYRIGHT

Copyright gives an author the legal right to control the copying of his or her work—visuals as well as text. The law makes a clear distinction between visuals used in documents prepared for school assignments and visuals used in documents that will be published. In general, you may use graphics from a source—print or electronic—as long as you document the source, just as you would any other source.

If you use visuals in documents that will be published, however, you must obtain permission in writing from the person or organization that holds the copyright. Sometimes the copyright holder will grant permission without charge, but often there will be a fee. Remember, it is your responsibility to determine whether or not permission is required.

CHECKLIST

USING VISUALS

When using visuals in your papers, follow these guidelines:
- ☐ Use a visual only when it contributes something important to the discussion, not simply for embellishment.
- ☐ Place the visual in the text only if you plan to refer to it in your paper (otherwise, place the visual in an appendix).

- ☐ Introduce each visual with a complete sentence.
- ☐ Follow each visual with a discussion of its significance.
- ☐ Leave wide margins around each visual.
- ☐ Place the visual as close as possible to the section of your document in which it is discussed.
- ☐ Label each visual appropriately.
- ☐ Document each visual borrowed from a source.

■ **EXERCISE 3**

Analyze the chart in Figure 30.8, noting the visual elements that are used to convey the billing costs of material, labor, and equipment on a construction project. Summarize the data in a brief paragraph. Then, list the advantages and disadvantages of presenting the data visually as opposed to verbally.

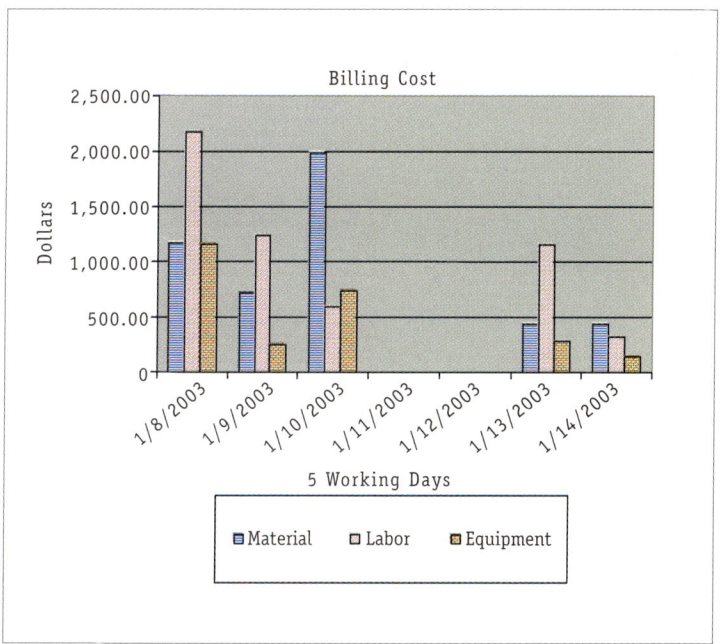

FIGURE 30.8 Billing cost chart.

30e Using Desktop Publishing

During your college career, you may be required to use your computer for **desktop publishing**—using graphics as well as words to produce documents. For example, you may produce a brochure or newsletter for a student organization to which you belong or as a service learning project for a course you are taking. (Figure 30.9 shows a sample student brochure.) Brochures and newsletters are frequently aimed at consumers of a product or service or at members of an organization. These documents may be informative, persuasive, or both.

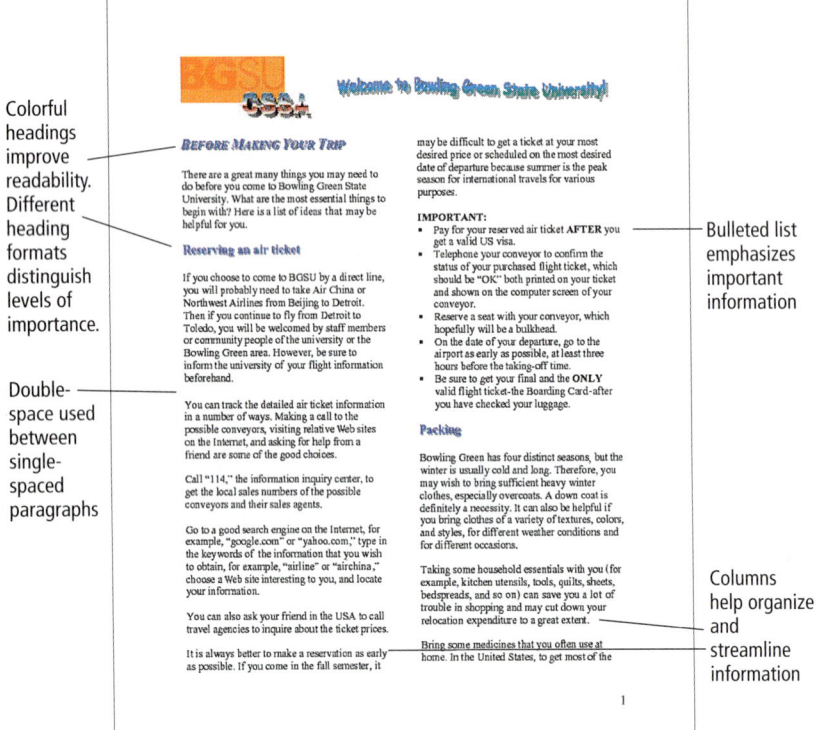

FIGURE 30.9 Sample student brochure.

Most word-processing programs, such as *Microsoft Word*, contain templates (see Figure 30.10, for example) that can help you design your newsletter or brochure. With these templates, you can select layout, color scheme, and typeface as well as document dimensions and paper size.

For more options, you can use one of the many desktop publishing software packages that are commercially available. *Microsoft Publisher*, like *Microsoft Word*, provides templates for a wide range of document types. More advanced desktop publishing programs include *Adobe PageMaker*, *QuarkXPress*, and *InDesign*, all of which are used extensively in business and industry.

Using Desktop Publishing 30e

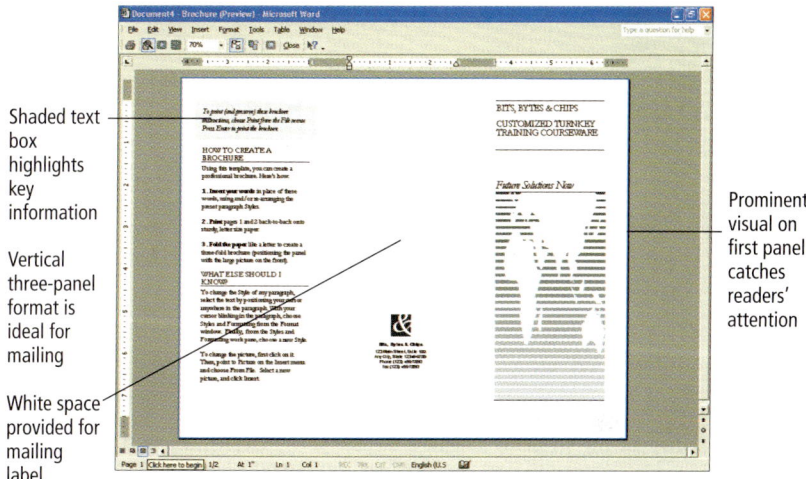

FIGURE 30.10 *Microsoft Word* brochure template.

■ EXERCISE 4

Create a promotional document for an organization on your campus. Before you begin the document-design process, interview someone affiliated with the organization to determine the type of information you will need, the format in which the information should be delivered, and the image the organization wishes to project to the campus community.

31

Designing a Web Site

❓ FAQs

What is the difference between a Web site and a Web page? (p. 456)
How do I include images on my Web site? (p. 458)
What is a splash page? (p. 460)
Do I need permission to use material from other Web sites? (p. 462)

See Ch. 30

At some point in your college career—for example, as a course assignment or as a way of marketing your job skills—you may be asked to create a Web page or even a full Web site. Like other documents, Web pages follow the conventions of <u>document design</u>. Because so much of the content is meant to be read online, your choices of text, color, and navigation strategy are especially important.

> **CLOSE-UP**
>
> ### COMPONENTS OF A WEB PAGE
>
> A **personal home page** usually contains information about how to contact the author, along with a brief biography. A home page can also be the first page of a **Web site,** a group of related **Web pages** focusing on a personal, professional, or academic topic. In this case, the home page contains **links**—highlighted words, images, or URLs—that allow users to move from one page to another or to another Web site.

31a Planning Your Web Site

See 1a–c

When you plan your Web site, you should consider your <u>purpose</u>, <u>audience</u>, and <u>tone</u>, just as you would when planning a print document. You should also consider what content to include. Finally, just as an essay or research paper may have a set page limit, your own Web site may have size and file-type limitations.

See 5d

Begin planning your Web site by sketching a basic plan or <u>storyboard</u> of your site's content (both text and visuals). Then, consider how your Web pages will be connected and what links you will provide to other Web sites. Because users will start with your home page and navigate from one part of your site to another, the home page should provide an overview of your site and give readers a clear sense of what material the site will contain. As you lay out the pages of your Web site, place related items together, and use text sparingly. Keep in mind that too many graphics and elaborate type styles will distract or confuse users.

As you plan your Web site, consider how your pages will be organized. If your site will have relatively few pages, you can arrange them so that one page leads sequentially to the next. If your site will include numerous pages, however, you will have to group pages under headings or categories in order of importance. For example, the home page of the student's Web site shown in Figure 31.1 indicates that information is grouped under the headings *About me*, *Résumé*, *Portfolio*, *Services*, and *Contact*.

FIGURE 31.1 Home page of student's Web site.

■ **EXERCISE 1**

Select three Web sites: one personal, one academic (such as your university's site), and one professional or organizational (such as that of the American Cancer Society). How do these sites differ in purpose, audience, and tone? How are these differences reflected in the designs of each site?

31b Creating Your Web Site

Once you have planned your Web site, you will need to select a method for actually creating the site. Essentially, there are three ways to do this: you can use Web authoring software packages; you can use

Web tools within your word-processing program; or you can create a page from scratch with a text editor that uses the programming language **HTML** (hypertext markup language) to convert standard documents into World Wide Web hypertext documents.

- **Web Authoring Packages**   Many Web authoring packages—for example, *Macromedia Dreamweaver* and *Microsoft FrontPage*—will automatically translate your pages into HTML. The advantage of an authoring package is that you do not have to have a working knowledge of HTML in order to develop your site. Some of these packages even make certain interactive functions—such as navigation bars, forms, or media effects—easier to implement.
- **Web Tools within Your Word-Processing Program**   Most word processors have an option under the File menu or the Save menu that automatically saves word-processed documents as HTML documents suitable for Web delivery. Although this option is appropriate for a single document, such as your résumé, it does not have the features you will need to create an entire Web site. For example, you cannot insert navigation buttons or include columns and tables that will transfer to the Web.
- **Text Editors**   If you have advanced knowledge of HTML, this is a good option. Text editors, including *Simple Text* for the Mac and *Notepad* for the PC, enable you to control all elements of your Web site design. The major drawback of using a text editor is that HTML coding can be confusing, and some special effects require complicated codes.

- **EXERCISE 2**

    Explore the Web tools within your word-processing program. What options do you have for creating individual Web pages?

31c   Selecting and Inserting Visuals

You can find visuals for your Web site by looking for sites on the Web that make visuals available for others to use. *Google*, for example, has an image directory at <http://images.google.com> that you can search. You can also create and upload visuals yourself by using either a digital camera or a scanner. Once a visual has been created and saved electronically, you can use a graphics package such as *Adobe Photoshop* to adjust the visual's size, contrast, or color scheme; to crop the image; or to add text. Other visual options include creating your own banners and backgrounds with special colors and textures. Figure 31.2 shows a Web page that includes a visual.

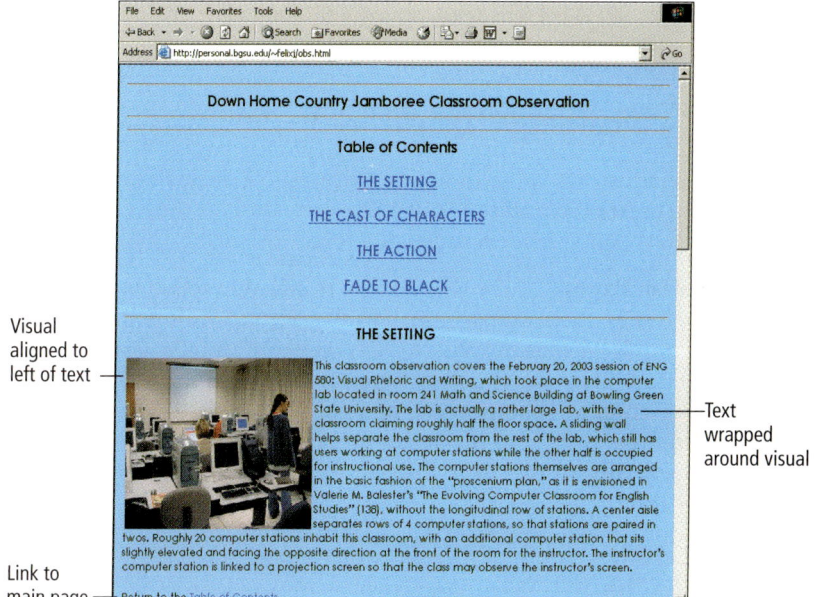

FIGURE 31.2 Web page with visual.

Once you have edited a visual, you will need to save it in one of two standard formats for the Web: JPG (for photographic images containing a wide range of colors) or GIF (for graphic files with fewer colors, line art, and text).

> **CLOSE-UP**
>
> **DETERMINING VISUAL FILE FORMAT AND SIZE**
>
> Before inserting a visual into a Web page, check the visual's size by clicking once on the file icon for the visual so that it is highlighted. Then, select Properties from the file menu. A small window will appear with information about the file's format and size.

■ **EXERCISE 3**

Select a visual you could include on a personal Web site. If you have access to *Netscape Composer* or another Web authoring package, practice inserting and aligning the visual near some text and adjusting its height and width in relation to the text. How well does the visual thematically and visually correspond to your written content and overall visual design? What alterations can you make to the visual before you reinsert it? What changes in size and alignment should you make once the visual is reinserted on the page?

31d Planning Navigation

Web sites use a number of design features to make navigation easier. As you create the pages of your Web site, consider the following options for helping readers navigate your site:

- **Splash Pages**   Many Web designers include a splash page on their Web sites. A splash page, such as the one shown in Figure 31.3, is more visual than textual, usually containing only limited background information and navigation features, such as links to the site's content. The purpose of a splash page is to create interest and draw users into the site; a more detailed overview of the site appears on another page that serves as the true home page.

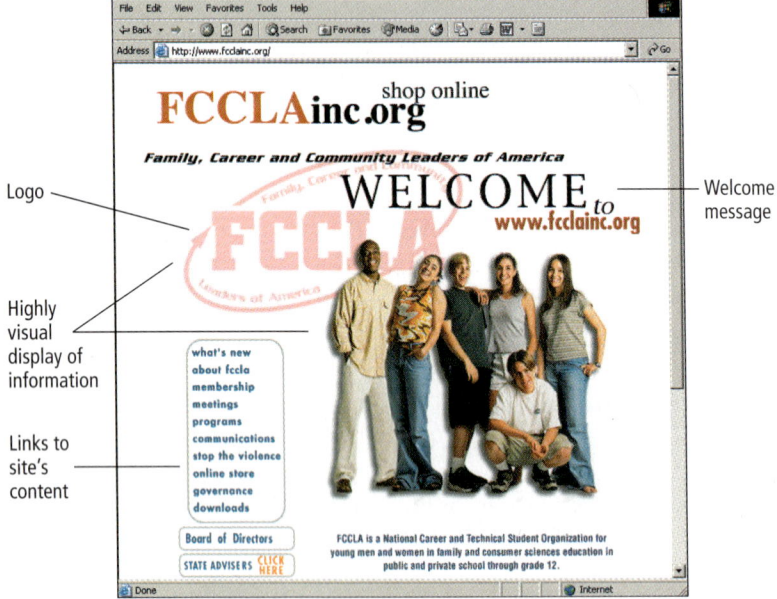

FIGURE 31.3 Splash page.

- **Navigation Links, Buttons, and Bars**   Navigation links, buttons, bars, and other graphic icons, such as arrows or pictures, enable readers to move from one page of a Web site to another (see Figure 31.4).
- **Anchors**   Anchors (or **relative links**) enable readers to jump from one part of a Web page to another (see Figure 31.4).

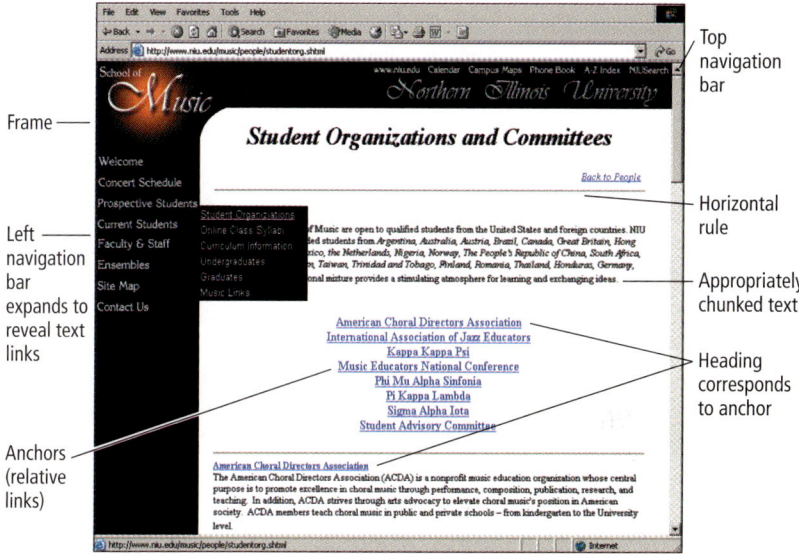

FIGURE 31.4 Web page with navigation links, anchors, and frames.

- **Horizontal Rules**   Horizontal rules divide sections and parts of a page (see Figure 31.4). You can use colored or patterned rules that coordinate with the color scheme of the Web site.
- **Chunking or Clustering**   Chunking or clustering means placing related items of text close to one another (see Figure 31.4). This technique cuts down on scrolling and helps users read content easily on the screen. By surrounding clusters of information with white space, you can create distinct areas of content.
- **Frames**   Like tables, frames organize text and graphics. Unlike tables, however, frames enable you to divide a single Web page into multiple windows (see Figure 31.4).
- **Text Formatting Features**   Like printed texts, Web texts follow the principles of **document design**, using design elements such as single-spaced text, headings, subheadings, and bulleted lists, as well as boldface and italics, to emphasize points. (Underlining is usually not used in Web texts because readers might mistake underlined text for a hyperlink.)

See Ch. 30

CHECKLIST

DESIGNING EFFECTIVE WEB PAGES

☐ Use the same type size and typeface for equivalent information. Keep headings consistent throughout your site.

(continued)

DESIGNING EFFECTIVE WEB PAGES (continued)

- ☐ Use text, buttons, and bars to facilitate navigation.
- ☐ Use special multimedia effects in moderation.
- ☐ Avoid pages so full of text, graphics, and navigation aids that they make reading difficult and increase loading time.
- ☐ For best visibility, use text and background colors that contrast well.
- ☐ Preview your Web site on multiple machines and browsers as well as on both high-speed networks and slower-speed modems.
- ☐ Provide your email address so you can receive feedback from users.

31e Linking Your Content

Links (short for **hyperlinks**) are obviously a very important part of Web design. When you provide a link, you are directing people to a particular Web site. For this reason, you should make sure that the site you link to is up and running and that the information appearing there is both accurate and reliable.

It is important to select a visible color for your text-based links to indicate that they are in fact links and not just highlighted text. You will need three colors to indicate the status of a link: one for the link before it is clicked; one for the active link (or the change in color as the link itself is being clicked); and one for the visited link (the color after the link has been successfully accessed).

Finally, make certain that you have the exact URL for the sites to which you are linking. The Web relies on exact URLs to deliver information; if even one letter or punctuation mark is incorrect, the page will not load.

CLOSE-UP

WEB SITES AND COPYRIGHT

As a rule, assume that any material on a Web site is **copyrighted** unless the author makes an explicit statement to the contrary. This means you must obtain written permission if you are going to reproduce this material on your Web site. The only exception to this rule is the **fair use doctrine,** which allows the use of copyrighted material for the purpose of commentary, parody, or research and education. (You are also allowed to provide a link to a Web site without permission.)

NOTE: Material you quote in a research paper for one of your classes falls under the fair use doctrine and does not require permission.

31f Editing and Proofreading Your Web Site

Before you post your Web site, you should edit and proofread it just as you would any other document. (Even if you run a spell check and a grammar check, you must still proofread carefully.)

See 6d

> **CHECKLIST**
>
> **STYLE CONVENTIONS OF WRITING FOR THE WEB**
>
> ☐ Avoid long, wordy sentences. Using active verbs will help keep your sentences short and concise.
> ☐ Avoid long paragraphs. Chunk content into small sections that are easy to read and access online.
> ☐ Speak directly to your audience, using the first person (*I*) and the second person (*you*) to establish a connection with readers.
> ☐ Avoid technical terminology that only a certain segment of your audience will understand.
> ☐ Choose your external links wisely. Do not provide so many that your audience is drawn away from your site.
> ☐ Use headings and bulleted lists to organize information visually and textually.
> ☐ Provide a title in the browser window for each page within your site to help users keep track of where they are.
> ☐ Proofread carefully offline before loading your content online.

31g Posting Your Web Site

Once you have designed a Web site, you will need to upload (**post**) it so you can view it on the Web. Most commonly, Web pages are posted with FTP (File Transfer Protocol) software.

To get your site up on the Web, you transfer your files to an **Internet server,** a computer that is connected at all times to the Internet. Your Internet service provider will instruct you on how to use FTP to transfer your files. Once your site is up and running, any mistakes you have made will be apparent as soon as you view your pages on the Web.

■ **EXERCISE 4**

Visit your university's Web site or Information Technology Center, and obtain a Web server account. What are your file size limitations, and what content guidelines are provided? What online training or tutorials are available to help you develop and upload your site?

32

Making Oral Presentations

❓ FAQs

What kind of notes should I use? (p. 466)
Should I use visual aids? (p. 467)

At school and on the job, you may be called on to make **oral presentations.** Although many people are uncomfortable about giving oral presentations, the guidelines that follow can make the experience easier and less stressful.

32a Getting Started

Just as with writing an essay, the preparation stage of an oral presentation is as important as the speech itself. The time you spend on this stage of the process will make your task easier later on.

Identify Your Topic. The first thing you should do is to identify the topic of your speech. Sometimes you are given a topic; at other times, you have the option of choosing your own. Once you have a topic, you will be able to decide how much information, as well as what kind of information, you will need.

Consider Your Audience. The easiest way to determine what kind of information you will need is to consider the nature of your audience. Is your audience made up of experts or of people who know little about your topic? How much background information will you have to provide? Can you use technical terms, or should you avoid them? Do you think your audience will be interested in your topic, or will you have to create interest? What opinions about your topic will the members of your audience bring with them?

> **ESL TIP**
>
> When making oral presentations, it is a good idea to choose topics related to your cultural background or home country. By doing so, you will be able to provide information on these topics that is new to your instructor and your classmates. If you choose such a topic, try to determine beforehand how much background your audience has by speaking with your instructor and classmates.

Consider Your Purpose. Your speech should have a specific purpose that you can sum up concisely. To help you zero in on your purpose, ask yourself what you are trying to accomplish with your presentation. It is a good idea to write out this purpose and to keep it in front of you as you plan your speech.

<u>Purpose</u>: to suggest ways to make registration easier for students

Consider Your Constraints. How much time do you have for your presentation? (Obviously, a ten-minute presentation requires more information and preparation than a three-minute presentation.) Do you already know enough about your topic, or will you have to do research?

> **CLOSE-UP**
>
> **GROUP PRESENTATIONS**
>
> Whether you are participating in a panel discussion or delivering one part of a long speech, you should be aware that group presentations require coordination. Before you begin planning, you should define your role as well as everyone else's. Who will be in charge? Who will be responsible for each part of the presentation? Who will prepare and display the visuals? In addition, all group members should understand that they must stick to a schedule.

32b Planning Your Speech

In the planning phase, you focus on your ideas about your topic and develop a thesis; then, you decide what specific points you will discuss and divide your speech into a few manageable sections.

Develop a Thesis Statement. Before you actually plan your speech, you need to develop a **thesis statement** that clearly and concisely presents your main idea—the key idea you want to communicate to your audience. If you know a lot about your topic, you can develop a thesis on your own. If you do not know a lot, you will have to gather information and review it before you can decide on a thesis.

See 5a–b

Decide on Your Points. Once you have developed a thesis, you can decide what points you will discuss. Unlike readers, who can read a passage again and again until they understand it, listeners must understand information the first time they hear it. For this reason, effective speeches focus on points that are clear and easy to follow. Your thesis statement should state (or at least strongly imply) these points.

Gather Support. You cannot expect your listeners to automatically accept what you say. You must supply details, facts, and examples that will convince them that what you are saying is both accurate and reasonable. You can gather this supporting material in the library, on the Web, or from your own experience.

Outline the Individual Parts of Your Speech. Every speech has a beginning, a middle, and an end. Your **introduction** should introduce your subject, engage your audience's interest, and state your thesis—but it should *not* present an in-depth discussion or summary of your topic. The **body,** or middle section, of your speech should present the points that support your thesis. It should also include the facts, examples, and other information that will clarify your points and help convince listeners your thesis is reasonable. Your **conclusion** should bring your speech to a definite end and reinforce your thesis.

32c Preparing Your Notes

Most people use notes of some form when they give a speech. Each system of notes has advantages and disadvantages.

Full Text. Some people like to write out the full text of their speech and refer to it during their presentation. If the type is large enough, and if you triple-space, this strategy can be useful. One disadvantage of using the full text of your speech is that it is easy to lose your place and become disoriented; another is that you may find yourself simply reading your speech.

Note Cards. Some people write important parts of their speech—for example, a list of key points or definitions—on note cards. Cards are portable, so they can be flipped through easily. They are also small, so they can be placed inconspicuously on a podium or a table. With some practice, you can learn to use note cards effectively. You have to be careful, however, not to become so dependent on the cards that you lose eye contact with your audience or begin fidgeting with the cards as you speak.

Outlines. Some people like to refer to an outline when they give a speech. As they speak, they can glance down at the outline to get their bearings or to remind themselves of a point they have to make. Because an outline does not contain the full text of a speech, the temptation to read is eliminated. However, if for some reason you draw a blank, an outline gives you very little to fall back on.

32d Preparing Visual Aids

1 Using Visuals

Visual aids, such as overhead transparencies or posters, can reinforce important information and make your speech easier to understand. For a simple speech, a visual aid may be no more than a definition or a few key terms, names, or dates written on the board or distributed in a handout. A more complicated presentation might require charts, graphs, diagrams, or photographs—or even objects. The major consideration for including a visual aid is whether it actually adds something to your speech.

If you are using equipment such as an overhead projector, make sure you know how to operate it—and have a contingency plan just in case the equipment does not work the way it should. If possible, visit the room in which you will be giving your speech ahead of time, and see whether it has the equipment you need (and whether the equipment works). Finally, make sure that whatever visual aid you use is large enough for everyone in your audience to see. Print or type should be neat and free of errors, and graphics should be clearly labeled and easy to see.

2 Using Presentation Software

Microsoft PowerPoint, the most commonly used **presentation software** package, enables you to organize an oral presentation and prepare attractive, professional slides (see Figure 32.1).

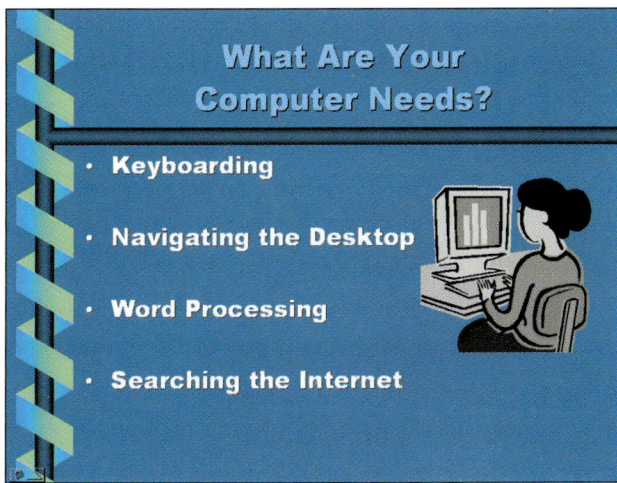

FIGURE 32.1 *PowerPoint* slide.

32d Making Oral Presentations

PowerPoint's more advanced features enable you to create multimedia presentations that combine images, video, audio, and animation. You can also use the Insert menu to insert various items—for example, clip art, word art, and image files you have created with a digital camera or scanner—into your slide templates (see Figure 32.2). You can also import charts and tables from *Microsoft Word* and *Excel* and download images from Internet sites directly into your slide templates.

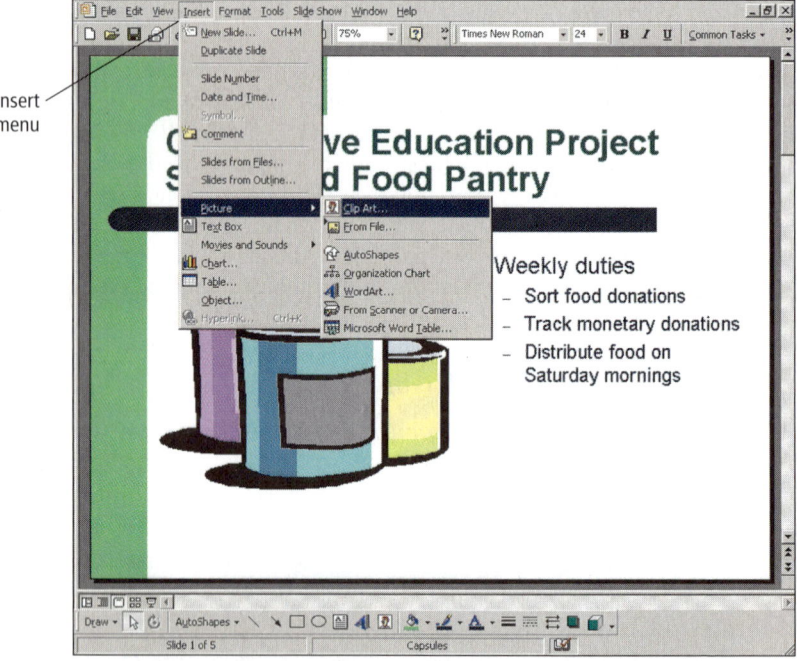

FIGURE 32.2 *Microsoft PowerPoint* **Insert menu.**

COMPUTER TIP academic.cengage.com/eng/kirsznermandell

USING *POWERPOINT*

If possible, use the computer that you used to prepare your *PowerPoint* slides when you deliver your speech. That way, you will be sure that you will be able to open your files and that all the multimedia effects you included with your slides will work.

Preparing Visual Aids **32d** 469

> **CHECKLIST**
>
> **DESIGNING VISUAL AIDS**
>
> - [ ] Do not put more than three or four major points on a single visual.
> - [ ] Use single words or short phrases, not sentences or paragraphs.
> - [ ] Limit the number of visuals. For a three- to five-minute presentation, five or six visuals are usually enough.
> - [ ] Use type that is large enough for your audience to see (44- to 50-point type for major headings and 30- to 34-point type for text).
> - [ ] Do not use elaborate graphics or special effects just because your computer software enables you to do so (this caution is especially relevant for users of *PowerPoint*).
> - [ ] Check your visuals carefully for typos, inaccurate captions or labels, or other errors.

USING VISUAL AIDS IN YOUR PRESENTATIONS

Visual Aid	Advantages	Disadvantages
Computer presentations	Clear Easy to read Professional Graphics, video, sound, and animated effects Portable (disk or CD-ROM)	Special equipment needed Expertise needed Special software needed Software might not be compatible with all computer systems
Overhead projectors	Transparencies are inexpensive Transparencies are easily prepared with computer or copier Transparencies are portable Transparencies can be written on during presentation Projector is easy to operate	Transparencies can stick together Transparencies must be placed on projector by hand Transparencies can be placed upside down Some projectors are noisy Speaker must avoid power cord to projector during presentation
Slide projector	Colorful Professional Projector is easy to use Order of slides can be reversed during presentation Portable (slide carousel)	Slides are expensive to produce Special equipment needed for lettering and graphics Dark room needed for presentation Slides can jam in projector

Visual Aid	Advantages	Disadvantages
Posters or flip charts	Low-tech and personal Good for small-group presentations Portable	May not be large enough to be seen in some rooms Artistic ability needed May be expensive if prepared professionally Must be secured to an easel
Chalkboards or whiteboards	Available in most rooms Easy to use Easy to erase or change information during presentation	Difficult to draw complicated graphics Handwriting must be legible Must catch errors while writing Cannot face audience when writing or drawing Very informal

■ **EXERCISE 1**

Create visuals for an oral presentation based on the content of a paper that you have just written for one of your classes. Begin by deciding which points need to be illustrated for your audience. Then, consulting the chart on pages 469–470, decide what kinds of visuals would be most effective.

32e Rehearsing Your Speech

You should practice your speech often—at least five times—and make sure you practice delivering your speech with your visuals. Do not try to memorize your entire speech, but be sure you know it well enough so you can move from point to point without constantly looking at your notes. If possible, rehearse your speech in the actual room you will be using, and try standing at the back of the room to make sure your visuals can be seen clearly. Finally, time yourself. Make certain your three-minute speech actually takes three minutes to deliver.

32f Delivering Your Speech

The most important part of your speech is your delivery. Remember that a certain amount of nervousness is normal, so try not to focus on it too much. Channel the nervous energy into your speech, and let it work for you.

CHECKLIST

DELIVERING YOUR SPEECH

As you deliver your speech, keep in mind the following tips on body language, eye contact, and pacing:
- ☐ Take your time before you begin.
- ☐ Make sure your visuals are positioned properly.
- ☐ Make sure your equipment is operating properly.
- ☐ Position yourself effectively.
- ☐ Stand straight.
- ☐ Speak slowly and clearly.
- ☐ Maintain eye contact with the audience.
- ☐ Use natural gestures.
- ☐ Face the audience at all times.
- ☐ Do not just show or read visuals to your audience. Tell your audience more than they can see or read for themselves.
- ☐ Do not block your visuals.
- ☐ Try to relax.
- ☐ Do not get flustered if something unexpected happens.
- ☐ If you forget something, don't let your audience know. Work the information in later.
- ☐ Do not sit down immediately after your speech. Leave time for questions.
- ☐ Distribute any handouts before or after the speech, not during it.

PART 8

Sentence Style

33 Building Simple Sentences 474
- **33a** Constructing Simple Sentences 474
- **33b** Identifying Phrases and Clauses 477
- **33c** Expanding Simple Sentences 479

34 Building Compound and Complex Sentences 488
- **34a** Building Compound Sentences 488
- **34b** Building Complex Sentences 491

35 Writing Varied Sentences 494
- **35a** Varying Sentence Length 494
- **35b** Combining Choppy Simple Sentences 495
- **35c** Breaking Up Strings of Compound Sentences 497
- **35d** Varying Sentence Types 498
- **35e** Varying Sentence Openings 500
- **35f** Varying Standard Word Order 501

36 Writing Emphatic Sentences 503
- **36a** Conveying Emphasis through Word Order 503
- **36b** Conveying Emphasis through Sentence Structure 506
- **36c** Conveying Emphasis through Parallelism and Balance 509
- **36d** Conveying Emphasis through Repetition 509
- **36e** Conveying Emphasis through Active Voice 510

37 Writing Concise Sentences 513
- **37a** Eliminating Wordiness 513
- **37b** Eliminating Unnecessary Repetition 516
- **37c** Tightening Rambling Sentences 517

33

Building Simple Sentences

❓ FAQs

What is a phrase? (p. 477)
What is a clause? (p. 477)
How can I use words and phrases to expand simple sentences? (p. 479)

A **sentence** is an independent grammatical unit that includes a subject and a predicate and expresses a complete thought.

   The quick brown fox jumped over the lazy dog.

   It came from outer space.

A **simple subject** is a noun or noun substitute (*fox, it*) that tells who or what the sentence is about. A **simple predicate** is a verb or verb phrase (*jumped, came*) that tells or asks something about the subject. The **complete subject** of a sentence includes the simple subject plus all its modifiers (*the quick brown fox*). The **complete predicate** includes the verb or verb phrase and all the words associated with it—such as modifiers, objects, and complements (*jumped over the lazy dog, came from outer space*).

See 33b1

> **ESL TIP**
>
> In some languages, such as Spanish and Italian, the subject of a sentence can sometimes be omitted (because the form of the sentence's verb clearly indicates who or what the subject of the sentence is). In English, however, every sentence must have a subject.

33a   Constructing Simple Sentences

A **simple sentence** consists of at least one subject and one predicate. Simple sentences conform to one of five basic patterns.

1 Subject + Intransitive Verb (s + v)

The most basic simple sentence consists of just a subject and a verb or **verb phrase** (the main verb plus all its auxiliary verbs).

See 46c1

    S   V
The price of gold rose.

    S   V
Stock prices may fall.

Here the verbs *rose* and *may fall* are **intransitive**—that is, they do not need an object to complete their meaning.

2 Subject + Transitive Verb + Direct Object (s + v + do)

Another kind of simple sentence consists of the subject, a verb, and a direct object.

  S   V   do
Van Gogh created *The Starry Night*.

  S   V   do
Caroline saved Jake.

Here the verbs *created* and *saved* are **transitive**—each requires an object to complete its meaning in the sentence. In each sentence, the **direct object** indicates where the verb's action is directed and who or what is affected by it.

> ### ESL TIP
>
> To determine whether a verb is intransitive or transitive, consult a dictionary. Remember, though, that some verbs, such as *write*, can be intransitive or transitive.
>
>   She wrote all night. (intransitive)
>
>   She wrote a paper about her semester in Spain. (transitive)

3 Subject + Transitive Verb + Direct Object + Object Complement (s + v + do + oc)

Some simple sentences include an **object complement**, a word or phrase that renames or describes the direct object.

   S   V   do   oc
The class elected Bridget treasurer. (Object complement *treasurer* renames direct object *Bridget*.)

S   V   do   oc
I found the exam easy. (Object complement *easy* describes direct object *exam*.)

4 Subject + Linking Verb + Subject Complement (s + v + sc)

Another kind of simple sentence consists of a subject, a **linking verb** (a verb that connects a subject to its complement), and the **subject complement** (the word or phrase that describes or renames the subject).

    s   v   sc
The injection was painless.

   s   v   sc
Tony Blair became prime minister.

Note that the linking verb is like an equal sign, equating the subject with its complement (*Tony Blair = prime minister*).

5 Subject + Transitive Verb + Indirect Object + Direct Object (s + v + io + do)

Some simple sentences include an **indirect object,** which indicates to whom or for whom the verb's action was done.

  s   v   io   do
Cyrano wrote Roxanne a poem. (Cyrano wrote a poem for Roxanne.)

     s   v   io   do
The officer handed Frank a ticket. (The officer handed a ticket to Frank.)

▪ EXERCISE 1

In each of the following sentences, underline the subject once and the predicate twice. Then, label direct objects, indirect objects, subject complements, and object complements.

                           sc
Example: Isaac Asimov was a science fiction writer.

1. Isaac Asimov first saw science fiction stories in his parents' Brooklyn store.
2. He practiced writing by telling his schoolmates stories.
3. Asimov published his first story in *Astounding Science Fiction*.
4. The magazine's editor, John W. Campbell, encouraged Asimov to continue writing.
5. The young writer researched scientific principles to make his stories more accurate.
6. Asimov's "Foundation" series of novels is a "future history."
7. The World Science Fiction Convention gave the series a Hugo Award.

8. Sometimes Asimov used "Paul French" as a pseudonym.
9. *Biochemistry and Human Metabolism* was Asimov's first nonfiction book.
10. Asimov coined the term *robotics*.

33b Identifying Phrases and Clauses

1 Identifying Phrases

A **phrase** is a group of related words that lacks a subject or predicate or both and functions as a single part of speech. It cannot stand alone as a sentence.

- A **verb phrase** consists of a main verb and all its auxiliary verbs.

  Time is flying.

- A **noun phrase** includes a noun or pronoun plus all related modifiers.

  I'll climb the highest mountain.

- A **prepositional phrase** consists of a preposition, its object, and any modifiers of that object.

  They discussed the ethical implications of the animal studies.

  He was last seen heading into the orange sunset.

- A **verbal phrase** consists of a **verbal** (participle, gerund, or infinitive) and its related objects, modifiers, or complements. A verbal phrase may be a **participial phrase**, a **gerund phrase**, or an **infinitive phrase**.

  Encouraged by the voter turnout, the candidate predicted a victory. (participial phrase)

  Taking it easy always makes sense. (gerund phrase)

  The jury recessed to evaluate the evidence. (infinitive phrase)

- An **absolute phrase** usually consists of a noun and a participle, accompanied by modifiers. It modifies an entire independent clause rather than a particular word or phrase.

  Their toes tapping, they watched the auditions.

2 Identifying Clauses

A **clause** is a group of related words that includes a subject and a predicate. An **independent** (main) **clause** can stand alone as a sentence, but

Building Simple Sentences

See 34b

a **dependent** (subordinate) **clause** cannot. It must always be combined with an independent clause to form a **complex sentence**.

[Lucretia Mott was an abolitionist.] [She was also a pioneer for women's rights.] (two independent clauses)

[Lucretia Mott was an abolitionist] [who was also a pioneer for women's rights.] (independent clause, dependent clause)

[Although Lucretia Mott is widely known for her support of women's rights,] [she was also a prominent abolitionist.] (dependent clause, independent clause)

Dependent clauses may be *adjective*, *adverb*, or *noun* clauses.

- **Adjective clauses**, sometimes called **relative clauses**, modify nouns or pronouns and always follow the nouns or pronouns they modify. They are introduced by relative pronouns—*that, what, whatever, which, who, whose, whom, whoever,* or *whomever*—or by the adverbs *where* or *when*.

  The television series *M*A*S*H*, which depicted life in an army hospital in Korea during the Korean War, ran for eleven years. (Adjective clause modifies the noun *M*A*S*H*.)

  William Styron's novel *Sophie's Choice* is set in Brooklyn, where the narrator lives in a house painted pink. (Adjective clause modifies the noun *Brooklyn*.)

  NOTE: Some adjective clauses, called **elliptical clauses**, are grammatically incomplete but nevertheless can be easily understood from the context of the sentence. Typically, a part of the subject or predicate (or the entire subject or predicate) is missing: *Although [they were] full, they could not resist dessert.*

- **Adverb clauses** modify single words (verbs, adjectives, or adverbs), entire phrases, or independent clauses. They are always introduced by subordinating conjunctions. Adverb clauses provide information to answer the questions *how? where? when? why?* and *to what extent?*

  Exhausted after the match was over, Kim decided to take a long nap. (Adverb clause modifies *exhausted*, telling *when* Kim was exhausted.)

  Mark will go wherever there's a party. (Adverb clause modifies *will go*, telling *where* Mark will go.)

  Because 75 percent of its exports are fish products, Iceland's economy is heavily dependent on the fishing industry. (Adverb clause modifies independent clause, telling *why* the fishing industry is so important.)

- **Noun clauses** function as subjects, objects, or complements. A noun clause may be introduced by a relative pronoun or by *whether, when, where, why,* or *how.*

  <u>What you see</u> is <u>what you get</u>. (Noun clauses serve as subject and subject complement.)

  They finally decided <u>which candidate was most qualified</u>. (Noun clause serves as direct object of verb *decided*.)

■ EXERCISE 2

Which of the following groups of words are independent clauses? Which are dependent clauses? Which are phrases? Label each word group *IC, DC,* or *P.*

Example: Coming through the rye. (P)

1. Beauty is truth.
2. When knights were bold.
3. In a galaxy far away.
4. He saw stars.
5. I hear a symphony.
6. Whenever you're near.
7. The clock struck ten.
8. The red planet.
9. Slowly I turned.
10. For the longest time.

33c Expanding Simple Sentences

A **simple sentence** is a single independent clause. A simple sentence can consist of just a subject and a verb.

  <u>Jessica</u> <u>fell</u>.

Or, a simple sentence can be expanded with modifying words and phrases.

  Jessica and her younger sister Victoria almost immediately fell hopelessly in love with the very mysterious Henry Goodyear.

NOTE: Joined with other clauses, simple sentences can be expanded into <u>compound and complex sentences</u>.

See Ch. 34

1 Expanding Simple Sentences with Adjectives and Adverbs

<u>Adjectives and adverbs</u> can expand a simple sentence by modifying nouns, verbs, or other adjectives or adverbs. Read this sentence again.

See 50a

  Jessica and her younger sister Victoria almost immediately fell hopelessly in love with the very mysterious Henry Goodyear.

33c adj/adv — Building Simple Sentences

In the last sentence on page 479, two adjectives describe nouns.

Adjective	Noun
younger	sister
mysterious	Henry Goodyear

Four adverbs describe the action of verbs or modify adjectives or other adverbs.

Adverb	
almost	immediately (adverb)
immediately	fell (verb)
hopelessly	fell (verb)
very	mysterious (adjective)

■ EXERCISE 3

Label all the adjectives and adverbs in the following simple sentences.

Example: Marge listened *secretly* (adv) to the *quiet* (adj) conversation at the *next* (adj) table.

1. John swallowed the last of his cold coffee and gently set the thermos down. (Sherman Alexie, *Indian Killer*)
2. Each year I watched the field across from the Store turn caterpillar green, then gradually frosty white. (Maya Angelou, *I Know Why the Caged Bird Sings*)
3. He gingerly held the box and studied the old, familiar pictures. (Alan Lightman, *Good Benito*)
4. Stealthy and alert, he hunkers down like a predator and sneaks right up behind the seal, climbs decisively onto its back, and grips its cheeks in both hands. (Diane Ackerman, *The Rarest of the Rare*)
5. In late mammal times, the body evidently added a third brain. (Robert Bly, *The Sibling Society*)

■ EXERCISE 4

Using the following sentences as models, write five original simple sentences. Use adverbs and adjectives where the model sentences use them, and then underline and label these modifiers.

Example: Manek gazed <u>shyly</u> (adv) at the <u>beautiful</u> (adj) girl.

The cat ran <u>wildly</u> (adv) around the <u>empty</u> (adj) house.

Expanding Simple Sentences **33c** 481

1. Walkways from the Washington Monument to the Lincoln Memorial quickly filled.
2. People, shrugging off their winter coats, seemed to step more lightly around the mall.
3. Some sat on benches in carefully pressed white shirts, holding half-eaten sandwiches in pale hands.
4. Others, dressed in shiny spandex or torn T-shirts, spun wildly by on bikes or Rollerblades, sweatily celebrating the first days of spring.
5. Finally, the cherry blossoms were in flower.

2 Expanding Simple Sentences with Nouns and Verbals

Nouns and verbals that serve as modifiers can help you build richer simple sentences.

Nouns. Nouns can act as adjectives modifying other nouns.

> He needed two cake pans for the layer cake.

Verbals. Some verbals (participles and infinitives) may also act as modifiers.

See 46c2

> All the living former presidents attended the funeral. (Present participle acts as adjective.)

> The Grand Canyon is the attraction to visit. (Infinitive acts as adjective.)

> The puzzle was impossible to solve. (Infinitive acts as adverb.)

CLOSE-UP

VERBALS USED AS NOUNS

A verbal may also act as a noun, serving as a subject, object, or complement in a sentence.

> The making of a motion picture can be a complex and lengthy process. (Gerund acts as noun.)

> To err is human. (Infinitive acts as noun.)

> It took me the entire lab period to identify my unknown. (Past participle acts as noun.)

EXERCISE 5

For additional practice in building simple sentences with individual words, combine each of the following groups of sentences into one simple sentence that contains several modifiers. You may have to add, delete, or reorder words.

Example: The ~~night was~~ cold, ~~The night was~~ wet, ~~The~~ night scared them, ~~They were~~ terribly scared.

1. The ship landed. The ship was from space. The ship was tremendous. It landed silently.
2. It landed in a field. The field was grassy. The field was deserted.
3. A dog appeared. The dog was tiny. The dog was abandoned. The dog was a stray.
4. The dog was brave. The dog was curious. He approached the spacecraft. The spacecraft was burning. He approached it carefully.
5. A creature emerged from the spaceship. The creature was smiling. He was purple. He emerged slowly.
6. The dog and the alien stared at each other. The dog was little. The alien was purple. They stared meaningfully.
7. The dog and the alien walked. They walked silently. They walked carefully. They walked toward each other.
8. The dog barked. He barked tentatively. He barked questioningly. The dog was uneasy.
9. The alien extended his hand. The alien was grinning. He extended it slowly. The hand was hairy.
10. In his hand was a bag. The bag was made of canvas. The bag was green. The bag was for laundry.

3 Expanding Simple Sentences with Prepositional Phrases

See 46f
ESL 63e

A **preposition** indicates the relationship between a noun or noun substitute and other words in a sentence. A **prepositional phrase** consists of the preposition, its object (the noun or noun substitute), and any modifiers of that object. Prepositional phrases can function in a sentence as adjectives or as adverbs.

                              prep   obj
Carry Nation was a crusader <u>for temperance</u>. (Prepositional phrase functions as adjective modifying the noun *crusader*.)

                         prep   mod   obj
The Madeira River flows <u>into the mighty Amazon</u>. (Prepositional phrase functions as adverb modifying the verb *flows*.)

EXERCISE 6

Read the following sentences. Underline each prepositional phrase, and then connect it with an arrow to the word it modifies. Label each prepositional phrase to indicate whether it functions as an adjective or an adverb.

Example: The porch <u>of her grandmother's house</u> [adj] wraps <u>around all three sides</u> [adv].

1. Carol sat on the front porch and rocked in her grandmother's chair.
2. Age had surprised her in the middle of her life, crept up behind her in the mirror, and attacked her at the joints of her knees and hips.
3. Now she sat on the porch and felt that it too creaked in its joints.
4. Inside the house, her grandmother slept in a narrow bed under a worn chenille spread, the mattress sagging and spilling over the edges of the frame.
5. The slow rocking of the chair soothed the worries from Carol's mind.

EXERCISE 7

For additional practice in using prepositional phrases, combine each of these sentence pairs to create one simple sentence that includes a prepositional phrase. You may add, delete, or reorder words. Some sentences may have more than one possible correct version.

Example: America's drinking water is being contaminated <ins>by toxic substances</ins>. ~~Toxic substances are contaminating it.~~

1. Toxic waste disposal presents a serious problem. Americans have this problem.
2. Hazardous chemicals pose a threat. People are threatened.
3. Some towns, such as Times Beach, Missouri, were completely abandoned. Their residents abandoned them.
4. Dioxin is one chemical. It has serious toxic effects.
5. Dioxin is highly toxic. The toxicity affects animals and humans.
6. Toxic chemical wastes like dioxin may be found. Over fifty thousand dumps have them.
7. Industrial parks contain toxic wastes. Open pits, ponds, and lagoons are where the toxic substances are.
8. Toxic wastes pose dangers. The land, water, and air are endangered.
9. In addition, toxic substances are a threat. They threaten our public health and our economy.
10. Continuing toxic waste cleanup should be a high priority. Americans are the ones who will benefit.

4 Expanding Simple Sentences with Verbal Phrases

See 33b1

A **verbal phrase** consists of a **verbal** (participle, gerund, or infinitive) and its related objects, modifiers, or complements.

- Some verbal phrases act as modifiers. **Participial phrases** always function as adjectives; **infinitive phrases** may function as adjectives or as adverbs.

  <u>Fascinated by Scheherazade's story</u>, they waited anxiously for the next installment. (Participial phrase modifies pronoun *they*.)

  It wasn't the ideal time <u>to do homework</u>. (Infinitive phrase modifies noun *time*.)

  Henry M. Stanley went to Africa <u>to find Dr. Livingstone</u>. (Infinitive phrase modifies verb *went*.)

> **CLOSE-UP**
>
> **USING MODIFIERS**
>
> *See Ch. 40*
>
> When you use verbal phrases as modifiers, be especially careful not to create **misplaced modifiers** or **dangling modifiers**.

- Other verbal phrases act as nouns. For example, **gerund phrases**, like gerunds themselves, are always used as nouns. **Infinitive phrases** may also be used as nouns.

  <u>Making a living</u> is not always easy. (Gerund phrase serves as sentence's subject.)

  Wendy appreciated <u>Tom's being honest</u>. (Gerund phrase serves as object of verb *appreciated*.)

  The entire town was shocked by <u>their breaking up</u>. (Gerund phrase is object of preposition *by*.)

  <u>To know him</u> is <u>to love him</u>. (Infinitive phrase *To know him* serves as sentence's subject; infinitive phrase *to love him* is subject complement.)

■ **EXERCISE 8**

For practice in using verbal phrases, combine each of these sentence pairs to create one simple sentence that contains a participial phrase, a gerund phrase, or an infinitive phrase. Underline the verbal phrase in your sentence. You may have to add, delete, or reorder words, and you may find more than one way to combine each pair.

Example: The American labor movement has helped millions of workers. ~~It has won~~ , winning them higher wages and better working conditions.

1. In 1912, the textile workers of Lawrence, Massachusetts, went on strike. They were demonstrating for "Bread and Roses, too."
2. The workers wanted higher wages and better working conditions. They felt trapped in their miserable jobs.
3. Mill workers toiled six days a week. They earned about $1.50 for this.
4. Most of the workers were women and children. They worked up to sixteen hours a day.
5. The mills were dangerous. They were filled with hazards.
6. Many mill workers joined unions. They did this to fight exploitation by their employers.
7. They wanted to improve their lives. This was their goal.
8. Finally, twenty-five thousand workers walked off their jobs. They knew they were risking everything.
9. The police and the state militia were called in. Attacking the strikers was their mission.
10. After sixty-three days, the American Woolen Company surrendered. This ended the strike with a victory for the workers.

(Adapted from William Cahn, *Lawrence 1912: The Bread and Roses Strike*)

5 Expanding Simple Sentences with Appositives

An **appositive** is a noun or a noun phrase that functions as an adjective, identifying or renaming an adjacent noun or pronoun.

> Farrington hated his boss, <u>a real tyrant</u>. (Appositive *a real tyrant* identifies noun *boss*.)

> <u>A barrier island off the coast of New Jersey</u>, Long Beach Island is a popular vacation spot. (Appositive *A barrier island off the coast of New Jersey* identifies noun *Long Beach Island*.)

CLOSE-UP

APPOSITIVES

An appositive is sometimes introduced by *such as, or, that is, for example, for instance, namely,* or *in other words*.

> A regional airline, <u>such as Southwest</u>, may account for more than half the departures at some second-tier airports.

> Rabies, or <u>hydrophobia</u>, was nearly always fatal until Pasteur's work.

NOTE: For information on punctuating sentences that include appositives, **see 52d1.**

EXERCISE 9

For practice in using appositives when you write, build five new simple sentences by combining each of the following pairs, turning one sentence in each pair into an appositive. (Note that each pair can be combined in a variety of different ways and that the appositive can precede or follow the noun it modifies.) You may need to delete or reorder words in some cases.

Example: ~~René Descartes was~~ a noted French philosopher, René Descartes is best known for his famous declaration, "I think, therefore I am."

1. *I Know Why the Caged Bird Sings* is the first book in Maya Angelou's autobiography. It deals primarily with her life as a young girl in Stamps, Arkansas.
2. Catgut is a tough cord generally made from the intestines of sheep. Catgut is used for tennis rackets, for violin strings, and for surgical stitching.
3. Hermes was the messenger of the Greek gods. He is usually portrayed as an athletic youth wearing a cap and winged sandals.
4. Emiliano Zapata was a hero of the Mexican Revolution. He is credited with effecting land reform in his home state of Morelos.
5. Pulsars are celestial objects that emit regular pulses of radiation. Pulsars were discovered in 1967.

6 Expanding Simple Sentences with Compound Constructions

See 41a

A **compound construction** consists of two or more grammatically parallel items that are equivalent in importance. Within simple sentences, compound words or phrases—subjects, predicates, complements, or modifiers—may be joined in one of three ways.

- With commas:

  He took one <u>long,</u> <u>loving</u> look at his '57 Chevy.

See 34a1

- With **coordinating conjunctions**:

  They <u>reeled</u>, <u>whirled</u>, <u>flounced</u>, <u>capered</u>, <u>gamboled</u>, <u>and</u> <u>spun</u>. (Kurt Vonnegut Jr., "Harrison Bergeron")

- With **correlative conjunctions** (*both/and, not only/but also, either/or, neither/nor, whether/or*):

Both milk and carrots contain Vitamin A.

Neither the twentieth-century poet Sylvia Plath nor the nineteenth-century poet Emily Dickinson achieved recognition during her lifetime.

EXERCISE 10

A. Expand each of the following sentences by using compound subjects and/or predicates.

Example: Bill played guitar. *and Juan* *and sang.*

B. Then, expand your simple sentence with modifying words and phrases, using compound constructions whenever possible.

Example: *Despite butterflies in their stomachs and a restless audience,* Bill and Juan played guitar and sang.

1. Cortés explored the New World.
2. Virginia Woolf wrote novels.
3. Edison invented the phonograph.
4. PBS airs educational television programming.
5. Thomas Jefferson signed the Declaration of Independence.

EXERCISE 11

To practice building sentences with compound subjects, predicates, and modifiers, combine each of the following groups of sentences into one.

Example: Marion studied. Frank studied. They studied quietly. They studied diligently.

1. Robert Ludlum writes best-selling spy thrillers. Tom Clancy writes best-selling spy thrillers. John le Carré writes best-selling spy thrillers.
2. Smoking can cause heart disease. A high-fat diet can cause heart disease. Stress can cause heart disease.
3. Walter Mosley and Sue Grafton write detective novels. They both write about "hard-boiled" detectives.
4. Successful rock bands give concerts. They record albums. They make videos. They license merchandise bearing their names and likenesses.
5. Sports superstars such as Tiger Woods and Michael Jordan earn additional income by making personal appearances. They earn money by endorsing products.

34

Building Compound and Complex Sentences

❓ FAQs

How do I create a compound sentence? (p. 488)
How do I create a complex sentence? (p. 491)

See Ch. 35

Writing that includes <u>varied sentences</u> is more interesting than writing that does not. One way to vary your sentences is to use compound and complex sentences along with simple sentences.

34a Building Compound Sentences

A **compound sentence** is created when two or more independent clauses are joined with *coordinating conjunctions, transitional words or phrases, correlative conjunctions, semicolons,* or *colons*.

1 Using Coordinating Conjunctions

You can join two independent clauses with a **coordinating conjunction**—*and, or, nor, but, for, so,* or *yet*—preceded by a comma.

> She carried a thin, small cane made from an umbrella, <u>and</u> with this she kept tapping the frozen earth in front of her. (Eudora Welty, "A Worn Path")

> In the fall the war was always there, <u>but</u> we did not go to it any more. (Ernest Hemingway, "In Another Country")

> **ESL TIP**
>
> Some languages, such as Arabic, typically use coordination more than English does. If you think you are overusing compound sentences, try experimenting with complex sentences **(see 35c)**.

2 Using Transitional Words or Phrases

You can join two independent clauses with a **transitional word or phrase,** preceded by a semicolon (and followed by a comma).

Aerobic exercise can help lower blood pressure; <u>however</u>, people with high blood pressure should still limit salt intake.

The saxophone does not belong to the brass family; <u>in fact</u>, it is a member of the woodwind family.

Commonly used <u>transitional words and phrases</u> include **conjunctive adverbs** like *however, therefore, nevertheless, consequently, finally, still,* and *thus* as well as expressions such as *for example, in fact, on the other hand,* and *for instance.*

See 7b2

3 Using Correlative Conjunctions

You can use <u>correlative conjunctions</u> to join two independent clauses into a compound sentence.

See 46g

Diana <u>not only</u> passed the exam, <u>but</u> she <u>also</u> passed the course.
<u>Either</u> he left his coat in his locker, <u>or</u> he left it on the bus.

4 Using Semicolons

A <u>semicolon</u> can join two closely related independent clauses into a compound sentence.

See 53a

Alaska is the largest state<u>;</u> Rhode Island is the smallest.

Theodore Roosevelt was president after the Spanish-American War<u>;</u> Andrew Johnson was president after the Civil War.

5 Using Colons

A <u>colon</u> can join two independent clauses into a compound sentence.

See 56a

He got his orders<u>:</u> he was to leave for Iraq on Sunday.

They thought they knew the outcome<u>:</u> Truman would lose to Dewey.

CLOSE-UP

USING COMPOUND SENTENCES

When you join independent clauses to create compound sentences, you help readers to see the relationships between your ideas. Compound sentences can indicate the following relationships:

- Addition (*and, in addition, not only . . . but also*)
- Contrast (*but, however*)
- Causal relationships (*so, therefore, consequently*)
- Alternatives (*or, either . . . or*)

34a Building Compound and Complex Sentences

■ EXERCISE 1

After reading the following paragraph, edit it to create as many compound sentences as you think your readers need to understand the relationships between ideas. When you have finished, bracket the independent clauses and underline the coordinating conjunctions, transitional words or phrases, correlative conjunctions, or punctuation marks that link clauses.

    Paolo Soleri came to the United States from Italy. He came as an apprentice to Frank Lloyd Wright. Frank Lloyd Wright's designs celebrate the suburban lifestyle, with stand-alone homes meant for single families. Soleri's Utopian designs celebrate the city. Soleri believes that suburban lifestyles separate people from true nature. He also believes that our lifestyle separates us from the energy of the city. His first theoretical design was called Mesa City. It proposed to house two million people. Soleri is currently building one of his dream cities, Arcosanti, in the desert outside of Scottsdale, Arizona. This project is funded privately by Soleri. He teaches design and building classes to students who help build the city. The students' tuition helps pay for construction. He also makes wind bells and chimes. He sells these all over the world. The profits further finance Arcosanti. The design for Arcosanti evokes images of colonies erected on space stations. It also resembles the hillside towns in Soleri's home country, Italy. The problems with our current city structures grow each year. People are looking for ways to revitalize the city. Some are looking at Soleri's Arcosanti as a model for sustainable urban development and renewal.

■ EXERCISE 2

Add appropriate coordinating conjunctions, transitional words or phrases, or correlative conjunctions as indicated to combine each pair of sentences into one well-constructed compound sentence that retains the meaning of the original pair. Be sure to use correct punctuation.

Example: The American population is aging./~~People~~ *, so people* seem to be increasingly concerned about what they eat. (coordinating conjunction)

1. The average American consumes 128 pounds of sugar each year. Most of us eat much more sugar than any other food additive, including salt. (transitional word or phrase)
2. Many of us are determined to reduce our sugar intake. We have consciously eliminated sweets from our diets. (transitional word or phrase)
3. Unfortunately, sugar is not found only in sweets. It is also found in many processed foods. (correlative conjunction)
4. Processed foods like puddings and cake contain sugar. Foods like ketchup and spaghetti sauce do too. (coordinating conjunction)

5. We are trying to cut down on sugar. We find limiting sugar intake extremely difficult. (coordinating conjunction)
6. Processors may use sugar in foods for taste. They may also use it to help prevent foods from spoiling and to improve the texture and appearance of food. (correlative conjunction)
7. Sugar comes in many different forms. It is easy to overlook on a package label. (coordinating conjunction)
8. Sugar may be called sucrose or fructose. It may also be called corn syrup, corn sugar, brown sugar, honey, or molasses. (coordinating conjunction)
9. No sugar is more nourishing than the others. It really does not matter which is consumed. (transitional word or phrase)
10. Sugars contain empty calories. Whenever possible, they should be avoided. (transitional word or phrase)

(Adapted from *Jane Brody's Nutrition Book*)

34b Building Complex Sentences

A **complex sentence** consists of one **independent clause** and at least one **dependent clause**.

A dependent clause cannot stand alone; it must be combined with an independent clause to form a sentence. A **subordinating conjunction** or **relative pronoun** links the independent and dependent clauses and indicates the relationship between them.

      dependent clause   independent clause
[After the town was evacuated,] [the hurricane began.]

  independent clause   dependent clause
[Officials watched the storm,] [which threatened to destroy the town.]

NOTE: Sometimes a dependent clause may be embedded within an independent clause: *Town officials, [who were very concerned,] watched the storm.*

Frequently Used Subordinating Conjunctions

after	in order that	unless
although	now that	until
as	once	when
as if	rather than	whenever
as though	since	where
because	so that	whereas
before	that	wherever
even though	though	while

34b Building Compound and Complex Sentences

RELATIVE PRONOUNS		
that	whatever	who (whose, whom)
what	which	whoever (whomever)

CLOSE-UP

USING COMPLEX SENTENCES

When you join clauses to create complex sentences, you help readers to see the relationships between your ideas. Complex sentences can indicate the following relationships:

- Time relationships (*before, after, until, when, since*)
- Contrast (*however, although*)
- Causal relationships (*therefore, because, so that*)
- Conditional relationships (*if, unless*)
- Location (*where, wherever*)
- Identity (*who, which, that*)

■ EXERCISE 3

Bracket the independent and dependent clauses in the following complex sentences. Then, using the five sentences as models, create two new complex sentences in imitation of each. For each pair of new sentences, use the same subordinating conjunction or relative pronoun that appears in the original sentence.

Example: [Although life is sweet,] [it is sometimes hard.]
Although chemistry is difficult, it is often rewarding.
Although a computer may become obsolete, it can often be upgraded.

1. I said what I meant.
2. Savion Glover is the dancer who best exemplifies the phrase "poetry in motion."
3. Because she was considered a heretic, Joan of Arc was burned at the stake.
4. The oracle at Delphi predicted that Oedipus would murder his father and marry his mother.
5. The ghost vanished before Hamlet could question him further.

■ EXERCISE 4

Use a subordinating conjunction or relative pronoun to combine each of the following pairs of sentences into one well-constructed complex sentence. Be sure to choose a connecting word that indicates the relationship between the two sentences. You may have to change or reorder words.

Example: ~~Some~~ *Because some* colleges are tightening admissions requirements**,** ~~Their~~ *their* pool of students is growing smaller.

1. Many high school graduates are currently out of work. They need new skills for new careers.
2. Talented high school students are usually encouraged to go to college. Some high school graduates are now starting to see that a college education may not guarantee them a job.
3. A college education can cost a student more than $100,000. Vocational education is becoming an increasingly attractive alternative.
4. Vocational students complete their work in less than four years. They can enter the job market more quickly.
5. Nurses' aides, paralegals, travel agents, and computer technicians do not need college degrees. They have little trouble finding work.
6. Some four-year colleges are experiencing growth. Public community colleges and private trade schools are growing much more rapidly.
7. The best vocational schools are responsive to the needs of local businesses. They train students for jobs that actually exist.
8. For instance, a school in Detroit might offer advanced automotive design. A school in New York City might focus on fashion design.
9. Other schools offer courses in horticulture, respiratory therapy, and computer programming. They are able to place their graduates easily.
10. Laid-off workers, returning housewives, recent high school graduates, and even college graduates are reexamining vocational education. They all hope to find rewarding careers.

CLOSE-UP

COMPOUND-COMPLEX SENTENCES

Another way to vary your sentences is to create an occasional compound-complex sentence. A **compound-complex sentence** consists of two or more independent clauses and at least one dependent clause.

dependent clause
[When small foreign imports began dominating the US automobile industry,] [consumers were very responsive,] but [American auto workers were dismayed.]
independent clause *independent clause*

35

Writing Varied Sentences

❓ FAQs

How do I combine choppy sentences to make my writing "flow"? (p. 496)

How do I revise a string of compound sentences? (p. 497)

How do I revise sentences when they all begin the same way? (p. 500)

Using **varied sentences** can help make your writing livelier and more interesting, and can also ensure that you emphasize the most important ideas in your sentences.

35a Varying Sentence Length

To add interest to your writing, try to mix sentences of different lengths.

1 Mixing Long and Short Sentences

A paragraph consisting entirely of short sentences (or entirely of long ones) can be dull.

> Drag racing began in California in the 1940s. It was an alternative to street racing. Street racing was illegal and dangerous. It flourished in the 1950s and 1960s. Eventually, it became almost a rite of passage. Then, during the 1970s, almost one-third of America's racetracks closed. Today, however, drag racing is making a comeback.

Combining some of the paragraph's short sentences into longer ones creates a more interesting passage.

> Drag racing began in California in the 1940s as an alternative to street racing, which was illegal and dangerous. It flourished in the 1950s and 1960s, eventually becoming almost a rite of passage. Then, during the 1970s, almost one-third of America's racetracks closed. Today, however, drag racing is making a comeback.

2 Following a Long Sentence with a Short One

Another way to add interest is to follow one or more long sentences with a short one. (This strategy also places emphasis on the short sentence.)

> Over the years, vitamin boosters say, a misconception has grown that as long as there are no signs or symptoms of, say, scurvy, then we have all of the vitamin C we need. Although we know how much of a particular vitamin or mineral will prevent clinical disease, we have practically no information on how much is necessary for peak health. In short, we know how sick is sick, but we don't know how well is well. (*Philadelphia Magazine*)

■ EXERCISE 1

Combine each of the following sentence groups into one long sentence. Then, compose a relatively short sentence to follow each long one. Finally, combine all the sentences into a paragraph, adding a topic sentence and any transitions necessary for coherence. Proofread your paragraph to be sure the sentences are varied in length.

1. Chocolate is composed of more than three hundred compounds. Phenylethylamine is one such compound. Its presence in the brain may be linked to the emotion of falling in love.
2. Americans now consume a good deal of chocolate. On average, they eat more than nine pounds of chocolate per person per year. The typical Belgian, however, consumes almost fifteen pounds per year.
3. In recent years, Americans have begun a serious love affair with chocolate. Elegant chocolate boutiques sell exquisite bonbons by the piece. At least one hotel offers a "chocolate binge" vacation. The bimonthly *Chocolate News* for connoisseurs is flourishing.

(Adapted from *Newsweek*)

35b Combining Choppy Simple Sentences

Strings of short simple sentences can be tedious—and sometimes hard to understand, as the following paragraph illustrates.

> John Peter Zenger was a newspaper editor. He waged and won an important battle for freedom of the press in America. He criticized the policies of the British governor. He was charged with criminal libel as a result. Zenger's lawyers were disbarred. Andrew Hamilton defended him. Hamilton convinced the jury that Zenger's criticisms were true. Therefore, the statements were not libelous.

You can revise choppy sentences like these by using *coordination*, *subordination*, or *embedding* to combine them with adjacent sentences.

1 Using Coordination

Coordination pairs similar elements—words, phrases, or clauses—giving equal weight to each. The following revision links two of the original paragraph's choppy simple sentences with *and* to create a compound sentence.

See 34a

> John Peter Zenger was a newspaper editor. He waged and won an important battle for freedom of the press in America. <u>He criticized the policies of the British governor, and as a result, he was charged with criminal libel.</u> Zenger's lawyers were disbarred. Andrew Hamilton defended him. Hamilton convinced the jury that Zenger's criticisms were true. Therefore, the statements were not libelous.

> **ESL TIP**
>
> Some ESL students rely on simple sentences and coordination in their writing because they are afraid of making sentence structure errors. The result is a monotonous style. To add variety, try using **subordination** and **embedding** in your sentences.

2 Using Subordination

Subordination places the more important idea in an independent clause and the less important idea in a dependent clause. The following revision of the preceding paragraph uses subordination to change two simple sentences into dependent clauses, creating two complex sentences.

See 34b

> <u>John Peter Zenger was a newspaper editor who waged and won an important battle for freedom of the press in America.</u> He criticized the policies of the British governor, and as a result, he was charged with criminal libel. <u>When Zenger's lawyers were disbarred, Andrew Hamilton defended him.</u> Hamilton convinced the jury that Zenger's criticisms were true. Therefore, the statements were not libelous.

3 Using Embedding

Embedding is the working of additional words and phrases into a sentence. In the following revision, the sentence *Hamilton convinced the jury* . . . has been reworded to create a phrase (*convincing the jury*) that is embedded into another sentence, where it now modifies the independent clause *Andrew Hamilton defended him*.

John Peter Zenger was a newspaper editor who waged and won an important battle for freedom of the press in America. He criticized the policies of the British governor, and as a result, he was charged with criminal libel. <u>When Zenger's lawyers were disbarred, Andrew Hamilton defended him, convincing the jury that Zenger's criticisms were true.</u> Therefore, the statements were not libelous.

This final revision of the original string of choppy sentences is interesting and readable because it is composed of varied and logically linked sentences. The final short simple sentence has been retained for emphasis.

■ **EXERCISE 2**

Using coordination, subordination, and embedding, revise this string of choppy simple sentences into a more varied and interesting paragraph.

The first modern miniature golf course was built in New York in 1925. It was an indoor course with 18 holes. Entrepreneurs Drake Delanoy and John Ledbetter built 150 more indoor and outdoor courses. Garnet Carter made miniature golf a worldwide fad. Carter built an elaborate miniature golf course. He later joined with Delanoy and Ledbetter. Together they built more miniature golf courses. They abbreviated playing distances. They highlighted the game's hazards at the expense of skill. This made the game much more popular. By 1930, there were 25,000 miniature golf courses in the United States. Courses grew more elaborate. Hazards grew more bizarre. The craze spread to London and Hong Kong. The expansion of miniature golf grew out of control. Then, interest in the game declined. By 1931, most miniature golf courses were out of business. The game was revived in the early 1950s. Today, there are between eight and ten thousand miniature golf courses. The architecture of miniature golf remains an enduring form of American folk art. (Adapted from *Games*)

35c Breaking Up Strings of Compound Sentences

When you write, try to avoid creating an unbroken series of compound sentences. A string of compound sentences can be extremely monotonous; moreover, if you connect clauses only with coordinating conjunctions, you may find it difficult to indicate exactly how ideas are related and which is most important.

All Compound Sentences:
A volcano that is erupting is considered *active*, but one that may erupt is designated *dormant*, and one that has not erupted for a long time is called *extinct*. Most active volcanoes are located in "The Ring of Fire," a belt that circles the Pacific Ocean, and

35d var ■ Writing Varied Sentences

they can be extremely destructive. Italy's Vesuvius erupted in AD 79, and it destroyed the town of Pompeii. In 1883, Krakatoa, located between the Indonesian islands of Java and Sumatra, erupted, and it caused a tidal wave, and more than 36,000 people were killed. Martinique's Mont Pelée erupted in 1902, and its hot gas and ash killed 30,000 people, and this completely wiped out the town of St. Pierre.

Varied Sentences:
A volcano that is erupting is considered *active*. (simple sentence) One that may erupt is designated *dormant*, and one that has not erupted for a long time is called *extinct*. (compound sentence) Most active volcanoes are located in "The Ring of Fire," a belt that circles the Pacific Ocean. (simple sentence with modifier) Active volcanoes can be extremely destructive. (simple sentence) Erupting in AD 79, Italy's Vesuvius destroyed the town of Pompeii. (simple sentence with modifier) When Krakatoa, located between the Indonesian islands of Java and Sumatra, erupted in 1883, it caused a tidal wave that killed 36,000 people. (complex sentence with modifier) The eruption of Martinique's Mont Pelée in 1902 produced hot gas and ash that killed 30,000 people, completely wiping out the town of St. Pierre. (complex sentence with modifier)

■ **EXERCISE 3**

Revise the compound sentences in this passage so the sentence structure is varied. Be sure that the writer's emphasis and the relationships between ideas are clear.

Dr. Alice I. Baumgartner and her colleagues at the Institute for Equality in Education at the University of Colorado surveyed two thousand Colorado schoolchildren, and they found some startling results. They asked, "If you woke up tomorrow and discovered that you were a (boy) (girl), how would your life be different?" and the answers were sad and shocking. The researchers assumed they would find that boys and girls would see advantages in being either male or female, but instead they found that both boys and girls had a fundamental contempt for females. Many elementary school boys titled their answers "The Disaster" or "Doomsday," and they described the terrible lives they would lead as girls, but the girls seemed to feel they would be better off as boys, and they expressed feelings that they would be able to do more and have easier lives. (Adapted from *Redbook*)

35d Varying Sentence Types

Another way to achieve sentence variety is to mix **declarative sentences** (statements) with occasional **imperative sentences** (com-

Varying Sentence Types ■ **var** **35d** 499

mands or requests), **exclamations,** and **rhetorical questions** (questions that readers are not expected to answer), as the following paragraph does.

> Local television newscasts seem to be delivering less and less news. Although we stay awake for the late news, hoping to be updated on local, national, and world events, only about 30 percent of most newscasts is devoted to news. Up to 25 percent of the typical program—even more during "sweeps weeks"—can be devoted to feature stories, with another 25 percent reserved for advertising. The remaining time is spent on weather, sports, and casual conversation between anchors. Given this focus on "soft" material, what options do those of us wishing to find out what happened in the world have? (rhetorical question) Critics of local television have a few suggestions. First, write to your local station's management voicing your concern and threatening to boycott the news if changes are not made; then, try to get others who feel the way you do to sign a petition. (imperatives) If changes are not made, try turning off your television and reading the newspaper! (exclamation)

CLOSE-UP

VARYING SENTENCE TYPES

Other options for varying sentence types include mixing simple, compound, and complex sentences **(see Chs. 33–34** and **35b–c)**; mixing cumulative and periodic sentences **(see 36b)**; and using balanced sentences **(see 36c)**.

■ **EXERCISE 4**

The following paragraph is composed entirely of declarative sentences. To make it more varied, add three sentences—one exclamation, one rhetorical question, and one imperative—anywhere in the paragraph. Be sure the new sentences are consistent with the paragraph's purpose and tone.

> When the Fourth of July comes around, the nation explodes with patriotism. Everywhere we look we see parades and picnics, firecrackers and fireworks. An outsider might wonder what all the fuss is about. We could explain that this is America's birthday party, and all the candles are being lit at once. There is no reason for us to hold back our enthusiasm—or to limit the noise that celebrates it. The Fourth of July is watermelon and corn on the cob, American flags and sparklers, brass bands and more. Everyone looks forward to this celebration, and everyone has a good time.

35e Varying Sentence Openings

Rather than beginning every sentence with the subject (*I* or *It*, for example), try beginning with a modifying *word*, *phrase*, or *clause*.

Beginning with Words

Proud and relieved, they watched their daughter receive her diploma. (adjectives)

Hungrily, he devoured his lunch. (adverb)

Beginning with Phrases

For better or worse, credit cards are now widely available to college students. (prepositional phrase)

Located on the west coast of Great Britain, Wales is part of the United Kingdom. (participial phrase)

His interests widening, Picasso designed ballet sets and illustrated books. (absolute phrase)

Beginning with Clauses

After President Woodrow Wilson was incapacitated by a stroke, his wife unofficially performed many presidential duties. (adverb clause)

GRAMMAR CHECKER

COORDINATING CONJUNCTIONS AND FRAGMENTS

If you begin a sentence with a coordinating conjunction, use your grammar checker to make sure that it is a complete sentence and not a fragment.

See Ch. 38

```
Spelling and Grammar: English (U.S.)         [?][X]
Fragment:
And then the speaker.              [Ignore]
                                   [Ignore Rule]
                                   [Next Sentence]
Suggestions:
Fragment (consider revising)       [Change]
```

■ **EXERCISE 5**

Each of these sentences begins with the subject. Revise each so that it has a different opening; then, identify your opening strategy.

Example: In *The Names,* ^N. Scott Momaday, the prominent Native American writer, tells the story of his first fourteen years ~~in *The Names*~~. (prepositional phrase)

1. Momaday was taken as a very young child to Devil's Tower, the geological formation in Wyoming that is called Tsoai (Bear Tree) in Kiowa, and there he was given the name Tsoai-talee (Bear Tree Boy).
2. The Kiowa myth of the origin of Tsoai is about a boy who playfully chases his seven sisters up a tree, which rises into the air as the boy is transformed into a bear.
3. The boy-bear becomes increasingly ferocious and claws the bark of the tree, which becomes a great rock with a flat top and deeply scored sides.
4. The sisters climb higher and higher to escape their brother's wrath, and eventually they become the seven stars of the Big Dipper.
5. This story, from which Momaday received one of his names, appears in his works *The Way to Rainy Mountain*, *House Made of Dawn*, and *The Ancient Child*.

35f Varying Standard Word Order

You can vary standard **word order** (subject-verb-object or subject-verb-complement) either by intentionally inverting this usual order or by inserting words between the subject and the verb.

1 Inverting Word Order

Sometimes you can place the complement or direct object *before* the verb instead of in its conventional position after the verb, or you can place the verb *before* the subject instead of after it. These strategies draw attention to the word or word group that appears in an unexpected place.

                   (subject)   (subject)
   (object)   ↓   (verb)   (object)   ↓   (verb)
The north wall he painted red; the other walls he painted white.

(complement)   (verb)   (subject)
   Crucial to the agreement is a clear understanding of the issues.

NOTE: Be careful to use inverted word order in moderation; when it is used in a series of sentences, inverted word order becomes distracting and hard to follow.

2 Separating Subject from Verb

You can also place words or phrases between subject and verb—but be sure that the word group does not obscure the connection between subject and verb or create an **agreement** error.

See 49a

> Many <u>states require</u> that infants and young children ride in government-approved child safety seats because they hope this regulation will reduce needless fatalities. (subject and verb together)

> Many <u>states</u>, hoping to reduce needless fatalities, <u>require</u> that infants and young children ride in government-approved child safety seats. (subject and verb separated)

■ EXERCISE 6

The following five sentences use conventional word order. To vary this standard word order, revise each sentence in one of two ways: either invert the sentence, or insert words between the subject and the verb. After you have completed your revisions, link all the sentences together to create a paragraph.

Example: Dada ʼwas an artistic and literary rebellion ʼthat defied the conventional values of the early twentieth century.
(words inserted between subject and verb)

1. The Dada movement first appeared in 1915 and effectively ended in 1925 with the rise of Surrealism.
2. The name *Dada,* French for "hobby horse," was selected at random from a dictionary.
3. The Dadaists ultimately rejected all traditional cultural values, and their goal became to destroy art as an aesthetic cult and replace it with "antiart" and "nonart."
4. The Dadaists rejected traditional art, and they substituted the nonsense poem, the ready-made object, and the collage.
5. The most notorious example of Dada art is the sculpture *Fountain* (1917), which was a urinal Marcel Duchamp found and signed *R. Mutt* and then entered into a gallery exhibit.

36

Writing Emphatic Sentences

❓ FAQs

Why shouldn't I begin a sentence with there is *or* there are*? (p. 504)*
Is repeating words and phrases ever a good idea? (p. 509)
When is it acceptable to use passive voice? (p. 510)

In speaking, we emphasize certain ideas and deemphasize others with intonation and gesture; in writing, we convey **emphasis**—the relative importance of ideas—through the selection and arrangement of words.

36a   Conveying Emphasis through Word Order

Because readers tend to focus on the beginning and end of a sentence, you should place the most important information there.

1   Beginning with Important Ideas

Placing key ideas at the beginning of a sentence stresses their importance. The unedited version of the following sentence places emphasis on the study, not on those who conducted it or on those who participated in it. Editing shifts this focus and puts the emphasis on the researcher, not on the study.

> ~~In a landmark study of alcoholism,~~ Dr. George Vaillant of Harvard ˄*, in a landmark study of alcoholism,* followed two hundred Harvard graduates and four hundred inner-city, working-class men from the Boston area.

Situations that demand a straightforward presentation—laboratory reports, memos, technical papers, business correspondence, and the like—call for sentences that present vital information first and qualifiers later.

> Treating cancer with interferon has been the subject of a good deal of research. (emphasizes the treatment, not the research)
>
> Dividends will be paid if the stockholders agree. (emphasizes the dividends, not the stockholders)

CLOSE-UP

WRITING EMPHATIC SENTENCES

Placing an empty phrase like *there is* or *there are* at the beginning of a sentence generally weakens the sentence.

> MIT places
> ~~There is~~ heavy emphasis on the development of computational skills ~~at MIT~~.

2 Ending with Important Ideas

Placing key elements at the end of a sentence is another way to convey their importance.

Using a Colon or a Dash. A colon or a dash can add emphasis by isolating an important word or phrase at the end of a sentence.

> Beth had always dreamed of owning one special car: a 1953 Corvette.

> The elderly need a good deal of special attention—and they deserve that attention.

CLOSE-UP

PLACING TRANSITIONAL WORDS AND PHRASES

When they are placed at the end of a sentence, conjunctive adverbs or other transitional words lose their power to indicate the relationship between ideas. Placed earlier in the sentence, transitional words and phrases can link ideas and add emphasis.

See 7b2

> however,
> Smokers do have rights; they should not try to impose their habit on others ~~, however~~.

Using Climactic Word Order. **Climactic word order,** the arrangement of a series of items from the least to the most important, places emphasis on the last item in the series.

> Binge drinking can lead to unwanted pregnancies, car accidents, and even death. (*Death* is the most serious consequence.)

■ EXERCISE 1

Underline the most important idea in each sentence of the following paragraph. Then, identify the strategy that the writer uses to emphasize each idea. Is the key idea placed at the beginning or the end of a sentence? Does the writer use climactic order?

> Listening to diatribes by angry callers or ranting about today's news, the talk radio host spreads ideas over the air waves. Every day at the same time, the political talk show host discusses national events and policies, the failures of the opposing view, and the foibles of the individuals who espouse those opposing views. Listening for hours a day, some callers become recognizable contributors to many different talk radio programs. Other listeners are less devoted, tuning in only when they are in the car and never calling to voice their opinions. Political radio hosts usually structure their programs around a specific agenda, espousing the party line and ridiculing the opponent's position. With a style of presentation aimed both at entertainment and information, the host's ideas become caricatures of party positions. Sometimes, in order to keep the information lively and interesting, a host may either state the issues too simply or deliberately mislead the audience. A host can excuse these errors by insisting that the show is harmless: it's for entertainment, not information. Many are concerned about how the political process is affected by this misinformation.

3 Experimenting with Word Order

ESL 63f

In English sentences, the most common **word order** is subject-verb-object (or subject-verb-complement). By intentionally departing from this expected word order, you can place emphasis on the word, phrase, or clause that you have relocated.

> More modest and less inventive than Turner's paintings are John Constable's landscapes.

Here the writer calls attention to the modifying phrase *more modest and less inventive than Turner's paintings* by **inverting word order**, placing the complement and the verb before the subject.

See 35f1

ESL TIP

If English is not your first language, you may be reluctant to experiment with word order. However, to keep your sentences from becoming monotonous, you need to experiment occasionally. When you do, check with a native English speaker or with your instructor if you are uncertain about whether or not your sentences are grammatical.

■ EXERCISE 2

Revise the following sentences to make them more emphatic. For each, decide which ideas should be highlighted, and place these key ideas at sentence beginnings or endings. Use climactic order or depart from conventional word order where appropriate.

1. Police want to upgrade their firepower because criminals are better armed than ever before.
2. A few years ago, felons used so-called Saturday night specials, small-caliber six-shot revolvers.
3. Now, semiautomatic pistols capable of firing fifteen to twenty rounds, along with paramilitary weapons like the AK-47, have replaced these weapons.
4. Police are adopting such weapons as new fast-firing shotguns and 9mm automatic pistols in order to gain an equal footing with their adversaries.
5. Faster reloading and a hair trigger are two of the numerous advantages that automatic pistols, the weapons of choice among law-enforcement officers, have over the traditional .38-caliber police revolver.

36b Conveying Emphasis through Sentence Structure

As you write, try to construct sentences that emphasize more important ideas and deemphasize less important ones.

1 Using Cumulative Sentences

A **cumulative sentence** begins with an independent clause, followed by additional words, phrases, or clauses that expand or develop it.

> She holds me in strong arms, arms that have chopped cotton, dismembered trees, scattered corn for chickens, cradled infants, shaken the daylights out of half-grown upstart teenagers. (Rebecca Hill, *Blue Rise*)

Because it presents its main idea first, a cumulative sentence tends to be clear and straightforward. (Most English sentences are cumulative.)

2 Using Periodic Sentences

A **periodic sentence** moves from supporting details, expressed in modifying phrases and dependent clauses, to the sentence's key idea, which is placed in the independent clause at the end of the sentence.

> Unlike World Wars I and II, which ended decisively with the unconditional surrender of the United States's enemies, the war in Vietnam did not end when American troops withdrew.

Conveying Emphasis through Sentence Structure ■ **emp** **36b**

NOTE: In some periodic sentences, the modifying phrase or dependent clause comes between subject and predicate: *Columbus, after several discouraging and unsuccessful voyages, finally reached America.*

■ **EXERCISE 3**

A. Bracket the independent clause(s) in each sentence, and underline each modifying phrase and dependent clause. Label each sentence cumulative or periodic.
B. Relocate the supporting details to make cumulative sentences periodic and periodic sentences cumulative, adding words or rephrasing to make your meaning clear.
C. Be prepared to explain how your revision changes the emphasis of the original sentence.

Example: Feeling isolated, sad, and frightened, [the small child sat alone in the train depot.] (periodic)

Revised: The small child sat alone in the train depot, feeling isolated, sad, and frightened. (cumulative)

1. However different in their educational opportunities, both Jefferson and Lincoln as young men became known to their contemporaries as "hard students." (Douglas L. Wilson, "What Jefferson and Lincoln Read," *Atlantic Monthly*)
2. The road came into being slowly, league by league, river crossing by river crossing. (Stephen Harrigan, "Highway 1," *Texas Monthly*)
3. Without willing it, I had gone from being ignorant of being ignorant to being aware of being aware. (Maya Angelou, *I Know Why the Caged Bird Sings*)

■ **EXERCISE 4**

Combine each of the following sentence groups into one cumulative sentence, subordinating supporting details to more important ideas. Then, combine each group into one periodic sentence. (Each group can be combined in a variety of ways, and you may have to add, delete, change, or reorder words.) How do the two versions of the sentence differ in emphasis?

Example: More women than ever before are running for office. They are encouraged by the success of other female candidates.

Cumulative: More women than ever before are running for office, encouraged by the success of other female candidates.

Periodic: Encouraged by the success of other female candidates, more women than ever before are running for office.

1. Some politicians opposed the prescription drug program. They believed it was too expensive. They felt that a smaller, more limited program was preferable.
2. Smoking poses a real danger. It is associated with various cancers. It is linked to heart disease and stroke. It threatens even non-smokers.
3. Infertile couples who want children sometimes go through a series of difficult processes. They may try adoption. They may also try artificial insemination or in vitro fertilization. They may even seek out surrogate mothers.
4. The Thames is a river that meanders through southern England. It has been the inspiration for such literary works as *Alice's Adventures in Wonderland* and *The Wind in the Willows*. It was also captured in paintings by Constable, Turner, and Whistler.
5. Black-footed ferrets are rare North American mammals. They prey on prairie dogs. They are primarily nocturnal. They have black feet and black-tipped tails. Their faces have raccoonlike masks.

■ EXERCISE 5

Combine each of the following sentence groups into one sentence that subordinates supporting details to the main idea. In each case, create either a periodic or a cumulative sentence, depending on which structure you think will best convey the sentence's emphasis. Add, delete, change, or reorder words when necessary.

Example: The fears of today's college students, that there are too many graduates and too few jobs, are based on reality. ~~They are afraid there are too many graduates and too few jobs.~~ (periodic)

1. Today's college students are under a good deal of stress. Job prospects in some fields are not very good. Financial aid is not as easy to come by as it was in the past.
2. Education has grown very expensive. The job market has become tighter. Pressure to get into graduate and professional schools has increased.
3. Family ties seem to be weakening. Students are not always able to count on family support.
4. College students have always had problems. Now, college counseling centers report more—and more serious—problems.
5. The term *student shock* was coined several years ago. This term describes a syndrome that may include depression, anxiety, headaches, and eating and sleeping disorders.
6. Many students are overwhelmed by the vast array of courses and majors offered at their colleges. They tend to be less decisive. They take longer to choose a major and to complete school.

7. Many drop out of school for brief (or extended) periods or switch majors several times. Many take five years or longer to complete their college education.
8. Some colleges are responding to the pressures that students feel. They hold stress-management workshops and suicide-prevention courses. They advertise the services of their counseling centers. They train students as peer counselors. They improve their vocational counseling services.

36c Conveying Emphasis through Parallelism and Balance

By reinforcing the similarity between grammatical elements, <u>parallelism</u> can help you convey information clearly and emphatically.   *See 41a*

> We seek an individual <u>who is</u> a self-starter, <u>who owns</u> a late-model automobile, and <u>who is</u> willing to work evenings. (classified advertisement)
>
> <u>Do not pass</u> Go; <u>do not collect</u> $200. (game instructions)
>
> The Faust legend is central <u>in Benét's *The Devil and Daniel Webster*</u>, <u>in Goethe's *Faust*</u>, and <u>in Marlowe's *Dr. Faustus*</u>. (examination answer)

A **balanced sentence** is neatly divided between two parallel structures—for example, two independent clauses in a compound sentence. The symmetrical structure of a balanced sentence adds emphasis by highlighting similarities or differences between the ideas in the two clauses.

> In the 1950s, the electronic miracle was the television; in the 1980s, the electronic miracle was the computer.
>
> Alive, the elephant was worth at least a hundred pounds; dead, he would only be worth the value of his tusks, five pounds, possibly. (George Orwell, "Shooting an Elephant")

36d Conveying Emphasis through Repetition

<u>Unnecessary repetition</u> makes sentences dull and monotonous as well as wordy.   *See 37b*

> He had a good pitching arm and <u>also</u> could field well and was <u>also</u> a fast runner.

Effective repetition, however, can place emphasis on key words or ideas.

They decided to begin again: <u>to begin</u> hoping, <u>to begin</u> trying to change, <u>to begin</u> working toward a goal.

During those years when I was just learning to speak, my mother and father addressed me only <u>in Spanish</u>; <u>in Spanish</u> I learned to reply. (Richard Rodriguez, *Aria: A Memoir of a Bilingual Childhood*)

■ EXERCISE 6

Revise the sentences in this paragraph, using parallelism and balance to highlight corresponding elements, and using repetition of key words and phrases to add emphasis. You may combine sentences and add, delete, or reorder words.

> Many readers distrust newspapers. They also distrust what they read in magazines. They do not trust what they hear on the radio and what television shows them, either. Of these media, newspapers have been the most responsive to audience criticism. Some newspapers even have ombudsmen. They are supposed to listen to readers' complaints. They are also charged with acting on these grievances. One complaint that many people have is that newspapers are inaccurate. Newspapers' disregard for people's privacy is another of many readers' criticisms. Reporters are seen as arrogant, and readers feel that journalists can be unfair. They feel that reporters tend to glorify criminals, and they believe there is a tendency to place too much emphasis on bizarre or offbeat stories. Finally, readers complain about poor writing and editing. Polls show that despite its efforts to respond to reader criticism, the press continues to face hostility. (Adapted from *Newsweek*)

36e   Conveying Emphasis through Active Voice

See 48d ESL 63a6

The <u>active voice</u> is generally more emphatic than the <u>passive voice</u>.

> **Passive:** The prediction that oil prices will rise is being made by economists.
>
> **Active:** Economists are predicting that oil prices will rise.

Notice that the passive voice focuses readers' attention on the action or on its recipient rather than on who is performing it. The recipient of the action (*The prediction*) is the subject of a passive sentence, so the actor fades into the background (*by economists*) or is omitted entirely (*the prediction . . . is being made*). The active voice, however, places the emphasis where it belongs: on the actor or actors (*Economists*).

 Sometimes, of course, you *want* to stress the action rather than the actor, so you intentionally use the passive voice.

Passive: The West was explored by Lewis and Clark. (stresses the exploration of the West, not who explored it)

Active: Lewis and Clark explored the West. (stresses the contribution of the explorers)

NOTE: Passive voice is also used when the identity of the person performing the action is irrelevant or unknown: *The course was canceled.* For this reason, the passive voice is frequently used in scientific and technical writing: *The beaker was filled with a saline solution.*

GRAMMAR CHECKER

USING PASSIVE VOICE

Your word processor's grammar checker will highlight passive voice constructions in your writing and offer revision suggestions. Sometimes, however, the clearest way to express your ideas is by using passive voice. For example, the use of passive voice in the sentence below is necessary for clarity. The grammar checker's suggestion is awkward—and incorrect.

Spelling and Grammar: English (U.S.)

Passive Voice:
The spreadsheet is sorted by number.

Suggestions:
Number sorts the spreadsheet

■ EXERCISE 7

Revise this paragraph to eliminate awkward or excessive use of passive constructions.

Jack Dempsey, the heavyweight champion between 1919 and 1926, had an interesting but uneven career. He was considered one of the greatest boxers of all time. Dempsey began fighting as "Kid Blackie," but his career did not take off until 1919, when Jack "Doc" Kearns became his manager. Dempsey won the championship when Jess Willard was defeated by him in Toledo, Ohio, in 1919. Dempsey immediately became a popular sports figure; President Franklin D. Roosevelt was one of his biggest fans. Influential friends were made by Jack Dempsey. Boxing lessons were given by him to the actor Rudolph

Valentino. He made friends with Douglas Fairbanks Sr., Damon Runyon, and J. Paul Getty. Hollywood serials were made by Dempsey, but the title was lost by him to Gene Tunney, and Dempsey failed to regain it the following year. After his boxing career declined, a restaurant was opened by Dempsey, and many major sporting events were attended by him. This exposure kept him in the public eye until he lost his restaurant. Jack Dempsey died in 1983.

37

Writing Concise Sentences

❓ FAQs

How can I tell which words I really need in my sentences and which can be deleted? (p. 513)

How do I revise a long, rambling sentence? (p. 517)

A sentence is not concise simply because it is short; a **concise** sentence contains only the words necessary to make its point.

37a   Eliminating Wordiness

A good way to find out which words are essential in a sentence is to underline the key words. Look carefully at the remaining words so you can determine which are unnecessary, and then eliminate wordiness by deleting them.

> It seems to me that it does not make sense to allow any <u>bail</u> to be <u>granted</u> to <u>anyone</u> who has ever been <u>convicted</u> of a <u>violent crime</u>.

The underlining shows you immediately that none of the words in the long introductory phrase are essential. The following revision includes just the words necessary to convey the key ideas.

> Bail should not be granted to anyone who has ever been convicted of a violent crime.

Whenever possible, delete nonessential words—*deadwood, utility words,* and *circumlocution*—from your writing.

1   Eliminating Deadwood

The term **deadwood** is used for unnecessary phrases that take up space and add nothing to meaning.

> ~~There were~~ ^{Many} ~~many~~ factors ~~that~~ influenced his decision to become a priest.

The two plots are ~~both~~ similar in ~~the way~~ that they trace the characters' increasing rage.

Shoppers ~~who are~~ looking for bargains often go to outlets.

They played a racquetball game ~~that was exhausting~~. [an exhausting inserted before "racquetball"]

~~In this~~ article ~~it~~ discusses lead poisoning. [This]

The only truly tragic character in *Hamlet* ~~would have to be~~ Ophelia. [is]

Deadwood also includes unnecessary statements of opinion, such as *I believe*, *I feel*, and *it seems to me*.

~~In my opinion, the~~ characters seem undeveloped. [The]

~~As far as I'm concerned, this~~ course looks interesting. [This]

2 Eliminating Utility Words

Utility words simply act as filler; they contribute nothing to the meaning of a sentence. **Utility words** include nouns with imprecise meanings (*factor*, *situation*, *type*, *aspect*, and so on); adjectives so general that they are almost meaningless (*good*, *bad*, *important*); and common adverbs denoting degree (*basically*, *actually*, *quite*, *very*, *definitely*). Often, you can just delete the utility word; if you cannot, replace it with a more precise word.

~~The registration situation~~ was disorganized. [Registration]

The scholarship ~~basically~~ offered Fran ~~a good~~ opportunity to study Spanish in Spain. [an]

It was ~~actually~~ a worthwhile book, but I didn't ~~really~~ finish it.

3 Avoiding Circumlocution

Circumlocution is taking a roundabout way to say something (using ten words when five will do). Instead of complicated constructions, use concise, specific words and phrases that come right to the point.

~~It is not unlikely that the~~ trend will continue. [The ... probably]

The curriculum was ~~of a~~ unique ~~nature~~.

Joe was in the army ~~during the same time that~~ I was in college. [while]

Eliminating Wordiness ▪ con/w **37a** **515**

> **CLOSE-UP**
>
> **REVISING WORDY PHRASES**
>
> A wordy phrase can almost always be replaced by a more concise, more direct term.
>
> | Wordy | Concise |
> |---|---|
> | at the present time | now |
> | at this point in time | now |
> | for the purpose of | for |
> | due to the fact that | because |
> | on account of | because |
> | until such time as | until |
> | in the event that | if |
> | by means of | by |
> | in the vicinity of | near |
> | have the ability to | be able to |

▪ **EXERCISE 1**

Revise the following paragraph to eliminate deadwood, utility words, and circumlocution. Whenever possible, delete wordy phrases or replace them with more concise expressions.

    For all intents and purposes, the shopping mall is no longer an important factor in the American cultural scene. In the '80s, shopping malls became gathering places where teenagers met, walkers came to get in a few miles, and shoppers who were looking for a wide selection and were not concerned about value went to shop. There are several factors that have worked to undermine the mall's popularity. First, due to the fact that today's shoppers are more likely to be interested in value, many of them have headed to the discount stores. Today's shopper is now more likely to shop in discount stores or bulk-buying warehouse stores than in the small, expensive specialty shops in the large shopping malls. Add to this a resurgence of the values of community, and we can see how mall shopping would have to be less attractive than shopping at local stores. Many malls actually have up to 20 percent empty storefronts, and some have had to close down altogether. Others have met the challenge by expanding their roles from shopping centers into community centers. They have added playgrounds for the children and more amusements and restaurants for the adults. They have also appealed to the growing sense of value shopping by giving gift certificates and discounts to shoppers who spend money in their stores. For a while it seemed as if the huge shopping malls that had become familiar cultural icons were dying out, replaced by catalog and Internet shopping. Now, however, it looks as if some of those icons just might make it and survive by reinventing themselves as more than just places to shop.

37b Eliminating Unnecessary Repetition

See 36d

Repetition can make your sentences more emphatic, but unnecessary repetition and **redundant** word groups (repeated words or phrases that say the same thing, such as *free gift* and *unanticipated surprise*) can lessen the impact of your writing.

You can correct unnecessary repetition by using one of the following strategies.

1 Deleting Redundancy

People's clothing ~~attire~~ can reveal a good deal about their personalities.

The twins kept having ~~recurring~~ cold symptoms.

The two candidates share several positions ~~in common.~~

GRAMMAR CHECKER

DELETING REDUNDANCY

Your word processor's grammar checker will highlight some redundant expressions and offer suggestions for revision.

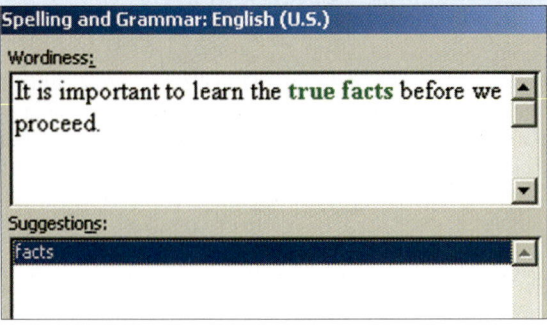

2 Substituting a Pronoun

Fictional detective Miss Marple has solved many crimes. *The Murder at the Vicarage* was one of ~~Miss Marple's~~ her most challenging cases.

Tightening Rambling Sentences ■ **con** **37c**   517

3 Creating an Appositive

Red Barber ˏwas a sportscaster./ˏHe was known for his colorful expressions.

4 Creating a Compound

John F. Kennedy was the youngest man ever elected president./
ˏand
He was the first Catholic to hold this office.

5 Creating a Complex Sentence

, which
Americans value freedom of speech./ ~~Freedom of speech~~ is guaranteed by the First Amendment.

■ **EXERCISE 2**

Eliminate any unnecessary repetition of words or ideas in this paragraph. Also, revise to eliminate deadwood, utility words, and circumlocution.

> For a wide variety of different reasons, more and more people today are choosing a vegetarian diet. There are three kinds of vegetarians: strict vegetarians eat no animal foods at all; lactovegetarians eat dairy products, but they do not eat meat, fish, poultry, or eggs; and ovolactovegetarians eat eggs and dairy products, but they do not eat meat, fish, or poultry. Famous vegetarians include such well-known people as George Bernard Shaw, Leonardo da Vinci, Ralph Waldo Emerson, Henry David Thoreau, and Mahatma Gandhi. Like these well-known vegetarians, the vegetarians of today have good reasons for becoming vegetarians. For instance, some religions recommend a vegetarian diet. Some of these religions are Buddhism, Brahmanism, and Hinduism. Other people turn to vegetarianism for reasons of health or for reasons of hygiene. These people believe that meat is a source of potentially harmful chemicals, and they believe meat contains infectious organisms. Some people feel meat may cause digestive problems and may lead to other difficulties as well. Other vegetarians adhere to a vegetarian diet because they feel it is ecologically wasteful to kill animals after we feed plants to them. These vegetarians believe we should eat the plants. Finally, there are facts and evidence to suggest that a vegetarian diet may possibly help people live longer lives. A vegetarian diet may do this by reducing the incidence of heart disease and lessening the incidence of some cancers. (Adapted from *Jane Brody's Nutrition Book*)

37c Tightening Rambling Sentences

The combination of nonessential words, unnecessary repetition, and complicated syntax creates **rambling sentences**. Revising rambling sentences frequently requires extensive editing.

1 Eliminating Excessive Coordination

When you string a series of independent clauses together with coordinating conjunctions, you create a rambling, unfocused compound sentence that presents your ideas as if they all have equal weight. To revise such sentences, identify the main idea or ideas, and then subordinate supporting details to that main idea.

See 34a

> **Wordy:** Benjamin Franklin was the son of a candlemaker, but he later apprenticed as a printer, and this experience led to his buying the *Pennsylvania Gazette*, and he managed this periodical with great success.
>
> **Concise:** Benjamin Franklin, the son of a candlemaker, later apprenticed as a printer, an experience that led to his buying the *Pennsylvania Gazette*, which he managed with great success. (Franklin's apprenticeship as a printer is the sentence's main idea.)
>
> **Wordy:** Puerto Rico is a large island in the Caribbean, and it is very mountainous, and it has steep slopes, and they fall to gentle plains along the coast.
>
> **Concise:** A large island in the Caribbean, Puerto Rico is very mountainous, with steep slopes falling to gentle plains along the coast. (Puerto Rico's mountainous terrain is the sentence's main idea.)

2 Eliminating Adjective Clauses

See 33b2

A series of adjective clauses is also likely to produce a rambling sentence. To revise, substitute more concise modifying words or phrases for the adjective clauses.

> **Wordy:** *Moby-Dick*, which is a novel about a white whale, was written by Herman Melville, who was friendly with Nathaniel Hawthorne, who urged him to revise the first draft.
>
> **Concise:** *Moby-Dick*, a novel about a white whale, was written by Herman Melville, who revised the first draft at the urging of his friend Nathaniel Hawthorne.

3 Eliminating Passive Constructions

See 48d1 ESL 63a6

Excessive use of the passive voice can create rambling sentences. Correct this problem when you revise by changing passive to active voice.

> ~~Water rights are being fought for in court by~~ Indian tribes, such as the Papago in Arizona and the Pyramid Lake Paiute in Nevada. *, are fighting in court for water rights.*

4 Eliminating Wordy Prepositional Phrases

When you revise, substitute adjectives or adverbs for wordy **prepositional phrases**.

See 33c3

The trip was ~~one of danger~~ *dangerous* but also ~~one of excitement~~ *exciting*.

He spoke ~~in a confident manner~~ *confidently* and ~~with a lot of authority~~ *authoritatively*.

5 Eliminating Wordy Noun Constructions

Substitute strong verbs for wordy **noun phrases**.

See 33b1

We have ~~made the decision~~ *decided* to postpone the meeting until ~~the appearance of~~ all the board members *appear*.

Sometimes ~~there is an accumulation of~~ water *accumulates* on the roof.

■ EXERCISE 3

Revise the rambling sentences in these paragraphs by eliminating excessive coordination; unnecessary use of the passive voice; and overuse of adjective clauses, prepositional phrases, and noun constructions. As you revise, make your sentences more concise by deleting nonessential words and unnecessary repetition.

>   Some colleges that have been in support of fraternities for a number of years are at this time in the process of conducting a reevaluation of the position of those fraternities on campus. In opposition to the fraternities are a fair number of students, faculty members, and administrators who claim fraternities are inherently sexist, which they say makes it impossible for the groups to exist in a coeducational institution, which is supposed to offer equal opportunities for members of both sexes. More and more members of the college community also see fraternities as elitist as well as sexist and favor their abolition. In addition, many point out that fraternities are associated with dangerous practices, such as hazing and alcohol abuse.
>   However, some students, faculty, and administrators remain wholeheartedly in support of traditional fraternities, which they believe are responsible for helping students make the acquaintance of people and learn the leadership skills that they believe will be of assistance to them in their future lives as adults. Supporters of fraternities believe that students should retain the right to make their own social decisions, and they think that joining a fraternity is one of those decisions, and they also believe fraternities are responsible for providing valuable services. Some of these are tutoring, raising money for charity, and running campus escort services. Therefore, these individuals are not of the opinion that the abolition of traditional fraternities makes sense.

PART 9

Solving Common Sentence Problems

38 Revising Sentence Fragments 522
- **38a** Recognizing Sentence Fragments 522
- **38b** Revising Dependent Clause Fragments 524
- **38c** Revising Phrase Fragments 525
- **38d** Revising Compounds 529
- **38e** Using Fragments Intentionally 530

39 Revising Run-ons 532
- **39a** Recognizing Comma Splices and Fused Sentences 532
- **39b** Revising with Periods 533
- **39c** Revising with Semicolons 533
- **39d** Revising with Coordinating Conjunctions 534
- **39e** Revising with Subordinating Conjunctions or Relative Pronouns 534

40 Revising Misplaced and Dangling Modifiers 537
- **40a** Revising Misplaced Modifiers 537
- **40b** Revising Intrusive Modifiers 541
- **40c** Revising Dangling Modifiers 542

41 Using Parallelism 544
- **41a** Using Parallelism Effectively 544
- **41b** Revising Faulty Parallelism 546

42 Revising Awkward or Confusing Sentences 548
- **42a** Revising Unwarranted Shifts 548
- **42b** Revising Mixed Constructions 551
- **42c** Revising Faulty Predication 552
- **42d** Revising Incomplete or Illogical Comparisons 553

38

Revising Sentence Fragments

❓ FAQs

What is a sentence fragment? (p. 522)
How do I turn a fragment into a complete sentence? (p. 523)
Can a list stand alone as a sentence? (p. 528)
Are sentence fragments ever acceptable? (p. 530)

38a Recognizing Sentence Fragments

A **sentence fragment** is an incomplete sentence—a phrase or clause that is punctuated as if it were a complete sentence. A sentence may be incomplete for any of the following reasons:

- **It lacks a subject.**

  Many astrophysicists now believe that galaxies are distributed in clusters. <u>And even form supercluster complexes.</u>

- **It lacks a verb.**

  Every generation has its defining moments. <u>Usually the events with the most news coverage.</u>

- **It lacks both a subject and a verb.**

  Researchers are engaged in a variety of studies. <u>Suggesting a link between alcoholism and heredity.</u> (*Suggesting* is a **verbal,** which cannot serve as a sentence's main verb.)

- **It is a dependent clause.**

  Bishop Desmond Tutu was awarded the 1984 Nobel Peace Prize. <u>Because he fought to end apartheid.</u>

  The pH meter and the spectrophotometer are two scientific instruments. <u>That changed the chemistry laboratory dramatically.</u>

NOTE: A sentence cannot consist of a single clause that begins with a subordinating conjunction (such as *because*) or a relative pronoun (such as *that*); moreover, unless it is a question, a sentence cannot consist of a single clause beginning with *when, where, who, which, what, why,* or *how.*

A fragment is especially confusing when it comes between two independent clauses and readers cannot tell which of the two clauses completes the fragment's thought. For instance, it is impossible to tell to which independent clause the underlined fragment in each of the following sequences belongs.

The course requirements were changed last year. <u>Because a new professor was hired at the very end of the spring semester.</u> I was unable to find out about this change until after preregistration.

In *The Ox-Bow Incident*, the crowd is convinced that the men are guilty. <u>Even though the men insist they are innocent and Davies pleads for their lives.</u> They are hanged.

> ### CLOSE-UP
>
> **REVISING SENTENCE FRAGMENTS**
>
> If you identify a fragment in your writing, use one of the following two strategies to revise it:
>
> 1. Attach the fragment to an adjacent independent clause.
>
>   According to German legend, Lohengrin is the son of Parzival. ~~And~~ *and* a knight of the Holy Grail.
>
>   Pioneers traveled west. ~~Because~~ *because* they hoped to find a better life.
>
> 2. Turn the fragment into a sentence.
>
>   Lancaster County, Pennsylvania, is home to many Pennsylvania Dutch. ~~Descended~~ *They are descended* from German immigrants. (missing subject and verb added)
>
>   Property taxes rose sharply. ~~Although~~ *City* services declined. (subordinating conjunction *although* deleted)

> ### GRAMMAR CHECKER
>
> **IDENTIFYING FRAGMENTS**
>
> Your grammar checker will identify many (although not all) sentence fragments. As you type, they will be underlined in green, and you will be prompted to revise them. However, not every word group identified as a fragment will actually be a fragment. You, not your grammar checker, will have to make the final decision about whether or not a sentence is grammatically complete—and decide how to correct it.
>
>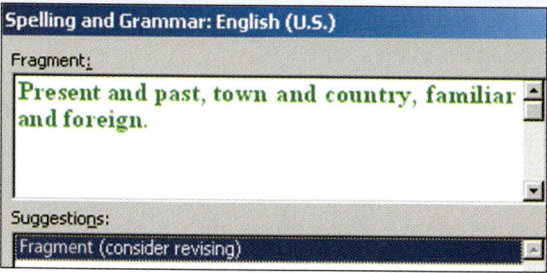

38b frag ■ Revising Sentence Fragments

■ **EXERCISE 1**

Identify each of the following word groups as either a sentence fragment or a complete sentence. Be prepared to explain why each fragment is not a complete sentence. When you have finished, type each sentence into your word-processing program, and use the grammar checker to check your responses.

1. Consisting of shortness of breath, a high fever, and a racing pulse.
2. Held in contempt of court by the presiding judge.
3. Walking to the end of the road and back is good exercise.
4. On her own at last, after many years of struggle for independence.
5. Because he felt torn between two cultures.
6. With boundaries extending from the ocean to the bay.
7. Although language study can be challenging.
8. In addition, a new point guard will be a valuable addition to the team.
9. Defeated by his own greed but not in the least regretful.
10. Moreover, the continued presence of troops in Iraq.

Sections 38b–d identify the grammatical structures most likely to appear as fragments and illustrate the most effective ways of revising each kind.

38b Revising Dependent Clause Fragments

A **dependent clause** contains both a subject and a verb, but it cannot stand alone as a sentence. Because it needs an independent clause to complete its meaning, a <u>dependent clause</u> (also called a *subordinate clause*) must always be attached to at least one independent clause to form a complete sentence. You can recognize a dependent clause because it is always introduced by a <u>subordinating conjunction</u> (*although, because,* and so on) or a <u>relative pronoun</u> (*that, which, who,* and so on).

See 34b

In most cases, the best way to correct a dependent clause fragment is to join the dependent clause to a neighboring independent clause, creating a complex sentence.

> The United States declared war. ~~Because~~ *because* the Japanese bombed Pearl Harbor. (Dependent clause has been attached to an independent clause, creating a complex sentence.)

> The battery is dead. ~~Which~~ *, which* means the car won't start. (Dependent clause has been attached to an independent clause, creating a complex sentence.)

Another way to correct a dependent clause fragment is to delete the subordinating conjunction or relative pronoun, turning the fragment into a complete sentence.

The United States declared war. ~~Because the~~ **The** Japanese bombed Pearl Harbor. (Subordinating conjunction *because* has been deleted; the result is a new sentence.)

The battery is dead. ~~Which~~ **This** means the car won't start. (Relative pronoun *which* has been replaced by *this*; the result is a new sentence.)

NOTE: Simply deleting the subordinating conjunction or relative pronoun, as in the two examples above, is usually the least desirable way to revise a dependent clause fragment because it is likely to create two choppy sentences.

■ EXERCISE 2

Identify the sentence fragments in the following paragraph. Then, correct each fragment either by attaching the fragment to an independent clause or by deleting the subordinating conjunction or relative pronoun to create a sentence that can stand alone. (In some cases, you will have to replace a relative pronoun with another word that can serve as the subject.)

The drive-in movie came into being just after World War II. When both movies and cars were central to the lives of many Americans. Drive-ins were especially popular with teenagers and young families during the 1950s. When cars and gas were relatively inexpensive. Theaters charged by the carload. Which meant that a group of teenagers or a family with several children could spend an evening at the movies for a few dollars. In 1958, when the fad peaked, there were over four thousand drive-ins in the United States. While today there are fewer than three thousand. Many of these are in the Sunbelt, with most in California. Although many Sunbelt drive-ins continue to thrive because of the year-round warm weather. Many northern drive-ins are in financial trouble. Because land is so expensive. Some drive-in owners break even only by operating flea markets or swap meets in daylight hours. While others, unable to attract customers, are selling their theaters to land developers. Soon, drive-ins may be a part of our nostalgic past. Which will be a great loss for many who enjoy them.

38c Revising Phrase Fragments

A **phrase** provides information—description, examples, and so on—about other words or word groups in a sentence. However, because it lacks a subject, a verb, or both, a phrase cannot stand alone as a sentence.

38c frag ▪ Revising Sentence Fragments

> **CLOSE-UP**
>
> ### FRAGMENTS INTRODUCED BY TRANSITIONS
>
> *See 7b2*
>
> Many phrase fragments are word groups that are introduced by transitional words and phrases, such as *also*, *finally*, *in addition*, and *now*, but are missing subjects and verbs. To correct such a fragment, you need to add the missing subject and verb.
>
> ~~Also~~ *It was also* a step in the right direction.
>
> Finally, *he found* a new home for the family.
>
> In addition, *we need* three new keyboards for the computer lab.
>
> Now, *I will explain* the first step.

1 Prepositional Phrases

See 33b1
ESL 63e

A **prepositional phrase** consists of a preposition, its object, and any modifiers of the object.

To correct a prepositional phrase fragment, attach it to the independent clause that contains the word or word group modified by the prepositional phrase.

President Lyndon Johnson did not seek reelection, ~~For~~ *for* a number of reasons. (Prepositional phrase has been attached to an independent clause, creating a complete sentence.)

He ran sixty yards for a touchdown, ~~In~~ *in* the final minutes of the game. (Prepositional phrase has been attached to an independent clause, creating a complete sentence.)

■ **EXERCISE 3**

Read the following passage, and identify the sentence fragments. Then, correct each one by attaching it to the independent clause that contains the word or word group it modifies.

> Most college athletes are caught in a conflict. Between their athletic and academic careers. Sometimes college athletes' responsibilities on the playing field make it hard for them to be good students. Often, athletes must make a choice. Between sports and a degree. Some athletes would not be able to afford college. Without athletic scholarships. Ironically, however, their commitments (training, exercise, practice, and travel to out-of-town games, for example) deprive athletes. Of valuable classroom time. The role of college athletes is constantly being questioned. Critics suggest that athletes exist only to participate in and promote college athletics. Because of the importance of this role to acade-

mic institutions, scandals occasionally develop. With coaches and even faculty members arranging to inflate athletes' grades to help them remain eligible. For participation in sports. Some universities even lower admissions standards. To help remedy this and other inequities. The controversial Proposition 48, passed at the NCAA convention in 1982, established minimum College Board scores and grade standards for student athletes. But many people feel that the NCAA remains overly concerned. With profits rather than with education. As a result, college athletic competition is increasingly coming to resemble pro sports. From the coaches' pressure on the players to win to the network television exposure to the wagers on the games' outcomes.

2 Verbal Phrases

A verbal phrase consists of a **verbal**—a present participle (*walking*), past participle (*walked*), infinitive (*to walk*), or gerund (*walking*)—plus related objects and modifiers (*walking along the lonely beach*). Because a verbal cannot serve as a sentence's main verb, a verbal phrase is not a complete sentence and should not be punctuated as one.

To correct a verbal phrase fragment, you can attach the verbal phrase to a related independent clause.

In 1948, India became an independent country. ~~Divided~~ *divided* into the nations of India and Pakistan. (Verbal phrase has been attached to a related independent clause, creating a complete sentence.)

A familiar trademark can increase a product's sales. ~~Reminding~~ *, reminding* shoppers that the product has a long-standing reputation. (Verbal phrase has been attached to a related independent clause, creating a complete sentence.)

Or, you can change the verbal to a verb and add a subject.

In 1948, India became an independent country. ~~Divided~~ *It was divided* into the nations of India and Pakistan. (Verb *was divided* has replaced verbal *divided*, and subject *it* has been added; the result is a complete sentence.)

A familiar trademark can increase a product's sales. ~~Reminding~~ *It reminds* shoppers that the product has a long-standing reputation. (Verb *reminds* has replaced verbal *reminding*, and subject *it* has been added; the result is a complete sentence.)

■ EXERCISE 4

Identify the sentence fragments in the following paragraph and correct each one. Either attach the fragment to a related independent clause, or add a subject and a verb to create a complete sentence.

Many food products have well-known trademarks. Identified by familiar faces on product labels. Some of these symbols have remained the same, while others have changed considerably. Products like Sun-Maid Raisins, Betty Crocker potato mixes, Quaker Oats, and Uncle Ben's Rice use faces. To create a sense of quality and tradition and to encourage shopper recognition of the products. Many of the portraits have been updated several times. To reflect changes in society. Betty Crocker's portrait, for instance, has changed many times since its creation in 1936. Symbolizing women's changing roles. The original Chef Boy-ar-dee has also changed. Turning from the young Italian chef Hector Boiardi into a white-haired senior citizen. Miss Sunbeam, trademark of Sunbeam Bread, has had her hairdo modified several times since her first appearance in 1942; the Blue Bonnet girl, also created in 1942, now has a more modern look, and Aunt Jemima has also been changed. Slimmed down a bit in 1965. Similarly, the Campbell's Soup kids are less chubby now than in the 1920s when they first appeared. Still, manufacturers are very careful about selecting a trademark or modifying an existing one. Typically spending a good deal of time and money on research before a change is made.

3 Appositives

An **appositive**—a noun or noun phrase that identifies or renames an adjacent noun or pronoun—cannot stand alone as a sentence.

To correct an appositive fragment, attach the appositive to the independent clause that contains the word the appositive renames.

Brian was the star forward of the Blue Devils⟨,⟩ ~~T~~he team with the best record. (Appositive has been attached to an independent clause, creating a complete sentence.)

Piero della Francesca was a leader of the Umbrian school of painting⟨,⟩ ~~A~~ school that remained close to the traditions of Gothic art. (Appositive has been attached to an independent clause, creating a complete sentence.)

> **CLOSE-UP**
>
> **LISTS**
>
> When an appositive fragment is in the form of a <u>list</u>, add a colon to connect the list to the independent clause that introduces it.
>
> Tourists often outnumber residents in four European cities⟨:⟩ Venice, Florence, Canterbury, and Bath.

See 56a1

Sometimes an appositive consists of a word or phrase like *that is, for example, for instance, namely,* or *such as,* followed by an example.

To correct this kind of appositive fragment, attach the appositive to the preceding independent clause.

Fairy tales are full of damsels in distress, ~~Such~~ *such* as Cinderella and Rapunzel.

NOTE: Sometimes you can correct an appositive fragment by embedding the appositive within an independent clause.

Some popular novelists —for example, Charles Dickens and Mark Twain— are highly respected in later generations. ~~For example, Charles Dickens and Mark Twain.~~

■ EXERCISE 5

Identify the fragments in this paragraph, and correct them by attaching each one to the independent clause containing the word the appositive identifies or renames.

> Until the early 1900s, communities in West Virginia, Tennessee, and Kentucky were isolated by the mountains that surrounded them. The great chain of the Appalachian Mountains. Set apart from the emerging culture of a growing America and American language, these communities retained a language rich with the dialect of Elizabethan English and sprinkled with hints of a Scotch-Irish influence. In the 1910s and '20s, the communities in these mountains began to long for a better future for their children. The key to that future, as they saw it, was education. In some communities, that education took the form of Settlement Schools. Schools led by idealistic young graduates of eastern women's colleges. These teachers taught the basic academic subjects. Such as reading, writing, and mathematics. They also schooled their students in the culture of the mountains. For example, the crafts, music, and folklore of the Appalachians. In addition, they taught them skills that would help them survive when the coal market began to decline. The Settlement Schools attracted artisans from around the world. Quilters, weavers, basketmakers, and carpenters. The schools also opened the mountains to the world, leading to the decline of the Elizabethan dialect.

38d Revising Compounds

The last part of a **compound predicate, compound object**, or **compound complement** cannot stand alone as a sentence.

To correct this type of fragment, connect the detached part of the compound to the sentence to which it belongs.

People with dyslexia have trouble reading, *and* ~~And~~ may also find it difficult to write. (Detached part of the compound predicate has been connected to the sentence to which it belongs.)

They took only a compass and a canteen, *and* ~~And~~ some trail mix. (Detached part of the compound object has been connected to the sentence to which it belongs.)

38e frag ■ Revising Sentence Fragments

When their supplies ran out they were surprised~~,~~ ~~And~~ *and* hungry.
(Detached part of the compound complement has been connected to the sentence to which it belongs.)

■ **EXERCISE 6**

Identify the sentence fragments in this passage, and correct them by attaching each detached compound to the sentence to which it belongs.

As more and more Americans discover the pleasures of the wilderness, our national parks are feeling the stress. Wanting to get away for a weekend or a week, hikers and backpackers stream from the cities into nearby state and national parks. They bring with them a hunger for the wilderness. But very little knowledge about how to behave ethically in the wild. They also do not know how to keep themselves safe. Some of them think of the national parks as inexpensive amusement parks. Without proper camping supplies and lacking enough food and water for their trip, they are putting at risk their lives and the lives of those who will be called on to save them. One family went for a hike up a desert canyon with an eight-month-old infant. And their seventy-eight-year-old grandmother. Although the terrain was difficult, they were not wearing the proper shoes. Or good socks. They did not even carry a first aid kit. Or a map or compass. They were on an unmarked trail in a little-used section of Bureau of Land Management lands. And following vague directions from a friend. Soon, they were lost. They had not brought water or food. Or even rain gear or warm clothes. Luckily for them, they had brought a cell phone. By the time they called for help, however, it was getting dark and a storm was building. A rescue plane eventually located the family. And brought them to safety. Still, a little planning before they hiked in an inhospitable area, and a little awareness and preparedness for the terrain they were traveling in, would have saved this family much worry. And the taxpayers a lot of money.

38e Using Fragments Intentionally

In professional and academic writing, sentence fragments are generally not acceptable.

> **CHECKLIST**
>
> **ACCEPTABLE FRAGMENTS**
>
> It is permissable to use fragments in the following special situations:
> ☐ In lists
> ☐ In captions that accompany visuals
> ☐ In topic outlines
> ☐ In quoted dialogue

- ☐ In *PowerPoint* presentations
- ☐ In titles and subtitles of papers and reports

Fragments are, however, often used in speech and in personal email and other informal writing—as well as in journalism, political slogans, bumper stickers, creative writing, and advertising. Magazine advertisements, such as the one for Orange Glo polishing cloths shown in Figure 38.1, often rely heavily on fragments to isolate (and thereby emphasize) key concepts about the product. Sometimes these fragments are formatted as bulleted lists of the product's key features; sometimes, as in the Orange Glo ad, the fragments are used in a central message or tag line (*Leaves other wipes in the dust*).

FIGURE 38.1 Magazine ad for Orange Glo polishing cloths.

■ EXERCISE 7

Select several advertisements from magazines, newspapers, or the Internet. Identify word groups that you think are fragments. Then, type each into your word processor, and run a grammar check. Keep in mind that some word groups may look like fragments but may in fact be <u>imperative</u> sentences (commands) that have an implied subject (*you*) and will therefore be recognized as grammatically correct sentences.

See 48c

Revise each fragment you identify so that it is a complete sentence. Then, decide which version—the fragment or your corrected sentence—is more effective for each advertisement's purpose and audience.

39

Revising Run-ons

❓ FAQs

What is a run-on? (p. 532)

What is the difference between a comma splice and a fused sentence? (p. 532)

How do I revise a comma splice or fused sentence? (p. 533)

39a Recognizing Comma Splices and Fused Sentences

❓ A **run-on** is an error that occurs when two **independent clauses** are joined incorrectly. There are two kinds of run-ons: *comma splices* and *fused sentences.*

See 33b2

❓ A **comma splice** is a run-on that occurs when two independent clauses are joined by just a comma. A **fused sentence** is a run-on that occurs when two independent clauses are joined with no punctuation.

> **Comma Splice:** Charles Dickens created the character of Mr. Micawber, he also created Uriah Heep.
>
> **Fused Sentence:** Charles Dickens created the character of Mr. Micawber he also created Uriah Heep.

GRAMMAR CHECKER

REVISING COMMA SPLICES

Your word processor's grammar checker will highlight comma splices and prompt you to revise them.

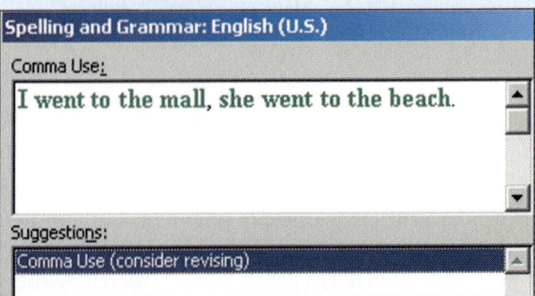

Your grammar checker may also highlight fused sentences, but it may identify them as long sentences that need revision. Moreover, it will not offer suggestions for revising fused sentences.

CLOSE-UP

REVISING COMMA SPLICES AND FUSED SENTENCES

To revise a comma splice or fused sentence, use one of the following four strategies:
1. Add a period between the clauses, creating two separate sentences.
2. Add a semicolon between the clauses, creating a compound sentence.
3. Add a coordinating conjunction between the clauses, creating a compound sentence.
4. Subordinate one clause to the other, creating a complex sentence.

39b Revising with Periods

You can revise a comma splice or fused sentence by adding a period between the independent clauses, creating two separate sentences. This is a good strategy to use when the clauses are long or when they are not closely related.

In 1894, Frenchman Alfred Dreyfus was falsely convicted of treason, his struggle for justice pitted the army against civil libertarians. *[edit: replace ", his" with ". His"]*

CLOSE-UP

COMMA SPLICES AND FUSED SENTENCES

Using a comma to punctuate an interrupted quotation that consists of two complete sentences creates a comma splice. Instead, use a period.

"This is a good course," Eric said, "in fact, I wish I'd taken it sooner." *[edit: replace ", "in" with ." "In"]*

39c Revising with Semicolons

You can revise a comma splice or fused sentence by adding a **semicolon** between two closely related clauses that convey parallel or contrasting information. The result will be a single compound sentence.

See 53a

In pre–World War II western Europe, only a small elite had access to a university education, this situation changed dramatically after the war. *[edit: replace "," with ";"]*

Chippendale chairs have straight legs, however, Queen Anne chairs have curved legs. *[edit: replace "," before "however" with ";"]*

NOTE: When you use a **transitional word or phrase** (such as *however*, *therefore*, or *for example*) to connect two independent clauses, the transitional element must be preceded by a semicolon and followed

See 7b2

by a comma. If you link the two clauses with just a comma, you create a comma splice; if you omit punctuation entirely, you create a fused sentence.

39d Revising with Coordinating Conjunctions

You can use a coordinating conjunction (*and, or, but, nor, for, so, yet*) to join two closely related clauses of equal importance into one **compound sentence**. The coordinating conjunction you choose indicates the relationship between the clauses: addition (*and*), contrast (*but, yet*), causality (*for, so*), or a choice of alternatives (*or, nor*). Be sure to include a comma before the coordinating conjunction.

See 34a1

> Elias Howe invented the sewing machine, *and* Julia Ward Howe was a poet and social reformer.

39e Revising with Subordinating Conjunctions or Relative Pronouns

When the ideas in two independent clauses are not of equal importance, you can use a subordinating conjunction or relative pronoun to join the clauses into one **complex sentence**, placing the less important idea in the dependent clause. The subordinating conjunction or relative pronoun you choose indicates how the clauses are related.

See 34b

> Stravinsky's ballet *The Rite of Spring* shocked Parisians in 1913, *because* its rhythms seemed erotic.

> Lady Mary Wortley Montagu, *who* had suffered from smallpox herself, ~~she~~ helped spread the practice of inoculation.

CLOSE-UP

ACCEPTABLE COMMA SPLICES

In a few special cases, comma splices are acceptable. For instance, a comma is conventionally used in dialogue between a statement and a tag question, even though each is a separate independent clause.

This is Ron's house, isn't it?

I'm not late, am I?

In addition, commas may be used to connect two short, balanced independent clauses or two or more short parallel independent clauses, especially when one clause contradicts the other.

Commencement isn't the end, it's the beginning.

EXERCISE 1

Identify the comma splices and fused sentences in the following paragraph. Correct each in two of the four possible ways listed in the Close-up box on page 533. If a sentence is correct, leave it alone.

Example: The fans rose in their seats, the game was almost over.

Revised: The fans rose in their seats; the game was almost over.
The fans rose in their seats because the game was almost over.

Entrepreneurship is the study of small businesses, college students are embracing it enthusiastically. Many schools offer one or more courses in entrepreneurship these courses teach the theory and practice of starting a small business. Students are signing up for courses, moreover, they are starting their own businesses. One student started with a car-waxing business, now he sells condominiums. Other students are setting up catering services they supply everything from waiters to bartenders. One student has a thriving cake-decorating business, in fact, she employs fifteen students to deliver the cakes. All over the country, student businesses are selling everything from tennis balls to bagels, the student owners are making impressive profits. Formal courses at the graduate as well as undergraduate level are attracting more business students than ever, several schools (such as Baylor University, the University of Southern California, and Babson College) even offer degree programs in entrepreneurship. Many business school students are no longer planning to be corporate executives instead, they plan to become entrepreneurs.

EXERCISE 2

Combine each of the following sentence pairs into one sentence without creating comma splices or fused sentences. In each case, subordinate one clause to the other to create a complex sentence. You may have to add, delete, reorder, or change words or punctuation.

Example: *Because* I grew up at the New Jersey shore, *people* think I'm lucky.

1. Other beach rats know better than to envy me. Inlanders romanticize life by the ocean.
2. The sound of the waves is comforting. The sand gets into everything.
3. In the summer, tourists clog the roads. In the winter, many of the locals are out of work.
4. Beach towns have a difficult time attracting industry. Taxes are often high.
5. After a while, going to the beach in the summer loses its charm. The beach in winter, empty of other people, is a beautiful sight.

EXERCISE 3

Combine each of the following sentence pairs into one sentence without creating comma splices or fused sentences. In each case, either connect the clauses into a compound sentence (with a semicolon or with a comma and a coordinating conjunction) or subordinate one clause to the other to create a complex sentence. You may have to add, delete, reorder, or change words or punctuation.

1. Several recent studies indicate that many American high school students have little knowledge of history. This is affecting our future as a democratic nation and as individuals.
2. Surveys show that nearly one-third of American seventeen-year-olds cannot identify the countries the United States fought against in World War II. One-third think Columbus reached the New World after 1750.
3. Several reasons have been given for this decline in historical literacy. The main reason is the way history is taught.
4. This problem is bad news. The good news is that there is increasing agreement among educators about what is wrong with current methods of teaching history.
5. History can be exciting and engaging. Too often, it is presented in a boring manner.
6. Students are typically expected to memorize dates, facts, and names. History as adventure—as a "good story"—is frequently neglected.
7. One way to avoid this problem is to use good textbooks. Textbooks should be accurate, lively, and focused.
8. Another way to create student interest in historical events is to use primary sources instead of so-called comprehensive textbooks. Autobiographies, journals, and diaries can give students insight into larger issues.
9. Students can also be challenged to think about history by taking sides in a debate. They can learn more about connections among historical events by writing essays than by taking multiple-choice tests.
10. Finally, history teachers should be less concerned about specific historical details. They should be more concerned about conveying the wonder of history.

40

Revising Misplaced and Dangling Modifiers

❓ FAQs

What are misplaced modifiers, and how do I revise them? (p. 537)
Is a split infinitive ever acceptable? (p. 541)
What are dangling modifiers, and how do I revise them? (p. 542)

A **modifier** is a word, phrase, or clause that describes, limits, or qualifies another word or word group in a sentence. A modifier should be placed close to the word it modifies. **Faulty modification** is the confusing placement of modifiers or the modification of nonexistent words.

GRAMMAR CHECKER

REVISING FAULTY MODIFICATION

Your grammar checker will identify some modification problems, including certain awkward split infinitives. However, the grammar checker will not offer revision suggestions.

See 40b

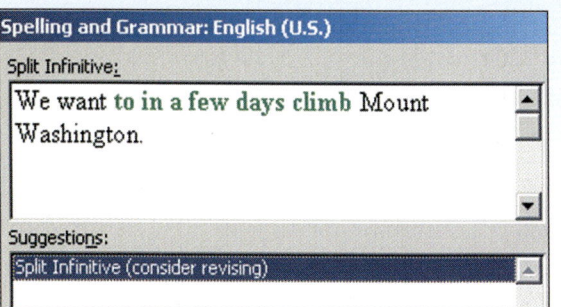

40a Revising Misplaced Modifiers

A **misplaced modifier** is a word or word group whose placement suggests that it modifies one word (or phrase or clause) when it is intended to modify another.

Wendy watched the storm, fierce
~~Fierce and threatening,~~ ~~Wendy watched the storm.~~ (The storm, not Wendy, was fierce and threatening.)

The lawyer argued that the defendant, with
With an IQ of just 52, ~~the lawyer argued that the defendant~~ should not get the death penalty. (The defendant, not the lawyer, had an IQ of 52.)

1 Placing Modifying Words Precisely

Limiting modifiers—such as *almost, only, even, hardly, merely, nearly, exactly, scarcely, simply,* and *just*—should always immediately precede the words they modify. A different placement will change the meaning of the sentence.

Nick *just* set up camp at the edge of town. (He did it just now.)

Just Nick set up camp at the edge of town. (He did it alone.)

Nick set up camp *just* at the edge of town. (His camp was precisely at the edge.)

When a limiting modifier is placed so that it is not clear whether it modifies a word before it or one after it, it is called a **squinting modifier**.

The life that everyone thought would fulfill her <u>totally</u> bored her.

To correct a squinting modifier, place the modifier so that it is clear which word it modifies.

The life that everyone thought would <u>totally</u> fulfill her bored her. (Everyone expected her to be totally fulfilled.)

The life that everyone thought would fulfill her bored her <u>totally</u>. (She was totally bored.)

■ EXERCISE 1

In the following sentence pairs, the modifier in each sentence points to a different word. Underline the modifier and draw an arrow to the word it modifies. Then, explain the meaning of each sentence.

Example: She <u>just</u> came in wearing a hat. (She just now entered.)

She came in wearing <u>just</u> a hat. (She wore only a hat.)

1. He wore his almost new jeans.
   He almost wore his new jeans.
2. He had only three dollars in his pocket.
   Only he had three dollars in his pocket.

3. I don't even like freshwater fish.
   I don't like even freshwater fish.
4. I go only to the beach on Saturdays.
   I go to the beach only on Saturdays.
5. He simply hated driving.
   He hated simply driving.

2 Relocating Misplaced Phrases

Placing a modifying phrase incorrectly can change the meaning of a sentence or create an unclear or confusing (or even unintentionally humorous) construction.

To avoid ambiguity, place phrases as close as possible to the words they modify.

- Place **verbal phrase** modifiers directly before or directly after the words or word groups they modify.

  Roller-skating along the shore,
  Jane watched the boats ~~roller-skating along the shore~~.

- Place **prepositional phrase** modifiers immediately after the words they modify.

  with no arms
  Venus de Milo is a statue created by a famous artist ~~with no arms~~.

■ EXERCISE 2

Underline the modifying verbal phrases or prepositional phrases in each sentence, and draw arrows to the words they modify.

Example: Calvin is the Democrat <u>running for town council</u>.

1. The bridge across the river swayed in the wind.
2. The spectators on the shore were involved in the action.
3. Mesmerized by the spectacle, they watched the drama unfold.
4. The spectators were afraid of a disaster.
5. Within the hour, the state police arrived to save the day.
6. They closed off the area with roadblocks.
7. Drivers approaching the bridge were asked to stop.
8. Meanwhile, on the bridge, the scene was chaos.
9. Motorists in their cars were paralyzed with fear.
10. Struggling against the weather, the police managed to rescue everyone.

■ EXERCISE 3

Use the phrase that follows each sentence as a modifier in that sentence. Then, underline the modifier, and draw an arrow to indicate the word it modifies.

Example: He approached the lion. (with fear in his heart)

With fear in his heart, he approached the lion.

1. The lion paced up and down in his cage, ignoring the crowd. (watching Jack)
2. Jack stared back at the lion. (in terror)
3. The crowd around them grew. (anxious to see what would happen)
4. Suddenly, Jack heard a terrifying growl. (from deep in the lion's throat)
5. Jack ran from the zoo, leaving the lion behind. (scared to death)

3 Relocating Misplaced Dependent Clauses

A dependent clause that serves as a modifier must be clearly related to the word it modifies.

- An **adjective clause** appears immediately *after* the word it modifies.

    During the Civil War, Lincoln was the president who governed the United States.

- An **adverb clause** can appear in any of several positions, as long as its relationship to the word or word group it modifies is clear.

    When Lincoln was president, the Civil War raged.

    The Civil War raged when Lincoln was president.

EXERCISE 4

Relocate the misplaced verbal phrases, prepositional phrases, or dependent clauses so that they clearly point to the words or word groups they modify.

Example: *Silent Running* is a film with Bruce Dern about a scientist left alone in space. ~~with Bruce Dern.~~

1. She realized that she had married the wrong man after the wedding.
2. *The Prince and the Pauper* is a novel about an exchange of identities by Mark Twain.
3. The energy was used up in the ten-kilometer race that he was saving for the marathon.
4. He loaded the bottles and cans into his new car, which he planned to leave at the recycling center.
5. The manager explained the sales figures to the board members using a graph.

40b Revising Intrusive Modifiers

An **intrusive modifier** awkwardly interrupts a sentence, making it difficult to understand.

Revise when a long modifying phrase comes between an auxiliary verb and a main verb.

> She ~~had, without~~ giving it a second thought or considering the consequences, ^*she had* planned to reenlist.
> *Without*

Revise when an adverb phrase or clause comes between a subject and a verb (or between a verb and its object or complement).

> The election ^*was contested* because officials discovered that some people had voted more than once~~, was contested~~.

Revise when a modifier creates an awkward **split infinitive**—that is, when a modifier comes between the word *to* and the base form of the verb.

> He hoped to^ quickly and easily ^*defeat his opponent* ~~defeat his opponent~~.

NOTE: A split infinitive is acceptable when the intervening modifier is short, especially if the alternative would be awkward or ambiguous: *She expected to almost beat her previous record.*

EXERCISE 5

Revise these sentences so that the modifying phrases or clauses do not interrupt an infinitive, separate an auxiliary verb from a main verb, or separate a subject from a verb or a verb from its object or complement.

Example: ^*Despite the playwright's best efforts, a* A play can sometimes be, ~~despite the playwright's best efforts,~~ mystifying to the audience.

1. The people in the audience, when they saw the play was about to begin and realized the orchestra had finished tuning up and had begun the overture, finally quieted down.
2. They settled into their seats, expecting to very much enjoy the first act.
3. However, most people were, even after watching and listening for twenty minutes and paying close attention to the drama, completely baffled.
4. In fact, the play, because it had nameless characters, no scenery, and a rambling plot that did not seem to be heading anywhere, puzzled even the drama critics.
5. Finally, one of the three major characters explained, speaking directly to the audience, what the play was really about.

40c Revising Dangling Modifiers

 A **dangling modifier** is a word or phrase that cannot logically modify any word in the sentence.

> **Dangling:** <u>Using this drug</u>, many undesirable side effects are experienced. (Who is using this drug?)

- One way to correct a dangling modifier is to **create a new subject** by adding a word or word group that *using this drug* can logically modify.

> **Revised:** Using a drug, patients experience many undesirable side effects.

- Another way to correct a dangling modifier is to **create a dependent clause**.

> **Revised:** Many undesirable side effects are experienced <u>when this drug is used</u>.

These two options for correcting dangling modifiers are further illustrated below.

1 Creating a New Subject

Using a pair of forceps, ^the technician lifted^ the skin of the rat's abdomen ~~was lifted~~. (Modifier cannot logically modify *skin*.)

With fifty more pages to read, ^Meg found^ *War and Peace* ~~was~~ absorbing. (Modifier cannot logically modify *War and Peace*.)

2 Creating a Dependent Clause

^Before^ ~~To implement~~ a plus/minus grading system, ^was implemented,^ all students were polled. (Modifier cannot logically modify *students*.)

^Because the magazine had been on^ ~~On~~ the newsstands only an hour, its sales surprised everyone. (Modifier cannot logically modify *sales*.)

CLOSE-UP

REVISING DANGLING ELLIPTICAL CLAUSES

See 33b2

<u>Elliptical clauses</u> are incomplete constructions. Typically, the writer has intentionally omitted part of the subject or predicate (or the entire subject or predicate) from a dependent clause in order to create a more

concise sentence. When such a clause cannot logically modify the subject of the sentence's main clause, it dangles. To revise a dangling elliptical clause, add a subject that the elliptical clause can logically modify.

> **Dangling:** While still in the Buchner funnel, you should press the crystals with a clear stopper to eliminate any residual solvent. (Elliptical clause cannot logically modify *you*.)
>
> **Revised:** While still in the Buchner funnel, the crystals should be pressed with a clear stopper to eliminate any residual solvent. (Subject of main clause has been changed from *you* to *crystals*, a word the elliptical clause can logically modify.)

■ EXERCISE 6

Eliminate the dangling modifier from each of the following sentences. Either supply a word or word group the dangling modifier can logically modify, or change the dangling modifier into a dependent clause.

Example: Skiing down the mountain, my hat flew off.
(dangling modifier)

Revised: Skiing down the mountain, I lost my hat.
(new subject added)

As I skied down the mountain, my hat flew off.
(dependent clause)

1. Writing for eight hours every day, her lengthy books are published every year or so.
2. As an out-of-state student without a car, it was difficult to get to off-campus cultural events.
3. To build a campfire, kindling is necessary.
4. With every step upward, the trees became sparser.
5. Being an amateur tennis player, my backhand is weaker than my forehand.
6. When exiting the train, the station will be on your right.
7. Driving through the Mojave, the bleak landscape was oppressive.
8. By requiring auto manufacturers to further improve emission-control devices, the air quality will get better.
9. Using a piece of filter paper, the ball of sodium is dried as much as possible and placed in a test tube.
10. Having missed work for seven days straight, my job was in jeopardy.

41

Using Parallelism

❓ FAQs

What is parallelism? (p. 544)
How can I use parallelism to improve my writing? (p. 544)
How can I correct faulty parallelism? (p. 546)

Parallelism—the use of matching words, phrases, or clauses to express equivalent ideas—adds unity, balance, and coherence to your writing. Effective parallelism can help you write clearer sentences, but faulty parallelism can create awkward sentences that obscure your meaning and confuse readers.

See 41b

41a Using Parallelism Effectively

Parallelism highlights the correspondence between *items in a series*, *paired items*, and elements in *lists and outlines*.

1 With Items in a Series

<u>Eat</u>, <u>drink</u>, and <u>be</u> merry.

<u>Baby food consumption</u>, <u>toy production</u>, and <u>school construction</u> are likely to decline as the US population ages.

Three factors influenced his decision to seek new employment: <u>his desire to relocate</u>, <u>his need for greater responsibility</u>, and <u>his dissatisfaction with his current job</u>.

NOTE: For information on punctuating items in a series, **see 52b** and **53c**.

2 With Paired Items

The thank-you note was <u>short</u> but <u>sweet</u>.

<u>Roosevelt represented the United States</u>, and <u>Churchill represented Great Britain</u>.

<u>Ask not what your country can do for you</u>; <u>ask what you can do for your country</u>. (John F. Kennedy)

Paired elements linked by **correlative conjunctions** (such as *not only/but also*, *both/and*, *either/or*, *neither/nor*, and *whether/or*) should always be parallel.

The design team paid close attention not only <u>to color</u> but also <u>to texture</u>.

Either <u>repeat physics</u> or <u>take calculus</u>.

Parallelism also highlights the contrast between paired elements linked by *than* or *as*.

Richard Wright and James Baldwin chose <u>to live in Paris</u> rather than <u>to remain in the United States</u>.

Success is as much <u>a matter of hard work</u> as <u>a matter of luck</u>.

3 In Lists and Outlines

Elements in a <u>list</u> should be parallel.

See 30c

The Irish potato famine had four major causes:

1. The establishment of the landlord-tenant system
2. The failure of the potato crop
3. The reluctance of England to offer adequate financial assistance
4. The passage of the Corn Laws

Elements in a <u>formal outline</u> should also be parallel.

See 6c4

■ EXERCISE 1

Identify the parallel elements in these sentences by bracketing parallel phrases and clauses.

Example: Manek spent six years in America [going to school] and [working for a computer company].

1. After he completed his engineering degree, Manek returned to India to visit his large extended family and to find a wife.
2. Unfamiliar with marriage practices in India and accustomed to the American notion of marriage for love, Manek's American friends disapproved of his plans.
3. Not only Manek but also his parents wanted an arranged marriage.
4. He didn't believe that either you married for love or you had a loveless marriage.
5. His parents' marriage, an arranged one, continues happily; his aunt's marriage, also arranged, has lasted thirty years.

■ EXERCISE 2

Combine each of the following sentence pairs or sentence groups into one sentence that uses parallel structure. Be sure all paired items and items in a series (words, phrases, or clauses) are expressed in parallel terms.

1. Originally, there were five performing Marx Brothers. One was nicknamed Groucho. The others were called Chico, Harpo, Gummo, and Zeppo.

2. Groucho was very well known. So were Chico and Harpo. Gummo soon dropped out of the act. And later Zeppo did too.
3. They began in vaudeville. That was before World War I. Their first show was called *I'll Say She Is*. It opened in New York in 1924.
4. The Marx Brothers' first movie was *The Cocoanuts*. The next was *Animal Crackers*. And this was followed by *Monkey Business, Horse Feathers*, and *Duck Soup*. Then came *A Night at the Opera*.
5. In each of these movies, the Marx Brothers make people laugh. They also exhibit a unique, zany comic style.
6. In their movies, each brother has a set of familiar trademarks. Groucho has a mustache and a long coat. He wiggles his eyebrows and smokes a cigar. There is a funny hat that Chico always wears. And he affects a phony Italian accent. Harpo never speaks.
7. Groucho is always cast as a sly operator. He always tries to cheat people out of their money. He always tries to charm women.
8. In *The Cocoanuts*, Groucho plays Mr. Hammer, proprietor of the run-down Coconut Manor, a Florida hotel. In *Horse Feathers*, his character is named Professor Quincy Adams Wagstaff. Wagstaff is president of Huxley College. Huxley also has financial problems.
9. In *Duck Soup*, Groucho plays Rufus T. Firefly, president of the country of Fredonia. Fredonia was formerly ruled by the late husband of a Mrs. Teasdale. Fredonia is now at war with the country of Sylvania.
10. Margaret Dumont is often Groucho's leading lady. She plays Mrs. Teasdale in *Duck Soup*. In *A Night at the Opera*, she plays Mrs. Claypool. Her character in *The Cocoanuts* is named Mrs. Potter.

41b Revising Faulty Parallelism

Faulty parallelism occurs when matching words, phrases, or clauses are not used to express equivalent ideas.

Many people in developing countries suffer because the countries lack sufficient housing, sufficient food, and ~~their~~ sufficient health-care facilities ~~are also insufficient~~.

To correct faulty parallelism, match nouns with nouns, verbs with verbs, and phrases or clauses with similarly constructed phrases or clauses.

Popular exercises for men and women include yoga, weight lifting ~~lifters~~, and jogging.

I look forward to hearing from you and to ~~have~~ having an opportunity to tell you more about myself.

CLOSE-UP

REPEATING KEY WORDS

Although the use of similar grammatical structures may sometimes be enough to convey parallelism, sentences are often clearer if certain key words (for example, articles, prepositions, and the *to* in infinitives) are also repeated in each element of a pair or a series. In the following sentence, repeating the preposition *by* makes it clear that *not* applies only to the first phrase.

Computerization has helped industry by not allowing labor costs to skyrocket, ^by^ increasing the speed of production, and ^by^ improving efficiency.

GRAMMAR CHECKER

REVISING FAULTY PARALLELISM

Grammar checkers are not very useful for identifying faulty parallelism. Although your grammar checker may highlight some nonparallel constructions, it may miss others.

■ EXERCISE 3

Identify and correct faulty parallelism in these sentences. Then, underline the parallel elements—words, phrases, and clauses—in your corrected sentences. If a sentence is already correct, mark it with a *C*, and underline the parallel elements.

Example: Alfred Hitchcock's films include <u>North by Northwest</u>, <u>Vertigo</u>, <u>Psycho</u>, ~~and he also directed~~ <u>Notorious</u>, and <u>Saboteur</u>.

1. The world is divided between those with galoshes on and those who discover continents.
2. World leaders, members of Congress, and religious groups are all concerned about global warming.
3. A national task force on education recommended improving public education by making the school day longer, higher teachers' salaries, and integrating more technology into the curriculum.
4. The fast food industry has expanded to include many kinds of restaurants: those that serve pizza, fried chicken chains, some offering Mexican-style menus, and hamburger franchises.
5. The consumption of Scotch in the United States is declining because of high prices, tastes are changing, and increased health awareness has led many whiskey drinkers to switch to wine or beer.

42
Revising Awkward or Confusing Sentences

❓ FAQs
What's the difference between direct and indirect discourse? (p. 549)
What's wrong with using the reason is . . . because? *(p. 552)*

The most common causes of awkward or confusing sentences are *unwarranted shifts, mixed constructions, faulty predication,* and *incomplete or illogical comparisons.*

> **ESL TIP**
>
> Some of the faulty example sentences in this chapter are similar to sentences that native English speakers sometimes use in conversation. Keep in mind, however, that although such constructions may be acceptable in informal speech, they are not acceptable in your writing.

42a Revising Unwarranted Shifts

1 Shifts in Tense

See 48b
ESL 63a2

Verb **tense** in a sentence or in a related group of sentences should not shift without good reason—to indicate changes of time, for example. Unwarranted shifts in tense can be confusing.

> I registered for the advanced philosophy seminar because I wanted a challenge. However, by the first week I ~~start~~ *started* having trouble understanding the reading. (unwarranted shift from past to present)
>
> Jack Kerouac's novel *On the Road* follows a group of friends who ~~drove~~ *drive* across the United States in the 1950s. (unwarranted shift from present to past)

See 23b

NOTE: The present tense is used in **writing about literature**.

2 Shifts in Voice

Unwarranted shifts from active to passive **voice** (or from passive to active) can be confusing. In the following sentence, for instance, the shift from active (*wrote*) to passive (*was written*) makes it unclear who wrote *The Great Gatsby*.

> F. Scott Fitzgerald wrote *This Side of Paradise*, and later The Great Gatsby ~~was written~~. [wrote]

NOTE: Sometimes a shift from active to passive voice within a sentence may be necessary to give the sentence proper emphasis: *Even though consumers protested, the sales tax was increased.* (To say *the legislature increased the sales tax* would draw the sentence's emphasis away from *consumers*.)

3 Shifts in Mood

Unwarranted shifts in **mood** can also create awkward sentences.

> Next, heat the mixture in a test tube, and ~~you should make~~ [be] sure it does not boil. (unwarranted shift from imperative to indicative)

4 Shifts in Person and Number

Person indicates who is speaking (first person—*I, we*), who is spoken to (second person—*you*), and who is spoken about (third person—*he, she, it, one,* or *they*). Unwarranted shifts between the second and the third person are most often responsible for awkward sentences.

> When ~~one looks~~ [you look] for a car loan, you compare the interest rates of several banks. (unwarranted shift from third to second person)

Number indicates one (singular—*novel, it*) or more than one (plural—*novels, they, them*). Singular pronouns should refer to singular **antecedents** and plural pronouns to plural antecedents.

> If a person does not study regularly, ~~they~~ [he or she] will have a difficult time learning a foreign language. (unwarranted shift from singular to plural)

5 Shifts from Direct to Indirect Discourse

Direct discourse reports the exact words of a speaker or writer. It is always enclosed in quotation marks and is often accompanied by an **identifying tag** (*he says, she said*). **Indirect discourse** summarizes

42a awk/shift ■ Revising Awkward or Confusing Sentences

the words of a speaker or writer. No quotation marks are used, and the reported words are often introduced with the word *that* or, in the case of questions, with *who, what, why, whether, how,* or *if.*

> **Direct Discourse:** My instructor said, "I want your paper by this Friday."
>
> **Indirect Discourse:** My instructor said that he wanted my paper by this Friday.

Unwarranted shifts between indirect and direct discourse can be confusing.

During the trial, John Brown repeatedly defended his actions and said that he was not guilty. (shift from indirect to direct discourse)

My mother asked, "Are you ever going to get a job?" (shift from direct to indirect discourse)

■ EXERCISE 1

Read the following sentences, and eliminate any shifts in tense, voice, mood, person, or number. Some sentences are correct, and some can be revised in more than one way.

Example: When you examines the history of the women's movement, you see that it had many different beginnings.

1. Some historians see World War II and women's work in the factories as the beginning of the push toward equal rights for women.
2. Women went to work in the textile mills of Lowell, Massachusetts, in the late 1800s, and her efforts at reforming the workplace are seen by many as the beginning of the equal rights movement.
3. Farm girls from New Hampshire, Vermont, and western Massachusetts came to Lowell to make money, and they wanted to experience life in the city.
4. The factories promised the girls decent wages, and parents were promised by them that their daughters would live in a safe, wholesome environment.
5. Dormitories were built by the factory owners; they are supposed to ensure a safe environment for the girls.
6. First, visit the loom rooms at the Boot Mills Factory, and then you should tour a replica of a dormitory.
7. When one visits the working loom room at the factory, you are overcome with a sense of the risks and dangers the girls faced in the mills.
8. For a mill girl, moving to the city meant freedom and an escape from the drudgery of farm life; it also meant they had to face many new social situations for which they were not always prepared.

9. Harriet Robinson wrote *Loom and Spindle*, the story of her life as a mill girl, and then a book of poems was published.
10. When you look at the lives of the loom girls, one can see that their work laid part of the foundation for women's later demands for equal rights.

■ **EXERCISE 2**

Change the direct discourse in the following sentences to indirect discourse.

Example: Anna Quindlen explained why she kept her maiden name when she married: "It was a political decision, a simple statement that I was somebody and not an adjunct of anybody, especially a husband."

Anna Quindlen explained that she kept her maiden name when she married as a political decision, a simple statement that she was somebody and not an adjunct of anybody, especially a husband.

1. Sally Thane Christensen, advocating the use of an endangered species of tree, the yew, as a treatment for cancer, asked, "Is a tree worth a life?"
2. Stephen Nathanson, considering the morality of the death penalty, asked, "What if the death penalty did save lives?"
3. Martin Luther King Jr. said, "I have a dream that one day this nation will rise up and live out the true meaning of its creed."
4. Benjamin Franklin once stated, "The older I grow, the more apt I am to doubt my own judgment of others."
5. Thoreau said, "The finest qualities of our nature, like the bloom on fruits, can be preserved only by the most delicate handling."

42b   Revising Mixed Constructions

A **mixed construction** is an error created when a dependent clause, prepositional phrase, or independent clause is incorrectly used as the subject of a sentence.

Because she studies every day, ~~explains why~~ she gets good grades. (dependent clause used as subject)

By calling for information, you can ~~is the way to~~ learn more about the benefits of ROTC. (prepositional phrase used as subject)

Being
~~He was~~ late ~~was what~~ made him miss Act 1. (independent clause used as subject)

42c awk ■ Revising Awkward or Confusing Sentences

■ **EXERCISE 3**

Revise the following mixed constructions so their parts fit together both grammatically and logically.

Example: ~~By investing~~ *Investing* in commodities made her rich.

1. In implementing the "motor voter" bill has made it easier for people to register to vote.
2. She sank the basket was the reason they won the game.
3. Just because situations change, does not change the characters' hopes and dreams.
4. By dropping the course would be his only chance to avoid a low GPA.
5. Even though she works for a tobacco company does not mean that she is against laws prohibiting smoking in restaurants.

42c Revising Faulty Predication

Faulty predication occurs when a sentence's predicate does not logically complete its subject.

1 Incorrect Use of *Be*

Faulty predication is especially common in sentences that contain a **linking verb**—a form of the verb *be*, for example—and a subject complement.

Mounting costs and decreasing revenues ~~were~~ *caused* the downfall of the hospital.

This sentence incorrectly states that mounting costs and decreasing revenues *were* the downfall of the hospital when, in fact, they were the *reasons* for its downfall.

2 *Is When* or *Is Where*

Faulty predication also occurs in one-sentence definitions that contain a construction like *is where* or *is when*. In a definition, *is* must be preceded and followed by a noun or noun phrase.

Taxidermy is ~~where you construct~~ *the construction of* a lifelike representation of an animal from its preserved skin.

3 *The Reason . . . Is Because*

A similar type of problem occurs when the phrase *the reason is* precedes *because*. In this situation, *because* (which means "for the reason that") is redundant and should be deleted.

The reason we drive is ~~because~~ *that* we are afraid to fly.

GRAMMAR CHECKER

REVISING FAULTY PREDICATION

Your word processor's grammar checker will highlight certain instances of faulty predication and offer suggestions for revision.

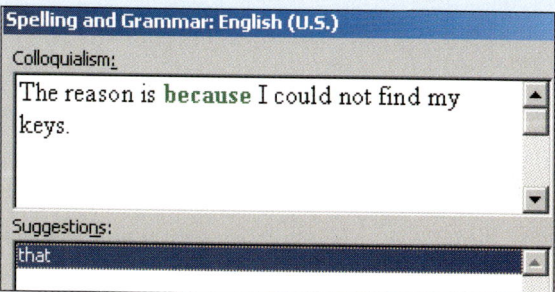

Your grammar checker will also highlight some other causes of awkward or confusing sentences, including shifts in voice, person, and number, and will frequently offer revision suggestions. However, the grammar checker will miss many unwarranted shifts, mixed constructions, and incomplete or illogical comparisons.

■ EXERCISE 4

Revise the following sentences to eliminate faulty predication. Keep in mind that each sentence may be revised in more than one way.

Example: ~~The reason~~ Traffic ~~traffic~~ jams occur at 9 a.m. and 5 p.m. ~~is~~ because too many people work traditional rather than staggered hours.

1. Inflation is when the purchasing power of currency declines.
2. Hypertension is where blood pressure is elevated.
3. Television and the Internet were the decline in students' reading scores.
4. Some people say the reason for the increasing violence in American cities is because guns are too easily available.
5. The reason for all the congestion in American cities is because too many people live too close together.

42d Revising Incomplete or Illogical Comparisons

A comparison tells how two things are alike or unlike. When you make a comparison, be sure it is *complete* (that readers can tell which two items are being compared) and *logical* (that it equates two comparable items).

My chemistry course is harder ^*than Nina's*. (What two things are being compared?)

A pig's intelligence is greater than a ^*dog's* ~~dog~~. (illogically compares *a pig's intelligence* to *a dog*)

■ EXERCISE 5

Revise the following sentences to correct any incomplete or illogical comparisons.

Example: Technology-based industries are concerned about inflation as much as service industries ^*are*.

1. Opportunities in technical writing are more promising than business writing.
2. Technical writing is more challenging.
3. In some ways, technical writing requires more attention to detail and is, therefore, more difficult.
4. Business writers are concerned about clarity as much as technical writers.
5. Technology-based industries may one day create more writing opportunities than any other industry.

PART 10

Using Words Effectively

43 Choosing Words 556
- **43a** Choosing an Appropriate Level of Diction 556
- **43b** Choosing the Right Word 559
- **43c** Using Figures of Speech 561
- **43d** Avoiding Inappropriate Language 563
- **43e** Avoiding Offensive Language 566

44 Using a Dictionary 570
- **44a** Understanding a Dictionary Entry 570
- **44b** Surveying Dictionaries 574

45 Improving Spelling 575
- **45a** Understanding Spelling and Pronunciation 575
- **45b** Learning Spelling Rules 577
- **45c** Developing Spelling Skills 581

43

Choosing Words

❓ FAQs

How formal should I be in my college writing? (p. 558)
How do I know whether I'm using exactly the right word? (p. 559)
What is a cliché? (p. 564)
What is sexist language, and how can I avoid it? (p. 567)

43a Choosing an Appropriate Level of Diction

Diction, which comes from the Latin word for *say,* refers to the choice and use of words. Different audiences and situations call for different levels of diction.

1 Formal Diction

Formal diction is grammatically correct and uses words familiar to an educated audience. A writer who uses formal diction often maintains emotional distance from the audience by using the impersonal *one* rather than the more personal *I* and *you*. In addition, the tone of the writing—as determined by word choice, sentence structure, and choice of subject—is dignified and objective.

> We learn to perceive in the sense that we learn to respond to things in particular ways because of the contingencies of which they are a part. We may perceive the sun, for example, simply because it is an extremely powerful stimulus, but it has been a permanent part of the environment of the species throughout its evolution, and more specific behavior with respect to it could have been selected by contingencies of survival (as it has been in many other species). (B. F. Skinner, *Beyond Freedom and Dignity*)

> **ESL TIP**
>
> Some of the expressions you learn from other students or from television are not appropriate for use in formal writing. When you hear new expressions, pay attention to the contexts in which they are used.

2 Informal Diction

Informal diction is the language that people use in conversation and in personal letters and informal emails. You should use informal diction in your college writing only to reproduce speech or dialect or to give a paper a conversational tone.

Colloquial Diction. **Colloquial diction** is the language of everyday speech. Contractions—*isn't, I'm*—are typical colloquialisms, as are **clipped forms**—*phone* for *telephone, TV* for *television, dorm* for *dormitory.* Other colloquialisms include placeholders such as *kind of* and utility words such as *nice* for *acceptable, funny* for *odd,* and *great* for almost anything. Colloquial English also includes expressions such as *get across* for *communicate, come up with* for *find,* and *check out* for *investigate.*

Slang. **Slang,** language that calls attention to itself, is used to establish or reinforce identity within a group—urban teenagers, rock musicians, or computer users, for example. One characteristic of slang vocabulary is that it is usually relatively short-lived, coming into existence and fading out much more quickly than other words do. Because slang terms can emerge and disappear so quickly, no dictionary—even a dictionary of slang—can list all or even most of the slang terms currently in use. Some slang words, however, eventually lose their slang status and become accepted as part of the language.

Regionalisms. **Regionalisms** are words, expressions, and idiomatic forms that are used in particular geographical areas but may not be understood by a general audience. In eastern Tennessee, for example, a paper bag is a *poke,* and empty soda bottles are *dope bottles.* In Lancaster, Pennsylvania, which has a large Amish population, it is not unusual to hear an elderly person say *darest* for *dare not* or *daresome* for *adventurous.* And New Yorkers stand *on line* for a movie, whereas people in most other parts of the country stand *in line.*

Nonstandard Diction. **Nonstandard diction** refers to words and expressions not generally considered a part of standard English—words such as *ain't, nohow, anywheres, nowheres, hisself,* and *theirselves.*

No absolute rules distinguish standard from nonstandard usage. In fact, some linguists reject the idea of nonstandard usage altogether, arguing that this designation relegates both the language and those who use it to second-class status.

NOTE: Keep in mind that colloquial expressions, slang, regionalisms, and nonstandard diction are almost always inappropriate in your college writing.

GRAMMAR CHECKER

SETTING THE WRITING STYLE LEVEL

To increase your grammar checker's ability to detect incorrect constructions in your college writing, you can change the writing style level from *Standard* to *Formal* or *Technical* (see Figure 43.1).

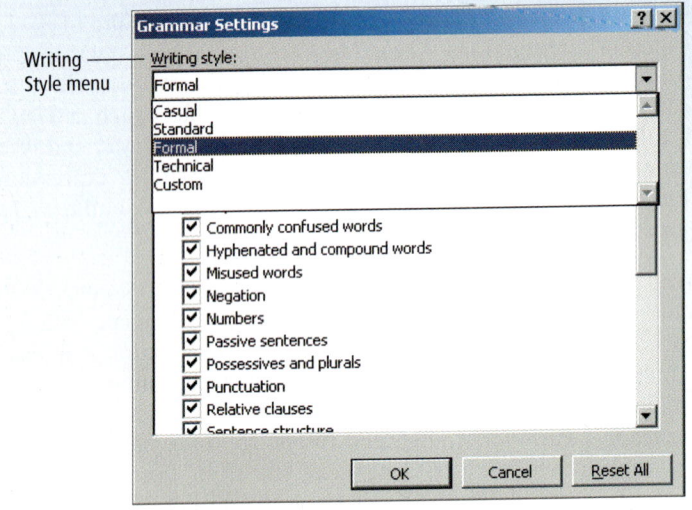

FIGURE 43.1 *Microsoft Word* Grammar Settings tool.

3 College Writing

The level of diction appropriate for college writing depends on your assignment and your audience. A personal-experience essay calls for a somewhat informal style, but a research paper, an exam, or a report requires a more formal level of diction. In general, most college writing falls somewhere between formal and informal English, using a conversational tone but maintaining grammatical correctness and using a specialized vocabulary when the situation requires it. (This is the level of diction that is used in this book.)

COMPUTER TIP   academic.cengage.com/eng/kirsznermandell

DICTION AND ELECTRONIC COMMUNICATION

In email, instant messages, and text messages, writers commonly use **emoticons**—typed characters, such as :-) or ;-), that indicate emotions or feelings—and **acronyms**, such as BTW (by the way) or LOL (laughing out loud). Although these typographical devices are common in informal electronic communication, they are inappropriate in formal electronic or print situations.

EXERCISE 1

The diction of this paragraph, from Toni Cade Bambara's short story "The Hammer Man," is informal. In order to represent the speech of a young girl, the writer intentionally uses slang expressions and nonstandard diction. Underline the words that identify the diction of this paragraph as informal. Then, rewrite the paragraph, using standard diction.

> Manny was supposed to be crazy. That was his story. To say you were bad put some people off. But to say you were crazy, well, you were officially not to be messed with. So that was his story. On the other hand, after I called him what I called him and said a few choice things about his mother, his face did go through some piercing changes. And I did kind of wonder if maybe he sure was nuts. I didn't wait to find out. I got in the wind. And then he waited for me on my stoop all day and all night, not hardly speaking to the people going in and out. And he was there all day Saturday, with his sister bringing him peanut-butter sandwiches and cream sodas. He must've gone to the bathroom right there cause every time I looked out the kitchen window, there he was. And Sunday, too. I got to thinking the boy was mad.

EXERCISE 2

After reading the following paragraph, underline the words and phrases that identify it as formal diction. Then, rewrite the paragraph, using the level of diction that you would use in your college writing. Consult a dictionary if necessary.

> In looking at many small points of difference between species, which, as far as our ignorance permits us to judge, seem quite unimportant, we must not forget that climate, food, etc., have no doubt produced some direct effect. It is also necessary to bear in mind that owing to the law of correlation, when one part varies and the variations are accumulated through natural selection, other modifications, often of the most unexpected nature, will ensue. (Charles Darwin, *The Origin of Species*)

43b Choosing the Right Word

Choosing the right word to use in a particular context is very important. If you use the wrong word—or even *almost* the right one—you run the risk of misrepresenting your ideas.

1 Denotation and Connotation

A word's **denotation** is its basic dictionary meaning, what it stands for without any emotional associations. A word's **connotations** are the emotional, social, and political associations it has in addition to its denotative meaning.

Word	Denotation	Connotations
politician	someone who holds a political office	opportunist; wheeler-dealer

Selecting a word with the appropriate connotation can be challenging. For example, the word *skinny* has negative connotations, whereas *thin* is neutral, and *slender* is positive. And words and expressions such as *mentally ill*, *insane*, *neurotic*, *crazy*, *psychopathic*, and *emotionally disturbed*, although similar in meaning, have different emotional, social, and political connotations that affect the way people respond. If you use terms without considering their connotations, you run the risk of undercutting your credibility, to say nothing of confusing and possibly angering your readers.

> **ESL TIP**
>
> Dictionary entries sometimes give a word's connotations as well as its denotations. You can also increase your understanding of a word's connotations by paying attention to the context in which the word appears.

■ EXERCISE 3

The following words have negative connotations. For each, list one word with a similar meaning whose connotation is neutral and another whose connotation is positive.

Example: *Negative*   skinny
Neutral   thin
Favorable   slender

1. deceive
2. antiquated
3. pushy
4. pathetic
5. cheap
6. blunder
7. weird
8. politician
9. shack
10. stench

2 Euphemisms

A **euphemism** is a polite term used in place of a blunt or harsh term that describes a subject that many people consider offensive or unpleasant. College writing is no place for euphemisms. Say what you mean—*pregnant*, not *expecting*; *died*, not *passed away*; and *strike*, not *work stoppage*.

3 Specific and General Words

Specific words refer to particular persons, items, or events; **general** words denote entire classes or groups. *Queen Elizabeth II*, for example, is more specific than *monarch*; *jeans* is more specific than *clothing*; and *SUV* is more specific than *vehicle*. You can use general words to describe entire classes of items, but you should use specific words to clarify such generalizations.

> **CLOSE-UP**
>
> **USING SPECIFIC WORDS**
>
> Take particular care to avoid general words such as *nice*, *great*, and *terrific* that say nothing and could be used in almost any sentence. These utility words convey only enthusiasm, not precise meanings. Replace them with more specific words.

See 37a2

4 Abstract and Concrete Words

Abstract words—*beauty*, *truth*, *justice*, and so on—refer to ideas, qualities, or conditions that cannot be perceived by the senses. **Concrete** words name things that readers can see, hear, taste, smell, or touch. As with general and specific words, whether a word is abstract or concrete is relative. The more concrete your words and phrases, the more vivid the image you evoke in the reader.

■ **EXERCISE 4**

Revise the following paragraph from a job application letter by substituting specific, concrete language for general or abstract words and phrases.

> I have had several part-time jobs lately. Some of them would qualify me for the position you advertised. In my most recent job, I sold products in a store. My supervisor said I was a good worker who had a number of valuable qualities. I am used to dealing with different types of people in different settings. I feel that my qualifications would make me a good candidate for your job opening.

43c Using Figures of Speech

Writers often use **figures of speech** (such as *similes* and *metaphors*) to go beyond the literal meanings of words. By doing so, they add interest and variety to their writing. Although you should not overuse figures of speech, do not be afraid to use them when you think they will help you communicate your ideas to your readers.

CLOSE-UP

COMMONLY USED FIGURES OF SPEECH

- A **simile** is a comparison between two essentially unlike things on the basis of a shared quality. A simile is introduced by *like* or *as*.

  Like travelers with exotic destinations on their minds, the graduates were remarkably forgetful. (Maya Angelou, *I Know Why the Caged Bird Sings*)

- A **metaphor** also compares two essentially dissimilar things, but instead of saying that one thing is *like* another, it *equates* them.

  Perhaps it is easy for those who have never felt the stings and darts of segregation to say, "Wait." (Martin Luther King Jr., "Letter from Birmingham Jail")

- An **analogy** explains an unfamiliar item or concept by comparing it to a more familiar one.

  According to Robert Frost, writing free verse is similar to playing tennis without a net.

- **Personification** gives an idea or inanimate object human attributes, feelings, or powers.

  Truth strikes us from behind, and in the dark, as well as from before in broad daylight. (Henry David Thoreau, *Journals*)

- **Hyperbole** (or overstatement) is an intentional exaggeration for emphasis. For example, Jonathan Swift uses hyperbole in his essay "A Modest Proposal" when he suggests that eating Irish babies would help the English solve their food shortage.

- **Understatement** intentionally downplays the seriousness of a situation or sentiment by saying less than is really meant.

  According to Mao Tse-tung, a revolution is not a tea party.

EXERCISE 5

Read the following paragraph from Mark Twain's *Life on the Mississippi*, and identify as many figures of speech as you can.

   Now when I had mastered the language of this water, and had come to know every trifling feature that bordered the great river as familiarly as I knew the letters of the alphabet, I had made a valuable acquisition. But I had lost something, too. I had lost something which could never be restored to me while I lived. All the grace, the beauty, the poetry, had gone out of the majestic river! I still keep in mind a certain wonderful sunset which I witnessed when steamboating was new to me. A broad expanse of the river was turned to blood; in the middle distance the red hue brightened into gold, through which a solitary log came floating black and conspicuous; in one place a long, slanting mark lay sparkling upon the water; in another the surface was broken by boiling, tumbling rings, that were as many-tinted as an opal; where the ruddy flush was faintest, was a smooth spot that was covered with graceful circles and radiating lines, ever so delicately traced; the shore on our left was densely wooded, and the somber shadow that fell from this forest was broken in one place by a long, ruffled trail that shone like silver; and high above the forest wall a clean-stemmed dead tree waved a single leafy bough that glowed like a flame in the unobstructed splendor that was flowing from the sun. There were graceful curves, reflected images, woody heights, soft distances; and over the whole scene, far and near, the dissolving lights drifted steadily, enriching it every passing moment with new marvels of coloring.

■ **EXERCISE 6**

Rewrite the following sentences, adding a figure of speech to each sentence to make the ideas more vivid and exciting. Identify each figure of speech you use.

Example: The room was cool and still✓ *like the inside of a cathedral.* (simile)

1. The last of the marathon runners limped toward the finish line.
2. The breeze gently stirred the wind chimes.
3. Jeremy has shoulder-length hair and a high forehead, and he wears small, red glasses.
4. The computer classroom was quiet.
5. The demolition crew worked slowly but efficiently.
6. Interstate highways often make for tedious driving.
7. Diego found calculus easy.
8. Music is essentially mathematical.
9. Katrina claims her dog is far more intelligent than her brother is.
10. Emotions are curious things.

43d Avoiding Inappropriate Language

1 Jargon

Jargon, the specialized or technical vocabulary of a trade, a profession, or an academic discipline, is useful for communicating in the field for which it was developed. Outside that field, however, it is often imprecise and confusing. For example, medical doctors may say that a procedure is *contraindicated* or that they are going to carry out a *differential diagnosis.* Business executives may want departments to *interface* effectively, and sociologists may identify the need for *perspectivistic thinking* to achieve organizational goals. If they are addressing other professionals in their respective fields, these terms can facilitate communication. If, however, they are addressing a general audience, these terms have the opposite effect and should therefore be avoided.

2 Neologisms

Neologisms are newly coined words that are not part of standard English. New situations call for new words, and frequently such words become part of the language—*email, carjack,* and *outsource,* for example. Others, however, are never fully accepted. For example, questionable neologisms are created when the suffix *-wise* is added to existing words—creating nonstandard words such as *weatherwise, sportswise, timewise,* and *productwise.*

See Ch. 44

If you are not sure whether to use a word, look it up in a current college **dictionary**. If the word is not there, you probably should not use it.

3 Pretentious Diction

Good writing is clear and direct, not pompous or flowery. Revise to eliminate **pretentious diction,** inappropriately elevated and wordy language.

As I fell ~~into slumber~~ *asleep*, I ~~cogitated~~ *thought* about my day ~~ambling~~ *hiking* through ~~the splendor of~~ the Appalachian Mountains.

> **CLOSE-UP**
>
> **PRETENTIOUS DICTION**
>
> Frequently, pretentious diction is formal diction used in a relatively informal situation. In such a context, it is always out of place. For every pretentious word, there is usually a clear and direct alternative.
>
> | Pretentious | Clear |
> |---|---|
> | ascertain | discover |
> | commence | start |
> | implement | carry out |
> | minuscule | small |
> | reside | live |
> | terminate | end |
> | utilize | use |

4 Clichés

Figures of speech, such as metaphors and similes, stimulate thought by calling up vivid images in a reader's mind. When overused, however, figures of speech lose their power and become clichés—pat, meaningless phrases.

off the beaten path	happy as a clam
sit on the fence	a shot in the arm
free as a bird	smooth sailing
spread like wildfire	fit like a glove
Herculean efforts	fighting like cats and dogs

Writers sometimes resort to clichés when they run out of ideas. If readers sense that you are filling your writing with empty, tired phrases, they will lose interest and disregard your ideas. To keep their attention, you should take the time to think of original expressions that will give your writing the impact and appeal your ideas deserve.

ESL TIP

Many ESL students learn a long list of English idioms in an ESL class. Some of these idioms, however, have become clichés. Although becoming familiar with these idioms can help you understand them when you encounter them, remember that college instructors discourage students from using clichés in their writing, preferring language that is more original and more precise.

5 Mixed Metaphors

A **mixed metapho**r is created when a writer combines two or more incompatible images. The result can be illogical, humorous, or both. For this reason, you should revise mixed metaphors to make your imagery consistent.

> **Mixed:** Management <u>extended an olive branch</u> in an attempt <u>to break some of the ice</u> between the company and the striking workers.
>
> **Revised:** Management extended an olive branch with the hope that the striking workers would take it.

■ EXERCISE 7

Rewrite the following passage, eliminating jargon, neologisms, pretentious diction, and clichés. Feel free to add words and phrases and to reorganize sentences to make their meaning clear. If you are not certain about the meaning or status of a word, consult a dictionary.

At a given point in time, there coexisted a hare and a tortoise. The aforementioned rabbit was overheard by the tortoise to be blowing his horn about the degree of speed he could attain. The latter quadruped thereupon put forth a challenge to the former by advancing the suggestion that they interact in a running competition. The hare acquiesced, laughing to himself. The animals concurred in the decision to acquire the services of a certain fox to act in the capacity of judicial refereee. This particular fox was in agreement, and, consequently, implementation of the plan was facilitated. In a relatively small amount of time, the hare had considerably outdistanced the tortoise and, after ascertaining that he himself was in a more optimized position distancewise than the tortoise, he arrived at the unilateral decision to avail himself of a respite. He made the implicit assumption in so doing that he would anticipate no difficulty in overtaking the tortoise when his suspension of activity ceased. An unfortunate development racewise occurred when the hare's somnolent state endured for a longer-than-anticipated time frame, facilitating the tortoise's victory in the contest and affirming the concept of unhurriedness and firmness triumphing in competitive situations. Thus, the hare was unable to snatch victory out of the jaws of defeat.

■ EXERCISE 8

Go through a newspaper or magazine, and list the examples of jargon, neologisms, pretentious diction, clichés, and mixed metaphors that you find. Then, substitute more appropriate words for the ones you identified. Be prepared to discuss your interpretation of each word and of the word you chose to put in its place.

43e Avoiding Offensive Language

Because the language you use not only expresses your ideas, but also shapes your thinking, you should avoid using words that insult or degrade others.

1 Stereotypes

Racial and Ethnic. When referring to any racial, ethnic, or religious group, use words with neutral connotations or words that the group uses in *formal* speech or writing to refer to itself.

Age. Avoid potentially offensive labels relating to age. Many older people like to call themselves *senior citizens* or *seniors*, and these terms are commonly used by the media and the government.

Class. Do not demean certain jobs because they are low paying or praise others because they have impressive titles. Similarly, do not use words—*hick, cracker, redneck,* or *trailer trash,* for example—that denigrate people based on their social class.

Sexual Orientation. Always use neutral terms (such as *gay* and *lesbian*), but do not mention a person's sexual orientation unless it is relevant to your discussion.

2 Sexist Language

Sexist language entails much more than the use of derogatory words, such as *hunk, chick,* and *bimbo.* Assuming that some professions are exclusive to one gender—for instance, that *nurse* denotes only women and that *doctor* denotes only men—is also sexist. So is the use of outdated job titles, such as *postman* for *letter carrier, fireman* for *firefighter,* and *stewardess* for *flight attendant.*

Sexist language also occurs when a writer fails to apply the same terminology to both men and women. For example, refer to two scientists with PhDs not as Dr. Sagan and Mrs. Yallow, but as Dr. Sagan and Dr. Yallow. Refer to two writers as James and Wharton, or Henry James and Edith Wharton, not James and Mrs. Wharton.

In your writing, always use *women*—not *girls, gals,* or *ladies*—when referring to adult females. Use *Ms.* as the form of address when a woman's marital status is unknown or irrelevant. (If the woman you are addressing refers to herself as *Mrs.* or *Miss,* however, use the form of address she prefers.) Finally, avoid using the generic *he* or *him* when your subject could be either male or female. Use the third-person plural (*they*) or the phrase *he or she* (not *he/she*).

> **Sexist:** Before boarding, each passenger should make certain that he has his ticket.
>
> **Revised:** Before boarding, passengers should make certain that they have their tickets.
>
> **Revised:** Before boarding, each passenger should make certain that he or she has a ticket.

NOTE: When trying to avoid sexist use of *he* and *him* in your writing, be careful not to use the plural pronoun *they* or *their* to refer to a singular antecedent.

> ~~Any driver~~ Drivers caught speeding should have their driving privileges suspended.

> **CLOSE-UP**
>
> **ELIMINATING SEXIST LANGUAGE**
>
> For every sexist usage, there is usually a nonsexist alternative.
>
> | Sexist Usage | Possible Revisions |
> |---|---|
> | Mankind | People, human beings |
> | Man's accomplishments | Human accomplishments |
> | Man-made | Synthetic |
> | Female engineer/lawyer/accountant, and so on; male model | Engineer/lawyer/accountant, and so on; model |
> | Policeman/woman | Police officer |
> | Salesman/woman/girl | Salesperson, sales representative |
> | Businessman/woman | Businessperson, executive |
> | <u>Everyone</u> should complete <u>his</u> application by Tuesday. | <u>Everyone</u> should complete <u>his or her</u> application by Tuesday. <u>All students</u> should complete <u>their</u> applications by Tuesday. |

■ EXERCISE 9

Suggest at least one alternative form for each of the following words or phrases. In each case, comment on the advantages and disadvantages of the alternative you recommend. If you feel that a particular term is not sexist, explain why.

forefathers	Girl Friday
man-eating shark	point man
manpower	draftsman
workman's compensation	man overboard
men at work	fisherman
waitress	foreman
first baseman	manned space program
congressman	gentleman's agreement
manhunt	no man's land
longshoreman	spinster
committeeman	old maid
(to) man the battle stations	old wives' tale

■ EXERCISE 10

Each of the following pairs of terms includes a feminine form that was at one time in wide use; most are still used to some extent. Which do you think are likely to remain in our language for some time, and which do you think will disappear? Explain your reasoning.

heir/heiress
benefactor/benefactress
murderer/murderess
actor/actress
hero/heroine
host/hostess
aviator/aviatrix
executor/executrix

author/authoress
poet/poetess
tailor/seamstress
comedian/comedienne
villain/villainess
prince/princess
widow/widower

44

Using a Dictionary

❓ FAQs

What kind of dictionary should I use? *(p. 570)*
Should I use a thesaurus? *(p. 572)*
Is an electronic dictionary better than a print dictionary? *(p. 574)*

44a Understanding a Dictionary Entry

Every writer should own a dictionary. The most widely used type of dictionary is a one-volume **desk dictionary** or **college dictionary**.

To fit a lot of information into a small space, dictionaries use a system of symbols, abbreviations, and typefaces (see Figure 44.1). Consult the preface of your dictionary to determine how its system operates.

1 Entry Word, Pronunciation Guide, and Part-of-Speech Label

The **entry word,** which appears in boldface at the beginning of the entry, gives the spelling of a word and indicates how the word is divided into syllables.

> col • or *n.* Also chiefly British col • our

The **pronunciation guide** appears in parentheses or between slashes after the main entry. Dictionaries use symbols to represent sounds, and an explanation of these symbols usually appears at the bottom of each page or across the bottom of facing pages throughout the alphabetical listing.

Abbreviations called **part-of-speech labels** indicate parts of speech and grammatical forms.

See 48a

If a verb is regular, the entry provides only the base form of the verb. If a verb is irregular, the part-of-speech label indicates the irregular principal parts of the verb.

> with • draw . . . *v.* -drew, -drawn, -drawing

In addition, the label indicates whether a verb is transitive (*tr.*), intransitive (*intr.*), or both.

570

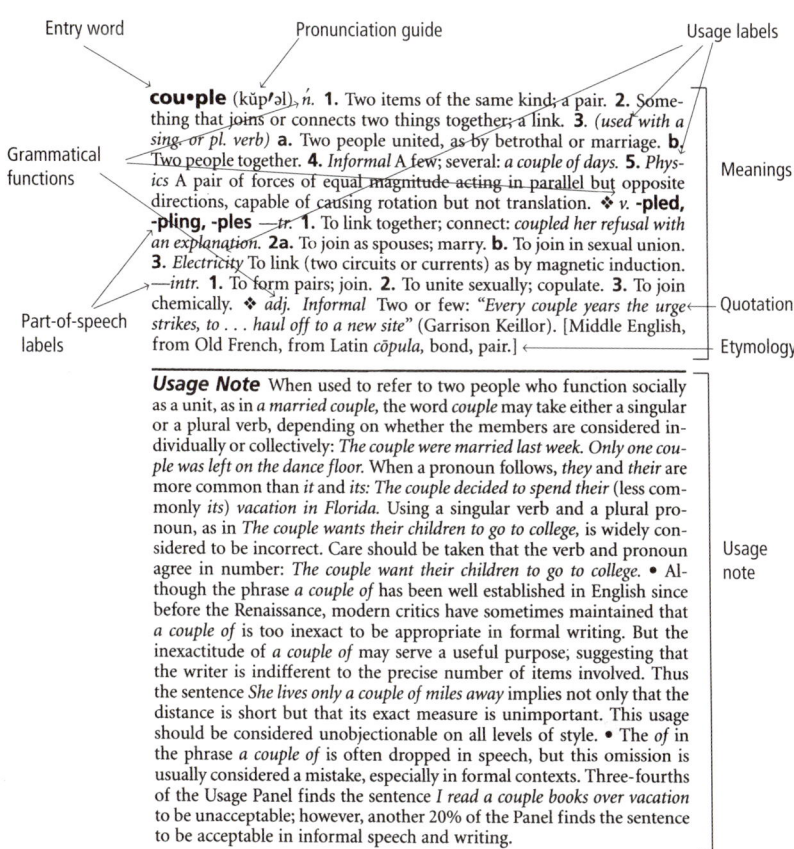

FIGURE 44.1 Entry from *The American Heritage Dictionary of the English Language*.

Part-of-speech labels also indicate the plural form of irregular nouns. (When the plural form is regular, it is not shown.)

child ... *n. pl.* chil · dren

Finally, part-of-speech labels indicate the <u>comparative and superlative forms</u> of both regular and irregular adjectives and adverbs.

See 50d

red ... *adj.* red · der; red · dest

2 Meanings

Some dictionaries give the most common meaning first and then list less common ones. Others begin with the oldest meaning and move to the most current ones. Check the preface of your dictionary to find out how its entries are arranged.

3 Etymology

The **etymology** of a word—its history, its evolution over the years—appears in brackets either before or after the list of meanings. For example, *The American Heritage Dictionary of the English Language* shows that *couple* came into Middle English from Old French and into Old French from Latin.

4 Synonyms and Antonyms

A dictionary entry often lists synonyms (and occasionally antonyms) in addition to definitions. **Synonyms** are words that have similar meanings, such as *well* and *healthy*. **Antonyms** are words that have opposite meanings, such as *courage* and *cowardice*.

CLOSE-UP

USING A THESAURUS

When you consult a print or online **thesaurus,** a list of synonyms and antonyms, remember that no two words have exactly the same meanings. Use synonyms carefully, checking your dictionary to make sure the connotation of the synonym is very close to that of the original word.

COMPUTER TIP academic.cengage.com/eng/kirsznermandell

USING AN ELECTRONIC THESAURUS

A good way to find synonyms is to use the Thesaurus tool in your word-processing program. With your cursor, highlight the word you want to find a synonym for, then select Language from the Tools menu, click Thesaurus, and then select a synonym from the list provided (see Figure 44.2). Before replacing the word, check the meaning of the synonym by clicking Look Up.

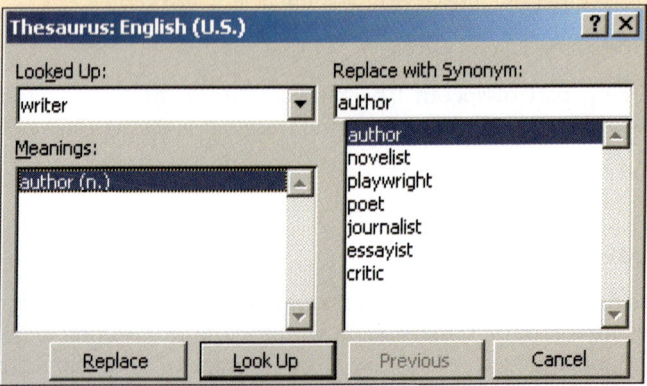

FIGURE 44.2 *Microsoft Word* Thesaurus tool.

5 Idioms

Dictionary entries often show how certain words are used in set expressions called **idioms**. The meaning of such phrases cannot always be determined from the words alone. For example, what would someone learning English make of the expressions "catch a cold" and "take a walk"?

Dictionaries also indicate the idiomatic use of prepositions.

ESL
63e

6 Usage Labels

Dictionaries use **usage labels** to indicate in what contexts words are acceptable. (Where such labels involve value judgments, dictionaries differ.) Among these labels are *nonstandard* (in wide use but not considered standard usage), *informal/colloquial* (part of the language of conversation and acceptable in informal writing), *slang* (appropriate only in extremely informal situations), *dialect/regional* (limited to a certain geographical region), *obsolete* (no longer in use), *archaic/rare* (once common but now seldom used), and *poetic* (common only in poetry).

■ EXERCISE 1

Use your college dictionary to help you answer the following questions about grammatical forms.

1. What are the principal parts of the following verbs: *drink*, *deify*, *carol*, *draw*, and *ring*?
2. Which of the following nouns can be used as verbs: *minister*, *council*, *command*, *magistrate*, *mother*, and *lord*?
3. What are the plural forms of these nouns: *silo*, *sheep*, *seed*, *scissors*, *genetics*, and *alchemy*?
4. What are the comparative and superlative forms of the following adverbs and adjectives: *fast*, *airy*, *good*, *mere*, *homey*, and *unlucky*?
5. Are the verbs *bias*, *halt*, *dissatisfy*, *die*, and *turn* transitive, intransitive, or both? Copy from the dictionary the phrase or sentence that illustrates the uses of each verb.

■ EXERCISE 2

Use your college dictionary to help you determine the restrictions on the use of the following words.

1. irregardless
2. apse
3. flunk
4. lorry
5. kirk
6. gofer
7. whilst
8. sine
9. bannock
10. blowhard

44b Surveying Dictionaries

An **abridged dictionary** is condensed from a more complete collection of words and meanings. Even so, a good hardback abridged dictionary will contain about 1,500 pages and about 150,000 entries. A paperback dictionary—which contains fewer entries, treated in less detail—is adequate for checking spelling, but for reference, you should consult a hardback abridged dictionary, such as *The American Heritage College Dictionary*, *The Concise Oxford Dictionary*, *The Random House College Dictionary*, *Merriam-Webster's Collegiate Dictionary*, or *Webster's New World College Dictionary*.

COMPUTER TIP   academic.cengage.com/eng/kirsznermandell

ELECTRONIC DICTIONARIES

Electronic dictionaries include the same amount of information that one-volume desk dictionaries have. Electronic dictionaries come in two forms—CD-ROM and online. Typically, you have to download a CD-ROM dictionary into your hard drive before you can use it with your word-processing program. To use an online dictionary, you have to log on to a Web site such as <http://www.merriam-webster.com>.

ESL TIP

A number of special dictionaries are designed to help ESL writers. Two useful dictionaries are *Heinle's Newbury House Dictionary of American English*, 4th edition (available online at <http://nhd.heinle.com>) and *Heinle's Basic Newbury House Dictionary of American English*, 2nd edition.

When you are looking for a detailed history of a word or when you want to look up a rare usage, you will need to consult an **unabridged dictionary**, which presents a comprehensive survey of all words in a language.

The Oxford English Dictionary (*OED*) is considered one of the foremost English-language dictionaries in the world. The *OED* (available in CD-ROM and online as well as in print) consists of twenty volumes plus four supplements and contains more than 500,000 definitions, chronologically arranged, and more than two million illustrative quotations.

45

Improving Spelling

❓ FAQs

Why do I still need to proofread if I use a spell checker? (p. 577)
Are there any spelling rules that I can memorize? (p. 577)
What can I do to become a better speller? (p. 581)

Most people can spell even difficult words "almost correctly"; usually only a letter or two are wrong. For this reason, memorizing a few rules and their exceptions and learning the correct spelling of the most commonly misspelled words can help you become a better speller.

45a Understanding Spelling and Pronunciation

Because pronunciation often provides few clues to English spelling, you need to memorize the spellings of many words and use a dictionary or spell checker regularly.

1 Vowels in Unstressed Positions

Many unstressed vowels sound exactly alike. For instance, it is hard to tell from pronunciation alone that the *i* in *terrible* is not an *a*. In addition, the unstressed vowels *a*, *e*, and *i* are impossible to distinguish in the suffixes *-able* and *-ible*, *-ance* and *-ence*, and *-ant* and *-ent*.

comfort<u>a</u>ble	brilli<u>a</u>nce	serv<u>a</u>nt
compat<u>i</u>ble	excell<u>e</u>nce	independ<u>e</u>nt

2 Silent Letters

Some English words contain silent letters, such as the *b* in *climb* and the *t* in *mortgage*.

ai<u>s</u>le	depo<u>t</u>	<u>p</u>neumonia
clim<u>b</u>	<u>k</u>night	si<u>l</u>houette
condem<u>n</u>	mor<u>t</u>gage	so<u>v</u>ereign

575

3 Words That Are Often Pronounced Carelessly

Most of us pronounce words rather carelessly in everyday speech. Consequently, when spelling, we may leave out, add, or transpose letters.

can<u>di</u>date	lib<u>r</u>ary	reco<u>g</u>nize
enviro<u>n</u>ment	light<u>n</u>ing	<u>s</u>pecific
Feb<u>r</u>uary	nuc<u>l</u>ear	suppose<u>d</u> to
gove<u>r</u>nment	pe<u>r</u>form	su<u>r</u>prise
hun<u>d</u>red	quan<u>t</u>ity	use<u>d</u> to

4 American and British Spellings

Some words are spelled one way in the United States and another way in Great Britain and the Commonwealth nations.

American	**British**
color	colour
defense	defence
honor	honour
judgment	judgement
theater	theatre
toward	towards
traveled	travelled

5 Homophones

Homophones are words—such as *accept* and *except*—that are pronounced alike but spelled differently.

accept	to receive
except	other than
affect	to have an influence on (*verb*)
effect	result (*noun*); to cause (*verb*)
its	possessive of *it*
it's	contraction of *it is*
principal	most important (*adjective*); head of a school (*noun*)
principle	a basic truth; rule of conduct

For a full list of these and other homophones, along with their meanings and sentences illustrating their use, **see the Glossary of Usage.**

> **CLOSE-UP**
>
> **ONE WORD OR TWO?**
>
> Some words may be written as one word or two, depending on meaning.

any way vs. *anyway*
The early pioneers made the trip west any way they could.
It began to rain, but the game continued anyway.

every day vs. *everyday*
Every day brings new opportunities.
John thought of his birthday as an everyday event.

Other words are frequently misspelled because people are not sure whether they are one word or two.

One Word	Two Words
already	a lot
cannot	all right
classroom	even though
overweight	no one

Consult a dictionary if you have any doubts about whether a word is written as one word or two.

> **COMPUTER TIP**   academic.cengage.com/eng/kirsznermandell
>
> **RUNNING A SPELL CHECK**
>
> You should always run a spell check, but keep in mind that it will not identify a word that is spelled correctly but used incorrectly—*then* for *than* or *its* for *it's*, for example—or a typo that creates another word, such as *form* for *from*. For this reason, always proofread your papers—even after you have run a spell check.

45b Learning Spelling Rules

Knowing a few reliable rules can help you overcome problems caused by the inconsistency between pronunciation and spelling.

1 The *ie/ei* Combinations

The old rule still stands: use *i* before *e* except after *c* (or when pronounced *ay*, as in *neighbor*).

i before *e*	*ei* after *c*	*ei* pronounced *ay*
belief	ceiling	weigh
chief	deceit	freight
niece	receive	eight

Exceptions: *either, neither, foreign, leisure, weird,* and *seize.* In addition, if the *ie* combination is not pronounced as a unit, the rule does not apply: *atheist, science.*

45b sp ■ Improving Spelling

■ **EXERCISE 1**

Fill in the blanks with the proper *ie* or *ei* combination. After completing the exercise, use your dictionary or spell checker to check your answers.

Example: conc _ei_ ve

1. rec____pt
2. var____ty
3. caff____ne
4. ach____ve
5. kal____doscope
6. misch____f
7. effic____nt
8. v____n
9. spec____s
10. suffic____nt

2 Doubling Final Consonants

The only words that double their consonants before a suffix that begins with a vowel (*-ed*, *-ing*) are those that pass the following three tests:

1. They have one syllable or are stressed on the last syllable.
2. They contain only one vowel in the last syllable.
3. They end in a single consonant.

The word *tap* satisfies all three conditions: it has only one syllable, it contains only one vowel (*a*), and it ends in a single consonant (*p*). Therefore, the final consonant doubles before a suffix beginning with a vowel (*tapped*, *tapping*). The word *relent* meets two of the three conditions: it is stressed on the last syllable, and it has one vowel in the last syllable, but it does not end in a single consonant. Therefore, its final consonant is not doubled (*relented*, *relenting*).

3 Prefixes

The addition of a prefix never affects the spelling of the root (*mis* + *spell* = *misspell*). Some prefixes can cause spelling problems, however, because they are pronounced alike although they are not spelled alike: *ante-/anti-*, *en-/in-*, *per-/pre-*, and *de-/di-*.

antebellum antiaircraft
encircle integrate
perceive prescribe
deduct direct

4 Silent *e* before a Suffix

When a suffix that begins with a consonant is added to a word ending in silent *e*, the *e* is generally kept: *hope/hopeful; lame/lamely; bore/boredom*. **Exceptions:** *argument, truly, ninth, judgment,* and *acknowledgment*.

When a suffix that starts with a vowel is added to a word that ends in a silent *e*, the *e* is generally dropped: *hope/hoping; trace/traced; grieve/grievance; love/lovable*. **Exceptions:** *changeable, noticeable,* and *courageous*.

■ EXERCISE 2

Combine the following words with the suffixes in parentheses. Keep or drop the silent *e* as you see fit; be prepared to explain your choices.

Example: fate (al)
fatal

1. surprise (ing)
2. sure (ly)
3. force (ible)
4. manage (able)
5. due (ly)
6. outrage (ous)
7. service (able)
8. awe (ful)
9. shame (ing)
10. shame (less)

5 *y* before a Suffix

When a word ends in a consonant plus *y*, the *y* generally changes to an *i* when a suffix is added (*beauty + ful = beautiful*). The *y* is kept, however, when the suffix *-ing* is added (*tally + ing = tallying*) and in some one-syllable words (*dry + ness = dryness*).

When a word ends in a vowel plus *y*, the *y* is retained (*joy + ful = joyful; employ + er = employer*). **Exception:** *day + ly = daily*.

■ EXERCISE 3

Add the endings in parentheses to the following words. Change or keep the final *y* as you see fit; be prepared to explain your choices.

Example: party (ing)
partying

1. journey (ing)
2. study (ed)
3. carry (ing)
4. shy (ly)
5. study (ing)
6. sturdy (ness)
7. merry (ment)
8. likely (hood)
9. plenty (ful)
10. supply (er)

6 *seed* Endings

Endings with the sound *seed* are nearly always spelled *cede*, as in *precede, intercede, concede,* and so on. **Exceptions:** *supersede, exceed, proceed,* and *succeed.*

7 -able, -ible

If the root of a word is itself an independent word, the suffix *-able* is most often used. If the root of a word is not an independent word, the suffix *-ible* is most often used.

*com*fort**able**   *com*pat**ible**
*a*gree**able**   *in*cred**ible**
*dr*y**able**   *plaus***ible**

8 Plurals

Most nouns form plurals by adding *s*: *savage/savages, tortilla/tortillas, boat/boats.* There are, however, a number of exceptions.

Words Ending in -f or -fe. Some words ending in *-f* or *-fe* form plurals by changing the *f* to *v* and adding *es* or *s*: *life/lives, self/selves.* Others add just *s*: *belief/beliefs, safe/safes.* Words ending in *-ff* take *s* to form plurals: *tariff/tariffs.*

Words Ending in -y. Most words that end in a consonant followed by *y* form plurals by changing the *y* to *i* and adding *es*: *baby/babies.* **Exceptions:** proper nouns, such as the *Kennedys* (never the *Kennedies*).
Words that end in a vowel followed by a *y* form plurals by adding *s*: *day/days, monkey/monkeys.*

Words Ending in -o. Words that end in a vowel followed by *o* form the plural by adding *s*: *radio/radios, stereo/stereos, zoo/zoos.* Most words that end in a consonant followed by *o* add *es* to form the plural: *tomato/tomatoes, hero/heroes.* **Exceptions:** *silo/silos, piano/pianos, memo/memos,* and *soprano/sopranos.*

Words Ending in -s, -ss, -sh, -ch, -x, and -z. These words form plurals by adding *es*: *Jones/Joneses, mass/masses, rash/rashes, lunch/lunches, box/boxes, buzz/buzzes.* **Exceptions:** Some one-syllable words that end in *-s* or *-z* double their final consonants when forming plurals: *quiz/quizzes.*

Compound Nouns. Compound nouns—nouns formed from two or more words—usually form the plural with the last word in the compound construction: *welfare state/welfare states; snowball/snowballs.*

However, where the first word of the compound noun is more important than the others, form the plural with the first word: *sister-in-law/sisters-in-law, attorney general/attorneys general, hole in one/holes in one.*

Foreign Plurals. Some words, especially those borrowed from Latin or Greek, keep their foreign plurals. Look up a foreign word's plural form in a dictionary if you do not know it.

Singular	Plural
basis	bases
criterion	criteria
datum	data
larva	larvae
medium	media
memorandum	memoranda
stimulus	stimuli

45c Developing Spelling Skills

In addition to studying the rules outlined in 45b, you can take some additional steps to help yourself become a better speller.

1 Making Your Own Spelling List

Keep a list of your own problem words. When you read through a first draft, circle any words whose spellings you are unsure of. Then, look them up in your dictionary or spell checker as you revise, and add them all (even those you have spelled correctly) to your list. When your instructor returns a paper, add to your list any words you have misspelled.

2 Uncovering Patterns of Misspelling

Do you consistently have a problem with plurals or with *-ible/-able* endings? If so, review the spelling rules that apply to these particular problems. By using this strategy, you can eliminate the need to memorize single words.

3 Fixing Each Word in Your Mind

Think of associations that will make the correct spellings stick in your mind. For example, you can remember the correct spelling of *definite* (often misspelled *definate*) by remembering that it contains the word *finite*, which suggests the concept of limit, as does *definite*.

You can recall the *a* in *brilliance* (often misspelled *brilli<u>ence</u>*) by remembering that brilliant people often get A's in their classes.

4 Learning to Distinguish Commonly Confused Words

See 45a5

Learn to distinguish commonly confused **homophones** (words that sound exactly alike but have different spellings and meanings, such as *night* and *knight*) and near-homophones (words that sound similar, such as *accept* and *except*). For a list of homophones, **see the Glossary of Usage.**

PART 11

Understanding Grammar

46 Using Parts of Speech 584
46a Using Nouns 584
46b Using Pronouns 584
46c Using Verbs 586
46d Using Adjectives 588
46e Using Adverbs 589
46f Using Prepositions 590
46g Using Conjunctions 591
46h Using Interjections 592

47 Using Nouns and Pronouns 593
47a Understanding Case 593
47b Determining Pronoun Case in Special Situations 594
47c Revising Pronoun Reference Errors 596

48 Using Verbs 600
48a Understanding Verb Forms 600
48b Understanding Tense 604
48c Understanding Mood 609
48d Understanding Voice 610

49 Revising Agreement Errors 613
49a Making Subjects and Verbs Agree 613
49b Making Pronouns and Antecedents Agree 619

50 Using Adjectives and Adverbs 623
50a Understanding Adjectives and Adverbs 623
50b Using Adjectives 623
50c Using Adverbs 624
50d Using Comparative and Superlative Forms 625
50e Avoiding Illogical Comparatives and Superlatives 627

46

Using Parts of Speech

❓ FAQs

How does a noun function in a sentence? (p. 584)
How does a pronoun function in a sentence? (p. 584)
How does a verb function in a sentence? (p. 586)
How does an adjective function in a sentence? (p. 588)
How does an adverb function in a sentence? (p. 589)
How does a preposition function in a sentence? (p. 590)
How does a conjunction function in a sentence? (p. 591)
How does an interjection function in a sentence? (p. 592)

The eight basic **parts of speech**—the building blocks for all English sentences—are *nouns, pronouns, verbs, adjectives, adverbs, prepositions, conjunctions,* and *interjections*. How a word is classified depends on its function in a sentence.

46a Using Nouns

ESL
63b

Nouns name people, animals, places, things, ideas, actions, or qualities.

A **common noun** names any one of a class of people, places, or things: *artist, judge, building, event, city*.

A **proper noun**, always capitalized, designates a particular person, place, or thing: *Mary Cassatt, World Trade Center, Crimean War*.

A **count noun** names something that can be counted: five *dogs*, two dozen *grapes*.

A **noncount noun** names a quantity that is not countable: *time, dust, work, gold*. Noncount nouns generally have only a singular form.

See
49a5

A **collective noun** designates a group thought of as a unit: *committee, class, navy, band, family*. Collective nouns are generally singular unless the members of the group are referred to as individuals.

An **abstract noun** designates an intangible idea or quality: *love, hate, justice, anger, fear, prejudice*.

46b Using Pronouns

ESL
63c

Pronouns are words used in place of nouns. The word for which a pronoun stands is called its **antecedent**.

Using Pronouns 46b

If you use a <u>quotation</u> in your paper, you must document <u>it</u>. (Pronoun *it* refers to antecedent *quotation*.)

A **personal pronoun** stands for a person or thing. Personal pronouns include *I, me, we, us, my, mine, our, ours, you, your, yours, he, she, it, its, him, his, her, hers, they, them, their,* and *theirs*.

<u>They</u> made <u>her</u> an offer <u>she</u> couldn't refuse.

An **indefinite pronoun** does not refer to any particular person or thing, so it does not require an antecedent. Indefinite pronouns include *another, any, each, few, many, some, nothing, one, anyone, everyone, everybody, everything, someone, something, either,* and *neither*.

See 49b3

<u>Many</u> are called, but <u>few</u> are chosen.

A **reflexive pronoun** ends with *-self* and refers to a recipient of the action that is the same as the actor. The reflexive pronouns are *myself, yourself, himself, herself, itself, oneself, themselves, ourselves,* and *yourselves*.

They found <u>themselves</u> in downtown Pittsburgh.

An **intensive pronoun** emphasizes a noun or pronoun that directly precedes it. (Intensive pronouns have the same form as reflexive pronouns.)

Darrow <u>himself</u> was sure his client was innocent.

A **relative pronoun** introduces an adjective clause or a noun clause in a sentence. Relative pronouns include *which, who, whom, that, what, whose, whatever, whoever, whomever,* and *whichever*.

Gandhi was the charismatic man <u>who</u> helped lead India to independence. (introduces adjective clause)

<u>Whatever</u> happens will be a surprise. (introduces noun clause)

An **interrogative pronoun** introduces a question. Interrogative pronouns include *who, which, what, whom, whose, whoever, whatever,* and *whichever*.

<u>Who</u> was that masked man?

A **demonstrative pronoun** points to a particular thing or group of things. *This, that, these,* and *those* are demonstrative pronouns.

<u>This</u> is one of Shakespeare's early plays.

A **reciprocal pronoun** denotes a mutual relationship. The reciprocal pronouns are *each other* and *one another*. *Each other* indicates a relationship between two individuals; *one another* denotes a relationship among more than two.

Romeo and Juliet declared their love for <u>each other</u>.

Concertgoers jostled <u>one another</u> in the ticket line.

NOTE: Although different types of pronouns may have exactly the same form, they are distinguished from one another by their function in a sentence.

46c Using Verbs

1 Recognizing Verbs

ESL
63a

A <u>verb</u> may express either action or a state of being.

He <u>ran</u> for the train. *(physical action)*

He <u>worried</u> about being late. *(emotional action)*

Elizabeth II <u>became</u> queen after the death of her father, George VI. *(state of being)*

Verbs can be classified into two groups: *main verbs* and *auxiliary verbs*.

Main Verbs. **Main verbs** carry most of the meaning in a sentence. Some main verbs are **action verbs.**

Emily Dickinson <u>wrote</u> poetry.

Other main verbs function as linking verbs. A **linking verb** does not show any physical or emotional action. Its function is to link the sentence's subject to a **subject complement,** a word or phrase that renames or describes the subject.

Carbon disulfide <u>smells</u> bad.

FREQUENTLY USED LINKING VERBS				
appear	believe	look	seem	taste
be	feel	prove	smell	turn
become	grow	remain	sound	

Auxiliary Verbs. **Auxiliary verbs** (also called **helping verbs**), such as *be* and *have,* combine with main verbs to form **verb phrases.** Auxiliary verbs indicate tense, voice, or mood.

[auxiliary] [main verb]   [auxiliary] [main verb]

The train <u>has started</u>. We <u>are leaving</u> soon.

[verb phrase]   [verb phrase]

Certain auxiliary verbs, known as **modal auxiliaries,** indicate necessity, possibility, willingness, obligation, or ability.

In the future, farmers <u>might</u> cultivate seaweed as a food crop.

Coal mining <u>would</u> be safer if dust were controlled in the mines.

MODAL AUXILIARIES			
can	might	ought [to]	will
could	must	shall	would
may	need [to]	should	

2 Recognizing Verbals

Verbals, such as *known* or *swimming* or *to go,* are verb forms that act as adjectives, adverbs, or nouns. A verbal can never serve as a sentence's main verb unless it is used with one or more auxiliary verbs (*has known, should be swimming*). Verbals include *participles, infinitives,* and *gerunds.*

Participles. Virtually every verb has a **present participle,** which ends in *-ing* (*loving, learning, going, writing*), and a **past participle**, which usually ends in *-d* or *-ed* (*agreed, learned*). Some verbs have <u>irregular</u> past participles (*gone, begun, written*). Participles may function in a sentence as adjectives or as nouns.

See 48a2

Twenty brands of <u>running</u> shoes were displayed at the exhibition. (Present participle *running* serves as adjective modifying noun *shoes.*)

The <u>crowded</u> bus went past those waiting at the corner. (Past participle *crowded* serves as adjective modifying noun *bus.*)

The <u>wounded</u> were given emergency first aid. (Past participle *wounded* serves as a noun, the sentence's subject.)

Infinitives. An **infinitive** is made up of *to* and the base form of the verb (*to defeat*). An infinitive may function as an adjective, an adverb, or a noun.

Ann Arbor was clearly the place <u>to be</u>. (Infinitive serves as adjective modifying noun *place.*)

They say that breaking up is hard <u>to do</u>. (Infinitive serves as adverb modifying adjective *hard.*)

Carla went outside <u>to think</u>. (Infinitive serves as adverb modifying verb *went.*)

>   To win was everything. (Infinitive serves as noun, the sentence's subject.)
>
> **Gerunds.** Gerunds (which, like present participles, end in *-ing*) always function as nouns.
>
>   Seeing is believing. (Gerund *seeing* serves as sentence's subject; gerund *believing* serves as subject complement.)
>
>   He worried about interrupting. (Gerund *interrupting* is object of preposition *about*.)
>
>   Andrew loves skiing. (Gerund *skiing* is direct object of verb *loves*.)
>
> **NOTE:** When the *-ing* form of a verb is used as a noun, it is a *gerund*; when it is used as an adjective, it is a *present participle*.

46d Using Adjectives

Adjectives describe, limit, qualify, or in some other way modify nouns or pronouns.

1 Descriptive Adjectives

Descriptive adjectives name a quality of the noun or pronoun they modify.

>   After the game, they were exhausted.
>   They ordered a chocolate soda and a butterscotch sundae.

Some descriptive adjectives are formed from common nouns or from verbs (*friend/friendly, agree/agreeable*). Others, called **proper adjectives,** are formed from proper nouns.

>   A Shakespearean sonnet consists of an octave and a sestet.

Two or more words may be joined (hyphenated before a noun, without a hyphen after a noun) to form a **compound adjective**: *His parents are very well-read people; most people are not so well read.*

2 Determiners

When articles, pronouns, numbers, and the like function as adjectives, limiting or qualifying nouns or pronouns, they are referred to as **determiners**.

> **Articles** (*a, an, the*)
>   The boy found a four-leaf clover.

Possessive nouns

Lesley's mother lives in New Jersey.

Possessive pronouns (the personal pronouns *my, your, his, her, its, our, their*)

Their lives depended on my skill.

Demonstrative pronouns (*this, these, that, those*)

This song reminds me of that song we heard yesterday.

Interrogative pronouns (*what, which, whose*)

Whose book is this?

Indefinite pronouns (*another, each, both, many, any, some*, and so on)

Both candidates agreed to return another day.

Relative pronouns (*what, whatever, which, whichever, whose, whoever*)

I forgot whatever reasons I had for leaving.

Numbers (*one, two, first, second*, and so on)

The first time I played baseball, I got only one hit.

46e Using Adverbs

ESL
63d

Adverbs describe the action of verbs or modify adjectives, other adverbs, or complete phrases, clauses, or sentences. They answer the questions "How?" "Why?" "Where?" "When?" "Under what conditions?" and "To what extent?"

He walked rather hesitantly toward the front of the room. (walked *how?*)

Let's meet tomorrow for coffee. (meet *when?*)

Adverbs that modify other adverbs or adjectives limit or qualify the words they modify.

He pitched an almost perfect game.

Interrogative adverbs—*how, when, why,* and *where*—introduce questions.

Why did the compound darken?

See 7b2

Conjunctive adverbs act as transitional words, joining and relating independent clauses. Conjunctive adverbs may appear in various positions in a sentence.

> Jason forgot to register for chemistry. However, he managed to sign up during the drop/add period.
>
> Jason forgot to register for chemistry; however, he managed to sign up during the drop/add period.
>
> Jason forgot to register for chemistry. He managed, however, to sign up during the drop/add period.
>
> Jason forgot to register for chemistry. He managed to sign up during the drop/add period, however.

FREQUENTLY USED CONJUNCTIVE ADVERBS

accordingly	furthermore	meanwhile	similarly
also	hence	moreover	still
anyway	however	nevertheless	then
besides	incidentally	next	thereafter
certainly	indeed	nonetheless	therefore
consequently	instead	now	thus
finally	likewise	otherwise	undoubtedly

46f Using Prepositions

ESL 63e

A preposition introduces a noun or pronoun (or a phrase or clause functioning in the sentence as a noun), linking it to other words in the sentence. The word or word group the preposition introduces is called its **object**.

> They received a postcard *from* Bobby telling *about* his trip *to* Canada.
> (prep) (obj) (prep) (obj) (prep) (obj)

FREQUENTLY USED PREPOSITIONS

about	around	beside	during
above	as	between	except
across	at	beyond	for
after	before	by	from
against	behind	concerning	in
along	below	despite	inside
among	beneath	down	into

like	out	through	until
near	outside	throughout	up
of	over	to	upon
off	past	toward	with
on	regarding	under	within
onto	since	underneath	without

46g Using Conjunctions

Conjunctions connect words, phrases, clauses, or sentences.
  Coordinating conjunctions (*and, or, but, nor, for, so, yet*) connect words, phrases, or clauses of equal weight.

  The choice was simple: chicken <u>or</u> fish. (*Or* links two nouns.)

  The United States is a government "of the people, by the people, <u>and</u> for the people." (*And* links three prepositional phrases.)

  Thoreau wrote *Walden* in 1854, <u>and</u> he died in 1862. (*And* links two independent clauses.)

Correlative conjunctions, always used in pairs, also link grammatically equivalent items.

  <u>Both</u> Hancock <u>and</u> Jefferson signed the Declaration of Independence. (Correlative conjunctions link two nouns.)

  <u>Either</u> I will renew my lease, <u>or</u> I will move. (Correlative conjunctions link two independent clauses.)

CORRELATIVE CONJUNCTIONS

both . . . and	neither . . . nor
either . . . or	not only . . . but also
just as . . . so	whether . . . or

  Subordinating conjunctions include *since, because, although, if, after, when, while, before, unless,* and so on. A subordinating conjunction introduces a dependent (subordinate) clause, connecting it to the sentence's independent (main) clause to form a complex sentence.

See 34b

  <u>Although</u> drug use is a serious concern for parents, many parents are afraid to discuss it with their children.

  It is best to diagram your garden <u>before</u> you start to plant it.

46h Using Interjections

Interjections are exclamations used to express emotion: *Oh! Ouch! Wow! Alas! Hey!* These words are grammatically independent; that is, they do not have a grammatical function in a sentence.

An interjection may be set off in a sentence by commas.

The message, <u>alas</u>, arrived too late.

For greater emphasis, an interjection can be punctuated as an independent unit, set off with an exclamation point.

<u>Alas</u>! The message arrived too late.

NOTE: Other kinds of words may also be used in isolation. These include *yes, no, hello, good-bye, please,* and *thank you.* All such words, including interjections, are collectively referred to as **isolates.**

47

Using Nouns and Pronouns

❓ FAQs

Is *I* always more appropriate than *me*? *(p. 594)*
How do I know whether to use *who* or *whom*? *(p. 595)*
What is an antecedent? *(p. 596)*
How do I know whether to use *who*, *which*, or *that*? *(p. 598)*

47a Understanding Case

Case is the form a noun or pronoun takes to indicate its function in a sentence. Nouns change form only in the possessive case: the *cat's* eyes, *Molly's* book. Pronouns, however, have three cases: *subjective*, *objective*, and *possessive*.

PRONOUN CASE FORMS						
Subjective						
I	he, she	it	we	you	they	who whoever
Objective						
me	him, her	it	us	you	them	whom whomever
Possessive						
my mine	his, her hers	its	our ours	your yours	their theirs	whose

1 Subjective Case

A pronoun takes the **subjective case** in the following situations.

Subject of a Verb: <u>I</u> bought a new mountain bike.
Subject Complement: It was <u>he</u> who volunteered to drive.

2 Objective Case

A pronoun takes the **objective case** in the following situations.

Direct Object: Our supervisor asked Adam and *me* to work on the project.

Indirect Object: The plumber's bill gave *him* quite a shock.

Object of a Preposition: Between *us*, we own ten shares of stock.

> **CLOSE-UP**
>
> **PRONOUN CASE IN COMPOUND CONSTRUCTIONS**
>
> *I* is not necessarily more appropriate than *me*. In compound constructions like the following, *me* is correct.
>
> > Just between you and *me* [not *I*], I think we're going to have a quiz. (*Me* is the object of the preposition *between*.)

3 Possessive Case

A pronoun takes the **possessive case** when it indicates ownership (*our* car, *your* book). The possessive case is also used before a **gerund**.

> Napoleon gave *his* approval to *their* ruling Naples. (*His* indicates ownership; *ruling* is a gerund.)

See 46c2

■ **EXERCISE 1**

Underline the correct form of the pronoun within the parentheses. Be prepared to explain why you chose each form.

Example: Toni Morrison, Alice Walker, and (<u>she</u>, her) are perhaps the most widely recognized African-American women writing today.

1. Both Walt Whitman and (he, him) wrote a great deal of poetry about nature.
2. Our instructor gave Matthew and (me, I) an excellent idea for our project.
3. The sales clerk objected to (me, my) returning the sweater.
4. I understand (you, your) being unavailable to work tonight.
5. The waiter asked Michael and (me, I) to move to another table.

47b Determining Pronoun Case in Special Situations

1 Comparisons with *Than* or *As*

When a comparison ends with a pronoun, the pronoun's function in the sentence dictates your choice of pronoun case. If the pronoun functions as a subject, use the subjective case; if it functions as an object, use the objective case. You can determine the function of the pronoun by completing the comparison.

> Darcy likes John more than I. (*I* is the subject: more than I like John)
>
> Darcy likes John more than me. (*Me* is the object: more than she likes me.)

2 *Who* and *Whom*

The case of the pronouns *who* and *whom* depends on their function *within their own clause*. When a pronoun serves as the subject of its clause, use *who* or *whoever*; when it functions as an object, use *whom* or *whomever*.

> The Salvation Army gives food and shelter to whoever is in need. (*Whoever* is the subject of the dependent clause *whoever is in need*.)
>
> I wonder whom jazz musician Miles Davis influenced. (*Whom* is the object of *influenced* in the dependent clause *whom jazz musician Miles Davis influenced*.)

> #### CLOSE-UP
>
> **PRONOUN CASE IN QUESTIONS**
>
> To determine whether to use subjective case (*who*) or objective case (*whom*) in a question, use a personal pronoun to answer the question. If the personal pronoun is the subject, use *who*; if the personal pronoun is the object, use *whom*.
>
> > Who wrote *The Age of Innocence?* She wrote it. (subject)
> >
> > Whom do you support for mayor? I support her. (object)

3 Appositives

An appositive is a noun or noun phrase that identifies or renames an adjacent noun or pronoun. The case of a pronoun in an appositive depends on the function of the word the appositive identifies or renames.

> We heard two Motown recording artists, Smokey Robinson and him. (*Artists* is the object of the verb *heard,* so the pronoun in the appositive *Smokey Robinson and him* takes the objective case.)
>
> Two Motown recording artists, Smokey Robinson and he, had contracts with Motown Records. (*Artists* is the subject of the

sentence, so the pronoun in the appositive *Smokey Robinson and he* takes the subjective case.)

4 *We* and *Us* before a Noun

When a first-person plural pronoun directly precedes a noun, the case of the pronoun depends on the way the noun functions in the sentence.

<u>We</u> women must stick together. (*Women* is the subject of the sentence, so the pronoun *we* must be in the subjective case.)

Teachers make learning easy for <u>us</u> students. (*Students* is the object of the preposition *for,* so the pronoun *us* must be in the objective case.)

■ EXERCISE 2

Using the word in parentheses, combine each pair of sentences into a single sentence. You may change word order and add or delete words.

Example: After he left the band The Police, bass player Sting continued as a solo artist. He once taught middle-school English. (who)

Revised: After he left the band The Police, bass player Sting, who once taught middle-school English, continued as a solo artist.

1. Herb Ritts has photographed world leaders, leading artistic figures in dance and drama, and a vanishing African tribe. He got his start by taking photographs of Hollywood stars. (who)
2. Tim Green has written several novels about a fictional football team. He played for the Atlanta Hawks and has a law degree. (who)
3. Some say Carl Sagan did more to further science education in America than any other person. He wrote many books on science and narrated many popular television shows. (who)
4. Jodie Foster has won two Academy Awards for her acting. She was a child star. (who)
5. Sylvia Plath met fellow poet Ted Hughes at Cambridge University in England. She later married him. (whom)

47c Revising Pronoun Reference Errors

An **antecedent** is the word or word group to which a pronoun refers. The connection between a pronoun and its antecedent should

Revising Pronoun Reference Errors ■ **ref** **47c**

always be clear. If the <u>pronoun reference</u> is not clear, you will need to revise the sentence.

1 Ambiguous Antecedent

Sometimes it is not clear to which antecedent a pronoun—for example, *this*, *that*, *which*, or *it*—refers. In such cases, eliminate the ambiguity by substituting a noun for the pronoun.

> The accountant took out his calculator and completed the tax return. Then, he put it into his briefcase. *[the calculator]* (The pronoun *it* can refer either to *calculator* or to *tax return*.)

> When you make a promise to give someone a gift, you should keep it. *[that promise]* (The pronoun *it* can refer either to *promise* or to *gift*.)

2 Remote Antecedent

If a pronoun is far from its antecedent, readers will have difficulty making a connection between them. To eliminate this problem, replace the pronoun with a noun.

> During the mid-1800s, many Czechs began to immigrate to America. By 1860, about 23,000 Czechs had left their country; by 1900, 13,000 Czech immigrants were coming to its shores *[America's]* each year.

3 Nonexistent Antecedent

Sometimes a pronoun—for example, *this*—refers to an antecedent that does not exist. In such cases, add a word that identifies the unstated antecedent.

> Some one-celled organisms contain chlorophyll yet are considered animals. This illustrates the difficulty of classifying *[paradox]* single-celled organisms. (Exactly what does *this* refer to?)

CLOSE-UP

PRONOUN REFERENCE

Colloquial expressions such as "*It* says in the paper" and "*He* said on the news," which refer to unidentified antecedents, are not acceptable

(continued)

> **PRONOUN REFERENCE** *(continued)*
> in college writing. Substitute the appropriate noun for the unclear pronoun: "The *article* in the paper says...."; "In his commentary, *Ted Koppel* observes...."

4 Who, Which, and That

In general, *who* refers to people or to animals that have names. *Which* and *that* refer to things or to unnamed animals. When referring to an antecedent, be sure to choose the appropriate pronoun (*who*, *which*, or *that*).

> David Henry Hwang, who wrote the Tony Award-winning play *M. Butterfly*, also wrote *Family Devotions* and *FOB*.
>
> The spotted owl, which lives in old growth forests, is in danger of extinction.
>
> Houses that are built today are usually more energy efficient than those built twenty years ago.

Never use *that* to refer to a person.

> The man ~~that~~ *who* holds the world record for eating hot dogs is my neighbor.

NOTE: Be sure to use *which* in nonrestrictive clauses, which are always set off with commas. In most cases, use *that* in restrictive clauses, which are not set off with commas. *Who* may be used in both restrictive and nonrestrictive clauses.

See 52d1

■ EXERCISE 3

Analyze the pronoun reference errors in each of the following sentences. After doing so, revise each sentence by substituting an appropriate noun or noun phrase for the underlined pronoun.

Example: Jefferson asked Lewis to head the expedition, and Lewis selected ~~him~~ *Clark* as his associate. (*Him* refers to a nonexistent antecedent.)

1. The purpose of the expedition was to search out a land route to the Pacific and to gather information about the West. The Louisiana Purchase increased the need for it.
2. The expedition was going to be difficult. They trained the men in Illinois, the starting point.

3. Clark and most of the men who descended the Yellowstone River camped on the bank. It was beautiful and wild.
4. Both Jefferson and Lewis had faith that he would be successful in this transcontinental journey.
5. The expedition was efficient, and only one man was lost. This was extraordinary.

48

Using Verbs

❓ FAQs

Which verbs are irregular? (p. 601)
What is the difference between lie *and* lay*? (p. 603)*
Is it always better to use the active voice? (p. 611)

48a Understanding Verb Forms

Every verb has four **principal parts:** a **base form** (the form of the verb used with *I, we, you,* and *they* in the present tense), a **present participle** (the *-ing* form of the verb), a **past tense form,** and a **past participle.**

NOTE: The verb *be* is so irregular that it is the one exception to this definition; its base form is *be*.

1 Regular Verbs

A **regular verb** forms both its past tense and its past participle by adding *-d* or *-ed* to the base form of the verb.

PRINCIPAL PARTS OF REGULAR VERBS		
Base Form	**Past Tense Form**	**Past Participle**
smile	smiled	smiled
talk	talked	talked
jump	jumped	jumped

2 Irregular Verbs

Irregular verbs do not follow the pattern discussed above. The chart that follows lists the principal parts of the most frequently used irregular verbs.

600

Understanding Verb Forms **48a** **601**

FREQUENTLY USED IRREGULAR VERBS

Base Form	Past Tense Form	Past Participle
arise	arose	arisen
awake	awoke, awaked	awoke, awaked
be	was/were	been
beat	beat	beaten
begin	began	begun
bend	bent	bent
bet	bet, betted	bet
bite	bit	bitten
blow	blew	blown
break	broke	broken
bring	brought	brought
build	built	built
burst	burst	burst
buy	bought	bought
catch	caught	caught
choose	chose	chosen
cling	clung	clung
come	came	come
cost	cost	cost
deal	dealt	dealt
dig	dug	dug
dive	dived, dove	dived
do	did	done
drag	dragged	dragged
draw	drew	drawn
drink	drank	drunk
drive	drove	driven
eat	ate	eaten
fall	fell	fallen
fight	fought	fought
find	found	found
fly	flew	flown
forget	forgot	forgotten, forgot
freeze	froze	frozen
get	got	gotten
give	gave	given
go	went	gone
grow	grew	grown
hang (execute)	hanged	hanged
hang (suspend)	hung	hung
have	had	had
hear	heard	heard
keep	kept	kept
know	knew	known
lay	laid	laid
lead	led	led

(continued)

Frequently Used Irregular Verbs *(continued)*

Base Form	Past Tense Form	Past Participle
lend	lent	lent
let	let	let
lie (recline)	lay	lain
lie (tell an untruth)	lied	lied
make	made	made
prove	proved	proved, proven
read	read	read
ride	rode	ridden
ring	rang	rung
rise	rose	risen
run	ran	run
say	said	said
see	saw	seen
set (place)	set	set
shake	shook	shaken
shrink	shrank, shrunk,	shrunk, shrunken
sing	sang	sung
sink	sank	sunk
sit	sat	sat
sneak	sneaked	sneaked
speak	spoke	spoken
speed	sped, speeded	sped, speeded
spin	spun	spun
spring	sprang	sprung
stand	stood	stood
steal	stole	stolen
strike	struck	struck, stricken
swear	swore	sworn
swim	swam	swum
swing	swung	swung
take	took	taken
teach	taught	taught
throw	threw	thrown
wake	woke, waked	waked, woken
wear	wore	worn
wring	wrung	wrung
write	wrote	written

GRAMMAR CHECKER

Using Correct Verb Forms

Your word processor's grammar checker will highlight incorrect verb forms in your writing and offer revision suggestions.

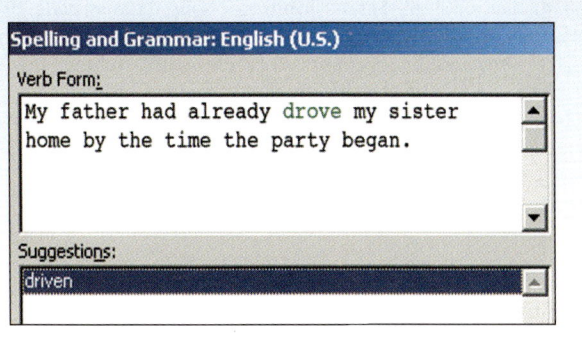

CLOSE-UP

LIE/LAY AND SIT/SET

Lie means "to recline" and does not take an object ("He likes to *lie* on the floor"); *lay* means "to place" or "to put" and does take an object ("He wants to *lay* a rug on the floor").

Base Form	Past Tense Form	Past Participle
lie	lay	lain
lay	laid	laid

Sit means "to assume a seated position" and does not take an object ("She wants to *sit* on the table"); *set* means "to place" or "to put" and usually takes an object ("She wants to *set* a vase on the table").

Base Form	Past Tense Form	Past Participle
sit	sat	sat
set	set	set

■ **EXERCISE 1**

Complete the sentences in the following paragraph with an appropriate form of the verbs in parentheses.

Example: An air of mystery surrounds many of those who have ____*sung*____ (sing) and played the blues.

The legendary bluesman Robert Johnson supposedly _____ (sell) his soul to the devil in order to become a guitar virtuoso. Myth has it that the young Johnson could barely play his instrument and annoyed other musicians by trying to sit in at clubs, where he _____ (sneak) onto the bandstand to play every chance he got. He disappeared for a short time, the story goes, and when he returned he was a phenomenal guitarist, having _____ (swear) a Faustian oath to Satan. Johnson's song "Crossroads Blues"—rearranged and recorded by the sixties band Cream as simply "Crossroads"—supposedly recounts this exchange, telling how Johnson _____ (deal) with the devil. Some of his other songs, such as "Hellhound on My Trail," are allegedly about the torment he suffered as he _____ (fight) for his soul.

EXERCISE 2

Complete the following sentences with appropriate forms of the verbs in parentheses.

Example: Mary Cassatt ____*laid*____ down her paintbrush. (lie, lay)

1. Impressionist artists of the nineteenth century preferred everyday subjects and used to _____ fruit on a table to paint. (sit, set)
2. They were known for their technique of _____ dabs of paint quickly on canvas, giving an "impression" of a scene rather than extensive detail. (lying, laying)
3. Claude Monet's *Women in the Garden* featured one woman in the foreground who _____ on the grass in a garden. (sat, set)
4. In Pierre Auguste Renoir's *Nymphs*, two nude figures talk while _____ on flowers in a garden. (lying, laying)
5. Paul Cézanne liked to _____ in front of his subject as he painted and often painted out of doors rather than in a studio. (sit, set)

48b Understanding Tense

Tense is the form a verb takes to indicate when an action occurred or when a condition existed.

ENGLISH VERB TENSES

Simple Tenses

Present (I *finish*, she or he *finishes*)
Past (I *finished*)
Future (I *will finish*)

Perfect Tenses

Present perfect (I *have finished*, she or he *has finished*)
Past perfect (I *had finished*)
Future perfect (I *will have finished*)

Understanding Tense 48b

> **Progressive Tenses**
> Present progressive (I *am finishing*, she or he *is finishing*)
> Past progressive (I *was finishing*)
> Future progressive (I *will be finishing*)
> Present perfect progressive (I *have been finishing*)
> Past perfect progressive (I *had been finishing*)
> Future perfect progressive (I *will have been finishing*)

1 Using the Simple Tenses

The **simple tenses** include *present*, *past*, and *future*.

The **present tense** usually indicates an action that is taking place at the time it is expressed in speech or writing. It can also indicate an action that occurs regularly.

> I <u>see</u> your point. (an action taking place when it is expressed)
>
> We <u>wear</u> wool in the winter. (an action that occurs regularly)

> **CLOSE-UP**
>
> **SPECIAL USES OF THE PRESENT TENSE**
>
> The present tense has four special uses.
>
> **To Indicate Future Time:** The grades <u>arrive</u> next Thursday.
>
> **To State a Generally Held Belief:** Studying <u>pays</u> off.
>
> **To State a Scientific Truth:** An object at rest <u>tends</u> to stay at rest.
>
> **To Discuss a Literary Work:** *Family Installments* <u>tells</u> the story of a Puerto Rican family.

The **past tense** indicates that an action has already taken place.

> John Glenn <u>orbited</u> the earth three times on February 20, 1962. (an action completed in the past)
>
> As a young man, Mark Twain <u>traveled</u> through the Southwest. (an action that occurred once or many times in the past but did not extend into the present)

The **future tense** indicates that an action will or is likely to take place.

> Halley's Comet <u>will reappear</u> in 2061. (a future action that will definitely occur)
>
> The land boom in Nevada <u>will</u> probably <u>continue</u>. (a future action that is likely to occur)

2 Using the Perfect Tenses

ESL 63a2

The perfect tenses designate actions that were or will be completed before other actions or conditions. The perfect tenses are formed with the appropriate tense form of the auxiliary verb *have* plus the past participle.

The **present perfect** tense can indicate two types of continuing action beginning in the past.

> Dr. Kim has finished studying the effects of BHA on rats. (an action that began in the past and is finished at the present time)

> My mother has invested her money wisely. (an action that began in the past and extends into the present)

The **past perfect** tense indicates an action occurring before a certain time in the past.

> By 1946, engineers had built the first electronic digital computer.

The **future perfect** tense indicates that an action will be finished by a certain future time.

> By Tuesday, the transit authority will have run out of money.

CLOSE-UP

COULD HAVE, SHOULD HAVE, AND WOULD HAVE

Do not use the preposition *of* after *would*, *should*, *could*, and *might*. Use the auxiliary verb *have* after these words.

> I should ~~of~~ *have* left for class earlier.

---

3 Using the Progressive Tenses

ESL 63a2

The progressive tenses express continuing action. They are formed with the appropriate tense of the verb *be* plus the present participle.

The **present progressive** tense indicates that something is happening at the time it is expressed in speech or writing.

> The volcano is erupting, and lava is flowing toward the town.

The **past progressive** tense indicates two kinds of past action.

> Roderick Usher's actions were becoming increasingly bizarre. (a continuing action in the past)

> The French revolutionary Marat was stabbed to death while he was bathing. (an action occurring at the same time in the past as another action)

The **future progressive** tense indicates a continuing action in the future.

The treasury secretary will be carefully monitoring the money supply.

The **present perfect progressive** tense indicates action continuing from the past into the present and possibly into the future.

Rescuers have been working around the clock.

The **past perfect progressive** tense indicates that a past action went on until another one occurred.

Before President Kennedy was assassinated, he had been working on civil rights legislation.

The **future perfect progressive** tense indicates that an action will continue until a certain future time.

By eleven o'clock we will have been driving for seven hours.

4 Using Verb Tenses in a Sentence

You use different tenses in a sentence to indicate that actions are taking place at different times. By choosing tenses that accurately express these times, you enable readers to follow the sequence of actions.

- When a **verb** appears in a dependent clause, its tense depends on the tense of the main verb in the independent clause. When the main verb in the independent clause is in the past tense, the verb in the dependent clause is usually in the past or past perfect tense. When the main verb in the independent clause is in the past perfect tense, the verb in the dependent clause is usually in the past tense. (When the main verb in the independent clause is in any tense except the past or past perfect, the verb in the dependent clause may be in any tense needed for meaning.)

Main Verb	Verb in Dependent Clause
George Hepplewhite was (past) an English cabinetmaker	who designed (past) distinctive chair backs.
The battle had ended (past perfect)	by the time reinforcements arrived. (past)

- When an **infinitive** appears in a verbal phrase, the tense it expresses depends on the tense of the sentence's main verb. The *present infinitive* (the *to* form of the verb) indicates an action happening at the same time as or later than the main verb. The *perfect infinitive* (*to have* plus the past participle) indicates action happening earlier than the main verb.

Main Verb	Infinitive
I <u>went</u>	<u>to see</u> the Rangers play last week. (The going and seeing occurred at the same time.)
I <u>want</u>	<u>to see</u> the Rangers play tomorrow. (Wanting occurs in the present, and seeing will occur in the future.)
I would <u>like</u>	<u>to have seen</u> the Rangers play. (Liking occurs in the present, and seeing would have occurred in the past.)

- *When a **participle** appears in a verbal phrase, its tense depends on the tense of the sentence's main verb.* The *present participle* indicates action happening at the same time as the action of the main verb. The *past participle* or the *present perfect participle* indicates action occurring before the action of the main verb.

Participle	Main Verb
<u>Addressing</u> the 1896 Democratic Convention,	William Jennings Bryan <u>delivered</u> his Cross of Gold speech. (The addressing and the delivery occurred at the same time.)
<u>Having written</u> her term paper,	Camille <u>studied</u> for her history final. (The writing occurred before the studying.)

■ **EXERCISE 3**

A verb is missing from each of the following sentences. Fill in the form of the verb indicated in parentheses.

Example: The Outer Banks ___*stretch*___ (stretch: present) along the North Carolina coast for more than 175 miles.

1. Many portions of the Outer Banks of North Carolina _____ (give: present) the visitor a sense of history and timelessness.
2. Many students of history _____ (read: present perfect) about the Outer Banks and its mysteries.
3. It was on Roanoke Island in the 1580s that English colonists _____ (establish: past) the first settlement in the New World.
4. That colony vanished soon after it was settled, _____ (become: present participle) known as the famous "lost colony."
5. By 1718, the pirate Blackbeard _____ (made: past perfect) the Outer Banks a hiding place for his treasures.

6. It was at Ocracoke, in fact, that Blackbeard _____ (meet: past) his death.
7. Even today, people _____ (search: present progressive) the Outer Banks for Blackbeard's hidden treasures.
8. The Outer Banks are also famous for Kitty Hawk; even as technology has advanced into the space age, the number of tourists flocking to the site of the Wright brothers' epic flight _____. (grow: present perfect progressive)
9. Long before that famous flight occurred, however, the Outer Banks _____ (claim: past perfect) countless ships along its ever-shifting shores, resulting in its nickname—the "Graveyard of the Atlantic."
10. If the Outer Banks continue to be protected from the ravages of overdevelopment and commercialization, visitors _____ (enjoy: future progressive) the mysteries of this tiny finger of land for years to come.

48c Understanding Mood

Mood is the form a verb takes to indicate whether a writer is making a statement or asking a question (*indicative mood*), giving a command (*imperative mood*), or expressing a wish or a contrary-to-fact statement (*subjunctive mood*).

- The **indicative** mood expresses an opinion, states a fact, or asks a question: Jackie Robinson <u>had</u> a great impact on professional baseball. (The indicative is the mood used in most English sentences.)
- The **imperative** mood is used in commands and direct requests. Usually, the imperative includes only the base form of the verb without a subject: <u>Use</u> a dictionary.
- The **subjunctive** mood was common in the past, but it now is used less and less often, and usually only in formal contexts.

1 Forming the Subjunctive Mood

The **present subjunctive** uses the base form of the verb, regardless of the subject. The **past subjunctive** has the same form as the past tense of the verb. (However, when *be* is used as an auxiliary verb, it takes the form *were* regardless of the number or person of the subject.)

Dr. Gorman suggested that I <u>study</u> the Cambrian Period. (present subjunctive)

The sign recommended that we <u>be</u> careful. (present subjunctive)

I wish I <u>were</u> going to Europe. (past subjunctive)

2 Using the Subjunctive Mood

The present subjunctive may be used in *that* clauses after words such as *ask, suggest, require, demand, recommend,* and *insist.*

> The report recommended that juveniles <u>be</u> given mandatory counseling.
>
> Captain Ahab insisted that his crew <u>hunt</u> the white whale.

The past subjunctive may be used in **conditional statements** (statements beginning with *if* that are contrary to fact, including statements that express a wish).

> If John <u>were</u> here, he could see Marsha. (John is not here.)
>
> The father acted as if he <u>were</u> having the baby. (The father couldn't be having the baby.)
>
> I wish I <u>were</u> more organized. (expresses a wish)

NOTE: In many situations, the subjunctive mood can sound stiff or formal. To eliminate the need for a subjunctive construction, rephrase the sentence.

> The group asked ~~that~~ the city council ^to ban smoking in public places.

■ EXERCISE 4

Complete the sentences in the following paragraph by inserting the appropriate form (indicative, imperative, or subjunctive) of the verb in parentheses. Be prepared to explain your choices.

> Harry Houdini was a famous escape artist. He _____ (perform) escapes from every type of bond imaginable: handcuffs, locks, straitjackets, ropes, sacks, and sealed chests underwater. In Germany, workers _____ (challenge) Houdini to escape from a packing box. If he _____ (be) to escape, they would admit that he _____ (be) the best escape artist in the world. Houdini accepted. Before getting into the box, he asked that the observers _____ (give) it a thorough examination. He then asked that a worker _____ (nail) him into the box. "_____ (place) a screen around the box," he ordered after he had been sealed inside. In a few minutes, Houdini _____ (step) from behind the screen. When the workers demanded that they _____ (see) the box, Houdini pulled down the screen. To their surprise, they saw the box with the lid still nailed tightly in place.

48d Understanding Voice

Voice is the form a verb takes to indicate whether its subject acts or is acted upon. When the subject of a verb does something—that is, acts—

the verb is in the **active voice.** When the subject of a verb receives the action—that is, is acted upon—the verb is in the **passive voice.**

Active Voice: Hart Crane <u>wrote</u> *The Bridge*.

Passive Voice: *The Bridge* <u>was written</u> by Hart Crane.

> **CLOSE-UP**
>
> **ACTIVE VS. PASSIVE VOICE**
>
> Because the active voice emphasizes the person or thing performing an action, it is usually briefer, clearer, and more emphatic than the passive voice. Some situations, however, require use of the passive voice. For example, you should use passive constructions when the actor is unknown or unimportant or when the recipient of an action should logically receive the emphasis.
>
> DDT <u>was found</u> in soil samples. (Passive voice emphasizes the discovery of DDT; who found it is not important.)
>
> Grits <u>are eaten</u> throughout the South. (Passive voice emphasizes the fact that grits are eaten, not those who eat them.)
>
> Still, whenever possible, you should use active constructions in your college writing.

1 Changing Verbs from Passive to Active Voice

You can change a verb from passive to active voice by making the subject of the passive verb the object of the active verb. The person or thing performing the action then becomes the subject of the new sentence.

Passive: The novel *Frankenstein* <u>was written</u> by Mary Shelley.

Active: Mary Shelley <u>wrote</u> the novel *Frankenstein*.

If a passive verb has no object, you must supply one that will become the subject of the active verb.

Passive: Baby elephants are taught to avoid humans. (By whom are baby elephants taught?)

Active: <u>Adult elephants</u> teach baby elephants to avoid humans.

■ EXERCISE 5

Determine which sentences in the following paragraph should be in the active voice, and rewrite those sentences.

Rockets were invented by the Chinese about AD 1000. Gunpowder was packed into bamboo tubes and ignited by means of a fuse. These rockets were fired by soldiers at enemy armies and usually caused panic. In thirteenth-century England, an improved form of gunpowder was introduced by Roger Bacon. As a result, rockets were used in battles and were a common—although unreliable—weapon. In the early eighteenth century, a twenty-pound rocket that traveled almost two miles was constructed by William Congreve, an English artillery expert. By the late nineteenth century, thought was given to supersonic speeds by the physicist Ernst Mach, and the sonic boom was predicted by him. The first liquid-fuel rocket was launched by the American Robert Goddard in 1926. A pamphlet written by him anticipated almost all future rocket developments. As a result of his pioneering work, he is known as the father of modern rocketry.

2 Changing Verbs from Active to Passive Voice

You can change a verb from active to passive voice by making the object of the active verb the subject of the passive verb. The subject of the active verb then becomes the object of the passive verb.

Active: Sir James Murray compiled *The Oxford English Dictionary*.

Passive: *The Oxford English Dictionary* was compiled by Sir James Murray.

Remember that an active verb must have an object or else it cannot be put into the passive voice. If an active verb has no object, supply one. This object will become the subject of the passive sentence.

Active: Jacques Cousteau invented.
Cousteau invented ____?____.

Passive: ____?____ was invented by Jacques Cousteau.
The scuba was invented by Jacques Cousteau.

■ EXERCISE 6

Determine which sentences in the following paragraph should be in the passive voice, and rewrite those sentences.

> The Regent Diamond is one of the world's most famous and coveted jewels. A slave discovered the 410-carat diamond in 1701 in an Indian mine. Over the years, people stole and sold the diamond several times. In 1717, the regent of France bought the diamond for an enormous sum, but during the French Revolution, it disappeared again. Someone later found it in a ditch in Paris. Eventually, Napoleon had the diamond set into his ceremonial sword. At last, when the French monarch fell, the government placed the Regent Diamond in the Louvre, where it remains today.

49

Revising Agreement Errors

❓ FAQs

What do I do if a phrase such as along with *comes between the subject and the verb? (p. 614)*
If a subject has two parts, is the verb singular or plural? (p. 614)
Do subjects such as anyone *take singular or plural verbs? (p. 615)*
Can I use they *and* their *to refer to words such as* everyone? *(p. 620)*

Agreement is the correspondence between words in number, gender, and person. Subjects and verbs agree in **number** (singular or plural) and **person** (first, second, or third); pronouns and their antecedents agree in number, person, and **gender** (masculine, feminine, or neuter).

ESL
63a1

49a Making Subjects and Verbs Agree

Singular subjects take singular verbs, and plural subjects take plural verbs.

Singular: Hydrogen peroxide is an unstable compound.
Plural: Characters are not well developed in O. Henry's short stories.

Present tense verbs, except *be* and *have*, add *-s* or *-es* when the subject is third-person singular. Third-person singular subjects include nouns; the personal pronouns *he, she, it,* and *one;* and many indefinite pronouns.

ESL
63a2

See
49a4

> The president has the power to veto congressional legislation.
> She frequently cites statistics to support her assertions.
> In every group, somebody emerges as a natural leader.

Present tense verbs do not add *-s* or *-es* when the subject is a plural noun, a first-person or second-person pronoun (*I, we, you*), or third-person plural pronoun (*they*).

> Experts recommend that dieters avoid salty processed meat.
> In our Bill of Rights, we guarantee all defendants the right to a speedy trial.

At this stratum, you see rocks dating back fifteen million years.

They say that some wealthy people default on their student loans.

In the following special situations, subject-verb agreement can cause problems for writers.

1 When Words Come between Subject and Verb

If a modifying phrase comes between subject and verb, the verb should agree with the subject, not with a word in the modifying phrase.

The sound of the drumbeats builds in intensity in Eugene O'Neill's play *The Emperor Jones*.

The games won by the intramural team are usually few and far between.

NOTE: When phrases introduced by *along with*, *as well as*, *in addition to*, *including*, and *together with* come between subject and verb, these phrases do not change the subject's number: Heavy rain, together with high winds, causes hazardous driving conditions.

2 When Compound Subjects Are Joined by *And*

Compound subjects joined by *and* usually take plural verbs.

Air bags and antilock brakes are standard on all new models.

There are, however, two exceptions to this rule. First, compound subjects joined by *and* that stand for a single idea or person are treated as a unit and used with singular verbs.

Rhythm and blues is a forerunner of rock and roll.

Second, when *each* or *every* precedes a compound subject joined by *and*, the subject takes a singular verb.

Every desk and file cabinet was searched before the letter was found.

3 When Compound Subjects Are Joined by *Or*

Compound subjects joined by *or* (or by *either . . . or* or *neither . . . nor*) may take singular or plural verbs.

If both subjects are singular, use a singular verb; if both subjects are plural, use a plural verb.

Either radiation or chemotherapy is combined with surgery for the most effective results. (Both *radiation* and *chemotherapy* are singular, so the verb is singular.)

Either radiation treatments or chemotherapy sessions are combined with surgery for the most effective results. (Both *treatments* and *sessions* are plural, so the verb is plural.)

If one subject is singular and the other is plural, the verb agrees with the subject that is nearer to it.

Either radiation treatments or chemotherapy is combined with surgery for the most effective results. (Singular verb agrees with *chemotherapy*.)

Either chemotherapy or radiation treatments are combined with surgery for the most effective results. (Plural verb agrees with *treatments*.)

4 When Indefinite Pronouns Serve as Subjects

Most indefinite pronouns—*another, anyone, everyone, one, each, either, neither, anything, everything, something, nothing, nobody,* and *somebody*—are always singular and take singular verbs.

ESL
63c3

Anyone is welcome to apply for this grant.

Each of the chapters includes a review exercise.

Some indefinite pronouns—*both, many, few, several, others*—are always plural and take plural verbs.

Several of the articles are useful for my research.

A few indefinite pronouns—*some, all, any, more, most,* and *none*—can be singular or plural, depending on the noun they refer to.

Of course, some of this trouble is to be expected. (*Some* refers to *trouble*.)

Some of the spectators are getting restless. (*Some* refers to *spectators*.)

GRAMMAR CHECKER

SUBJECT-VERB AGREEMENT

Your word processor's grammar checker will highlight and offer revision suggestions for many subject-verb agreement errors, including errors in sentences that have indefinite pronoun subjects.

(continued)

SUBJECT-VERB AGREEMENT *(continued)*

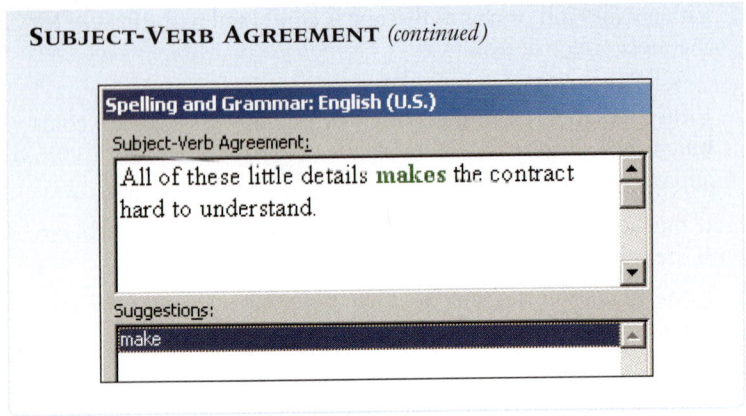

5 When Collective Nouns Serve as Subjects

A **collective noun** names a group of persons or things—for instance, *navy, union, association, band*. When it refers to a group as a unit (as it usually does), a collective noun takes a singular verb; when it refers to the individuals or items that make up the group, it takes a plural verb.

> To many people, the royal family symbolizes Great Britain. (The family, as a unit, is the symbol.)

> The family all eat at different times. (Each member eats separately.)

NOTE: If a plural verb sounds awkward with a collective noun, reword the sentence: *Family members all eat at different times.*

ESL TIP

In British English, which you may have learned if you took ESL classes outside the United States, collective nouns tend to take plural verbs more often than they do in American English: *Management are considering giving workers a bonus.*

Phrases that name fixed amounts—*three-quarters, twenty dollars, the majority*—are treated like collective nouns. When the amount denotes a unit, it takes a singular verb; when it denotes part of the whole, it takes a plural verb.

> Three-quarters of his usual salary is not enough to live on. (*Three-quarters* denotes a unit.)

> Three-quarters of workshop participants improve dramatically. (*Three-quarters* denotes part of the group.)

NOTE: *The number* is always singular, and *a number* is always plural: <u>The number</u> of voters <u>has</u> declined. <u>A number</u> of students <u>have</u> missed the opportunity to preregister.

6 When Singular Subjects Have Plural Forms

A singular subject takes a singular verb, even if the form of the subject is plural.

> <u>Politics</u> <u>makes</u> strange bedfellows.
>
> <u>Statistics</u> <u>deals</u> with the collection, classification, analysis, and interpretation of data.

When such a word has a plural meaning, however, use a plural verb.

> Her <u>politics</u> <u>are</u> too radical for her parents. (*Politics* refers not to the science of political government but, rather, to political principles or opinions.)
>
> The <u>statistics</u> <u>prove</u> him wrong. (*Statistics* denotes not a body of knowledge but the numerical facts or data themselves.)

NOTE: Some words retain their Latin <u>plural</u> forms, which do not look like English plural forms. Be particularly careful to use the correct verbs with such words: <u>criterion is</u>, <u>criteria are</u>; <u>medium is</u>, <u>media are</u>; <u>bacterium is</u>, <u>bacteria are</u>.

See 45b8

7 When Subject-Verb Order Is Inverted

Even when <u>word order</u> is inverted so that the verb comes before the subject (as it does in questions and in sentences beginning with *there is* or *there are*), the subject and verb must agree.

ESL 63f

> <u>Is</u> <u>either</u> answer correct?
>
> There <u>is</u> a <u>monument</u> to Emiliano Zapata in Mexico City.
>
> There <u>are</u> currently thirteen federal <u>circuit courts</u> of appeals.

8 With Linking Verbs

A <u>linking verb</u> should agree with its subject, not with the subject complement.

See 46c1

> The <u>problem</u> <u>was</u> termites.

Here, the verb *was* correctly agrees with the subject *problem*, not with the subject complement *termites*. If *termites* were the subject, the verb would be plural.

> <u>Termites</u> <u>were</u> the problem.

49a agr ■ Revising Agreement Errors

9 With Relative Pronouns

See 46b

When you use a **relative pronoun** (*who*, *which*, *that*, and so on) to introduce a dependent clause, the verb in that clause should agree in number with the pronoun's **antecedent** (the word to which the pronoun refers).

> The farmer is among the ones who suffer during a grain embargo. (Verb *suffer* agrees with plural antecedent *ones*.)

> The farmer is the only one who suffers during the grain embargo. (Verb *suffers* agrees with singular antecedent *one*.)

■ **EXERCISE 1**

Each of these ten correct sentences illustrates one of the conventions just explained. Read each sentence carefully, and explain why each verb form is used.

Example: Obedience in our schools is at an all-time low. (The verb is singular because *obedience*, not *schools*, is the subject.)

1. Jack Kerouac, along with Allen Ginsberg and William S. Burroughs, was a major figure in the "beat" movement.
2. Every American boy and girl needs to learn basic computational skills.
3. Aesthetics is not an exact science.
4. The audience was restless.
5. The Beatles' *Sergeant Pepper* album is one of those albums that remain popular long after they are issued.
6. All is quiet.
7. The subject was contagious diseases.
8. When he was young, Benjamin Franklin's primary concern was books.
9. Eighty dollars is too much to spend on one concert ticket.
10. "There are more things in heaven and earth, Horatio, than are dreamt of in your philosophy."

■ **EXERCISE 2**

Some of the following sentences are correct, but others contain common errors in subject-verb agreement. If a sentence is correct, mark it with a *C*; if it has an error, correct it.

1. *I Love Lucy* is one of those television shows that almost all Americans have seen at least once.
2. The committee presented its findings to the president.
3. Neither Western novels nor science fiction appeal to me.

4. Stage presence and musical ability makes a rock performer successful today.
5. *It's a Wonderful Life*, like many old Christmas movies, seems to be shown on television every year.
6. Hearts are my grandmother's favorite card game.
7. The best part of B. B. King's songs are the guitar solos.
8. Time and tide waits for no man.
9. Sports are my main pastime.
10. *Vincent and Theo* is Robert Altman's movie about the French Impressionist painter Vincent van Gogh and his brother.

49b Making Pronouns and Antecedents Agree

A **pronoun** must agree with its **antecedent**—the word or word group to which the pronoun refers. Singular pronouns—such as *he, him, she, her, it, me, myself,* and *oneself*—should refer to singular antecedents. Plural pronouns—such as *we, us, they, them,* and *their*—should refer to plural antecedents.

In the following special situations, pronoun-antecedent agreement can cause problems for writers.

1 With Compound Antecedents

In most cases, use a plural pronoun to refer to a **compound antecedent** (two or more antecedents connected by *and* or *or*).

Mormonism and Christian Science were influenced in their beginnings by Shaker doctrines.

However, this rule has several exceptions:

- If a compound antecedent denotes a single unit—one person, thing, or idea—use a singular pronoun to refer to the compound antecedent.

    In 1904, the husband and father brought his family from Germany to the United States.

- Use a singular pronoun when a compound antecedent is preceded by *each* or *every*.

    Every programming language and software package has its limitations.

- Use a singular pronoun to refer to two or more singular antecedents linked by *or* or *nor*.

    Neither Thoreau nor Whitman lived to see his work read widely.

- When one part of a compound antecedent is singular and one part is plural, the pronoun agrees in person and number with the antecedent that is nearer to it.

    Neither Dana nor her parents had their seatbelts fastened.

2 With Collective Noun Antecedents

If the meaning of the collective noun antecedent is singular (as it will be in most cases), use a singular pronoun. If the meaning is plural, use a plural pronoun.

The nurses' union announced its plan to strike. (All the members acted as one.)

The team ran onto the court and took their positions. (Each member acted individually.)

3 With Indefinite Pronoun Antecedents

See 49a4

ESL 63c3

Most indefinite pronouns—*each, either, neither, one, anyone,* and the like—are singular and require singular pronouns.

Neither of the men had his proposal ready by the deadline.

Each of these neighborhoods has its own traditions and values.

> **CLOSE-UP**
>
> **PRONOUN-ANTECEDENT AGREEMENT**
>
> In speech and in informal writing, many people use the plural pronouns *they* or *their* with singular indefinite pronouns that refer to people, such as *someone, everyone,* and *nobody*.
>
> Everyone can present their own viewpoint.
>
> In college writing, however, you should try to avoid using a plural pronoun to refer to a singular subject. Instead, you can use both the masculine and the feminine pronoun.
>
> Everyone can present his or her own viewpoint.

Or, you can make the sentence's subject plural.

> All participants can present their own viewpoints.

The use of *his* alone to refer to a singular indefinite pronoun (Everyone can present *his* own viewpoint) is considered sexist language.

See 43e2

GRAMMAR CHECKER

PRONOUN-ANTECEDENT AGREEMENT

Your word processor's grammar checker will highlight and offer revision suggestions for many pronoun-antecedent agreement errors.

```
Spelling and Grammar: English (U.S.)
Pronoun Use:
Someone should take responsibility for their
actions.

Suggestions:
his or her
```

EXERCISE 3

In the following sentences, find and correct any errors in subject-verb or pronoun-antecedent agreement.

1. The core of a computer is a collection of electronic circuits that are called the central processing unit.
2. Computers, because of advanced technology that allows the central processing unit to be placed on a chip, a thin square of semiconducting material about one-quarter of an inch on each side, has been greatly reduced in size.
3. Computers can "talk" to each other over phone lines through a modem, an acronym for *modulator-demodulator*.
4. Pressing keys on keyboards resembling typewriter keyboards generate electronic signals that are input for the computer.
5. Computers have built-in memory storage, and equipment such as disks or tapes provide external memory.
6. RAM (random-access memory), the erasable and reusable computer memory, hold the computer program, the computations executed by the program, and the results.
7. After computer programs are "read" from a disk or tape, the computer uses the instructions as needed to execute the program.

49b agr ■ Revising Agreement Errors

8. ROM (read-only memory), the permanent memory that is "read" by the computer but cannot be changed, are used to store programs that are needed frequently.
9. A number of video games with impressive graphics, sound, and color is available for home computers.
10. Although some computer users write their own programs, most buy ready-made software programs such as the ones that allows a computer to be used as a word processor.

■ EXERCISE 4

The following ten sentences illustrate correct subject-verb and pronoun-antecedent agreement. Following the instructions in parentheses after each sentence, revise each so its verbs and pronouns agree with the newly created subject.

Example: One child in ten suffers from a learning disability. (Change *One child in ten* to *Ten percent of all children*.)

Revised: Ten percent of all children suffer from a learning disability.

1. The governess is seemingly pursued by evil as she tries to protect Miles and Flora from those she feels seek to possess the children's souls. (Change *The governess* to *The governess and the cook*.)
2. Insulin-dependent diabetics are now able to take advantage of new technology that can help alleviate their symptoms. (Change *diabetics* to *the diabetic*.)
3. All homeowners in coastal regions worry about the possible effects of a hurricane on their property. (Change *All homeowners* to *Every homeowner*.)
4. Federally funded job-training programs offer unskilled workers an opportunity to acquire skills they can use to secure employment. (Change *workers* to *the worker*.)
5. Foreign imports pose a major challenge to the American textile market. (Change *Foreign imports* to *The foreign import*.)
6. *Brideshead Revisited* tells how one family and its devotion to its Catholic faith influence Charles Ryder. (Delete *and its devotion to its Catholic faith*.)
7. *Writer's Digest* and *The Writer* are designed to aid writers as they seek markets for their work. (Change *writers* to *the writer*.)
8. Most American families have access to television; in fact, more have televisions than have indoor plumbing. (Change *Most American families* to *Almost every American family*.)
9. In Montana, it seems as though every town's elevation is higher than its population. (Change *every town's elevation* to *all the towns' elevations*.)
10. A woman without a man is like a fish without a bicycle. (Change *A woman/a man* to *Women/men*.)

50

Using Adjectives and Adverbs

❓ FAQs

What's the difference between an adjective and an adverb? (p. 623)
How do I know when to use more *and when to use an* -er *ending? (p. 625)*
How do I know when to use most *and when to use an* -est *ending? (p. 626)*
What's wrong with most unique? *(p. 627)*

50a Understanding Adjectives and Adverbs

Adjectives modify nouns and pronouns. **Adverbs** modify verbs, adjectives, or other adverbs—or entire phrases, clauses, or sentences. Both adjectives and adverbs describe, limit, or qualify other words, phrases, or clauses.

The function of a word in a sentence, not its form, determines whether it is an adjective or an adverb. Although many adverbs (such as *immediately* and *hopelessly*) end in *-ly*, others (such as *almost* and *very*) do not. Moreover, some words that end in *-ly* (such as *lively*) are adjectives.

ESL TIP

For information on correct placement of adjectives and adverbs in a sentence, **see 63d1**. For information on correct order of adjectives in a series, **see 63d2**.

50b Using Adjectives

Be sure to use an **adjective**—not an adverb—as a subject complement. A subject complement is a word that follows a linking verb and modifies the sentence's subject, not its verb. A **linking verb** does not show physical or emotional action. *Seem, appear, believe, become, grow, turn, remain, prove, look, sound, smell, taste, feel,* and the forms of the verb *be* are (or can be used as) linking verbs.

See 33a4

623

Michelle seemed <u>brave</u>. (*Seemed* shows no action, so it is a linking verb. Because *brave* is a subject complement that modifies the subject *Michelle*, it takes the adjective form.)

Michelle smiled <u>bravely</u>. (*Smiled* shows action, so it is not a linking verb. *Bravely* modifies *smiled*, so it takes the adverb form.)

NOTE: Sometimes the same verb can function as either a linking verb or an action verb: *He remained <u>stubborn</u>.* (He was still stubborn.) *He remained <u>stubbornly</u>.* (He remained, in a stubborn manner.)

Also, be sure to use an adjective—not an adverb—as an **object complement,** a word that follows a sentence's direct object and modifies that object and not the verb. Objects are nouns or pronouns, so their modifiers must be adjectives.

Most people called him <u>timid</u>. (People consider him to be timid; here *timid* is an object complement that modifies *him*, the sentence's direct object, so the adjective form is correct.)

Most people called him <u>timidly</u>. (People were timid when they called him; here *timidly* modifies the verb *called*—not the object—so the adverb form is correct.)

50c Using Adverbs

Be sure to use an **adverb**—not an adjective—to modify verbs, adjectives, or other adverbs—or entire phrases, clauses, or sentences.

Most students did ~~great~~ *very well* on the midterm.

My parents dress a lot more ~~conservative~~ *conservatively* than my friends do.

CLOSE-UP

USING ADJECTIVES AND ADVERBS

In informal speech, adjective forms such as *good, bad, sure, real, slow, quick,* and *loud* are often used to modify verbs, adjectives, and adverbs. Avoid these informal modifiers in college writing.

The program ran ~~real good~~ *really well* the first time we tried it, but the new system performed ~~bad~~ *badly*.

■ **EXERCISE 1**

Revise each of the incorrect sentences in the following paragraph so that only adjectives modify nouns and pronouns and only adverbs modify verbs, adjectives, or other adverbs.

A popular self-help trend in the United States today is subliminal tapes. These tapes, with titles like *How to Attract Love*, *Freedom from Acne*, and *I Am a Genius*, are intended to address every problem known to modern society—and to solve these problems quick and easy. The tapes are said to work because their "hidden messages" bypass conscious defense mechanisms. The listener hears only music or relaxing sounds, like waves rolling slow and steady. At decibel levels perceived only subconsciously, positive words and phrases are embedded, usually by someone who speaks deep and rhythmic. The top-selling cassettes are those that help listeners lose weight or quit smoking. The popularity of such tapes is not hard to understand. They promise easy solutions to complex problems. But the main benefit of these tapes appears to be for the sellers, who are accumulating profits real fast.

■ **EXERCISE 2**

Being careful to use adjectives—not adverbs—as subject complements and object complements, write five sentences in imitation of each of the following sentences. Consult the list of linking verbs in 46c1, and use a different linking verb in each of your sentences.

1. Julie looked worried.
2. Dan considers his collection valuable.

50d Using Comparative and Superlative Forms

Most adjectives and adverbs have **comparative** and **superlative** forms that can be used with nouns to indicate degree.

COMPARATIVE AND SUPERLATIVE FORMS

Form	Function	Example
Positive	Describes a quality; does not indicate a comparison	big, lovely
Comparative	Indicates a comparison between *two* qualities (greater or lesser)	bigger, lovelier
Superlative	Indicates a comparison among *more than two* qualities (greatest or least)	biggest, loveliest

1 Regular Comparative Forms

To form the comparative, all one-syllable adjectives and many two-syllable adjectives (particularly those that end in -*y*, -*ly*, -*le*, -*er*, and

-ow) add *-er*: slow<u>er</u>, funn<u>ier</u>. (Note that a final *y* becomes *i* before *-er* is added.)

Other two-syllable adjectives and all long adjectives form the comparative with *more*: <u>more</u> famous, <u>more</u> incredible.

Adverbs ending in *-ly* also form the comparative with *more*: <u>more</u> slowly. Other adverbs use the *-er* ending to form the comparative: soon<u>er</u>.

All adjectives and adverbs indicate a lesser degree with *less*: <u>less</u> lovely, <u>less</u> slowly.

2 Regular Superlative Forms

Adjectives that form the comparative with *-er* add *-est* to form the superlative: nic<u>est</u>, funni<u>est</u>. Adjectives that indicate the comparative with *more* use *most* to indicate the superlative: <u>most</u> famous, <u>most</u> challenging.

The majority of adverbs use *most* to indicate the superlative: <u>most</u> quickly. Others use the *-est* ending: soon<u>est</u>.

All adjectives and adverbs use *least* to indicate the least degree: <u>least</u> interesting, <u>least</u> willingly.

> **CLOSE-UP**
>
> **USING COMPARATIVES AND SUPERLATIVES**
>
> - Never use both *more* and *-er* to form the comparative or both *most* and *-est* to form the superlative.
>
>   Nothing could have been ~~more~~ easier.
>
>   Jack is the ~~most~~ meanest person in town.
>
> - Never use the superlative when comparing only two things.
>
>   older
>   Stacy is the oldest of the two sisters.
>
> - Never use the comparative when comparing more than two things.
>
>   earliest
>   We chose the ~~earlier~~ of the four appointments.

3 Irregular Comparatives and Superlatives

Some adjectives and adverbs have irregular comparative and superlative forms. Instead of adding a word or an ending to the positive form, they use different words to indicate the comparative and the superlative.

Avoiding Illogical Comparatives and Superlatives ■ adj/adv **50e**

IRREGULAR COMPARATIVES AND SUPERLATIVES

	Positive	Comparative	Superlative
Adjectives:	good	better	best
	bad	worse	worst
	a little	less	least
	many, some, much	more	most
Adverbs:	well	better	best
	badly	worse	worst

50e Avoiding Illogical Comparatives and Superlatives

Many adjectives and adverbs can logically exist only in the positive degree. For example, words such as *perfect, unique, excellent, impossible,* and *dead* can never be used in the comparative or superlative degree.

> I read ~~the most~~ *an* excellent story.

> The vase in the museum's collection is ~~very~~ unique.

These words can, however, be modified by words that suggest approaching the absolute state—*nearly* or *almost,* for example.

> He revised until his draft was <u>almost perfect</u>.

NOTE: Some adverbs, particularly those indicating time, place, and degree (*almost, very, here,* and *immediately*), do not have comparative or superlative forms.

■ EXERCISE 3

Supply the correct comparative and superlative forms for each of the following adjectives or adverbs. Then, use each form in a sentence.

Example: strange   stranger   strangest

> The story had a *strange* ending.
> The explanation sounded *stranger* each time I heard it.
> This is the *strangest* gadget I have ever seen.

1. difficult
2. eccentric
3. confusing
4. bad
5. mysterious
6. softly
7. embarrassing
8. well
9. often
10. tiny

PART 12

Understanding Punctuation and Mechanics

51 Using End Punctuation 630
51a Using Periods 630
51b Using Question Marks 632
51c Using Exclamation Points 633

52 Using Commas 634
52a Setting Off Independent Clauses 634
52b Setting Off Items in a Series 635
52c Setting Off Introductory Elements 637
52d Setting Off Nonessential Material 639
52e Using Commas in Other Conventional Contexts 643
52f Using Commas to Prevent Misreading 645
52g Editing Misused Commas 646

53 Using Semicolons 649
53a Separating Independent Clauses 649
53b Separating Independent Clauses Introduced by Transitional Words and Phrases 651
53c Separating Items in a Series 652
53d Editing Misused Semicolons 654

54 Using Apostrophes 656
54a Forming the Possessive Case 656
54b Indicating Omissions in Contractions 658
54c Forming Plurals 660
54d Editing Misused Apostrophes 661

55 Using Quotation Marks 663
55a Setting Off Quoted Speech or Writing 663
55b Setting Off Long Prose Passages and Poetry 665
55c Setting Off Titles 667
55d Setting Off Words Used in Special Ways 668
55e Using Quotation Marks with Other Punctuation 668
55f Editing Misused Quotation Marks 669

56 Using Other Punctuation Marks 672

56a Using Colons 672
56b Using Dashes 674
56c Using Parentheses 675
56d Using Brackets 677
56e Using Slashes 677
56f Using Ellipses 678

57 Knowing When to Capitalize 681
57a Capitalizing the First Word of a Sentence 681
57b Capitalizing Proper Nouns 681
57c Capitalizing Important Words in Titles 685
57d Capitalizing the Pronoun *I*, the Interjection *O*, and Other Single Letters in Special Constructions 685
57e Capitalizing Salutations and Closings of Letters 686
57f Editing Misused Capitals 686

58 Using Italics 688
58a Setting Off Titles and Names 688
58b Setting Off Foreign Words and Phrases 689
58c Setting Off Elements Spoken of as Themselves and Terms Being Defined 689
58d Using Italics for Emphasis 690

59 Using Hyphens 691
59a Breaking a Word at the End of a Line 691
59b Dividing Compound Words 691

60 Using Abbreviations 695
60a Abbreviating Titles 695
60b Abbreviating Organization Names and Technical Terms 695
60c Abbreviating Dates, Times of Day, and Temperatures 696
60d Editing Misused Abbreviations 697

61 Using Numbers 700
61a Spelled-Out Numbers versus Numerals 700
61b Conventional Uses of Numerals 701

51

Using End Punctuation

❓ FAQs

Do abbreviations always include periods? (p. 631)
How are periods used in electronic addresses? (p. 631)
Can I use exclamation points for emphasis? (p. 633)

51a Using Periods

1 Ending a Sentence

Use a period to signal the end of a statement, a mild command or polite request, or an indirect question.

> Something is rotten in Denmark. (statement)
>
> Be sure to have the oil checked before you start out. (mild command)
>
> When the bell rings, please exit in an orderly fashion. (polite request)
>
> They wondered whether the water was safe to drink. (indirect question)

2 Marking an Abbreviation

Use a period in most abbreviations.

> Mr. Spock   1600 Pennsylvania Ave.   9 p.m.
> Dr. Who   Aug.   etc.

If an abbreviation ends the sentence, do not add another period.

> He promised to be there at 6 a.m./

However, do add a question mark if the sentence is a question.

> Did he arrive at 6 p.m.?

If the abbreviation falls *within* a sentence, use normal punctuation after the period.

> He promised to be there at 6 p.m., but he forgot.

Using Periods ■ . **51a**

> **CLOSE-UP**
>
> **ABBREVIATIONS WITHOUT PERIODS**
>
> Abbreviations composed of all capital letters do not usually require periods unless they are the initials of people's names (E. B. White).
>
> MD   RN   BC
>
> Familiar abbreviations of the names of corporations or government agencies and abbreviations of scientific and technical terms do not require periods.
>
> IBM   EPA   DNA   CD-ROM
>
> **Acronyms**—new words formed from the initial letters or first few letters of a series of words—do not include periods.
>
> modem   op-ed   scuba   radar
> OSHA   AIDS   NAFTA   CAT scan
>
> **Clipped forms** (commonly accepted shortened forms of words, such as *flu*, *dorm*, *math*, and *fax*) do not include periods.
>
> **Postal abbreviations** do not include periods.
>
> NY   CA   MS   FL   TX

3 Marking Divisions in Dramatic, Poetic, and Biblical References

Use periods to separate act, scene, and line numbers in plays; book and line numbers in long poems; and chapter and verse numbers in biblical references. (Do not space between the periods and the elements they separate.)

Dramatic Reference: *Hamlet* 2.2.1–5
Poetic Reference: *Paradise Lost* 7.163–67
Biblical Reference: Judges 4.14

NOTE: In MLA parenthetical references, titles of literary and biblical works are often abbreviated: (***Ham.** 2.2.1-5*); (***Judg.** 4.14*).

4 Marking Divisions in Electronic Addresses

Periods, along with other punctuation marks (such as slashes and colons), are frequently used in electronic addresses (URLs).

http://academic.cengage.com/eng/kirsznermandell

NOTE: When you type a URL, do not end it with a period; do not add spaces after periods within the address.

EXERCISE 1

Correct these sentences by adding missing periods and deleting unnecessary ones. If a sentence is correct, mark it with a *C*.

Example: Their mission changed the war.

1. Julius Caesar was killed in 44 B.C.
2. Dr. McLaughlin worked hard to earn his Ph.D..
3. Carmen was supposed to be at A.F.L.-C.I.O. headquarters by 2 p.m.; however, she didn't get there until 10 p.m.
4. After she studied the fall lineup proposed by N.B.C., she decided to work for C.B.S.
5. Representatives from the U.M.W. began collective bargaining after an unsuccessful meeting with Mr. L Pritchard, the coal company's representative.

51b Using Question Marks

1 Marking the End of a Direct Question

Use a question mark to signal the end of a direct question.

> Who was at the door?

2 Marking Questionable Dates or Numbers

Use a question mark in parentheses to indicate uncertainty about a date or number.

> Aristophanes, the Greek playwright, was born in 448 (?) BC and died in 380 (?) BC.

3 Editing Misused Question Marks

Use a period, not a question mark, with an **indirect question** (a question that is not reproduced word for word).

> The personnel officer asked whether he knew how to type.

Do not use a question mark to convey sarcasm. Instead, suggest your attitude through your choice of words.

> I refused his ~~generous (?)~~ *not very* generous offer.

NOTE: Never use more than one consecutive question mark.

EXERCISE 2

Correct the use of question marks and other punctuation in the following sentences.

Example: She asked whether Freud's theories were accepted during his lifetime?.

1. He wondered whether he should take a nine o'clock class?
2. The instructor asked, "Was the Spanish-American War a victory for America."
3. Are they really going to China??!!
4. He took a modest (?) portion of dessert—half a pie.
5. "Is *data* the plural of *datum*?," he inquired.

51c Using Exclamation Points

Use an exclamation point to signal the end of an emotional or emphatic statement, an emphatic interjection, or a forceful command.

Remember the *Maine*!

"No! Don't leave!" he cried.

NOTE: Except for recording dialogue, exclamation points are almost never appropriate in college writing. Even in informal writing, use exclamation points sparingly—and never use more than one in a row.

EXERCISE 3

Add appropriate punctuation to this passage.

    Dr Craig and his group of divers paused at the shore, staring respectfully at the enormous lake Who could imagine what terrors lay beneath its surface Which of them might not emerge alive from this adventure Would it be Col Cathcart Capt Wilks, the MD from the naval base Her husband, P L Fox Or would they all survive the task ahead Dr Craig decided some encouraging remarks were in order

    "Attention divers," he said in a loud, forceful voice "May I please have your attention The project which we are about to undertake—"

    "Oh, no" screamed Mr Fox suddenly "Look out It's the Loch Ness Monster"

    "Quick" shouted Dr Craig "Move away from the shore" But his warning came too late

52

Using Commas

❓ FAQs

Do I need a comma before the word and *when it comes between the last two items in a series? (p. 635)*

How do I know whether to put a comma after a word or phrase that opens a sentence? (p. 637)

How do I use commas with that *and* which*? (p. 640)*

How do I use commas with words and phrases such as however *and* in fact*? (p. 641)*

How do I use commas with quotations? (p. 643)

Should I always use a comma before the words and *and* but*? (p. 648)*

52a Setting Off Independent Clauses

Use a comma when you form a compound sentence by linking two independent clauses with a **coordinating conjunction** or a pair of **correlative conjunctions**.

See 46g

> The House approved the bill**,** but the Senate rejected it.
>
> **Either** the hard drive is full**,** or the modem is too slow.

NOTE: You may omit the comma if two clauses connected by a coordinating conjunction are very short: *Seek and ye shall find. Love it or leave it.*

CLOSE-UP

SEPARATING INDEPENDENT CLAUSES

See 53b

Use a **semicolon**—not a comma—to separate two independent clauses linked by a coordinating conjunction when at least one of the clauses already contains a comma or when the clauses are especially complex.

> The tourists visited Melbourne, the capital of Australia, for three days**;** and they toured Wellington, New Zealand, for two.

EXERCISE 1

Combine each of the following sentence pairs into one compound sentence, adding commas where necessary.

Example: Emergency medicine became an approved medical specialty in 1979. Now, pediatric emergency medicine is becoming increasingly important. (and)

[Edit marks show: comma after "1979", "Now" changed to "and now"]

1. The Pope did not hesitate to visit Cuba. He did not hesitate to meet with President Fidel Castro. (nor)
2. Agents place brand-name products in prominent positions in films. The products are seen and recognized by large audiences. (and)
3. Unisex insurance rates may have some drawbacks for women. These rates may be very beneficial. (or)
4. Cigarette advertising no longer appears on television. It does appear in print media. (but)
5. Dorothy Day founded the Catholic Worker movement in the 1930s. Her followers still dispense free food, medical care, and legal advice to the needy. (and)

52b Setting Off Items in a Series

1 Coordinate Elements

Use commas between items in a series of three or more **coordinate elements** (words, phrases, or clauses joined by a coordinating conjunction).

<u>Chipmunk</u>, <u>raccoon</u>, and <u>Mugwump</u> are Native American words.

You may pay <u>by check</u>, <u>with a credit card</u>, or <u>in cash</u>.

<u>Brazilians speak Portuguese</u>, <u>Colombians speak Spanish</u>, and <u>Haitians speak French and Creole</u>.

NOTE: If phrases or clauses in a <u>series</u> already contain commas, use semicolons to separate the items.

See 53c

Do not use a comma to introduce or to close a series.

Three important criteria are, fat content, salt content, and taste.

Quebec, Ontario, and Alberta, are Canadian provinces.

NOTE: To avoid ambiguity, always use a comma before the *and* (or other coordinating conjunction) that separates the last two items in a series: *The downtown area includes a bakery, a florist, a small supermarket with an excellent butcher, and a bookstore.*

adj/∧ ■ Using Commas

2 Coordinate Adjectives

Use a comma between items in a series of two or more **coordinate adjectives**—adjectives that modify the same word or word group—unless they are joined by a conjunction.

> She brushed her long, shining hair.
>
> The baby was tired and cranky and wet. (no commas required)

CHECKLIST

PUNCTUATING ADJECTIVES IN A SERIES

☐ If you can reverse the order of the adjectives or insert *and* between the adjectives without changing the meaning, the adjectives are coordinate, and you should use a comma.

> She brushed her long, shining hair.
> She brushed her shining, long hair.
> She brushed her long [and] shining hair.

☐ If you cannot reverse the order of the adjectives or insert *and*, the adjectives are not coordinate, and you should not use a comma.

> Ten red balloons fell from the ceiling.
> Red ten balloons fell from the ceiling.
> Ten [and] red balloons fell from the ceiling.

NOTE: Numbers—such as *ten*—are not coordinate with other adjectives.

ESL TIP

If you have difficulty determining the correct order of adjectives in a series, **see 63d2.**

■ EXERCISE 2

Correct the use of commas in the following sentences, adding or deleting commas where necessary. If a sentence is punctuated correctly, mark it with a *C*.

Example: Neither dogs, snakes, bees, nor dragons frighten her.

1. Seals, whales, dogs, lions, and horses, all are mammals.
2. Mammals are warm-blooded vertebrates that bear live young, nurse them, and usually have fur.

3. Seals are mammals, but lizards, and snakes, and iguanas are reptiles, and salamanders are amphibians.
4. Amphibians also include frogs, and toads and newts.
5. Eagles geese ostriches turkeys chickens and ducks are classified as birds.

■ **EXERCISE 3**

Add two coordinate adjectives to modify each of the following phrases, inserting commas where required.

Example: *strong, beautiful* classical music

1. distant thunder
2. silver spoon
3. New York Yankees
4. miniature golf
5. Rolling Stones
6. loving couple
7. computer science
8. wheat bread
9. art museum
10. new math

52c Setting Off Introductory Elements

In most cases, an introductory element is followed by a comma. If the sentence's meaning will be clear without it, the comma can be omitted. When in doubt, however, you should include the comma.

1 Dependent Clauses

An introductory dependent clause is generally set off from the rest of the sentence by a comma.

> Although the CIA used to call undercover agents *penetration agents*, they now routinely refer to them as *moles*.
>
> When war came to Baghdad, many victims were children.

If a dependent clause is short and designates time, you may omit the comma—provided the sentence will be clear without it.

> When I exercise I drink plenty of water.

NOTE: Do not use a comma to set off a dependent clause at the *end* of a sentence.

2 Verbal and Prepositional Phrases

An introductory **verbal phrase** is usually set off by a comma.

> Thinking that this might be his last chance, Peary struggled toward the North Pole. (participial phrase)
>
> To write well, one must read a lot. (infinitive phrase)

An introductory **prepositional phrase** is also usually set off by a comma.

<u>During the Depression</u>, movie attendance rose. (prepositional phrase)

However, if an introductory prepositional phrase is short and no ambiguity is possible, you may omit the comma.

<u>After lunch</u> I took a four-hour nap.

> **CLOSE-UP**
>
> **USING COMMAS WITH VERBAL PHRASES**
>
> See 33b1
>
> A **verbal phrase** that serves as a subject is not set off by a comma.
>
> Laughing out loud, can release tension. (gerund phrase)
> To know him, is to love him. (infinitive phrase)

3 Transitional Words and Phrases

See 7b2

When a **transitional word or phrase** begins a sentence, it is usually set off from the rest of the sentence with a comma.

<u>However</u>, any plan that is enacted must be fair.

<u>In other words</u>, we cannot act hastily.

■ **EXERCISE 4**

Add commas in the following paragraph where necessary to set off an introductory element from the rest of a sentence.

While childhood is shrinking adolescence is expanding. Whatever the reason girls are maturing earlier. The average onset of puberty is now two years earlier than it was only forty years ago. What's more both boys and girls are staying in the nest longer. At present, it is not unusual for children to stay in their parents' home until they are twenty or twenty-one, delaying adulthood and extending adolescence. To some who study the culture this increase in adolescence portends dire consequences. With teenage hormones running amuck for longer the problems of teenage pregnancy and sexually transmitted diseases loom large. Young boys' spending long periods of their lives without responsibilities is also a recipe for disaster. However others see this "youthing" of American culture in a more positive light. Without a doubt adolescents are creative, lively, and more willing to take risks. If we channel their energies carefully they can contribute, even in their extended adolescence, to American culture and technology.

52d Setting Off Nonessential Material

Sometimes words, phrases, or clauses *contribute* to the meaning of a sentence but are not *essential* for conveying the sentence's main point. Use commas to set off such **nonessential material** whether it appears at the beginning, in the middle, or at the end of a sentence.

1 Nonrestrictive Modifiers

Use commas to set off **nonrestrictive modifiers,** which supply information that is not essential to the meaning of the word or word group they modify. (Do *not* use commas to set off **restrictive modifiers,** which supply information that is essential to the meaning of the word or word group they modify.)

> **Nonrestrictive (commas required):** Actors, who have inflated egos, are often insecure. (*All* actors—not just those with inflated egos—are insecure.)
>
> **Restrictive (no commas):** Actors who have inflated egos are often insecure. (Only those actors with inflated egos—not all actors—are insecure.)

In the following examples, commas set off only nonrestrictive modifiers—those that supply nonessential information. Commas do not set off restrictive modifiers, which supply essential information.

Adjective Clauses

> **Nonrestrictive:** He ran for the bus, which was late as usual.
>
> **Restrictive:** Speaking in public is something that most people fear.

Prepositional Phrases

> **Nonrestrictive:** The clerk, with a nod, dismissed me.
>
> **Restrictive:** The man with the gun demanded their money.

Verbal Phrases

> **Nonrestrictive:** The marathoner, running her fastest, beat her previous record.
>
> **Restrictive:** The candidates running for mayor have agreed to a debate.

Appositives

> **Nonrestrictive:** *Citizen Kane,* Orson Welles's first film, made him famous.
>
> **Restrictive:** The film *Citizen Kane* made Orson Welles famous.

CHECKLIST

RESTRICTIVE AND NONRESTRICTIVE MODIFIERS

To determine whether a modifier is restrictive or nonrestrictive, ask yourself these questions:

- ☐ Is the modifier essential to the meaning of the noun it modifies (*The man with the gun*, not just any man)? If so, it is restrictive and does not take commas.
- ☐ Is the modifier introduced by *that* (*something that most people fear*)? If so, it is restrictive. *That* cannot introduce a nonrestrictive clause.
- ☐ Can you delete the relative pronoun without causing ambiguity or confusion (*something [that] most people fear*)? If so, the clause is restrictive.
- ☐ Is the appositive more specific than the noun that precedes it (*the film Citizen Kane*)? If so, it is restrictive.

CLOSE-UP

USING COMMAS WITH *THAT* AND *WHICH*

That introduces only restrictive clauses, which are not set off by commas.

Restrictive (no comma): I bought a used car that cost $2,000.

Which can introduce both restrictive and nonrestrictive clauses.

Restrictive (no comma): I bought a used car which cost $2,000.
Nonrestrictive (commas needed): The used car I bought, which cost $2,000, broke down after a week.

NOTE: Many writers prefer to use *which* to introduce only nonrestrictive clauses.

GRAMMAR CHECKER

THAT OR *WHICH*

Your word processor's grammar checker may label the use of *which* as an error when it introduces a restrictive clause. It will prompt you to add commas, using *which* to introduce a nonrestrictive clause, or to change *which* to *that*. Review the meaning of your sentence, and revise accordingly.

(continued)

THAT OR *WHICH* (continued)

> **Spelling and Grammar: English (U.S.)**
>
> "That" or "Which":
>
> Only the **books which are in the attic** must be moved.
>
> Suggestions:
>
> books, which are in the attic,
>
> —— OR ——
>
> books that are in the attic

■ EXERCISE 5

Insert commas where necessary to set off nonrestrictive modifiers.

The Statue of Liberty which was dedicated in 1886 has undergone extensive renovation. Its supporting structure whose designer was the French engineer Alexandre Gustave Eiffel is made of iron. The Statue of Liberty created over a period of nine years by sculptor Frédéric-Auguste Bartholdi stands 151 feet tall. The people of France who were grateful for American help in the French Revolution raised the money to pay the sculptor who created the statue. The people of the United States contributing over $100,000 raised the money for the pedestal on which the statue stands.

2 Transitional Words and Phrases

<u>Transitional words and phrases</u>—which include conjunctive adverbs like *however*, *therefore*, *thus*, and *nevertheless* as well as expressions like *for example* and *on the other hand*—qualify, clarify, and make connections. However, they are not essential to the sentence's meaning. For this reason, they are always set off by commas when they interrupt a clause or when they begin or end a sentence.

See 7b2

The Outward Bound program<u>, for example,</u> is considered safe.

<u>In fact,</u> Outward Bound has an excellent reputation.

Other programs are not so safe<u>, however</u>.

NOTE: When a transitional word or phrase joins two independent clauses, it must be preceded by a semicolon and followed by a comma: *Laughter is the best medicine<u>; of course,</u> penicillin also comes in handy sometimes.*

3 Contradictory Phrases

A phrase that expresses contradiction is usually set off by commas.

> This medicine is taken after meals, never on an empty stomach.
>
> Mark McGwire, not Sammy Sosa, was the first to break Roger Maris's home-run record.

4 Absolute Phrases

An **absolute phrase,** which usually consists of a noun plus a participle and modifies an entire independent clause, is always set off by a comma from the independent clause it modifies.

> His fear increasing, he waited to enter the haunted house.
>
> Many soldiers were lost in Southeast Asia, their bodies never recovered.

5 Miscellaneous Nonessential Material

Other nonessential material usually set off by commas includes tag questions, names in direct address, mild interjections, and *yes* and *no*.

> This is your first day on the job, isn't it?
>
> I wonder, Mr. Honeywell, whether Mr. Albright deserves a raise.
>
> Well, it's about time.
>
> Yes, that's what I thought.

■ EXERCISE 6

Set off the nonessential elements in these sentences with commas. If a sentence is correct, mark it with a *C*.

Example: Piranhas, like sharks, will attack and eat almost anything if the opportunity arises.

1. Kermit the Frog is a Muppet a cross between a marionette and a puppet.
2. The common cold a virus is frequently spread by hand contact not by mouth.
3. The account in the Bible of Noah's Ark and the forty-day flood may be based on an actual deluge.
4. Many US welfare recipients, such as children, the aged, and the severely disabled, are unable to work.
5. The submarine *Nautilus* was the first to cross under the North Pole wasn't it?

6. The 1958 Ford Edsel was advertised with the slogan "Once you've seen it, you'll never forget it."
7. Superman was called Kal-El on the planet Krypton; on earth however he was known as Clark Kent not Kal-El.
8. Its sales topping any of his previous singles "Heartbreak Hotel" was Elvis Presley's first million-seller.
9. Two companies Nash and Hudson joined in 1954 to form American Motors.
10. A firefly is a beetle not a fly and a prairie dog is a rodent not a dog.

52e Using Commas in Other Conventional Contexts

1 With Direct Quotations

In most cases, use commas to set off a direct quotation from the **identifying tag**—the phrase that identifies the speaker (*he said*, *she answered*, and so on).

Emerson said to Whitman, "I greet you at the beginning of a great career."

"I greet you at the beginning of a great career," Emerson said to Whitman.

"I greet you," Emerson said to Whitman, "at the beginning of a great career."

When the identifying tag comes between two complete sentences, however, the tag is introduced by a comma but followed by a period.

"Winning isn't everything," Coach Vince Lombardi once said. "It's the only thing."

If the first sentence of an interrupted quotation ends with a question mark or exclamation point, do not use commas.

"Should we hold the front page?" she asked. "It's a slow news day."

"Hold the front page!" he cried. "There's breaking news!"

2 With Titles or Degrees Following a Name

Hamlet, prince of Denmark, is Shakespeare's most famous character.

Michael Crichton, MD, wrote *Jurassic Park*.

3 In Addresses and Dates

When a date or an address falls within a sentence, use a comma after the last element.

On August 30, 1983, the space shuttle *Challenger* was launched.

Do not use a comma to separate the street number from the street or the state name from the ZIP code.

Her address is 600 West End Avenue, New York, NY 10024.

NOTE: Do not use a comma to separate the month from the year: *August 1983*.

4 In Salutations and Closings

In informal correspondence, use commas following salutations and closings. Also use commas in both informal and business correspondence following the complimentary close.

Dear John,   Love,
Dear Aunt Sophie,   Sincerely,

See 29a

NOTE: In business letters, always use a colon, not a comma, after the salutation.

5 In Long Numbers

For a number of four digits or more, place a comma before every third digit, counting from the right.

1,200   120,000
12,000   1,200,000

NOTE: Commas are not used in long page and line numbers, address numbers, telephone numbers, or ZIP codes (or in four-digit year numbers).

ESL TIP

In some countries, writers use commas in decimal numbers where US writers use periods. When writing in English, remember to use periods in decimal numbers.

The total bill was $53.75.

The number 1¾ can be represented as the decimal number 1.75.

EXERCISE 7

Add commas where necessary to set off quotations, names, dates, addresses, and numbers.

1. India became independent on August 15 1947.
2. The UAW has more than 1500000 dues-paying members.
3. Nikita Khrushchev, former Soviet premier, once said "We will bury you!"
4. Mount St. Helens, northeast of Portland Oregon, began erupting on March 27 1980 and eventually killed at least thirty people.
5. Located at 1600 Pennsylvania Avenue Washington DC, the White House is a popular tourist attraction.
6. In 1956, playing before a crowd of 64519 fans in Yankee Stadium in New York New York, Don Larsen pitched the first perfect game in World Series history.
7. Lewis Thomas MD was born in Flushing New York and attended Harvard Medical School in Cambridge Massachusetts.
8. In 1967 2000000 people worldwide died of smallpox, but in 1977 only about twenty people died.
9. "The reports of my death" Mark Twain remarked "have been greatly exaggerated."
10. The French explorer Jean Nicolet landed at Green Bay Wisconsin in 1634, and in 1848 Wisconsin became the thirtieth state; it has 10355 lakes and a population of more than 4700000.

52f Using Commas to Prevent Misreading

In some cases, you need to use a comma to avoid ambiguity. For example, consider the following sentence.

> Those who can, sprint the final lap.

Without the comma, *can* appears to be an auxiliary verb ("Those who can sprint . . ."), and the sentence seems incomplete. Because the comma tells readers to pause, it eliminates confusion.

Also use a comma to acknowledge the omission of a repeated word, usually a verb, and to separate words repeated consecutively.

> Pam carried the box; Tim, the suitcase.

> Everything bad that could have happened, happened.

EXERCISE 8

Add commas where necessary to prevent misreading.

Example: Whatever will be, will be.

1. According to Bob Frank's computer is obsolete.
2. Da Gama explored Florida; Pizarro Peru.
3. By Monday evening students must begin preregistration for fall classes.
4. Whatever they built they built with care.
5. When batting practice carefully.
6. Brunch includes warm muffins topped with whipped butter and freshly brewed coffee.
7. Students go to school to learn not to play sports.
8. Technology has made what once seemed not possible possible.

EXERCISE 9

Add commas to the following sentences where needed, and be prepared to explain why each is necessary. If a sentence is correct, mark it with a *C*.

Example: Once again, Congress is looking to make changes in immigration law.

1. According to some critics this test which new citizens must take before they are naturalized is simple and shallow.
2. Others claim that making the test more difficult would be unfair because many graduates of American high schools cannot answer the basic civics questions about the design of the American flag the structure of the US government and the events of American political history required by the test.
3. Some fear that too many new citizens from foreign countries will undermine core American values but others argue that those values came from earlier immigrants and that change is not necessarily bad.
4. Fear of immigrants while seemingly unfounded is not new.
5. In the 1940s the American government forced immigrants from Japan and their American-born children into internment camps after the Japanese bombed Pearl Harbor initiating America's involvement in World War II.

52g Editing Misused Commas

Do not use commas in the following situations.

1 To Join Two Independent Clauses

See 39a

A comma alone cannot join two independent clauses; it must be followed by a coordinating conjunction. Using just a comma to connect two independent clauses creates a **comma splice**.

The season was unusually cool, *but* the orange crop was not seriously harmed.

2 To Set Off Restrictive Modifiers

Commas are not used to set off **restrictive modifiers**.

See
52d1

Women⁄ who seek to be equal to men⁄ lack ambition.

The film⁄ *Malcolm X*⁄ was directed by Spike Lee.

3 Between Inseparable Grammatical Constructions

Do not place a comma between grammatical elements that cannot be logically separated: a subject and its predicate, a verb and its complement or direct object, a preposition and its object, or an adjective and the word or phrase it modifies.

A woman with dark red hair⁄ opened the door. (comma incorrectly placed between subject and predicate)

Louis Braille developed⁄ an alphabet of raised dots for the blind. (comma incorrectly placed between verb and object)

They relaxed somewhat during⁄ the last part of the obstacle course. (comma incorrectly placed between preposition and object)

Wind-dispersed weeds include the well-known and plentiful⁄ dandelions, milkweed, and thistle. (comma incorrectly placed between adjective and words it modifies)

4 Between a Verb and an Indirect Quotation or Indirect Question

Do not use commas between a verb and an indirect quotation or between a verb and an indirect question.

General Douglas MacArthur vowed⁄ that he would return. (comma incorrectly placed between verb and indirect quotation)

The landlord asked⁄ if we would sign a two-year lease. (comma incorrectly placed between verb and indirect question)

5 Between Phrases Linked by Correlative Conjunctions

Commas are not used to separate two phrases linked by **correlative conjunctions**.

See
46g

Forty years ago, most college students had access to neither photocopiers⁄ nor pocket calculators.

Both typewriters⁄ and tape recorders were generally available, however.

6 In Compounds That Are Not Composed of Independent Clauses

Do not use commas before coordinating conjunctions like *and* or *but* when they join two elements of a compound subject, predicate, object, complement, or auxiliary verb.

> Plagues,/ and pestilence were common during the Middle Ages. (compound subject)
>
> Many women thirty-five and older are returning to college,/ and tend to be good students. (compound predicate)
>
> Mattel has marketed a doctor's lab coat,/ and an astronaut suit for its Barbie doll. (compound object)
>
> People buy bottled water because it is pure,/ and fashionable. (compound complement)
>
> She can,/ and will be ready to run in the primary. (compound auxiliary verb)

7 Before a Dependent Clause at the End of a Sentence

Commas are generally not used before a dependent clause that falls at the end of a sentence.

> Jane Addams founded Hull House,/ because she wanted to help Chicago's poor.

■ EXERCISE 10

Unnecessary commas have been intentionally added to some of the sentences that follow. Delete any unnecessary commas. If a sentence is correct, mark it with a *C*.

Example: Spring fever,/ is a common ailment.

1. A book is like a garden, carried in the pocket. (Arab proverb)
2. Like the iodine content of kelp, air freight, is something most Americans have never pondered. (*Time*)
3. Charles Rolls, and Frederick Royce manufactured the first Rolls-Royce Silver Ghost, in 1907.
4. The hills ahead of him were rounded domes of grey granite, smooth as a bald man's pate, and completely free of vegetation. (Wilbur Smith, *Flight of the Falcon*)
5. Food here is scarce, and cafeteria food is vile, but the great advantage to Russian raw materials, when one can get hold of them, is that they are always fresh and untampered with. (Andrea Lee, *Russian Journal*)

53

Using Semicolons

❓ FAQs

When do I use a semicolon? (p. 649)
Do I introduce a list with a semicolon or a colon? (p. 655)

A **semicolon** is used only between items of equal grammatical rank: two independent clauses, two phrases, and so on.

53a Separating Independent Clauses

Use a semicolon between closely related independent clauses that convey parallel or contrasting information but are not joined by a coordinating conjunction.

> Paul Revere's *The Boston Massacre* is traditional American protest art**;** Edward Hicks's paintings are socially conscious art with a religious strain.

NOTE: Using only a comma or no punctuation at all between independent clauses creates a **run-on**.

See Ch. 39

■ EXERCISE 1

Add semicolons where necessary to separate independent clauses. Then, reread the paragraph to make certain no run-ons remain.

Example: *Birth of a Nation* was one of the earliest epic movies**;** it was based on the book *The Klansman*.

During the 1950s movie attendance declined because of the increasing popularity of television. As a result, numerous gimmicks were introduced to draw audiences into theaters. One of the first of these was Cinerama, in this technique three pictures were shot side by side and projected onto a curved screen. Next came 3-D, complete with special glasses, *Bwana Devil* and *The Creature from the Black Lagoon* were two early 3-D ventures. *The Robe* was the first picture filmed in Cinemascope in this technique a shrunken image was projected on a screen twice as wide as it was tall. Smell-O-Vision (or Aroma-rama) enabled audiences to smell the scenes, it was impossible to get one odor out of the theater in time for the next smell to be introduced. William Castle's

Thirteen Ghosts introduced special glasses for cowardly viewers, the red part of the glasses was the "ghost viewer," and the green part was the "ghost remover." Perhaps the ultimate in movie gimmicks accompanied the film *The Tingler* seats in the theater were wired to generate mild electric shocks. Unfortunately, the shocks set off a chain reaction that led to hysteria in the theater. During the 1960s, such gimmicks all but disappeared, viewers were able once again to simply sit back and enjoy a movie. In 1997, *Mr. Payback*, a short interactive film, introduced a new gimmick, it allowed viewers to vote on how they wanted the plot to unfold.

■ EXERCISE 2

Combine each of the following sentence groups into one sentence that contains only two independent clauses. Use a semicolon to join the two clauses. You will need to add, delete, relocate, or change some words; keep experimenting until you find the arrangement that best conveys the sentence's meaning.

Example: The Congo River Rapids is a ride at the Dark Continent in Tampa, Florida. ; riders / ~~Riders~~ raft down the river. , gliding / ~~They glide~~ alongside jungle plants and animals.

1. Theme parks offer exciting rides. They are thrill packed. They flirt with danger.
2. Free Fall is located in Atlanta's Six Flags over Georgia. In this ride, riders travel up a 128-foot-tall tower. They plunge down at fifty-five miles per hour.
3. In the Sky Whirl, riders go 115 feet up in the air and circle about seventy-five times. This ride is located in Great America. Great America parks are in Gurnee, Illinois, and Santa Clara, California.
4. The Kamikaze Slide can be found at the Wet'n Wild parks in Arlington, Texas, and Orlando, Florida. This ride is a slide three hundred feet long. It extends sixty feet into the air.
5. Viper is an exciting ride. It is found at Six Flags Great Adventure in Jackson, New Jersey. Its outside loop has a 360-degree spiral.
6. Astroworld in Houston, Texas, boasts Greezed Lightnin'. This ride is an eighty-foot-high loop. The ride goes from zero to sixty miles per hour in four seconds and moves forward and backward.
7. The Beast is at Kings Island near Cincinnati, Ohio. The Beast is a wooden roller coaster. It has a 7,400-foot track and goes seventy miles per hour.
8. Busch Gardens in Williamsburg, Virginia, features Escape from Pompeii. This is a water ride. It allows riders to explore ruins and see Mount Vesuvius.

Separating Independent Clauses ■ ; **53b** **651**

9. Wild Arctic is at Sea World in Orlando, Florida. This ride includes a simulated helicopter flight. The flight goes to Base Station Wild Arctic. The ride also goes to a wrecked ship.
10. At Busch Gardens Tampa Bay in Tampa, Florida, Egypt is a thrill-packed attraction. It features an inverted roller coaster with cars hanging from the top. A replica of King Tut's tomb is also featured.

53b Separating Independent Clauses Introduced by Transitional Words and Phrases

Use a semicolon before a <u>transitional word or phrase</u> that joins two independent clauses. (The transitional element is followed by a comma.)

See 7b2

> Thomas Jefferson brought two hundred vanilla beans and a recipe for vanilla ice cream back from France; thus, he gave America its all-time favorite ice-cream flavor.

■ EXERCISE 3

Combine each of the following sentence groups into one sentence that contains only two independent clauses. Use a semicolon and the transitional word or phrase in parentheses to join the two clauses, adding commas within clauses where necessary. You will need to add, delete, relocate, or change some words. There is no one correct version; keep experimenting until you find the arrangement you feel is most effective.

Example: The Aleutian Islands are located off the west coast of Alaska. They are an extremely remote chain of islands; in fact, they They are sometimes called America's Siberia. (in fact)

1. The Aleutians lie between the North Pacific Ocean and the Bering Sea. The weather there is harsh. Dense fog, 100-mph winds, and even tidal waves and earthquakes are not uncommon. (for example)
2. These islands constitute North America's largest network of active volcanoes. The Aleutians boast some beautiful scenery. The islands are relatively unexplored. (still)
3. The Aleutians are home to a wide variety of birds. Numerous animals, such as fur seals and whales, are found there. These islands may house the largest concentration of marine animals in the world. (in fact)
4. During World War II, thousands of American soldiers were stationed on Attu Island. They were stationed on Adak Island. The Japanese eventually occupied both islands. (however)

5. The islands' original population of native Aleuts was drastically reduced in the eighteenth century by Russian fur traders. Today, the total population is only about 8,500. US military employees comprise more than half of this. (consequently)

(Adapted from *National Geographic*)

53c Separating Items in a Series

Use semicolons between items in a series when one or more of these items include commas.

> Three papers are posted on the bulletin board outside the building: a description of the exams; a list of appeal procedures for students who fail; and an employment ad from an automobile factory, addressed specifically to candidates whose appeals are turned down. (Andrea Lee, *Russian Journal*)

> Laramie, Wyoming; Wyoming, Delaware; and Delaware, Ohio, were three of the places they visited.

■ EXERCISE 4

Replace commas with semicolons where necessary to separate internally punctuated items in a series. (For information on use of semicolons with quotation marks, **see 55e2.**)

Example: Luxury automobiles have some strong selling points: they are status symbols; some, such as the Corvette, appreciate in value; and they are usually comfortable and well appointed.

1. The history of modern art seems at times to be a collection of "isms": Impressionism, a term that applies to painters who attempted to depict contemporary life by reproducing an "impression" of what the eye sees, Abstract Expressionism, which applies to artists who stress emotion and the unconscious in their nonrepresentational works, and, more recently, Minimalism, which applies to painters and sculptors whose work reasserts the physical reality of the object.
2. Although the term *Internet* is widely used to refer only to the World Wide Web and email, the Internet consists of a variety of discrete elements, including newsgroups, which allow users to post and receive messages on an unbelievably broad range of topics, interactive communication forums, such as blogs, discussion forums, and chat rooms, and FTP, which allows users to download material from remote computers.

3. Three of rock and roll's best-known guitar heroes played with the "British Invasion" group The Yardbirds: Eric Clapton, the group's first lead guitarist, went on to play with John Mayall's Bluesbreakers, Cream, and Blind Faith, and is now a popular solo act, Jeff Beck, the group's second guitarist, though not as visible as Clapton, made rock history with the Jeff Beck Group and inventive solo albums, and Jimmy Page, the group's third and final guitarist, transformed the remnants of the original group into the premier heavy metal band, Led Zeppelin.
4. Some of the most commonly confused words in English are *aggravate*, which means "to worsen," and *irritate*, which means "to annoy," *continual*, which means "recurring at intervals," and *continuous*, which means "an action occurring without interruption," *imply*, which means "to hint, suggest," and *infer*, which means "to conclude from," and *compliment*, which means "to praise," and *complement*, which means "to complete or add to."
5. Tennessee Williams wrote *The Glass Menagerie*, which is about Laura Wingfield, a disabled young woman, and her family, *A Streetcar Named Desire*, which starred Marlon Brando, and *Cat on a Hot Tin Roof*, which won a Pulitzer Prize.

■ EXERCISE 5

Combine each of the following sentence groups into one sentence that includes a series of items separated by semicolons. You will need to add, delete, relocate, or change words. Try several versions of each sentence until you find the most effective arrangement.

Example: Collecting baseball cards is a worthwhile hobby~~.~~ ^because it^ ~~It~~ helps children learn how to bargain and trade~~.~~ ^; it^ ~~It also~~ encourages them to compare data about ballplayers~~.~~ ^; and, most^

~~Most~~ important, it introduces them to positive role models.

1. A good dictionary offers definitions of words, including some obsolete and nonstandard words. It provides information about synonyms, usage, and word origins. It also offers information on pronunciation and syllabication.
2. The flags of the Scandinavian countries all depict a cross on a solid background. Denmark's flag is red with a white cross. Norway's flag is also red, but its cross is blue, outlined in white. Sweden's flag is blue with a yellow cross.
3. Over one hundred international collectors' clubs are thriving today. One of these associations is the Cola Clan, whose members buy, sell, and trade Coca-Cola memorabilia. Another is the Citrus Label Society. There is also a Cookie Cutter Collectors' Club.

4. Listening to the radio special, we heard "Shuffle Off to Buffalo" and "Moon over Miami," both of which are about eastern cities. We heard "By the Time I Get to Phoenix" and "I Left My Heart in San Francisco," which mention western cities. Finally, we heard "The Star-Spangled Banner," which seemed to be an appropriate finale.
5. There are three principal types of contact lenses. Hard contact lenses, also called "conventional lenses," are easy to clean and handle and quite sturdy. Soft lenses, which are easily contaminated and must be cleaned and disinfected daily, are less durable. Gas-permeable lenses, sometimes advertised as "semihard" or "semisoft" lenses, look and feel like hard lenses but are more easily contaminated and less durable.

53d Editing Misused Semicolons

Do not use semicolons in the following situations.

1 Between a Dependent and an Independent Clause

Use a comma, not a semicolon, between a dependent and an independent clause.

> Because new drugs can now suppress the body's immune reaction; fewer organ transplants are rejected by the body.

GRAMMAR CHECKER

EDITING MISUSED SEMICOLONS

Your word processor's grammar checker will highlight certain misused semicolons and frequently offer suggestions for revision.

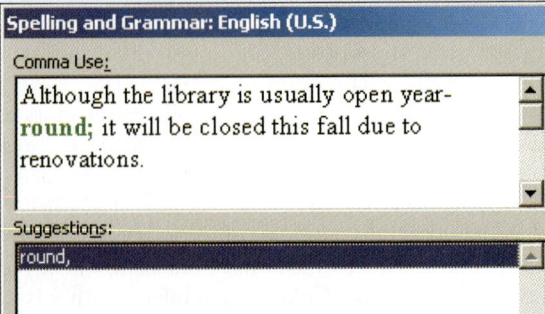

Editing Misused Semicolons ; **53d**

2 Between a Phrase and a Clause

Use a comma, not a semicolon, between a phrase and a clause.

Increasing rapidly*,* computer crime poses a challenge for government, financial, and military agencies.

3 To Introduce a List

Use a colon, not a semicolon, to introduce a **list**.

See 56a1

Despite the presence of CNN and Fox News, the evening news remains a battleground for the three major television networks*:* CBS, NBC, and ABC.

NOTE: Always introduce a list with a complete sentence followed by a colon.

4 To Introduce a Quotation

Do not use a semicolon to introduce **quoted speech or writing**.

See 55a

Marie Antoinette may not have said*,* "Let them eat cake."

■ EXERCISE 6

Read the following paragraph carefully. Then, add semicolons where necessary, and delete incorrectly used ones, substituting other punctuation where necessary.

> Barnstormers were aviators; who toured the country after World War I, giving people short airplane rides and exhibitions of stunt flying, in fact, the name *barnstormer* was derived from the use of barns as airplane hangars. Americans' interest in airplanes had all but disappeared after the war. The barnstormers helped popularize flying; especially in rural areas. Some were pilots who had flown in the war; others were just young men with a thirst for adventure. They gave people rides in airplanes; sometimes charging a dollar a minute. For most passengers, this was their first ride in an airplane, in fact, sometimes it was their first sight of one. After Lindbergh's 1927 flight across the Atlantic; Americans suddenly needed no encouragement to embrace aviation. The barnstormers had outlived their usefulness; and an era ended. (Adapted from William Goldman, *Adventures in the Screen Trade*)

54

Using Apostrophes

❓ FAQs
How do I form the possessive of a singular word that already ends in -s? (p. 656)
How do I form the possessive of plural words that end in -s? (p. 657)
What's the difference between its *and* it's*? (p. 659)*

Use an apostrophe to form the possessive case, to indicate omissions in contractions, and to form certain plurals.

54a Forming the Possessive Case

The possessive case indicates ownership. In English, the possessive case of nouns and indefinite pronouns is indicated either with a phrase that includes the word *of* (the hands *of* the clock) or with an apostrophe and, in most cases, an *s* (the clock's hands).

1 Singular Nouns and Indefinite Pronouns

To form the possessive case of singular nouns and indefinite pronouns, add -'s.

> "The Monk's Tale" is one of Chaucer's *Canterbury Tales.*
> When we would arrive was anyone's guess.

2 Singular Nouns Ending in -s

❓ To form the possessive case of singular nouns that end in -s, add -'s in most cases.

> Reading Henry James's *The Ambassadors* was not Maris's idea of fun.
> The class's time was changed to 8 a.m.

NOTE: With some singular nouns that end in -s, pronouncing the possessive ending as a separate syllable can sound awkward. In such cases, it is acceptable to use just an apostrophe: Crispus Attucks' death, Aristophanes' *Lysistrata.*

An apostrophe is not used to form the possessive case of a title that already contains an -'s ending; use a phrase instead.

> The staging of
> ~~A Midsummer Night's Dream's staging~~ presents a challenge.

3 Plural Nouns Ending in -s

To form the possessive case of regular plural nouns (those that end in -s or -es), add only an apostrophe.

> The Readers' Guide to Periodical Literature is available online.
>
> Laid-off employees received two weeks' severance pay and three months' medical benefits.
>
> The Lopezes' three children are triplets.

4 Irregular Plural Nouns

To form the possessive case of nouns that have irregular plurals, add -'s.

> Long after they were gone, the geese's honking could still be heard.
>
> The Children's Hour is a play by Lillian Hellman; The Women's Room is a novel by Marilyn French.
>
> The two oxen's yokes were securely attached to the cart.

5 Compound Nouns or Groups of Words

To form the possessive case of compound nouns or of word groups, add -'s to the last word.

> The editor-in-chief's position is open.
>
> He accepted the secretary of state's resignation under protest.
>
> This is someone else's responsibility.

6 Two or More Items

To indicate individual ownership of two or more items, add -'s to each item.

> Ernest Hemingway's and Gertrude Stein's writing styles have some similarities. (Hemingway and Stein have two separate writing styles.)

To indicate joint ownership, add -'s only to the last item.

> Gilbert and Sullivan's operettas include *The Pirates of Penzance* and *The Mikado*. (Gilbert and Sullivan collaborated on both operettas.)

54b Using Apostrophes

EXERCISE 1

Change the modifying phrases that follow the nouns to possessive forms that precede the nouns.

Example: the pen belonging to my aunt
            my aunt's pen

1. the songs recorded by Ray Charles
2. the red glare of the rockets
3. the idea that Warren had
4. the housekeeper Rick and Leslie hired
5. the first choice of everyone
6. the dinner given by Harris
7. furniture designed by William Morris
8. the climate of the Virgin Islands
9. the sport the Russells play
10. the role created by the French actress

EXERCISE 2

Change each word or phrase in parentheses to its possessive form. In some cases, you may have to use a phrase to indicate the possessive.

Example: The (children) toys were scattered all over their (parents) bedroom.

   The children's toys were scattered all over their parents' bedroom.

1. Jane (Addams) settlement house was called Hull House.
2. (*A Room of One's Own*) popularity increased with the rise of feminism.
3. The (chief petty officer) responsibilities are varied.
4. Vietnamese (restaurants) numbers have grown dramatically in ten (years) time.
5. (Charles Dickens) and (Mark Twain) works have sold millions of copies.

54b Indicating Omissions in Contractions

1 Omitted Letters

Apostrophes replace omitted letters in contractions that combine a pronoun and a verb (*he* + *will* = *he'll*) or the elements of a verb phrase (*do* + *not* = *don't*).

FREQUENTLY USED CONTRACTIONS	
it's (it is, it has)	let's (let us)
he's (he is, he has)	we've (we have)

Indicatng Omissions in Contractions ■ ✓ **54b**   **659**

wouldn't (would not)
couldn't (could not)
don't (do not)
won't (will not)
she's (she is, she has)
who's (who is, who has)
isn't (is not)

we're (we are)
you'd (you would)
we'd (we would)
they'd (they had)
they're (they are)
we'll (we will)
I'm (I am)

NOTE: Contractions are generally too informal for use in college writing.

GRAMMAR CHECKER

REVISING CONTRACTIONS

If you set your word processor's writing style to Formal or Technical, the grammar checker will highlight contractions and offer suggestions for revision.

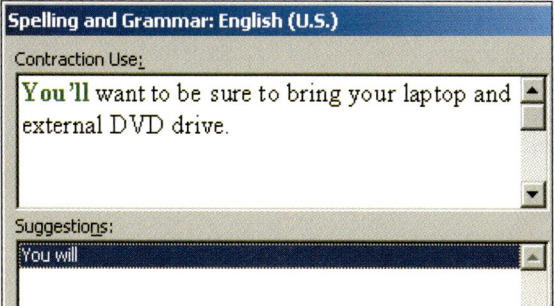

CLOSE-UP

USING APOSTROPHES

Be careful not to confuse contractions (which always include apostrophes) with the possessive forms of personal pronouns (which never include apostrophes).

Contractions	Possessive Forms
Who's on first?	Whose book is this?
They're playing our song.	Their team is winning.
It's raining.	Its paws were muddy.
You're a real pal.	Your résumé is very impressive.

2 Omitted Numbers

In informal writing, an apostrophe may be used to represent the century in a year.

　　　Crash of '29　　　class of '06　　　'57 Chevy

In college writing, however, write out the year in full: *the Crash of 1929, the class of 2006, a 1957 Chevrolet.*

■ EXERCISE 3

In the following sentences, correct any errors in the use of apostrophes. (Remember, apostrophes are used in contractions but not in possessive pronouns.) If a sentence is correct, mark it with a *C*.

Example:　~~Who's~~ *Whose* troops were sent to Afghanistan?

1. Its never easy to choose a major; whatever you decide, your bound to have second thoughts.
2. Olive Oyl asked, "Whose that knocking at my door?"
3. Their watching too much television; in fact, they're eyes are glazed.
4. Whose coming along on the backpacking trip?
5. The horse had been badly treated; it's spirit was broken.
6. Your correct in assuming its a challenging course.
7. Sometimes even you're best friends won't tell you your boring.
8. They're training had not prepared them for the hardships they faced.
9. It's too early to make a positive diagnosis.
10. Robert Frost wrote the poem that begins, "Who's woods these are I think I know."

54c Forming Plurals

In a few special situations, add -'s to form plurals.

FORMING PLURALS WITH APOSTROPHES

Plurals of Letters

　　The Italian language has no *j*'s, *k*'s, or *w*'s.

Plurals of Words Referred to as Words

　　The supervisor would accept no *if*'s, *and*'s, or *but*'s.

NOTE: Elements spoken of as themselves (letters, numerals, or words) are set in italic type; the plural ending, however, is not.

See 58c

NOTE: Apostrophes are not used in plurals of abbreviations (including acronyms) or numbers.

DVDs   PACs   1960s

■ EXERCISE 4

In the following sentences, form correct plurals for the letters and words in parentheses. Underline to indicate italics where necessary.

Example: The word *bubbles* contains three (b).
                        The word *bubbles* contains three *b*'s.

1. She closed her letter with a row of (x) and (o) to indicate kisses and hugs.
2. The three (R) are reading, writing, and 'rithmetic.
3. The report included far too many (maybe) and too few (definitely).
4. The word bookkeeper contains two (o), two (k), and three (e).
5. His letter included many (please) and (thank you).

54d Editing Misused Apostrophes

Do not use apostrophes with plural nouns that are not possessive.

   The Thompson's are not at home.

   Down vest's are very warm.

   The Philadelphia Seventy Sixer's have had good years and bad.

Do not use apostrophes to form the possessive case of personal pronouns.

   This ticket must be your's or her's.

   The next turn is their's.

   Her doll had lost it's right eye.

   The next great moment in history is our's.

NOTE: Be especially careful not to confuse the possessive forms of personal pronouns with **contractions**.

See 54b1

■ EXERCISE 5

In the following sentences, correct all errors in the use of apostrophes to form noun plurals or the possessive case of personal pronouns.

Example: Dr. Sampson's lecture's were more interesting than her's.

1. The Schaefer's seats are right next to our's.
2. Most of the college's in the area offer computer courses open to outsider's as well as to their own students.

3. The network completely revamped it's daytime programming.
4. Is the responsibility for the hot dog concession Cynthia's or your's?
5. Romantic poets are his favorite's.
6. Debbie returned the books to the library, forgetting they were her's.
7. Cultural revolution's do not occur very often, but when they do they bring sweeping change's.
8. Roll-top desk's are eagerly sought by antique dealer's.
9. A flexible schedule is one of their priorities, but it isn't one of our's.
10. Is your's the red house or the brown one?

55

Using Quotation Marks

❓ FAQs

How do I punctuate quotations that are introduced by phrases such as he said? *(p. 663)*
Do I use quotation marks with a long quotation? (p. 665)
Are lines of poetry always set off with quotation marks? (p. 667)
Which titles require quotation marks? (p. 667)
Do I put commas and periods inside or outside quotation marks? (p. 668)
What do I do about a quotation inside another quotation? (p. 669)

Use quotation marks to set off brief passages of quoted speech or writing, to set off certain titles, and to set off words used in special ways. Do not use quotation marks when quoting long passages of prose or poetry.

55a Setting Off Quoted Speech or Writing

When you quote a word, phrase, or brief passage of someone else's speech or writing, enclose the quoted material in a pair of quotation marks.

> Gloria Steinem observed, "We are becoming the men we once hoped to marry."

> Galsworthy writes that Aunt Juley is "prostrated by the blow" (329). (Note that in this example from a student paper, the end punctuation follows the parenthetical documentation.)

CLOSE-UP

USING QUOTATION MARKS WITH DIALOGUE

When you record **dialogue** (conversation between two or more people), enclose the quoted words in quotation marks. Begin a new paragraph each time a new speaker is introduced.

When you are quoting several paragraphs of dialogue by one speaker, begin each new paragraph with quotation marks. However, use closing quotation marks only at the end of the *entire quoted passage*, not at the end of each paragraph.

Special rules govern the punctuation of a quotation when it is used with an **identifying tag,** a phrase (such as *he said*) that identifies the speaker or writer. Punctuation guidelines for various situations involving identifying tags are outlined below.

1 Identifying Tag in the Middle of a Quoted Passage

Use a pair of commas to set off an identifying tag that interrupts a quoted passage.

"In the future**,**" pop artist Andy Warhol once said**,** "everyone will be world famous for fifteen minutes."

If the identifying tag follows a completed sentence but the quoted passage continues, use a period after the tag; begin the new sentence with a capital letter, and enclose it in quotation marks.

"Be careful**,**" Erin warned**.** "Reptiles can be tricky."

2 Identifying Tag at the Beginning of a Quoted Passage

Use a comma after an identifying tag that introduces quoted speech or writing.

The Raven repeated**,** "Nevermore."

See 56a3

Use a **colon** instead of a comma before a quotation if the identifying tag is a complete sentence.

She gave her final answer**:** "No."

> **GRAMMAR CHECKER**
>
> **CHECKING PUNCTUATION WITH QUOTATION MARKS**
>
> Your word processor's grammar checker will often highlight missing punctuation in sentences containing quotation marks and offer suggestions for revision.
>
>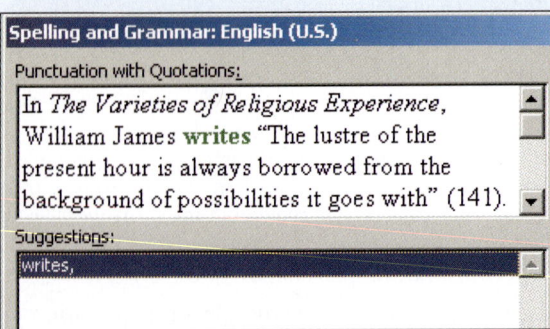

3 Identifying Tag at the End of a Quoted Passage

Use a comma to set off a quotation from an identifying tag that follows it.

"Be careful out there," the sergeant warned.

If the quotation ends with a question mark or an exclamation point, use that punctuation mark instead of the comma. In this situation, the tag begins with a lowercase letter even though it follows end punctuation.

"Is Ankara the capital of Turkey?" she asked.

"Oh boy!" he cried.

NOTE: Commas and periods are always placed *inside* quotation marks. For information on placement of other punctuation marks with quotation marks, **see 55e**.

■ EXERCISE 1

Add quotation marks to these sentences where necessary to set off quotations from identifying tags.

Example: Wordsworth's phrase "splendour in the grass" was used as the title of a movie about young lovers.

1. Few people can explain what Descartes's words I think, therefore I am actually mean.
2. Gertrude Stein said, You are all a lost generation.
3. Freedom of speech does not guarantee anyone the right to yell fire in a crowded theater, she explained.
4. There's no place like home, Dorothy insisted.
5. If everyone will sit down the teacher announced the exam will begin.

55b Setting Off Long Prose Passages and Poetry

1 Long Prose Passages

Do not enclose a **long prose passage** (a passage of more than four lines) in quotation marks. Instead, set it off by indenting the entire passage one inch from the left-hand margin. Treat the quoted passage like regular text: double-space above and below it, and double-space between lines within it. Introduce the passage with a colon, and place parenthetical documentation one space after the end punctuation.

The following portrait of Aunt Juley illustrates several of the devices Galsworthy uses throughout *The Forsyte Saga*, such as a journalistic detachment that is almost cruel in its scrutiny, a subtle sense of the grotesque, and an ironic stance:

> Aunt Juley stayed in her room, prostrated by the blow. Her face, discoloured by tears, was divided into compartments by the little ridges of pouting flesh which had swollen with emotion. . . . At fixed intervals she went to her drawer, and took from beneath the lavender bags a fresh pocket-handkerchief. Her warm heart could not bear the thought that Ann was lying there so cold. (329)

Many similar portraits of characters appear throughout the novel.

CLOSE-UP

QUOTING LONG PROSE PASSAGES

When you quote a long prose passage that is a single paragraph, do not indent the first line. When quoting two or more paragraphs, however, indent the first line of each paragraph (including the first) an additional one-quarter inch. If the first sentence of the quoted passage does not begin a paragraph in the source, do not indent—but do indent the first line of each subsequent paragraph. If the passage you are quoting includes material set in quotation marks, keep the quotation marks.

NOTE: APA guidelines differ from those set forth here, which follow MLA style.

2 Poetry

Treat one line of poetry like a short prose passage: enclose it in quotation marks, and run it into the text.

> One of John Donne's best-known poems begins with the line, "Go and catch a falling star."

If you quote two or three lines of poetry, separate the lines with **slashes** (/), and run the quotation into the text. (Leave one space before and one space after the slash.)

> Alexander Pope writes, "True Ease in Writing comes from Art, not Chance, / As those move easiest who have learned to dance."

If you quote more than three lines of poetry, set them off like a **long prose passage**. (For special emphasis, you may set off fewer lines in this manner.) Do not use quotation marks, and be sure to reproduce punctuation, spelling, capitalization, and indentation *exactly* as they appear in the poem.

> Wilfred Owen, a poet who was killed in action in World War I, expresses the horrors of war with vivid imagery:
>
>> Bent double, like old beggars under sacks.
>>
>> Knock-kneed, coughing like hags, we cursed through sludge.
>>
>> Till on the haunting flares we turned our backs
>>
>> And towards our distant rest began to trudge. (lines 1-4)

55c Setting Off Titles

Titles of short works and titles of parts of long works are enclosed in quotation marks. Other titles are *italicized*.

See 58a

TITLES REQUIRING QUOTATION MARKS

Articles in Magazines, Newspapers, and Professional Journals
"Why Johnny Can't Write"

Essays, Short Stories, Short Poems, and Songs
"Fenimore Cooper's Literary Offenses"   "Flying Home"
"The Road Not Taken"   "The Star-Spangled Banner"

Chapters or Sections of Books
"Miss Sharp Begins to Make Friends"

Episodes of Radio or Television Series
"Lucy Goes to the Hospital"

See 58a for a list of titles that require italics.

■ EXERCISE 2

Add quotation marks to the following sentences where necessary to set off titles. If italics are incorrectly used, substitute quotation marks. Place commas and periods inside quotation marks.

Example: Margaret Atwood has written stories, such as
             "Rape Fantasies,"   "   "
             ~~Rape Fantasies,~~ and poems, such as You Fit Into Me.
                     ^   ^   ^

1. One of the essays from her new book *Good Bones and Simple Murder* was originally published in Harper's magazine.
2. Her collection of poems, *Morning in the Burned House*, contains the moving poem *In the Secular Night*.
3. You may have seen the movie *The Handmaid's Tale*, starring Robert Duvall, based on her best-selling novel.
4. *Surfacing* was the first book of hers I read, but my favorite work of hers is the short story Hair Ball.
5. I wasn't surprised to find her poems The Animals in the Country and This Is a Photograph of Me in our English textbook last year.

55d Setting Off Words Used in Special Ways

Enclose a word used in a special or unusual way in quotation marks. (If you use *so-called* before an unusual usage, do not use quotation marks as well.)

> It was clear that adults approved of children who were "readers," but it was not at all clear why this was so. (Annie Dillard)

Also enclose a **coinage**—an invented word—in quotation marks.

> After the twins were born, the minivan became a "babymobile."

55e Using Quotation Marks with Other Punctuation

At the end of a quotation, punctuation is sometimes placed before the closing quotation marks and sometimes placed after them.

1 With Final Commas or Periods

At the end of a quotation, place the quotation marks *after* a comma or a period.

> Many, like the poet Robert Frost, think about "the road not taken," but not many have taken "the one less traveled by."

2 With Final Semicolons or Colons

At the end of a quotation, place the quotation marks *before* a semicolon or colon.

> Students who do not pass the test receive "certificates of completion"; those who pass are awarded diplomas.

> Taxpayers were pleased with the first of the candidate's promised "sweeping new reforms": a balanced budget.

3 With Question Marks, Exclamation Points, and Dashes

If a question mark, exclamation point, or dash is part of the quotation, place the quotation marks *after* the punctuation.

"Who's there?" she demanded.

"Stop!" he cried.

"Should we leave now, or—" Vicki paused, unable to continue.

If a question mark, exclamation point, or dash is *not* part of the quotation, place the quotation marks *before* the punctuation.

Did you finish reading "The Black Cat"?

Whatever you do, don't yell "Uncle"!

The first story—Updike's "A&P"—provoked discussion.

If both the quotation and the sentence are questions or exclamations, place the quotation marks *before* the punctuation mark.

Who asked, "Is Paris burning"?

CLOSE-UP

QUOTATIONS WITHIN QUOTATIONS

Use *single* quotation marks to enclose a quotation within a quotation.

Claire noted, "Liberace always said, 'I cried all the way to the bank.'"

Also use single quotation marks within a quotation to indicate a title that would normally be enclosed in double quotation marks.

I think what she said was, "Play it, Sam. Play 'As Time Goes By.'"

Use *double* quotation marks around quotations or titles within a long prose passage.

See 55b1

55f Editing Misused Quotation Marks

Do not use quotation marks in the following situations.

1 To Convey Emphasis

Do not use quotation marks to convey emphasis.

William Randolph Hearst's "fabulous" home is a castle called San Simeon.

2 To Set Off Slang or Technical Terms

Do not use quotation marks to set off slang or technical terms. (Note that slang is almost always inappropriate in college writing.)

Dawn is "~~into~~" *very involved in* running.

"Biofeedback" is sometimes used to treat migraine headaches.

3 To Enclose Titles of Long Works

See 58a

Titles of long works are italicized, not set in quotation marks.

> The classic novel "*War and Peace*" is even longer than the epic poem "*Paradise Lost*."

NOTE: Do not use quotation marks (or italics) to set off titles of your own papers.

4 To Set Off Terms Being Defined

Terms being defined are italicized.

> The word "*tintinnabulation*," meaning the ringing sound of bells, is used by Poe in his poem "The Bells."

5 To Set Off Indirect Quotations

Quotation marks should not be used to set off **indirect quotations** (someone else's written or spoken words that are not quoted exactly).

Freud wondered "what a woman wanted."

■ EXERCISE 3

In the following paragraph, correct the use of single and double quotation marks to set off direct quotations, titles, and words used in special ways. Supply quotation marks where they are required, and delete those that are not required, substituting italics where necessary.

> In her essay 'The Obligation to Endure' from the book "Silent Spring," Rachel Carson writes: As Albert Schweitzer has said, 'Man can hardly even recognize the devils of his own creation.' Carson goes on to point out that many chemicals have been used to kill insects and other organisms which, she writes, are "described in the modern vernacular as pests." Carson believes such "advanced" chemicals, by contaminating our environment, do more harm than good. In addition to "Silent Spring," Carson is also the author of the book "The Sea Around Us." This work, divided into three sections (Mother Sea, The Restless Sea, and Man and the Sea About Him), was published in 1951.

EXERCISE 4

Correct the use of quotation marks in the following sentences. If a sentence is correct, mark it with a *C*.

Example: The "Watergate" incident brought many new expressions into the English language.

1. Kilroy was here and Women and children first are two expressions Bartlett's Familiar Quotations attributes to "Anon."
2. Neil Armstrong said he was making a small step for man but a giant leap for mankind.
3. "The answer, my friend", Bob Dylan sang, "is blowin' in the wind".
4. The novel was a real "thriller," complete with spies and counterspies, mysterious women, and exotic international chases.
5. The sign said, Road liable to subsidence; it meant that we should look out for potholes.
6. One of William Blake's best-known lines—To see a world in a grain of sand—opens his poem Auguries of Innocence.
7. In James Thurber's short story The Catbird Seat, Mrs. Barrows annoys Mr. Martin by asking him silly questions like Are you tearing up the pea patch? Are you scraping around the bottom of the pickle barrel? and Are you lifting the oxcart out of the ditch?
8. I'll make him an offer he can't refuse, promised "the godfather" in Mario Puzo's novel.
9. What did Timothy Leary mean by "Turn on, tune in, drop out?"
10. George, the protagonist of Bernard Malamud's short story, A Summer's Reading, is something of an "underachiever."

56

Using Other Punctuation Marks

❓ FAQs

When should I use a colon to introduce a quotation? (p. 673)
Are dashes acceptable in college writing? (p. 675)
When should I use parentheses? (p. 675)
When should I use brackets? (p. 677)
What kind of punctuation do I use when I delete words from a quotation? (p. 678)

56a Using Colons

The **colon** is a strong punctuation mark that points readers ahead to the rest of the sentence. When a colon introduces a list or series, explanatory material, or a quotation, it must be preceded by a complete sentence.

1 Introducing Lists or Series

Use a colon to set off a list or a series, including one introduced by a phrase such as *the following* or *as follows*.

> Waiting tables requires three skills**:** memory, speed, and balance.

2 Introducing Explanatory Material

Use a colon to introduce material that explains, exemplifies, or summarizes. Frequently, this material is presented in the form of an **appositive**, a word group that identifies or renames an adjacent noun or pronoun.

> Diego Rivera painted a controversial mural**:** the one commissioned for Rockefeller Center in the 1930s.

> She had one dream**:** to play professional basketball.

Sometimes a colon separates two independent clauses, the second illustrating or explaining the first.

A *U.S. News & World Report* survey revealed a surprising fact: Americans spend more time at malls than anywhere else except at home and at work.

> **CLOSE-UP**
>
> **USING COLONS**
>
> When a complete sentence follows a colon, it may begin with either a capital or a lowercase letter. However, if the sentence is a quotation, the first word is always capitalized (unless it was not capitalized in the source).

3 Introducing Quotations

When you quote a long prose passage, always introduce it with a colon. Also use a colon before a short quotation when it is introduced by a complete sentence.

See 55b1

> With dignity, Bartleby repeated the familiar words: "I prefer not to."

OTHER CONVENTIONAL USES OF COLONS

To Separate a Title from a Subtitle

> *Family Installments: Memories of Growing Up Hispanic*

To Separate Minutes from Hours

> 6:15 a.m.

After the Salutation in a business letter

See 29a

> Dear Dr. Evans:

To Separate Place of Publication from Name of Publisher in a Works-Cited List

See 18a2

> Boston: Wadsworth, 2008

---

4 Editing Misused Colons

Do not use colons in the following situations.

***After Expressions Like* Such As *and* For Example.** Do not use colons after the expressions *such as, namely, for example,* and *that is.* Remember that when a colon introduces a list or series, a complete sentence must precede the colon.

The Eye Institute treats patients with a wide variety of conditions, such as: myopia, glaucoma, and cataracts.

In Verb and Prepositional Constructions. Do not place colons between verbs and their objects or complements or between prepositions and their objects.

James A. Michener wrote: *Hawaii, Centennial, Space,* and *Poland.*

Hitler's armies marched through: the Netherlands, Belgium, and France.

■ EXERCISE 1

Add colons where appropriate in the following sentences, and delete any misused colons.

Example: There was one thing he really hated getting up at 7:00 every morning.

1. Books about the late John F. Kennedy include the following *A Hero for Our Time; Johnny, We Hardly Knew Ye; One Brief Shining Moment;* and *JFK: Reckless Youth.*
2. Only one task remained to tell his boss he was quitting.
3. The story closed with a familiar phrase "And they all lived happily ever after."
4. The sergeant requested: reinforcements, medical supplies, and more ammunition.
5. She kept only four souvenirs a photograph, a matchbook, a theater program, and a daisy pressed between the pages of *William Shakespeare The Complete Works.*

56b Using Dashes

1 Setting Off Nonessential Material

See 52d

Like commas, **dashes** can set off <u>nonessential material</u>, but unlike commas, dashes call attention to the material they set off. Indicate a dash with two unspaced hyphens (which your word-processing program will automatically convert to a dash).

For emphasis, you may use dashes to set off explanations, qualifications, examples, definitions, and appositives.

Neither of the boys—both nine-year-olds—had any history of violence.

Too many parents learn the dangers of swimming pools the hard way—after their toddler has drowned.

2 Introducing a Summary

Use a dash to introduce a statement that summarizes a list or series before it.

> "Study hard," "Respect your elders," "Don't talk with your mouth full"—Sharon had often heard her parents say these things.

3 Indicating an Interruption

In dialogue, a dash can mark a hesitation or an unfinished thought.

> "I think—no, I know—this is the worst day of my life," Julie sighed.

4 Editing Overused Dashes

Too many dashes can make your writing seem disorganized and out of control, so you should be careful not to overuse them.

> Registration was a nightmare~~—most~~ . Most of the courses I wanted to take—geology and conversational Spanish, for instance—met at inconvenient times~~—~~, or were closed by the time I tried to sign up for them~~—it~~ . It was really depressing~~—~~, even for registration.

■ EXERCISE 2

Add dashes where needed in the following sentences. If a sentence is correct, mark it with a *C*.

Example: World War I̲ called "the war to end all wars"̲ was, unfortunately, no such thing.

1. Tulips, daffodils, hyacinths, lilies all these flowers grow from bulbs.
2. St. Kitts and Nevis two tiny island nations are now independent after 360 years of British rule.
3. "But it's not" She paused and thought about her next words.
4. He considered several different majors history, English, political science, and business before deciding on journalism.
5. The two words added to the Pledge of Allegiance in the 1950s "under God" remain part of the Pledge today.

56c Using Parentheses

1 Setting Off Nonessential Material

Use **parentheses** to enclose material that expands, clarifies, illustrates, or supplements.

56c ( ) ■ Using Other Punctuation Marks

In some European countries (notably Sweden and France), high-quality day care is offered at little or no cost to parents.

When a complete sentence set off by parentheses falls within another sentence, it should not begin with a capital letter or end with a period.

The region is so cold (temperatures average in the low twenties) that it is virtually uninhabitable.

If the parenthetical sentence does *not* fall within another sentence, however, it must begin with a capital letter and end with appropriate punctuation.

The region is very cold. (Temperatures average in the low twenties.)

CLOSE-UP

USING PARENTHESES WITH OTHER PUNCTUATION

When parentheses fall within a sentence, punctuation never immediately precedes the opening parenthesis. Punctuation may follow the closing parenthesis, however.

George Orwell's *1984* (1949), which focuses on the dangers of a totalitarian society, is required reading.

---

2 Using Parentheses in Other Situations

Use parentheses around letters and numbers that identify points on a list, dates, cross-references, and documentation.

All reports must include the following components: (1) an opening summary, (2) a background statement, and (3) a list of conclusions.

Russia defeated Sweden in the Great Northern War (1700–1721).

Other scholars also make this point (see p. 54).

One critic has called the novel "puerile" (Arvin 72).

■ **EXERCISE 3**

Add parentheses where appropriate in the following sentences. If a sentence is correct, mark it with a *C*.

Example: The greatest battle of the War of 1812 (the Battle of New Orleans) was fought after the war was declared over.

1. During the Great War 1914–1918, Britain censored letters written from the front lines.

2. Those who lived in towns on the southern coast such as Dover could often hear the mortar shells across the channel in France.
3. Wilfred Owen wrote his most famous poem "Dulce et Decorum Est" in the trenches in France.
4. The British uniforms with bright red tabs right at the neck were responsible for many British deaths.
5. It was difficult for the War Poets as they are now called to return to writing about subjects other than the horrors of war.

56d Using Brackets

Use brackets in the following situations.

1 Setting Off Comments within Quotations

Brackets within quotations tell readers that the enclosed words are yours and not those of your source. You can bracket an explanation, a clarification, a correction, or an opinion.

> "Even at Princeton he [F. Scott Fitzgerald] felt like an outsider."

If a quotation contains an error, indicate that the error is not yours by following the error with the Latin word *sic* ("thus") in brackets.

> "The octopuss [sic] is a cephalopod mollusk with eight arms."

NOTE: Use brackets to indicate changes that you make in order to fit a quotation smoothly into your sentence.

See 16d1

2 Replacing Parentheses within Parentheses

When one set of parentheses falls within another, use brackets in place of the inner set.

> In her study of American education between 1945 and 1960 (*The Trouble Crusade* [New York: Basic, 1963]), Diane Ravitch addresses issues such as progressive education, race, educational reforms, and campus unrest.

56e Using Slashes

Use slashes in the following situations.

1 Separating One Option from Another

When separating one option from another with a **slash**, do not leave a space before or after the slash.

The either/or fallacy is a common error in logic.

Writer/director Spike Lee will speak at the film festival.

2 Separating Lines of Poetry Run Into the Text

When separating lines of poetry run into the text, leave one space before and one space after the slash.

> The poet James Schevill writes, "I study my defects / And learn how to perfect them."

56f Using Ellipses

Use ellipses in the following situations.

1 Indicating an Omission in Quoted Prose

Use an **ellipsis**—three *spaced* periods—to indicate that you have omitted words from a prose quotation. Note that an ellipsis in the middle of a quoted passage can indicate the omission of a word, a sentence or two, or even a whole paragraph or more. When deleting material from a quotation, be very careful not to change the meaning of the original passage.

> **Original:** "When I was a young man, being anxious to distinguish myself, I was perpetually starting new propositions." (Samuel Johnson)
>
> **With Omission:** "When I was a young man, ... I was perpetually starting new propositions."

Note that when you delete words immediately after an internal punctuation mark (such as the comma in the above example), you retain the punctuation before the ellipsis.

When you delete material at the end of a sentence, place the sentence's period or other end punctuation before the ellipsis.

> According to humorist Dave Barry, "from outer space Europe appears to be shaped like a large ketchup stain. ... " (period followed by ellipses)

NOTE: Never begin a quoted passage with an ellipsis.

When you delete material between sentences, any punctuation should precede the ellipsis.

> **Deletion from Middle of One Sentence to End of Another**
> According to Donald Hall, "Everywhere one meets the idea that

reading is an activity desirable in itself. ... People surround the idea of reading with piety and do not take into account the purpose of reading." (period followed by ellipses)

Deletion from Middle of One Sentence to Middle of Another "When I was a young man, ... I found that generally what was new was false." (Samuel Johnson) (comma followed by ellipses)

NOTE: If a quoted passage already contains an ellipsis, MLA recommends that you enclose your own ellipses in brackets to distinguish them from those that appear in the original quotation.

> **CLOSE-UP**
>
> **USING ELLIPSES**
>
> If a quotation ending with an ellipsis is followed by parenthetical documentation, the final punctuation comes *after* the documentaton.
>
> As Jarman argues, "Compromise was impossible . . ." (161).

2 Indicating an Omission in Quoted Poetry

Use an ellipsis when you omit a word or phrase from a line of poetry. When you omit one or more lines of poetry, use a line of spaced periods. (The length may be equal either to the line above it or to the missing line—but it should not be longer than the longest line of the poem.)

Original:
> Stitch! Stitch! Stitch!
> In poverty, hunger, and dirt,
> And still with a voice of dolorous pitch,
> Would that its tone could reach the Rich,
> She sang this "Song of the Shirt!"
>
> (Thomas Hood)

With Omission:
> Stitch! Stitch! Stitch!
> In poverty, hunger, and dirt,
> . . . .
> She sang this "Song of the Shirt!"

■ **EXERCISE 4**

Read the following paragraph, and follow the instructions after it, taking care in each case not to delete essential information.

> The most important thing about research is to know when to stop. How does one recognize the moment? When I was eighteen or thereabouts, my mother told me that when out with a young man I should always leave a half-hour before I wanted to. Although I was not sure how this might be accomplished, I recognized the advice as sound, and exactly the same rule applies to research. One must stop *before* one has finished; otherwise, one will never stop and never finish. (Barbara Tuchman, *Practicing History*)

1. Delete words from the middle of one sentence to the end of another, marking the omission with ellipses.
2. Delete words from the middle of one sentence to the middle of another, marking the omission with ellipses.
3. Delete words at the end of any sentence, marking the omission with ellipses.
4. Delete one complete sentence from the middle of the passage, marking the omission with ellipses.

■ EXERCISE 5

Add appropriate punctuation—colons, dashes, parentheses, brackets, or slashes—to the following sentences. If a sentence is correct, mark it with a *C*.

Example: There was one thing she was sure of ; if she did well at the interview, the job would be hers.

1. Mark Twain Samuel L. Clemens made the following statement "I can live for two months on a good compliment."
2. Liza Minnelli, the actress singer who starred in several films, is the daughter of legendary singer Judy Garland.
3. Saudi Arabia, Oman, Yemen, Qatar, and the United Arab Emirates all these are located on the Arabian Peninsula.
4. John Adams 1735–1826 was the second president of the United States; John Quincy Adams 1767–1848 was the sixth.
5. The sign said, "No tresspassing sic."
6. *Checkmate* a term derived from the Persian phrase meaning "the king is dead" announces victory in chess.
7. The following people were present at the meeting the president of the board of trustees, three trustees, and twenty reporters.
8. Before the introduction of the potato in Europe, the parsnip was a major source of carbohydrates in fact, it was a dietary staple.
9. In the well-researched book *Crime Movies* (New York Norton, 1980), Carlos Clarens studies the gangster genre in film.
10. I remember reading though I can't remember where that Upton Sinclair sold plots to Jack London.

57

Knowing When to Capitalize

❓ FAQs
Is the first word of a line of poetry always capitalized? (p. 681)
Are east *and* west *capitalized? (p. 682)*
Are brand names always capitalized? (p. 684)
Which words in titles are not *capitalized? (p. 685)*
Are the names of seasons capitalized? (p. 686)

57a Capitalizing the First Word of a Sentence

Capitalize the first word of a sentence, including a sentence of quoted speech or writing.

<u>A</u>s Shakespeare wrote, "<u>W</u>ho steals my purse steals trash."

Do not capitalize a sentence set off within another sentence by dashes or parentheses.

Finding the store closed—it was a holiday—they went home.

The candidates are Frank Lester and Jane Lester (they are not related).

> **CLOSE-UP**
>
> **USING CAPITAL LETTERS IN POETRY**
>
> Remember that the first word of a line of poetry is generally capitalized. If the poet uses a lowercase letter to begin a line, however, you should follow that style when you quote the line.   ❓

57b Capitalizing Proper Nouns

Proper nouns—the names of specific persons, places, or things—are capitalized, and so are adjectives formed from proper nouns.

> **ESL TIP**
>
> If you are not sure whether a noun should be capitalized, look it up in a dictionary. Do not capitalize a word simply because you want to emphasize its importance.

57b cap ■ Knowing When to Capitalize

1 Specific People's Names

Franklin D. Roosevelt   Medgar Evers   Eudora Welty

Capitalize a title when it precedes a person's name (Senator Olympia Snowe) or is used instead of the name (Dad). Do not capitalize titles that *follow* names (Olympia Snowe, the senator from Maine) or those that refer to the general position, not the particular person who holds it (a stay-at-home dad).

You may, however, capitalize titles that indicate very high-ranking positions even when they are used alone or when they follow a name: the Pope; George W. Bush, President of the United States. Never capitalize a title denoting a family relationship when it follows an article or a possessive pronoun (an uncle, his mom).

Capitalize titles that represent academic degrees or abbreviations of those degrees even when they follow a name: Dr. Benjamin Spock; Benjamin Spock, MD.

2 Names of Particular Structures, Special Events, Monuments, and So On

the Brooklyn Bridge   the Taj Mahal
the Eiffel Tower   Mount Rushmore
the World Series   the *Titanic*

NOTE: Capitalize a common noun, such as *bridge*, *river*, *county*, or *lake*, when it is part of a proper noun (Lake Erie, Kings County).

3 Places and Geographical Regions

Saturn   the Straits of Magellan
Budapest   the Fiji Islands
Walden Pond   the Western Hemisphere

Capitalize *north*, *south*, *east*, and *west* when they denote particular geographical regions but not when they designate directions.

> There are more tornadoes in Kansas than in the East. (*East refers to a specific region.*)
>
> Turn west at Broad Street and continue north to Market. (*West and north refer to directions, not specific regions.*)

4 Days of the Week, Months, and Holidays

Saturday   Cinco de Mayo
January   Rosh Hashanah

Capitalizing Proper Nouns ▪ **cap** **57b**

5 Historical Periods, Events, Documents, and Names of Legal Cases

the Industrial Revolution   the Treaty of Versailles
the Reformation   the Voting Rights Act
the Battle of Gettysburg   *Brown* v. *Board of Education*

NOTE: Names of court cases are italicized (or underlined to indicate italics) in the text of your papers, but not in works-cited entries.

6 Philosophic, Literary, and Artistic Movements

Naturalism   Dadaism
Neoclassicism   Expressionism

7 Races, Ethnic Groups, Nationalities, and Languages

African American   Korean
Latino/Latina   Dutch

NOTE: When the words *black* and *white* denote races, they have traditionally not been capitalized. Current usage is divided on whether to capitalize *black*.

8 Religions and Their Followers; Sacred Books and Figures

Islam   the Koran   Buddha
the Talmud   the Scriptures   God

NOTE: It is not necessary to capitalize pronouns referring to God (although some people do so as a sign of respect).

9 Specific Groups and Organizations

the Democratic Party
the International Brotherhood of Electrical Workers
the New York Yankees
the American Civil Liberties Union
the National Council of Teachers of English
the Rolling Stones

NOTE: When the name of a group or organization is abbreviated, the abbreviation uses capital letters in place of the capitalized words.

See 60b

IBEW   ACLU   NCTE

10 Businesses, Government Agencies, and Other Institutions

General Electric   Lincoln High School
the Environmental Protection   the University of Maryland
Agency

11 Brand Names and Words Formed from Them

Velcro   Coke   Post-it   Rollerblades   Astroturf

NOTE: Brand names that over long use have become synonymous with the product—for example, *nylon* and *aspirin*—are no longer capitalized. (Consult a dictionary to determine whether to capitalize a familiar brand name.)

CLOSE-UP

USING BRAND NAMES

In general, use generic references, not brand names, in college writing—*photocopy*, not *Xerox*, for example. These generic names are not capitalized.

---

12 Specific Academic Courses

Sociology 201   English 101

NOTE: Do not capitalize a general subject area (sociology, zoology) unless it is the name of a language (English, Spanish).

13 Adjectives Formed from Proper Nouns

Freudian slip   Elizabethan era
Platonic ideal   Shakespearean sonnet
Aristotelian logic   Marxist ideology

When words derived from proper nouns have lost their original associations, do not capitalize them: <u>c</u>hina bowl, <u>f</u>rench fries.

GRAMMAR CHECKER

RECOGNIZING PROPER NOUNS

Your word processor's spell checker may not recognize many of the proper nouns you use in your documents, particularly those that require irregular capitalization, such as *Leonardo da Vinci*, and therefore will identify these nouns as spelling errors. To solve this problem, click Ignore Once to instruct the spell checker to ignore the word one time, and Ignore All to instruct the spell checker to ignore all uses of the word in your document.

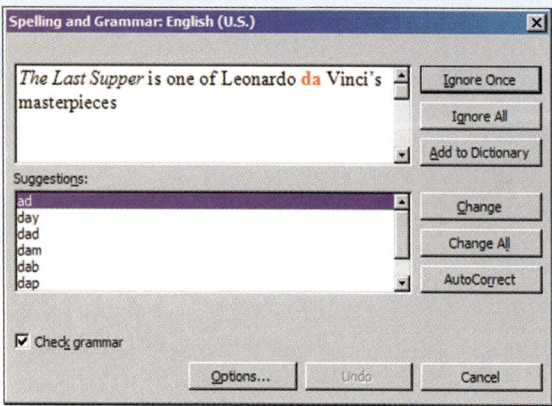

57c Capitalizing Important Words in Titles

In general, capitalize all words in titles with the exception of articles (*a*, *an*, and *the*), prepositions, coordinating conjunctions, and the *to* in infinitives (unless they are the first or last word in the title or subtitle).

"Dover Beach" *On the Waterfront*
The Declaration of Independence *Madame Curie: A Biography*
Across the River and into the Trees "What Friends Are For"

57d Capitalizing the Pronoun *I*, the Interjection *O*, and Other Single Letters in Special Constructions

Always capitalize the pronoun *I* even if it is part of a contraction (*I'm, I'll, I've*).

Sam and I finally went to Mexico, and I'm glad we did.

Always capitalize the interjection *O*.

Give us peace in our time, O Lord.

However, capitalize the interjection *oh* only when it begins a sentence.

NOTE: Many other single letters are capitalized in certain usages: an A in history, vitamin B, C major. Check your dictionary to determine whether or not to use a capital letter.

57e Capitalizing Salutations and Closings of Letters

See 29a

Always capitalize the first word of the salutation of a personal or business letter.

    Dear Fred,   Dear Mr. Reynolds:

Always capitalize the first word of the complimentary close.

    Sincerely,   Very truly yours,

57f Editing Misused Capitals

Do not capitalize words for emphasis or as an attention-getting strategy. If you are uncertain about whether or not a word should be capitalized, consult a dictionary.

1 Seasons

Do not capitalize the names of the seasons—summer, fall, winter, spring—unless they are personified, as in *Old Man Winter*.

2 Centuries and Loosely Defined Historical Periods

Do not capitalize the names of centuries or general historical periods.

    seventeenth-century poetry   the automobile age

Do, however, capitalize names of specific historical, anthropological, and geological periods: *Iron Age; Renaissance; Paleozoic Era*

3 Diseases and Other Medical Terms

See 51a2

Do not capitalize names of diseases or medical tests or conditions unless a proper noun is part of the name or unless the name of the disease is an **acronym**.

    smallpox   Apgar test   AIDS
    Lyme disease   mumps   SIDS

Editing Misused Capitals ■ **cap/lc**

■ **EXERCISE 1**

Capitalize words where necessary in these sentences.

Example: John F. Kennedy won the *P*ulitzer *P*rize for his book *P*rofiles in *C*ourage.

1. Two of the brontë sisters wrote *jane eyre and wuthering heights,* nineteenth-century novels that are required reading in many english classes that focus on victorian literature.
2. It was a beautiful day in the spring—it was april 15, to be exact—but all Ted could think about was the check he had to write to the internal revenue service and the bills he had to pay by friday.
3. Traveling north, they hiked through british columbia, planning a leisurely return on the cruise ship *canadian princess.*
4. Alice liked her mom's apple pie better than aunt nellie's rhubarb pie, but she liked grandpa's punch best of all.
5. A new elective, political science 30, covers the vietnam war from the gulf of tonkin to the fall of saigon, including the roles of ho chi minh, the viet cong, and the buddhist monks; the positions of presidents johnson and nixon; and the influence of groups like the student mobilization committee and vietnam veterans against the war.
6. When the central high school drama club put on a production of shaw's *pygmalion,* the director xeroxed extra copies of the parts for eliza doolittle and professor henry higgins so he could give them to the understudies.
7. Shaking all over, Bill admitted, "driving on the los angeles freeway is a frightening experience for a kid from brooklyn, even in a bmw."
8. The new united federation of teachers contract guarantees teachers many paid holidays, including columbus day, veterans day, and washington's birthday; a week each at christmas and easter; and two full months (july and august) in the summer.
9. The sociology syllabus included the books *beyond the best interests of the child, regulating the poor: the functions of public welfare,* and *a welfare mother;* in anthropology, we were to begin by studying the stone age; and in geology, we were to focus on the Mesozoic era.
10. Winners of the nobel peace prize include lech walesa, former leader of the polish trade union solidarity; the reverend dr. martin luther king jr., founder of the southern christian leadership conference; and archbishop desmond tutu of south africa.

58

Using Italics

❷ FAQs

What kinds of titles are italicized? (p. 688)
Should I use italics in my papers, or should I underline to indicate italics? (p. 689)
Can I use italics to emphasize certain words or phrases? (p. 690)

58a Setting Off Titles and Names

See 55c

Use italics for the titles and names listed in the following box. Most other titles are set off with **quotation marks**.

> ### TITLES AND NAMES SET IN ITALICS
>
> **Books:** *David Copperfield, The Bluest Eye*
>
> **Newspapers:** the *Washington Post,* the *Philadelphia Inquirer* (According to MLA style, the word *the* is not italicized in titles of newspapers.)
>
> **Magazines and Journals:** *Rolling Stone, Scientific American*
>
> **Online Magazines and Journals:** *salon.com, theonion.com*
>
> **Web Sites or Home Pages:** *urbanlegends.com, movie-mistakes.com*
>
> **Pamphlets:** *Common Sense*
>
> **Films:** *The Matrix, Citizen Kane*
>
> **Television Programs:** *60 Minutes, The Apprentice, Fear Factor*
>
> **Radio Programs:** *All Things Considered, A Prairie Home Companion*
>
> **Long Poems:** *John Brown's Body, The Faerie Queen*
>
> **Plays:** *Macbeth, A Raisin in the Sun*
>
> **Long Musical Works:** *Rigoletto, Eroica*
>
> **Software Programs:** *Microsoft Word, PowerPoint*
>
> **Search Engines and Web Browsers:** *Google, Netscape Communicator*
>
> **Databases:** *Academic Search Premier, Expanded Academic ASAP Plus*
>
> **Paintings and Sculpture:** *Guernica, Pietà*
>
> **Ships:** *Lusitania,* U.S.S. *Saratoga* (S.S. and U.S.S. are not italicized.)

Trains: *City of New Orleans, The Orient Express*

Aircraft: *The Hindenburg, Enola Gay* (Only particular aircraft, not makes or types such as Piper Cub or Airbus, are italicized.)

Spacecraft: *Challenger, Enterprise*

NOTE: Names of sacred books, such as the Bible and the Koran, and well-known documents, such as the Constitution and the Declaration of Independence, are neither italicized nor placed within quotation marks.

> **CLOSE-UP**
>
> **USING ITALICS**
>
> MLA guidelines now recommend that you italicize rather than underline to indicate italics.

58b Setting Off Foreign Words and Phrases

Italics are often used to set off foreign words and phrases that have not become part of the English language.

"*C'est la vie*," Madeline said when she saw the long line for the concert.

Spirochaeta plicatilis is a corkscrewlike bacterium.

If you are not sure whether a foreign word has been assimilated into English, consult a dictionary.

58c Setting Off Elements Spoken of as Themselves and Terms Being Defined

Use italics to set off letters, numerals, and words that refer to the letters, numerals, and words themselves.

Is that a *p* or a *g*?

I forget the exact address, but I know it has a *3* in it.

Does *through* rhyme with *cough*?

Also use italics to set off words and phrases that you go on to define.

A *closet drama* is a play meant to be read, not performed.

NOTE: When you quote a dictionary definition, put the word you are defining in italics and the definition itself in quotation marks.

> To *infer* means "to draw a conclusion"; to *imply* means "to suggest."

58d Using Italics for Emphasis

Italics can occasionally be used for emphasis.

> Initially, poetry might be defined as a kind of language that says *more* and says it *more intensely* than does ordinary language. (Lawrence Perrine, *Sound and Sense*)

However, overuse of italics is distracting. Instead of italicizing, try to indicate emphasis with word choice and sentence structure.

■ **EXERCISE 1**

Underline to indicate italics where necessary, and delete any italics that are incorrectly used. If a sentence is correct, mark it with a *C*.

Example: <u>However</u> is a conjunctive adverb, not a coordinating conjunction.

1. I said Carol, not Darryl.
2. A *deus ex machina*, an improbable device used to resolve the plot of a fictional work, is used in Charles Dickens's novel Oliver Twist.
3. He dotted every i and crossed every t.
4. The Metropolitan Opera's production of Carmen was a tour de force for the principal performers.
5. *Laissez-faire* is a doctrine holding that government should not interfere with trade.
6. Antidote and anecdote are often confused because their pronunciations are similar.
7. Hawthorne's novels include Fanshawe, The House of the Seven Gables, The Blithedale Romance, and The Scarlet Letter.
8. Words such as mailman, policeman, and fireman have been replaced by nonsexist terms such as letter carrier, police officer, and firefighter.
9. A classic black tuxedo was considered de rigueur at the charity ball, but Jason preferred to wear his *dashiki*.
10. Thomas Mann's novel Buddenbrooks is a bildungsroman.

59

Using Hyphens

❓ FAQs

Where do I put the hyphen if I divide a compound word at the end of a line? (p. 691)

Should I use a hyphen to divide an electronic address at the end of a line? (p. 691)

Hyphens have two conventional uses: to break a word at the end of a line and to link words in certain compounds.

59a Breaking a Word at the End of a Line

A computer never breaks a word at the end of a line; if the full word will not fit, it is brought down to the next line. Sometimes, however, you will want to break a word with a hyphen—for example, to fill in space at the end of a line.

When you break a word at the end of a line, divide it only between syllables, consulting a dictionary if necessary. Never divide a word at the end of a page, and never hyphenate a one-syllable word. In addition, never leave a single letter at the end of a line or carry only one or two letters to the next line.

If you divide a **compound word** at the end of a line, put the hyphen between the elements of the compound (*snow-mobile*, not *snowmo-bile*).

See 59b

COMPUTER TIP   academic.cengage.com/eng/kirsznermandell

DIVIDING ELECTRONIC ADDRESSES (URLs)

Never insert a hyphen to divide an electronic address (URL) at the end of a line. (Readers might think the hyphen is part of the address.) MLA style recommends that you break the URL after a slash. If this is not possible, break it in a logical place—after a period, for example—or avoid the problem altogether by moving the entire URL to the next line.

59b Dividing Compound Words

A **compound word** consists of two or more words. Some familiar compound words are always hyphenated: *no-hitter*, *helter-skelter*. Other compounds are always written as one word: *fireplace, peacetime*. Finally, some compounds are always written as two separate words: *labor relations, bunk bed*. Your dictionary can tell you whether a particular compound requires a hyphen.

> **GRAMMAR CHECKER**
>
> **HYPHENATING COMPOUND WORDS**
>
> Your word processor's grammar checker will highlight certain compound words with incorrect or missing hyphenation and offer suggestions for revision.

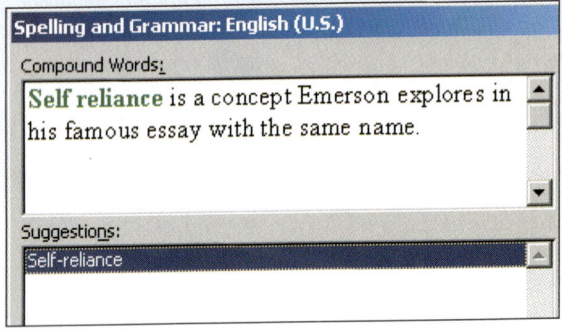

1 Hyphenating with Compound Adjectives

A **compound adjective** is a series of two or more words that function together as an adjective. When a compound adjective *precedes* the noun it modifies, use hyphens to join its elements.

> The research team tried to use nineteenth-century technology to design a space-age project.

When a compound adjective *follows* the noun it modifies, do not use hyphens to join its elements.

> The three government-operated programs were run smoothly, but the one that was not government operated was short of funds.

NOTE: A compound adjective formed with an adverb ending in *-ly* is not hyphenated, even when it precedes the noun.

> Many upwardly mobile families are on tight budgets.

Use **suspended hyphens**—hyphens followed by a space or by appropriate punctuation and a space—in a series of compounds that modify the same word.

Graduates of two- and four-year colleges were eligible for the grants.

The exam called for sentence-, paragraph-, and essay-length answers.

2 Hyphenating with Certain Prefixes and Suffixes

Use a hyphen between a prefix and a proper noun or proper adjective.

    mid-July   pre-Columbian

Use a hyphen to connect the prefixes *all-*, *ex-*, *half-*, *quarter-*, *quasi-*, and *self-* and the suffix *-elect* to a noun.

    ex-senator   self-centered   president-elect

NOTE: The words *selfhood*, *selfish*, and *selfless* do not include hyphens. In these words, *self* is the root, not a prefix.

3 Hyphenating in Compound Numerals and Fractions

Hyphenate compounds that represent numbers below one hundred (even if they are part of a larger number).

    the twenty-first century   three hundred sixty-five days

Also hyphenate the written form of a fraction when it modifies a noun.

    a two-thirds share of the business

4 Hyphenating for Clarity

Hyphenate to prevent readers from misreading one word for another.

    Before we can reform criminals, we must re-form our ideas about prisons.

Hyphenate to avoid hard-to-read combinations, such as two *i*'s (*semi-illiterate*) or more than two of the same consonant (*shell-less*).

In most cases, hyphenate between a capital initial and a word when the two combine to form a compound: *A-frame*, *T-shirt*, *D-day*.

5 Hyphenating in Coined Compounds

A **coined compound**, one that uses a new combination of words as a unit, requires hyphens.

    He looked up with a who-do-you-think-you-are expression.

Using Hyphens

■ **EXERCISE 1**

Form compound adjectives from the following word groups, inserting hyphens where necessary.

Example: a ~~three-year~~ contract ~~for three years~~

1. a relative who has long been lost
2. someone who is addicted to video games
3. a salesperson who goes from door to door
4. a display calculated to catch the eye
5. friends who are dearly beloved
6. a household that is centered on a child
7. a line of reasoning that is hard to follow
8. the border between New York and New Jersey
9. a candidate who is thirty-two years old
10. a computer that is friendly to its users

■ **EXERCISE 2**

Add hyphens to the compounds in these sentences wherever they are required. Consult a dictionary if necessary.

Example: Alaska was the forty-ninth state to join the United States.

1. One of the restaurant's blue plate specials is chicken fried steak.
2. Virginia and Texas are both right to work states.
3. He stood on tiptoe to see the near perfect statue, which was well hidden by the security fence.
4. The five and ten cent store had a self service makeup counter and stocked many up to the minute gadgets.
5. The so called Saturday night special is opposed by pro gun control groups.
6. He ordered two all beef patties with special sauce, lettuce, cheese, pickles, and onions on a sesame seed bun.
7. The material was extremely thought provoking, but it hardly presented any earth shattering conclusions.
8. The Dodgers Phillies game was rained out, so the long suffering fans left for home.
9. Bone marrow transplants carry the risk of what is known as a graft versus host reaction.
10. The state funded child care program was considered a highly desirable alternative to family day care.

60

Using Abbreviations

❓ FAQs

Can I abbreviate technical terms? (p. 696)
Can I use abbreviations such as e.g. *and* etc. *in college writing? (p. 697)*

Generally speaking, **abbreviations** are not appropriate in college writing except in tables, charts, and works-cited lists. Some abbreviations are acceptable only in scientific, technical, or business writing, or only in a particular <u>discipline</u>. If you have any questions about the appropriateness of a particular abbreviation, check a style manual in your field.

See Pt. 6

> **COMPUTER TIP** academic.cengage.com/eng/kirsznermandell
>
> **ABBREVIATIONS IN ELECTRONIC COMMUNICATIONS**
>
> Like emoticons and acronyms, which are popular in email and instant messages, shorthand abbreviations and symbols—such as GR8 (great) and 2NITE (tonight)—are common in text messages. Although they are acceptable in informal electronic communication, such abbreviations are not appropriate in college writing or in business communication.

60a Abbreviating Titles

Titles before and after proper names are usually abbreviated.

Mr. Homer Simpson	Rep. Chaka Fattah
Henry Kissinger, PhD	Prof. Elie Weisel

Do not, however, use an abbreviated title without a name.

The ~~Dr.~~ *doctor* diagnosed tuberculosis.

60b Abbreviating Organization Names and Technical Terms

You may refer to well-known businesses and to government, social, and civic organizations by capitalized initials. These <u>abbreviations</u>

See 51a2

fall into two categories: those in which the initials are pronounced as separate units (MTV) and **acronyms,** in which the initials are pronounced as a word (FEMA).

To save space, you may use accepted abbreviations for complex technical terms that are not well known, but be sure to spell out the full term the first time you mention it, followed by the abbreviation in parentheses.

> Citrus farmers have been using ethylene dibromide (EDB), a chemical pesticide, for more than twenty years. Now, however, EDB has contaminated water supplies.

CLOSE-UP

ABBREVIATIONS IN MLA DOCUMENTATION

See 18a

MLA documentation style requires abbreviations of publishers' company names—for example, **Columbia UP** for *Columbia University Press*—in the works-cited list. Do not, however, use such abbreviations in the body of your paper.

MLA style also permits the use of abbreviations that designate parts of written works (**ch. 3, sec. 7**)—but only in the works-cited list and parenthetical documentation.

Finally, MLA recommends abbreviating literary works and books of the Bible in parenthetical citations: **Oth.** (*Othello*), **Exod.** (Exodus). These words should not be abbreviated in the text of your paper or in the works-cited list.

60c Abbreviating Dates, Times of Day, and Temperatures

Dates, times of day, and temperatures are often abbreviated.

50 BC (*BC* follows the date.)   AD 432 (*AD* precedes the date.)
6 a.m.   3:03 p.m.
20°C (Centigrade or Celsius)   180°F (Fahrenheit)

Always capitalize *BC* and *AD*. (The alternatives *BCE,* for "before the common era," and *CE,* for "common era," are also capitalized.) Use lowercase letters for a.m. and p.m., but use these abbreviations only when they are accompanied by numbers.

We will see you in the ~~a.m.~~ *morning*.

NOTE: Avoid the abbreviation *no.* (written either *no.* or *No.*), except in technical writing, and then use it only before a specific number: *The unidentified substance was labeled no. 52.*

60d Editing Misused Abbreviations

In college writing, abbreviations are not used in the following cases.

1 Names of Days, Months, or Holidays

Do not abbreviate days of the week, months, or holidays.

On ~~Sat., Dec.~~ 23, I started my ~~Xmas~~ shopping.
    Saturday, December   *Christmas*

2 Names of Streets and Places

In general, do not abbreviate names of streets and places.

He lives on Riverside ~~Dr.~~ in ~~NYC.~~
       Drive   *New York City.*

Exceptions: The abbreviation *US* is often acceptable (*US Coast Guard*), as is *DC* in *Washington, DC*. Also permissible are *Mt.* before the name of a mountain (*Mt. Etna*) and *St.* in a place name (*St. Albans*).

3 Names of Academic Subjects

Do not abbreviate names of academic subjects.

~~Psych.~~ and English ~~lit.~~ are required courses.
Psychology   *literature*

4 Names of Businesses

Write company names exactly as the firms themselves write them, including the distinction between the ampersand (&) and the word *and*: *AT&T, Charles Schwab & Co., Inc.* Abbreviations for *company, corporation*, and the like are used only along with a company name.

The ~~corp.~~ merged with a ~~co.~~ in Ohio.
   corporation   *company*

5 Latin Expressions

Abbreviations of the common Latin phrases *i.e.* ("that is"), *e.g.* ("for example"), and *etc.* ("and so forth") are generally not appropriate in college writing except in notes and bibliographic citations.

Other musicians (~~e.g.,~~ Bruce Springsteen) have also been influenced by Bob Dylan.
             for example,

Poe wrote "The Raven," "Annabel Lee," ~~etc.~~
                                   and other poems.

6 Units of Measurement

In technical writing, some units of measurement are abbreviated when they are preceded by a numeral.

> The hurricane had winds of 35 mph.
>
> One new Honda gets over 50 mpg.

However, MLA style requires that you write out units of measurement and spell out words such as *inches, feet, years, miles, pints, quarts,* and *gallons*.

7 Symbols

The symbols =, +, and # are acceptable in technical and scientific writing but not in nontechnical college writing. The symbols % and $ are acceptable only when used with **numerals** (15%, $15,000), not with spelled-out numbers.

See 61b4, 7

■ EXERCISE 1

Correct any incorrectly used abbreviations in the following sentences, assuming that all are intended for a college audience. If a sentence is correct, mark it with a *C*.

Example: Romeo *&* Juliet is a play by Shakespeare.
　　　　　　　　　　　and

1. The committee meeting, attended by representatives from Action for Children's Television (ACT) and NOW, Sen. Putnam, & the pres. of ABC, convened at 8 A.M. on Mon. Feb. 24 at the YWCA on Germantown Ave.
2. An econ. prof. was suspended after he encouraged his students to speculate on securities issued by a corp. under investigation by the SEC.
3. Benjamin Spock, who wrote *Baby and Child Care*, was a respected dr. known throughout the USA.
4. The FDA banned the use of Red Dye no. 2 in food in 1976, but other food additives are still in use.
5. The Rev. Dr. Martin Luther King Jr., leader of the SCLC, led the famous Selma, Ala., march.
6. Wm. Golding, a novelist from the U.K., won the Nobel Prize in lit.
7. The adult education center, financed by a major computer corp., offers courses in basic subjects such as introductory bio. and tech. writing as well as teaching HTML and XML.
8. All the fraternity brothers agreed to write to Pres. Dexter appealing their disciplinary probation under Ch. 4, Sec. 3, of the IFC constitution.

9. A 4 qt. (i.e., 1 gal.) container is needed to hold the salt solution.
10. According to Prof. Morrison, all those taking the exam should bring two sharpened no. 2 pencils to the St. Joseph's University auditorium on Sat.

61

Using Numbers

❓ FAQ

When do I spell out a number, and when do I use a numeral? (p. 700)

Convention determines when to use a **numeral** (22) and when to spell out a number (twenty-two). Numerals are commonly used in scientific and technical writing and in journalism, but they are used less often in the humanities.

NOTE: The guidelines in this chapter are based on the *MLA Handbook for Writers of Research Papers*, 7th ed. (2009). APA style, however, requires that all numbers below ten be spelled out if they do not represent specific measurements and that numbers ten and above be expressed in numerals.

61a Spelled-Out Numbers versus Numerals

Unless a number falls into one of the categories listed in 61b, spell it out if you can do so *in one or two words*.

> The Hawaiian alphabet has only twelve letters.
> Class size stabilized at twenty-eight students.
> The subsidies are expected to total about two million dollars.

Numbers *more than two words* long are expressed in figures.

> The dietitian prepared 125 sample menus.
> The developer of the community purchased 300,000 doorknobs and 153,000 faucets.

Never begin a sentence with a numeral. If necessary, reword the sentence.

> **Faulty:** 250 students are currently enrolled in World History 106.
> **Revised:** Current enrollment in World History 106 is 250 students.

NOTE: When one number immediately precedes another in a sentence, spell out the first, and use a numeral for the second: *five 3-quart containers.*

GRAMMAR CHECKER

SPELLED-OUT NUMBERS VERSUS NUMERALS

Your word processor's grammar checker will often highlight numerals in your writing and suggest that you spell them out. Before clicking Change, be sure that the number does not fall into one of the categories listed in 61b.

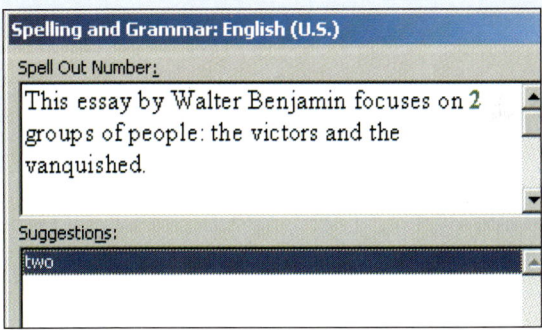

61b Conventional Uses of Numerals

1 Addresses

111 Fifth Avenue, New York, NY 10003

2 Dates

January 15, 1929   1914–1919

3 Exact Times

9:16   10 a.m. (or 10:00 a.m.)

Exceptions: Spell out times of day when they are used with *o'clock: eleven o'clock*, not *11 o'clock*. Also spell out times expressed in quarter and half hours: *half-past eight, a quarter to ten*.

4 Exact Sums of Money

$25.11 $6,752.00

NOTE: Always use a numeral (not a spelled-out number) with a $ symbol. You may spell out a round sum of money if you use sums infrequently in your paper, provided you can do so in two or three words: *five dollars; two thousand dollars*.

61b num ■ Using Numbers

5 Divisions of Written Works

Use arabic (not roman) numerals for chapter and volume numbers; acts, scenes, and lines of plays; chapters and verses of the Bible; and line numbers of long poems.

6 Measurements before an Abbreviation or Symbol

12″	55 mph
32°	15 cc

7 Percentages and Decimals

80%   3.14

NOTE: You may spell out a percentage (*eighty percent*) if you use percentages infrequently in your paper, provided the percentage can be expressed in two or three words. Always use a numeral (not a spelled-out number) with a % symbol.

8 Ratios, Scores, and Statistics

See Ch. 19, Ch. 21

In a paper that follows APA or CSE style, use numerals for numbers presented as a comparison.

Children preferred Fun Flakes over Graino by a ratio of 20 to 1.

The Orioles defeated the Phillies 6 to 0.

The median age of the patients was 42; the mean age was 40.

9 Identification Numbers

Route 66   Track 8   Channel 12

NOTE: When writing large numbers, insert a comma every three digits from the right, beginning after the third digit.

3,000   25,000   6,751,098

Do not, however, use commas in four-digit page and line numbers, addresses, or year numbers.

page 1202   3741 Laurel Ave.   1968

■ **EXERCISE 1**

Following MLA guidelines, revise the use of numbers in these sentences, making sure usage is correct and consistent. If a sentence uses numbers correctly, mark it with a *C*.

Example: The Empire State Building is ~~one hundred and two~~ 102 stories high.

1. *1984*, a novel by George Orwell, is set in a totalitarian society.
2. The English placement examination included a 30-minute personal-experience essay, a 45-minute expository essay, and a 150-item objective test of grammar and usage.
3. In a control group of two hundred forty-seven patients, almost three out of four suffered serious adverse reactions to the new drug.
4. Before the Thirteenth Amendment to the Constitution, slaves were counted as $3/5$ of a person.
5. The intensive membership drive netted 2,608 new members and additional dues of over 5 thousand dollars.
6. They had only 2 choices: either they could take the yacht at Pier Fourteen, or they could return home to the penthouse at Twenty-seven Harbor View Drive.
7. The atomic number of lithium is three.
8. Approximately 3 hundred thousand schoolchildren in District 6 were given hearing and vision examinations between May third and June 26.
9. The United States was drawn into the war by the Japanese attack on Pearl Harbor on December seventh, 1941.
10. An upper-middle-class family can spend more than 250,000 dollars to raise each child up to age 18.

PART 13

Bilingual and ESL Writers

62 Adjusting to the US Classroom 706
- **62a** Understanding the Writing Process 706
- **62b** Understanding English Language Basics 708
- **62c** Learning to Edit Your Work 708

63 Grammar and Style for ESL Writers 713
- **63a** Using Verbs 713
- **63b** Using Nouns 720
- **63c** Using Pronouns 723
- **63d** Using Adjectives and Adverbs 726
- **63e** Using Prepositions 727
- **63f** Understanding Word Order 730

62

Adjusting to the US Classroom

❓ FAQs

How is writing taught in the United States? (p. 706)
Should I use my native language when I write? (p. 707)
What is the best way to edit my paper? (p. 709)
How can I get help with editing my paper? (p. 709)

❓ If you went to school outside of the United States, you may not be familiar with the way writing is taught in US composition classes.

> **CLOSE-UP**
>
> ### CHARACTERISTICS OF US CLASSROOMS
>
> Here are some aspects of US classrooms that may be unfamiliar to you:
>
> - **Punctuality** Students are expected to be in their seats and ready to begin class at the scheduled time. If you are late repeatedly, your grade may be lowered.
> - **Student–Instructor Relationships** The relationship between students and instructors may be more casual and friendly than what you are used to. However, instructors still expect students to abide by the rules they set.
> - **Class Discussion** Instructors typically expect students to volunteer ideas in class and may even enjoy it when students disagree with instructors' opinions (as long as the students can make good arguments for their positions). Rather than being seen as a sign of disrespect, this is usually considered to be evidence of interest and involvement in the topic under discussion.

62a Understanding the Writing Process

See Chs. 4–6

Typically, US composition instructors teach writing as a process. This process usually includes the following components:

- **Planning and shaping your writing** Your instructor will probably help you get ideas for your writing by assigning relevant readings, conducting class discussions, and asking you to keep a journal or engage in freewriting, brainstorming, or clustering.

- **Writing multiple drafts** After you write your paper, you will probably get feedback from your teacher or your classmates so that you can **revise** (improve) your paper before receiving a grade on it. Instructors expect students to use the suggestions they receive to make significant improvements to their papers. (For more information on the drafting process, **see Chapter 6.**)
- **Looking at sample papers** Your instructor may provide the class with sample student papers of the type that he or she has assigned. Such samples can help you understand how to complete the assigned paper. Sometimes the samples are strong papers that can serve as good examples of what to do. However, most samples will have both strengths and weaknesses, so be sure you understand your instructor's opinion of the samples he or she provides.
- **Engaging in** peer review (sometimes called peer editing) Your instructor may ask the class to work in small groups or individually to exchange ideas about an assigned paper. You will be expected to provide other students with feedback on the strengths and weaknesses of their papers. Afterward, you should think carefully about your classmates' comments and make changes to improve your paper.
- **Attending conferences** Your instructor may schedule one or more appointments with you to discuss your writing and may ask you to bring a draft of the paper you are working on. Your instructor may also be available to help you with your paper without an appointment during his or her office hours. In addition, many educational institutions have **writing centers,** where tutors help students get started on their papers or improve their drafts. When you meet with your instructor or writing center tutor, bring a list of specific questions about your paper, and be sure to make careful notes about what you discuss. You can refer to these notes when you revise your paper.

> **CLOSE-UP**
>
> **USING YOUR NATIVE LANGUAGE**
>
> Depending on your language background and skills, you may find it helpful to use your native language in some stages of your writing.
>
> When you are making notes about the content of your paper, you may be able to generate more ideas and record them more quickly if you do some of the work in your native language. Additionally, when you are drafting your paper and cannot think of a particular word in English, it may be better simply to write the word in your native language (and come back to it later) so you do not lose your train of thought.
>
> *(continued)*

> **USING YOUR NATIVE LANGUAGE** *(continued)*
>
> However, if you use another language a great deal as you draft your writing and then try to translate your work into English, the English may sound awkward or be hard to understand. The best strategy when you draft your papers is to write in English as much as you can, using the vocabulary and structures that you already know.

62b Understanding English Language Basics

Getting used to writing and editing your work in English will be easier if you understand a few basic principles:

ESL 63a
- **In English, words may change their form according to their function.** For example, verbs change form to communicate whether an action is taking place in the past, present, or future.
- **In English, context is extremely important to understanding function.** In the following sentences, for instance, the word *walk* performs different functions according to its relationships to other words.

   Juan and I are taking a walk. (*Walk* is a noun, a direct object of the verb *taking*, witn an article, *a*, attached to it.)

   If you walk instead of driving, you will help conserve the Earth's resources. (*Walk* is a verb, the predicate of the subject *you*.)

See Ch. 45
- **Spelling in English is not always phonetic and sometimes may seem illogical.** Spelling in English may be related more to the history of the word and to its origins in other languages than to the way the word is pronounced. Therefore, learning to spell correctly is often a matter of memorization, not of sounding out the word phonetically. For example, "ough" is pronounced differently in *tough*, *though*, and *thought*.

ESL 63f
- **Word order is extremely important in English sentences.** In English sentences, word order may indicate which word is the subject of the sentence and which is the object, whether the sentence is a question or a statement, and so on.

62c Learning to Edit Your Work

See 6d

Editing your paper involves focusing on grammar, spelling, punctuation, and mechanics. The approach you take to editing for grammar errors should depend on your strengths and weaknesses in English.

CHECKLIST

EDITING STRATEGIES

☐ **If you learned English mostly by speaking it, if you have strong oral skills, and if you usually make correct judgments about English by instinct,** the best approach for you may be reading your paper aloud and listening for mistakes, correcting them by deciding what sounds right. You may even find that as you read aloud, you automatically correct your written mistakes as you speak. (Be sure to transfer those corrections to your paper.) In addition to proofreading your paper from beginning to end, you might find it helpful to start from the end of the paper, reading and proofreading sentence by sentence. This strategy can keep you from being distracted by your ideas, allowing you to focus on grammar alone.

☐ **If you learned English mostly by reading, studying grammar rules, and/or translating between your native language and English,** you may not feel that you have good instincts about what sounds right in English. If this is the case, you should take a different approach to editing your papers. First, identify the errors you make most frequently by looking at earlier papers your instructor has marked or by asking your instructor for help. Once you have identified your most common errors, read through your paper, checking each sentence for these errors. Try to apply the grammar and mechanics rules you already know, or check the relevant grammar explanations in Chapter 63 for help.

After you check your paper for grammar errors, you should check again to make sure that you have used proper punctuation, capitalization, and spelling. If you have difficulty with spelling, you can use a spell checker to help you, but remember that spell checkers cannot catch every error. After you have made grammar and mechanics corrections on your own, you can seek outside help in identifying errors you might have missed. You should also keep a notebook with a list of your most frequent grammatical errors and review these errors regularly.

CHECKLIST

GETTING OUTSIDE HELP WITH EDITING

☐ **Ask a tutor or a friend for help.** After you have done your best to edit your own paper, you may want to ask for help from a Writing Center tutor, from your instructor, or from a friend whose English skills you trust. Ask your helper to point out any errors. Then, try to correct these errors.

(continued)

62c ESL ■ Adjusting to the US Classroom

> **GETTING OUTSIDE HELP WITH EDITING** *(continued)*
>
> ☐ **Use a grammar checker.** Your computer's grammar checker may give you some help with editing, but you may not find it very helpful since such grammar checkers are usually not designed to catch the types of errors typically made by ESL students.
>
> ☐ **Use a dictionary.** The dictionary can also be a good source of grammar help, especially if you use a dictionary designed for non-native English speakers.

■ EXERCISE 1

This exercise is designed to familiarize you with an online dictionary for ESL learners so that you can use such a dictionary to help you edit your writing. To complete this exercise, you will need to log on to the online version of *Heinle's Newbury House Dictionary of American English*, 4th edition <http://nhd.heinle.com>.

A. Examine the online dictionary entry for the word tuition (see Figure 62.1).

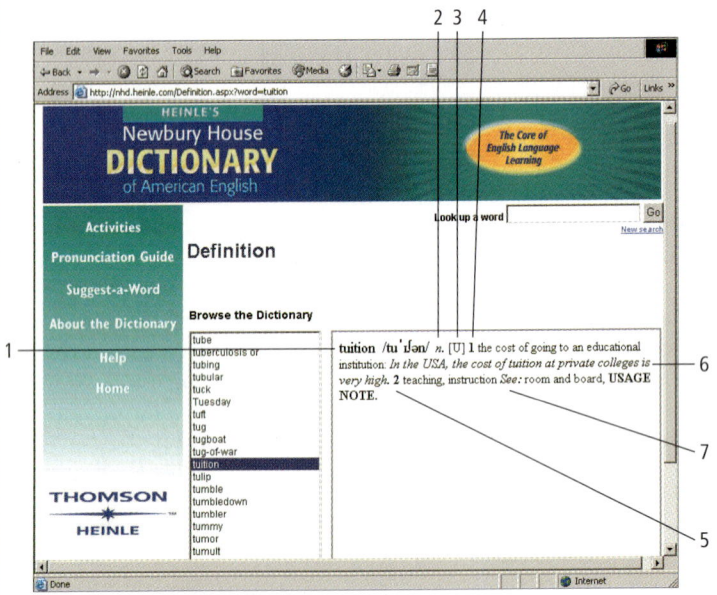

FIGURE 62.1 Online dictionary entry for *tuition*.

This entry gives you several pieces of information:

1. spelling
2. indication (with the abbreviation *n*.) that the word is a noun

3. indication (with the abbreviation [U]) that this noun is uncountable—that is, it is a **noncount noun**.
4., 5. definitions of the word
6. example sentence
7. usage note about the related phrase *room and board*

Now, look up the online dictionary entry for *room and board*, and write an explanation of the difference between *tuition* and *room and board*.

B. Examine the online dictionary entry for the word *ride* (see Figure 62.2).

This entry gives you the following information:

1. indication (with the abbreviation *v.*) that the word can be used as a verb
2. that the simple past form of *ride* is *rode:* I rode my bike yesterday.
3. that the past participle of *ride* is *ridden:* She has ridden the same bike for ten years.
4. that the present participle of *ride* is *riding*: He's out riding his horse.
5. that the third person conjugation of *ride* is *rides:* He rides to school with the neighbors.
6. indication (with the abbreviation *n.*) that *ride* can also be used as a noun

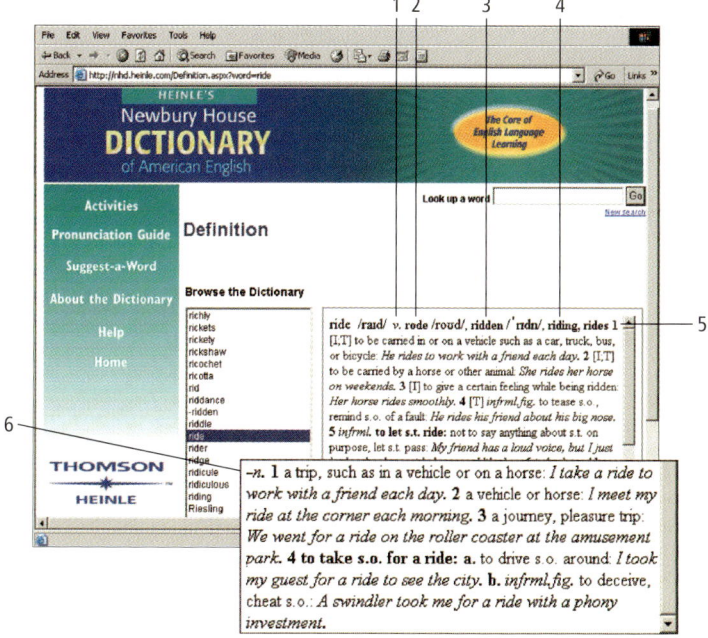

FIGURE 62.2 Online dictionary entry for *ride*.

Now, go to <http://nhd.heinle.com> to read the complete entry for *ride*, and answer the following questions:

1. What does the sentence, "The teacher rode them about their poor attendance." mean?
2. If someone calls "Shotgun!" on the way to the car, what does it mean?
3. If I say my investment advisor "took me for a ride," what do I probably mean?

C. Using the online version of *Heinle's Newbury House Dictionary of American English*, 4th edition <http://nhd.heinle.com>, look up the answers to the following questions:

1. What does the word *paternalistic* mean? (You will need to look up its root word, *paternalism*, to find out.)
2. Which preposition—*at*, *with*, or *in*—is usually used with the verb *participate*?
3. Should the season *spring* be capitalized? Should the days of the week be capitalized?
4. Have you ever had *cabin fever*? What does it mean?

63

Grammar and Style for ESL Writers

❓ FAQs

When do English verbs change form? (p. 713)
What are phrasal verbs, and how do I use them? (p. 716)
Why can't I write clothings *or* informations? *(p. 720)*
What is the difference between a *and* the? *(p. 721)*
If several adjectives modify one noun, which adjective comes first?
   (p. 727)
How do I know which preposition to use? (p. 727)

For ESL writers (as for many native English writers), grammar can be a persistent problem. Grammatical knowledge in a second language usually develops slowly, with time and practice, and much about English is idiomatic (not subject to easy-to-learn rules). This chapter is designed to provide you with the tools you will need to address some of the most common grammatical problems ESL writers face.

63a   Using Verbs

1 Subject-Verb Agreement

English **verbs** change their form according to person, number, and tense. The verb in a sentence must **agree** with the subject in both person and number. Person refers to *who* or *what* is performing the action of the verb (for example, *I, you,* or someone else), and number refers to *how many* people or things are performing the action (one or more than one).

See
Ch. 48

In English, the rules for **subject-verb agreement** are very important. Unless you use the correct person and number in the verbs in your sentences, you will confuse your English-speaking audience by communicating meanings you do not intend.

See
49a

2 Tense

Tense refers to *when* the action of the verb takes place. One problem that many nonnative speakers of English have with English verb

See
48b

See 48a2

tenses results from the large number of irregular verbs in English. For example, the first-person singular present tense of *be* is not "I be" but "I am," and the past tense is not "I beed" but "I was."

> **CLOSE-UP**
>
> **CHOOSING THE SIMPLEST VERB FORMS**
>
> Some nonnative English speakers use verb forms that are more complicated than they need to be. They may do this because their native language uses more complicated verb forms than English does or because they "overcorrect" their verbs into complicated forms. Specifically, nonnative speakers tend to use progressive tenses and perfect tenses instead of simple verb forms. To communicate your ideas clearly to an English-speaking audience, choose the simplest possible verb form.

See 48b2–3

3 Auxiliary Verbs

The **auxiliary verbs** (also known as **helping verbs**) *be*, *have*, and *do* are used to create some present, past, and future forms of verbs in English: "Julio is taking a vacation"; "I have been tired lately"; "He does not need a license." The auxiliary verbs *be*, *have*, and *do* change form to reflect the time frame of the action or situation and to agree with the subject; however, the main verb remains in simple present or simple past form.

> **CLOSE-UP**
>
> **AUXILIARY VERBS**
>
> Only auxiliary verbs, not the verbs they "help," change form to indicate person, number, and tense.
>
> **Present:** We have to eat.
>
> **Past:** We had to eat. (*not* "We had to ate.")
>
> Modal auxiliaries (such as *can* and *should*) do not change form to indicate tense, person, or number.

See 46c1

■ EXERCISE 1

A student wrote the following two paragraphs as part of a paper for his ESL composition class. He was asked to write about several interviews he conducted with people in his future profession, hotel management. The paragraphs contain errors in subject-verb agreement and verb tense, which the student's instructor underlined. Correct the underlined verbs by changing their form: begin by considering when the action took place, and then choose the simplest appropriate verb form to express that time. (Be sure to pay attention to the meaning and context of the sentences to determine which verb form is appropriate.)

In the past, when someone (1) <u>ask</u> me why I was interested in the hotel business, I always (2) <u>have</u> a hard time answering that question. I do not know exactly when and why I (3) <u>decide</u> to be a hotel manager. The only reason I can think of is my father. In his current job, he (4) <u>travel</u> a lot, and I have had a few chances to follow him and see other cities. Every time I went with him on a business trip, we (5) <u>spended</u> the night in a hotel, and I was surprised at how much hotels (6) <u>does</u> to satisfy their customers. All the employees are always friendly and polite. This gave me a positive image of hotels that made me (7) <u>decided</u> that the hotel business would be right for me.

For this paper, I (8) <u>spended</u> almost two weeks interviewing department heads at a local Hilton Hotel. Mr. Andrew Plain, the person who (9) <u>spend</u> the most time with me, (10) <u>share</u> an experience related to when he first got into the business. One of his first jobs was to plan a wedding, and he (11) <u>feel</u> a lot of responsibility because he (12) <u>believe</u> that a wedding is a one-time life experience for most people. So he wanted to take care of everything and make sure that everything was on track. To prepare for the wedding, he (13) <u>need</u> to work almost every Sunday, and one night he even (14) <u>have</u> to sleep in his office to attend the early wedding ceremony the next morning. From my experience with this interview, I realized that the people who are interested in the hotel business (15) <u>needs</u> great dedication to their career.

GETTING HELP FROM THE DICTIONARY

You may have trouble with items 5, 8, and 9 of Exercise 1 if you do not know the correct past tense forms of the verb *spend*, which is irregular. For help, look up the word *spend* in the dictionary. The first word after the word *spend* is the simple past form of *spend*.

4 Negative Verbs

The meaning of a verb may be made negative in English in a variety of ways, chiefly by adding the words *not* or *does not* to the verb (is, is *not*; can ski, *cannot* ski; drives a car, *does not* drive a car).

CLOSE-UP

CORRECTING DOUBLE NEGATIVES

A **double negative** occurs when the meaning of a verb is negated not just once but twice in a single sentence.

(continued)

CORRECTING DOUBLE NEGATIVES (continued)

Henry doesn't have ~~no~~ *any* friends. (*or* Henry ~~doesn't have~~ *has* no friends.)

I looked for articles in the library, but there weren't ~~none~~. (*or* I looked for articles in the library, but there weren't *any* ~~none~~.)

5 Phrasal Verbs

Many verbs in English are composed of two or more words—for example, *check up on, run for, turn into,* and *wait on.* These verbs are called **phrasal verbs.** It is important to become familiar with phrasal verbs and their definitions so you will recognize these verbs as phrasal verbs (instead of as verbs that are followed by prepositions).

Sometimes the words that make up a phrasal verb can be separated from each other by a direct object. In these **separable phrasal verbs,** the object can come either before or after the preposition. For example, "Ellen turned down the job offer" and "Ellen turned the job offer down" are both correct. However, when the object is a pronoun, the pronoun must come before the preposition. Therefore, "Ellen turned it down" is correct, but "Ellen turned down it" is incorrect.

CLOSE-UP

SEPARABLE PHRASAL VERBS

Verb	Definition
call off	cancel
carry on	continue
cheer up	make happy
clean out	clean the inside of
cut down	reduce
figure out	solve
fill in	substitute
find out	discover
give back	return something
give up	stop doing something or stop trying
leave out	omit
pass on	transmit
put away	place something in its proper place
put back	place something in its original place
put off	postpone

start over	start again
talk over	discuss
throw away/out	discard
touch up	repair

However, some phrasal verbs—such as *look into*, *make up for*, and *break into*—consist of words that can never be separated. With these **inseparable phrasal verbs,** you do not have a choice about where to place the object; the object must always follow the preposition. For example, "Anna cared for her niece" is correct, but "Anna cared her niece for" is incorrect.

CLOSE-UP

INSEPARABLE PHRASAL VERBS

Verb	Definition
come down with	develop an illness
come up with	produce
do away with	abolish
fall behind in	lag
get along with	be congenial with
get away with	avoid punishment
keep up with	maintain the same achievement or speed
look up to	admire
make up for	compensate
put up with	tolerate
run into	meet by chance
see to	arrange
show up	arrive
stand by	wait or remain loyal to
stand up for	support
watch out for	beware of or protect

6 Voice

Verbs may be in either active or passive <u>voice</u>. When the subject of a sentence performs the action of the verb, the verb is in **active voice.** When the action of the verb is performed on the subject, the verb is in **passive voice.**

See 48d

Karla and Miguel <u>purchased</u> the tickets. (active voice)

The tickets <u>were purchased</u> by Karla and Miguel. (passive voice)

Because your writing will usually be clearer and more concise if you use the active voice, you should use the passive voice only when you have a good reason to do so.

7 Transitive and Intransitive Verbs

Many nonnative English speakers find it difficult to decide whether or not a verb needs an object and in what order direct and indirect objects should appear in a sentence. Learning the difference between transitive verbs and intransitive verbs can help you with such problems.

A **transitive verb** is a verb that has a direct object: "<u>My father asked</u> a question" (subject + verb + direct object). In this example, *asked* is a transitive verb; it needs an object to complete its meaning.

An **intransitive verb** is a verb that does not take an object: "<u>The doctor smiled</u>" (subject + verb). In this example, *smiled* is an intransitive verb; it does not need an object to complete its meaning.

A transitive verb may be followed by a direct object or by both an indirect object and a direct object. (An indirect object answers the question "To whom?" or "For whom?") The indirect object may come before or after the direct object. If the indirect object follows the direct object, the preposition *to* or *for* must precede the indirect object.

    s   v   do
<u>Keith</u> <u>wrote</u> a letter. (subject + verb + direct object)

    s   v   io   do
<u>Keith</u> <u>wrote</u> his friend a letter. (subject + verb + indirect object + direct object)

    s   v   do   io
<u>Keith</u> <u>wrote</u> a letter to his friend. (subject + verb + direct object + *to/for* + indirect object)

Some verbs in English look similar and have similar meanings, except that one is transitive and the other is intransitive. For example, *lie* is intransitive, *lay* is transitive; *sit* is intransitive, *set* is transitive; *rise* is intransitive, *raise* is transitive. Knowing whether a verb is transitive or intransitive will help you with troublesome verb pairs such as these and will help you place words in the correct order.

NOTE: It is also important to know whether a verb is transitive or intransitive because only transitive verbs can be used in the **passive voice**. To determine whether a verb is transitive or intransitive—that is, to determine whether or not it needs an object—consult the example phrases in a dictionary.

See 48d

8 Infinitives and Gerunds

In English, two verb forms may be used as nouns: **infinitives,** which always begin with *to* (as in *to work, to sleep, to eat*), and **gerunds,** which always end in *-ing* (as in *working, sleeping, eating*).

> To bite into this steak requires better teeth than mine. (infinitive used as a noun)
>
> Cooking is one of my favorite hobbies. (gerund used as a noun)

Sometimes the gerund and the infinitive form of the same verb can be used interchangeably. For example, "He continued *to sleep*" and "He continued *sleeping*" convey the same meaning. However, this is not always the case. Saying, "Marco and Lisa stopped *to eat* at Julio's Café" is not the same as saying, "Marco and Lisa stopped *eating* at Julio's Café." In this example, the meaning of the sentence changes depending on whether a gerund or infinitive is used.

9 Participles

In English, verb forms called **present participles** and **past participles** are frequently used as adjectives. Present participles usually end in *-ing*, as in *working, sleeping,* and *eating,* and past participles usually end in *-ed, -t,* or *-en,* as in *worked, slept,* and *eaten*.

> According to the Bible, God spoke to Moses from a burning bush. (present participle used as an adjective)
>
> Some people think raw fish is healthier than cooked fish. (past participle used as an adjective)

A **participial phrase** is a group of words consisting of the participle plus the noun phrase that functions as the object or complement of the action being expressed by the participle. To avoid confusion, the participial phrase must be placed as close as possible to the noun it modifies.

> Having visited San Francisco last week, Jim and Lynn showed us pictures from their vacation. (The participial phrase is used as an adjective that modifies *Jim and Lynn*.)

NOTE: When a participial phrase falls at the beginning of a sentence, a comma is used to set it off. When a participial phrase is used in the middle of a sentence, commas should be used only if the phrase is *not* essential to the meaning of the sentence. No commas should be used if the participial phrase is essential to the meaning of the sentence.

See 52d

10 Verbs Formed from Nouns

In English, nouns can sometimes be used as verbs, with no change in form (other than the addition of an *-s* for agreement with third-person singular subjects or the addition of past tense endings). For example, the nouns *chair, book, frame,* and *father* can all be used as verbs.

> She <u>chairs</u> a committee on neighborhood safety.
>
> We <u>booked</u> a flight to New York for next week.
>
> I will <u>frame</u> my daughter's diploma after she graduates.
>
> He <u>fathered</u> several children out of wedlock.

63b Using Nouns

See 46a

A <u>noun</u> names things: people, animals, objects, places, feelings, ideas. If a noun names one thing, it is singular; if a noun names more than one thing, it is plural.

1 Noncount Nouns

Some English nouns do not have a plural form. These are called **noncount nouns** because what they name cannot be counted.

> **CLOSE-UP**
>
> **NONCOUNT NOUNS**
>
> The following commonly used nouns are noncount nouns. These words have no plural forms. Therefore, you should never add *-s* to them.
>
> | | |
> |---|---|
> | advice | homework |
> | clothing | information |
> | education | knowledge |
> | equipment | luggage |
> | evidence | merchandise |
> | furniture | revenge |

■ **EXERCISE 2**

An ESL student wrote the following paragraph as part of a composition paper about her experiences learning English. Read the paragraph, and decide which of the underlined words need to be made plural and which should remain unchanged. If a word should be made plural, make the necessary correction. If a word is correct as is, mark it with a *C*.

Visiting Ireland for three (1) <u>month</u> expanded my (2) <u>knowledge</u> of English. I took a part-time English (3) <u>course</u>, which was the key to improving my writing. The (4) <u>course</u> helped me understand the essential (5) <u>rule</u> of English, and I learned a lot of new (6) <u>vocabulary</u> and expressions. In the first three (7) <u>lecture</u>, the teacher, Mr. Nelson, explained the fundamentals of writing in English. My (8) <u>enthusiasm</u> for the English language increased because I realized the importance of this (9) <u>language</u> for my (10) <u>future</u>. Mr. Nelson recommended that I read more English (11) <u>book</u>. I took his advice, and my English got better.

GETTING HELP FROM THE DICTIONARY

Some of the nouns in Exercise 2 are noncount nouns, which cannot be made plural. If you are not sure whether a noun is countable or not, look it up in a dictionary.

2 Articles Used with Nouns

English has two kinds of **articles,** indefinite and definite.

Use an **indefinite article** (*a* or *an*) with a noun when readers are not familiar with the noun you are naming—for example, when you are introducing a noun for the first time. To say, "Jatin entered *a* building," signals to the audience that you are introducing the idea of the building for the first time. The building is indefinite, or not specific, until it has been identified.

The indefinite article *a* is used when the word following it (which may be a noun or an adjective) begins with a consonant or with a consonant sound: *a tree, a onetime offer*. The indefinite article *an* is used if the word following it begins with a vowel (*a, e, i, o,* or *u*) or with a vowel sound: *an apple, an honor*.

Use the **definite article** (*the*) when the noun you are naming has already been introduced, when the noun is already familiar to readers, or when the noun to which you refer is specific. To say, "Jatin entered *the* building," signals to readers that you are referring to the same building you mentioned earlier. The building has now become specific and may be referred to by the definite article.

CLOSE-UP

USING ARTICLES WITH NOUNS

There are three main exceptions to the rules governing the use of articles with nouns:

1. **A plural noun** does not require an indefinite article: "I love horses," not "I love *a* horses." (A plural noun does, however, require a definite article when you have already introduced the noun

(continued)

USING ARTICLES WITH NOUNS (continued)

to your readers or when you are referring to a specific plural noun: "I love *the* horses in the national park near my house.")

2. **A noncount noun** may or may not require an article.

   "Love conquers all," not "*A* love conquers all" or "*The* love conquers all."

   "*A* good education is important," not "Good education is important."

   "*The* homework is difficult" or "Homework is difficult," not "*A* homework is difficult."

   To help determine whether or not a noncount noun requires an article, look up that noun in a dictionary and consult the sample sentences provided.

3. **A proper noun,** which names a particular person, place, or thing, sometimes takes an article and sometimes does not. When you use an article with a proper noun, do not capitalize the article unless the article is the first word of the sentence.

   "*The* Mississippi River is one of the longest rivers in the world," not "Mississippi River is one of the longest rivers in the world."

   "Teresa was born in *the* United States," not "Teresa was born in United States."

   "China is the most populous nation on earth," not "*The* China is the most populous nation on earth."

   To find out whether or not a proper noun requires an article, look up that noun in a dictionary, and consult the sample sentences provided.

■ EXERCISE 3

The following introductory paragraph of a paper about renewable energy power sources was written for an ESL composition course. Read the paragraph, and decide whether or not each of the underlined noun phrases requires an article. If a noun phrase is correct as is, mark it with a *C*. If a noun phrase needs an article, indicate whether that article should be *a*, *an*, or *the*.

(1) <u>Use of electrical power</u> has increased dramatically over (2) <u>last thirty years</u> and continues to rise. (3) <u>Most ordinary sources</u> of (4) <u>electricity</u> require (5) <u>oil</u>, (6) <u>gas</u>, or (7) <u>uranium</u>, which are not (8) <u>renewable resources</u>. Living without (9) <u>electrical power</u> is not feasible as long as everything in our lives depends on (10) <u>electricity</u>, but (11) <u>entire world</u> will be in (12) <u>big crisis</u> if (13) <u>ignorance regarding renewable energy</u> continues. (14) <u>Renewable energy</u>, including (15) <u>solar energy</u>, (16) <u>wind energy</u>, (17) <u>hydro energy</u>, and (18) <u>biomass energy</u>, need (19) <u>more attention</u> from (20) <u>scientists</u>.

GETTING HELP FROM THE DICTIONARY

If you are uncertain whether or not to use an article with a certain noun, look up that noun in a dictionary, and use the sample sentences provided as a guide. When dealing with a noun phrase, be sure to look up the main noun. For example, in item 1, look up *use*, and in item 2, look up *year*.

3 Other Determiners Used with Nouns

Determiners are words that function as adjectives to limit or qualify the meaning of nouns. In addition to articles, **demonstrative pronouns, possessive nouns and pronouns, numbers** (both **cardinal** and **ordinal**), and other words indicating number and order can function in this way.

See 46d2

CLOSE-UP

USING OTHER DETERMINERS WITH NOUNS

- **Demonstrative pronouns** (*this*, *that*, *these*, *those*) communicate the following:
  1. the relative nearness or farness of the noun from the speaker's position (*this* and *these* for things that are *near*; *that* and *those* for things that are *far*): *this* book on my desk, *that* book on your desk; *these* shoes on my feet, *those* shoes in my closet.
  2. the number of things indicated (*this* and *that* for *singular* nouns, *these* and *those* for *plural* nouns): *this* (or *that*) flower in the vase, *these* (or *those*) flowers in the garden.
- **Possessive nouns** and **possessive pronouns** (*Ashraf's*, *his*, *their*) show who or what the noun belongs to: *Maria's* courage, *everybody's* fears, the *country's* natural resources, *my* personality, *our* groceries.
- **Cardinal numbers** (*three*, *fifty*, *a thousand*) indicate how many of the noun you mean: *seven* continents. **Ordinal** numbers (*first*, *tenth*, *thirtieth*) indicate in what order the noun appears among other items: *third* planet.
- Words other than numbers may indicate **amount** (*many*, *few*) and **order** (*next*, *last*) and function in the same ways as cardinal and ordinal numbers: *few* opportunities, *last* chance.

63c Using Pronouns

Any English noun may be replaced by a pronoun. Pronouns enable you to avoid repeating a noun over and over. For example, *doctor* may be replaced by *he* or *she*, *books* by *them*, and *computer* by *it*.

See 46b, Ch. 47

1 Pronoun Reference

See 47c

Pronoun reference is very important in English sentences, where the noun the pronoun replaces (the **antecedent**) must be easily identified. In general, you should place the pronoun as close as possible to the noun it replaces so the noun to which the pronoun refers is clear. If this is impossible, use the noun itself instead of replacing it with a pronoun.

> **Unclear:** When Tara met Emily, she was nervous. *(Does she refer to Tara or to Emily?)*
>
> **Clear:** When Tara met Emily, Tara was nervous.
>
> **Unclear:** Stefano and Victor love his DVD collection. *(Whose DVD collection—Stefano's, Victor's, or someone else's?)*
>
> **Clear:** Stefano and Victor love Emilio's DVD collection.

2 Pronoun Placement

Never use a pronoun immediately after the noun it replaces. For example, do not say, "Most of my classmates they are smart"; instead, say, "Most of my classmates are smart." The only exception to this rule occurs with an **intensive pronoun**, which ends in *-self* and emphasizes the preceding noun or pronoun: *Marta herself was eager to hear the results.*

3 Indefinite Pronouns

Unlike **personal pronouns** (*I, you, he, she, it, we, they, me, him, her, us, them,* and so on), **indefinite pronouns** do not refer to a particular person, place, or thing. Therefore, an indefinite pronoun does not require an antecedent. **Indefinite pronoun subjects** (*anybody, nobody, each, either, someone, something, all, some*), like personal pronouns, must

See 49a4

agree in number with the sentence's verb.

> Nobody have failed the exam. *(Nobody is a singular subject and requires a singular verb.)*
>
> [has — correction above "have"]

4 Appositives

Appositives are nouns or noun phrases that identify or rename an adjacent noun or pronoun. An appositive usually follows the noun it explains or modifies but can sometimes precede it.

> My parents, Mary and John, live in Louisiana. *(Mary and John identifies parents.)*

NOTE: The <u>case</u> of a pronoun in an appositive depends on the case of the word it identifies.

See 47b3

If an appositive is *not* essential to the meaning of the sentence, use commas to set off the appositive from the rest of the sentence. If an appositive *is* essential to the meaning of the sentence, do not use commas.

His aunt <u>Trang</u> is in the hospital. (*Trang* is necessary to the meaning of the sentence because it identifies which aunt is in the hospital.)

Akta's car, <u>a 1997 Jeep</u>, broke down last night, so she had to walk home. (*a 1997 Jeep* is not essential to the meaning of the sentence.)

5 Pronouns and Gender

A pronoun must agree in **gender** with the noun to which it refers.

My sister sold <u>her</u> old car.

Your uncle is walking <u>his</u> dog.

NOTE: In English, most nonhuman nouns are referred to as *it* because they do not have grammatical gender. However, exceptions are sometimes made for pets, ships, and countries. Pets are often referred to as *he* or *she*, depending on their sex, and ships and countries are sometimes referred to as *she*.

■ EXERCISE 4

There are no pronouns in the following passage. The repetition of the nouns again and again would seem strange to a native English speaker. Rewrite the passage, replacing as many of the nouns as possible with appropriate pronouns. Be sure that the connection between the pronouns and the nouns they replace is clear.

> The young couple seated across from Daniel at dinner the night before were newlyweds from Tokyo. The young couple and Daniel ate together with other guests of the inn at long, low tables in a large dining room with straw mat flooring. The man introduced himself immediately in English, shook Daniel's hand firmly, and, after learning that Daniel was not a tourist but a resident working in Osaka, gave Daniel a business card. The man had just finished college and was working at the man's first real job, clerking in a bank. Even in a sweatsuit, the man looked ready for the office: chin closely shaven, bristly hair neatly clipped, nails clean and buffed. After a while the man and Daniel exhausted the man's store of English and drifted into Japanese.

The man's wife, shy up until then, took over as the man fell silent. The woman and Daniel talked about the new popularity of hot springs spas in the countryside around the inn, the difficulty of finding good schools for the children the woman hoped to have soon, the differences between food in Tokyo and Osaka. The woman's husband ate busily. From time to time the woman refilled the man's beer glass or served the man radish pickles from a china bowl in the middle of the table, and then returned to the conversation.

63d Using Adjectives and Adverbs

See Ch. 50

Adjectives and adverbs are words that **modify** (describe, limit, or qualify) other words.

1 Position of Adjectives and Adverbs

Adjectives in English usually appear *before* the nouns they modify. A native speaker of English would not say, "Cars *red and black* are involved in more accidents than cars *blue or green*" but would say instead, "*Red and black* cars are involved in more accidents than *blue or green* cars."

However, adjectives may appear *after* linking verbs ("The name seemed *familiar*"), *after* direct objects ("The coach found them *tired* but *happy*."), and *after* indefinite pronouns ("Anything *sad* makes me cry.").

Adverbs may appear before or after the verbs they describe, but they should be placed as close to the verb as possible: not "I *told* John that I couldn't meet him for lunch *politely*," but "I *politely told* John that I couldn't meet him for lunch" or "I *told* John *politely* that I couldn't meet him for lunch." When an adverb describes an adjective or another adverb, it usually comes *before* that adjective or adverb: "The essay has *basically sound* logic"; "You must express yourself *absolutely clearly*." Never place an adverb between the verb and the direct object.

Incorrect: Rolf *drank quickly* the water.

Correct: Rolf *drank* the water *quickly* (or, Rolf *quickly* drank the water).

Incorrect: Suong *took quietly* the test.

Correct: Suong *quietly* took the test (or, Suong *took* the test *quietly*).

2 Order of Adjectives

A single noun may be modified by more than one adjective, perhaps even by a whole list of adjectives. Given a list of three or four adjectives, most native speakers would arrange them in a sentence in the same order. If, for example, shoes are to be described as *green* and *big*, numbering *two*, and of the type worn for playing *tennis*, a native speaker would say "two big green tennis shoes." Generally, the adjectives that are most important in completing the meaning of the noun are placed closest to the noun.

> **CLOSE-UP**
>
> **ORDER OF ADJECTIVES**
>
> 1. Articles (*a*, *the*), demonstratives (*this*, *those*), and possessives (*his*, *our*, *Maria's*, *everybody's*)
> 2. Amounts (*one*, *five*, *many*, *few*), order (*first*, *next*, *last*)
> 3. Personal opinions (*nice*, *ugly*, *crowded*, *pitiful*)
> 4. Sizes and shapes (*small*, *tall*, *straight*, *crooked*)
> 5. Age (*young*, *old*, *modern*, *ancient*)
> 6. Colors (*black*, *white*, *red*, *blue*, *dark*, *light*)
> 7. Nouns functioning as adjectives to form a unit with the noun (*soccer* ball, *cardboard* box, *history* class)

■ **EXERCISE 5**

Write five original sentences in which two or three adjectives describe a noun. Be sure that the adjectives are in the correct order.

63e Using Prepositions

See 46f

In English, <u>prepositions</u> (such as *to*, *from*, *at*, *with*, *among*, *between*) give meaning to nouns by linking them with other words and other parts of the sentence. Prepositions convey several different kinds of information:

- Relations to **time** (*at* nine o'clock, *in* five minutes, *for* a month)
- Relations of **place** (*in* the classroom, *at* the library, *beside* the chair) and **direction** (*to* the market, *onto* the stage, *toward* the freeway)
- Relations of **association** (go *with* someone, the tip *of* the iceberg)
- Relations of **purpose** (working *for* money, dieting *to* lose weight)

1 Commonly Used Prepositional Phrases

In English, the use of prepositions is often idiomatic rather than governed by grammatical rules. In many cases, therefore, learners of English as a second language need to memorize which prepositions are used in which phrases.

In English, some prepositions that relate to time have specific uses with certain nouns, such as days, months, and seasons:

63e ESL ▪ Grammar and Style for ESL Writers

- *On* is used with days and specific dates: *on* Monday, *on* September 13, 1977.
- *In* is used with months, seasons, and years: *in* November, *in* the spring, *in* 1999.
- *In* is also used when referring to some parts of the day: *in* the morning, *in* the afternoon, *in* the evening.
- *At* is used to refer to other parts of the day: *at* noon, *at* night, *at* seven o'clock.

> **CLOSE-UP**
>
> **DIFFICULT PREPOSITIONAL PHRASES**
>
> The following phrases (accompanied by their correct prepositions) sometimes cause difficulties for ESL writers:
>
> | | | |
> |---|---|---|
> | according *to* | *at* least | relevant *to* |
> | apologize *to* | *at* most | similar *to* |
> | appeal *to* | refer *to* | subscribe *to* |
> | different *from* | | |

2 Commonly Confused Prepositions

The prepositions *to*, *in*, *on*, *into*, and *onto* are very similar to one another and are therefore easily confused.

> **CLOSE-UP**
>
> **USING COMMON PREPOSITIONS**
>
> - *To* is the basic preposition of direction. It indicates movement toward a physical place: "She went *to* the restaurant"; "He went *to* the meeting." *To* is also used to form the infinitive of a verb: "He wanted *to deposit* his paycheck before noon"; "Irene offered *to drive* Maria to the baseball game."
> - *In* indicates that something is within the boundaries of a particular space or period of time: "My son is *in* the garden"; "I like to ski *in* the winter"; "The map is *in* the car."
> - *On* indicates position above or the state of being supported by something: "The toys are *on* the porch"; "The baby sat *on* my lap"; "The book is *on* top of the magazine."
> - *Into* indicates movement to the inside or interior of something: "She walked *into* the room"; "I threw the stone *into* the lake"; "He put the photos *into* the box." Although *into* and *in* are sometimes interchangeable, note that usage depends on whether the subject is stationary or moving. *Into* usually indicates movement, as in "I jumped *into* the water." *In* usually indicates a stationary position relative to the object of the preposition, as in "Mary is swimming *in* the water."

- *Onto* indicates movement to a position on top of something: "The cat jumped *onto* the chair"; "Crumbs are falling *onto* the floor." Both *on* and *onto* can be used to indicate a position on top of something (and therefore they can sometimes be used interchangeably), but *onto* specifies that the subject is moving to a place from a different place or from an outside position.

CLOSE-UP

PREPOSITIONS IN IDIOMATIC EXPRESSIONS

Many nonnative speakers use incorrect prepositions in idiomatic expressions. Compare the incorrect expressions in the left-hand column below with the correct expressions in the right-hand column.

Incorrect	Correct
according *with*	according *to*
apologize *at*	apologize *to*
appeal *at*	appeal *to*
believe *at*	believe *in*
different *to*	different *from*
for least, *for* most	*at* least, *at* most
refer *at*	refer *to*
relevant *with*	relevant *to*
similar *with*	similar *to*
subscribe *with*	subscribe *to*

EXERCISE 6

An ESL student in a composition class wrote the following paragraphs as part of a paper about her experiences learning to write in English. In several cases, she chose the wrong prepositions. The student's instructor has underlined the misused prepositions. Your task is to replace each underlined preposition with a correct preposition. (In some cases, there may be more than one possible correct answer.) If you have trouble, see the "Getting Help from the Dictionary" box, which follows the exercise.

My first experience writing (1) of English took place (2) at my early youth. I don't remember what the experience was like, but I do know that I have improved my writing skills since then. The improvement stems from various reasons. One major impact (3) to my writing was the fact that I attended an American school (4) of my country. This helped a lot because the first language (5) to the school was English. Being surrounded (6) in English helped me improve both my verbal skills and my writing skills. Another major factor that helped me develop my English writing skills, especially my grammar and vocabulary, was reading novels.

(7) <u>At</u> the future, I plan to improve my writing skills in English by participating (8) <u>to</u> several activities. I plan to read more novels so I can further develop the grammar and vocabulary skills that will help me earn my degree. I also plan to communicate verbally with native speakers and to listen (9) <u>at</u> public speeches (such as the president's state of the union address), which usually contain rich vocabulary. But my main plan is to keep writing more papers and discussing my writing (10) <u>to</u> my instructor. The more I write, the more confident I will become and the more my writing will improve. And there is always room for improvement.

GETTING HELP FROM THE DICTIONARY

In some cases, you can determine which preposition to use by consulting a dictionary. For example, you can find the answers to items 3, 6, 7, 8, 9, and 10 in Exercise 6 by consulting a dictionary. Look up a noun or verb that is part of the phrase in question, and within the dictionary entry for each of these words, you will find example phrases containing the correct preposition. *Hint:* For item 3, look up the word *impact*, and for item 6, look up *surround*.

63f Understanding Word Order

In English, word order is extremely important, contributing a good deal to the meaning of a sentence.

1 Standard Word Order

Like Chinese, English is an "SVO" language, or one in which the most typical sentence pattern is "subject-verb-object." (Arabic, by contrast, is an example of a "VSO" language.)

2 Word Order in Questions

Word order in questions can be particularly troublesome for speakers of languages other than English, partly because there are so many different ways to form questions in English.

CLOSE-UP

WORD ORDER IN QUESTIONS

1. To create a **yes/no question** from a statement using the verb *be*, simply invert the order of the subject and the verb.

   Rasheem is researching the depletion of the ozone layer.

   Is Rasheem researching the depletion of the ozone layer?

2. To create a **yes/no question** from a statement using a verb other than *be*, use a form of the auxiliary verb *do* before the sentence without inverting the subject and verb.

   Does Rasheem want to research the depletion of the ozone layer?

   Do Rasheem's friends want to help him with his research?

   Did Rasheem's professors approve his research proposal?

3. You can also form a question by adding a **tag question**—such as *won't he?* or *didn't I?*—to the end of a statement. If the verb of the main statement is *positive*, then the verb of the tag question is *negative*; if the verb of the main statement is *negative*, then the verb of the tag question is *positive*.

   Rasheem is researching the depletion of the ozone layer, isn't he?

   Rasheem doesn't intend to write his dissertation about the depletion of the ozone layer, does he?

4. To create a **question asking for information,** use interrogative words (*who, what, where, when, why, how*), and invert the order of the subject and verb. (Note that *who* functions as the subject of the question in which it appears.)

   Who is researching the depletion of the ozone layer?

   What is Rasheem researching?

   Where is Rasheem researching the depletion of the ozone layer?

Glossary of Usage

This glossary of usage lists words and phrases that writers often find troublesome and explains how they are used.

a, an   Use *a* before words that begin with consonants and words with initial vowels that sound like consonants: *a* person, *a* historical document, *a* one-horse carriage, *a* uniform. Use *an* before words that begin with vowels and words that begin with a silent *h*: *an* artist, *an* honest person.

accept, except   *Accept* is a verb that means "to receive"; *except* as a preposition or conjunction means "other than" and as a verb means "to leave out": The auditors will *accept* all your claims *except* the last two. Some businesses are *excepted* from the regulation.

advice, advise   *Advice* is a noun meaning "opinion or information offered"; *advise* is a verb that means "to offer advice to": The broker *advised* her client to take his attorney's *advice*.

affect, effect   *Affect* is a verb meaning "to influence"; *effect* can be a verb or a noun—as a verb it means "to bring about," and as a noun it means "result": We know how the drug *affects* patients immediately, but little is known of its long-term *effects*. The arbitrator tried to *effect* a settlement between the parties.

all ready, already   *All ready* means "completely prepared"; *already* means "by or before this or that time": I was *all ready* to help, but it was *already* too late.

all right, alright   Although the use of *alright* is increasing, current usage calls for *all right*.

allusion, illusion   An *allusion* is a reference or hint; an *illusion* is something that is not what it seems: The poem makes an *allusion* to the Pandora myth. The shadow created an optical *illusion*.

a lot   *A lot* is always two words.

among, between   *Among* refers to groups of more than two things; *between* refers to just two things: The three parties agreed *among* themselves to settle the case. There will be a brief intermission *between* the two acts. (Note that *amongst* is British, not American, usage.)

amount, number   *Amount* refers to a quantity that cannot be counted; *number* refers to things that can be counted: Even a small *amount* of caffeine can be harmful. Seeing their commander fall, a large *number* of troops ran to his aid.

an, a See **a, an**.

and/or In business or technical writing, use *and/or* when either or both of the items it connects can apply. In college writing, however, avoid the use of *and/or*.

as . . . as . . . In such constructions, *as* signals a comparison; therefore, you must always use the second *as:* John Steinbeck's *East of Eden* is *as* long *as* his *The Grapes of Wrath.*

as, like *As* can be used as a conjunction (to introduce a complete clause) or as a preposition; *like* should be used as a preposition only: In *The Scarlet Letter*, Hawthorne uses imagery *as* (not *like*) he does in his other works. After classes, Fred works *as* a manager of a fast food restaurant. Writers *like* Carl Sandburg appear once in a generation.

at, to Many people use the prepositions *at* and *to* after *where* in conversation: *Where* are you working *at? Where* are you going *to?* This usage is redundant and should not appear in college writing.

awhile, a while *Awhile* is an adverb; *a while,* which consists of an article and a noun, is used as the object of a preposition: Before we continue, we will rest *awhile.* (modifies the verb *rest*) Before we continue, we will rest for *a while.* (object of the preposition *for*)

bad, badly *Bad* is an adjective, and *badly* is an adverb: The school board decided that *Huckleberry Finn* was a *bad* book. American automobile makers did not do *badly* this year. After verbs that refer to any of the senses or after any other linking verb, use the adjective form: He looked *bad.* He felt *bad.* It seemed *bad.*

being as, being that These awkward phrases add unnecessary words, thereby weakening your writing. Use *because* instead.

beside, besides *Beside* is a preposition meaning "next to"; *besides* can be either a preposition meaning "except" or "other than" or an adverb meaning "as well": *Beside* the tower was a wall that ran the length of the city. *Besides* its industrial uses, laser technology has many other applications. Edison invented not only the lightbulb but the phonograph *besides.*

between, among See **among, between**.

bring, take *Bring* means "to transport from a farther place to a nearer place"; *take* means "to carry or convey from a nearer place to a farther place": *Bring* me a souvenir from your trip. *Take* this message to the general, and wait for a reply.

can, may *Can* denotes ability; *may* indicates permission: If you *can* play, you *may* use my piano.

capital, capitol *Capital* refers to a city that is an official seat of government; *capitol* refers to a building in which a legislature meets: Washington, DC, is the *capital* of the United States. When we were there, we visited the *Capitol* building.

center around This imprecise phrase is acceptable in speech and informal writing but not in college writing. Use *center on* instead.

cite, site *Cite* is a verb meaning "to quote as an authority or example"; *site* is a noun meaning "a place or setting"; it is also a shortened form of *Web site:* Jeff *cited* five sources in his research paper. The builder cleared the *site* for the new bank. Marisa uploaded her *site* to the Web.

climactic, climatic *Climactic* means "of or related to a climax"; *climatic* means "of or related to climate": The *climactic* moment of the movie occurred unexpectedly. If scientists are correct, the *climatic* conditions of Earth are changing.

coarse, course *Coarse* is an adjective meaning "inferior" or "having a rough, uneven texture"; *course* is a noun meaning "a route or path," "an area on which a sport is played," or "a unit of study": *Coarse* sandpaper is used to smooth the surface. The *course* of true love never runs smoothly. Last semester I had to drop a *course*.

complement, compliment *Complement* means "to complete or add to"; *compliment* means "to give praise": A double-blind study would *complement* their preliminary research. My instructor *complimented* me on my improvement.

conscious, conscience *Conscious* is an adjective meaning "having one's mental faculties awake"; *conscience* is a noun that means the moral sense of right and wrong: The patient will remain *conscious* during the procedure. His *conscience* would not allow him to lie.

continual, continuous *Continual* means "recurring at intervals"; *continuous* refers to an action that occurs without interruption: A pulsar is a star that emits a *continual* stream of electromagnetic radiation. (It emits radiation at regular intervals.) A small battery allows the watch to run *continuously* for five years. (It runs without stopping.)

could of, should of, would of The contractions *could've, should've*, and *would've* are often misspelled as the nonstandard constructions *could of, should of,* and *would of.* Use *could have, should have,* and *would have* in college writing.

council, counsel A *council* is "a body of people who serve in a legislative or advisory capacity"; *counsel* means "to offer advice or guidance": The city *council* argued about the proposed ban on smoking. The judge *counseled* the couple to settle their differences.

couple, couple of *Couple* means "a pair," but *couple of* is often used colloquially to mean "several" or "a few." In your college writing, specify "four points" or "two examples" rather than using "a couple of."

criterion, criteria *Criteria,* from the Greek, is the plural of *criterion,* meaning "standard for judgment": Of all the *criteria* for hiring graduating seniors, class rank is the most important *criterion.*

data *Data* is the plural of the Latin *datum,* meaning "fact." In everyday speech and writing, *data* is often used as the singular as well as the plural form. In college writing, use *data* only for the plural: The *data* discussed in this section *are* summarized in Appendix A.

different from, different than *Different than* is widely used in American speech. In college writing, use *different from*.

discreet, discrete *Discreet* means "careful or prudent"; *discrete* means "separate or individually distinct": Because Madame Bovary was not *discreet*, her reputation suffered. Atoms can be broken into hundreds of *discrete* particles.

disinterested, uninterested *Disinterested* means "objective" or "capable of making an impartial judgment"; *uninterested* means "indifferent or unconcerned": The American judicial system depends on *disinterested* jurors. Finding no treasure, Hernando de Soto was *uninterested* in going farther.

don't, doesn't *Don't* is the contraction of *do not*; *doesn't* is the contraction of *does not*. Do not confuse the two: My dog *doesn't* (not *don't*) like to walk in the rain. (Note that contractions are generally not acceptable in college writing.)

effect, affect See **affect, effect.**

e.g. *E.g.* is an abbreviation for the Latin *exempli gratia*, meaning "for example" or "for instance." In college writing, do not use *e.g.* Instead, use *for example* or *for instance*.

emigrate from, immigrate to To *emigrate* is "to leave one's country and settle in another"; to *immigrate* is "to come to another country and reside there." The noun forms of these words are *emigrant* and *immigrant*: My great-grandfather *emigrated from* Warsaw along with many other *emigrants* from Poland. Many people *immigrate to* the United States for economic reasons, but such *immigrants* still face great challenges.

eminent, imminent *Eminent* is an adjective meaning "standing above others" or "prominent"; *imminent* means "about to occur": Oliver Wendell Holmes Jr. was an *eminent* jurist. In ancient times, a comet signaled *imminent* disaster.

enthused *Enthused*, a colloquial form of *enthusiastic*, should not be used in college writing.

etc. *Etc.*, the abbreviation of *et cetera*, means "and the rest." Do not use it in your college writing. Instead, use *and so on*—or, better yet, specify exactly what *etc.* stands for.

everyday, every day *Everyday* is an adjective that means "ordinary" or "commonplace"; *every day* means "occurring daily": In the Gettysburg Address, Lincoln used *everyday* language. She exercises almost *every day*.

everyone, every one *Everyone* is an indefinite pronoun meaning "every person"; *every one* means "every individual or thing in a particular group": *Everyone* seems happier in the spring. *Every one* of the packages had been opened.

except, accept See **accept, except**.

explicit, implicit *Explicit* means "expressed or stated directly"; *implicit* means "implied" or "expressed or stated indirectly": The director *explicitly* warned the actors to be on time for rehearsals. Her *implicit* message was that lateness would not be tolerated.

farther, further *Farther* designates distance; *further* designates degree: I have traveled *farther* from home than any of my relatives. Critics charge that welfare subsidies encourage *further* dependence.

fewer, less Use *fewer* with nouns that can be counted: *fewer* books, *fewer* people, *fewer* dollars. Use *less* with quantities that cannot be counted: *less* pain, *less* power, *less* enthusiasm.

firstly (secondly, thirdly, . . .) Archaic forms meaning "in the first . . . second . . . third place." Use *first, second, third* instead.

further, farther See **farther, further**.

good, well *Good* is an adjective, never an adverb: She is a *good* swimmer. *Well* can function as an adverb or as an adjective. As an adverb, it means "in a good manner": She swam *well* (not *good*) in the meet. *Well* is used as an adjective meaning "in good health" with verbs that denote a state of being or feeling: I feel *well*.

got to *Got to* is not acceptable in college writing. To indicate obligation, use *have to, has to,* or *must*.

hanged, hung Both *hanged* and *hung* are past participles of *hang*. *Hanged* is used to refer to executions; *hung* is used to mean "suspended": Billy Budd was *hanged* for killing the master-at-arms. The stockings were *hung* by the chimney with care.

he, she Traditionally, *he* has been used in the generic sense to refer to both males and females. To acknowledge the equality of the sexes, however, avoid the generic *he*. Use plural pronouns whenever possible. See **43e2**.

hopefully The adverb *hopefully*, meaning "in a hopeful manner," should modify a verb, an adjective, or another adverb. Do not use *hopefully* as a sentence modifier meaning "it is hoped." Rather than "*Hopefully,* scientists will soon discover a cure for AIDS," write "*People hope* scientists will soon discover a cure for AIDS."

i.e. *I.e.* is an abbreviation for the Latin *id est*, meaning "that is." In college writing, do not use *i.e.* Instead, use its English equivalent.

if, whether When asking indirect questions or expressing doubt, use *whether*: He asked *whether* (not *if*) the flight would be delayed. The flight attendant was not sure *whether* (not *if*) it would be delayed.

illusion, allusion See **allusion, illusion**.

immigrate to, emigrate from See **emigrate from, immigrate to**.

implicit, explicit See **explicit, implicit**.

imply, infer *Imply* means "to hint" or "to suggest"; *infer* means "to conclude from": Mark Antony *implied* that the conspirators had murdered Caesar. The crowd *inferred* his meaning and called for justice.

infer, imply See **imply, infer**.

inside of, outside of *Of* is unnecessary when *inside* and *outside* are used as prepositions. *Inside of* is colloquial in references to time: He waited *inside* (not *inside of*) the coffee shop. He could run a mile in *under* (not *inside of*) eight minutes.

irregardless, regardless *Irregardless* is a nonstandard version of *regardless*. Use *regardless* or *irrespective* instead.

is when, is where These constructions are faulty when they appear in definitions: A playoff is (not *is when* or *is where*) an additional game played to establish the winner of a tie.

its, it's *Its* is a possessive pronoun; *it's* is a contraction of *it is*: *It's* no secret that the bank is out to protect *its* assets.

kind of, sort of *Kind of* and *sort of* to mean "rather" or "somewhat" are colloquial and should not appear in college writing: It is well known that Napoleon was *rather* (not *kind of*) short.

lay, lie See **lie, lay**.

leave, let *Leave* means "to go away from" or "to let remain"; *let* means "to allow" or "to permit": *Let* (not *leave*) me give you a hand.

less, fewer See **fewer, less**.

let, leave See **leave, let**.

lie, lay *Lie* is an intransitive verb (one that does not take an object) meaning "to recline." Its principal forms are *lie, lay, lain, lying*: Each afternoon she would *lie* in the sun and listen to the surf. *As I Lay Dying* is a novel by William Faulkner. By 1871, Troy had *lain* undisturbed for two thousand years. The painting shows a nude *lying* on a couch.
 Lay is a transitive verb (one that takes an object) meaning "to put" or "to place." Its principal forms are *lay, laid, laid, laying*: The Federalist Papers *lay* the foundation for American conservatism. In October 1781, the British *laid* down their arms and surrendered. He had *laid* his money on the counter before leaving. We watched the stonemasons *laying* a wall.

like, as See **as, like**.

loose, lose *Loose* is an adjective meaning "not rigidly fastened or securely attached"; *lose* is a verb meaning "to misplace": The marble facing of the building became *loose* and fell to the sidewalk. After only two drinks, most people *lose* their ability to judge distance.

lots, lots of, a lot of These words are colloquial substitutes for *many, much*, or *a great deal of*. Avoid their use in college writing: The students had *many* (not *lots of* or *a lot of*) options for essay topics.

man Like the generic pronoun *he*, *man* has been used in English to denote members of both sexes. This usage is being replaced by *human beings, people*, or similar terms that do not specify gender. See **43e2**.

may, can See **can, may**.

may be, maybe *May be* is a verb phrase: *maybe* is an adverb meaning "perhaps": She *may be* the smartest student in the class. *Maybe* her experience has given her an advantage.

media, medium *Medium*, meaning "a means of conveying or broadcasting something," is singular; *media* is the plural form and requires a plural verb: The *media have* distorted the issue.

might have, might of *Might of* is a nonstandard spelling of the contraction of *might have (might've)*. Use *might have* in college writing.

number, amount See **amount, number**.

OK, O.K., okay All three spellings are acceptable, but this term should be avoided in college writing. Replace it with a more specific word or words: The lecture was *adequate* (not *okay*), if uninspiring.

outside of, inside of See **inside of, outside of**.

passed, past *Passed* is the past tense of the verb *pass; past* means "belonging to a former time" or "no longer current": The car must have been going eighty miles per hour when it *passed* us. In the envelope was a bill marked *past* due.

percent, percentage *Percent* indicates a part of a hundred when a specific number is referred to: "*10 percent* of his salary." *Percentage* is used when no specific number is referred to: "a *percentage* of next year's receipts." In technical and business writing, it is permissible to use the % sign after percentages you are comparing. Write out the word *percent* in college writing.

phenomenon, phenomena A *phenomenon* is a single observable fact or event. It can also refer to a rare or significant occurrence. *Phenomena* is the plural form and requires a plural verb: Many supposedly paranormal *phenomena are* easily explained.

plus As a preposition, *plus* means "in addition to." Avoid using *plus* as a substitute for *and*: Include the principal, *plus* the interest, in your calculations. Your quote was too high; *moreover* (not *plus*), it was inaccurate.

precede, proceed *Precede* means "to go or come before"; *proceed* means "to go forward in an orderly way": Robert Frost's *North of Boston* was *preceded* by an earlier volume. In 1532, Francisco Pizarro landed at Tumbes and *proceeded* south.

principal, principle As a noun, *principal* means "a sum of money (minus interest) invested or lent" or "a person in the leading position"; as an adjective, it means "most important"; a *principle* is a noun meaning a rule of conduct or a basic truth: He wanted to reduce the *principal* of the loan. The *principal* of the high school is a talented administrator.

Women are the *principal* wage earners in many American households. The Constitution embodies certain fundamental *principles*.

quote, quotation *Quote* is a verb. *Quotation* is a noun. In college writing, do not use *quote* as a shortened form of *quotation*: Scholars attribute these *quotations* (not *quotes*) to Shakespeare.

raise, rise *Raise* is a transitive verb, and *rise* is an intransitive verb—that is, *raise* takes an object, and *rise* does not: My grandparents *raised* a large family. The sun will *rise* at 6:12 tomorrow morning.

real, really *Real* means "genuine" or "authentic"; *really* means "actually." In your college writing, do not use *real* as an adjective meaning "very."

reason is that, reason is because *Reason* should be used with *that* and not with *because*, which is redundant: The *reason* he left is *that* (not *because*) you insulted him.

regardless, irregardless See **irregardless, regardless**.

respectably, respectfully, respectively *Respectably* means "worthy of respect"; *respectfully* means "giving honor or deference"; *respectively* means "in the order given": He skated quite *respectably* at his first Olympics. The seminar taught us to treat others *respectfully*. The first- and second-place winners were Tai and Kim, *respectively*.

rise, raise See **raise, rise**.

set, sit *Set* means "to put down" or "to lay." Its principal forms are *set* and *setting*: After rocking the baby to sleep, he *set* her down carefully in her crib. After *setting* her down, he took a nap.

Sit means "to assume a sitting position." Its principal forms are *sit*, *sat*, and *sitting*: Many children *sit* in front of the television five to six hours a day. The dog *sat* by the fire. We were *sitting* in the airport when the flight was canceled.

shall, will *Will* has all but replaced *shall* to express all future action.

should of See **could of, should of, would of**.

since Do not use *since* for *because* if there is any chance of confusion. In the sentence "*Since* President Nixon traveled to China, trade between China and the United States has increased," *since* could mean either "from the time that" or "because." To be clear, use *because*.

sit, set See **set, sit**.

so Avoid using *so* as a vague intensifier meaning "very" or "extremely." Follow *so* with *that* and a clause that describes the result: She was *so* pleased with their work *that* she took them out to lunch.

sometime, sometimes, some time *Sometime* means "at some time in the future"; *sometimes* means "now and then"; *some time* means "a period of time": The president will address Congress *sometime* next week. All automobiles, no matter how reliable, *sometimes* need repairs. It has been *some time* since I read that book.

Glossary of Usage 741

sort of, kind of See **kind of, sort of.**

stationary, stationery *Stationary* means "staying in one place"; *stationery* means "materials for writing" or "letter paper": The communications satellite appears to be *stationary* in the sky. The secretaries supply departmental offices with *stationery*.

supposed to, used to *Supposed to* and *used to* are often misspelled. Both verbs require the final *d* to indicate past tense.

take, bring See **bring, take.**

than, then *Than* is a conjunction used to indicate a comparison; *then* is an adverb indicating time: The new shopping center is bigger *than* the old one. He did his research; *then*, he wrote a report.

that, which, who Use *that* or *which* when referring to a thing; use *who* when referring to a person: It was a speech *that* inspired many. The movie, *which* was a huge success, failed to impress her. Anyone *who* (not *that*) takes the course will benefit.

their, there, they're *Their* is a possessive pronoun; *there* indicates place and is also used in the expressions *there is* and *there are*; *they're* is a contraction of *they are:* Watson and Crick did *their* DNA work at Cambridge University. I love Los Angeles, but I wouldn't want to live *there*. *There* is nothing we can do to resurrect an extinct species. When *they're* well treated, rabbits make excellent pets.

themselves, theirselves, theirself *Theirselves* and *theirself* are nonstandard variants of *themselves*.

then, than See **than, then.**

till, until, 'til *Till* and *until* have the same meaning, and both are acceptable. *Until* is preferred in college writing. *'Til*, a contraction of *until*, should be avoided.

to, at See **at, to.**

to, too, two *To* is a preposition that indicates direction; *too* is an adverb that means "also" or "more than is needed"; *two* expresses the number 2: Last year we flew from New York *to* California. "Tippecanoe and Tyler, *too*" was William Henry Harrison's campaign slogan. The plot was *too* complicated for the average reader. Just north of *Two* Rivers, Wisconsin, is a petrified forest.

try to, try and *Try and* is the colloquial equivalent of the more formal *try to:* He decided to *try to* (not *try and*) do better. In college writing, use *try to*.

-type Deleting this empty suffix eliminates clutter and clarifies meaning: Found in the wreckage was an *incendiary* (not *incendiary-type*) device.

uninterested, disinterested See **disinterested, uninterested.**

unique Because *unique* means "the only one"—not "remarkable" or "unusual"—never use constructions like *the most unique* or *very unique*.

until See **till, until, 'til.**

used to See **supposed to, used to.**

utilize In most cases, replace *utilize* with *use* (*utilize* often sounds pretentious).

wait for, wait on To *wait for* means "to defer action until something occurs." To *wait on* means "to act as a waiter": I am *waiting for* (not *on*) dinner.

weather, whether *Weather* is a noun meaning "the state of the atmosphere"; *whether* is a conjunction used to introduce an alternative: The *weather* will improve this weekend. It is doubtful *whether* we will be able to ski tomorrow.

well, good See **good, well.**

were, we're *Were* is a verb; *we're* is the contraction of *we are:* The Trojans *were* asleep when the Greeks attacked. We must act now if *we're* going to succeed.

whether, if See **if, whether.**

which, who, that See **that, which, who.**

who, whom When a pronoun serves as the subject of its clause, use *who* or *whoever;* when it functions in a clause as an object, use *whom* or *whomever:* Sarah, *who* is studying ancient civilizations, would like to visit Greece. Sarah, *whom* I met in France, wants me to travel to Greece with her. See **47b2.**

who's, whose *Who's* means "who is" or "who has"; *whose* indicates possession: *Who's* going to take calculus? *Who's* already left for the concert? The writer *whose* book was in the window was autographing copies.

will, shall See **shall, will.**

would of See **could of, should of, would of.**

your, you're *Your* indicates possession; *you're* is the contraction of *you are*: You can improve *your* stamina by jogging two miles a day. *You're* certain to be the winner.

Glossary of Grammatical and Rhetorical Terms

absolute phrase See **phrase**.

abstract noun See **noun**.

acronym A word formed from the first letters or initial sounds of a group of words: <u>NATO</u> = <u>N</u>orth <u>At</u>lantic <u>T</u>reaty <u>O</u>rganization.

active voice See **voice**.

adjective A word that describes, limits, qualifies, or in any other way modifies a noun or pronoun. A **descriptive adjective** names a quality of the noun or pronoun it modifies: <u>junior</u> year. A **proper adjective** is formed from a proper noun: <u>Hegelian</u> philosophy. **46d, 50b**

adjective clause See **clause**.

adverb A word that describes the action of verbs or modifies adjectives, other adverbs, or complete phrases, clauses, or sentences. Adverbs answer the questions "How?" "Why?" "Where?" "When?" and "To what extent?" Adverbs are formed from adjectives, many by adding *ly* to the adjective form (*dark/darkly, solemn/solemnly*), and may also be derived from prepositions (*Joe carried <u>on</u>*.). Other adverbs that indicate time, place, condition, cause, or degree are not derived from other parts of speech: *then, never, very,* and *often*, for example. The words *how, why, where,* and *when* are classified as **interrogative adverbs** when they ask questions (<u>How</u> *did we get into this mess?*). See also **conjunctive adverb. 46e, 50c**

adverb clause See **clause**.

adverbial conjunction See **conjunctive adverb**.

agreement The correspondence among words in number, person, and gender. Subjects and verbs must agree in number (singular or plural) and person (first, second, or third): <u>Soccer</u> <u>is</u> *a popular European sport;* <u>I</u> <u>play</u> *soccer too.* **49a** Pronouns and their antecedents must agree in number, person, and gender (masculine, feminine, neuter): <u>Lucy</u> *loaned Charlie* <u>her</u> *car.* **49b**

allusion A reference to a well-known historical, literary, or biblical person or event that readers are expected to recognize.

analogy   A kind of comparison in which the writer explains an unfamiliar idea or object by comparing it to a more familiar one: *Sensory pathways of the central nervous system are bundles of nerves rather like telephone cables that feed information about the outside world into the brain for processing.*

antecedent   The word or word group to which a pronoun refers: <u>Brian</u> *finally bought the car he had always wanted.* (*Brian* is the antecedent of the pronoun *he*.)

appositive   A noun or noun phrase that identifies or renames an adjacent noun or pronoun: *Columbus,* <u>the capital of Ohio</u>, *is in the central part of the state.* Appositives may be used without special introductory phrases, as in the preceding example, or they may be introduced by *such as, or, that is, for example,* or *in other words: Japanese cars,* <u>such as Hondas</u>, *now have a large share of the US automobile market.* **33c5** In a **restrictive appositive,** the appositive precedes the noun or pronoun it modifies: <u>Singing cowboy</u> *Gene Autry was once the owner of the California Angels.* **52d1**

article   The word *a, an,* or *the.* Articles signal that a noun follows and are classified as **determiners. 63b2–3**

auxiliary verb   See **verb.**

balanced sentence   A sentence neatly divided between two parallel structures. Balanced sentences are typically **compound sentences** made up of two parallel clauses (*The telephone rang, and I answered*), but the parallel clauses of a **complex sentence** can also be balanced. **36c**

base form   See **principal parts.**

cardinal number   A number that expresses quantity—*seven, thirty, one hundred.* (Contrast **ordinal number.**)

case   The form a noun or pronoun takes to indicate how it functions in a sentence. English has three cases. A pronoun takes the **subjective** (or **nominative**) **case** when it acts as the subject of a sentence or a clause: <u>I</u> *am an American.* **47a1** A pronoun takes the **objective case** when it acts as the object of a verb or of a preposition: *Fran gave* <u>me</u> *her dog.* **47a2** Both nouns and pronouns take the **possessive case** when they indicate ownership: <u>My</u> *house is brick,* <u>Brandon's</u> *T-shirt is red.* This is the only case in which nouns change form. **47a3**

clause   A group of related words that includes a subject and a predicate. An **independent (main) clause** may stand alone as a sentence (*Yellowstone is a national park in the West*), but a **dependent (subordinate) clause** must always be accompanied by an independent clause (*Yellowstone is a national park in the West* <u>that is known for its geysers</u>). Dependent clauses are classified according to their function in a sentence. An **adjective clause** (sometimes called a **relative clause**) modifies a noun or pronoun: *The ficus,* <u>which grew to be twelve feet tall</u>, *finally died* (the clause modifies *ficus*). An **adverb clause** modifies a single word (verb, adjective, or adverb) or an entire phrase or clause: *The film was exposed <u>when Bill opened the camera</u>* (the clause modifies *exposed*). A **noun clause** acts as a noun (as subject, direct object, indirect object, or complement) in a sentence: <u>*Whoever arrives first*</u> *wins the prize* (the clause is the subject of the sentence). An **elliptical clause** is grammatically incomplete—that is, part or all of the subject or predicate is missing. If the missing part can be inferred from the context of the sentence, such a construction is acceptable: <u>*When*</u> *(they are)* <u>*pressed*</u>, *the committee members will act.* **33b2**

climactic word order The writing strategy of moving from the least important to the most important point in a sentence and ending with the key idea. **36a2**

collective noun See **noun**.

comma splice A type of run-on created when two independent clauses are incorrectly joined by just a comma. Correct comma splices by separating the independent clauses with a period, a semicolon, or a comma and a coordinating conjunction, or by using subordination. **Ch. 39**

Comma Splice: The Mississippi River flows south, the Nile River flows north.

Revised: The Mississippi River flows south. The Nile River flows north.

Revised: The Mississippi River flows south; the Nile River flows north.

Revised: The Mississippi River flows south, and the Nile River flows north.

Revised: Although the Mississippi River flows south, the Nile River flows north.

common noun See **noun**.

comparative degree See **degree**.

complement A word or word group that describes or renames a subject, an object, or a verb. A **subject complement** is a word or phrase that follows a linking verb and renames the subject. It can be an adjective (called a **predicate adjective**) or a noun (called a **predicate nominative**): *Clark Gable was a <u>movie star</u>.* An **object complement** is a word or phrase that describes or renames a direct object. Object complements can be either adjectives or nouns: *We call the treehouse our <u>hideout</u>.*

complete predicate See **predicate**.

complete subject See **subject**.

complex sentence See **sentence**.

compound Two or more words that function as a unit, such as **compound nouns:** *attorney-at-law, boardwalk;* **compound adjectives:**

hardhitting editorial; **compound prepositions:** *by way of, in addition to;* **compound subjects:** *April and May are spring months.;* and **compound predicates:** *Many try and fail to climb Mount Everest.*

compound adjective   See **compound.**

compound noun   See **compound.**

compound predicate   See **compound.**

compound preposition   See **compound.**

compound sentence   See **sentence.**

compound subject   See **compound.**

compound-complex sentence   See **sentence.**

conjunction   A word or words used to connect single words, phrases, clauses, and sentences. **Coordinating conjunctions** (*and, or, but, nor, for, so, yet*) connect words, phrases, or clauses of equal weight: *crime and* punishment (coordinating conjunction *and* connects two words). **Correlative conjunctions** (*both . . . and, either . . . or, neither . . . nor,* and so on), always used in pairs, also link items of equal weight: *Neither Texas nor Florida crosses the Tropic of Cancer.* **Subordinating conjunctions** (*since, because, although, if, after,* and so on) introduce adverb clauses: *You will have to pay for the tickets now because I will not be here later.* **46g**

conjunctive adverb   An adverb that joins and relates independent clauses in a sentence (*also, anyway, besides, hence, however, nevertheless, still,* and so on): *Howard tried out for the Yankees; however, he didn't make the team.* **46e**

connotation   The emotional associations that surround a word. (Contrast **denotation.**) **43b1**

contraction   The combination of two words with an apostrophe replacing the missing letters: *We + will = we'll; was + not = wasn't.*

coordinate adjective   One of a series of adjectives that modify the same word or word group: *The park was quiet, shady, and cool.* **52b2**

coordinating conjunction   See **conjunction.**

coordination   The pairing of similar elements (words, phrases, or clauses) to give equal weight to each. Coordination is used in simple sentences to link similar elements into compound subjects, predicates, complements, or modifiers. It can also link two independent clauses to form a compound sentence: *The sky was cloudy, and it looked like rain.* (Contrast **subordination.**)

correlative conjunction   See **conjunction.**

count noun   See **noun.**

cumulative sentence   A sentence that begins with a main clause followed by additional words, phrases, or clauses that expand or develop it: *On the hill stood a schoolhouse, paint peeling, windows boarded, playground overgrown with weeds.* **36b1**

dangling modifier A word or phrase that cannot logically modify any word in the sentence. To correct dangling modifiers, either create a new subject that the dangling modifier can logically modify, or change the dangling modifier into a dependent clause.

Thinking about their destination, *they continued the trip.* ~~the trip continued.~~ **40b**

deductive argument An argument that begins with a general statement or proposition and establishes a chain of reasoning that leads to a conclusion. **9b**

degree Most adjectives and adverbs change form to indicate degree. The **positive degree** describes a quality without indicating a comparison (*Frank is tall*). The **comparative degree** indicates a comparison between two persons or things (*Frank is taller than John*). The **superlative degree** indicates a comparison between one person or thing and two or more others (*Frank is the tallest boy in his scout troop*). **50d**

demonstrative pronoun See **pronoun**; see also **determiner**.

denotation The dictionary meaning of a word. (Contrast **connotation**.) **43b1**

dependent clause See **clause**.

descriptive adjective See **adjective**.

determiner Determiners are words that function as adjectives to limit or qualify nouns. Determiners include **articles** (*a, an, the*): *the book, a peanut;* **possessive nouns** (*Janet's*): *Janet's dog;* **possessive pronouns** (*my, your, his,* and so on): *their apartment, my house;* **demonstrative pronouns** (*this, these, that, those*): *that table, these chairs;* **interrogative pronouns** (*what, which, whose,* and so on): *Which car is yours?;* **indefinite pronouns** (*another, each, both, many,* and so on): *any minute, some day;* **relative pronouns** (*what, whatever, which, whichever, whose, whosoever*): *Bed rest was what the doctor ordered;* and **ordinal** and **cardinal numbers** (*one, two, first, second,* and so on): *Claire saw two robins.* **46d2; 50a; 63b2–3**

direct object See **object**.

direct quotation See **quotation**.

documentation The formal acknowledgment of the sources used in a piece of writing. **Pt. 3**

documentation style A format for providing information about the sources used in a piece of writing. Documentation formats vary from discipline to discipline. **Pts. 4–5**

double negative A nonstandard combination of two negative words:

Double Negative: She didn't have no time.

Revised: She had no time *or* She didn't have any time. **63a4**

ellipsis   Three spaced periods used to indicate the omission of a word or words from a quotation: *"The time has come . . . and we must part."* **56f**

elliptical clause   See **clause.**

embedding   A strategy for varying sentence structure that involves changing some sentences into modifying phrases and working them into other sentences. **35b3**

enthymeme   A syllogism in which one of the premises—usually the major premise—is implied rather than stated. **9b3**

faulty parallelism   See **parallelism.**

figurative language   Language that departs from the literal meaning or order of words to create striking effects or new meanings. Types of figurative language (called **figures of speech**) include **simile, metaphor,** and **personification. 43c**

figure of speech   See **figurative language.**

finite verb   A verb that can serve as the main verb of a sentence. Unlike **participles, gerunds,** and **infinitives** (see also **verbal**), finite verbs do not require an auxiliary in order to function as the main verb: *The rooster crowed.*

fragment   See **sentence fragment.**

function word   An article, a preposition, a conjunction, or an auxiliary verb that indicates the function of and the grammatical relationships among the nouns, verbs, and modifiers in a sentence.

fused sentence   A type of **run-on** created when two independent clauses are joined without punctuation. Correct fused sentences by separating the independent clauses with a period, a semicolon, or a comma and a coordinating conjunction, or by using **subordination. Ch. 39**

Fused Sentence: Protein is needed for good nutrition lipids and carbohydrates are too.

Revised: Protein is needed for good nutrition. Lipids and carbohydrates are too.

Revised: Protein is needed for good nutrition; lipids and carbohydrates are too.

Revised: Protein is needed for good nutrition, but lipids and carbohydrates are too.

Revised: Although protein is needed for good nutrition, lipids and carbohydrates are too.

gender   The classification of nouns and pronouns as masculine (*father, boy, he*), feminine (*mother, girl, she*), or neuter (*radio, kitten, them*).

gerund   A special verb form ending in *-ing* that is always used as a noun: *Fishing is relaxing* (gerund *fishing* serves as subject; gerund *relaxing* serves as subject complement). **NOTE:** When the *-ing* form of a verb is used as a modifier, it is considered a **present participle**. See also **verbal**.

gerund phrase   See **phrase**.

helping verb   See **verb**.

idiom   An expression that is characteristic of a particular language and whose meaning cannot be predicted from the meaning of its individual words: *lend a hand*.

imperative mood   See **mood**.

indefinite pronoun   See **pronoun**; see also **determiner**.

independent clause   See **clause**.

indicative mood   See **mood**.

indirect object   See **object**.

indirect question   A question that tells what has been asked but, because it does not report the speaker's exact words, does not take quotation marks or end with a question mark: *He asked whether he could use the family car.*

indirect quotation   See **quotation**.

inductive argument   An argument that begins with observations or experiences and moves toward a conclusion. **9a**

infinitive   The base form of the verb preceded by *to*. An infinitive can serve as an adjective (*He is the man to watch*), an adverb (*Chris hoped to break the record*), or a noun (*To err is human*). See also **verbal**.

infinitive phrase   See **phrase**.

intensifier   A word that adds emphasis but not additional meaning to words it modifies. *Much, really, too, very,* and *so* are typical intensifiers.

intensive pronoun   See **pronoun**.

interjection   A grammatically independent word, expressing emotion, that is used as an exclamation. An interjection can be set off by a comma, or, for greater emphasis, it can be punctuated as an independent unit, set off by an exclamation point: *Ouch! That hurt.* **46h**

interrogative adverb   See **adverb**.

interrogative pronoun   See **pronoun**; see also **determiner**.

intransitive verb   See **verb**.

irregular verb   A verb that does not form both its past tense and past participle by adding *-d* or *-ed* to the base form of the verb. **48a2**

isolate   Any word, including an **interjection**, that can be used in isolation: *Yes. No. Hello. Good-bye. Please. Thanks.*

linking verb   A verb that connects a subject to its complement: *The crowd became quiet.* Words that can be used as linking verbs include *seem, appear, believe, become, grow, turn, remain, prove, look, sound, smell, taste, feel,* and forms of the verb *be.*

main clause See **clause.**

main verb See **verb.**

metaphor A **figure of speech** in which the writer makes an implied comparison between two unlike items, equating them in an unexpected way: *The subway coursed through the arteries of the city.* (Contrast **simile.**) **43c**

misplaced modifier A modifier whose placement suggests that it modifies one word or word group when it is intended to modify another. **40a**

Dan smiled at his baby son, finally
‸Finally asleep in his crib.∕ ‸D̶a̶n̶ ̶s̶m̶i̶l̶e̶d̶ ̶a̶t̶ ̶h̶i̶s̶ ̶b̶a̶b̶y̶ ̶s̶o̶n̶.̶

mixed construction A sentence made up of two or more parts that do not fit together grammatically. **42b**

Mixed: The Great Chicago Fire caused terrible destruction was what prompted changes in the fire code. (independent clause used as a subject)

Revised: The terrible destruction of the Great Chicago Fire prompted changes in the fire code.

Revised: Because of the terrible destruction of the Great Chicago Fire, the fire code was changed.

mixed metaphor The combination of two or more incompatible images in a single figure of speech: *During the race, John kept a stiff upper lip as he ran like the wind.* **43d5**

modal auxiliary See **verb.**

modifier A word, phrase, or clause that acts as an adjective or an adverb, describing, limiting, or qualifying another word or word group in the sentence.

mood The verb form that indicates the writer's basic attitude. There are three moods in English. The **indicative mood** is used for statements and questions: *Nebraska <u>became</u> a state in 1867.* The **imperative mood** specifies commands or requests and is often used without a subject: (*You*) <u>Pay</u> *the rent.* The **subjunctive mood** expresses wishes or hypothetical conditions: *I wish the sun <u>were</u> shining.* **48c**

nominal A word, phrase, or clause that functions as a noun.

nominative case See **case.**

noncount noun See **noun.**

nonfinite verb See **verbal.**

nonrestrictive modifier A modifying phrase or clause that does not limit or particularize the words it modifies, but rather supplies additional information about them. Nonrestrictive modifiers are set off by commas: *Oregano, also known as marjoram or suganda, is a member of the mint family.* (Contrast **restrictive modifier.**) **52d1**

noun A word that names people, places, things, ideas, actions, or qualities. A **common noun** names any of a class of people, places, or things: *lawyer, town, bicycle.* A **proper noun,** always capitalized, refers to a particular person, place, or thing: *Mother Teresa, Chicago, Schwinn.* A **count noun** names something that can be counted: *a dozen eggs, two cats in the yard.* A **noncount noun** names a quantity that is not countable: *sand, time, work.* An **abstract noun** refers to an intangible idea or quality: *bravery, equality, hunger.* A **collective noun** designates a group of people, places, or things thought of as a unit: *Congress, police, family.* **46a**

noun clause   See **clause.**

noun phrase   See **phrase.**

number The form taken by a noun, pronoun, or verb to indicate one (**singular**): *car, he, this, boast,* or many (**plural**): *cars, they, those, boasts.* **42a4**

object A noun, pronoun, or other noun substitute that receives the action of a **transitive verb, verbal,** or **preposition.** A **direct object** indicates where the verb's action is directed and who or what is affected by it: *John caught a butterfly.* An **indirect object** tells to or for whom the verb's action was done: *John gave Nancy the butterfly.* An **object of a preposition** is a word or word group introduced by a preposition: *John gave Nancy the butterfly for an hour.*

object complement   See **complement.**

object of a preposition   See **object.**

objective case   See **case.**

ordinal number A number that indicates position in a series: *seventh, thirtieth, one-hundredth.* (Contrast **cardinal number.**)

parallelism The use of similar grammatical elements in sentences or parts of sentences: *We serve beer, wine, and soft drinks.* Words, phrases, clauses, or complete sentences may be parallel, and parallel items may be paired or presented in a series. When elements that have the same function in a sentence are not presented in the same terms, the sentence is flawed by **faulty parallelism. 36c; Ch. 41**

participial phrase   See **phrase.**

participle A verb form that generally functions in a sentence as an adjective. Virtually every verb has a **present participle,** which ends in *-ing* (*breaking, leaking, taking*), and a **past participle,** which usually ends in *-d* or *-ed* (*agreed, walked, taken*). (See also **verbal.**) *The heaving seas swamped the dinghy* (present participle *heaving* modifies noun *seas*); *Aged people deserve respect* (past participle *aged* modifies noun *people*).

parts of speech The eight basic building blocks for all English sentences: *nouns, pronouns, verbs, adjectives, adverbs, prepositions, conjunctions,* and *interjections.*

passive voice See **voice.**

past participle See **participle.**

periodic sentence A sentence that moves from a number of specific examples to a conclusion, gradually building in intensity until a climax is reached in the main clause: *Sickly and pale and looking ready to crumble, the marathoner headed into the last mile of the race.* **36b2**

person The form a pronoun or verb takes to indicate the speaker (**first person**): *I am/we are;* those spoken to (**second person**): *you are;* and those spoken about (**third person**): *he/she/it is; they are.* **42a4**

personal pronoun See **pronoun.**

personification A form of **figurative language** in which the writer describes an idea or inanimate object in human terms: *The big feather bed beckoned to my tired body.* **43c**

phrase A grammatically ordered group of related words that lacks a subject or a predicate or both and functions as a single part of speech. A **verb phrase** consists of an auxiliary (helping) verb and a main verb: *The wind was blowing hard.* A **noun phrase** includes a noun or pronoun plus all related modifiers: *She broke the track record.* A **prepositional phrase** consists of a preposition, its object, and any modifiers of that object: *The ball sailed over the fence.* A **verbal phrase** consists of a verbal and its related objects, modifiers, or complements. A verbal phrase may be a **participial phrase** (*Undaunted by the sheer cliff, the climber scaled the rock*), a **gerund phrase** (*Swinging from trees is a monkey's favorite way to travel*), or an **infinitive phrase** (*Wednesday is Bill's night to cook spaghetti*). An **absolute phrase** includes a noun and a participle, accompanied by modifiers: *His heart racing,* he dialed her number. It modifies an entire independent clause. **33b1**

plural See **number.**

positive degree See **degree.**

possessive case See **case.**

possessive noun See **determiner.**

possessive pronoun See **determiner.**

predicate A verb or verb phrase that tells or asks something about the subject of a sentence is called a **simple predicate:** *Well-tended lawns grow green and thick.* (*Grow* is the simple predicate.) A **complete predicate** includes all the words associated with the predicate: *Well-tended lawns grow green and thick.* (*Grow green and thick* is the complete predicate.)

predicate adjective See **complement.**

predicate nominative See **complement.**

prefix A letter or group of letters put before a root or a word that adds to, changes, or modifies it.

preposition A part of speech that introduces a noun or pronoun (or a phrase or clause functioning in the sentence as a noun), linking it to other words in the sentence: *Jeremy crawled under the bed.* **46f**

prepositional phrase See **phrase**.

present participle See **participle**.

principal parts The forms of a verb from which all other forms can be derived. The principal parts are the **base form** (*give*), the **present participle** (*giving*), the **past tense** (*gave*), and the **past participle** (*given*).

pronoun A word that may be used in place of a noun in a sentence. The noun for which a pronoun stands is called its **antecedent**. There are eight types of pronouns. Some have the same form but are distinguished by their function in the sentence. A **personal pronoun** stands for a person or thing: *I, me, we, us, my,* and so on (*They broke the window*). A **reflexive pronoun** ends in *-self* or *-selves* and refers to the subject of the sentence or clause: *myself, yourself, himself,* and so on (*They painted the house themselves*). An **intensive pronoun** ends in *-self* or *-selves* and emphasizes a preceding noun or pronoun (*Custer himself died in the battle*). A **relative pronoun** introduces an adjective or noun clause in a sentence: *which, who, whom,* and so on (*Sitting Bull was the Sioux chief who defeated Custer*). An **interrogative pronoun** introduces a question: *who, which, what, whom,* and so on (*Who won the lottery?*). A **demonstrative pronoun** points to a particular thing or group of things: *this, that, these, those* (*Who was that on the phone?*). A **reciprocal pronoun** denotes a mutual relationship: *each other, one another* (*We still have each other*). An **indefinite pronoun** refers to persons or things in general, not to specific individuals. Most indefinite pronouns are singular—*anyone, everyone, one, each*—but some are always plural—*both, many, several* (*Many are called, but few are chosen*). **46b**

proper adjective See **adjective**.

proper noun See **noun**.

quotation The use of the written or spoken words of others. A **direct quotation** is a passage borrowed word for word from another source. Quotation marks (" ") establish the boundaries of a direct quotation: "*Those tortillas taste like cardboard,*" *complained Beth.* **55a** An **indirect quotation** reports someone else's written or spoken words without quoting that person directly. Quotation marks are not used: *Beth complained that the tortillas tasted like cardboard.*

reciprocal pronoun See **pronoun**.

reflexive pronoun See **pronoun**.

regular verb A verb that forms both its past tense and past participle by the addition of *-d* or *-ed* to the base form of the verb. **48a1** *relative clause* See **clause.**

relative pronoun See **pronoun.**

restrictive appositive See **appositive.**

restrictive modifier A modifying phrase or clause that limits the meaning of the word or word group it modifies. Restrictive modifiers are not set off by commas: *The Ferrari that ran over the fireplug was red.* (Contrast **nonrestrictive modifier.**) **52d1**

root A word from which other words are formed. An understanding of a root word increases a reader's ability to understand unfamiliar words that incorporate the root.

run-on An incorrect construction that results when the proper connective or punctuation does not appear between independent clauses. A run-on occurs either as a **comma splice** or as a **fused sentence. Ch. 39**

sentence An independent grammatical unit that contains a *subject* and a *predicate* and expresses a complete thought: *Carolyn sold her car.* A **simple sentence** consists of one subject and one predicate: *The season ended.* **33a;** a **compound sentence** is formed when two or more simple sentences are connected with coordinating conjunctions, conjunctive adverbs, semicolons, or colons: *The rain stopped, and the sun began to shine.* **34a;** a **complex sentence** consists of one simple sentence, which functions as an independent clause in the complex sentence, and at least one dependent clause, which is introduced by a subordinating conjunction or a relative pronoun: *When he had sold three boxes* [dependent clause], *he was halfway to his goal.* [independent clause] **34b;** and a **compound-complex sentence** consists of two or more independent clauses and at least one dependent clause: *After he prepared a shopping list* [dependent clause], *he went to the store* [independent clause], *but it was closed.* [independent clause] **34b**

sentence fragment An incomplete sentence; a phrase or clause that is punctuated as if it were a complete sentence. **Ch. 38**

shift A change of *tense, voice, mood, person, number,* or *type of discourse* within or between sentences. Some shifts are necessary, but problems occur with unnecessary or illogical shifts. **42a**

simile A **figure of speech** in which the writer makes a comparison, introduced by *like* or *as,* between two unlike items on the basis of a shared quality: *Like sands through the hourglass, so are the days of our lives. The wind was as savage as his neighbor's Doberman.* (Contrast **metaphor.**) **43c**

simple predicate See **predicate.**

simple sentence See **sentence.**

simple subject See **subject.**

singular See **number.**

split infinitive An infinitive whose parts are separated by a modifier. She expected ~~to~~ one day soon ^to^ swim the channel. **40b**

squinting modifier A modifier that seems to modify either a word before it or one after it and that conveys a different meaning in each case. **40a1**

subject A noun or noun substitute that tells who or what a sentence is about is called a **simple subject:** *Healthy thoroughbred <u>horses</u> run like the wind.* (*Horses* is the simple subject.) The **complete subject** of a sentence includes all the words associated with the subject: *<u>Healthy thoroughbred horses</u> run like the wind.* (*Healthy thoroughbred horses* is the complete subject.) **33a**

subject complement See **complement.**

subjective case See **case.**

subjunctive mood See **mood.**

subordinate clause See **clause.**

subordinating conjunction See **conjunction.**

subordination Making one or more clauses of a sentence grammatically dependent upon another element in a sentence: *Preston was only eighteen when he joined the firm.* (Contrast **coordination.**) **34b**

suffix A syllable added at the end of a word or root that changes its part of speech.

superlative degree See **degree.**

suspended hyphen A hyphen followed by a space or by the appropriate punctuation and a space: *The wagon was pulled by a two-, four-, or six-horse team.*

syllogism A three-part set of statements or propositions, devised by Aristotle, that contains a major premise, a minor premise, and a conclusion. **9b2**

tag question A question, consisting of an auxiliary verb plus a pronoun, that is added to a statement and set off by a comma: *You know it's going to rain, <u>don't you</u>?*

tense The form of a verb that indicates when an action occurred or when a condition existed. **48b**

transitive verb See **verb.**

verb A word or phrase that expresses action (*He <u>painted</u> the fence*) or a state of being (*Henry <u>believes</u> in equality*). A **main verb** carries most of the meaning in the sentence or clause in which it appears: *Winston Churchill <u>smoked</u> long, thick cigars.* A main verb is a **linking verb** when it is followed by a **subject complement:** *Dogs <u>are</u> good pets.* An **auxiliary verb** (sometimes called a **helping verb**) combines with the main verb to form a **verb phrase:** *Graduation day <u>has arrived</u>.* The auxiliaries *be* and *have* are used to indicate the tense and voice of the main verb. The auxiliary *do* is used for asking questions and forming negative statements. Other auxiliary verbs, known as **modal auxiliaries** (*must, will, can, could, may, might, ought* [*to*], *should,* and *would*), indicate necessity, possibility, willingness, obligation, and ability: *It might rain next Tuesday.* A **transitive verb** requires an **object** to complete its meaning in the sentence: *Pete drank all the wine* (*wine* is the direct object). An **intransitive verb** has no direct object: *The candle flame glowed.* **46c1; Ch. 48**

verb phrase See **phrase.**

verbal **(nonfinite verb)** Verb forms—**participles, infinitives,** and **gerunds**—that are used as nouns, adjectives, or adverbs. Verbals do not behave like verbs. Only when used with an auxiliary can such a verb form serve as the main verb of a sentence. *The wall painted* is not a sentence; *The wall was painted* is. **46c2**

verbal phrase See **phrase.**

voice The form that determines whether the subject of a verb is acting or is acted upon. When the subject of a verb performs the action, the verb is in the **active voice:** *Tiger Woods sank a thirty-foot putt.* When the subject of a verb receives the action—that is, is acted upon—the verb is in the **passive voice:** *A thirty-foot putt was sunk by Tiger Woods.* **36e; 42a2; 48d, 63a6**

Credits

This page constitutes an extension of the copyright page. We have made every effort to trace the ownership of all copyrighted material and to secure permission from copyright holders. In the event of any question arising as to the use of any material, we will be pleased to make the necessary corrections in future printings. Thanks are due to the following authors, publishers, and agents for permission to use the material indicated.

Text and Illustrations

p. 3: "Aria: Memoir of a Bilingual Childhood" by Richard Rodriguez. Copyright © 1980 by Richard Rodriguez. Originally appeared in *The American Scholar*. Reprinted by permission of Georges Borchardt, Inc. for the author.

p. 4: Review by Charles Peterson of *The King of Torts* by John Grisham. Reprinted by permission of the author.

p. 7: "What Makes a Credit Score Rise or Fall?" by Jennifer Bayot from *The New York Times*, June 29, 2003. Copyright © 2003 The New York Times Co. Reprinted by permission.

pp. 17–19: "The Case Against Joe Nocera: How People Like Me Helped Ruin the Public Schools" by Joseph Nocera reprinted with permission from *The Washington Monthly*, September/October 1989. Copyright by Washington Monthly Publishing, LLC, 1319 F St. NW, Suite 710, Washington, DC 20004. (202) 393-5155. Web site: http://www.washingtonmonthly.com.

pp. 19–21: "Undecided—and Proud of It" by Michael Finkel. Originally published in *The New York Times*. Reprinted with permission of the Stuart Krichevsky Literary Agency, Inc.

p. 23: Reprinted by permission of Jen Sorensen.

p. 25: Figure 3.2. Reprinted by permission of New Balance.

p. 33: From *Born on the Fourth of July* by Ron Kovic. Copyright © 1976. Reprinted by permission of The McGraw-Hill Companies.

p. 79: "Aria: Memoir of a Bilingual Childhood" by Richard Rodriguez. Copyright ©1980 by Richard Rodriguez. Originally appeared in *The American Scholar*. Reprinted by permission of Georges Borchardt, Inc. for the author.

pp. 111–112: "Questioning the Motives of Home-Schooling Parents" by Froma Harrop as appeared in *The Seattle Times*, June 28, 2001. Reprinted by permission of The Providence Journal Company.

pp. 118–119: "English Comes First" by Richard D. Lamm from *The New York Times*, July 1, 1986. Copyright © 1986 by Richard D. Lamm. Reprinted by permission of The New York Times.

pp. 123–124: Excerpt from article, "The World of Hunting," by William R. Quimby. From *Safari Magazine*, July/August 1992. Copyright © 1992 by William R. Quimby. Reprinted courtesy of Safari Club International.

p. 143: Figure 11.3. Reprinted by permission of Dick Adair.

p. 144: Figure 11.4. © North America Syndicate.

p. 148: Figure 11.10. Salary chart from the CPIT Maths2Go, New Zealand, www.cpit.ac.nz/maths2go. Reprinted by permission.

p. 148: Figure 11.11. Salary chart from the CPIT Maths2Go, New Zealand, www.cpit.ac.nz/maths2go. Reprinted by permission.

p. 151: "Do More Guns Mean Less Crime?" A REASON ONLINE Debate. Reprinted by permission of Reason.

p. 214: "Freedom of Hate Speech?" by Phil Sudo from *Scholastic Update*, 1992. Copyright © 1992 by Scholastic Inc. Reprinted by permission of Scholastic Inc.

p. 225: "The Red Wheelbarrow" by William Carlos Williams from *Collected Poems: 1909–1939*, Volume I, copyright 1938 by New Directions Publishing Corp. Reprinted by permission of New Directions Publishing Corp. and Carcanet Press Limited.

p. 242: "A Song in the Front Yard" by Gwendolyn Brooks. Reprinted by consent of Brooks Permissions.

p. 252: Figure 18.3. From "The Reception of Reader Response Theory" by Patricia Harkin from *CCC* 56:3, February 2005, p. 410. Copyright © 2005 by the National Council of Teachers of English. Reprinted with permission.

p. 338: Graph from http://www.cru.uea.uk/cru/data/temperature. Reprinted by permission of Climatic Research Unit, School of Environmental Sciences, University of East Anglia.

pp. 355–356: "The True-Blue American" by Delmore Schwartz, from *Selected Poems: Summer Knowledge*, copyright © 1959 by Delmore Schwartz. Reprinted by permission of New Directions Publishing Corp. and Pollinger Limited.

p. 449: Figure 30.3. Reprinted by permission of 90.9 WBUR-FM, Boston's NPR News Station.

p. 571: Figure 44.1. Copyright © 2006 by Houghton Mifflin Company. Reproduced by permission from *The American Heritage Dictionary of the English Language*, Fourth Edition.

Photos

Part and Chapter opener graphic: Robert Stahl/Getty Images

p. 8 top: Figure 1.1. Bill Aron/PhotoEdit

p. 8 center: Figure 1.2. EPA/Andrew Booher/FEMA/Corbis

p. 8 bottom: Figure 1.3. The Advertising Archive

p. 22 left: © MAPS.com/Corbis

p. 22 right: © Jeff Greenberg/Getty Images

p. 23 center left: Private Collection © Christie's Image/Bridgeman Art Library

p. 23 center right: Courtesy of Mercedes-Benz USA, LLC

p. 23 bottom right: © Don Bishop/Getty Images

p. 24: Figure 3.1. Photo by Bryan Grigsby

p. 28: Figure 3.4. Michael Newman/PhotoEdit

p. 34: Figure 4.1. Rolf Bruderer/Corbis

p. 76: © 2003 Heinle Division of Thomson Learning

p. 91 top: Figure 7.1. Philip Gould/Corbis

p. 91 bottom: Figure 7.2. Buddy Mays/Corbis

p. 92: Figure 7.3. Art Montes de Oca/Taxi/Getty Images

p. 93: Figure 7.4. Bettmann/Corbis

p. 94 top: Figure 7.5. Richard T. Nowitz/Corbis

p. 94 bottom: Figure 7.6. Bettmann/Corbis

p. 95 top left and right: Figure 7.7. Corbis

p. 95 bottom: Figure 7.8. © Images.com/Corbis

p. 96 top: Figure 7.9. Anthony Bannister/Gallo Images/Corbis

p. 96 bottom: Figure 7.10. Jim Zuckerman/Corbis

p. 97 top: Figure 7.11. Peabody Museum, Harvard University 97-39-70/72853 T13

p. 97 bottom: Figure 7.12. Alan Schein Photography/Corbis

p. 99 top left: Figure 7.13. Steve Prezant/Corbis

p. 99 top right: Figure 7.14. Leonard de Selva/Corbis

p. 99 bottom left: Figure 7.15. Gideon Mendel/Corbis

p. 99 bottom right: Figure 7.16. Bettmann/Corbis

p. 142: Figure 11.1. U.S. Department of Transportation

p. 145: Figure 11.5. © Chris Hamilton/Aurora Photos

p. 146 left: Figure 11.6. Joe Rosenthal/Corbis

p. 146 right: Figure 11.7. Bettmann/Corbis

p. 147 top: Figure 11.8. Stephanie Maze/Corbis

p. 147 bottom: Figure 11.9. Stephanie Maze/Corbis

p. 158: Figure 13.1. Courtesy, Google.com

p. 159: Figure 13.2. Screen shot from InfoTrac® by Gale Group. Reprinted by permission of The Gale Group.

p. 176: Figure 13.3. Courtesy, Google.com

p. 182: Figure 14.1. Courtesy Sims Memorial Library/Southeastern Louisiana University

p. 184: Figure 14.2. Courtesy Sims Memorial Library/Southeastern Louisiana University

p. 186: Figure 14.3. Courtesy Sims Memorial Library/Southeastern Louisiana University

p. 187: Figure 14.4. "The Supply Side of the Digital Divide: Is There Equal Availability in the Broadband Internet Access Market?" by James E. Prieger from *Economy Inquiry*, April 2003, Vol. 41, No. 2, p. 346. Reprinted by permission of Oxford University Press.

p. 188: Figure 14.5. Copyright 2007 LexisNexis, a division of Reed Elsevier Inc. All Rights Reserved. LexisNexis and the Knowledge Burst logo are registered trademarks of Reed Elsevier Properties Inc. and are used with permission of LexisNexis.

p. 200: Figure 15.2. © 2005 Netscape Communications Corporation. Screen shot used with permission.

p. 202: Figure 15.3. Reproduced with permission of Yahoo! Inc. © 2006. Yahoo! and the Yahoo! logo are trademarks of Yahoo!, Inc.

p. 203: Figure 15.4. Courtesy, Google.com

p. 211: Figure 15.5. Screen shot copyright © 2003, The Washington Post, reprinted with permission.

p. 212: Figure 15.6. Used with the permission of the American Cancer Society, Inc. All rights reserved.

p. 212: Figure 15.7. Screen shot courtesy of CancerSource/MediMedia Oncology

p. 451: Figure 30.6. Reprinted with permission of Lyric Opera of Waco, Education Department

p. 460: Figure 31.3. Screen shot reprinted with permission from National Family, Career & Community Leaders of America, Inc.

p. 531: Figure 38.1. Courtesy, Orange Glo International

Index

Note: Page numbers in blue indicate definitions.

A

A, an, use as artices, 733
A lot, 733
A lot of, lot, lots of, 738
A number, the number, 617
Abbreviation(s), 695–98. *See also* Acronym(s)
   of academic degrees, capitalizing, 682
   in addresses, 630, 631, 697
   in APA-style reference list, 289, 290, 293
   business names, 696, 697
   capitalizing, 682, 683
   dates, 660, 696
   defined, 695
   editing misused, 697–98
   measurements before, 702
   in MLA-style paper, 240, 243, 246, 251, 270, 631, 696, 698
   organization names, 695–96, 697
   with periods, 630–31
   technical terms, 695–96
   temperatures, 696
   times of day, 696
   titles of people, 695
   without periods, 558, 631, 683, 695–96, 697
-able, -ible endings, 580
Abridged dictionary(ies), 574
Absolute phrase(s)
   commas with, 642
   defined, 477, 642, 752
Abstract(s)
   APA reference list, 294
   APA-style paper, 299
   CSE-style paper, 335
   defined, 15, 395
   in the humanities, 350
   in the natural and applied sciences, 395–96
   in online databases, 186
Abstract noun(s), 584, 751
Abstract word(s)
   concrete words versus, 561
   defined, 561
Academic course(s)
   abbreviating, 695, 697
   capitalizing names of, 684
   in Chicago manuscript style, 324
   home page, MLA works-cited list, 258
   in MLA works-cited list, 258
Academic degrees
   capitalizing, 682
   commas with, 643
Academic success, 401–14
   active learning, 407–09
   checklist, 414
   college services, 409–10
   contacts, 412–13

Academic success (*continued*)
  library resources, 410–11
  lifelong learning, 413
  school and course requirements, 405–07
  study as priority, 404–05
  technological competence, 411–12
  time management, 402–04
Accept, except, 576, 733
Accuracy
  defined, 108, 209
  of evidence, 108
  of Web site content, 209
Acronym(s)
  defined, 558, 631, 696, 743
  in email, 558, 695
  in instant messaging, 558, 695
  using, 631
Action verb(s)
  recognizing, 586
  in résumés, 433
Active learning, 407–09
  in the classroom, 407–08
  outside the classroom, 408–09
Active reading, 15, 25, 407
Active voice
  conveying emphasis through, 510–11
  defined, 610–11, 717–18, 756
  passive voice versus, 510–11
  shift from or to passive voice, 549, 611–12
AD, 696
Ad hominem (argument to the person) fallacy, 122
Ad populum (argument to the people) fallacy, 122
Addition
  compound sentences to signal, 489
  words and phrases to signal, 83

Address(es). *See also* Electronic address
  abbreviations in, 630, 631, 697
  commas in, 644
  numbers in, 701
Adjective(s)
  comparative degree, 625–27
  compound, 588, 692–93, 745–46
  coordinate, 636, 746
  defined, 588, 623, 726, 743
  descriptive, 588, 743
  double negatives, 715–16, 747
  ESL writers and, 623, 636, 726–27
  expanding simple sentences with, 479–80
  indefinite phrases as, 484
  as object complements, 624
  order of, 727
  as part of speech, 588–89, 743
  proper, 588, 684, 743
  in series, 636
  as subject complements. *See* Predicate adjective(s)
  superlative degree, 625, 626–27, 747
  understanding, 623
  using, 623–24
Adjective (relative) clause(s)
  commas with nonrestrictive, 598, 639
  in complex sentences, 534
  defined, 478, 744–45
  eliminating, 518
  interrupted, 542–43
  misplaced, revising, 540, 542–43
Adjective phrase(s), interrupted, 542–43
Adobe Acrobat Reader, 436
Adobe PageMaker, 454

Index 763

Adobe Photoshop®, 146, 389, 458
Adverb(s)
  comparative degree, 625–27
  conjunctive, 489, 590, 746
  defined, 589, 623, 624, 726, 743
  in describing action of verbs, 480
  ESL writers and, 623, 726
  expanding simple sentences with, 479–80
  indefinite phrases as, 484
  interrogative, 589, 743
  as part of speech, 589–90, 743
  superlative degree, 625, 626–27, 747
  understanding, 623
  using, 624
Adverb clause(s)
  defined, 478–79, 745
  interrupted, 542–43
  misplaced, revising, 540, 542–43
Adverb phrase(s), interrupted, 542–43
Adverbial conjunction(s). *See* Conjunctive adverb(s)
Advertisement(s)
  interpreting, 25
  MLA works-cited list, 256
  reading, 23
Advice, advise, 733
Affect, effect, 576, 733
Afterword
  APA reference list, 289
  MLA works-cited list, 248
Age stereotypes, 566
Agreement, 613–21
  defined, 613, 743
  in gender, 613
  in number, 613–18, 713, 743
  in person, 613–18, 713, 743
  pronoun-antecedent, 549, 596–98, 618, 619–21, 743

  subject-verb, 613–18, 713, 743
Aircraft, italicizing names of, 689
All ready, already, 733
All right, alright, 733
Allsearchengines.com, 205
AllTheWeb, 204
Allusion(s), 743
Allusion, illusion, 733
Almanacs, 189
Almost, as limiting modifier, 538
AltaVista, 204
Alternatives, compound sentences to signal, 489
a.m., 696
Ambiguous antecedent(s), 597
American English spelling(s), 576
American Psychological Association (APA), 284. *See also* APA documentation style
Among, between, 733
Amount, number, 723, 733
Ampersand
  in APA parenthetical references, 285
  in APA reference list, 288
  in business names, 697
An, a, use as articles, 733
Analogy(ies)
  in comparisons, 96
  defined, 96, 562, 744
  false, 121
Analysis
  defined, 353
  of literature. *See* Literary analysis
Analysis essay, 346–47
Anchors, in Web site design, 460
And
  with compound antecedents, 619

And (continued)
    compound subjects joined by, 614
    as coordinating conjunction, 488
    in series, comma with, 635
AND, as Boolean operator, 183, 187, 203
And/or, 734
Angle bracket(s), for electronic addresses, 257, 266
Annotated bibliography
    defined, 161, 385
    sample, 161–62, 344–46, 385
Annotation, of text, 16–19
    defined, 16, 26
    example of, 17–19
    visual text, 26
Anonymous/unsigned work(s)
    APA parenthetical references, 286
    APA reference list, 288, 293
    Chicago documentation style, 316–17
    CSE reference list, 334
    determining credibility of, 210
    MLA parenthetical references, 241
    MLA works-cited list, 250, 253–54
Antecedent(s)
    agreement with pronouns, 549, 596–98, 618, 619–21, 743
    ambiguous, 597
    collective noun, 620
    compound, 619–20
    defined, 584, 596, 618, 724, 744, 753
    indefinite pronoun, 615, 620
    nonexistent, 597
    relative pronoun, 618
    remote, 597

Anthology(ies)
    APA reference list, 289
    Chicago documentation style, 314
    MLA works-cited list, 249, 250
Anthropology. *See also* Social science(s)
    sample personal experience essay, 381–82
Antithesis, 126, 366–67
Antonym(s)
    defined, 572
    in dictionary entry, 572
Any way, anyway, 576
APA documentation style, 282–307
    checklists, 295–97
    content footnotes, 294
    defined, 284
    in-text citations, 282, 284–87
    manuscript guidelines, 294–97, 388
    parenthetical references, 282, 284–87
    reference list, 282–83, 287–94, 296–97, 307
    sample research paper, 297–307
Apostrophe(s), 656–61
    editing misused, 661
    in forming plurals, 660–61
    to indicate omissions, 658–60
    in possessive case, 656–57, 659, 661
Appeals, unfair, 132, 370–71
Appositive(s), 724–25
    commas with nonrestrictive, 598, 639
    creating, for concise sentences, 517
    defined, 485, 528, 595, 672, 724, 744
    expanding simple sentences with, 485

Index **765**

explanatory material, 595–96
fragments, revising, 528–29
introducing, 485
pronoun case in, 595–96, 725
restrictive, 744
Argument(s)
  deductive, 115–16, 747
  inductive, 113–14, 132, 749
  Toulmin model of, 117–18
Argument to ignorance fallacy, 122
Argument to the people *(ad populum)* fallacy, 122
Argument to the person *(ad hominem)* fallacy, 122
Argumentative essay(s), 125–48. *See also* Critical thinking; Essay(s)
  audience for, 127, 367–68
  checklists on, 139–40, 144
  defined, 106
  defining key terms in, 126–27, 367
  elements of, 132–33, 140, 366–71, 371–72
  evidence in, 129–32
  fairness in, 131–32, 370–71
  literary argument, 366–79
  logic in, 113
  organizing, 132–33, 140, 368–71
  planning, 125–28, 366–68
  refuting opposing arguments in, 128, 133, 140, 368, 372
  revising, 139–40
  sample, 134–39, 372–79
  thesis statement in, 125–26, 133, 140, 366–67, 371
  tone of, 130–31, 369–70
  topic selection for, 125–26
  visuals in, 142–48
  writing, 133–39
Argumentative thesis, 126, 133, 366–67, 371

Art. *See also* Humanities
  italicizing names of, 688
  MLA works-cited list, 256, 260
Article(s) (grammatical)
  defined, 744
  as determiners, 588, 744, 747
  ESL writers and, 721–22
  with nouns, 721–22
  order of adjectives, 727
  in titles of works, 685, 688
Article(s) (publications). *See also* Journal article(s); Magazine article(s); Newsletter article(s); Newspaper article(s)
  quotation marks with titles, 286
Artistic movements, capitalizing names of, 683
Arts and Humanities Citation Index, 350
As
  comparisons with, 594–95
  paired elements linked by, 545
As, like, 734
As . . . as . . . , in comparisons, 734
Ask.com, 204
Assertions, 129, 368–69
Assignment(s)
  analyzing, 31, 155–56
  essay, 31–32
  humanities writing assignments, 343–47
  natural and applied sciences writing assignments, 393–96
  research paper, 155–56
  social sciences writing assignments, 381–87
Association, prepositions and, 727
At, as preposition, 728

At, to, 734
Athletic groups, capitalizing names of, 683
Atlases
    CSE reference list, 334
    defined, 189
Audience
    accommodating, 127, 367–68
    for argumentative essay, 127, 367–68
    for college writer, 9–11
    defined, 9
    for essay, 9–11, 31, 127, 367–68
    for essay exam, 417
    in the humanities, 342–43
    identifying, 9–11, 31
    in the natural and applied sciences, 392
    for oral presentation, 464
    in the social sciences, 380–81
    types of, 464
    for Web site, 456
    well-developed paragraph and, 88
    writing for, 9
Audiocassette recording(s)
    APA reference list, 292
    CSE reference list, 334
Aural learners, 404
Author name(s)
    APA parenthetical references, 284–87
    APA reference list, 288–91
    Chicago bibliography, 311–21
    Chicago endnotes and footnotes, 311–21
    CSE in-text citations, 330–31
    CSE reference list, 332–34
    MLA parenthetical references, 240–44
    MLA-style paper, 267
    MLA works-cited list, 245–63
AutoCorrect tool, 266

Auxiliary (helping) verb(s)
    defined, 586, 714, 755
    to form past, present, and future verbs, 714
    in forming verb phrases, 586–87
    modal, 587, 714, 756
    in simple sentences, 474–75
Awhile, a while, 734
Awkward sentence(s), 548–54
    faulty predication in, 552–53
    illogical comparisons in, 553–54
    incomplete comparisons in, 553–54
    mixed constructions in, 551
    unwarranted shifts in, 548–50

B

Background section, argumentative essay, 371
Backing, in Toulmin logic, 117–18
Bad, badly, 734
Balanced sentence(s)
    conveying emphasis through, 509
    defined, 509, 744
Bandwagon fallacy, 122
Bartlett's Familiar Quotations, 189
Base form, 600–03, 753
BC, 696
Be
    faulty predication, 552
    in subjunctive mood, 609
Begging the question fallacy, 121
Being as, being that, 734
Beside, besides, 734
Between, among, 733
Bias
    avoiding in argumentative essays, 131–32, 370–71
    defined, 109
    detecting, 109–10

kinds of, 109–10
stereotypes and, 566–67
Bible
　abbreviating books of, 696
　capitalizing, 683
　Chicago documentation style, 314
　CSE reference list, 333
　MLA parenthetical references, 242, 249
　periods to mark divisions in, 631
Bibliographic essay, 344–46
Bibliography(ies) (documentation styles)
　APA reference list, 282–83, 287–94, 296–97, 307
　Chicago bibliography, 308–09, 311–21, 323, 328
　CSE reference list, 329, 331–35, 336, 339
　MLA works-cited list, 234–37, 244–63, 266, 278–79, 365
Bibliography(ies) (reference tools)
　general, 185
　specialized, 184
Bibliography(ies) (student)
　annotated, 161–62, 344–46, 385
　formatting, 161
　working, 159–61
Bilingual writer(s). *See* ESL (English as a Second Language) tip(s); ESL (English as a Second Language) writer(s)
Biographical essay(s), 396–97
Biographical references, general, 185
Biology. *See* Natural and applied science(s)
Blackboard™, 30
Blogs, 209

Body paragraph(s), 78–103
　coherent, 82–86
　defined, 41, 99
　of essay exam, 420
　of oral presentation, 466
　patterns of development, 44–45, 82, 90–97, 175
　of research paper, 174–75
　unified, 79–81
　well-developed, 88–90
Book(s)
　APA reference list, 288–89
　Chicago documentation style, 311–14
　CSE reference list, 332–33, 335
　in the humanities, 350
　italicizing titles of, 688
　in library research, 182–84, 189–90
　missing, locating, 190
　MLA parenthetical references, 240–43
　MLA works-cited list, 246–50, 259
　in online catalogs, 182–84, 189–90
　previewing, 15
　in working bibliography, 160
Book review(s)
　defined, 382
　in evaluating sources, 194
　MLA works-cited list, 254, 259
　in the social sciences, 382–83
　sources of, 194
Bookmark, 206–07
Boolean operators, 187, 203–04, 206
Boolean search, 183
Border(s), in document design, 443
Bracket(s)
　angle, for electronic addresses, 257, 266

Bracket(s) *(continued)*
    with ellipses, 221, 679
    to indicate substitutions within quotations, 220–21
    to replace parentheses within parentheses, 677
    to set off comments with quotations, 677
Brainstorming
    defined, 37
    for essay exams, 418–19
    in idea generation, 36–37, 38, 353
    in literary analysis, 353
Brand names
    capitalizing, 684
    generic names versus, 684
Bring, take, 734
British English
    collective nouns in, 616
    spelling in, 576
Brochure(s), desktop publishing and, 454, 455
Bullets, 447
Bullets and Numbering feature, 65
Business and economics. *See also* Social science(s); Workplace communication
    abbreviating business names, 696, 697
    capitalizing business names, 684
Business letter(s). *See also* Letter(s) (correspondence); Workplace communication
    format of, 429, 644, 673, 686
    job application letters, 428–30
    sample, 429
But, as coordinating conjunction, 488
Byline(s), APA-style paper, 388

C

Call number(s), 189
Can, may, 734
Capital, capitol, 734
Capitalization, 681–86. *See also* Proper noun(s)
    of abbreviations, 682, 683
    APA parenthetical references, 285–87
    APA reference list, 288–91
    changing, in quotations, 221
    Chicago bibliography, 311–21
    Chicago footnotes and endnotes, 311–21
    of closings, 686
    with colons, 673
    CSE in-text citations, 330–31
    CSE reference list, 331–35
    editing misused, 686
    ESL writers and, 681
    of first word of line of poetry, 681
    of first word of sentence, 681
    of *I*, 685
    of important words in titles, 685
    MLA parenthetical references, 240–43
    MLA-style paper, 265
    MLA works-cited list, 245–63
    of *O* (interjection), 685
    of proper adjectives, 588, 684, 743
    of salutations, 686
    of single letters in special constructions, 685–86, 693
    of structure names, 682
Caption(s), in APA-style paper, 296, 306
Cardinal number(s)
    defined, 744
    as determiners, 723, 747
Cartoon(s)
    MLA works-cited list, 256, 260
    in persuasive writing, 143

Index

Case, 593–96, 725. *See also specific types of case*
  defined, 593, 744
  list of cases, 744
Case study(ies)
  defined, 383
  in the social sciences, 383–84
Causal relationships
  complex sentences to signal, 492
  compound sentences to signal, 489
Cause and effect
  as pattern of development, 45, 93–94
  words and phrases to signal, 84
Cause-and-effect paragraphs
  causes in, 93
  defined, 93
  effects in, 94
CBE documentation style. *See* CSE documentation style
CD(s), APA reference list, 292
CD-ROMs
  dictionaries on, 574
  MLA works-cited list, 262–63
  subscription databases on, 185–87, 190
CE, 696
Center around, 735
Century(ies), names of, 686
-ch endings, plurals with, 580
Chalkboard(s), 470
Chapter(s)
  APA parenthetical references, 286
  Chicago documentation style, 314
  CSE reference list, 332
  quotation marks for titles, 667
Chart(s), misleading, 147–48

Chat rooms, ideas and, 30
Chemistry. *See also* Natural and applied science(s)
  style manual, 339, 397
Chicago documentation style, 308–28
  bibliography, 308–09, 311–21, 323, 328
  checklists, 321–23
  defined, 310
  endnotes and footnotes, 308–09, 322–23, 327
  in the humanities, 348
  manuscript guidelines, 321–23
Chicago Manual of Style, 310, 311, 322. *See also* Chicago documentation style
Chronological order
  defined, 82
  of paragraphs, 82, 90–91, 92
  résumé, 430, 431
  sample résumé, 431
Chunking, in Web site design, 461
Circumlocution
  avoiding, 514
  defined, 514
Citation-name format, CSE documentation style, 331
Citation-sequence format, CSE documentation style, 330–31
Cite, site, 735
Cited in, in APA-style paper, 286, 301
Civic groups, capitalizing names of, 683
Claim, in Toulmin logic, 117–18
Class stereotypes, 567
Classification
  defined, 96
  as pattern of development, 96–97

Clause(s). *See also specific types of clause*
  beginning sentences with, 500
  commas between phrases and, 655
  defined, 477, 744–45
  elliptical, 478, 542–43, 745
  identifying, 477–79
  nonrestrictive, 598, 639
  restrictive, 598, 639
  in series, 544
  types of, 744–45
Clichés, 564–65
Climactic, climatic, 735, 745
Climactic word order, 504
Clipped form(s), 557, 631
Closed-ended question(s), 197
Closing(s)
  capitalization of, 686
  punctuation of, 644
Clustering
  defined, 37
  in idea generation, 37–38
  in Web site design, 461
CMS style. *See* Chicago documentation style
Coarse, course, 735
Coherent paragraphs, 82–86
  achieving coherence between paragraphs, 85–86
  arranging details in, 82
  coherence, defined, 82
  key words and phrases in, 85
  parallel structure in, 85
  transitional words and phrases in, 82–84, 90–91, 92
Coinage, 668, 693
Coined compound(s), 693
Collaborative work
  checklist, 405
  group presentations, 465
  plagiarism avoidance, 226
  study groups, 405
Collection of work(s), MLA works-cited list, 249–50

Collective noun(s)
  as antecedents, 620
  defined, 584, 616, 751
  fixed amounts as, 616–17
  subject-verb agreement with, 616–17
College dictionaries, 570
College services, 409–10
Colloquial diction, 557
Colloquial expressions, 597–98
Colon(s), 672–74
  in biblical citations, 242, 314
  capitalization with, 673
  in compound sentences, 489
  defined, 672
  editing misused, 673–74
  for emphasis, 504
  with identifying tags for quoted passages, 664
  to introduce lists, 528, 655, 672
  to introduce quotations, 655, 673
  to introduce series, 672
  in letters, 644, 673
  with quotation marks, 668
  to set off explanations, 672–73
Color, in document design, 443, 444
Comic strip(s), MLA works-cited list, 256
Comma(s), 634–48
  in addresses, 644
  in APA parenthetical references, 287
  in closings, 644
  in compound constructions, 486, 488–89, 648
  with coordinating conjunctions, 488, 635
  in dates, 644
  editing misused, 646–48
  grammar checkers and, 654
  with identifying tags, 220, 664

in large numbers, 644, 645, 702
in letters, 644
with nonrestrictive clauses, 598, 639
with personal titles, 643
between phrases and clauses, 655
to prevent misreading, 645
to punctuate interrupted quotations, 533
with quotation marks, 220, 643, 664, 665, 668
in salutations, 644
to set off independent clauses, 534, 634, 646, 648
to set off introductory elements, 637–38
to set off items in series, 635–36, 652
to set off nonessential material, 639–42
to set off participial phrases, 719
with transitional elements, 533, 638, 641
Comma splice, 532–34, 646
acceptable use of, 534
correcting, 745
defined, 532, 745
Command(s), exclamation points for, 633
Comment(s)
brackets to set off, 677
of instructor, 9–10, 61–63, 177
in peer review, 10–11, 59–61, 178–79
Comment feature, 59, 62, 177, 398
Common ground, in establishing credibility, 130
Common knowledge, 225–26, 348

Common noun(s)
defined, 584, 751
as part of proper noun, capitalizing, 682
Common sentence problem(s), 521–54
awkward sentences, 548–54
comma splices, 532–34
comparisons, incomplete or illogical, 553–54
compound constructions standing alone, 529–30
confusing sentences, 548–54
dangling modifiers, 542–43
dependent clause fragments, 522, 524–25
faulty modification, 537–43
faulty parallelism, 546–47
faulty predication, 552–53
fused sentences, 532–34
incomplete or illogical comparisons, 553–54
misplaced modifiers, 537–40
mixed constructions, 551
phrase fragments, 524–29
run-on sentences, 532–34
sentence fragments, 522–31
shifts, unwarranted, 548–50
Comparative degree, 625–27
adjective, 625–27
adverb, 625–27
defined, 625, 747
dictionary part-of-speech labels, 571
illogical, 627
irregular, 626–27
using, 625–26
Compare Drafts feature, 58, 59
Comparison(s). *See also* Analogy(ies)
defined, 94, 553
revising incomplete or illogical, 553–54
with *than* or *as*, 594–95
words and phrases to signal, 84

Comparison and contrast, as
    pattern of development,
    45, 82, 94–96
Comparison-and-contrast
    paragraphs, 94–96
  defined, 94
  logical order in, 82
  point-by-point comparisons
    in, 94
  subject-by-subject
    comparisons in, 95–96
Complement(s), 745. *See also*
    Object complement(s);
    Subject complement(s)
Complement, compliment, 735
Complete predicate(s), 474,
    752
Complete subject, 474, 755
Complex sentence(s), 491–92
  as balanced sentences, 744
  to break up strings of
    compound sentences, 498
  as concise sentences, 517
  constructing, 491–92, 534
  defined, 491, 754
  expanding simple sentences
    into, 479–87
  relative clauses in formation
    of, 534
  subordinating conjunctions
    in formation of, 534
  using, 492
Complimentary close
  capitalization of, 686
  punctuation of, 644
Compound adjective(s)
  defined, 588, 692, 745–46
  hyphenating, 692–93, 745–46
Compound antecedents,
    619–20
Compound complement(s), as
    sentence fragments,
    529–30
Compound-complex
    sentence(s), 493, 754

Compound construction(s). *See
    also specific types*
  commas in, 486, 488–89, 648
  defined, 486
  expanding simple sentences
    with, 486–87
  objective case in, 594
Compound noun(s)
  defined, 580–81, 745
  forming, 580–81
  forming possessive case of,
    657
Compound object(s), as sentence
    fragments, 529–30
Compound predicate(s)
  defined, 746
  as sentence fragments,
    529–30
Compound preposition(s), 746
Compound sentence(s), 488–89
  as balanced sentences, 744
  breaking up strings of,
    497–98
  commas in, 488–89
  constructing, 488–89, 496,
    517, 634
  defined, 488, 754
  excessive coordination,
    eliminating, 518
  expanding simple sentences
    into, 479–87
  using, 489
Compound subject(s)
  defined, 746
  joined by *and*, 614
  joined by *or*, 614–15
  subject-verb agreement with,
    614–15
Compound word(s), 745–46
  adjectives, 692–93
  coined, 693
  defined, 691
  dividing, 691–93
  fractions, 693
  numerals, 693

Computer(s). *See also* Computer software; Computer tip(s)
  managing printouts, 168–69
  technological competence and, 411–12
Computer software. *See also* Grammar checker(s); Spell checker(s); *specific software names*
  APA reference list, 292
  in document design, 443
  italicizing titles of, 688
  outlining with, 49
  personal organizer, 402–04
  presentation, 30, 49, 412, 443, 444, 449, 467–68, 469
  in revision process, 58–59, 62
  types of, 30
  visuals and, 58, 388–89, 449–50
  Web authoring, 457–58
  in Web site design, 457–58
  writing process and, 30
Concession, words and phrases to signal, 84
Concise sentence(s), 513–19
  adjective (relative) clauses, eliminating, 518
  appositives, creating, 517
  circumlocution, avoiding, 514
  complex sentences, creating, 517
  compound sentences, creating, 517
  deadwood, eliminating, 513–14
  excessive coordination, eliminating, 518
  passive construction, eliminating, 518
  rambling, tightening, 517–19
  redundancy, deleting, 516
  repetition, eliminating unnecessary, 516–17
  utility words, eliminating, 514, 561
  wordiness, eliminating, 513–15, 518–19
Concluding paragraph(s), 102–03
  of argumentative essay, 133, 140, 372
  defined, 41
  of essay exam, 420
  importance of, 103
  of oral presentation, 466
  of research paper, 175
  strategies for effective, 102–03
  support, 133, 140
Conclusion(s)
  in argumentative essay, 372
  in deductive reasoning, 115, 116
  of essay exams, 420
  quotations in, 133
  words and phrases to signal, 84, 116
Concrete word(s)
  abstract words versus, 561
  defined, 561
Conditional relationships, complex sentences to signal, 492
Conditional statements, 610
Conferences
  with instructor, 62–64, 408, 706, 707
  online, 63–64
  writing center, 63, 409–10, 707
Confusing sentence(s), 548–54
  faulty predication in, 552–53
  illogical comparisons in, 553–54
  incomplete comparisons in, 553–54
  mixed constructions in, 551
  unwarranted shifts in, 548–50

Conjunction(s). *See also specific types of conjunction*
    defined, 591, 746
    as part of speech, 591, 746
    types of, 746
Conjunctive adverb(s)
    in compound sentences, 489
    defined, 489, 590, 746
    list of, 489, 590
    as transitional words, 590
Connotation
    defined, 559, 746
    denotation versus, 559–60
Conscious, conscience, 735
Consequently, as conjunctive adverb, 489
Contacts, 412–13
Content note(s)
    APA documentation style, 294
    MLA documentation style, 242, 264, 266, 277
    sample, 277
Context, quotation out of, 131–32, 370
Continual, continuous, 735
Continuous pagination, 253, 262, 290, 315, 333
Contraction(s)
    defined, 746
    formation of, 658–59
    list of, 658–59
    possessive form versus, 659, 661
Contradiction, commas with contradictory phrases, 642
Contradictory phrase(s)
    commas with, 642
    defined, 642
Contrast
    complex sentences to signal, 492
    compound sentences to signal, 489
    defined, 94
    words and phrases to signal, 84
Controversial statement, in introductions, 101 02
Coordinate adjective(s)
    commas with, 636
    defined, 636, 746
Coordinate elements. *See also* Coordination; *specific types*
    commas between, 635–36
    defined, 635
    parallelism of, 544
Coordinating conjunction(s)
    avoiding commas before, 648
    commas with, 488, 635
    in compound sentences, 486, 488, 634
    defined, 488, 591, 746
    grammar checkers and, 500
    list of, 534, 591
    in revising comma splices, 534
    in revising fused sentences, 534
    in revising run-on sentences, 534
    in titles of works, 685
Coordination
    to combine sentences, 496
    defined, 496, 746
    excessive, eliminating, 518
Copyright
    defined, 452
    visuals and, 452
    Web site design and, 462
Corporate author(s)
    APA parenthetical references, 286
    APA reference list, 288–89
    Chicago documentation style, 313
    MLA parenthetical references, 243
    MLA works-cited list, 247

Correlative conjunction(s)
in compound constructions, 486–87, 489, 634
defined, 591, 746
list of, 544, 591
paired items linked by, 544–45, 647
Could have, should have, would have, 606
Could of, should of, would of, 735
Council, counsel, 735
Council of Science Editors (CSE), 330, 392. *See also* CSE documentation style
Count noun(s), 584, 751
Couple, couple of, 735
Course names
abbreviating, 695, 697
capitalizing, 684
in Chicago manuscript style, 324
in MLA works-cited list, 258
Coverage
defined, 210
of Web site content, 210
Credibility
defined, 129, 209
establishing, 129–31, 330, 369–70
of Web site content, 209, 210
Criterion, criteria, 735
Critical thinking, 105–48
bias and, 109–10
checklists on, 144
deductive reasoning in, 115–18, 132
defined, 106
in essay exams, 415
fact versus opinion and, 106–07
inductive reasoning in, 113–14, 132, 749
logical fallacies in, 120–22
in reading process, 17
supporting evidence and, 108–09, 117–18, 129–31, 368–69
text annotation and, 17
Toulmin logic in, 117–18
in visuals evaluation, 143, 145–46
in writing process, 10, 29
Cross-references, parentheses with, 676
CSE documentation style, 329–39, 397
checklists, 335–36
defined, 330
in-text, 330–31
manuscript guidelines, 335–36
reference list, 329, 331–35, 336, 339
sample research paper, 337–39
Cumulative sentence(s)
conveying emphasis through, 506
defined, 506, 746–47
Currency
defined, 210
of Web site content, 210

D

-*d*, -*ed* ending, in past participles, 587
Dangling modifier(s)
creating dependent clause, 542
creating new subject, 542
defined, 542, 747
elliptical clauses, 542–43
passive voice with, 542
revising, 542–43
Dash(es), 674–75
capitalizing sentences set off within another sentence, 681
editing misused, 675
for emphasis, 504
to indicate interruptions, 675

Dash(es) *(continued)*
  with quotation marks, 669
  to set off nonessential material, 674
  to set off summaries, 675
Data, 735–36
Database(s). *See* Online database(s)
Date(s)
  abbreviating, 660, 696
  commas in, 644
  numbers in, 701
  parentheses in, 676
  questionable, marking, 632
Days of the week
  abbreviating, 697
  capitalizing names of, 682
Deadwood
  defined, 513
  eliminating, 513–14
Debatable topic, 125–26, 366
Decimal(s), numbers in, 702
Declarative sentence(s), 498–99
Deductive argument(s)
  deductive reasoning in, 115–18, 132
  defined, 747
  syllogism in, 115, 116, 117
Definite article(s), 721
Definition(s)
  in introductions, 101
  italics or underlining in, 670, 689
  of key terms in argumentative essay, 126–27, 367
  MLA works-cited list, 250
  as pattern of development, 45, 97, 101
  quotation marks with, 690
Definition paragraphs, defined, 97
Degree
  comparative, 571, 625–27, 747
  defined, 747
  positive, 747
  superlative, 571, 625–27, 747
Demonstrative article(s), 727
Demonstrative pronoun(s)
  defined, 585, 753
  as determiners, 589, 723, 747
  list of, 585, 589
Denotation
  connotation versus, 559–60
  defined, 559, 747
Dependent (subordinate) clause(s)
  avoiding commas before, 648
  commas with introductory, 637, 654
  in complex sentences, 491
  in compound-complex sentences, 493
  creating, to correct dangling modifier, 542
  defined, 477–78, 524, 744
  at end of sentence, commas with, 648
  misplaced, revising, 540
  as modifiers, 540
  semicolons to set off, 654
  as sentence fragments, 522, 524–25
  between subject and predicate, 507
  verbs in, 607
Description, as pattern of development, 44, 82, 91–92
Descriptive adjective(s), 588, 743
Descriptive paragraphs, 91–92
  defined, 91
  spatial order in, 82
Design. *See* Document design; Web site design
Desk dictionaries, 570
Desktop publishing, 453–55
Determiner(s)
  defined, 588, 723, 747

list of, 588–89, 723
using with nouns, 723
Diagram(s)
  reading, 23
  as visual aids, 450, 451
Dialogue. *See also* Quotation(s); Quotation mark(s)
  defined, 663
  exclamation points in, 633
  interruptions in, 643, 675
Diction, 556–58
  choosing appropriate level, 556–58
  for college writing, 558
  defined, 556
  formal, 556, 564
  informal, 557–58, 624, 660
  pretentious, 564
Dictionary(ies), 570–74
  abridged, 574
  college, 570
  connotation and denotation in, 560
  definitions in MLA works-cited list, 250
  desk, 570
  electronic, 574, 710, 711
  entry components, 570–73
  ESL writers and, 710, 711, 715, 723, 730
  sample entries, 571, 710, 711
  specialized, 184, 189, 574
  unabridged, 189, 574
Different from, different than, 736
Direct address, commas with names in, 642
Direct discourse
  defined, 549
  shift to indirect discourse, 549–50
Direct object(s)
  defined, 475, 751
  objective case with, 594, 744
Direct question(s), question marks with, 632

Direct quotation(s). *See also* Quotation(s); Quotation mark(s)
  colons to introduce, 655, 673
  commas with, 643
  defined, 753
  ellipses in, 679
  introductory tags with, 643
  quotation marks with, 663–65
  when to use, 217–18, 229, 663–65
Direction
  prepositions and, 727
  thesis statement in setting, 42–43
Discipline(s), 341–400. *See also* Humanities; Natural and applied science(s); Social science(s); *specific discipline names*
  abbreviations and, 695
  essay exams and, 417
  style manuals, 339–40
Discourse
  direct, 549–50
  indirect, 549–50
  shift from direct to indirect, 549–50
Discreet, discrete, 736
Discussion(s), classroom, participation in, 407, 408, 706
Discussion list(s), 207
Disease(s), capitalizing names of, 686
Disinterested, uninterested, 736
Dissertation(s), MLA works-cited list, 250–51, 262
Distortion, 131, 370
Division, 96
Division and classification, as pattern of development, 45, 96–97
Division-and-classification paragraphs, 96–97
  classification in, 96–97

Division-and-classification paragraphs *(continued)*
  defined, 96–97
  division in, 96
Document design, 442–63. *See also* Web site design
  APA manuscript guidelines, 294–97, 388
  checklists for, 447
  Chicago manuscript guidelines, 321–23
  CSE manuscript guidelines, 335–36
  defined, 442
  desktop publishing in, 453–55
  effective format on, 442–45
  headings in, 445–46
  in the humanities, 348–49
  lists in, 447–48
  MLA manuscript guidelines, 264–66
  in the natural and applied sciences, 392, 397, 398
  in the social sciences, 388–89
  visuals in, 449–53
Document names, capitalizing, 683
Documentation, 10. *See also* Documentation style
  to avoid plagiarism, 90, 225, 230, 348
  defined, 239, 747
  in demonstrating knowledge, 130, 369
  in establishing credibility, 130, 369
  in idea generation, 34
  of visuals, 57
Documentation style, 339–40, 747. *See also* APA documentation style; Chicago documentation style; CSE documentation style; MLA documentation style

Doesn't, don't, 736
Dogpile, 205
Domain(s), Web site, 210
Dominant impression, 91
Don't, doesn't, 736
Double negative(s), 715–16, 747
Dow Jones Interactive, 191
Drafting
  defined, 29
  ESL writers and, 52, 707
  essay, 52–61
  final draft, 71–77, 180
  instructor comments in, 61–63, 177
  peer review in, 10, 59–61, 178–79
  research paper, 173–80
  rough draft, 52–57, 173–79
  strategies for, 52–57
  understanding, 52
  in writing process, 29
Dramatic work(s). *See also* Humanities; Literature
  italicizing titles of, 688
  MLA parenthetical references, 242
  MLA works-cited list, 249
  periods to mark divisions in, 631
DVD(s) (digital videodiscs)
  Chicago documentation style, 318
  CSE reference list, 334
  MLA works-cited list, 255, 262–63
  subscription databases on, 185–87, 190

E

-*e* endings, 579
Each
  with compound antecedent, 619
  with compound subject, 614

Earth sciences. *See also* Natural
and applied science(s)
style manual, 339
EBSCOhost, 191
Ecology. *See also* Natural and
applied science(s)
sample observation essay,
393–94
Ed. (edited by), MLA works-
cited list, 247
Edited work(s)
APA reference list, 289
Chicago documentation
style, 313
CSE reference list, 332
MLA works-cited list, 247
Editing
defined, 29, 68
ESL writers and, 51, 708–10
essay, 68–69
Web site, 463
in writing process, 29
Editorial(s), MLA works-cited
list, 254
Editorials on File, 189
Eds. (editors), MLA works-cited
list, 247
Effect, affect, 576, 733
e.g. (for example), 697, 736
ei, ie combinations, 577
Either/or fallacy, 121
Either . . . or, compound subjects
joined by, 614–15
Electronic address. *See also* URL
(uniform resource locator)
angle brackets in, 257, 266
divisions of, 257, 631, 691
entering, 199–201, 208
MLA works-cited list
punctuation, 257
slashes in, 257, 631, 691
Electronic bulletin board(s),
APA parenthetical
references, 286
Electronic portfolio(s), 437

Electronic résumés, 433–34
Electronic source(s), 182–87.
See also Internet research;
Online database(s);
Source(s)
APA parenthetical references,
286–87
APA reference list, 292–94
CD-ROMs, 185–87, 190,
262–63, 574
Chicago documentation
style, 318–21
CSE reference list, 335
dictionaries, 574, 710, 711
DVDs, 185–87, 190, 255,
262–63, 318, 334
evaluating, 193–95, 199
italicizing names of, 688
in library research, 182–87,
193–95
MLA documentation style,
360, 363
MLA parenthetical
references, 243–44
MLA works-cited list,
256–63, 260–63
in the natural and applied
sciences, 399–400
online catalogs, 182–84,
189–90
in the social sciences, 390–91
Electronic version, APA
documentation style, 293
Ellipses, 678–79
brackets with, 221, 679
defined, 678, 748
to indicate omissions within
quotations, 221, 678–79
MLA-style paper, 269
Elliptical clause(s)
dangling, revising, 542–43
defined, 478, 745
Email
APA parenthetical references,
286

Email *(continued)*
  APA reference list, 293
  attachments to, 207, 433
  checklist, 440
  Chicago documentation style, 320
  diction in, 558
  instant messaging, 207–08, 558, 695
  interviews, 197
  MLA works-cited list, 258
  netiquette for, 208, 411–12
  as research tool, 207
  shorthand abbreviations, 695
  in the workplace, 440
Embedding
  to combine sentences, 496–97
  defined, 496, 748
  to revise appositive fragments, 529
Emigrate from, immigrate to, 736
Eminent, imminent, 736
Emoticon(s), 558
Emotional appeals, 132
Emphasis
  colons for, 504
  dashes for, 504
  defined, 503
  emphatic order and, 430, 432
  exclamation points for, 633
  headings and, 443–44, 445, 446
  with interjections, 592, 749
  italics for, 690
  with quotation marks, avoiding, 669
  thesis statement in setting, 42–43
  through active voice, 510–11
  through parallelism and balance, 509
  through repetition, 509–10
  through sentence structure, 506–07
  through word order, 503–05

Encyclopedia(s)
  general, 184, 185
  MLA works-cited list, 260
  specialized, 184, 185
End punctuation. *See* Exclamation point(s); Period(s); Question mark(s)
Endnote(s)
  Chicago-style paper, 308–09, 310–11, 322–23, 327
  MLA-style paper, 264, 277
Engineering. *See also* Natural and applied science(s)
  style manual, 397
English as a Second Language (ESL). *See* ESL (English as a Second Language) tip(s); ESL (English as a Second Language) writer(s)
Enthused, 736
Enthymeme(s), 116, 748
Entry word(s), in dictionary entry, 570–73
Equivocation, 121
-er, in comparative degree, 625–27
ERIC, 191
ESL (English as a Second Language) writer(s), 705–31. *See also* ESL (English as a Second Language) tip(s)
  articles, 721–22
  characteristics of classrooms, 706
  checklists, 709–10
  dictionaries and, 710, 711, 715, 723, 730
  editing by, 708–10
  English language basics and, 708
  grammar checkers and, 710
  nouns, 720–23

prepositions, 727–29
pronouns, 723–24
spelling issues, 708
using native language, 707–08, 709
verbs and, 713–20
word order, 708, 730–31
writing process and, 706–08
Essay(s). *See also* Argumentative essay(s)
  audience for, 9–11, 31, 127, 367–68
  bibliographic, 344–46
  biographical, 396–97
  Chicago documentation style, 314
  drafting, 52–61
  editing, 68–69
  in the humanities, 343–47
  idea generation for, 34–40, 53
  MLA works-cited list, 249–50
  in the natural and applied sciences, 393–94, 396–97
  observation, 393–94
  outlines of, 46–49, 64–65
  paragraphs, 66, 78–103
  patterns of development, 44–45, 82, 90–97, 101, 175
  peer review of, 59–61
  personal experience, 381–82
  planning, 29–30, 46–49, 64–65, 125–28, 366–68
  proofreading, 69–70
  purpose of, 2–5, 31
  quotation marks for titles, 667
  reading to write, 15–27
  review-of-research, 385–86
  revising, 53, 55–58, 65–67, 139–40
  sample essays, 72–77, 134–39
  shaping, 41–51
  in the social sciences, 381–82, 385–86
  storyboarding, 49–51
  thesis and support in, 41–51, 133, 140, 368–72
  title selection for, 67–68
  tone of, 12–13, 130–31
  topic selection for, 32, 125–26, 366–67
  visuals in, 57–58, 142–48, 371
  writing process and, 29–30
Essay exam(s), 415–27
  audience for, 417
  brainstorming for, 418–19
  informal outline of, 419–20
  key words in, 418
  paragraph-length, 426–27
  planning, 416–19
  purpose of, 417
  reading entire exam, 417–18
  review of material for, 416–17
  samples of effective answers, 421–24, 426–27
  samples of ineffective answers, 424–26, 427
  shaping answers to, 419–20
  structure of, 420
  thesis of, 419
  writing and revising, 420–26
-est, in superlative degree, 625, 626–27
Et al.
  APA documentation style, 285, 302
  Chicago documentation style, 313
  MLA documentation style, 241, 247
Etc. (and so forth), 697, 736
Ethical appeals, 132
Ethnic group(s)
  capitalizing names of, 683
  ethnic stereotypes, 566
Etymology, 572
Euphemism(s), 560

Evaluation
　defined, 193
　instructor comments in, 9–10, 61–63, 177
　in peer review, 10–11, 59–61, 178–79
　of sources, 193–95, 199, 208–11
　of visuals, 143, 145–46
　of Web site content, 208–11
Evaluative writing, 2, 4
Even, as limiting modifier, 538
Event names, capitalizing, 683
Every
　with compound antecedent, 619
　with compound subject, 614
Everyone, every one, 736
Everyday, every day, 577, 736
Evidence
　in argumentative essays, 129–32
　bias and, 109–10
　defined, 108
　distorting, 131
　in general-to-specific order, 82, 115–16
　in specific-to-general order, 82, 113–14
　supporting, 108–09, 117–18, 129–31, 368–69
　visuals as, 142, 371
Exact time(s), numbers in, 701
Exactly, as limiting modifier, 538
Example(s)
　appositive fragments to introduce, 528–29
　supporting, 89
　in supporting opinions, 107
　well-developed paragraph and, 89
　words and phrases to introduce, 84
Excel. See Microsoft Excel
Except, accept, 576, 733

Excite, 204
Exclamation(s). *See also* Interjection(s)
　defined, 499
　interrupted, punctuating, 643
Exclamation point(s)
　with interjections, 592, 633, 749
　with quotation marks, 633, 665, 669
　using, 633
Exemplification, as pattern of development, 44, 82, 92
Exemplification paragraphs
　defined, 92
　logical order in, 82
Expanded Academic ASAP, 191
Expert opinion
　bias and, 110
　in supporting opinions, 89–90, 107
　well-developed paragraph and, 89–90
Explanation(s), colons to set off, 672–73
Explicit, implicit, 737
Exploratory research, 163–64
　defined, 158
　in library, 181–87
　research question in, 158, 162, 181–82
　working bibliography in, 159–61

F

-f, -fe endings, plurals with, 580
Fact
　defined, 106
　opinion versus, 106–07
Facts on File, 189
Factual assertions, 129, 369
Factual statement(s), 366
Fair use doctrine, 462
Fairness, 131–32, 370–71

Fallacies, logical, 120–22, 132, 370–71
False analogy, 121
Farther, further, 737
Faulty modification, 537–43
　dangling modifiers, 542–43, 747
　defined, 537
　misplaced modifiers, 537–40, 750
　revising, 537–43
Faulty parallelism, 546–47
　defined, 544, 546, 751
　revising, 546–47
Faulty predication
　be, 552
　defined, 552
　is when, is where, 552, 738
　the reason . . . is because, 552, 740
　revising, 552–53
Favorites list, 206–07
Faxes, in the workplace, 440–41
FedWorld, 206
Fewer, less, 737
Fiction. *See also* Literature
　MLA parenthetical references, 242
　sample literary analysis, 359–65
　writing about, 359–65
Field research
　defined, 389
　in the social sciences, 389, 391
Fig. (Figure), with MLA-style visuals, 266, 271
Figurative language, 561–62, 748
　defined, 561
　list of, 562
Figure(s)
　in APA-style paper, 296, 305–06
　in Chicago-style paper, 322
　in CSE-style paper, 335, 338
　in MLA-style paper, 266, 271
Figures of speech. *See* Figurative language
Film(s). *See also* Humanities
　APA reference list, 292
　CSE reference list, 334
　italicizing titles of, 688
　MLA works-cited list, 255
　search engine, 206
Final draft
　essay, 71–77
　research paper, 180
Finally, as conjunctive adverb, 489
Find command, 68
FindLaw, 206
Finite verb(s), 748
First person
　defined, 549, 752
　in establishing credibility, 131
　in the humanities, 348
　in the natural and applied sciences, 393–94
　present-tense verbs in, 613–14
　in the social sciences, 381–82
Firstly (secondly, thirdly, . . .), 737
FirstSearch, 191
Fixed amounts, as collective nouns, 616
Flaming, 208
Flip chart(s), 470
Focused freewriting, defined, 35
Focused research, 163–64. *See also* Research
　defined, 163, 187–88
　in library, 187–93
　note-taking in, 164–69
　primary sources in, 163–64
　reading sources in, 163
　secondary sources in, 163–64
Follow-up letter(s), 430

Footnote(s), Chicago-style paper, 308–09, 310–11, 322–23
For, as coordinating conjunction, 488
For example, 673–74
   as conjunctive adverb, 489
   to introduce appositives, 485, 528
For instance
   as conjunctive adverb, 489
   to introduce appositives, 485, 528
Foreign plural(s), 581
Foreign words and phrase(s). *See also* Latin expression(s)
   British versus American English, 576, 616
   foreign plurals, 581
   italics to set off, 689
Foreword
   APA reference list, 289
   MLA works-cited list, 248
Formal diction, 556, 564
Formal outline(s)
   defined, 47
   of essays, 47–49, 64–65
   parallelism in, 545
   of research papers, 171–73
   sentence, 48–49, 171, 176–77
   topic, 48, 171
Formal writing assignment(s)
   defined, 342, 380
   in the humanities, 342–43
   in the social sciences, 380–81
Format
   of APA-style research paper, 294–307
   of business letters, 429, 644, 673, 686
   of Chicago-style research paper, 321–28
   of CSE-style research paper, 335–39
   heading, 446
   of job application letters, 429
   of long quotations within paper, 221–22, 240, 285
   of memos, 438–39
   of MLA-style research paper, 264–79
   of résumés, 430–37
   text formatting features in Web site design, 461
   of visual files, 459
Fraction(s), hyphenating compound, 693
Fragment(s). *See* Sentence fragment(s)
Frames, in Web site design, 461
Freewriting
   defined, 35
   in idea generation, 35–36, 38
   sample, 36
FrontPage. *See* Microsoft *FrontPage*®
FTP (file transfer protocol) site(s), for Web site publishing, 463
Function word(s), 748
Further, *farther*, 737
Fused sentence(s), 754
   defined, 532, 748
   revising, 532–34
Future perfect progressive tense, 607
Future perfect tense, 606
Future progressive tense, 607
Future tense, 605

G

Gender
   agreement in, 613
   defined, 613, 748
   pronoun, 725
   sexist language, 68, 110, 567–68
General BusinessFile ASAP, 191
General encyclopedias, 184, 185
General indexes to periodicals, 191

General-purpose search
   engines, 204–05
General reference works,
   184–85, 193
   defined, 184
   types of, 184–85
General-to-specific order, 82,
   115–16
General word(s), 560–61
Generalization(s)
   hasty generalization, 114, 121
   sweeping generalization, 121
Generic *he, him,* 567
Genetics, documentation style.
   See CSE documentation
   style
Geographic regions, capitalizing
   names of, 682
Geology. *See also* Natural and
   applied science(s)
   style manual, 339
Geometry, sample biographical
   essay, 396–97
Gerund(s)
   defined, 588, 748–49
   as nouns, 719
   possessive case before, 594
   recognizing, 588
   as verbals, 588, 756
Gerund phrase(s), 477
   defined, 752
   as nouns, 484
GIF (graphic file format), 459
Glossary(ies)
   grammatical and rhetorical
      terms, 743–56
   usage, 733–42
Go, 204
God, capitalizing pronouns
   referring to, 683
Good, well, 737
Google, 158–59, 203, 204, 458
Got to, 737
Government agencies,
   capitalizing names of, 684

Government document(s)
   APA reference list, 289
   Chicago documentation
      style, 317
   finding, 193
   MLA parenthetical
      references, 243
   MLA works-cited list, 251,
      260
   as primary source material,
      192
   in the social sciences, 390
   style manual, 339–40
Grammar. *See* Parts of speech;
   specific concepts
Grammar checker(s)
   avoiding passive voice, 511
   checking quotation marks, 664
   comma splices, 532
   coordinating conjunctions
      and, 500
   defined, 70
   diction, 558
   ESL writers and, 710
   faulty modification, 537
   faulty parallelism, 547
   faulty predication, 553
   hyphenating compound
      words, 692
   pronoun-antecedent
      agreement, 621
   redundancy, deleting, 516
   revising contractions, 659
   semicolons, misused, 654
   sentence fragments, 523
   sentence fragments and, 500
   spelled-out numbers, 701
   subject-verb agreement,
      615–16
   that and *which,* 640–41
   using, 70, 500
   verb forms, 602–03
   writing style levels, 558
Grammatical terms, glossary of,
   743–56

Graph(s)
  in document design, 450
  misleading, 147–48
  reading, 23
  as visual aids, 451
Group presentation(s), 465

H

Handwriting
  marginal comments, 62
  in revision process, 57, 62
Hanged, hung, 737
Hardly, as limiting modifier, 538
Hasty generalization, 114, 121
He, him, generic, 567
He or she, 567
He, she, 737
Header/Footer option, 295
Heading(s)
  APA-style paper, 294, 388, 389
  consistency of, 446
  in document design, 445–46
  indentation of, 446
  number of, 445
  phrasing of, 445–46
  previewing, 16
  research paper, 174
  résumé, 431, 432, 435
  sample formats, 446
  typographical emphasis in, 443–44, 446
  uses of, 445
Headword(s), misplaced modifiers, 750
HealthFinder, 206
Helping verbs. *See* Auxiliary (helping) verb(s)
Highlighting
  defined, 16, 26
  example of, 17–19
  of text, 16
  of visual text, 26
Him, he, generic, 567
His or her, 567

Historical periods
  capitalizing names of, 683
  names of, 686
History, documentation styles. *See* Chicago documentation style
Hits, 202
Holiday(s)
  abbreviating, 697
  capitalizing names of, 682
Home page(s), 199
  Chicago documentation style, 319
  italicizing, 688
  MLA works-cited list, 258
  personal, 258, 457
Homophone(s), 576–77, 582
Hopefully, 737
Horizontal rule(s), in document design, 443
HotBot, 205
However, as conjunctive adverb, 489
HTML (hypertext markup language), 458
Humanities, 342–51. *See also* Literature
  analysis essay, 346–47
  annotated bibliography, 344–46
  audience in, 342–43
  bibliographic essay, 344–46
  defined, 342
  documentation styles, 348–49. *See also* Chicago documentation style; MLA documentation style
  format of writing, 348
  overview of, 342
  plagiarism, avoiding, 348
  purpose in, 342–43
  research sources, 349–51, 354
  response essay, 343–44
  style of writing, 348
  summary essay, 344

tone in, 342–43
visuals and technology in, 348–49
writing assignments, 343–47
Humanities Index, 349–50
Hung, hanged, 737
Hyperbole, 562
Hyperlinks, hypertext link(s), 199, 210, 266, 456, 460, 462
Hyphen(s), 691–93
  to break word at end of line, 691
  for clarity, 693
  in coined compounds, 693
  in compound adjectives, 692–93, 745–46
  defined, 691
  to divide compound words, 691–93
  to form dashes, 674
  MLA works-cited list, 247, 251
  suspended, 692–93, 755
Hypothesis, 380, 392
  in the natural and applied sciences, 392
  in the social sciences, 380

I

I. *See also* First person
  capitalizing, 685
I, me, in compound constructions, 594
Ibid. (in the same place), 327
-ible, -able endings, 580
Idea(s). *See also* Main idea
  beginning with important, 503–04
  ending with important, 504
  generating, 34–40, 53
  plagiarism avoidance, 228–29
Identification number(s), 702
Identifying tag(s)
  at beginning of quoted passage, 643, 664

defined, 219, 643, 663–64
  at end of quoted passage, 643, 665
  to introduce source material, 219, 220, 222
  location of, 219
  in middle of quoted passage, 664
  for paraphrases, 219, 222
  punctuating, 220, 664
  for quotations, 219, 540, 663–64, 731
  for summaries, 219, 222
Identity, complex sentences to signal, 492
Idiom(s), 565, 573, 729, 749
i.e. (that is), 697, 737
ie, ei combinations, 577
If, in conditional statements, 610
If, whether, 737
Illogical comparisons, 553–54
Illusion, allusion, 733
Immigrate to, emigrate from, 736
Imminent, eminent, 736
iMovie, 389
Imperative mood
  defined, 609, 750
  exclamation points for, 633
  in instructions, 93
Imperative sentence(s), 498–99
Implicit, explicit, 737
Imply, infer, 738
In, as preposition, 728
In-depth questions, 39–40
In fact, as conjunctive adverb, 489
In other words, to introduce appositives, 485
In-text citation(s). *See* Parenthetical reference(s)
Inappropriate language, 563–65
  clichés, 564–65
  jargon, 563–64
  neologisms, 564

Inappropriate language, *(continued)*
  pretentious diction, 564
Indefinite article(s), 721
Indefinite pronoun(s), 613
  as antecedents, 615, 620
  defined, 585, 753
  as determiners, 589, 747
  forming possessive case of, 656
  list of, 585, 589, 615, 724
  subject-verb agreement with, 615–16
Indefinite pronoun subject(s), 724
Indentation
  in APA manuscript style, 295
  in Chicago manuscript style, 321, 325
  in CSE manuscript style, 337
  of first line of paragraph, 78
  of headings, 446
  of lists, 447
  of long prose passages, 665–66
  in MLA manuscript style, 268
Independent (main) clause(s)
  commas to set off, 534, 634, 646, 648
  in complex sentences, 491
  in compound-complex sentences, 493
  defined, 477–78, 744
  semicolons to set off, 634, 649, 651, 654–55
  transitional words and phrases to connect, 533–34, 641, 651
  verbs in, 607
InDesign, 454
Index(es)
  in the humanities, 349–50
  in the natural and applied sciences, 399
  periodical, 190–91
  in the social sciences, 390

Index card(s)
  note-taking, 165
  oral presentation notes on, 466
  working bibliography, 160
Indicative mood, defined, 609, 750
Indirect discourse
  defined, 549
  shift from direct discourse, 549–50
Indirect object(s)
  defined, 476, 718, 751
  objective case with, 594, 744
  in simple sentences, 476
Indirect question(s)
  commas in, 647
  defined, 749
  periods in, 632
Indirect quotation(s)
  commas in, 647
  defined, 670, 753
Indirect source(s)
  APA parenthetical references, 286, 301
  MLA parenthetical references, 241, 273
Inductive argument(s)
  defined, 749
  inductive reasoning in, 113–14, 132, 749
Inductive leap, 114
Inductive reasoning, 113–14, 132, 749
  defined, 113
  inferences in, 114
  specific to general in, 82, 113–14
Infer, imply, 738
Inference, 114
Infinitive(s)
  defined, 587, 749
  recognizing, 587–88
  split, 541, 755
  in titles of works, 685

use in sentences, 607–08, 719
as verbals, 587–88, 756
Infinitive phrase(s), 477
as adjectives or adverbs, 484
defined, 752
as nouns, 484
Informal diction, 557–58
adjective forms in, 624
adverb forms in, 624
apostrophe in dates, 660
colloquial diction, 557
defined, 557
nonstandard diction, 557
regionalisms, 557
slang, 557, 670
Informal outline(s)
defined, 46
of essay exams, 419–20
of essays, 46–47, 48, 53
Informal writing assignment(s)
defined, 342, 380
in the humanities, 342
in the social sciences, 380
Information Please Almanac, 189
Informative writing, 2, 3
content of, 4
in the social sciences, 380–81
tone in, 12
InfoTrac® College Edition, 159, 224–25
-ing ending
in gerunds, 588
in present participles, 587, 600
Inseparable phrasal verb(s)
defined, 717
list of, 717
Inside of, outside of, 738
InSite, 224–25
Instant messaging
diction in, 558, 695
as research tool, 207–08
Instruction(s)
defined, 93
in process paragraphs, 93

Instructor
as audience for essay, 9–11
as audience for essay exam, 417
comments of, 9–10, 61–63, 177
conferences with, 62–64, 408, 706, 707
course requirements, 405–07
emailing, 411–12
expectations of, 9–10
as mentor, 413
topic of essay and, 32
Integrating source material, 219–22
identifying tags, 219, 222
paraphrases, 219, 222
quotations, 220–22
summaries, 219, 222
visuals, 175–76
Intensifier(s), 749
Intensive pronoun(s), 585, 724, 753
Intentional plagiarism, 224
Interjection(s)
capitalizing *O*, 685
commas with, 642
defined, 592, 749
exclamation points for, 592, 633, 749
as part of speech, 592, 749
Interlibrary loan, 193
Internal heading(s), APA-style paper, 295, 388
Internet, 30, 199. *See also* Internet research
defined, 198
printing source material from, 168, 198
Internet Movie Database, The, 206
Internet research, 181, 198–212. *See also* Electronic source(s)
email, 207
evaluating sources, 193–95, 199

Internet research (*continued*)
  instant messaging, 207–08
  Internet, defined, 198
  IRCS, 207–08
  limitations of, 198–99
  listservs, 120, 207
  MOOS, 207–08, 258–59
  MUDS, 207–08, 258–59
  netiquette, 208
  newsgroups, 207, 258–59, 293
  plagiarism avoidance, 224–25, 227
  resources for, 199
  scholarly journals in, 190
  in the social sciences, 390
  technological competence and, 411–12
  Telnet, 207–08, 258–59
  users with disabilities, 199, 200
  Web sites. *See* Web site(s)
  World Wide Web, 199–207
Internet server(s), 463
Internships, 409
Interpretation
  defined, 353
  of literature, 353
  of visuals, 24–25
Interrogative adverb(s)
  defined, 589, 743
  list of, 589
Interrogative pronoun(s)
  defined, 585, 753
  as determiners, 589, 747
  list of, 585
Interruption(s), 542–43
  avoiding commas with, 643
  commas to punctuate, 533
  dashes to punctuate, 675
Interview(s)
  APA parenthetical references, 286
  Chicago documentation style, 317
  defined, 196
  email, 197
  in the humanities, 351
  MLA works-cited list, 254
  in the social sciences, 389, 391
  transcription of, 389
Into, as preposition, 728
Intransitive verb(s)
  in basic simple sentence, 474–75
  defined, 475, 718, 756
  in simple sentences, 474–75
Introductory element(s)
  commas to set off, 637–38
  dependent clauses, 637, 654
  prepositional phrases, 638
  transitional words and phrases, 638
  verbal phrases, 637, 638
Introductory paragraph(s), 100–02
  of argumentative essay, 132
  defined, 41, 100
  of essay exam, 420
  of oral presentation, 466
  of research paper, 174
  strategies for effective, 101–02
Introductory tags, with direct quotations, 643
Intrusive modifier(s), 541
  defined, 541
  misplaced, revising, 541
  split infinitives, 541, 755
  subjects and verbs, interrupted, 542–43
  verb phrases, interrupted, 541
  verbs and objects or complements, interrupted, 542–43
Inversion, of word order, 501–02, 505, 617
IRCS, as research tool, 207–08

Irregardless, regardless, 738
Irregular verb(s)
  defined, 600, 713–14, 749
  principal parts of, 600–03
Is when, is where, 552, 738
Isolate(s), 592, 749
It, for nonhuman subjects, 725
Italic(s), 688–90. *See also* Underlining
  in APA parenthetical references, 286
  in APA reference list, 288–94
  in Chicago-style papers, 311
  for emphasis, 690
  with names of court cases, 683
  to set off foreign words and phrases, 689
  to set off letters as letters, 660, 689
  to set off numerals as numerals, 660, 689
  to set off titles and names, 667, 688–89
  to set off words as words, 660, 668, 689–90
  for terms being defined, 670, 689
  underlining versus, in MLA works-cited list, 245–63, 670, 689
Its, it's, 576, 738
Ixquick, 205

J

Jargon, 563–64
Job application letter(s), 428–30
Journal(s)
  defined, 35
  in idea generation, 35
  italicizing titles of, 688
  sample, 35
Journal article(s)
  APA reference list, 290, 293
  Chicago documentation style, 315, 318–19, 320–21
  continuous pagination, 253, 262, 290, 315, 333
  CSE reference list, 333–34, 335
  in library research, 190–91
  MLA parenthetical references, 240–43
  MLA works-cited list, 252–53, 259, 261–62
  in periodical indexes, 190–91
  previewing, 15–16
  quotation marks with, 667
  separate pagination, 253, 261–62, 290, 315, 333
  in subscription databases, 185–87, 190
  in working bibliography, 160
Journalism, style manual, 340
Journalistic questions
  defined, 38
  in idea generation, 38
  in-depth, 39–40
JPG (photographic image format), 459
Just, as limiting modifier, 538
Justification, document, 442–43

K

Key terms, defining, 126–27, 367
Key words and phrases
  defined, 85
  essay exam, 418
  repeating, 85, 547
Keyword search
  Boolean operators in, 183, 187, 203–04, 206
  defined, 183
  electronic subscription service, 261
  MLA works-cited list, 261
  of online catalogs, 182, 183
  of online databases, 187, 261
  search engine, 202–04, 206–07

Keyword search (*continued*)
　subject search versus, 183
Kind of, sort of, 738

L

Label(s)
　in APA-style paper, 296, 306
　in CSE-style paper, 338
　for visuals in essay, 57–58
Laboratory report, 393
Language(s). *See also* Foreign words and phrase(s); Humanities; Latin expression(s)
　capitalizing names of, 683
　documentation style, 348. *See also* MLA documentation style
Laser disc(s), MLA works-cited list, 255
Latin expression(s)
　ad hominem (argument to the person) fallacy, 122
Latin expression(s) (*continued*)
　e.g. (for example), 697, 736
　et al. (and others), 241, 247, 285, 302, 313
　etc. (and so forth), 697, 736
　ibid. (in the same place), 327
　i.e. (that is), 697, 737
　plural forms versus English plurals, 617
　sic (thus), 677
Law. *See also* Legal sources; Social science(s)
　legal case names, 683
　style manual, 340
Lay, lie, 603, 738
Learning styles, 404
Leave, let, 738
Lecture(s). *See also* Oral presentation(s)
　MLA works-cited list, 254
Legal case names, capitalizing, 683

Legal sources
　MLA parenthetical references, 243
　MLA works-cited list, 251
　search engine, 206
Length, varying sentence, 494–95
Less, fewer, 737
Let, leave, 738
Letter(s) (of alphabet)
　apostrophes for omitted, 658–59
　apostrophes in plurals of, 660
　capitalizing, in special constructions, 685–86, 693
　as letters, setting off, 660, 689
Letter(s) (correspondence)
　APA parenthetical references, 286
　APA reference list, 291
　business, writing, 428–30, 644, 673, 686
　capitalization in, 686
　Chicago documentation style, 317
　job application, 428–30
　MLA works-cited list, 255
　punctuation of, 644, 673
Letter(s) of application, 428–30
　defined, 428
　follow-up letters for, 430
　sample, 429
　templates, 430
Letters to the editor
　APA reference list, 291
　MLA works-cited list, 254, 259
LexisNexis Academic Universe, 188, 191
Library of Congress Classification System, 183
Library research, 181–97
　advantages of, 410–11
　books, 182–84, 189–90

circulating collection, 189–90
defined, 389
electronic sources, 182–87, 193–95
evaluating sources, 193–95
exploratory, 181–87
focused, 187–93
in the humanities, 349–50
library classification systems, 189
library resources, 410–11
library Web sites, 185, 188
in the natural and applied sciences, 398–99
online catalogs, 182–84
periodicals, 190–91
popular publications, 194–95
primary sources, 191–92
print sources, 184–85, 188–95
reference collection, 184–85
scholarly publications, 194–95
secondary sources, 191–92
in the social sciences, 389–91
special resources, 193
using the library, 410–11
Library subscription services, 260
   Chicago documentation style, 320–21
   MLA works-cited list, 261
Lie, lay, 603, 738
Life science(s). *See* Natural and applied science(s)
Lifelong learning, 413
Like, as, 734
Limiting modifier(s)
   defined, 538
   list of, 538
   placing, 538
Line/lines, MLA parenthetical references, 357
Line spacing
   in APA-style paper, 287, 294, 296

   in Chicago-style paper, 321, 325, 328
   in CSE-style paper, 335, 338
   in document design, 444–45
   in MLA-style paper, 267
Link(s), in Web site design, 199, 210, 266, 456, 460, 462
Linking verb(s)
   defined, 476, 586, 749–50, 755
   incorrect use of *be*, 552
   list of, 586
   in simple sentences, 476
   subject complements and, 476, 586, 623–24
   subject-verb agreement with, 617
List(s)
   in APA-style paper, 303
   appositive fragments as, 528
   colons to introduce, 528, 655, 672
   constructing, 447–48
   in document design, 447–48
   parallelism in, 447, 545
   parentheses for points on, 676
   spelling, 581
Listserv(s)
   Chicago documentation style, 320
   defined, 207
Literary analysis, 352–65
   analysis essay, 346–47
   defined, 352
   of fiction, 359–65
   of poetry, 355–59
   reading literature, 352
   research sources, 354, 365
   sample papers, 355–59
   writing about literature, 353–54
Literary argument, 366–79
   credibility in, 369–70
   organization of, 371–72

Literary argument (*continued*)
  planning, 366–68
  sample essay, 372–79
  supporting, 368–71
Literary movements, capitalizing names of, 683
Literature. *See also* Humanities; Literary analysis; Literary argument; Poetry; Prose
  abbreviating works of, 696
  CSE reference list, 333
  documentation styles, 348. *See also* Chicago documentation style; MLA documentation style
  long quotations of. *See* Long quotation(s)
  MLA parenthetical references, 221–22, 240, 242
  MLA works-cited list, 249–50
  past tense in writing about, 353
  periods to mark divisions in, 631
  present tense in writing about, 353, 548
  sample analysis essay, 346–47
  sample annotated bibliography, 345–46
  sample bibliographic essay, 345–46
Literature survey(s)
  defined, 394
  in the natural and applied sciences, 394–95
  in the social sciences, 385–86
Local organizing principle, 86
Location, complex sentences to signal, 492
Logic, 113–22
  deductive reasoning, 115–18, 132, 747
  defined, 113
  fallacies in, 120–22, 132

inductive reasoning, 82, 113–14, 132, 749
Toulmin, 117–18
Logical appeals, 132, 370–71
Logical fallacies, 120–22, 132, 370–71
Logical order
  defined, 82
  of paragraphs, 82
Long quotation(s)
  colons to introduce, 673
  of poetry, 221–22, 240, 666–67
  of prose, 221–22, 240, 274, 285, 321, 361, 665–66, 673
Loose, lose, 738
Lose, loose, 738
Lots, lots of, a lot of, 738
Lotus, 449
-ly, in comparative degree, 625–27
Lycos, 205

M

Macromedia Dreamweaver, 458
Magazine article(s)
  APA reference list, 290
  Chicago documentation style, 315–16, 319
  CSE reference list, 334
  in library research, 190–91
  MLA parenthetical references, 240–43
  MLA works-cited list, 253–54, 259, 262
  in periodical indexes, 190–91
  previewing, 15–16
  quotation marks with, 667
  in subscription databases, 185–87, 190
  in working bibliography, 160
Magazine(s), italicizing titles of, 688
Main clause(s). *See* Independent (main) clause(s)

Main idea. *See also* Thesis; Topic
   sentence(s)
 implied, 79–80
 well-developed paragraph
   and, 88
Main verb(s), 474, 586, 755
Major premise, in deductive
   reasoning, 115, 116
Man, 739
Map(s)
 CSE reference list, 334
 MLA works-cited list, 260
 reading, 22
Margin(s)
 APA-style paper, 295
 Chicago-style paper, 321
 MLA-style paper, 265
Margin(s), in document design,
   442–43
Mathematics. *See also* Natural
   and applied science(s)
 style manual, 340, 397
May be, maybe, 739
May, can, 734
Me, I, in compound
   constructions, 594
Meaning(s), in dictionary entry,
   571
Measurement(s). *See also* Time
   measure(s)
 abbreviating, 698
 numbers in, 702
Media, medium, 739
Medicine. *See also* CSE
   documentation style
 medical terms, 686
 style manual, 340
Medium, media, 739
Memo(s), 438–39
 APA parenthetical references,
   286
 format of, 438–39
 sample, 439
Mentor(s), 413
Merely, as limiting modifier, 538

Metacrawler, 205
Metacrawler engine(s), 205
Metaphor(s)
 defined, 562, 750
 mixed, 565, 750
Metasearch engine(s), 205
Microfilm, MLA works-cited
   list, 250–51
Microsoft Excel, 412, 449, 468
Microsoft FrontPage®, 30, 458
Microsoft Internet Explorer, 199
Microsoft Notepad, 458
Microsoft Outlook, 403
Microsoft PowerPoint®, 30, 49,
   412, 443, 444, 467–68
Microsoft Publisher®, 30, 454
Microsoft Word. See also
   Grammar checker(s); Spell
   checker(s)
 AutoCorrect tool, 266
 Bullets and Numbering
   feature, 65
 Comment feature, 59, 62,
   177, 398
 Compare Drafts feature, 58,
   59
 formatting visuals, 449, 468
 outlining with, 49, 173
 Save/Save As option, 53
 Search or Find command, 68
 templates, 430, 443, 454,
   455
 Track Changes feature,
   58–59, 178–79, 398
 visuals and, 57
Might have, might of, 739
Minor premise, in deductive
   reasoning, 115, 116
- (minus sign), as Boolean
   operator, 204
Misplaced modifier(s), 537–40
 defined, 537, 750
 dependent clauses, 540
 intrusive modifiers, 541
 limiting modifiers, 538

Misplaced modifier(s) (*continued*)
  modifying words, 538
  phrases, 539
  revising, 537–40
  squinting modifiers, 538, 755
Miss, Ms. Mrs., 567
Mixed construction
  defined, 551, 750
  revising, 551
Mixed metaphor(s), 565, 750
MLA documentation style, 233–79
  checklists, 265–66
  content notes, 242, 264, 266, 277
  defined, 239
  in the humanities, 348
  manuscript guidelines, 264–66
  parenthetical references, 234, 239–44, 269, 362
  sample essays, 72–77, 134–39
  sample research papers, 266–79, 359–65
  works-cited list, 234–37, 244–63, 266, 278–79, 365
MLA Handbook for Writers of Research Papers, 239, 256, 264, 700. *See also* MLA documentation style
Modal auxiliary(ies), 714
  defined, 587, 756
  list of, 587
Modern Language Association (MLA), 239. *See also* MLA documentation style
Modifier(s). *See also* Adjective(s); Adverb(s)
  dangling, 542–43, 747
  defined, 750
  faulty modification, revising, 537–43
  intrusive, 541
  limiting, 538
  misplaced, 537–40, 750

nonrestrictive, 639–41, 750–51
phrases, 484, 539, 614
restrictive, 639–41, 647, 754
squinting, 538, 755
using, 484
Money amounts, numbers in, 701
Month(s)
  abbreviating, 697
  capitalizing names of, 682
Monthly calendar, 402–04
Monument names, capitalizing, 682
MOO(s)
  MLA works-cited list, 258–59
  as research tool, 207–08
Mood, 609–10. *See also specific types of mood*
  defined, 609, 750
  shift in, 549, 754
  types of, 609–10, 750
Movie(s). *See* Film(s)
Mrs., Miss, Ms., 567
MUD(s)
  MLA works-cited list, 258–59
  as research tool, 207–08
Multiple author(s)
  APA parenthetical references, 285, 302
  APA reference list, 288, 289
  Chicago documentation style, 312–13
  CSE reference list, 332
  MLA parenthetical references, 240–41
  MLA works-cited list, 246–47
Multiple citations
  MLA content notes, 264
  MLA parenthetical references, 241–42
Multivolume work(s)
  APA reference list, 289
  Chicago documentation style, 314

MLA parenthetical
    references, 241
MLA works-cited list, 248
MultiWeb browser, 200
Music. *See also* Humanities
    APA reference list, 292
    Chicago documentation
        style, 318
    CSE reference list, 334
    italicizing titles of long
        works, 688
    MLA works-cited list, 255
    quotation marks for titles, 667
    sample response essay, 343–44
    style manual, 340
Musical(s). *See* Dramatic work(s)

N

Name(s). *See* Author name(s);
    Place name(s); Proper
    noun(s); Publisher's name
Name-year format, CSE
    documentation style, 331
Namely, to introduce
    appositives, 485, 528
Narration, as pattern of
    development, 44, 82,
    90–91
Narrative paragraph(s), 82, 90–91
Narrator
    reliable, 367
    unreliable, 367
Narrowing of focus
    for essay topic, 32
    words and phrases to
        introduce, 84
*National Geographic Atlas of the
    World*, 189
Nationalities
    capitalizing names of, 683
    stereotypes, 566
Natural and applied science(s),
    392–400
    abstract, 395–96
    audience in, 392

biographical essay, 396–97
documentation styles, 392,
    397, 398. *See also* CSE
    documentation style
format of writing, 397
laboratory report, 393
literature survey, 394–95
observation essay, 393–94
plagiarism, avoiding, 398
purpose in, 392
reference books, 399
research sources, 398–400
style manual, 340
style of writing, 397
tone in, 392
visuals and technology in,
    398
writing assignments, 393–96
Navigation links, buttons, bars,
    460, 461
n.d. (no date), APA
    documentation style, 293
Nearly, as limiting modifier, 538
Negative verb(s), 715–16
Neither . . . nor, compound
    subjects joined by, 614–15
Neologisms, 564
Net meeting software, 30
Netiquette
    defined, 208
    observing, 208, 411–12
Netscape Navigator, 199, 200
Nevertheless, as conjunctive
    adverb, 489
News service(s), MLA works-
    cited list, 262
News wire, MLA works-cited
    list, 262
Newsgroup(s), 207
    APA reference list, 293
    MLA works-cited list, 258
Newsletter article(s), MLA
    works-cited list, 259
Newsletter(s), desktop
    publishing and, 454

Newspaper article(s)
  APA reference list, 291, 294
  Chicago documentation style, 316–17, 319
  CSE reference list, 334
  in library research, 190–91
  MLA parenthetical references, 240–43
  MLA works-cited list, 253–54, 259, 262
  in periodical indexes, 190–91
  previewing, 15–16
  quotation marks with, 667
  in the social sciences, 390
  in subscription databases, 185–87
  in working bibliography, 160
Newspaper(s), italicizing titles of, 688
No., 696
No, commas with, 642
Nominal, 750
Nominative case, 744
Non sequitur, 121
Noncount noun(s)
  articles with, 722
  defined, 584, 720, 751
  list of, 720
Nonessential material
  commas to set off, 639–42
  dashes to set off, 674
  defined, 639
  nonrestrictive modifiers, 639–41
  parentheses to set off, 675–76
Nonexistent antecedent(s), 597
Nonfinite verb(s). *See* Verbal(s)
Nonrestrictive clause(s), 598, 639
Nonrestrictive modifier(s)
  commas to set off, 639–41
  defined, 639, 750–51
  types of, 639–41
Nonstandard diction, 557

Nor
  with compound antecedents, 620
  as coordinating conjunction, 488
NOT, as Boolean operator, 183, 187, 204
Note(s). *See* Content note(s); Endnote(s); Footnote(s); Note-taking
Note-taking
  to avoid plagiarism, 229
  in the classroom, 407
  computer printouts in, 161, 166–69
  index cards in, 165
  notes for oral presentation, 466
  photocopies in, 168–69
  recording source information, 164–68
Notepad. *See* Microsoft Notepad
Noun(s). *See also specific types of noun*
  articles with, 721–22
  case, 593–96, 744
  defined, 584, 720, 751
  ESL writers and, 720–23
  expanding simple sentences with, 481
  forming possessive case of, 656–57, 659, 661
  gerund phrases as, 484
  gerunds as, 719
  infinitives as, 719
  noncount, 584, 720, 722, 751
  other determiners with, 723
  as part of speech, 584, 593–98, 751
  plural. *See* Plural(s)
  possessive, 589, 723, 747
  prepositions to introduce, 590
  singular-plural distinction, 613–14

as subject complements. *See*
Predicate nominative(s)
types of, 584, 751
using, 584, 593–96
verbal phrases as, 484
verbals used as, 481
verbs formed from, 720
we, us before, 596
Noun clause(s), 479, 745
Noun phrase(s)
defined, 477, 752
in rambling sentences, 519
in simple sentence, 477
wordy constructions, eliminating, 519
Number
agreement in, 613–18, 713, 743
defined, 549, 613, 751
plural, 613–14, 751. *See also* Plural(s)
shift in, 549
singular, 613–18, 743, 751
Number(s), 700–02
in addresses, 701
APA-style paper, 700
apostrophes for omitted, 660
cardinal, 723, 744, 747
in dates, 701
in decimals, 702
as determiners, 589, 723, 744, 747
in divisions of written works, 702
in exact times, 701
hyphenating compound, 693
identification, 702
in lists, 447
long, commas in, 644, 645, 702
in measurements before abbreviations, 702
in measurements before symbols, 702
MLA-style paper, 700–02
in money amounts, 701
noncoordination with other adjectives, 636
as numbers, setting off, 660, 689
ordinal, 723, 747, 751
paragraph, 243–44
in percentages, 702
questionable, marking, 632
in ratios, 702
in scores, 702
shift in, 599, 754
spelled-out, versus numerals, 700–01
in statistics, 702
Number, amount, 723, 733
Numeral(s). *See* Number(s)

O

O, capitalizing, 685
-o endings, plurals with, 580
Object(s)
compound, as sentence fragments, 529–30
defined, 751
direct, 475, 594, 744, 751
indirect, 476, 718, 751
interrupted, 542–43
of transitive verbs, 756
Object complement(s)
defined, 475, 624, 745
interrupted, 542–43
in simple sentences, 475
Object of preposition
defined, 590, 751
objective case with, 593–94, 744
Objective case, 593–94, 744
Objectivity
defined, 209
of Web site content, 209
Observation essay, 393–94
Observing, in idea generation, 34

O'clock, 701
Offensive language
   racist language, 110
   sexist language, 68, 110, 567–68
   stereotypes, 566–67
OK, O.K., okay, 739
Omission(s)
   apostrophes to indicate, 658–60
   ellipsis to indicate, 221, 678–79
On, as preposition, 728
On the other hand, as conjunctive adverb, 489
One-page article(s), MLA parenthetical references, 241
Online catalog(s), 182–84, 189–90
   defined, 182
   keyword searches of, 182, 183
   subject searches in, 182, 183–84
Online database(s), 185–87
   APA reference list, 294
   Chicago documentation style, 320–21
   defined, 185
   in the humanities, 350
   italicizing names of, 688
   list of, 185
   in the natural and applied sciences, 399
   searching, 186–87
   in the social sciences, 390–91
   types of, 185–86
Online forum(s), MLA works-cited list, 258
Only, as limiting modifier, 538
Onto, as preposition, 729
Open-ended question(s), 196–97
Opinion. *See also* Expert opinion
   defined, 106
   fact versus, 106–07

   supported, 89–90, 107, 354
   unsupported, 107
Or
   and/or, 734
   with compound antecedents, 619, 620
   compound subjects joined by, 614–15
   as coordinating conjunction, 488
   to introduce appositives, 485
OR, as Boolean operator, 183, 187, 203
Oral presentation(s), 464–71
   checklists for, 471
   defined, 464
   delivering, 470, 471
   getting started, 464–65
   group presentations, 465
   notes for, 466
   planning, 465–66
   presentation software, 30, 49, 412, 443, 444, 449, 467–68, 469
   rehearsing, 470
   visual aids for, 449–53, 467–70
Ordinal number(s)
   defined, 751
   as determiners, 723, 747
Organization
   of APA-style paper, 295
   of argumentative essay, 132–33, 140, 371–72
   of research paper, 174–75
Organization name(s)
   abbreviating, 695–96, 697
   capitalizing, 683
Outline(s). *See also* Formal outline(s); Informal outline(s)
   defined, 46
   essay, 46–49, 64–65
   essay exam, 419–20
   oral presentation, 466

parallelism in, 48, 545
research paper, 171–73
Outlining, computer tips for, 49, 173
Outlook. *See* Microsoft Outlook
Outside of, inside of, 738
Overhead projector(s), 469
Oxford English Dictionary (OED), 189, 574

P

P., pp.
  APA parenthetical references, 286
  APA reference list, 289, 290
  MLA works-cited list, 252
Page header(s), APA-style paper, 295, 388
Page number(s)
  APA parenthetical references, 284–87
  APA reference list, 288–91
  APA-style paper, 295
  Chicago bibliography, 315
  Chicago endnotes and footnotes, 311–21
  Chicago-style paper, 321, 322
  CSE reference list, 331–33
  CSE-style paper, 336, 338
  in literary analysis, 354
  MLA parenthetical references, 240–44
  MLA-style paper, 265, 269
  MLA works-cited list, 245–56, 252–54, 261–62
Painting(s)
  italicizing names of, 688
  MLA works-cited list, 256, 260
  reading, 23
Paired items
  linked by correlative conjunctions, 544–45, 647
  parallelism of, 544–45

Pamphlet(s)
  italicizing titles of, 688
  MLA works-cited list, 251
Paper(s). *See* Essay(s); Research paper(s)
Paragraph(s), 78–103
  achieving coherence between paragraphs, 85–86
  APA parenthetical references, 286–87, 300
  arranging details in, 44–45, 82, 90–97
  beginning new, 78
  body. *See* Body paragraph(s)
  checklists on, 66, 78
  coherent, 82–86
  concluding. *See* Concluding paragraph(s)
  defined, 78
  exemplification, 82, 92
  introductory. *See* Introductory paragraph(s)
  key words and phrases in, 85
  parallel structure in, 85
  patterns of development, 44–45, 82, 90–97, 101, 175
  revising, 66, 80–81, 83, 88–90
  topic sentences in, 79
  transitional, 85–86, 99–100
  transitional words and phrases in, 82–84, 90, 92
  types of, 41
  unified, 79–81
  well-developed, 88–90
Paragraph number(s), MLA parenthetical references, 243–44
Parallelism, 544–47
  in coherent paragraphs, 85
  conveying emphasis through, 509
  defined, 85, 544, 751
  effective, 544–45
  faulty, 544, 546–47, 751
  in lists, 447, 545

Parallelism (*continued*)
  in outlines, 48, 545
  in paired items, 544–45
  parallel elements in, 547
  repeating key words in, 547
  repeating relative pronouns in, 547
  in series, 544
Paraphrase(s)
  to avoid plagiarism, 228–29
  characteristics of, 216
  defined, 215
  identifying tags to introduce, 219, 222
  integrating, 219, 222
  MLA parenthetical references for, 240
  sample, 216–17
  of source information, 164–68, 215–17
  writing, 215–17
Parentheses, 675–76
  capitalizing sentences set off within another sentence, 681
  for cross-references, 676
  with other punctuation marks, 676
  within parentheses, brackets for, 677
  with points on list, 676
  question marks in, 632
  to set off nonessential material, 675–76
Parenthetical reference(s)
  APA documentation style, 282, 284–87
  CSE documentation style, 330–31
  defined, 239
  formatting, 161
  MLA documentation style, 234, 239–44, 269, 362
  placement of, 240

Participial phrase(s), 477
  defined, 719, 752
  as modifiers, 484, 614
Participle(s). *See also specific types of participle*
  defined, 587, 751
  recognizing, 587
  types of, 751
  as verbals, 587, 756
Parts of speech, 584–92. *See also specific parts of speech*
  defined, 584, 752
  list of, 584, 752
  part-of-speech label, in dictionary entry, 570–71
Passed, past, 739
Passive voice, 717
  active voice versus, 510–11
  with dangling modifiers, 542
  defined, 611, 756
  eliminating, 518
  intentional use of, 381, 397, 511, 611
  in rambling sentences, 518
  shift from or to active voice, 549, 611–12
Past participle(s). *See also* Verbal(s)
  defined, 587, 719, 751, 753
  formation of, 608
  in principal parts, 753
  in verb forms, 600–03
Past, passed, 739
Past perfect progressive tense, 607
Past perfect tense, 606
Past progressive tense, 606
Past subjunctive mood, 609, 610
Past tense
  defined, 605, 753
  principal parts, 600–03
  in résumés, 433
  in verb forms, 600–03
  in writing about literature, 353

in writing about social science research, 301, 303
Path, MLA works-cited list, 261
Patterns of development, 44–45, 82, 90–97, 101, 175
PDF (portable document format), 436, 437
Peak, 389
Peer review
   audience in, 10–11
   comments in, 10–11, 59–61, 178–79
   defined, 10, 59
   drafts in, 10, 59–61, 178–79
   ESL writers and, 707
Percent, percentage, 739
Percentages, numbers in, 702
Perfect infinitive, 607–08
Perfect tense(s), 604
   defined, 606
   ESL writers and, 714
   types of, 606
Period(s), 630–31
   abbreviations without, 558, 631, 683, 695–96, 697
   with ellipses, 678–79
   to end a sentence, 630
   with identifying tags for quoted passages, 664
   in indirect questions, 632
   to mark abbreviations, 630–31
   to mark divisions in electronic addresses, 631
   to mark divisions in literary works, 631
   with quotation marks, 665, 668
   in revising comma splices, 533
   in revising fused sentences, 533
   in revising run-on sentences, 533
Periodic sentence(s)
   conveying emphasis through, 506–07
   defined, 506, 752

Periodical(s), 190–91. *See also* Journal article(s); Magazine article(s); Newspaper article(s)
   previewing, 15–16
Periodical index(es), 190–91
Person
   agreement in, 613–18, 713, 743
   defined, 549, 613, 752
   first. *See* First person
   second, 549, 613–14, 752
   shift in, 549, 754
   third, 549, 613–14, 752
Personal communication. *See also* Business letter(s); Email; Letter(s) (correspondence)
   APA parenthetical references, 286
   APA reference list, 291
   Chicago documentation style, 317, 320
   MLA works-cited list, 255, 258–59
Personal experience essay(s), 381–82
Personal home page(s), 457
   MLA works-cited list, 258
Personal organizer, 402–04
Personal pronoun(s)
   avoiding apostrophes with plural, 661
   defined, 585, 753
   list of, 585, 724
Personal subscription services, 260
   MLA works-cited list, 261
Personal title(s). *See* Titles of people
Personification, 562, 752
Persuasive writing, 2, 3. *See also* Argumentative essay(s)
   content of, 4
   in the social sciences, 385–86

Persuasive writing (*continued*)
   tone in, 12
   visuals to support, 143
Phenomenon, phenomena, 739
Philosophic movements, capitalizing names of, 683
Philosophy. *See also* Humanities
   sample summary essay, 344
Photocopies, managing, 168–69
Photograph(s)
   interpreting, 24–25
   misleading, 145–46
   MLA works-cited list, 256, 260
   reading, 22
   staged, 146
   as visual aids, 450–52
Photoshop. See Adobe Photoshop®
Phrasal verb(s), 716–17
Phrase(s). *See also specific types of phrase;* Transitional words and phrase(s)
   beginning sentences with, 500
   commas between clauses and, 655
   contradictory, commas with, 642
   defined, 477, 525, 752
   identifying, 477
   key, 85, 547
   misplaced, relocating, 539
   nonrestrictive, commas with, 639
   phrase fragments, 524–29
   plagiarism avoidance, 227–28
   in series, 544
   to signal conclusions, 84, 116
   between subject and verb, 614
   types of, 477, 752
   wordy, eliminating, 515
Phrase fragment(s), 524–29
   appositive, 528–29
   causes of, 525
   introduced by transitions, 526
   prepositional phrase, 526
   revising, 525–29
   verbal phrase, 527
Phrasing
   of headings, 445–46
   in plagiarism avoidance, 227–28
Physics. *See also* Natural and applied science(s)
   style manual, 340
Physiology, documentation style. *See* CSE documentation style
Pilot-Search.com, 206
Place name(s)
   abbreviating, 630, 631, 697
   capitalizing, 682
   numbers in, 701
   prepositions and, 727
Plagiarism, 224–30
   avoiding, 90, 169, 213, 224–30, 348, 388, 398
   defined, 224
   detecting, 224–25
   examples of, 226–30
   idea generation and, 34
   intentional, 224
   revising to eliminate, 226–30
   unintentional, 224, 225–26
Planning
   analyzing assignment in, 31
   defined, 29, 31
   ESL writers and, 706–07
   of essay, 29–30, 46–49, 64–65, 125–28, 366–68
   of essay exam answer, 416–19
   idea generation in, 34–40
   of oral presentation, 465–66
   of research paper, 156–57
   topic selection in, 32
   in Web site design, 456–57, 460–62
   in writing process, 29
Play(s). *See* Dramatic work(s)
Plot summary, avoiding, in literary analysis, 354

Plural(s)
    apostrophes in, 660–61
    articles with, 721–22
    defined, 613, 751
    foreign, 581
    forming, 580–81, 660
    forming possessive case of, 657
    forms of, 613–14
    subject-verb agreement,
        613–18, 713, 743
Plus, 739
+ (plus sign), as Boolean
    operator, 204
p.m., 696
Poetry. *See also* Literature
    capitalizing first word of line
        of, 681
    indicating omissions in, 679
    italicizing titles of long
        poems, 688
    long quotations of, 221–22,
        240, 666–67
    MLA parenthetical references,
        221–22, 240, 242
    MLA works-cited list, 249
    periods to mark divisions in,
        631
    quotation marks for titles, 667
    slashes to separate lines of,
        357, 678
    writing about, 355–59
Point(s)
    in document design, 443–44
    in oral presentations, 465–66
Point-by-point comparisons, 94
Political groups, capitalizing
    names of, 683
Political science. *See also* Social
    science(s)
    sample book review, 382–83
Popular publication(s). *See also*
    Magazine article(s)
    defined, 194
    scholarly publications versus,
        194–95

Portals, 412
Portfolio(s)
    electronic, 437
    of work, 406–07
Positive degree, 747
Possessive article(s), 727
Possessive case
    defined, 594, 744
    forming, 656–57, 659, 661
Possessive noun(s), as
    determiners, 589, 723, 747
Possessive pronoun(s)
    as determiners, 589, 723, 747
    forming, 656–57, 659, 661
    list of, 589
Post hoc fallacy, 121
Postal abbreviation(s), 631
Poster(s), 470
Posting, Web site, 463
*PowerPoint®. See Microsoft
    PowerPoint®*
Precede, proceed, 739
Predicate(s)
    complete, 474, 752
    compound, 529–30, 746
    defined, 752
    simple, 474, 752
Predicate adjective(s), 745
Predicate nominative(s), 745
Predication. *See* Faulty
    predication
Prediction, in conclusions,
    102–03
Preface
    APA reference list, 289
    MLA works-cited list, 248
Prefix(es)
    defined, 753
    hyphenating with, 693
    spelling rules, 578
Preposition(s)
    compound, 746
    defined, 482, 590, 727, 753
    ESL writers and, 727–29
    in idiomatic expressions, 729

806 Index

Preposition(s) (*continued*)
list of, 590–91, 727–29
object, 594, 744, 751
as part of speech, 590–91, 753
in titles of works, 685
Prepositional phrase(s)
commas with introductory, 638
commas with nonrestrictive, 639
commonly confused, 728–29
commonly used, 727–28
defined, 477, 482, 752
difficult, 728
expanding simple sentences with, 482
fragments, revising, 526
misplaced, 539
as modifiers, 539
in rambling sentences, 519
in simple sentence, 477
wordy, eliminating, 519
Present infinitive, 607–08
Present participle(s)
defined, 587, 719, 751
formation of, 608
principal parts, 753
in verb forms, 600–03
Present perfect participle(s), 608
Present perfect progressive tense, 607
Present perfect tense, 606
Present progressive tense, 606
Present subjunctive mood, 609
Present tense
defined, 605
in résumés, 433
special uses of, 605
in verb forms, 600–03, 613
in writing about literature, 353, 548
Presentation(s). *See* Oral presentation(s)

Presentation software, 30, 49, 412, 443, 444, 449, 467–68, 469
Pretentious diction, 564
Previewing
defined, 15, 25
of text, 15–16
of visual text, 25
of Web site, 463
Prewriting stage, 34–40
Primary source(s), 163–64
defined, 163, 191, 342
finding, 191–92
in the humanities, 342, 349
interviews, 196–97
list of, 164
Principal part(s), 600
defined, 753
irregular verbs, 600–03
Principal, principle, 576, 739–40
Principle, principal, 576, 739–40
Print résumés, 430–33
Print source(s). *See also* Source(s); *specific print sources*
APA parenthetical references, 285–86
APA reference list, 288–91
Chicago documentation style, 311–17
CSE reference list, 331–34
evaluating, 193–95
in the humanities, 349–50
in library research, 184–85, 188–95
MLA parenthetical references, 240–43
MLA works-cited list, 245–55
in the natural and applied sciences, 398–99
in the social sciences, 389–90
Proceed, precede, 739
Process, as pattern of development, 44, 82, 92–93

Process paragraphs, 92–93
  chronological order in, 82
  defined, 92
Professor. *See* Instructor
Profusion, 205
Progressive tense(s), 605, 606–07
  defined, 606
  ESL writers and, 714
  simplest verb forms, 714
  types of, 606–07
Pronoun(s). *See also* Antecedent(s); Indefinite pronoun(s); *specific types*
  case, 593–96, 725, 744
  defined, 584, 753
  ESL writers and, 723–24
  forming possessive case of, 656–57, 659, 661
  gender, 725
  as part of speech, 584, 593–98, 753
  placement in sentence, 724
  prepositions to introduce, 590
  reference, 596–98, 724
  revising reference errors, 596–98
  sexist use of, 567–68
  subject-verb agreement with, 618
  substituting, for concise sentences, 516–17
  types of, 585–86, 753
  using, 584–86
Pronoun-antecedent agreement, 549, 596–98, 618, 619–21, 743
Pronoun reference, 596–98, 724
Pronunciation guide, in dictionary entry, 570
Pronunciation, spelling and, 575–77
Proofreading
  defined, 29, 69
  email, 208, 440
  essay, 69–70
  strategies for, 70
  Web site, 463
  in writing process, 29
Proper adjective(s), 588, 684, 743
Proper noun(s), 681–85
  adjectives formed from, 588, 684, 743
  articles with, 722
  artistic movements, 683
  athletic groups, 683
  brand names, 684
  business names, 684
  civic groups, 683
  days of the week, 682
  defined, 584, 681, 751
  documents, 683
  ethnic groups, 683
  events, 683
  geographical regions, 682
  government agencies, 684
  historical periods, 683
  holidays, 682
  languages, 683
  legal case names, 683
  literary movements, 683
  months, 682
  monument names, 682
  nationalities, 683
  organizations, 683
  particular structures, 682
  philosophic movements, 683
  place names, 682
  political groups, 683
  races, 683
  religions, 683
  religious works and figures, 683, 689
  sacred books, 683, 689
  social groups, 683
  special event names, 682
  specific academic courses, 684
  specific people, 682

Proposal(s), 386–87
Prose
 fiction, writing about, 359–65
 indicating omissions in, 678–79
 long quotations of, 221–22, 240, 274, 285, 321, 361, 665–66, 673
 MLA parenthetical references, 221–22, 240, 242
 MLA works-cited list, 249
PsychINFO, 191
Psychology. *See also* Social science(s)
 sample case study in, 383–84
 sample proposal, 386–87
Publication date(s)
 APA parenthetical references, 285
 APA reference list, 288–94
 CSE in-text citations, 332
 CSE reference list, 331–35
 MLA parenthetical references, 240–44
 MLA works-cited list, 245–63
Publication Manual of the American Psychological Association, 284, 294. *See also* APA documentation style
Publisher's name
 APA reference list, 288–89
 colons to separate publication place from, 673
 MLA works-cited list, 246, 696
PubMed (MEDLINE), 191
Punctuation, 629–79. *See also specific punctuation marks*
 APA parenthetical references, 286
 APA reference lists, 288–94
 Chicago endnotes and footnotes, 311–21
 CSE in-text citations, 330–31
 CSE reference list, 331–35
 in editing essays, 69
 end punctuation, 630–33
 for identifying tags, 220, 664
 to indicate changes to quotations, 220–21
 of lists, 447
 MLA parenthetical references, 240, 274
 MLA works-cited list, 245–63
Purpose
 defined, 2
 of essay, 2–5, 31
 of essay exam, 417
 in the humanities, 342–43
 in the natural and applied sciences, 392
 of oral presentation, 465
 prepositions and, 727
 in previewing, 15–16, 25
 in the social sciences, 380–81
 tone and, 12–13
 of visual text, 25
 of Web site, 456
 well-developed paragraph and, 88
 of writer, 2–5, 31

Q

Qtd. in (quoted in), MLA parenthetical references, 241, 273
Qualifiers, in Toulmin logic, 117–18
Qualitative data, 380
Quantitative data, 380
QuarkXPress, 454
Question(s)
 closed-ended, 197
 conferences with instructor, 63
 essay exam, 417–18
 in idea generation, 38–40, 53

in-depth, 39–40
indirect, 632, 647, 749
interrupted, punctuating, 643
in introductions, 101
journalistic, 38–40
open-ended, 196–97
peer review, 60–61
pronoun case in, 595
research, 158, 162, 181–82
rhetorical, 499
tag, 642, 731, 755
word order in, 730–31
Question mark(s), 632
and abbreviations with periods, 630
editing misused, 632
at end of direct question, 632
to mark questionable dates or numbers, 632
with quotation marks, 665, 669
Quotation(s), 217–18. *See also* Direct quotation(s); Long quotation(s); Quotation mark(s)
additions within, 220–21
APA parenthetical references, 284–85, 295
colons to introduce, 655, 673
comments within, 677
in conclusions, 103
defined, 217, 753
identifying tags for, 219, 540, 663–64, 731
indirect, 647, 670, 753
integrating, 220–22
interrupted, commas with, 533
in introductions, 101
MLA parenthetical references, 240, 274
MLA-style paper, 240, 265, 274, 358
omissions within, 221, 678–79

out of context in argumentative essays, 131–32
of poetry, 221–22, 240, 358, 666–67
of prose, 221–22, 240, 274, 285, 321, 361, 665–66, 673
quotation marks with, 663–65
within quotations, 669
run in with text, 240, 268
set off from text, 240, 274, 358
of sources, 164–68, 217–18
substitutions within, 220–21
when to quote, 217–18, 663–65
Quotation book(s), 189
Quotation mark(s), 663–70. *See also* Direct quotation(s); Quotation(s)
for borrowed words, 226–27, 229
for coined or borrowed words, 668
colons with, 668
double, 669
editing misused, 669–70
with other punctuation marks, 643, 664–65, 668–69, 677
as search operators online, 202, 203
single, 669
for titles of chapters, 667
for titles of periodical articles, 252, 667
for titles of unpublished dissertations, 251
for titles within titles, 249, 254, 669
when to use, 226–27, 229, 663
for words being defined, 690
Quotation, quote, 740
Quote, quotation, 740

R

Race(s)
  capitalizing names of, 683
  racial stereotypes, 566
  racist language, 110
Radio program(s)
  italicizing titles of, 688
  MLA works-cited list, 255, 258
  quotation marks for episodes, 667
Raise, rise, 740
Rambling sentence(s)
  adjective (relative) clauses, 518
  defined, 517
  excessive coordination, 518
  passive constructions, 518
  tightening, 517–19
  wordy noun constructions, 519
  wordy prepositional phrases, 519
Rand McNally Cosmopolitan World Atlas, 189
Ratio(s), numbers in, 702
Readers' Guide to Periodical Literature, 191
Reading, 15–27
  active reading, 15, 25, 407
  of essay exams before completing, 417–18
  in idea generation, 34
  of texts, 15–19
  of visual texts, 22–27
Real, really, 740
Reason is that, reason is because, 552, 740
Reciprocal pronoun(s)
  defined, 585, 753
  list of, 585–86
Recommendations for action, in conclusions, 103
Recording(s)
  APA reference list, 292
  Chicago documentation style, 318

CSE reference list, 334
MLA works-cited list, 255
Red herring fallacy, 122
Redundancy
  defined, 516
  deleting, 516
Refereed Web sites, 209
Reference
  parenthetical. *See* Parenthetical reference(s)
  pronoun, 596–98, 724
Reference list(s). *See also* Bibliography(ies) (reference tools)
  APA-style, 282–83, 287–94, 296–97, 307
  CSE-style, 329, 331–35, 336, 339
  defined, 287
Reference work(s)
  APA reference list, 289
  general, 184–85, 193
  in the humanities, 350
  list of, 189
  MLA works-cited list, 250
  in the natural and applied sciences, 399
  in the social sciences, 390
  specialized, 184, 188–89, 193, 350
  Web sites, 208–11
Reflective writing, 2–3, 4
Reflexive pronoun(s)
  defined, 585, 753
  list of, 585
Refutation
  in argumentative essay, 128, 133, 140, 368, 372
  defined, 128
Regardless, irregardless, 738
Regionalisms, 557
Regular verb(s)
  defined, 600, 753
  principal parts of, 600

Rehearsal, of oral presentation, 470
Relative clause(s). *See* Adjective (relative) clause(s)
Relative link(s), in Web site design, 460
Relative pronoun(s)
   in complex sentences, 491, 492
   defined, 585, 753
   in dependent clause fragments, 524–25
   as determiners, 589, 747
   to introduce adjective (relative) clauses, 478
   to introduce noun clauses, 479
   list of, 492, 585, 589
   repeating, 547
   in revising comma splices, 534
   in revising fused sentences, 534
   in revising run-on sentences, 534
   subject-verb agreement with, 618
Relevance
   defined, 109
   of evidence, 109
Reliable narrator, 367
Religion(s). *See also* Humanities
   capitalizing names of, 683
Religious work(s)
   capitalizing, 683, 689
   Chicago documentation style, 314
   CSE reference list, 333
   MLA parenthetical references, 242, 249
   names of, 683, 689
Remote antecedent(s), 597
Repetition
   conveying emphasis through, 509–10
   eliminating unnecessary, 516–17
   parallelism and, 547
Representativeness
   defined, 109
   of evidence, 109
Republished work(s), MLA works-cited list, 248
Requirements, school and course, 405–07
Research, 181–212. *See also* Exploratory research; Focused research; Internet research; Library research
   for argumentative essay, 130, 369
   defined, 154
   Internet research, 193–95, 198–212
   interviews, 196–97
   library research, 181–97
   sources in the humanities, 349–51
   sources in the social sciences, 389–91
Research notebook, 157
Research paper(s), 153–279
   checklists on, 155, 156–57, 167–68, 169, 179
   drafting, 173–80
   exploratory research, 158, 163–64, 181–87
   final draft, 180
   focused research, 163–64
   note-taking, 164–69
   organizing, 174–75
   outlines, 171–73
   plagiarism avoidance, 224–30
   planning, 156–57
   research notebook, 157
   research question, 158, 162, 181–82
   revising, 176–79
   rough draft, 173–79

Research paper(s) (*continued*)
  sample papers, 266–79, 294–307, 321–28, 335–39
  search strategy, 158–59, 163–64, 181–97
  sources for, 159–61, 163–64, 175–76
  systematic process for, 154
  thesis statement, 162, 169–70, 176
  titles of, 180
  topic selection, 156–57
  visuals in, 175–76
  working bibliography, 159–61
  writing assignment for, 155–56
Research question, 158, 162, 181–82
Respectably, respectfully, respectively, 740
Response essay, 343–44
Restrictive appositive(s), 744
Restrictive clause(s), 598, 639
Restrictive modifier(s)
  defined, 639, 754
  using, 639–41, 647
Résumé(s), 430–37
  chronological order, 430, 431
  electronic, 433–34
  emphatic order, 430, 432
  PDF (portable document format), 436, 437
  print, 430–33
  sample, 431, 432, 435
  scannable, 433–34, 435
  typeface for, 13
  Web-based, 436–37
Review(s). *See also* Book review(s)
  MLA works-cited list, 254, 259
Review of literature essay(s). *See* Review-of-research essay(s)
Review-of-research essay(s)
  defined, 385
  sample, in the social sciences, 385–86

Revision
  of agreement errors, 613–21
  of awkward sentences, 548–54
  checklists for, 65–67, 139–40, 179
  of comma splices, 532–34
  of confusing sentences, 548–54
  of dangling modifiers, 542–43
  defined, 29, 55–56
  to eliminate plagiarism, 226–30
  ESL writers and, 707
  of essay exams, 420–26
  of essays, 53, 55–58, 65–67, 139–40
  of faulty modification, 537–43
  of faulty parallelism, 546–47
  of faulty predication, 552–53
  of fused sentences, 532–34
  handwritten revisions, 57
  of incomplete and illogical comparisons, 553–54
  instructor's comments in, 9–10, 61–63, 177
  of misplaced modifiers, 537–40
  of misused abbreviations, 697–98
  of misused apostrophes, 661
  of misused capitalization, 686
  of misused colons, 673–74
  of misused commas, 646–48
  of misused dashes, 675
  of misused question marks, 632
  of misused quotation marks, 669–70
  of misused semicolons, 654–55
  of mixed constructions, 551
  of paragraphs, 66, 80–81, 83, 88–90

peer review in, 10–11, 59–61, 178–79
of phrase fragments, 525–29
of pronoun reference errors, 596–98
of research papers, 176–79
of run-on sentences, 532–34
of sentence fragments, 522–31
of sentences, 66–67
of thesis statement, 43–44
with Track Changes, 58–59, 178–79, 398
understanding, 53
of unwarranted shifts, 548–50
visuals in, 57–58
word-processing tools for, 58–59, 65
of words, 67
in writing process, 29
Rhetorical questions, 499
Rhetorical terms, glossary of, 743–56
Rise, raise, 740
Rogerian argument, 130
Root, 754
Rough draft. *See also* Revision
defined, 52
essay, 52–57
research paper, 173–79
Run-on sentence(s)
comma splice, 532–34, 754
creating, 649
defined, 532, 754
fused sentences, 532–34, 748, 754
revising, 532–34
Running head(s), APA-style paper, 295, 388

S

-s, -ss endings, plurals with, 580, 613–14
-s, possessive form of nouns ending in, 657

Sacred books, capitalizing names of, 683, 689
Salutation(s)
capitalization of, 686
punctuation of, 644, 673
Sarcasm, 632
-'s
in forming plurals, 660–61
in forming possessive case, 656–57
Save/Save As option, 53
Scannable résumés, 433–34, 435
Scarcely, as limiting modifier, 538
Scholarly journal(s). *See also* Journal article(s)
defined, 190
Scholarly publication(s)
defined, 194
popular publications versus, 194–95
Science. *See* Natural and applied science(s); *specific sciences*
Scientific method, 392
Scientific writing
style manual, 340
symbols in, 698
units of measurement, abbreviating, 698
Scope
defined, 209
of essay, 42–43
thesis statement in setting, 42–43
of Web site content, 209
Score(s), numbers in, 702
Sculpture, italicizing names of, 688
Search command, 68
Search engine(s), 199–207
choosing the right, 204–07
defined, 199
entering electronic address, 199–201
general-purpose, 204–05

Search engine(s) (*continued*)
  italicizing names of, 688
  keyword searches, 202–04, 206–07
  lists of, 201, 202, 203, 204–06
  metasearch/metacrawler, 205
  in publicizing Web site, 463
  specialized, 205–06
  subject guides, 156, 201–02
Search Engine Watch, 205
Search operators, 202–04
Search strategy, 158–59
  exploratory research, 158, 163–64, 181–87
  focused research, 163–64, 187–93
Season(s), names of, 686
Second person
  defined, 549, 752
  present-tense verbs in, 613–14
Secondary source(s), 163–64
  defined, 163, 191, 342
  finding, 191–92
  in the humanities, 342, 349
  list of, 164
-*seed* endings, 580
Self-evident assertions, 129, 369
Semicolon(s), 649–55
  in APA parenthetical references, 287
  in compound sentences, 488, 489, 634
  defined, 649
  editing misused, 654–55
  with quotation marks, 668
  in revising comma splices, 533–34
  in revising fused sentences, 533–34
  in revising run-on sentences, 533–34
  to separate independent clauses, 634, 649, 651, 654–55
  in series, 652

  with transitional elements connecting independent clauses, 533–34, 641, 651
Senior citizens, seniors, 566
Sentence(s). *See also* Common sentence problem(s); Complex sentence(s); Compound-complex sentence(s); Compound sentence(s); Punctuation; Simple sentence(s); Subject of sentence; Topic sentence(s)
  agreement errors, 613–21
  awkward, 548–54
  balanced, 744
  capitalizing first word of, 681
  checklists for, 66–67
  concise, 513–19
  confusing, 548–54
  cumulative, 506, 746–47
  declarative, 498–99
  defined, 474, 754
  emphatic, 503–11
  end punctuation, 630–33
  fused, 532–34, 748, 754
  imperative, 498–99
  mixed construction, 551, 750
  periodic, 506–07, 752
  periods to end, 630
  rambling, tightening, 517–19
  revising, 66–67, 503–11, 522–31, 532–34, 537–43, 544–47, 548–54
  run-on, 532–34, 649, 748
  tenses in, 607–08
  types of, 498–99
  varied, 488, 494–502
  wordiness, eliminating, 513–15, 518, 519
Sentence fragment(s), 522–31
  causes of, 522–23
  checklist, 530
  compound fragments, 529–30

defined, 522, 754
dependent clause fragments, 522, 524–25
grammar checkers and, 500
intentional use of, 530–31
phrase fragments, 524–29
recognizing, 522–23
revising, 522–31, 524–30
Sentence outline(s), 171
defined, 48
essay, 48–49
research paper, 176–77
sample, 176–77
Sentence structure, conveying emphasis through, 506–07
Separable phrasal verb(s)
defined, 716–17
list of, 716–17
Separate pagination, 253, 261–62, 290, 315, 333
Sequence, words and phrases to signal, 83
Series
adjectives in, 636
clauses in, 544
colons to introduce, 672
commas in, 635–36, 652
MLA works-cited list, 248
parallelism in, 544
of questions, in introductions, 101
of quotations, in introductions, 101
semicolons in, 652
Server(s), 463
Service learning, 409
Set, sit, 603, 740
Sexist language, 68, 110, 567–68
Sexual orientation stereotypes, 567
-sh endings, plurals with, 580
Shading, in document design, 443
Shall, will, 740
Shaping
defined, 29, 41

ESL writers and, 706–07
essay, 41–51
essay exam answer, 419–20
research paper, 174–75
in writing process, 29
She, he, 737
Shift(s)
defined, 754
from direct to indirect discourse, 549–50
in mood, 549, 754
in number, 549, 754
in person, 549, 754
in tense, 548, 754
unwarranted, revising, 548–50
in voice, 549, 611–12, 754
Ship(s), italicizing names of, 688
Short story(ies)
MLA works-cited list, 249
quotation marks for titles, 667
Short works, MLA parenthetical references, 241, 242
Should have, could have, would have, 606
Should of, could of, would of, 735
[Sic] (thus), 677
Signal words and phrases, 83–84, 116
Silent letter(s), 575, 579
Simile(s), 562, 754
Simple predicate(s), 474, 752
Simple sentence(s), 474–87
to break up strings of compound sentences, 497–98
clauses in, 477–79
combining choppy, 495–97
constructing, 474–76
defined, 479, 754
expanding, 479–87
patterns of, 474–76
phrases in, 477
Simple subject, 474, 755

Simple tenses, 604, 605
  defined, 605
  types of, 605
Simple Text, 458
Simply, as limiting modifier, 538
Since, 740
Singular
  defined, 613, 751
  forming possessive case of, 656–57, 659
Singular (*continued*)
  forms of, 613–14
  subject-verb agreement, 613–18, 713, 743
Sit, set, 603, 740
Site, cite, 735
Slang, 557, 670
Slanted language
  avoiding, 132, 370
  defined, 110
Slash(es)
  in electronic addresses, 257, 631, 691
  in quotes of poetry, 357, 666, 678
  to separate options, 677–78
Slide projector(s), 469
So, 488, 740
Social groups, capitalizing names of, 683
Social science(s), 380–91
  annotated bibliography, 385
  audience in, 380–81
  book review, 382–83
  case study, 383–84
  defined, 380
  documentation styles, 388–89. See also APA documentation style; Chicago documentation style
  field research in, 389
  format of writing, 388
  overview of, 380
  past tense in writing about, 301, 303
  personal experience essay, 381–82
  plagiarism, avoiding, 388
  proposal, 386–87
  purpose in, 380–81
  reference books, 390
  research sources, 389–91
  review-of-research essay, 385–86
  style of writing, 388
  tone in, 380–81
  visuals and technology in, 388–89
  writing assignments, 380–87
Sociological Abstracts, 191
Sociology. *See also* Social science(s)
  sample annotated bibliography, 385
Software. *See* Computer software
Sometime, sometimes, some time, 740
Song(s), quotation marks for titles, 667
Sort of, kind of, 738
Sound Forge, 389
Sound syllogisms, 116
Source(s). *See also* Documentation; Electronic source(s); Print source(s)
  evaluating, 193–95, 199, 208–11
  integrating into paper, 175–76, 219–22
  note-taking from, 164–69
  paraphrasing, 164–68, 215–17
  plagiarism avoidance, 224–30
  primary, 163–64, 191–92, 196–97
  quoting, 164–68, 217–18
  reading, 163
  recording, 164–68
  secondary, 163–64, 191–92
  summarizing, 164–68

synthesizing, 213, 223
types of, 163–64
working bibliography for, 159–61
Spacecraft, italicizing names of, 689
Spatial order
 defined, 82
 of paragraphs, 82
Special collections, 193
Special dictionaries, 184, 189, 574
Special event names, capitalizing, 682
Specialized indexes to periodicals, 191
Specialized reference works, 184, 185, 188–89, 193, 350
Specialized search engines, 205–06
Specific-to-general order, 82, 113–14
Specific word(s)
 defined, 560–61
 using, 560–61
Speech(s). *See* Oral presentation(s)
Spell checker(s)
 defined, 70
 proper nouns, 684–85
 running, 577
 spelling lists and, 581
 using, 70
Spelling, 575–82. *See also* Spell checker(s)
 -able, -ible endings, 580
 American versus British, 576
 developing skill in, 581–82
 in editing essays, 69
 ESL writers and, 708
 final consonants, doubling, 578
 homophones, 576–77, 582
 ie/ei combinations, 577
 plurals, 580–81

prefixes, 578
pronunciation and, 575–77
rules of, 577–82
-seed endings, 580
silent *e* before suffix, 579
silent letters, 575, 579
vowels in unstressed positions, 575
y before suffix, 579
Spelling list, 581
Splash page(s), 460
Split infinitive(s)
 defined, 541, 755
 separated by modifiers, 541
SportQuest, 206
Squinting modifier(s)
 defined, 538, 755
 placing, 538
Stability
 defined, 211
 of Web site content, 211
Staged photographs, 146
Stationary, stationery, 741
Statistic(s)
 documenting, 228
 numbers in, 702
 in the social sciences, 389–90
 in supporting opinions, 89–90, 107
 well-developed paragraph and, 89–90
Statistical Abstract of the United States, 189
Stereotypes, 566–67
Still, as conjunctive adverb, 489
Storyboarding
 constructing a storyboard, 49–51
 defined, 49
 in Web site design, 456–57
Straw man, 128
Street name(s), abbreviating, 697
Structure names, capitalizing, 682

Study groups
  checklist, 405
  defined, 405
Study schedule, 404–05
Style, documentation. *See*
  Documentation style
Style manuals, in various fields, 339–40
Subject-by-subject comparisons, 95–96
Subject complement(s), 623–24
  defined, 476, 586, 745, 755
  linking verbs and, 476, 586, 623–24
  in simple sentences, 476
  in subjective case, 593
Subject guide(s), search engine, 156, 201–02
Subject headings, 186
Subject of sentence
  agreement with verb, 613–18, 713, 743
  collective nouns as, 616–17
  complete, 474, 755
  compound, 614–15, 746
  creating new, to correct dangling modifier, 542
  defined, 755
  indefinite pronouns as, 615
  interrupted, 542–43
  lack of, in sentence fragments, 522
  omitting, 474
  separating from verb, 502
  simple, 474, 755
  simple sentence, 474–76
  singular subjects with plural forms, 617
  words between verb and, 614
Subject of verb, subjective case with, 593, 744
Subject search, 182, 183–84
  defined, 182, 183–84
  keyword search versus, 183
  of online database, 186

search engine, 201–02
subject headings in, 186–87
Subject-verb agreement, 613–18, 713, 743
Subjective (nominative) case, 593, 744
Subjective expressions, in literary analysis, 354
Subjunctive mood
  defined, 609, 750
  forming, 609
  using, 610
Subordinate clause(s). *See*
  Dependent (subordinate) clause(s)
Subordinating conjunction(s)
  in complex sentences, 491
  defined, 591, 746
  in dependent clause fragments, 524–25
  to introduce adverb clauses, 478–79
  list of, 491, 591
  in revising comma splices, 534
  in revising fused sentences, 534
  in revising run-on sentences, 534
Subordination
  to combine sentences, 496
  defined, 496, 755
Subscription database(s), 185–87, 190
  Chicago documentation style, 320–21
  library, 260–61
  MLA works-cited list, 260–61
  personal, 260–61
Subsequent edition(s)
  Chicago documentation style, 313
  MLA works-cited list, 248
Subsequent references to same work, Chicago documentation style, 311

Subtitles, colons to separate
    titles from, 673
Success. *See* Academic success
Such as, 673–74
    to introduce appositives, 485,
    528–29
Sufficiency
    defined, 108–09
    of evidence, 108–09
Suffix(es)
    -able, *-ible*, 580
    defined, 755
    doubling final consonants
        before, 578
    hyphenating with, 693
    -seed, 580
    silent *e* before, 579
    spelling rules, 578–80
    vowels in unstressed
        positions, 575
    y before, 579
Summary(ies), 164–68. *See also*
    Abstract(s)
    to avoid plagiarism, 229
    characteristics of, 214–15
    dashes to punctuate, 675
    defined, 213
    identifying tags to introduce,
        116, 222
    integrating, 219, 222
    MLA parenthetical
        references for, 240
    sample, 214–15
    of source information, 164–66
    words and phrases to signal,
        84
    writing, 213–15
Summary essay, 344
Superlative degree
    defined, 625, 626–27, 747
    dictionary part-of-speech
        labels, 571
    illogical, 627
    irregular, 626–27
    using, 626

Superscript(s)
    APA documentation style, 294
    Chicago documentation
        style, 321, 325
    CSE in-text citations, 330, 337
    defined, 264, 294, 330
    MLA documentation style,
        264, 269, 275
Supported opinions, 89–90, 107,
    354
Supporting evidence, 108–09,
    117–18, 129–31, 368–69
Supposed to, *used to*, 741
Suspended hyphen(s), 692–93,
    755
Sweeping generalization, 121
Syllabus, 406
Syllogism(s), 115, 116
    constructing valid, 116
    defined, 115, 755
    enthymemes and, 116, 748
    parts of, 115, 116
    problems of, 117
Symbol(s)
    as abbreviations, 698
    correction, 61
    in highlighting text, 16
    measurements before, 702
    in revision process, 61
Synchronous communication
    defined, 207–08
    MLA works-cited list, 258–59
    types of, 207–08
Synonym(s)
    defined, 572
    in dictionary entry, 572
    in thesaurus entries, 572
Syntax, plagiarism avoidance,
    227–28
Synthesis
    defined, 213, 223
    in essay exams, 415
    of source material in paper,
        213, 223
Synthesizing source(s), 213, 223

T

Table(s)
  in APA-style paper, 287, 296, 304–05
  in Chicago-style paper, 322
  in CSE-style paper, 335
  in document design, 449–50
  in MLA-style paper, 265
  reading, 23
Tag question(s), 731
  commas with, 642
  defined, 755
Take, bring, 734
Technical terms
  abbreviating, 695–96
  quotation marks with, 670
Technical writing
  abbreviations in, 698
  style manual, 340
  symbols in, 698
  units of measurement, abbreviating, 698
Technological competence, 411–12. *See also* Computer(s); Computer tip(s)
Television program(s)
  APA reference list, 291
  italicizing titles of, 688
  MLA works-cited list, 255
  quotation marks for episodes, 667
Temperature(s), abbreviating, 696
Tense, 604–08, 713–14
  defined, 604, 713, 755
  in the natural and applied sciences, 397
  perfect tenses, 604, 606, 714
  principal parts, 753
  progressive tenses, 605, 606–07, 714
  in résumés, 433
  shift in, 548
  simple tenses, 604, 605
  use in sentences, 607–08

Tentative thesis, 170
  defined, 162
  developing, 162
Teoma, 205
Text editors, 458
Than
  comparisons with, 594–95
  paired elements linked by, 545
Than, then, 741
That clauses, in subjunctive mood, 610
That, commas with, 640–41
That is, to introduce appositives, 485, 528
That, which, who, 598, 741
The number, a number, 617
The, omitting in Chicago documentation style, 317
The reason . . . is because, faulty predication, 552, 740
Their, in eliminating sexist language, 567
Their, there, they're, 741
Theirselves, theirself, themselves, 741
Themselves, theirselves, theirself, 741
Then, than, 741
There is, there are, 504, 617
There, their, they're, 741
Therefore, as conjunctive adverb, 489
Thesauri
  defined, 572
  electronic, 572
  using, 572
Thesis
  argumentative, 126, 133, 366–67
  defined, 41
  of essay, 41–51, 125–26, 366–67, 371
  of essay exam, 419
  patterns of development, 82, 90–97

Index **821**

of research paper, 162, 169–70
structure of, 41
tentative, 162, 170
Thesis and support
 defined, 41
 essay, 41–51, 133, 140, 368–72
 oral presentation, 465–66
Thesis statement
 argumentative essay, 125–26, 133, 140, 366–67, 371
 characteristics of effective, 42–43
 defined, 100
 essay, 41–45, 100, 125–26, 133, 366–67
 essay exam, 421
 fine-tuning, 169–70
 oral presentation, 465
 in outline, 172
 patterns of development, 44–45
 research paper, 162, 169–70, 176
 revising, 43–44
 in shaping essay, 44–45
 structure of, 43
They, in eliminating sexist language, 567
They're, their, there, 741
Thinking critically. *See* Critical thinking
Third person, 613, 752
 defined, 549
 present-tense verbs in, 613–14
Thus, as conjunctive adverb, 489
Till, until, 'til, 741
Time management, 402–04
Time measure(s)
 abbreviating, 696
 capitalizing, 682
 colons in expressions of, 673
 numbers in, 701

prepositions and, 727
words and phrases to signal, 83–84
Time relationship, complex sentences to signal, 492
Title page(s)
 APA-style paper, 298
 books in MLA style, 245–46
 Chicago-style paper, 321, 324
 MLA-style paper, 265, 267, 360
Titles of people
 abbreviating, 695
 capitalizing, 682
 commas with, 643
 Miss, Ms., Mrs., 567
 sexist language, avoiding, 567, 568
Titles of work(s)
 APA-style paper, 298, 300, 388
 articles in, 685, 688
 capitalizing important words in, 685
 Chicago-style paper, 321, 324
 colons to separate subtitles from, 673
 CSE-style paper, 337
 infinitives in, 645
 italicizing, 667, 670
 in literary analysis, 354
 long, italics or underlining for, 670
 MLA-style paper, 265, 266, 631
 quotation marks with, 251, 286, 667, 669
 short, quotation marks for, 251, 667
 shortened, in MLA parenthetical references, 240, 270
 student essays, 67–68
 student research papers, 180
 within titles, in MLA works-cited list, 249, 254

Titles of work(s) (*continued*)
  within titles, quotation marks with, 249, 254, 669
  underlined, in MLA works-cited list, 245–63, 670, 689
To
  in forming infinitives, 607–08, 749
  as preposition, 728
To, at, 734
To, too, two, 741
Tone
  of argumentative essay, 130–31, 369–70
  bias and, 110
  defined, 12, 110
  of essay, 12–13, 130–31
  establishing, 12–13
  in the humanities, 342–43
  in the natural and applied sciences, 392
  netiquette and, 208
  purpose and, 12–13
  in the social sciences, 380–81
  of Web site, 456
Too, two, to, 741
Topic labels
  electronic subscription service, 261
  MLA works-cited list, 261
Topic outline(s), 48, 171
  essay, 64–65
  research paper, 172–73
  sample, 172–73
Topic selection
  debatable topic, 125–26, 366
  essay, 32, 125–26, 366–67
  idea generation and, 34–40
  narrowing, 32
  oral presentation, 464
  research paper, 156–57
Topic sentence(s)
  at beginning of paragraph, 79
  defined, 79
  at end of paragraph, 79

main idea implied, 79–80
placement of, 79
in unified paragraphs, 79
Toulmin logic, 117–18
Track Changes feature, 58–59, 178–79, 398
Train(s), italicizing names of, 689
Transitional paragraph(s), 85–86, 99–100
Transitional words and phrase(s), 56
  in argumentative essays, 140
  in coherent paragraphs, 82–84, 90–91, 92
  commas with, 533–34, 638, 641
  in compound sentences, 488–89
  conjunctive adverbs as, 590
  to connect independent clauses, 533–34, 641, 651
  ending sentences with, 504
  list of, 83–84
  in paragraph development, 82–84, 90, 92
  phrase fragments introduced by, 526
  placing, 504
  semicolons with, 533–34, 641, 651
Transitive verb(s)
  defined, 718, 756
  in simple sentences, 475, 476
Translation(s), MLA works-cited list, 247, 249
True by definition assertions, 129
True syllogisms, 116
Try to, try and, 741
Tutoring programs, 409–10, 709
Two, to, too, 741
Type size, in document design, 444
-type, 741

Typeface
  in conveying tone, 13
  in document design, 443–44, 446

U

Unabridged dictionary(ies), defined, 189, 574
Underlining. *See also* Italic(s)
  in Chicago-style papers, 311
  to eliminate wordiness, 513
  in highlighting text, 16
  in MLA-style papers, 245–63, 670, 689
  for terms being defined, 670
Understatement, 562
Unfair appeals, 132, 370–71
Unified paragraphs, 79–81
  defined, 79
  testing for unity, 80–81
  topic sentences in, 79
Unintentional plagiarism
  avoiding, 225–26
  defined, 224
Uninterested, disinterested, 736
Unique, 741
Units of measurement, abbreviating, 698
University Microfilms International (UMI), 250–51
Unreliable narrator, 367
Unsigned work(s). *See* Anonymous/unsigned work(s)
Unsupported opinions, 107
Until, 'til, till, 741
URL (uniform resource locator), 199–201
  APA reference list, 292–94
  division of, 257, 631, 691
  domain types, 210
  entering, 257
  entering electronic address, 199–201, 257

MLA works-cited list, 256–63
understanding, 201, 210
Us, we, before a noun, 596
Usage, glossary of, 733–42
Usage labels, in dictionary entries, 573
Used to, supposed to, 741
Usenet newsgroup(s), 207
  MLA works-cited list, 258–59
Utility word(s)
  defined, 514
  eliminating, 514, 561
Utilize, 742

V

Vague wording, 42, 127
Valid syllogisms, 116
Varied sentence(s), 488, 494–502
  breaking up strings of compound sentences in, 497–98
  combining choppy simple sentences in, 495–97
  defined, 494
  length in, 494–95
  sentence openings in, 500
  sentence types in, 498–99
  word order in, 501–02
Verb(s), 600–612. *See also* Tense; Verbal(s); Voice; *specific types of verb*
  action, 433, 586
  agreement with subject, 613–18, 713, 743
  defined, 586, 755
  ESL writers and, 713–20
  finite, 748
  formed from nouns, 720
  infinitives, 749
  interrupted, 542–43
  to introduce source material, 219

Verb(s) (*continued*)
   irregular, 600–03, 713–14, 749
   lack of, in sentence fragments, 522
   mood, 609–10
   negative, 715–16
   as part of speech, 586–88, 755–56
   phrasal, 716–17
   principal parts, 600–03, 753
   recognizing, 586–87
   regular, 600, 753
   separating from subject, 502
   simplest forms, 714
   types of, 755–56
   using, 586–88, 713–20
   words between subject of sentence and, 614
Verb phrase(s)
   defined, 477, 752
   forming, 586–87, 755–56
   interrupted, 541
   in simple sentences, 474–75
Verbal(s). *See also* Past participle(s); *specific types of verbal*
   defined, 477, 481, 527, 587, 756
   expanding simple sentences with, 481
   recognizing, 587–88
   types of, 756
   used as nouns, 481
   in verbal phrases, 484
Verbal phrase(s)
   commas with introductory, 637, 638
   commas with nonrestrictive, 639
   defined, 477, 484, 527, 752
   expanding simple sentences with, 484
   fragments, revising, 527
   misplaced, 539
   as modifiers, 484, 539, 614

   as nouns, 484
   in simple sentence, 477
Vertical file, 193
Videotape(s)
   Chicago documentation style, 318
   CSE reference list, 334
   MLA works-cited list, 255
Visual(s). *See also* Document design; Visual text(s); Web site design
   in APA-style paper, 296, 388–89
   checklists, 58, 144, 296, 452–53
   in Chicago-style paper, 322
   computer tips for, 49, 146
   copyright and, 452
   in CSE-style paper, 335, 338
   defined, 57, 142, 449
   in document design, 449–53
   in essays, 57–58, 142–48, 371
   evaluating, 143, 145–46
   as evidence, 142, 371
   file format, 459
   in the humanities, 348–49
   list of, 469–70
   misleading charts and graphs, 147–48
   misleading photographs, 145–46
   in MLA-style paper, 265–66, 271
   in the natural and applied sciences, 398
   presentation software, 443, 449, 467–68, 469
   in research papers, 175–76
   in the social sciences, 388–89
   using, 449–53
   visual aids for oral presentations, 449–53, 467–70
   in Web site design, 458–59

Visual aid(s), 449–53, 467–70
  checklist for, 469
  using, 469–70
Visual cues, in writing, 16
Visual learners, 404
Visual text(s). *See also* Visual(s)
  annotating, 26
  defined, 2
  highlighting, 26
  interpreting, 24–25
  previewing, 25
  reading, 22–27
  storyboarding, 49–51
  types of, 22–23
Voice, 610–12, 717–18. *See also* Active voice; Passive voice
  defined, 610, 756
  shift in, 549, 611–12, 754
Voice mail, 441
Voice of the Shuttle, 206
Vowel(s), in unstressed positions, 575

W

Wait for, wait on, 742
Warning, in conclusions, 103
Warrant, in Toulmin logic, 117–18
We the People, 189
We, us, before a noun, 596
Weather, whether, 742
Web. *See* World Wide Web
Web authoring software, 457–58
Web browser(s), 199, 200
  Bookmarks and Favorites, 206–07
  italicizing names of, 688
Web page(s), 199, 456
Web site(s)
  APA reference list, 293
  Chicago documentation style, 319
  connection problems, 201
  defined, 199, 456
  design of. *See* Web site design
  evaluating content of, 208–11
  in the humanities, 350
  italicizing, 688
  library, 185, 188
  MLA works-cited list, 256–63, 258
  in the natural and applied sciences, 399
  in the social sciences, 391
  Web-based résumés, 436–37
Web site design, 456–63
  checklists, 461–62, 463
  components of, 456
  copyright, 462
  creating Web site, 457–58
  editing in, 463
  linking content, 462
  planning in, 456–57, 460–62
  planning navigation, 460–62
  previewing in, 463
  proofreading, 463
  selecting and inserting visuals, 458–59
  style conventions, 463
  uploading, 463
WebCrawler, 205
WebCT™, 30
Well-developed paragraphs, 88–90
  characteristics of, 88–90
  defined, 88
  revising underdeveloped paragraphs, 88–90
  testing for adequate development, 88
Well, good, 737
Were, we're, 742
Whether, if, 737
Whether, weather, 742
Which, commas with, 640–41
Which, who, that, 598, 741
White space, in document design, 443
Whiteboard(s), 470

Who, that, which, 598, 741
Who? What? Why? Where? When? and *How?* questions, 38
Who, whom, 595, 742
Whoever, whomever, 595
Who's, whose, 742
Will, shall, 740
Word. See Microsoft Word
Word(s), 555–82. *See also* Figurative language; Parts of speech; Transitional words and phrase(s); Word order
   abstract, 561
   beginning sentences with, 500
   borrowed, 226–27, 229
   breaking at end of line, 691
   capitalizing first, 681
   checklists for, 67
   choosing right, 556–68
   clichés, 564–65
   coined words, quotation marks with, 668
   compound, 691–93, 745–46
   concrete, 561
   connotation, 559–60
   denotation, 559–60
   diction, 556–58
   euphemisms, 560
   function, 748
   general, 560–61
   inappropriate, 563–65
   isolates, 592, 749
   jargon, 563–64
   key, 85, 547
   mixed metaphor, 565, 750
   neologisms, 564
   plagiarism avoidance, 226–27, 228–29
   pretentious diction, 564
   revising, 67
   in series, 544
   sexist language, 68, 110, 567–68
   to signal conclusions, 84, 116
   specific, 560–61
   stereotypes, 566–67
   between subject and verb, 614
   utility, eliminating, 514
   as words, apostrophes in plurals of, 660
   as words, setting off, 660, 668, 689–90
Word order
   beginning with important ideas, 503–04
   climactic, 504, 745
   conveying emphasis through, 503–05
   ESL writers and, 708, 730–31
   experimenting with, 505
   inverting, 501–02, 505, 617
   in questions, 730–31
   separating subject from verb, 502
   standard, 501, 505, 730
Word processor(s). *See* Computer tip(s); Grammar checker(s); *Microsoft Word;* Spell checker(s)
Wordiness, eliminating, 513–15
   circumlocution, 514
   deadwood, 513–14
   excessive coordination, 518
   noun constructions, 519
   prepositional phrases, 519
   utility words, 514
   wordy phrases, 515, 519
Wording
   of thesis, 42
   of thesis statement, 44–45
   vague, 42, 127
Working bibliography, 159–61
   computer file, 161
   index card, 160
Workplace communication, 428–41. *See also* Business letter(s)
   computers in, 30

emails, 440
faxes, 440–41
memos, 438–39
résumés, 430–37
voice mail, 441
Works-cited list(s). *See also*
    Bibliography(ies)
    (documentation styles)
  checklists, 266
  defined, 244
  in literary analysis, 354, 365
  MLA style, 234–37, 244–63,
    266, 278–79, 365
  sample, 278–79
World Almanac, 189
World Wide Web, 199–207. *See
    also* Web site(s)
  connection problems, 201
  defined, 199
  plagiarism avoidance,
    224–25, 227
  search engines, 199–207
  URLs, 199–201. *See also*
    URL (uniform resource
    locator)
  Web browsers, 199, 200
*Would have, should have, could
    have*, 606
Would of, should of, could of, 735
WriteNote, 161
Writer's block, 53
Writing. *See also* ESL (English
    as a Second Language)
    writer(s); Essay(s);
    Research paper(s)
  about fiction, 352–65
  about poetry, 355–59
  argumentative essay, 133–39
  reflective, 2–3, 4
Writing center
  conferences, 63
  ESL writers and, 707
  using facilities of, 409–10
Writing process
  computers and, 30

ESL writers and, 706–08
stages of, 29–30
word-processing tools for,
    58–59

X
-*x* endings, plurals with, 580

Y
-*y* endings, 580
  plurals with, 580
  suffixes with, 579
Yahoo!, 202, 205
Yearbooks, 189
Yes, commas with, 642
Yes/no question(s), 731
Yet, as coordinating conjunction,
    488
Your; you're, 742

Z
-*z* endings, plurals with, 580
Zoology, documentation style.
    See CSE documentation
    style
Zworks, 205

Checklist(s)
  academic success, 414
  adjectives in series, 636
  analysis of writing
    assignment, 31
  anonymous or questionable
    sources, 210
  APA documentation style,
    295–97
  argumentative essays,
    139–40, 144
  assignment analysis, 155
  audience in peer review, 11
  becoming a successful
    student, 414
  bias detection, 144
  Chicago documentation
    style, 321–23

Checklist(s) (*continued*)
  collaborative work, 405
  computer printouts, 169
  conferences with instructor, 63
  constructing lists, 447
  credibility of anonymous
    Web source, 210
  critical thinking, 144
  CSE documentation style,
    335–36
  determining purpose of essay,
    5
  document design, 447
  drafting strategies, 52–53
  editing and proofreading, 69
  editing strategies for ESL
    writers, 709–10
  electronic arguments, writing
    and revising, 152
  email, writing, 440
  formal outlines, 171–72
  highlighting symbols, 16
  inserting visuals, 58
  interviews, 197
  keyword search tips, 183,
    206–07
  library books, locating
    missing, 190
  library research tips, 181
  for lists, 447
  MLA documentation style,
    265–66
  netiquette, 208
  note-taking, 167–68
  oral presentations, 471
  paraphrase writing, 217
  peer-review questions, 60–61
  photocopies, 169
  plagiarism avoidance, 229–30
  primary sources, 192
  quotations, 218
  reading texts, 21
  reading visual texts, 27
  research papers, 155, 156–57,
    167–68, 169, 179
  restrictive and nonrestrictive
    modifiers, 640
  revising argumentative
    essays, 139–40
  revising paragraphs, 66
  revising research paper, 179
  revising sentences, 66–67
  revising words, 67
  search engine tips, 206–07
  secondary sources, 192
  selecting visuals, 144
  sentence fragments, 530–31
  shaping essay with thesis
    statement, 44
  storyboarding, 50–51
  strategies for revising, 65–67
  summary writing, 215
  topic selection for research
    paper, 156–57
  visual aids, 469
  visuals in MLA-style paper,
    265–66
  visuals in papers, 296, 452–53
  voice mail, 441
  Web site design, 461–62,
    463
  when to paragraph, 78
  writing about literature,
    353–54

Computer Tip(s)
  breaking URLs, 691
  checking proper nouns,
    684–85
  checking quotation marks,
    664
  comma splices, 532
  contractions, revising, 659
  coordinating conjunctions
    and fragments, 500
  Copy, Cut, and Paste feature,
    56
  diction, 558
  document design, 443
  drafting, 174

Edit menu, 56
editing, 68
electronic dictionaries, 574
electronic organizers, 403
electronic thesauri, 572
email interviews, 197
emailing instructor, 411–12
emoticons, 558
faulty modification, 537
faulty parallelism, 547
faulty predication, 553
fax messages, 440–41
formatting an outline, 65
grammar checkers, 70
Header/Footer option, 295
hyphenating compound
  words, 692
idea generation, 38
letter templates, 430
note-taking, 161, 167
outline file, 173
outline formatting, 65
outlining, 49
passive voice, 511
PDF résumés, 436
peer review, 60
plagiarism avoidance,
  224–25, 227
PowerPoint®, 468
pronoun-antecedent
  agreement, 621
proofreading, 68
redundancy, deleting, 516
refuting opposing arguments,
  128
résumés, 433
revising, 56, 59, 179
semicolons, misused, 654
sentence fragments, 523
shorthand abbreviations, 695
spell checkers, 70, 577
spelled-out numbers, 701
subject-verb agreement,
  615–16
that and *which*, 640–41

tone, conveying, 13
URLs, 201
using search operators,
  203–04
verb forms, 602–03
visuals, 58
visuals, altering, 146
working bibliography, 161

ESL Tips
  See also ESL (English as a
  Second Language)
  writer(s)
  academic honors in other
    countries, 433
  adjective use, 623, 636,
    726–27
  adverb use, 623, 726
  annotating text, 17
  argumentative essay topics,
    127
  capitalization issues, 681
  class discussions, 408
  collective nouns, 616
  commas in numbers, 644
  connotations, 560
  coordination, 488
  critical thinking, 106
  drafting, 52
  editing, 52
  essay exams, 415–16, 418,
    421
  expectations of instructor, 10
  faulty sentences, 548
  idea generation, 34, 39
  idioms, 565
  indenting paragraphs, 78
  informal diction, 556
  instructor expectations, 406,
    408
  logical fallacies, 120
  note-taking, 168
  omitting subject of sentence,
    474
  oral presentations, 464

ESL Tip(s) (*continued*)
  plagiarism avoidance, 225
  reading text, 15
  special dictionaries, 574
  thesis statement, 100
  transitive versus intransitive verbs, 475
  varying sentences, 496
  word order, 505
  writing about poetry, 355
  writing center participation, 410
  writing process, 30
  writing response essays, 343

CHECKLIST

AVOIDING PLAGIARISM

- [ ] **Take careful notes.** Be sure you have recorded information from your sources carefully and accurately.
- [ ] **In your notes, clearly identify borrowed material.** In handwritten notes, put all words borrowed from your sources inside circled quotation marks, and enclose your own comments within brackets. If you are taking notes on a computer, boldface all quotation marks.
- [ ] **In your paper, differentiate your ideas from those of your sources** by clearly introducing borrowed material with an identifying tag and by following it with documentation.
- [ ] **Enclose all direct quotations** used in your paper within quotation marks.
- [ ] **Review all paraphrases and summaries** in your paper to make certain they are in your own words and that any distinctive words and phrases from a source are quoted.
- [ ] **Document all quoted material and all paraphrases and summaries** of your sources.
- [ ] **Document all information** that is open to dispute or that is not common knowledge.
- [ ] **Document all opinions, conclusions, figures, tables, statistics, graphs, and charts** taken from a source.
- [ ] **Never submit the work of another person as your own.** Do not buy a paper from an online paper mill or use a paper written by a friend. In addition, never include in your paper passages that have been written by a friend, relative, or writing tutor.
- [ ] **Never use sources that you have not actually read** (or invent sources that do not exist).

THE RESEARCH PROCESS		
Activity	**Date Due**	**Date Completed**
Move from an Assignment to a Topic, **13a**		
Do Exploratory Research and Formulate a Research Question, **13b**		
Assemble a Working Bibliography, **13c**		
Develop a Tentative Thesis, **13d**		
Do Focused Research, **13e**		
Take Notes, **13f**		
Fine-Tune Your Thesis, **13g**		
Outline Your Paper, **13h**		
Draft Your Paper, **13i**		
Revise Your Paper, **13j**		
Prepare Your Final Draft, **13k**		